UNORTHODOX LIFE

UNORTHODOX LIFE

RUDY ROSENBERG

authorHOUSE®

AuthorHouse™
1663 Liberty Drive
Bloomington, IN 47403
www.authorhouse.com
Phone: 1-800-839-8640

Published by AuthorHouse   03/27/2013

ISBN: 978-1-4817-1209-5 (sc)

Library of Congress Control Number: 2013902522

Any people depicted in stock imagery provided by Thinkstock are models, and such images are being used for illustrative purposes only.
Certain stock imagery © Thinkstock.

This book is printed on acid-free paper.

Because of the dynamic nature of the Internet, any web addresses or links contained in this book may have changed since publication and may no longer be valid. The views expressed in this work are solely those of the author and do not necessarily reflect the views of the publisher, and the publisher hereby disclaims any responsibility for them.

CONTENTS

Volume One—Part Three

Lopuszno, Poland. Only known photo of Lea Gittel Okawita Rozenberg, mother of Hillel (Hilaire). Note the obvious wig Lea is wearing, a sign of orthodoxy. There are no known photos of Mordecai Rozenberg, the Father of Hillel.

Russian, circa 1906. Gershen Rozenberg, Hillel's eldest brother in Russian uniform during Russo/Japanese war. Possibly taken in Port Arthur, Manchuria (now part of China).

VOLUME ONE
PART ONE

MEMOIRS OF RUDY ROSENBERG

Germany, Köln (Cologne) Probably 1912. The Friedemann Family. Frieda, 10 (?); Philip, Emma, Richard, 12 (?). Missing: Paul, 8 (?).

1922, Summer. Altena, Germany. Hillel (Hilaire) 20; (bareheaded, extreme right, hod carrier for a group of Germany masons, 18 months after the end of WWI.

PROLOGUE: I AM ABORTED (almost)

(With apologies to Charles Dickens and "David Copperfield")

I always knew I was supposed to be aborted. My Mother, Frieda, never made a secret of it. Often, as she held me in her arms, she would softly repeat:

"*On ne l'avait pas voulu*". We had not wanted him.

Somehow, over the years, it had come to my knowledge that when my Mother found out she was pregnant, both she and my Father, Hilaire, had decided that I was not wanted and that an abortion would be required. In Charleroi, in the middle of the Borinage, a miserable section of Belgium, abortions, although illegal in this Catholic country, were readily available, even under the care and supervision of regular doctors. I had been told that at the last moment my Father had changed his mind and sent the doctors away. The true circumstances were unknown to me.

In 1988, my Father, Hilaire Rosenberg, who still lived in Brussels, Belgium, was spending a few weeks at my house on Long Island. We had taken some time to go and visit Washington DC, where he had never been. As we walked through the city, we passed by the window of a hardware store, where my Father noticed a carpenter's folding yardstick. Pointing to it he said:

"If it weren't for this, you would not be here."

He went on to relate that sometime in 1929 he was driving to Marcinelle, a suburb of Charleroi, to measure a dining room in the home of Monsieur L'Hermite, an agronomy engineer. At the time my parents had a small furniture-interior decoratoration business called Maison Hilaire, and it was customary for my Father to travel here and there in his Fiat or Bedford truck to deliver furniture to clients.

Halfway to Marcinelle, my Father realized that he had forgotten his "*double mètre*", the folding yardstick. He turned around and drove back to his house, Rue de Marcinelle in Charleroi. He entered by the back door into the kitchen and found my Mother attended by two doctors who were about to perform an abortion. My Mother was already under the ether and was laid out on the kitchen table.

My Father paid off the doctors and when my Mother came to, she was still pregnant.

After relating this to me, my Father said:

> "If it wasn't for this *double mètre*, you would not be here and I would never have known you and I would have missed a wonderful son."

With that, we embraced on the streets of Washington. A week later, Hilaire was dead.

And so it was that on February 26, 1930 I was born in Charleroi.

3

1927, July. The Synagogue, Köln (Cologne) Germany. Frieda Friedemann and Hilaire
Rosenberg. Just married. Both are a month shy of 25.

Loverval, Belgium; 1932Frieda's
brother (Richard or Paul?), Frieda,
30; Hilaire, 30; Ruth, 4; Rudy,
2. After Frieda tried to commit
suicide, Hilaire rented a villa in
Loverval to get Frieda away from
the gloom of Charleroi.

PREFACE: POLAND AND GERMANY

My Father Hillel Rosenberg (or Rozenberg), was born in Lopuszno, Poland on August 13, 1902 to well-to-do-farmers. Seven days later, my Mother Frieda Friedemann, was born in Köln (Cologne), Germany on August 20, 1902 to wealthy merchants. Both families were Jewish, but Hillel's was Orthodox while Frieda's was more assimilated, as were the majority of Jewish families in Germany.

HILLEL'S STORY

Hillel was born into a family of eleven children. The eldest brother had fought in the Russo-Japanese war in 1906 and there was always a photograph of the handsome soldier in his Russian uniform in our home. Another brother, Moishe, was sent to Krakow to study with a rabbi and become a cantor. However, Moishe did not have any desire for that profession and one day took off for parts unknown. It was rumored that he fought in the Spanish Civil War and wound up in America but that was never confirmed and no further trace of him was ever uncovered. When Moishe left, it was up to my Father, Hillel, to fill the void. He left home and went to the rabbi to become a cantor.

It was not long before Hillel realized that he did not have any more of an inclination to become a clergyman than did Moishe and one day, Hillel cut his *payes*, long side curly locks and his long black coat and he was gone. "From that day forward, I became a modern Jew!" He explained.

Hillel never found his way home again and traveled from town to town, country to country, job to job. He was about thirteen at the time and as far as I know never saw his family again.

By then, the Great War had broken out and the borders of Eastern Europe were changing daily. In 1917, Hillel found himself, at fifteen, near the Austrian City of Przemysl (Pzermichel), where the Russians had besieged the Austrian troops. Hillel and another Jew by the name of Cohen made money ferrying horses into the besieged city for the Austrians. This was extremely dangerous, as this had to be done under fire and by riding and guiding the horses through gullies and exposed terrain. After a while, Cohen decided that there would be more profit and less risk if they simply sold the horses and harness to whomever. With the money they made from the sale, Hillel and Cohen took off for Germany just as the Russian revolution of October 1917 erupted.

Hillel hid in farms, traveled by freight train, worked wherever he could find a job, in salt mines, as hod carrier, saddler, coach maker, electrician . . . .

He loved to tell the story of a ride in the brake house of the train and how one morning he was awakened by a loud "Rosenberg *aussteigen!*" (Rosenberg, get off). He was sure he had been uncovered until he peered from his hideaway and saw that the train had arrived in a town called Rosenberg and that the trainmaster was just notifying passengers who wanted to get off there that they had arrived.

Along the way, Hillel picked up some German to go along with the Polish, Russian and Yiddish that he knew from his native land. I never knew if he spoke Hebrew, I only know that Hillel had no formal education and could not write. However, he was very bright and over the years was able to teach himself to read in several languages and to sign his name.

The Great War (it would later be called WW1, but at the time no one knew that there would be a need to number it) had ended and Hillel found himself in Germany in the midst of the terrible depression of the early twenties. Money was worthless and lost more and more of its value each day.

Hillel had found work dismantling a huge industrial smokestack brick by brick. As usual it was dangerous work, as he had to climb to the top of the structure and chisel each brick and drop it below onto a straw mattress so that the bricks could be reused for some other project. He had struck a deal with the boss that in exchange for this work, instead of money, he would be paid with a train ticket to Paris, or at least to France.

When the work was done, a ticket was purchased, but to Charleroi, which Hillel thought was in France. He had taken up with two Poles who had heard that there was work in Charleroi and that it was the place to go. Charleroi turned out to be in Belgium, not far from the French border but definitively not in France.

When the three of them arrived in Charleroi, there was indeed work, but it was in the coal mines. The coal mines of the Borinage were very dangerous and none of the trio wanted to work below. The manager agreed to let two of the men work above ground as long as one of them would work below. Hillel made knots in the corners of a handkerchief and they drew corners to see who would go down. He lost.

Hilaire was teamed up with Joseph, a Flemish miner. Together they could converse by mixing Flemish and German. They soon developed a bond of sorts, working side by side each day under perilous conditions where they depended on each other for their daily survival. One day, Hilaire decided to take a couple of days off and told Joseph that he would be taking the train for Antwerp. Joseph was very interested and asked Hilaire to look for Jews in Antwerp. "I understand that Jews have horns in the middle of their forehead, he said" Hilaire said nothing and left for Antwerp. When he returned, Joseph excitingly wanted to know if he had seen any Jews while in Antwerp. Hilaire stared at Joseph and pressed him to take a good look at his forehead. "Do you see any horns? Well, I am a Jew and you have been working side by side with a Jew for months "Joseph was dumbfounded and never brought up the subject again. However, Joseph would often peer at Hilaire's forehead, mutter something and shake his head in frustration.

The working conditions in the mine were terrible. The filthy surroundings, the heat, and the stench soon depressed my Father. The sight of blinded horses working in the dark made him think back to his youth on his Father's farm and the horses they kept there. He thought about the clean and beautiful salt mines, cut like cathedrals, where he had worked as a child. The coal mines of Charleroi were not for him and after a couple of near fatal accidents, he wanted out. To the end of his days, he retained a small chip of coal embedded in his flesh to which he would always point with pride.

Hillel had not yet learned to speak French but he shared a room with Max, a friend. One day, as they walked in the streets of Charleroi, they passed by a furniture store. In the workshop you could see men busy sewing and setting leather to the couches and armchairs. Hillel gestured to his friend that he should go in and tell the owners that he knew how to do that. He had learned to sew and decorate coaches in Germany and saw that the work of building furniture was basically the same. He was hired on the spot.

This was the furniture business of Madame Cousins. The first thing she did was to change Hillel's name to Hilaire. This would make him more acceptable to the customers with whom he would come in contact. Soon, Hilaire was the star of the shop. He had found his calling as an interior decorator with skills to match his talent and imagination. The customers wanted no one else to work on their furnishings and Hilaire was in constant demand to decorate homes all through the area.

Mme Cousins was very satisfied with the quality of his work and the echoes she heard about his work from the customers. She did not hide the fact that she would like very much for Hilaire to marry her niece, Liliane, who would one day inherit the whole business. In Charleroi this was known "as falling with your ass in butter". However, Hilaire knew of no one in his family to have ever transgressed the old tradition and it was always understood that no one should marry outside of his religion. What's more, he was not particularly attracted to the young girl and did not feel motivated or bold enough to break with the tradition.

Hilaire took French lessons, was named first decorator, bought his first car, a racing car, then an Imperia "with a beautiful copper radiator". This enabled him to prance about in the streets of Charleroi to impress pretty girls. He cut quite a handsome figure, with a fedora, a cane and soft leather gloves. A picture taken at the time gives him a distinct George Raft appearance.

There was a furniture exhibit in Germany and thanks to his knowledge of German, Mme Cousins chose Hilaire to go to the Düsseldorf fair to learn about the latest fashions in furniture. My Father, though born in Poland, was without a nationality or passport, an *apatride*, stateless. So, he went to find Mr Homburg who earlier, had helped him pass into Belgium so that he could arrange to help Hilaire cross the border again, this time into Germany and to assist him again when the time came to return to Charleroi after the fair.

While in Germany, Hilaire made a detour to Altena because he kept a very nice souvenir of the gentle Irma Friedenberg, the butcher's daughter, whom he had met while working in Germany and had always thought of asking her to marry him. Wearing his most beautiful blue suit, he went to visit the Friedenbergs, shared a meal and talk turned to a mutual future. That night Hilaire went back to his hotel with the firm intention to ask for Irma's hand the next day. During the night there was a fire in the butcher shop and all of Hilaire's plans fell in the water in the hours that followed. Gone was the dowry. Gone was the marriage. Hilaire would never see Irma again. Years later, long after the war, Hilaire visited Altena and learned that the whole Friedenberg family had been arrested, deported and disappeared without a trace. Only the eldest daughter managed to survive and emigrated to England.

At the time Hilaire felt that destiny was against all his projects. However, had he married Irma and moved back to Germany, he would most likely not have survived the Hitler years and I would never have seen the light of day.

Before leaving Altena, Hilaire went to see his friend Rudi Wolf who asked him if he could bring a small parcel for his Aunt Emma Friedemann who had a poultry store in Cologne. Little did he imagine that his life would take another turn just for doing a friend a favor.

Thus, Hilaire passed through Cologne and while he was sitting with Mrs Friedemann, having a cup of coffee, in came her daughter Frieda, back from a stay in Blankenese, a beach resort on the North Sea coast of Germany. She was prettily sun tanned and in full form. By coincidence they had a mutual friend, Roman Topf and she had a picture of Roman with Hilaire.

In his memoirs Hilaire, states that the moment Frieda laid eyes on him, he was the only man for her and that Frieda and her Mother kept him in the house until way past midnight when he finally had to excuse himself, because he had to get up early the next day to return to Charleroi.

Frieda's memoirs, on the other hand, recall that once Hilaire laid eyes on her, there was no way he could be gotten rid off. He stayed and stayed well past midnight until he had to be urged to leave and return to his hotel. Before he left, Hilaire gave Frieda his address and urged her to come and visit him in Belgium.

In Charleroi, Mme Cousins decided to terminate her business. Having worked there five years Hilaire felt confident that he could establish his own shop and started looking for a place. His French was good enough to speak with the customers. Of course, there was the problem of having to write and do the accountings, but his friend Max agreed to try the experiment with him.

A small house was found in Marcinelle, a suburb of Charleroi, which would be an excellent place to start. There were two rooms upstairs, which Hilaire and Max took for themselves. Downstairs was the store with just a few symbolic samples of armchairs that had been repaired and reupholstered.

Mme Cousins referred some of her customers to the new enterprise, the "Maison Hilaire" which so soon after the Great War sounded much better than Maison Rosenberg, which would have sounded too German. After a few false starts and learning experiences, the shop began to prosper and Hilaire settled down to what promised to be a bright future.

FRIEDA'S STORY

Frieda was the second child of Phillip and Emma (nee Wolff) Friedemann. She had an older brother, Richard, born in 1896, and a younger one, Paul born in 1906. Frieda was born on August 20th, 1902. Her parents had a prosperous wholesale and retail poultry business in Köln (Cologne), the beautiful German city on the Rhine River. Their home and shop was on Rudolfplatz, until 1917, when they moved to 44 Mittelstrasse, within sight of the monumental Dom (Cathedral) of Cologne.

In the early 1890's, while still a young man, Phillip had emigrated to the United States of America. However, his Mother missed him so much that she pleaded for him to return to Cologne. He remained in the USA a very short time before returning to Germany. There he met and married Karolia (Emma) Wolff. Had he remained in the USA (Chicago?) I and all that followed would have been altered considerably.

The Friedemann family was Jewish, but if they were practicing their religion, its members were by no mean Orthodox or deeply religious. Phillip would serve in the German army during the Great War, and would be stationed and see action in France. Things were so bad in the trenches, that Phillip, in order to be sent back to the rear, resorted to fakery. He threaded woolen strands on a huge needle, and ran the thick thread under the skin of his feet, at several places, leaving the wool to decompose and rot. After a while, his feet got infected and started to swell to the point he could not wear his boots and barely walk. He never got to the front lines again and survived the war.

Frieda grew up with an independent streak, which she was to keep all of her life. Richard was talented, outgoing, loved to gamble, learned to box with Max Schmeling and befriended opera singers. Paul was the youngest and always sickly.

Phillip Friedemann died shortly after The Great War. This was a great shock to Frieda who adored her Father. Her relationship with her Mother was difficult, as Emma was a hard working stern disciplinarian. All three children went to school, but also had to work in the store and deliver the poultry to the various stores and hotels that made up most of the clientele. The three children would strap on their roller skates and, lugging large bags filled with the poultry, would skate all over the city of Cologne to bring the chicken to the customers. Cologne's streets were already covered with macadam and you could skate from one end of the city to the other.

Frieda would tell of her adventures and those of her brothers. Among other souvenirs was the time she had to deliver chicken for the Prince of Wales, who was staying at one of the major hotels during the British occupation of the city, after the armistice of 1918. At the time, Frieda was nearly 17 and had to run a gauntlet of flirtatious British soldiers in order to deliver her precious cargo of chicken.

Once, Richard, having delivered chicken throughout the day, found himself fascinated on the way home, by a sidewalk dice game. He watched for a while, when suddenly, he put his hand in his pocket where he found a large sum of money, the proceeds of his day's deliveries. According to Richard, at the time he could not remember how all that money had gotten there. So, he joined in the game. In a short while, he had lost all his "found" money. Needless to say, this made a big to do when he got back to Mittelstrasse.

Paul, the youngest, was not in the best of health. On one of his deliveries, a man tried to rob him and Paul resisted. In the struggle, the robber pushed Paul down an elevator shaft and the fall and the experience, left him with a stutter that was to last for several years. He also had bouts with diabetes or bones attacked by TB and periodically had a leg in a cast. When that would happen, he could not deliver chicken. Instead, one of the store employees would take him to the nearby park, where Paul would sit on a bench and read or play the flute. One day, he sat at his usual place, set his cap on the bench near him and played the flute. People came by and dropped coins in his cap, feeling sorry for this poor child with the bad leg. When he got home that evening, he proudly showed his charity money. His parents, especially Emma, were mortified.

Frieda was petite but attractive, with jet-black hair, very dark brown eyes and alabaster skin. As a child, she had been made fun of by other kids, for having crooked legs. They would call her "bull". Frieda was put on a special diet of crushed egg shells to remedy her bad bones; apparently it worked. By the time she grew up, nature had remedied her problem and she was growing pretty. Frieda enjoyed traveling, went to Paris and Holland on her own and spent her summers at seaside resorts on the German north coast or on the Lake of Constance (Bodensee) on the German/Swiss border.

Frieda had learned to swim in the Rhine River, against the wishes of her Mother, who had also refused to pay for swimming lessons. Undaunted, Frieda, had a smith solder several cookies metal tins shut and strung these up in a buoy to fit around her waist and plunged on into the Rhine. She actually became quite a strong swimmer, a skill my sister Ruth inherited later while I inherited the swimming skills of Hilaire, my Father, which were not very good at all.

When Frieda met Hilaire, she immediately decided that he was the man she would marry. Unfortunately, when they met for the second time, she had just as quickly decided that she would have nothing further to do with him. Hilaire had crossed back into Germany to see Frieda again, but having no papers, he had asked her to meet him in Aachen, the border town where the *passeur d'hommes*, Mr Homburg, would arrange to smuggle him across for a few hours. Hilaire was insistent and kept imploring Frieda to see him again and to come to Charleroi. They had corresponded by letters written by Max as Hilaire was illiterate. She remembered how he had placed his hands around her shoulders, had shaken her and said "You must come, Fraulein, you must come". However, by that time, Frieda had already fallen out of love with Hilaire. If she gave him any hope, it must have been a scant one.

It is fair to note that, according to Hilaire's memoirs, his visit to Aachen was at the request of Frieda and that she had told him that her Mother wanted her to marry a big Dutchman, but that there was no other man in her dreams but Hilaire. Hilaire had been sensitive to this type of flattery, especially since it came from a pretty young lady, daughter of rich German/Jewish shopkeepers. Even though "he had absolutely no romantic feelings for her", it pleased his old Polish/Jewish complex. Frieda had also complained that she had had a fight with her brother Richard, during which she threw a coffeepot at his head. Hilaire, who abhorred violence, was taken aback and thought that he would not like to be in the skin of her future husband and become the target for a similar incident.

Meanwhile, Frieda took the train to Amsterdam to meet with her Hollander, whom her Mother wanted her to marry. Frieda rode all night and arrived in Amsterdam in the early hours of the morning. Her Dutch "fiancé" welcomed her at the train and asked in Dutch: *"Will U wat hebben?"* Which translated as "do you want to have something?". For Frieda, that was enough. He should not have asked her if she wanted something, but rather "What do you want to eat", not after a whole night's journey. Confronted with this lack of solicitude, she could not contemplate marriage to such a boor and took the very next train back to Cologne.

Back in Cologne, Emma Friedemann was very determined that Frieda should marry the Dutchman. Frieda was just as determined that she loathed him and would not consider marrying him. "It must be noted that when we speak of a "Dutchman", we are talking about a Jew living in Holland, who may or may not have been a Dutch citizen. His name was never known to me and I can only hope that he eventually found someone to marry and that he was able to survive the Holocaust that was to follow a dozen years later.

And so, Frieda sent a telegram to Hilaire, saying that she would arrive by train in Charleroi, at two in the morning and asking that he come and pick her up at the train station.

HILAIRE AND FRIEDA

Hilaire went to the station where Frieda came out and declared that she could not live without him and that she had run away from home to be with him and to get away from her Mother and the big Dutchman. All Hilaire could do was to give her one of the two rooms in the house he shared with Max and wait for the morning.

In the morning, when the two bachelors woke up, breakfast was ready and they found this much nicer that just the coffee they normally drank. Hilaire insisted that Frieda call her Mother, to reassure her, but once on the phone, Frieda announced that she had just become engaged to Hilaire. Hilaire found himself submerged; nobody seemed to pay any attention to his point of view. Of course, he was flattered to be distinguished by such a pretty girl, coming from a family much better off than his was. Hilaire still pined for Irma. According to him, he felt no irresistible attraction for Frieda.

Emma Friedemann urged the couple to come back to Cologne for a feast and betrothal. Hilaire was introduced as a rich Russian Jew, which flattered everyone's vanity. The civil marriage would take place in Charleroi, as soon as Hilaire were able to regularize his legal situation there.

Hilaire's birth certificate was sent for and translated and some papers finally put in order. On the 28th of July 1927, Frieda and Hilaire were married in Charleroi. Shortly thereafter, the religious ceremony was performed in the Glockengasse synagogue in Cologne. An immediate problem developed with the dowry, which turned out to be much smaller than what had been discussed. From then on a cold relation ensued with Frieda's family.

The newlyweds honeymooned in Ostende, a sea resort on the Belgian coast, known for its gambling casino. While there, they noticed couples in evening toilettes going in the *Kursaal,* the casino. Frieda remarked that when they became rich, they also would visit the Ostende *Kursaal* and mingle with the wealthy.

They settled down in Charleroi, where the house was now too small and they moved to Rue de L'Ecluse, in a three-story house, where Hilaire opened a luxury store, with modern furniture coming from Germany. He now drove a Fiat Prècis.

RUTH

There is little known to me about their first year together. Hilaire, worked hard to develop the business and Frieda helped out more and more. What is sure is that Frieda was homesick for her beautiful Cologne. She did not speak French and Charleroi was not a cheerful place. The air was filled with smoke and soot from the coal, glass and steel industries that surrounded the city. Around the outskirts of town and in the suburbs, coal miners, their lungs burned out, sat on stoops and coughed and spit out black or bloodstained saliva. The skies were traversed by smoke that rose from the factories and a dusty film was forever present. Like most towns in the Walloon area of Belgium, Mardi-Gras and Carnival were fully celebrated. However, the celebrations paled in comparison with the famed *Rosenmontag* celebrations of Cologne. Frieda's homesickness would always peak in that season.

Soon, Frieda became pregnant. Her Mother, Emma, wanted Frieda to come to Cologne for the birth. The reason being that Cologne and Germany were more advanced medically than Charleroi and Belgium. More to the point was the desire of Emma to show her friends that the child would be born after a full term, thus demonstrating the chastity of her daughter at the time of the marriage.

So, in July, Frieda left Charleroi and on July 31ˢᵗ 1928, she gave birth to a baby girl they named Ruth. Shortly thereafter, Frieda and Ruth moved back to Charleroi. Yet Ruth was issued a German birth certificate.

The relationship between Frieda and Hilaire soon became strained. It would be difficult to blame one or the other for the first misdeeds. Hilaire had a roving eye and Frieda was fond of men. Now and then, when Hilaire decorated a house, the lady of the house did not always pay him in money but in amorous affection. This did not help the financial situation of the business. At about the same time Hilaire became suspicious that Frieda was having an affair with an accountant by the name of Vandenbranden. Whether this happened early on or not, the fact is that Mr Vandenbranden surfaced now and again in the years that followed.

Frieda became more and more unhappy, spending hours crying and calling for her dead Father. She referred to Charleroi as *un trou* (a hole) and Belgium as "The pisspot of Europe", a reference, no doubt to the rainy weather that greeted every season.

I AM BORN

Around August 1929, Frieda and Hilaire drove to Waterloo, halfway to Brussels, for a few hours of sightseeing. The battlefield is about 30 kilometers north of Charleroi and a favorite weekend destination. In the middle of the plain that saw the defeat of Napoléon, the victorious allies erected a large mound topped by an enormous bronze lion made from melted French guns. Steep stairways rise along the man-made mountain and tourists can climb all the way to the lion.

Frieda and Hilaire climbed all the way up to view the panorama of the battlefield. On the way down Frieda felt faint and threw up. That was the first indication that she was pregnant again.

For Frieda, this was a catastrophe. Bad enough to be stuck with one child in a place like Charleroi, but to be stuck with two children was more than she could contemplate. This new life that began to stir in her body was for her yet another nail in her coffin. If she was ever to escape from this "hole", the pregnancy had to be terminated. She would find two doctors to perform an abortion. It was not difficult in Charleroi. Was Hilaire told of the second pregnancy? It is doubtful. However, as he walked in on the scene of the scheduled abortion, it must have become quite clear that another child was under way.

After Hilaire paid off the doctors and Frieda found herself still pregnant, life settled in again and all was made ready for the new birth. Whatever the reason, Frieda did not try to abort again. And so, on Mardi-Gras 1930, she entered the clinic and on Wednesday, February 26th, 1930, at three fifteen in the morning, I was born. I was named Rodolphe in French, or Rudolph in German.

At ten, the next morning, a Maria Dechevez, master midwife of the maternity who had assisted with the birth, appeared before the Charleroi authorities and declared, "In the absence of the Father" a child of the masculine sex had been born to Frieda Friedemann, wife of Hilaire Rosenberg and to whom she had given the name of Rodolphe. The name was chosen for Rudolph Valentino, the movie star, or Rudolph von Habsburg, a tragic and romantic figure of Imperial Austria/Hungary, or after Rudi, one of Frieda's heartthrobs of her youth. Frieda gave all three reasons for my name at various times.

Hilaire was full of joy. A son had been born. He blessed the good fortune that made him turn around and stop the abortion. A few days later, a "bris" was performed, a circumcision and I was given the Hebrew name of Mordecai.

Alida, a nursemaid, was hired. She was a large Flemish woman with generous breasts. I understand that we became inseparable. I was content to spend hours on end happily sucking away while resting my head on her chest. "This one, she used to say, he will love women".

I was born with distinctively Hebraic features. As a boy, my curly hair was so black that it reflected light in deep blue tones. My Mother always joked that my curly hair was the result of the winter cold in Charleroi, because during the final months of her pregnancy, her physician, Dr Matteau would place his cold ear on her belly to listen for my fetal heartbeat. Dr. Matteau had black curly hair and the shock of his frigid ear would make my Mother jump. Thus, my curly hair was a combined result of his cold ear and his curly black hair.

LIÈGE

For as long as my sister and I could remember, there was always a dark cloud about the city of Liège, a large industrial town near the German border. Whenever there was a fight between my parents or when Frieda wanted to say something negative about Hilaire, Liége was sure to come up. Usually, it was a sentence like "you don't know what your Father did to me in Liége". And, since Hilaire and Frieda had slugged it out about all subjects, one worse than the other, Ruth and I did not have enough imagination to conjure up what awful thing had happened in Liége.

When Frieda was in her late seventies, I was taping her memoirs and I asked her about that terrible Liége episode. She looked at me for a while. Then, she said "Ah, Liége, I recall, can you imagine?".

"It was about 1931 and there was a German film I wanted very much to see. It was "The Blue Angel" with Marlene Dietrich and Emil Jannings. The film, directed by Joseph von Sternberg had received great reviews but was also criticized for its immorality. Apparently, the film was not going to be shown in Charleroi. A dozen years after the Kaiser's troops had ravaged the town, there was no way a German film was going to be shown there and this was also a valid reason to bar the film without having to address the question of immorality. Liége was a larger city with perhaps broader views and Hilaire and I decided to go and see The Blue Angel there. We left Ruth and Rudy in the capable hands of Alida and drove to Liége. We had dinner, saw the film, but when we came out of the cinema, it was late, dark and raining hard. We decided that it would be dangerous to drive the few hours back to Charleroi that night and went about looking for a hotel where we could spend the night.

We found a small hotel which probably was used more for fast rendezvous than for all night stays. The clerk took one look at Hilaire and me and guessed that we were both there for a quick tryst, after all, we were both about twenty-eight and attractive. So, the clerk inquired "Is it for a couple of hours or for the night?"

I was mortified, this had never happened to me before. What kind of a place had Hilaire taken me to? Had he been there before and with whom?

Can you imagine?"

That was it? The dark mystery that we had wondered about all these years, that was it? I could not help to remark that Frieda, in subsequent years had surely spent many hours in "rendezvous" hotels that rented by the hour. Frieda agreed, but made the point of how naïve she had been as a young woman. "I was a virgin until the day I married. Can you imagine? How stupid I was! Besides, she continued, she had always preferred to make love in her own bed, in her own home."

And so, the dark mystery of Liége was lifted.

DEPRESSION

Violetta, Viole-e-tta,

Si je chante, c'est pour toi (La Traviata).

In the movie "A Lust for Life", the story of the Dutch painter Vincent Van Gogh, after finding out that he had no gift for the priesthood, yet wanting to minister to the poor, Van Gogh asked one of the church elders where he might go to find poor people he could help. The churchman points to a region on the wall map and says, "There, is a place where people are as miserable as in any other place on earth!" And the place he points to is the Borinage Region of Charleroi.

My Mother battled bouts of depression, although this mental illness was not as commonly diagnosed as it is today. She would spend hours sitting in a corner, facing the wall and crying out loud for her dead Father. "*Mein Papa, mein Papa*" she would cry out for hours at a time.

My memory of a particularly painful episode may have resulted from hearing stories when I grew older, but a vivid image remains in my mind's eye of a suicide attempt by my distraught Mother when I was about two years old. She had turned on the gas stove without lighting the burners, allowing toxic, deadly fumes to fill the kitchen and spread throughout the apartment.

Ruth would remember (she was nearly 4 years old). Mother was lying on a bed and Ruth practically sat on her and was trying to open Mother's eyes and crying "maman, maman". We are not supposed to remember what has happened when one is four or five years old but that was so traumatic that it has a special niche in my brain.

I do not know what happened next, whether others were in other rooms or had arrived home in time, but I can still picture Alida, our Flemish nursemaid, holding my sister and me in a tight grip as we were perched on the window ledge, overlooking the Rue de Marcinelle and breathing fresh air as our legs dangled above the street below.

Mother, depressed, had decided to kill herself by putting her head in the gas oven, a popular way of doing it in those early days of modern kitchens. She had every intention of taking her two beloved children, Ruth and Rudy to the grave with her. Only the lucky intervention by Alida had saved all three of us. The memory is vivid, even though no one ever mentioned the event to Ruth or me. It was only many years later that the story came to be repeated and during one of the many times Hilaire and Frieda fought in our presence. (*Hilaire wrote about it in his memoirs.*)

For the most part though, as I grew a little older, my Mother's temperament changed. I always felt loved as a child. She would hug me often and tell me that although I once was not wanted, I was now very important to her. I could remain in her arms, or Alida's, for hours, content and comfortable. Ruth, on the contrary, could not sit still for more than five minutes. Ruth would run away claiming she was too warm.

Hilaire was very upset when he got the news of the suicide attempt. Sure, he and Frieda had their differences, but he loved his children and was not a mean man. He worked hard, was absent a lot. There was a sharp contrast between their characters; Hilaire was calm, measured and a perfect gentleman. Frieda had a sharp tongue, quick temper and spoke faster than she could think. She also had the memory of an elephant and would never forget a slight, real or imagined.

In an effort to make Frieda's life more agreeable, Hilaire rented a small villa in Loverval, a pretty town within a short driving distance of Charleroi. We would go there mostly on Sundays. There were trees and a small garden around the house. I do not have any memory of the inside of the house but remember the house and the grounds quite well. There was also a public outdoor swimming pool in Loverval where Ruth and Mother would swim at length. Hilaire and I would watch, as we were the non-swimmers of the family. Frieda would swim from end to end for hours, bellowing like a seal at each turn. When dusk would fall, she was usually still there, swimming, turning, and bellowing. I remember being embarrassed by Frieda's showoff behavior, but in retrospect these were times when Mother was happy, proud of her figure, her athletic ability and the full measure of her femininity.

Although Frieda continued to be depressed, she never again tried to put an early end to her life. However, despite a mushroom-shaped, gold IUD (which she referred to as her *bague,* her ring), Frieda would get pregnant often. She would visit the *Maternite Reine Astrid* about once a year for an abortion.

THE CASINO

In Charleroi, life settled down. Hilaire was working hard at his trade and becoming more and more in demand, both for the quality of his work and for the tender ministration he was suited for. At the time, I was not aware of this side of my Father's, but Frieda had a great number of male friends who were introduced to Ruth and me as "Uncles".

The furniture business was known as Maison Hilaire, with Monsieur and Madame Hilaire. Ruth was *la petite Hilaire* and I was *le petit Hilaire.* No mention of Rosenberg appeared anywhere except on official papers and when Ruth and I began to go to school.

In the shop, my Father employed Alphonse, a Flemish cabinetmaker and polisher. Alphonse could curse bilingually, first in Flemish, then in French. He was short and stocky and had a bristling mustache that made him look like a French *Poilu* of the Great War. Once, while he was polishing some wood, I took a little hammer, and lightly struck the wood here and there, creating some dents. "*Gottferdekker van de nom de dieu*", he cursed, thus teaching me not only my first Flemish word but also my first profanity. I still have the hammer and the fateful double meter, for, through thick and thin, my Father kept most of his tools.

Hilaire and Frieda kept up a constant verbal battle, sometimes resorting to blows. This was done in our presence and Ruth and I spent many a tearful day trying to reason with these two belligerent adults. They argued mostly in German, this being the language in which they both could communicate best. German also had a special harshness to it and seemed ideally suited for their battles. Hilaire would call Mother a *sale Boche*, supreme insult in Belgium for someone coming from Germany. Frieda would retaliate by calling Hilaire a *dirty Polack*, an insult to which he was very sensitive. These words were heavy-duty artillery reserved toward the climax of a fight, when the need was felt to score a heavy blow.

As I said, Hilaire and Frieda also argued in German, as they did not want Ruth or me to understand what they were saying. As a result, we had a pretty good education in German, which became our second language, as we were treated to these lessons almost on a daily basis.

One day, after a particularly upsetting argument with Hilaire, Frieda left home and decided to get away for a while. She took the train to Ostende, the sea resort where they had spent their honeymoon only a few years earlier.

My Mother has always maintained that, as she walked along the *digue* (stone boardwalk) by the shore, the casino doorman invited her in. She sat down at a crowded roulette table. She had never been in such a gambling place before and was looking around, trying to figure out what to do next. The croupiers did not always pay close attention to which players were betting what and relied on the gamblers to keep track of their bets and when a pile of chips remained unclaimed, the croupier would inquire: *"A qui est ça?"* (Whose is this?). Frieda had replied *"A moi!* (Mine)." With that the croupier had pushed a huge pile of chips towards her with his *rateau*, the flat pusher used to rake in or push out the chips. She had grabbed the windfall, exchanged the chips at the cashier's window and left the casino. She had left so quickly; she did not even give the croupier a tip.

"Actually Frieda had been in a Casino at least once previously. Frieda together with her friend Rika from Hamburg (the same one who had informed Frieda that she was leaving for Paris) had previously visited the Kursaal in Wiesbaden, Germany but never shared any details with Ruth and me."

After purchasing a dress for herself and presents for Ruth and me, Frieda took the train back to Charleroi. As the business was in need of money, she gave the considerable remainder of her winnings to Hilaire, explaining how she came to get all that money. Hilaire, though happy to get the money, did not believe her story and accused her of having *fait Le Boulevard* (streetwalked). Frieda did not help matters by replying that if it was indeed that easy, she was sure to repeat it.

Hilaire, shortly thereafter, was introduced to gambling, as attested to in the following extract from his memoirs.

"One day, I had finished work in Lustin. On my way back to Charleroi, I drove through Namur to see the newly opened casino, which was decorated by De Coene. Everybody talked about it in Charleroi and I decided that I would go and take a look for myself. It would be my very first visit to a casino. Many others will follow, which could be, by themselves, the object of a much longer chapter before I decided with wisdom never to put my feet again in this type of establishment. On that day, I had only more or less one hundred francs in my pocket and to enter would cost twenty-five francs. So, I wound up with about seventy-five francs of chips, and I went to the gambling tables.

At the roulette, a big winner is being brought champagne buckets to put in his chips. Since I don't have the slightest idea what the game is about, I put my chips following the example of this winning person. By midnight, I have already won twelve thousand five hundred francs. Meanwhile, the director is consulted to find out if the table should be closed, or if this big winner should be allowed to continue. The director simply asked whether he is sitting or standing. Being told that he is sitting; he feels that he will not get up so soon and that he will continue to play. The sign is to let him continue and so they let him play on.

At about four o'clock in the morning, I had only eight thousand francs left and I decided to leave. According to witnesses that I saw later, the big winner lost everything and after that, they even had to lend him money so that he could take a streetcar."

Hilaire was hooked. Frieda and Hilaire had at last found something in common, gambling. They began to commute by train almost daily to Namur. One by one, all the casinos of Belgium became their enticers. Ruth and I began to know the map of Belgium by the proximity of the Casinos, besides Ostende and Namur; there was Dinant, Spa, Chaufontaine and the ones along the coast, Blankenberge, Knokke. But, by far, the most popular with my parents was Namur, only an hour from Charleroi by train.

Mother had developed a simple system which enabled her to eke out a meager living. It was a system that demanded discipline and patience and she had strangely found those two virtues when it came to gambling. Hilaire, on the other hand, soon tired of the roulette wheel, finding it too slow. He liked *Baccarat* and *Chemin de Fer* where an entire fortune could be made or lost with one turn of the cards, something he did quite often, unfortunately, mostly on the losing side.

Hilaire would see good omens everywhere. If he saw two nuns walking together, that was a good sign and he would drop whatever he was doing and was on his way to Namur. A single nun was bad luck, but as nuns were not allowed to travel alone, they always showed up in pairs. Hunchbacks were lucky signs too, one often stood outside the Namur Casino and the gamblers would rub his hunch before going in. If they won, he was sure to receive a big tip as they came out.

On one occasion, Hilaire made a killing in Ostende. When he returned to Charleroi he decided to purchase the house we lived in. He gave the owner a fifty thousand franc deposit and took on a mortgage for the balance. A few days later, he got cold feet and sold the mortgage to Monsieur Hecht, who had the *bonneterie* (hosiery) store next to us at the Rue de Marcinelle. There was a combination of needing the money back and Hilaire's basic feeling of insecurity. The memories of tales of pogroms in his native Poland would remain with him always and he never really wanted to own anything that was not liquid and that he could not stash in his pockets if he had to make a sudden exit.

The Depression hit Europe in the early thirties; the neglected business began to deteriorate. The stable life of the Famille Hilaire began to totter. In the years that followed, gambling became a destructive factor, but by a twist of fate, it eventually became one of the instruments that ensured our survival during the war years that would follow.

1934

C'etait un musicien qui jouait dans une boite de nuit'
Et toutes les jolies femmes venaient s'assoir autour de lui . . .
"He was a musician who played in night clubs
And all the pretty girls would come and sit around him . . ."

Although there was a lot of strife at home, I felt loved, especially by my Mother and I felt secure in my own little world. I was a strikingly beautiful child, I remember going to the Innovation, a department store in Charleroi, where the female store clerk would fill my cap, my casquette, with cookies and candy. I went to kindergarten, where I had a crush on little Christiane Fontaine, who looked just like Shirley Temple, with reddish blond hair she wore in ringlets. Sometime, when our Mothers took us shopping and we met in town, we would greet each other with big hugs and kisses. My Mother once joked to Christiane's Mother that, no doubt, these two would get married someday. That was not to be. One of those shopping trip meetings was the last time I ever saw her. She died while only five years old of what must have been leukemia.

I was only a few days shy of four years old at the time, but I still remember February 17th, 1934, the day King Albert of Belgium died in a mountaineering accident. He apparently fell from a cliff while doing some alpine climbing alone at Marche Les Dames, in the Belgian Ardennes; a place forever embedded in the folklore of Belgium. I was on the Place de la Ville Basse, market day, just a half-block away from our apartment, when the news spread like wildfire among the farmers selling their wares of the day. The crowd of shoppers reacted with an uproar when the news arrived that the king was dead. King Albert had been a hero of the Great War, standing up to the German invaders. He had even managed to keep a section of Belgium around the Yser River unoccupied by the Germans for the duration of the war. He was known as the Roi Chevalier, the Knight King and was widely adored, as was his wife Elizabeth, even though she was born a German Princess. There was a certain ironic coincidence that my Mother's Father, Phillip Friedemann, had fought in Belgium on the German side. King Albert's death struck the country in a stunning fashion, similar to the way the assassination of President Kennedy would, years later, affect the American population.

Not surprisingly, people wondered about the possibility of a conspiracy behind King Albert's death. Hitler had risen to power in Germany and his plan to dominate Europe was forming. There was concern that Albert, a nationalist who would undoubtedly strongly resist any advance by Hitler, may actually have been pushed over the cliff by Hitler operatives. Many people believed that Albert was too experienced an alpinist and the slopes he was climbing not unusually difficult, for him to have fallen accidentally. Still, to this day, no one knows what really happened.

Albert's son became King Léopold III. My memory is that he was not as loved as his Father had been. He had married Astrid, a Swedish princess, and they had two sons; Baudoin, who was my age, and Albert. There was also the eldest child, a daughter, Josephine-Charlotte. I also remember, but for reasons I can't recall, there were suspicions about Astrid's death in 1935, the year after her husband became king. The two of them were vacationing in Kussnach, Switzerland. He was driving an open car when he went off the road. Astrid was thrown out of the car and killed instantly. He escaped with a broken arm. Her death was traumatic for the country, as she was very beloved by all. I remember pictures and newsreels of King Léopold at the funeral, grief stricken, with his broken right arm in a sling and wearing a black armband over his army uniform. Memorial pictures of Astrid began to appear everywhere, from postage stamps to cookie tins. Schoolchildren across the country were saddened and special memorial events were organized for us, including a parade in Astrid's honor. The maternity hospital where I was born was renamed after Astrid. As I grew older and learned more, I abandoned the idea that Léopold was at fault. I came to realize that accidents do happen.

The fact was that in pre-war Belgium, a small nation, people felt a personal connection with the Royal family.

<u>1935</u>

La musique vient par ici,
Ohohoho hoho et sort par la . . .
"The music goes 'round and 'round
And it comes out here . . ."

We became aware of Hitler. Mother had a friend in Gilly, a suburb of Charleroi. Her name was Madame Lobet. She had a daughter, Rita, who was older than my sister Ruth. Madame Lobet was born in Germany and had married a Belgian. I never knew where Monsieur Lobet was, dead, divorced, he never appeared. Madame Lobet, still a German, had become enthralled with the Fuehrer and insisted that Frieda listen to his radio speeches. Madame Lobet felt he was a great man and would swoon at hearing him speak. Mother, while a born German, must have been aware of the anti-Semitic nature of Hitler's views and did not agree with the content of Hitler's speeches; however, she too was impressed by his spellbinding oratory.

My first memory of becoming aware of my Jewishness was in the fall of 1935. I remember sitting in the balcony with my Mother, at the Cinema Eden. Monsieur Den Hartog, a Jewish owner of all the movie theatres in Charleroi, had allowed the Eden to be converted into a temple for the Jewish High Holidays. I was sitting with my Mother in the balcony for the orthodox services—in which men and women were segregated—and looking down at the men with their prayer shawls, rocking back and forth in the almost musical recitation of the scriptures.

Such observances were rare for us as a family; for the most part, my parents did not promote their Jewishness in any way. My Father did observe some kosher dietary rules, but very loosely.

Most of my classmates were Christians. We were so immersed in Belgium's Catholic culture that we even celebrated Christmas. Indeed, one of the biggest holidays for me was December 6th, Saint Nicolas, celebrated mostly around the legend of Saint Nicolas and his miraculous reconstruction of three children, who had been chopped up by a butcher. We sang a lovely song based on the story in which one of the children says, "I thought I was in Heaven". The double doors of our school always seemed huge to me and I remember the arrival of Saint Nicolas, accompanied by a shower of "knickknacks", little, hard cookie, baked in all the letters of the alphabet, which we gathered and used to spell words. I always hesitated to eat my cookies because my words would then disappear. The magic disappeared one holiday, I was walking to the bathroom and noticed the fifth-grade teacher donning his Saint Nicolas costume. The Americanized myth of Santa Claus was not known in Belgium in those days and "Noel" (Christmas) was celebrated mostly by grownups.

My Mother sang "*Oh, Tannenbaum*" and "*Heilige Nacht*" (Holy Night) in German and always wound up crying and calling for her dead Father. My Father usually set up a little spindly Christmas tree on which he put some candles. He would light them and blow them out quickly before the tree caught on fire.

My parents had a few Jewish friends, mostly merchants. Monsieur and Madame Hecht had the hosiery store next to our store. Max Furst and his brother were fine tailors for men, but they also made suits for women, much to the delight of Frieda who enjoyed wearing neat, sharply tailored suits. Monsieur Khakoun, a tall, handsome North African Jew had a carpet store. He boasted that he had had every woman in Charleroi as a mistress. Frieda always made it a point of honor to remark that Khakoun had not had her. People would see me in the street and ask if I were the "*petit Khakoun*"? I'd answer: no, I am the "*petit Hilaire*". As far as I knew, the Jewish population of Charleroi was small. Of course, as always, Jews did not advertise that they were Jewish. They often used their first names instead of their last ones, so as not to be noticed. In school, I was close to Paulette Redlich, who was small and pretty, but I lost track of her and figured that she too had perished in the Holocaust that was to follow. I was to meet her again sixty-five years later, living in Brussels. She did not remember me, but we had coffee and sweets and a lovely afternoon.

My world revolved around the Rue de Marcinelle. Madame Nisole had a butcher shop, the *Boucherie* Nisole, across the street from where we lived. She was kind to my Mother. When we had no money, she provided food on credit or sometimes as a gift. With great care, I would cross the Rue de Marcinelle to go visit Madame Nisole, and she would reward my trip with cuts of *boudin noir* (black blood pudding), which I would eat with a little bit of white bread. This was almost pure pig blood and the best time to get some was on Tuesdays as by tradition, the pigs were usually slaughtered on Mondays. It was dangerous to cross the street, as the Rue de Marcinelle was one of the most commercial streets of Charleroi, wide and full of vehicular traffic. I returned there, decades later and was surprised to see how narrow the street was, with cars parked partway on the sidewalks so that one car could pass through the street.

Madame Marin operated a *friture* on the *Place de la Ville Basse*, where the specialty was *Moules & frites,* the traditional Belgian dish, always served *mariniere*, where the mussels swam mostly in an onion and celery broth. There are many ways to prepare mussels, but my favorite will always be *mariniere*. Madame Marin had a son, Maurice Marin, about my age and I would visit the restaurant and be treated with a free serving of *Moules & Frites.*

Of course, mussels and black blood pudding were not kosher, but I knew nothing about dietary restrictions, or even about the word *kosher*. Even today, the odor of mussels triggers a flood of memories. As Proust had his Madeleines, I have my mussels.

As a boy, I was not allowed to wander far afield in the city on my own. We lived on the Rue de Marcinelle, downtown, a few blocks from the Sambre River, not far from the railroad station. The place de la Ville Basse was the heart of Charleroi, where each February, they had the carnival feast procession, which I loved. Besides the many floats, my favorites were the Gilles de Binche, traditional Mardi Gras figures. Although the center for the Gilles was the nearby town of Binche, most towns in the Borinage had their own version and group and the Gilles would come to town and dance mightily for Carnival.

The origin of the Gilles came from the Incas of South America. Their costumes had been brought back after the first explorations of the New World. The Gilles wore white costumes, decorated with red and black motifs. They had a large hump in front and in back. Huge ostrich plumed hats crowned their heads and wooden *sabots* (clogs) clapped on the cobblestones as they danced. The dance was a slow, rhythmical turning, in cadence with the music played by a small band of musicians. The Gilles carried oranges in long, cylindrical wicker baskets, as they danced, they would toss oranges into the crowd, this in memory of the strange fruit, guavas and mangoes, brought back from the Americas, hundreds of years ago.

The snare drum would roll out a few beats. The trumpet followed with a few notes of the tune to be played next, from a tight group of ten or a dozen Gilles songs. Then the few brass instruments would blare out the tune, punctuated by the snare drum and the strong beat of a bass drum. The moment was electric, the crowd would cheer, the Gilles would dance, the oranges would fly in the air. If you were lucky, the music would play as the procession passed near you.

My Mother, who remembered the immense carnival festivals of her native Cologne, was always disappointed by the carnival of Charleroi and would usually be in a deep depression about that time.

Crossing the bridge over the Sambre River, you came to the *Rue de la Montagne,* "the Mountain Street". You could walk up to the Boulevard de l'Yser, where the middle city was laid out and continue on to the upper city, where the City Hall towered over the *Place de la Ville Haute.* Horse chestnut trees lined the boulevards. The carillon played the song of Charleroi on the hour, the words of which we had learned in school "Land of Charleroi, it is you that I prefer, the nicest place on earth, it is you, yes, it is you." My Mother always found it ironic. As for me, years after leaving Charleroi, tears would flood my eyes just at the thought of the song. As Frieda longed for Cologne, I would come to long for Charleroi.

At the base of the Rue de la Montagne, there was a small newspaper stand. In front of it, rolled a *homme-tronc,* a "trunk-man" on a small wooden platform fitted with four tiny wheels He was placed on this platform, had no legs, and seemed to have been cut below the hips. He wore a cap, a dirty gray jacket over an open shirt and fingerless black gloves. Two blocks of wood, strapped to his hands, made clacking sounds as he stroked them on the pavement to propel himself around the newspaper stand. I guessed he was a beggar, perhaps a wounded veteran of the Great War.

I never saw him get any money, but he was at his post, Rue de la Montagne, each day, summer and winter. He would occupy my thoughts, late in the evening, as I would wonder about how he got dressed, went to the bathroom, got into bed. I would see him in my nightmares, rolling full speed after me, his wheeled platform flying in the air, barely missing my head. One day, I asked my Mother all the questions I had about him. She told me he was a poor man and that I should stop thinking about him. Like magic, the nightmares left me, even though the *homme-tronc* kept up his vigil next to the newspaper stand.

King Charles of France had created Charleroi in the sixteenth century, as a fortified tow to prevent access to France from armies coming from Germany. It had substantial hills and sat strategically on the Sambre River, but it failed every time an army came through. Charleroi was pretty much destroyed by the Germans in the Great War, and would be severely damaged again during the Second World War that was looming on the horizon.

Situated in the heart of the Wallonia, the French speaking half of Belgium, its population spoke French, but also the Walloon dialect of the region. Although I was born in Charleroi, the dialect was not familiar to me, as my parents had enough trouble getting along in French to bother with the dialect. I knew a few bad words and expressions, but not to the point where I could converse with my school friends. However, in 1935, there was to be a Festival of the Walloon Rooster, (as opposed to the Lion of Flanders). The school children of Charleroi were to be assembled on the Place de la Ville Basse, and sing traditional songs of Wallonia. We learned about a dozen songs in Walloon, songs that I remember to this day. These were the only formal words and phrases I ever learned in the language of my place of birth.

In June, as the school year ended, we had to participate in a graduation ceremony prior to which all the children were to perform on the school stage. I do not remember what I was involved in, but I do recall that I was on the stage, next to Paulette Redlich, pretty Paulette, whose family of Jewish origin came from Poland, as did my Father.

My sister Ruth had been enlisted for a musical number where all the girls performed on stage and danced, lifting colored balloons over their heads. It was a dreamy number, danced to slow music. Ruth had been rehearsing in our home for several days. She would pretend to be carrying a balloon over her head, singing *"Les reves, sont des bulles de savon, qui montent vers le ciel comme un air de chanson"*. (Dreams are soap bubbles that climb towards the heavens like a song.).

On the big day, Ruth and the other girls in her class entered the stage, lined up and began to sing, the colored balloons held high over their head. The auditorium was filled with friends and parents. I sat near the front, with our Mother, very proud to see Ruth dancing in the middle of the first row of girls. "Dreams are soap bubbles, that . . ." POW!' Ruth's balloon exploded with a huge bang. Ruth stood there, arms extended over her head, holding on to nothing but air. Her eyes got bigger, her mouth turned down and crying very loudly, she ran off the stage. At the age of seven, that was the end of her stage career.

PAUL

The store in the Rue de Marcinelle was much nicer than the old place, Rue de L'Ecluse. There was the storefront and a showroom on the second floor. There was also a sewing *atelier* and the living quarters. In the back of the store, Hilaire had installed a decorating shop, a shop for polishing and an office. The kitchen was in the back, overlooking a garden with a hawthorn tree.

Frieda worked hard in the store, took care of the children, cleaned, cooked and did the bookkeeping. At night, she was tired and not always in an amorous mood. Hilaire, absorbed by the business, seemed unable to perceive to what extent Frieda became unhappy. Up until his marriage,

Hilaire had known only easy loves, encounters without tomorrows, hurried embraces which had not prepared him in any way to become a partner, if not ideal, at least acceptable to Frieda.

Without being aware of his own failings, Hilaire reproached Frieda for her lack of enthusiasm and soon, her coldness. Each one nursed his own reproaches, sure of his righteousness and blaming the other for this fiasco.

Frieda found special rewards in the construction and decoration of large salon dolls, a popular item assembled from prefabricated arms, legs and heads sewn into fancy dresses for display on sofas in the petit salons of Charleroi homes. These were very popular and sold well. Displayed in the storefront window, they attracted customers, who would come in, leading to the purchase of larger items of furniture One of our neighbors in Loverval ordered a dining room, but it had to be of smaller dimensions because she lived in a small house. She came to the store just as the furniture was being unpacked, where it sat pell-mell in the entrance. She told Hilaire of her strong disappointment. "That furniture is hideous ". Hilaire pretended that it must have been a mistake, because a second dining room would be arriving soon, probably the one that was destined for her.

Meanwhile, Hilaire displayed this "hideous" dining room set in the *vitrine,* the shop window. Sommetime later Hilaire advised the lady that the second dining room had just been delivered and that she should come and take a look at it. She saw the set in the window and told Hilaire that it was exactly what she wanted and what a difference it was from the other one. Hilaire agreed with her, the dining room set was delivered to her home in Loverval to everyone's satisfaction.

In late summer, Paul, my Mother's younger brother, arrived from Cologne to stay with us in Charleroi. Although we were not a party to the discussions, Ruth and I became aware that, because of the worsening situation for Jews in Hitler's Germany, Paul had decided to leave Germany and try to make it to the United States of America. Paul had married a woman, whose name was Mossbach, who came from one of the best families in Cologne and she now lived in New York, but he had not been able to rejoin her. He had a visa to travel from Cologne to Charleroi and a visa to go from Holland to New York. However, he had no visa to travel from Belgium to Holland, where he would have to find passage on a ship from Rotterdam to New York. Paul had said that once in New York, he would divorce Mossbach.

Not knowing how long he would have to wait, Paul would stay with us Rue de Marcinelle. In the meantime, he would learn the interior decorating trade from Hilaire. Unfortunately and despite a lot of good will, Hilaire soon realized that Paul was absolutely not suited for this trade and that handling a hammer would always be a mystery for him.

I came to like my uncle Paul. He was very quiet; never spoke much, unlike his older brother Richard, who had chosen to remain in Cologne and unlike Frieda who would plunge with enthusiasm into any subject of conversation. Frieda spoke with a heavy German accent and readily mixed German and French with some Yiddish. Mr LeMaitre, who would become an assiduous visitor of my Mother's in the years to come, was fond to say that, if MmeHilaire were to lose her accent, she would lose fifty percent of her charm.

Uncle Paul had picked up a few words of French and would amuse Ruth and me with short, funny phrases. He was also able to purse his lips and emit a high-pitched sound akin to a cat's meow that would send me into laughter. Paul would sing parts of the Belgian national anthem, substituting Ruth's name for a few key words. This always annoyed Ruth, who would protest good-naturedly. I did appreciate his jokes, as these were a relief from the tensions that were generated every time our parents got together.

In early fall each year, Charleroi held a *Braderie,* a street fair during which the stores sold products in front of their windows, on the sidewalk. For the *Braderie,* Hilaire would buy from Villeroy & Boch, a truckload of vases and other decorative objects that had been unsuitable for sale at the factory because of minor defects. Large quantities of pillows were fashioned with leftover cloth accumulated during the year. This gave the customers the illusion that they had made a wonderful buy, while providing a good profit to the store.

Mother's salon dolls were the chief attraction and sold at a fast pace. These were beautiful, decorative and quite fragile. Paul churned up the sales with a good-natured *"incassable, pas laisser tomber"* (Unbreakable, do not drop.)

Paul was anxious to leave for America and at night discussed the various means by which he might be able to cross the border into Holland. From Rotterdam, he would be free to board a ship to New York and rejoin his American wife. One morning, he kissed us "goodbye" and with his suitcase in hand, left for Rotterdam. The following day he returned, having been refused entry into Holland and expelled back to Belgium. Several times over the following weeks, he would leave us again, each time we'd find Paul back in Charleroi after a short absence. Our emotional "Goodbye" became more and more routine, as we felt that Paul would always reappear the next day.

On the sixth or seventh departure, we gave Paul a distracted sendoff. He never showed up again. We heard that he made it to Brooklyn, in America and settled in with his wife. In due time, he learned the trade of watch making and repairing, using tiny hammers, which proved that we must not be hasty in concluding of someone's lack of skill, when they simply are confronted by a trade they are not suited for.

<u>1936, BOULEVARD DE L'YSER</u>

Ah, sweet mystery of life,
At last I found you . . .

Whatever the reason, the end of 1935 saw the bankruptcy of the Maison Hilaire. We had to abandon the house and the store in the Rue de Marcinelle. Hilaire was able to repay most of his creditors, thanks to a combination of luck at the casino and being retained by Mr Hecht to decorate his newest store location, which turned out to be in the house we had just vacated.

My Father found a house to rent at 36, Blvd de l'Yser. The boulevard cut the city in two between the lower and higher areas of town. It was lined with huge horse chestnut trees. They dropped their spiked fruit on the center concourse, which ran between the two sides of the street. I found the house to be fabulous. It had three stories, a veranda above the street and my parent's interior decorating store on the street level. In the back, behind the kitchen, ran a long garden with a brick path all enclosed by a red brick wall topped with red tiles.

Mother's most frequent dessert was pudding, I can still remember walking in the house and being entranced by the smell of vanilla as the pudding cooled, still steaming, lined up on the kitchen window sill to dry in little yellow bowls with blue, red or black polka dots. My great pleasure was breaking the skin of the cooling pudding and dipping into the delicious soft center. Another favorite was milk soup, a combination of milk, tapioca and raisins.

Next to our house stood a church, which was reputed for being a center for miraculous occurrences, from healing the afflicted to resolving personal problems, especially marriage difficulties. I must say that being next to that church did not seem to have any beneficial effect on the relationship between Hilaire and Frieda.

The caretaker for the church had a son, Albert Coquet and we became good friends, almost inseparable. Poor Albert was slightly off, I did not know if he was retarded, but he did have a speech impediment. He was unable to pronounce my name correctly. Instead of "Rodolphe" the best he could manage was "Lugo". Albert had a little bicycle with training wheels that he let me ride. The trouble was that the training wheels were all crooked and would sometimes hit the ground at the worst possible time, sending the bike out of control. On one occasion, as I was racing down the brick path in the garden, going full speed, in imitation of Romain Maes, a Belgian cyclist who had just won the Tour de France, the third wheel locked and propelled the bike towards the right brick wall. I could not stop. I careened for a few painful meters, scraping my right arm against the rough bricks and leaving long strips of my skin bleeding on the wall.

Albert started to scream and cry. I was just numb, looking at the raw flesh of my right arm. Mother ran out of the kitchen, armed with a towel and a bowl of vanilla pudding which she proceeded to spoon into my mouth. Then, after dabbing the blood off my arm, we went to the nearby clinic for summary repairs. I remember nothing more about the incident, except the sweet taste and aroma of the vanilla pudding.

As there is the "five o'clock tea" in England, in Belgium, there is the *goûter*. At four in the afternoon, tradition dictates that one have a cup of coffee, with a sandwich, or more properly a *tartine,* a slice of white bread with butter and *confiture*. Grownups usually had some dry cookies with their coffee. On one occasion, as Albert and I were playing on the sidewalk in front of the store, *goûter* time came around and we ran into the kitchen where Mother was busy pouring the vanilla pudding into the polka dot bowls. The aroma of the vanilla had invaded the whole house. As I entered the kitchen, I asked my Mother for a *tartine*. Albert was right behind me. In an imploring tone he said *"Mange un pudding, Lugo, mange un pudding!"* Although he was a bit retarded, he was not dumb. And he knew that if I got to eat a pudding, he would surely get to eat one too. Mother laughed and we each received a pudding for our *goûter.* In the years that followed, neither my Mother nor I ever forgot Albert Coquet and *"mange un pudding, Lugo".*

THE MAID LEONA, *LA SERVANTE*

At the house, Frieda was working harder and harder. We had two seamstresses and one *garnisseur* whose main task was to cover and finish armchairs. Mother cooked, cleaned the large house, kept the books for the business, still produced the salon dolls and took care of the two children. In addition to these tasks, she would be the one who would change and maintain the window display. And despite all these occupations, Frieda and Hilaire still found time to escape to the casinos, mostly the one in Namur. As far as I know, they went there separately, as they would get into frequent arguments if they were together.

One day, a friend, Madame Den Hartog, walked into the store as Frieda was working and cleaning the window display. Madame Den Hartog remarked that Frieda should not be working so hard and since the business was doing well, it would be a good idea to hire a maid. And she knew just the person Mother should hire. She recommended a maid by the name of Léona Kohlen. She did not tell Frieda that her husband, Monsieur Den Hartog, had been having an affair with this Léona. She also omitted to mention that her son had been sleeping with the maid whenever her husband was away. She was glad to get rid of her and to pass her on to my Mother. Léona was to prove attractive to my Father too.

Léona was a very attractive wench. Healthy dark brown hair flowed around her dark skinned face. Her body was well formed, her breasts well delineated. She wore mostly black short-sleeved dresses and exuded sensuality. By then, although I was only six or seven, she held a fascination for me. Often, as we sat at the dining table, Léona would take a sip of water from her glass, toss her head back, open her mouth and with a spasm of her throat she would propel a fine mist of water in the air. The mist would arc in the air and sprinkle back to the table to the delight of Ruth and me. If we sat close enough, we could feel the mist settling on our faces. I could have sat there for hours and would beg Léona to do it again and again. Léona must have had other talents my Father was aware of, but for me, I was conquered by what was, in retrospect, an ability to spit water in a fine mist.

Father and Léona soon began an affair that went on secretly for a while. If Frieda had any suspicion, we were not aware of it. One day, we had all been on an excursion trip to Dinant, near Namur. We had driven there in the black 1930 Plymouth sedan Hilaire had bought from the lawyer who had prepared his bankruptcy papers. I had wanted something, which both my parents refused to buy. I was disconsolate, until Léona spoke up. She told me that I should not worry, that as soon as we were back in Charleroi, she, Léona, would prevail upon Hilaire and he would buy me what I had been refused in Dinant.

This statement, that attitude, struck Frieda like a bolt of lightning. At that moment, she understood that Hilaire was sleeping with Léona. A monstrous fight broke out, in front of Ruth and me. Frieda, Hilaire and Léona got out of the car and a violent argument ensued, until, in a total fit of exasperation, in a symbolic gesture, Hilaire threw his wedding ring from the bridge into the Meuse River below.

Things got a bit calmer after that and we drove back to Charleroi. The day had turned to night; the rain was pelting the windshield of the Plymouth. The two tiny wipers were streaking the windshield in separate rhythms. Hilaire was driving. Léona sat on the passenger side, next to him. Ruth and I were sitting in the back with Mother who cried and called for her dead Father all the way back to the Boulevard de l'Yser.

The next day, Hilaire and Léona drove away together in the 1930 Plymouth. They had gone on to Liége, where Léona came from. As it turned out, Hilaire found out that Léona had another boyfriend in Liége. Two weeks later he returned to our house in Charleroi, his ego well bruised and quite bitter about the whole escapade. Mother greeted his discomfiture with the appropriate sarcasm and another big argument erupted. In a fit, Hilaire declared that all women were whores.

Frieda, never at a loss for counter punches, fired back "And so is your Mother". This was a terrible blow to Father who idolized his Mother. He broke off the fight, leaving Frieda to savor her retort over and over again. For years afterwards, she would repeat "And so is your Mother" savoring each word with obvious delight. When I recorded Frieda's memoirs more than forty years later, she relished the phrase as much as she had on that day in 1936.

The fight over Léona Kohlen had ended, but the memory of the incident would linger on for decades and in the fights that followed through the years, the recriminations about *la servante,* the maid, would surface again and again. Hilaire's relationship with Leona continued for at least six more years although she had stopped working for us in 1936.

The breakdown of the relationship between our parents was almost complete now and Father would disappear, going off to live elsewhere for short periods at first, but longer as time went on. This left Frieda unable to pay bills and we depended again on the generosity of shopkeepers who would give Mother Credit or outright gifts of food.

At her wit's end, Frieda took us, by train, to visit her Aunt Rosa, who lived in Amsterdam. I remember her as a smiling, heavy set, friendly and kind woman. She was the sister of Emma Friedemann my GrandMother. While in Holland, we took a side trip to Vollendam, where even in 1936 Dutch villages still existed in the old fashion, albeit for tourists. Ruth and I were photographed in traditional Dutch costumes with wooden shoes. At several dikes, old fishermen, carrying large whicker baskets, offered freshly smoked eels we ate with delight.

We were to stay there a couple of days. However, Ruth and I quickly became aware that Frieda had decided to leave us there. Frieda made ready to return to Charleroi, while Ruth and I were to stay with *Tante* Rosa. We wanted nothing of that. In a scene reminiscent of a Dickens novel, we began to cry and carry on with such theatrical skills that Frieda relented and took us back to Belgium with her. We never saw *Tante* Rosa again. She was to perish in the Holocaust, deported to Poland like so many other Dutch Jews. Poor *Tante* Rosa, so kind, so loving, how we must have wounded her heart. And yet, had we stayed with her, we would have perished with her, just a bare five years later.

In school, we talked about the Civil War in Spain. Franco was the villain. We played "war" during *recreation* (recess) and the bad guys were the German and Italian "volunteers" fighting to help Generalissimo Franco. Mussolini and Italy were subjects of derision for their handling of the war in Ethiopia. Emperor Haile Selassie became a hero to us, although we did not know what to think about a black man walking around in a black bed sheet.

Charleroi was a center of Socialism. On May Day, a large gathering of workers paraded through the streets and on the Boulevard de l'Yser, in front of our store. The majority of the merchants was conservative and resented the power of the syndicates. So, while the parade was marching by, the merchants would scrub the sidewalk in front of their shops. With huge scrubbing brooms and soapy water, they would force the water into the marching workers. Somehow, it never turned ugly.

In Charleroi, Mother had befriended Mr and Mme Pesch. Monsieur Jean Pesch was the director of the Glassworks of Charleroi. In the mid-thirties, he had been named director of the Glassworks factory in Zeebruge and had moved to Blankenberge on the seacoast of Belgium. Monsieur and Madame Pesch were of Luxembourg origin and Madame Pesch was my Mother's confidante. She spoke perfect French and German, as well as Letzeberger, the dialect of Luxembourg. They had three children, Jean, the eldest, probably ten years older than I, Claudie, who was maybe three or four years older than my sister and Colette, my favorite, about the same age as Ruth.

To us, the Peschs were wealthy, they lived in a big house, had nice furniture and a stable home. Behind the house, was a large garden with a brook running alongside the property. Everyone would swim there, while mostly I stood on the bank and watched and ogled Colette. When my parent's marriage began to deteriorate and erupt in disagreement, Mother would pack my sister and me and take us by train to Blankenberge to stay at the Pesch house. I loved to go there because we could go to the seashore. Jean was especially solicitous to me, like a Father figure. Madame Pesch was a heavy chain smoker; I do not recall ever seeing her without a cigarette. She had a thin bony face and wore a scarf as a turban over her head. She had the habit of constantly biting her lower lip with her upper teeth, a little like a chipmunk. The only time she would stop was to take puffs from her cigarette. The Peschs attended Catholic Church regularly and on Sunday we would join them in the services.

On the beach, we would be treated to *Boules de l'Yser*. These were large doughnuts, filled with jelly and covered with powdered sugar. On windy days, you did not know if you were eating the sugar or the sand. Whatever, it tasted just grand. These used to be called *Boules de Berlin,* however after the Great War the name had been changed to *Yser,* in memory of the gallant four-year battle of the Belgian army under King Albert. Men, carrying large baskets on their heads, would peddle these pastries, hawking them with heavy foreign accents. For a few francs, you could savor one *Boule de l'Yser,* dough, jelly, sugar and sand.

There, I saw my first Orthodox Jews. In the hot sun, the bearded man wore a long black coat, black shoes laced very high and a black fur hat. His wife was fully covered with clothing. They had a little girl who kept running away. And the man was running after her, calling "*Kim, Charlotte, Charlotte kim"* in Yiddish. They must have been refugees from Germany or Jews from Antwerp. They seemed a Jewish world away from us.

Sometimes, we were allowed to visit the glass factory, a huge industrial complex where rolled glass was being produced. There were high mountains of coke (high temperature distilled coal) all over the factory grounds used in the glass manufacture. Though black on the outside, an inferno raged on the inside as the red-hot slag took weeks to cool off. Jean had shown me how one could insert a stick in its innards and watch as the stick began to smoke and burst into flames. We would walk along dodging the little locomotives that traveled along narrow rails, shuttling loads of sand or coal between buildings. The drivers would toll the bells to warn us as they passed by. There and then I made up my mind that this would be my job when I grew up.

The Pesches had two dogs, Tommy, a little tan and white wire-haired fox terrier and a German shepherd named Djahli. They would always accompany us on our visits to the factory. On one of our visits, Tommy, the terrier, jumped into a mountain of leftover burning coal that was cooling off. It was like a volcano, black on the outside, white hot, glowing, on the inside. Tommy was horribly burned. Djahly jumped after him and grabbed him in his jaws and pulled him out. But, Tommy was beyond saving. We spent a couple of days in the Pesch home, watching poor Tommy die. We were all around him, all the children and Djahly, crying. That was to be my first memory of death.

About the time of the Leona Kohlen affair, Mother took Ruth and me to visit her Mother Emma Friedemann and her brother Richard in Cologne. I have almost no recollection of that visit. I remember that there was a lot of whispering. In hindsight, I imagine that there must have been many discussions about our life in Charleroi. Surely, they could not have contemplated that we move back to Germany where the political situation was very tense. It would have been crazy for Jews to move to Germany where repression against Jews increased with each passing week.

We did receive two huge Teddy bears, which we carried in our arms back to the train as we left to return to Charleroi. At the border, two German customs officers, in their military uniform, seized the two Teddy bears, not allowing us to take them to Belgium with us. Ruth and I cried all the way back to Charleroi.

After the summer, we were back in school, a great refuge from the daily strife at home. Now and then, we would go and visit Max and Siegfried Furst. We'd spent many a happy hour in their tailor shop. Max was tall and handsome in a craggy way. He looked like Arthur Miller of later days. Leo was less striking, being more portly, but both were always impeccably dressed. They wore snappy Homburgs and were never without a cigarette. Their entire house was filled with the odor of tobacco and it was somehow pleasing to my senses. Whenever we had raffle tickets to sell for school, we would make a beeline for their shop, as they would always generously buy a book or two.

The only drawback was that they did not have indoor toilets. There was an outhouse. It was dark and smelly. The bench with a hole in it was too high for me and I had to make great feats of skill to arc my pee in such a way that it went in the hole. This, of course without touching the black, wet wood. Doing anything else, which would have required that I sit on the board, was out of the question.

I had also discovered the movies. My favorite *Cinema* was in the Rue de la Montagne, halfway between the Sambre River and the Boulevard de l'Yser. The spectacle was *continu*. You could go in early, pay only once and see the same movie over and over again. I'd often fall asleep and would wake up only when the action got violent and very noisy. Sometimes I'd only remember one or two scenes that I had seen time and again between snoozes. I cannot remember where I got the money; perhaps it was thanks to the generosity of Max Furst.

Now and then, during intermission, talking color slides were projected, advertising various stores. They were introduced by another slide, showing a black Congolese bellboy, with a pillbox hat. A poor-sounding ditty would play asking for the viewer's attention. Then the slides were projected. The slides were made of glass and usually showed cracks or missing corners. There was still one for the Maison Hilaire, our furniture store, although it still showed our old address, Rue de Marcinelle. It made me feel very special to see our name on the screen. After the last slide, the saluting *Sambo* would reappear, the ditty would play, and the lips would move and shout "*Werci*". This I guessed was for *Merci*, which the Congolese were not supposed to pronounce correctly.

Here I was, waking up in the middle of the Indians attacking the cowboys, or was it General Custer? Anyway, it was Gary Cooper (as Wild Bill Hickok) in "The Plainsman", except that it was called "Buffalo Bill" in the dubbed version. He got shot in the end. A scene in Michel Strogoff, with Anton Walbrook also impressed me. When enemy agents capture the hero, they torture him by placing a red-hot iron bar on his eyes. At that moment, he thinks about his Mother and tears protect him from being burned and losing his eyesight! It was terrific! Or it was Tarzan, the only one, Johnny Weissmuller and Maureen O'Sullivan. It was always the same scene, the savages are attacking and they give them salt, lots of salt, which seems to be the only thing they are after. They never ran out of salt, no matter how many times I slept through the rest of the movie. And Cheetah, finding a box of Kleenex and pulling them out, one at a time. This really fascinated me. I had never seen a paper tissue, or a Kleenex, or a dispensing box.

And after the movie, I'd walk back up the Rue de la Montagne, my head full of dreams of Wild Bill Hickok and Buffalo Bill and America. And often, as I walked, rain would be my companion, beating on the wings of my ears not well covered by my *casquette*.

1937

Bei Mir Bist Du Scheen
Bei Mir Bist Du Scheen

Our Father was to continue his affair with Léona Kohlen for several years. Now and then he would disappear for weeks, usually taking whatever money was available at the time. Once, we had sold a dining room and Frieda had put all the money in a drawer. Hilaire found the money, took it and left for Liège and Léona for several weeks. We had absolutely no money and there was a butcher and a baker who lived nearby. They would put food at the door of our house and leave it there for us.

At least, when Father was away, there was no fighting at home. Mother would prepare whatever food was available; it must have been very hard on her. If we had meager rations, there was always a little something to eat, like the milk, tapioca and raisins soup, which I loved.

At the corner of the Rue *de la Montagne* and the *Boulevard de l'Yser,* stood the *Bon Marché,* a large department store. I was intrigued by the corner, which had been draped over for several weeks. Then, one day, as I was returning from school, the draperies had been removed and the most fabulous windows dazzled my eyes. *Blanche Neige et les Sept Nains,* Snow White and the Seven Dwarfs, had been produced by Walt Disney and the *Bon Marché* had devoted three large windows to the promotion of the picture. The first window featured a road leading to a cave in a high mountain. A parade of dwarfs marched into the cave, singing "Hi Ho, Hi Ho". The second window opened inside the cave and was filled with glittering diamonds of all colors. The seven dwarfs worked there, with picks and shovels, loading diamonds onto wheeled carts, singing about the joys of working in the diamond mines. In the third window, the dwarfs were leaving the mine and the mountain, going home again, all the while singing "Hi Ho, Hi Ho". It was marvelous. I would stand there for hours, slipping from one window to the other, my nose and hands glued to the shop windows. It was a world of fantasy, full of beauty and light, so much in contrast with the drab sooty surroundings of Charleroi.

Frieda was less and less at home, taking the train for Namur and its gambling casino almost daily. There would be a set of regular cronies she would travel with. Among these, Bernard Horowitz, a childhood friend from Cologne. He and his wife had taken refuge from Hitler in Belgium and wound up in Charleroi. Late at night, the gamblers would take the last train back to Charleroi and if they had any money left, would sit in the *Wagon Restaurant* and order food. One night, the only food left were ham sandwiches. Upon hearing the news, Bernard complained to the waiter that ham was not kosher. The waiter shot back "One of these days, you will be happy to eat *merde*(shit)". These were prophetic words, as Bernard Horowitz wound up as a slave laborer, slaving on the Atlantic Wall for the Germans in the later years of the war.

There were times when Hilaire and Frieda went together to the casino to gamble, it was a passion they had in common. Yet, there was a basic difference in their approach to the games. Frieda would follow her little system and eke out a few dozen francs. Hilaire went in with the purpose of breaking the bank, making the big score. On one such occasion, they had driven to Namur in the Plymouth. Mother just wanted to go and have dinner, while Father decided to go in and play *Baccarat*. Frieda sat in the car for a while and a valet came and told her that Mr Hilaire was asking for her, inside. And she went inside and he was broke. And there they were in Namur, with no money, no food. And they drove back to Charleroi in the Plymouth. And then, they lost the store on the *Boulevard de l'Yser,* because they had no money left and could not pay the rent anymore. Most of our belongings were seized by the local *huissier* baliff, to be sold to pay our debts. By law, the beds were exempt from confiscation and we piled clothes and useful items, such as cooking pots, on top of the bed. The *huissier* seemed like a decent man, but my sister and I were traumatized by the event. We clung to our Mother while watching the eviction. Hilaire was not there.

We moved to a house at 7 *Rue d'Orleans*, a street on a steep incline, in the upper part of Charleroi. The house was very dark and narrow, with circular stairs connecting one floor to the next. We occupied only one floor, shared one bedroom, which was sufficient since Hilaire was away most of the time. We had a big Singer sewing machine and Frieda made a living sewing. When she was not working, I spent long hours playing with the sewing machine, pretending it was my automobile. I'd be pumping the pedals furiously, making car noises. Sometimes I took a chair, laid it flat on the floor, straddling the back of it and holding on to the seat with my feet stretched out as though I were in a racing car. The chair's back was curved, and it tipped when I made turns. In my imagination, I achieved fantastic speeds very safely, unless I took a turn too fast and toppled over.

Father was seldom there, when he was at home for short periods, he and Frieda argued often and loudly. Besides the *servante,* Mother would complain that Hilaire liked to play *Grand Seigneur,* big shot and took people out to eat, with butter, while we had to content ourselves with margarine. One memorable dispute happened, about the time Hilaire had purchased a new green felt fedora. My Mother had learned that he was going out to see a girlfriend. She took his new hat and burned it in the coal stove of our apartment. My sister had witnessed the burning of the green hat. Frieda warned Ruth not to tell Hilaire where the hat was. When Hilaire looked for his hat, no one would answer him. He got furious, created a scene, yelling at Ruth too and hitting her in a vain attempt to get her to tell where the hat was hidden. Mother was yelling "Don't touch her!" We all got hysterical, even me, although I was not in the know about the hat. Hilaire left, slamming the door and we did not see him for quite a while after that. Actually, Hilaire seldom, if ever hit us. Instead, it was Frieda who had a light hand and would serve us generous portions of *giffles,* slaps in the face, at the slightest provocation.

On the first Sunday in May, it got to be Mother's Day. Ruth desperately wanted to offer a bouquet of flowers to Frieda. There was a problem. If Mother was always short of money, Ruth and I had none. As the day got closer and closer Ruth had tried any which way to get her hands on a few centimes. One day, Ruth got a break. Mother had left her handbag on the kitchen counter and the ceiling light reflected the glint of a several coins onto Ruth's eyes. I never knew if Ruth agonized long over what she was about to do but steal the money she did.

On Mother's Day, there was a small bouquet of flowers to present to Mother. Somehow I had become aware of Ruth's "theft" and I seized the occasion to mercilessly blackmail Ruth into becoming my slave. No longer would I have to submit to her orders and requests; Ruth was now at my mercy and I was not inclined to show her any!

Whenever there were chores to be done or shared, I could now pass them on to Ruth, all of them! If Ruth asked me to do anything, I needed only to hint at "the money" and the work disappeared as if by magic. The same threat of "telling Mother" enticed Ruth to do my bidding in a multitude of ways. I do not recall how long I was able to keep my big sister on a leash but it was not sitting right with her. Even Mother had begun to notice that something was no longer the same in our "big sister-little brother" act. Ruth had always been somewhat domineering toward me. Now I seemed to be able to wrap her around my finger.

So, Ruth eventually had to confess to Mother that she had stolen the flower money out of her purse. I do not recall what happened next. I am sure that Mother understood Ruth's motivation. As for me, I soon found myself at the bottom of the totem pole that was not such a bad place to be.

I had relegated the Mother's Day "stolen money" incident to a forgotten corner of my mind until I went to visit my sister Ruth in her California mountain home in Valley Center in 2009. Ruth had been reading "And Somehow We Survive" and this was the first time we had a chance to remix our memories. From the expression in her eyes it was clear she had not forgotten the incident. I promised her it would be inserted in the second book, "An Unorthodox Life" and give her credit for reviving the episode.

It was not long after, that we were thrown out of our home, once again, for non-payment of rent.

We found a place to stay on the *Quai de Sambre*. At the time, the Sambre River was being filled out in order to turn the area into a boulevard. The Sambre would continue under the street level, but most of it would be diverted into a canal that rerouted the water around the city. In 1937, about half the river was filled in, leaving half the area as a river, the other half as a long, unfinished dirt area. Long underground tunnels of sewers ran along the entire length. It made a wonderful, if dangerous playground.

My parents knew a Monsieur Lemaitre. He represented *Delaise Le Lion,* a large Belgian grocery chain, for their wine business. He allowed us to move to an apartment on the third floor of his wine store on the *Quai de Sambre*. Mr Lemaitre looked like a functionary, with a short mustache and usually wearing a black bowler hat. He had six children. Frieda would mockingly call him a "good Catholic". He had indeed saddled Madame Lemaitre with a child each year. He had been compelled to stop at six. His first daughter had been born with a slight crease in her upper lip and with each succeeding child, the lip problem had gotten more severe. The last boy had a full Harelip, a cleft palate and could not speak. The doctors had warned him that the next child might be born without a palate or worse. So, Monsieur Lemaitre had consented not to have any more children.

The rent must have been very reasonable, as Monsieur Lemaitre found Frieda quite attractive. He would in later years be a steady visitor to our home in Brussels.

The house had a basement where the inventory of wine was being stored. There was a helper, Lucien, in his early teens. One day, he asked me to help him clean the coal-fired boiler. We worked for several hours, taking all the ashes out. By then, we were caked with gray ashes and I had ashes down my throat. Lucien pulled a bottle from the huge wine collection. It was Chassard, 45 degrees, maybe 90 proof. He poured a water glass full for me. "Take this" he said, "It is very good for dust". I drank the whole glass and in no time at all, I was drunk. I couldn't walk straight, but I had enough sense that I did not want to be punished, so I told my Mother, "I'm pretending to be drunk." I got quite sick and the next morning, I had the hangover of my life. I didn't touch alcohol again until I was sixteen, when I got sick again.

My parents did not drink alcohol or smoke. My friend Lucien procured some cigarettes, which I smoked. These were ladies cigarettes, in various pastel colors. They were so pretty, irresistible.

My Mother discovered that I was smoking and said, "You want to smoke? Smoke!" So, I quit! Then someone gave me a pipe. I smoked one huge pipeful of tobacco and got sick, dizzy and nauseous. That was the last time I ever smoked. My Mother knew what she was doing. I was seven. I can still taste that pipe.

One morning, a group of kids decided that we were going to explore the sewers running under the filled-in Sambre. All of the kids were older than I, but they allowed me to come along anyway. Large torches had been fashioned out of rolled newspaper dipped in tar we found on the construction sites. We descended in the manholes and walked along the tiny path walks running along the trough that carried the sewage. We could see the light coming from the next manholes. This allowed us to travel with caution, without having to use our torches. It stank in there, but we continued, walking perhaps five or six kilometers underground. When night fell, we lit our torches so we could continue on. Somehow, the torches burned at a faster rate than we had anticipated and after a while, we had nothing left to guide us in the sewers.

We turned around, and groped our way back to the place where we had started our expedition. We could see nothing, had no idea of the time. All we could do was to feel with our shoes the rim of the path walk lining the trench where the manure was flowing. Now and then, one of us would slip and splash in the stinking liquid. There was a lot of moaning and cursing. I was scared silly. We finally saw the entrance where we had entered the tunnel. Someone had dropped a light to show us the way.

When we got out, a whole crowd had gathered, the police, ambulances and lots of parents. We had been missing for about 14 hours. It was nearly midnight. And in the forefront of everyone, my nine-year-old sister Ruth, very angry, very concerned. "*C'est mon frère*" (He's my brother) she replied when my Mother asked why she was so upset.

Jeanine was the daughter of a Notary. A Notary is an important personage in Belgium. There might be just one or two in a town the size of Charleroi. A Notary is just one small notch under a judge. Jeanine appeared out of nowhere. One afternoon, as I was playing on the Sambre fill-up, there was Jeanine. She was pretty, with very white skin, long flowing light brown hair. She smiled at me and I could see her small white teeth. I was smitten and so was she. It was just so natural. She flirted with me and I responded shyly. I guess we were both seven at the time. She wore white ankle socks and white shoes with a button strap. A white blouse was tucked in her pleated yellow skirt, held over her blouse with yellow straps. Suddenly, Jeanine picked up the sides of her skirt and lifted it way up, showing me her white panties. She twirled and turned, all the while revealing all that had been hidden before. I was delighted; charmed by the natural way she behaved. She was so pretty. Then, she was gone.

However, someone had seen us and had reported this to her Father, the Notary. And the Notary had gotten in touch with my Father. And my Father was furious. It was my bad luck that for once, he had been home. As I came in the house, he cursed me out. The Notary had called and had threatened some legal action. Hilaire, who was not a Belgian citizen and who had enough problems with bankruptcies, did not want to get involved with a Notary. He lunged at me, but I was too quick for him and I ran up to the first landing where the bathroom offered a safe sanctuary. I locked myself in. Outside, pleading or threatening, Father wanted me to come out. I knew that if I came out, he would beat me up. I also knew that if I stayed longer, he would beat me up. I do not have any recollection of the final outcome. I know that I did not stay in there forever. I also do not remember Father ever hitting me. I guess his anger must have subsided. I eventually came out. I never saw Jeanine again.

I was in the second grade. One afternoon, I returned home from the school Rue de Marcinelle. I was dragging my right leg with increasing pains of muscle spasms. By the next morning, my right leg was paralyzed and I couldn't walk. At first, Mother thought I might have contracted polio, even though it was considered an American disease and virtually unseen in Europe. The fear loomed large, though, because in newsreels at the movie theatre, we had seen pictures of American children afflicted and being treated in huge ominous-looking iron lungs. Only the head was sticking out of the contraptions.

It was very painful, sharp pains were shooting from my right hip to my right foot. The doctor could not reach a diagnosis. Later in life, I thought that my paralysis might have been a psychosomatic reaction to the turmoil between my parents. I missed more than six weeks of school until I regained strength in my leg. That 1937 Charleroi was hit by a slight earthquake. I remember my bed shaking from the tremors.

When I returned to school, I was still not able to rejoin the other children at recess. I was given the duty of monitoring the kids in the punishment room where pupils who misbehaved had to stay and study during recess. I sat at the teacher's desk, but soon enough, I was joining in the chalk-throwing bedlam when the actual teacher had left the room. One day the teacher came back into the room and my new job was short-lived.

And yet, despite of all the turmoil and the difficulties we faced daily, Frieda, now and then, could find a special time for Ruth and me. On a late fall evening, the three of us went to a local theater to see a performance of *L'Auberge du Cheval Blanc,* The White Horse's Inn. It was a Viennese operetta by Stoltz and Benatsky, made famous in Vienna and Germany by the tenor Richard Tauber. Besides Stoltz and Benatsky, there were other contributors to the music and lyrics, but those two had gotten the major share of the credit. By that time, since they were Jews, Tauber and Benatsky had been forced to leave Germany. Tauber continuing his career mostly in England, Benatsky working first in France and then fleeing to the USA where he continued his career, writing hundreds of numbers for the movies of Hollywood.

My introduction to live theatre was, for me, a revelation. I could not get enough of the spectacle. The sets, lighting and costumes captivated me. Translated to French, the many songs, lilting and melodious delighted my young ears. In the Tyrolean number, a group of dancers in colorful dresses and short *lederhosen* danced and slapped their thighs and ankles. While this was going on, yodels and loud yells would erupt from the throat of one and then the other of the performers. In frustration, I tried in vain to detect from which mouth sprang each sound, but it was of no avail. I left the theater starry-eyed and forever in love with *L'Auberge du Cheval Blanc.*

On another occasion, we were taken to see *La Mascotte,* The Mascot, a French operetta about a geese guardian who falls in love with a shepherd. The plot revolves around the fact that the townspeople discover that the girl is a mascot. That is, she will bring luck to whoever owns her as long as she remains a virgin. Endless machinations ensue to prevent the romance, the marriage and the eventual consummation of the union. There is a charming duet between the two lovers. I sang both voices for a long time, until my voice changed.

1938, RUE DE MARCINELLE

Petit Homme tu pleures, j'connais ton chagrin
(Little man you're crying, I know who's to blame . . .)

My parents reunited early in 1938 and we moved back to the Rue de Marcinelle, in the same house that we had briefly owned. This time, instead of occupying the whole house, we rented a small apartment on the second floor. Mr Hecht, the haberdasher, was our landlord. He had bought the house from Hilaire a few years before and now we were his tenants. I was happy Rue de Marcinelle. It was only a small walk from the Quai de Sambre, but it was full of activity and near to the *Place de la Ville Basse.* My best friends were Franz and Marcel Bouret, sons of the Post Office caretaker. They thought that because I was Jewish, I was rich. Sometimes on weekends I would go by streetcar with Franz and Marcel to Marcinelle, a suburb where they visited their *marraine and parrain,* their godparents. They lived in a typical miner's house, small and simple, with whitewashed walls and a cobblestone walkway. Inside, white lace curtains hung at each window, a huge pot of coffee permanently steaming on the coal-fired stove. The boys always received *Dimanche,* a traditional allowance. I thought it was wondrous. I couldn't figure out why I wasn't privileged to have a *Marraine et Parrain.* This experience did give me an inkling of the cultural difference between Catholics and Jews.

Once in a while I would go to the small Bouret apartment, in the basement of the Post Office building. There Mr Bouret sat dying of cancer. He was emaciated and frail. He spoke in a death rattle, rasping voice greeting me, forcing a smile. I guess that he saw my revulsion and he wanted to reassure me of his friendliness for me. His black, marble-like eyes rolling in their saucer-sized sockets fascinated me. As he sat in his chair, head tilted backwards, I had visions of the eyes rolling off his face and bouncing on the floor. I could see me running on the black and white tile floor, trying to catch his eyes and having to replace them in their sockets. Oh, how I hated being there at all.

We liked to play on the *Place de la Ville Basse,* where the morning outdoor market was held. The merchandise was laid out on boards propped up on sawhorses. Afterwards, the sawhorses were stacked up on big *charettes,* or carts, which my friends and I climbed as though these were mountains.

One day, when I arrived at the square, I asked Marcel where Franz was. Marcel pointed to the top of a stack of sawhorses, atop a cart. Franz was standing at the very top and proceeded to urinate on me, wetting my hair, my face and my shoulders. I ran home crying and told my Mother who grabbed a broomstick, ran to the square and chased the two laughing brothers. Ten minutes later, I was playing with them again.

By now, I was in the third grade. Study was something I never had to do. I seemed to absorb all the lessons by just sitting in class. As my name began with an "R", and since the teachers would ask questions in alphabetical order, it was easy. In this French speaking section of Belgium, most of the family names ran from A to N. By the time the questions came to Rosenberg, I had already absorbed the answers delivered by the other boys in the class. The school on the *Rue de Marcinelle* catered to boys and girls, however, the classes were segregated. Only during recess were we able to play together.

I had come to know Rachelle who was in Ruth's class. She was older than Ruth, probably eleven or twelve. Like us, she was the daughter of a Polish Jew who had immigrated to Charleroi. On occasion, Rachelle would invite me to her home after school. She and her Father lived in a dark, dank warehouse-like room. There were no windows and no electricity. A large kerosene lantern and a stove provided heat and light. A narrow metal chimney that ran through the wall to the outside vented the stove. Rachelle was very tall, with legs that seemed to go on forever. She wore olive colored, knit body stockings. The whole place reeked of kerosene, so did Rachelle. I was only eight at the time; no sexual thoughts entered my mind. However, there emanated such a feeling of sensuality from Rachelle and her kerosene-scented woolen stockings! Even decades later, when I would ride a bus, the odor of kerosene would always bring me back to the dank, dark warehouse and Rachelle. I never did find out if Rachelle and her family survived the war years.

Whenever our parents got together, which was not that often, violent arguments would break out punctuated with recriminations going back to Léona Kohlen *"La Servante"* and the insults would fly, *"Sale Boche"* from my Father and *"Sale Pollack"* from my Mother. We would get out of the apartment and seek refuge in the house of a woman who lived on the Boulevard de l'Yser, where Frieda had placed us each weekday, for a few hours. We were supposed to go there, be quiet and sleep for a couple of hours, from 1 to 3, in a large bed set near the window. Ruth and I had never been used to sleeping in mid-day and we'd simply sit up, lift the lace curtains and watch the goings-on on the boulevard.

One day, as we were walking up the *Rue de la Montagne,* there was a commotion. Léon Degrelle, the head of the Belgian *Rexist* Party, was walking by, visiting Charleroi. Degrelle had become notorious for his support of the ideas advanced by Adolf Hitler. He was to figure prominently in the war years that lay ahead.

But it was gambling that gave Mother the courage to continue and go on with her miserable life. When she had no money, there was only one goal in her life: make money so she could buy a commuting ticket to go to Namur and gamble. There were three women and Frieda and they would go and gamble. At three o'clock and seven o'clock, the casino would draw a lottery, the four women would pool their tickets and whenever one would win, they would split the money. And all Frieda needed for the next day was to buy something to eat for Ruth and me. It was not always easy for Mother to find a guy who would give her money, but once in a while the *croupier* at the roulette wheel was nice and he would let her claim the betting on a number which was not hers and push the chips her way

Once, the casino drew a lottery and Frieda was in the group of 36 selected. Four weeks later, they called Frieda's name and asked her to come up to the office and pick a number. If the number she had picked came out, she could win the first prize, a new Ford automobile. And Frieda told her friend, Mme DeKnibber, that she had dreamed that the winning number would be "9". Frieda went to the office of the secretary of the casino, a very nice man and he asked her to pick a number. An hour later, there was a special spin of the roulette wheel for the Ford and number "9" came out. Mme DeKnibber yelled out "You have the nine! You told me you dreamed it was going to be the nine!" And Frieda began to cry; she had changed her mind and had picked "17" instead. She could have hit herself. As a consolation prize, she was given a book with pictures of Namur in it. The person who had won the car was a woman who was just passing through Namur with her son and who did not know anything about gambling or the lottery. And Mother was broke, she did not even have a phony win with the *croupier* and it was the man in the checkroom who loaned her twenty francs. And the next day, she was supposed to bring him back twenty-five, as he did not give twenty francs for nothing.

That summer of '38, Ruth and I were sent each morning to *Camp Bon Air,* a day camp. We'd take the streetcar and ride to a suburb where there were trees and grass. A Catholic group ran the day camp. There, Ruth and I were introduced to Catholicism. We learned to bray prayers three times a day, like donkeys, without knowing what it was all about. We would recite "*Notre père qui êtes aux cieux*" Our Father who art in heaven and "*Je vous salue Marie*" Hail Mary. We stumbled through the prayers, faltering and mumbling our way through the text. Nonetheless, the Catholic prayers, even badly recited, did little to foster our Jewish identity. By the end of the summer, we had both become quite familiar with the words and could recite them from memory.

Ruth and I were quite independent. We walked alone to the streetcar and back home again; a much safer proposition in pre-war Belgium than any urban place today. With both parents away a lot, we learned to take care of ourselves, eating whatever food might be available. Sometimes, when both parents were gone, we would visit the butcher shop, where Mme Nisolle would give us a favorite, *boudin noir, pig* blood pudding with applesauce.

Paul was our monitor at *Camp Bon Air.* He must have been sixteen and held the power of life or death over us. Imagine my surprise at the end of the summer when I ran into Paul, near the Rue de Marcinelle. He was working in a fruit store, arranging the apples and pears in the wooden boxes lining the storefront. I leaped on his back and screamed in his ear. He could do nothing about it. At the time, that simple encounter changed my views on authority.

Still, our parents, when they were together, fought every day, throwing things at each other and yelling in German. They even argued in the street, where their loud German epithets, hurled at each other, drew the attention of others, embarrassing my sister and me. We were sensitive to the Belgian animus towards things German. It had remained from the German occupation of the country during the First World War, barely twenty years before. The public discord made Ruth and me want to keep our distances from these "foreigners" when others stared at them. We pleaded with our parents not to speak German in public. I must admit, though, that Ruth and I did learn a lot of German, which still serves us as a third language, after English and French. One must be thankful for something.

When Germany invaded the Sudetenland in Czechoslovakia in 1938, Belgium mobilized its military. Troops were deployed at strategic points throughout the country. This included the Trezignie Bridge over the Sambre River, in Charleroi. The crossing over the Sambre was a turn-bridge maneuvered by a manual crank to rotate the structure and allow boats and barges to pass. As schoolchildren, we had been told the story of how soldier Trezignie had hindered the German's advance in August 1914 by furiously cranking to move the bridge away from the enemy soldiers on the opposite bank. He kept on cranking even after being mortally wounded by gunfire.

He died at the bridge. He was then made a corporal posthumously. After the war the bridge was named *Pont Caporal Trezignie.* Such history served to reinforce Belgian resentment against the Germans, still regarded as the enemy.

Watching the deployment of soldiers at the bridge, I imagined the hero's last stand, kneeling, bleeding and still turning the crank to his last breath.

The Belgian soldiers had built a little sandbag fortress around a machine gun to protect the Trezignie Bridge. I spent many hours sitting with them and talking. I imagined hordes of Germans approaching the river, trying to cross the bridge all over again. Nothing ever happened, though. The fighting didn't come to Belgium in 1938 and the citizens of Charleroi returned to their daily routines although the German threat seemed always to be hanging over us. The radio voice of Adolf Hitler and his appearances in newsreels were a constant evil presence. He was spellbinding. Today, he looks a little silly in historic newsreels, but at the time, his charisma was magnetic, drawing the German nation to him. To me, the son of a German Mother and of two Jewish parents, the sound of his voice was both fascinating and frightening, even though I was still too young to fully understand what was happening.

In November 1938, the German people, with the blessing of the Hitler government, began a mob action throughout Germany against Jewish businesses, synagogues and homes. During the nights of the ninth and tenth, synagogues were set afire and destroyed. Jewish stores were looted and all the windows broken. Jewish homes were ransacked and the furniture thrown out of the windows and set on fire. Thousands of Jews were beaten, at least 90 were killed. Thousands more were sent to Dachau and other concentration camps. The German police made sure that no one would interfere with the mob's action. The fire brigades watched the conflagrations and intervened only when the spreading fires threatened non-Jewish property. In the aftermath, the German government levied fines of one billion marks, not against the perpetrators, but against the Jewish victims of these attacks. Nearly a thousand synagogues were destroyed or badly damaged. It was further decreed that all insurance payments would be paid to the German government, instead of to the Jewish merchants that had carried such insurance. There was so much broken glass in the streets that Herman Goehring laughingly referred to it as *Kristallnacht,* the night of the crystal.

The Friedemann store at 44 Mittelstrasse, in Cologne, was thus sacked and looted and soon my grandMother Emma and my uncle Richard would be thrown out of their home and relegated to a small apartment in Cologne. Surely Frieda found out about *Kristallnacht,* the savagery of which was broadcast all over the world. However she did manage to keep it from Ruth and me. Immersed as we were in our relocation to Namur and later to Brussels, we managed to keep mostly detached and ignorant of this terrible disaster.

As an eight-year-old boy, I was less distressed by global events than I was by troubles within my own family. My Father was not the only one straying from the marriage. My Mother, in retaliation for Léona Kohlen, as she always claimed, had her own succession of boyfriends. At this time, it was René DeLange, or "de L'Ange". I learned much later that he was only a gigolo, who took advantage of women. DeLange told my Mother that he had a wealthy uncle who was near death, after which DeLange would inherit a great deal of money. In the meantime, DeLange borrowed from my Mother, promising to repay her when his uncle died. My Mother never received any money from him, but she still spoke glowingly of the man, always referring to him as "fantastic". Even in her nineties, when I would ask her who had been her best lover, she would reply "DeLange" without any hesitation.

Before DeLange, Mother would regularly go to the casino in Namur in the company of a Mr Rakowsky, whom she had met in the Namur Casino. He would give her some money to gamble with and she could keep all her winnings. Rakowsky was a refugee; he worked in the Antwerp diamond exchange and spoke not a word of French. Frieda always claimed she felt he was a homosexual, even though in those days, she was not sure what it meant. Rakowsky enjoyed the company of Frieda, who gave him a measure of respectability, being able to appear at the casino with an attractive woman at his side. The first night she stayed with him, he placed his ring on the night table. It had a diamond which must have been five or six carats. With this ring, he had explained, he would be able to leave for America, because to go to America, you needed money. Frieda left the room at about two or three in the morning to return to Charleroi. When Rakowsky woke up and found that Frieda had left, he almost had a heart attack, thinking that his "ticket" to America had gone with her. But Frieda had never taken anything and the ring was still there, on the night table, after she left.

Frieda would pick him up at the railroad station and one day he said, "Don't be surprised if someday I don't' show up because I have just received my affidavit to go to America." Like most Jews, Rakowsky was aware of the dangers that awaited him in Europe. One day, he told Frieda that he was leaving for America. She never saw him again, nor did she ever find out what became of him. But before he left, he gave her some money and he said "Here, that's for you and I want you to move to Namur.

My Mother was not a prostitute, but she had a code. If she was going to be helped by men and she was going to go to bed with a man, except for René DeLange, he had to give her something in return, even if it was only a dinner, or a drink. She felt it was the gentlemanly thing to do. If the man just took her and did not leave her something in return, that was improper. Long before the Léona Kohlen affair, she had slept with a Dutch Jew. What she remembered most about him was that he did not even offer her a drink or a cup of coffee. And when they were finished making love and he was getting dressed, he said, "Now I think I am going to go and eat a *filet Americain!* And nothing for her, so she crossed him off her list. To my Mother, that was unforgivable.

After Rakowsky left her, Mother had no one left who could support her. As Mother was walking back towards the Namur Railroad station to return to Charleroi, a taxi drove by, with its window rolled down. A man was leaning out the window. He asked the driver to stop the car and to go and ask "The pretty Japanese" if she would come to the Dinant casino with him. Frieda, whose guiding principle had always been "why not" agreed and stepped into the cab. The man was a doctor who treated patients with syphilis. So they drove to Dinant. Once in the Casino, the doctor gave her fifty francs and he said "change this" and "good luck". The first thing she did was to put away twenty francs for the next day so we could eat. And there was a man sitting at the bar, he said to Frieda "Would you like to have a drink?" "No, I don't drink," replied Frieda. And the man went away, a half-hour later he came back and asked her again if she wanted something to drink. When she again said no, the man suggested that they go and have dinner together. And so, they left the Casino and went into Dinant and had a big dinner. It was the first time in her life that she had eaten snails. Frieda never saw the doctor again, but that was how she met René DeLange, a gentleman who always traveled second class, at a time when Frieda was happy to be traveling third class on the train to Charleroi. And René DeLange got Mother a second class ticket and paid the difference between Frieda's third class ticket and the second class one.

And DeLange said "I have been observing you before, I saw that when that man gave you money, you put some aside, do you need money?" And Frieda replied, "Yes, we have to eat. DeLange gave her a sum of money. And Frieda cried and cried because she had the two children to take care of. René said, "Let's go and sleep together" and Frieda replied "Why not?" They got off the train in Namur and went to the Grand Hotel, *Place de la Gare*, right next door to where we would move to when we later left Charleroi for Namur. And that was how they began an affair that was to last about seven years, at least for quite a long time.

DeLange sent postcards to my Mother, signing them "Renée", with an extra "e" at the end as though it were a woman's name. My Father, although illiterate, discovered the ruse and the relationship. He may have been told about it by a third party. Another big argument ensued and fighting between Frieda and Hilaire renewed in intensity.

We were now in early 1939. In Germany, the situation for Jews became worrisome; the hunt for Jews began to take on the allures of a pogrom. In Charleroi, the Jewish merchants didn't feel at ease. Hilaire sold what remained of the store on the Rue de Marcinelle and left for Brussels, for a variety of reasons, including Léona Kohlen who had moved to Brussels to be near him. Frieda, Ruth and I were left to fend for ourselves.

With Hilaire gone, the store liquidated, no income, there was not much to hold Mother back in Charleroi. A gambling friend, Mme DeKnibber, also suggested that we move to Namur so that Frieda would not have to commute by train to the casino every day. Frieda asked me if I knew the way to Namur. I recalled having seen a road sign, near the Boulevard de l'Yser, pointing to an uphill street, indicating the road to Jambe, which was in the vague direction of Namur. I proudly told her the way. We hired a truck with a chauffeur and loaded what was left of our meager possessions. As we left our apartment at the Rue de Marcinelle, the lady who lived above us looked down into the stairwell from her landing and yelled out *"Délivrance!"* She was glad to see us go, having endured the fights between my parents for all the time we had been living there.

Mother had not understood the woman's French, later on, in the truck; she asked Ruth "What did she say?" When Ruth translated, Mother replied angrily, "She's lucky I didn't understand what she said, because I would have gone up there and thrown her down the stairs!"

The road out of Charleroi was mostly uphill and the growling of the transmission, in low gear, was unhappy music to my ears. For years afterwards, I associated such engine sounds with having to leave my beloved Charleroi. The attachment to the only town I had ever known, of course was strong. I had my friends and Charleroi was familiar turf; I knew every nook and cranny of the small town. My homesickness for Charleroi lasted for years and never quite left me. Even at the age of eight I felt that I was leaving unrecoverable happiness behind.

<u>1939, NAMUR</u>

Un Jour Mon Prince Viendra.
Some Day My Prince Will Come

In Namur, we moved into the second-story apartment across from the train station at 6, Place de la Gare, next to the Grand Hotel, above a hairdresser store. The owner's husband had a couple of shares in the Namur Casino and soon began to make trouble for Frieda, as she was a woman living alone with two children. Living in Namur, she was not allowed to enter the Casino.

Despite my chagrin about the move to Namur, I did well in school. I was a bright student. I had been in the third grade in Charleroi. In Namur I continued at the same level, except that the school placed me in the fourth grade for math. My new teachers were greatly interested in a multi-subject textbook I had brought from Charleroi. It included history, math, poetry, science and other topics. One section of the book was devoted to Abraham Lincoln, about whom I read avidly; my first strong connection to matters American.

In a small town like Namur, the train stationmaster, the *Chef de Gare,* was an important person in the community. Shortly after we moved to Namur, the stationmaster was shot and killed, apparently by his mistress (or by his wife, because he had a mistress). There was a big funeral, which I watched from our upstairs window as the procession marched mournfully past the station. The Railway Band played the slow Chopin Funeral March. A scandalous death like that, was parodied by onlookers who were singing softly *"Il est crevé, plus moyen d'le réparer",* meaning : He had a blowout, there's no way it can be fixed.

Ruth and I wondered if Mother was going to be able to repair our lives. Father was gone and Frieda was seeing René DeLange and going to the casino every night. Residents of Namur, at least those who were not wealthy, were prohibited from going to the casino. The city Fathers did not want the town's laborers to gamble away their monthly pay. Since she was now a Namur resident, Mother was subject to the prohibition, but she had made friends with some people who had a casino membership or were shareholders; she went as their guest. As far as Ruth and I knew, Mother's only source of income was gambling.

And René DeLange came every day. He wore tortoise shell glasses and always met Mother by the right portal in front of the train station. We would be watching from our window upstairs hoping that maybe he would not show up and Mother would come home. He and Mother would make love in the Grand Hotel, *place de la Gare*, right next door to where we lived, until he was broke, having lost everything at the gambling tables. Frieda, who always managed to win a little each day in Dinant, thanks to her little system, would make some *Tartines,* bread with butter and jelly, for us and for René DeLange. The four of us would go up to the Citadel of Namur (a strong fort overlooking the Meuse River) and would sit there, at the Namur Citadel and eat the *Tartines.*

The relationship with DeLange ended after we had been in Namur a few months. He had taken up with Mme Den Hartog, a wealthy acquaintance of my Mother's back in Charleroi. That relationship did not last either; the woman caught DeLange rifling through her handbag one day, stealing her jewelry, and she kicked him out.

We had neighbors who ran a newsstand at the *Place de la Gare*. At the end of the week, they would bring us the unsold magazines, which we would devour. Ruth read all the movie magazines and I concentrated on the sports and anything that had to do with aviation. I also got my first taste of the adventures of *Tintin et Milou*. The neighbors kind of kept an eye on us while Mother was away.

Ruth and I had one wish: that Mother be successful at the gaming table. If she won, we would be able to eat. Every night, when our Mother was out, Ruth and I knelt in front of the fireplace in our little apartment overlooking the railroad station and recited the prayers we had learned at the Catholic summer camp. For about one hour, we would pray out loud, "*Notre père qui ètes aux cieux*" and "*Je vous salue Marie, pleine de grâce*", the Lord's Prayer and the Hail Mary. Our prayers were being answered, because every night, Mother came home with at least enough money for food. Years later, when we lived in Brooklyn, we had the visit of a woman who had lived in the apartment next to ours in Namur. She told us how she used to hear Ruth and me praying each night. We were so mortified that someone had overheard us reciting prayers so that Mother could win at the gambling tables.

Later, Ruth came to the conclusion that the money came from boyfriends. Actually, Mother would be picked up by men who were going to the casino and they would give her fifty francs to gamble with. She would always put twenty francs aside, "so the children can eat".

Mother was an attractive woman with jet-black hair that she rolled in an elastic band to create almost a halo around the back and side of the head. With vivacious beautiful dark eyes, lovely hands with manicured nails and a nice figure, she had an engaging personality and presented herself well. She was outgoing and would initiate conversations with others. In French, one would have said of her, "*Elle n'avait pas froid aux yeux*", she was not one to be intimidated.

A few months after we moved to Namur, there was a big scandal involving Mr Toussaint, the Director of the casino and Belgium's Attorney General who had gambled away all the money that belonged to the Veterans of World War I. Mr Toussaint was jailed and replaced by Mr and Mrs Engelman. Soon afterward, the casino of Namur was forced to close and the closest casino was now in Dinant, some twenty kilometers away. This made it more difficult for Mother to go and gamble, but she did manage; and with the continued help of our prayers, Frieda was able to keep us fed.

Bernard Horowitz, Mother's Cologne childhood friend, came to find us in Namur. Somehow he had found out about our plight. He told Frieda that his wife Leah had left him and he wanted us to come and live in his house in Jette, a suburb of Brussels. He lived there with his parents and his two children. He said, "Take a truck, load up everything you own and come to Brussels." And since DeLange was not showing up anymore and we had no money and the Namur casino was closed, we moved to Brussels. The Namur interlude had lasted six months.

BRUXELLES—BRUSSELS

Belgium is a country divided between the Dutch-speaking Flemish citizens and the French-speaking Walloons. Brussels is an island of French-speaking *Bruxellois* in the Flemish area of the country. Along its suburbs, Flemish is spoken, but it is mostly a *patois, Brusselleer,* which owes as much to French as to Flemish.

So, in early 1939, we took up residence in the Jette suburb of Brussels, where small, squat houses with peaked, red-tiled roofs lined the street where we lived. We had found an apartment in the *Rue Léon Théodore,* close to the house where Bernard Horowitz lived. There was a neighbor, an old woman, who greeted me daily by saying, in Flemish, *"Gooien dag, mennekke"* Good day, little man. In school, where we were placed upon our arrival, most of the kids spoke Flemish. I felt out of place, because I only spoke French and I was still homesick for Charleroi. I was lost in a strange city. Mother took me to the largest department store in Brussels, *Au Bon Marché* and standing in the store crowded with people, I felt alone and very unhappy and I was crying "Mamma, let's go back to Charleroi, there are too many people in Brussels."

Meanwhile, Father was again working at his interior decorator trade. An old customer from the Charleroi days, who took care of import-export and was associated with the Baron d'Annis in the Belgian and Colonial Bank, was in Brussels and seemed very willing to help Hilaire find work suitable for him. Mr L'Hermitte, recommended a cousin to Hilaire, he was an *Aide de Camp* of King Léopold III. Hilaire was hired to execute several works in Brussels. As Father also needed to find a place to stay in Brussels, Bernard Horowitz contacted him and we all moved to *Rue Ferdinand Lenoir,* in Jette, the house where Horowitz and his parents resided.

As we were in the process of moving, Uncle Paul, Mother's brother, showed up again and helped us move our few meager possessions. Paul now lived in Brooklyn USA and had managed to obtain a temporary visa from the German government to allow him to go back to Germany. Neither Ruth nor I have any recollection of his visit. Frieda never spoke much about it, as she had enough other problems to keep her occupied at the time. The purpose of his trip was surely to visit his Mother Emma, and his brother Richard, in Cologne. He must have made a last attempt to persuade them to leave Germany. Even if he was able to convince them, the means and the opportunity to escape from Hitler's Germany in 1939, were then no longer available. It was a brave attempt to go into the lion's den, to save his family. Thus, he saw his sister Frieda again briefly in Jette and returned to America. *(It is possible that Ruth and I were already placed in the orphanage when Uncle Paul came to Brussels. That would explain why we recollect nothing about his visit.)*

It was early 1939 and we heard a lot about a Polish city, Danzig (Gdansk) and the need for Germany to have a corridor leading to East Prussia. On September 1st 1939, we learned that the German army had invaded Poland and that England and France had declared war on Germany. A Second World War had begun. In less that a month, Poland had surrendered and had been partitioned between Germany and Russia. In France, the French Army took up positions behind the Maginot Line and the Germans behind their Siegfried Line.

On October 12th, 1939, the first deportation of Austrian and Czech Jews to Poland began. Although Ruth and I were blissfully unaware of it at the time, our parents took notice of an influx of Polish Jew refugees into Belgium in the weeks that followed.

Hilaire would begin to work for the King's *Aide de Camp* just as the officer had to leave for the mobilization of the Belgian Army. He paid Hilaire in advance and asked him to carefully close the door after he was through with the work entrusted to him.

We were thus reunited as a family and moved together. We lived on the second floor of the house in the *Rue Ferdinand Lenoir, in Jette.* A bakery operated on the ground floor. Bernard Horowitz, an electrician by trade, lived on the first floor, with his parents, German Jew refugees from Cologne. Bernard had two daughters, but there is no recollection of them in my memory. Did they move out with Leah, his estranged wife, or remain with the old parents? My only clear memory of the period was of Bichka-Bichka, Bernard's Mother and Feibish, Bernard's Father, always wanting to lure me into the *cott.* "*Kom in de cott!*" he would tease at me, inviting me to come in the shed, in the back of the house at the end of the little garden. My imagination would invent all sorts of terrors hiding in that shed and I would run away from Feibish, much to his great amusement.

Bernard Horowitz was talking to Frieda about the plight he was in, with his two children now that his wife had left him. He had heard about an orphanage in the borough of Uccle, just south of the center of Brussels; he was considering placing his daughters there. Bernard never did place his daughters in the orphanage. At that time, Hilaire was again nowhere to be found and since she found herself once again without money, Frieda reasoned that placing Ruth and me in that orphanage was the proper and the only thing to do. Thus, on the first of December 1939, she placed Ruth and me in the *Foyer des Enfants,* the orphanage on the *Rue Beeckman,* in Uccle. I would not remember actually arriving at the institution, just that we were suddenly there. Although we knew we had been placed there for financial reasons that everyone hoped would be temporary, Ruth and I still worried that we might never see our parents again. I was nine years old and Ruth just reaching eleven.

With us in the orphanage, Hilaire and Frieda got back together under the Horowitz roof, but their financial condition did not improve to the point where they might have considered rescuing Ruth and me from our unhappy state. Whatever the reason, they were satisfied to know we were taken care of, without worrying about a situation where the children suffered from a great sense of insecurity.

In Brussels, bordering the center of town runs the *Boulevard du Jardin Botanique,* known simply as *Le Botanique.* It is a beautiful wide avenue topped by the *Rue Royale* and running down to the *Place Rogier* where stood the imposing *Gare du Nord,* the North Station and across, the large department store *Au Bon Marché.* Bordering the North side of the boulevard, the beautiful and imposing Botanical Garden provided an oasis of peace and greenery. Today, much of the *Jardin Botanique* has been sacrificed to accommodate the system of tunnels pierced in the boulevard to try to ease traffic.

One day, as Frieda and Hilaire were walking down the *Botanique,* who should walk by, René DeLange. Frieda told Hilaire that she had to go and buy something at the *Bon Marché.* Then she dumped Hilaire in the department store and went to rejoin DeLange. And nothing had changed,

Frieda was still in love with René and René was still broke. When he asked her, she told him where she lived in Jette and he came to see her every day. He had a girlfriend who gave him pocket money every day. And every day, after leaving the girlfriend, he was at the apartment Rue Léon Théodore at about two in the afternoon. He would stay with Frieda until four o'clock. After that, Frieda would walk him back as far as the *Pont de Laeken,* the bridge that led in the general direction of the King's Palace.

And downstairs, in the house, there was the bakery where the woman didn't like Frieda because she never bought her bread there. She would buy her bread at the bakery that was a little further away, because the bread was better. And one day, the woman waited until Hilaire came home. And when Hilaire came in, she said, "You know, every time you leave, there is another guy who comes in and goes to see your wife". At that time, Hilaire was still seeing Léona Kohlen. He looked at the woman and replied "Madame that is none of your business."

Then one day, Frieda had some money on her, probably gotten from Hilaire who was again working in his trade. DeLange came in and announced that his uncle had finally dropped dead and that he was the sole inheritor. He was the only one who had the right to the money, but he did not have the money to go to the Notary Public. So, Frieda gave him whatever money he needed to go to the Notary, who was a heavy fellow living in Dinant. And again, it was the last she saw of René DeLange. Well, not quite, he turned up one more time as described in Frieda's memoirs.

"And one day, I was at the Boulevard Adolphe Max in Brussels, when I spotted DeLange and I went to him and I said, "René, I need some of the money I have given you." And he looked at me and he said, "Madame, I do not wish to know you anymore." What a scum! And I said to DeLange, "Well, you may not want to know me anymore, but I still want to know you." And so he left and I followed him and he went to the Café des Jardins, in the street parallel to the Boulevard Adolphe Max and he went in and I went in. I asked the waiter for a beer. The waiter was happy to have a customer. And I said to the waiter when he brought me my "demi", "Don't be surprised if I leave without paying, because that man there is the one who should pay. I have paid enough for him." And I drank my beer and left without paying. What did I have to lose? And I did not see DeLange anymore or heard anything about that.

One day I went to Dinant, to see the Notary Public whose bill I had paid when I gave money to DeLange. And I told the Notary that the money DeLange had used to pay for all the formalities to inherit was money that I had given him. DeLange had said that one-day, when he inherits, that I would get a lot of money from him because I had been so helpful when he did not have any money. And the Notary, who was a big fellow, like an elephant, takes me in his arms and says, "I will come to see you next week and I will bring you money." And I noticed that he was smoking cigarettes with a ball in the middle, terrible Belgian cigarettes, very strong, called" Boules d'Or"

So, with the last of my money, I bought a sack of coal (for the stove and heat) and a pack of cigarettes and I waited for the Notary to come. And this elephant comes in and he pushes me onto the sofa. But I was quicker back on my feet than he had thought and I said," Monsieur le Notaire, let us talk about what you promised. Where is the money?" And he said, "The money is not ready yet." And I told him "When the money is ready, you come back." And I stood there with my sack of coal and my pack of "Boules d'Or "cigarettes. Can you imagine?"

As for Hilaire, he was looking for a job, an occupation that would pay. He went to find a MrDeferre, in the bank on the *Rue d'Arlon.* Mr Deferre was seeking to sell a wagonload of matches. Hilaire had never in his life taken care of such a transaction, but necessity being the law, he would have to dream of something to supplement his lack of experience in this matter. What's more, he did once get rid of a carload of rabbit skins in Charleroi, it had been for export. This would have been simpler.

The lure of a ten-percent commission was enough of an incentive for Hilaire to look for a buyer. A former client that he met near the *Bourse,* the stock exchange, referred him to a wholesaler who would have been interested in this kind of merchandise. The referral was good; the whole wagonload of matches was sold. Hilaire, happy and proud, informed Mr Deferre of the good news. Deferre paid him a good commission and proposed that he now try to sell a lot of sardines in cans, under the same conditions. All Hilaire had to do was to visit the same wholesaler in Jette and the deal was done.

Hilaire had found a new trade that would change and save our lives in the turmoil that was about to rage around us.

Ruth and I did not know what was happening with our parents in that fall of 1939, until years later. Now, we would try to fit in our new environment in the orphanage.

LE FOYER DES ENFANTS.—
THE CHILDREN'S HOME

The directress of *Le Foyer des Enfants,* was Mme Kerremans, a decent woman, but who seemed to care little about what happened to the sixty children living there when Ruth and I arrived. At the front of the attractive orphanage grounds was a big house, mansion-like, where Mme Kerremans had her office. There was also a huge dining room and some smaller rooms with windows overlooking the backyard. These smaller rooms were used as studies and breakfast rooms. When the weather was bad, they were converted into play areas. Pastor Van Gouthem, a Methodist minister, who lived on the upper floor of the main house with his wife, his daughter and his son, supervised day-to-day operations. Under the Van Gouthem floor, the girls' dormitory stretched the whole length of the house. Almost every night, the Van Gouthem son would visit the girls' dormitory and have his way with whoever was willing and quiet. The boys were housed in a large double dormitory built to the right of the main house. The two rooms rose all the way to the high ceilings and high French windows gracefully curved all along the inner side, from ground up to the ceiling.

In back of the main building, a large courtyard stretched to a low wall, topped with spiked bars. A double spiked gate marked the middle of the wall. Beyond the wall, a vegetable garden was laid out in well-cultivated rows.

The day we arrived, I was taken to a whitewashed bathroom, told to undress and plunged into a huge bathtub filled with a pink liquid. A strong, blond woman, wearing a blue and white striped apron proceeded to scrub every part of my body with a large brush. It had short sharp bristles and its shape, in the form of an 8, made it easy for my tormentor to apply great force to the brushing.

After about ten minutes, the woman seemed satisfied that I was now clean and deloused; she vigorously dried me with a harsh brown towel. I was then instructed to get dressed again.

Quickly, I slipped on my underwear and socks. I tucked my white shirt in my knee-length grey pants and slipped on my matching grey jacket. The woman motioned for me to follow her. Struggling to put my shoes on, I grabbed my grey *casquette* and kept up after her as well as possible, across the courtyard, into the dormitory. Walking was a chore; every inch of my body was stiff from the scrubbing, my skin being swollen from head to toe. This delousing ritual would be repeated often in the months to follow, as it was one of the favorite forms of punishment for bad behavior.

In the dormitory, I was assigned a bed and told to be ready for the evening meal. I sat on the dark grey blanket of the metal military bed and contemplated my surroundings. My bed was in the middle of a row of ten beds laid out against the far wall. Facing me another ten beds stretched along the French windows facing the courtyard and the main building. At the far right, a door led to the bathrooms, a series of sinks and the exit to the courtyard. To the left, stood a wall and a door leading to another room with a dozen beds.

With my legs dangling over the side of the bed, I tried to ignore the discomfort of my body and thought about running away right there and then. It would have been easy, no one was around me, the courtyard seemed deserted; it was tempting. Then I thought about Ruth. I had not seen her since we had arrived in the orphanage and I remembered I had not eaten since morning. I decided to wait until the next day.

At dinner, I saw Ruth. We waved at each other, but we did not talk. The dining room seating was segregated; she sat with the girls and I sat with the boys. The *refectoire*-dining hall was very large, with long tables covered with red-checkered tablecloths, seating was on wooden benches.

The meal was served by several attendants, but no one began to eat. I followed the example of the other boys and waited. Seated at a shorter table, a woman wearing a dark blue nurse's uniform was opening a very large book. She was pretty, with long dark hair. Her face was kind and smiling. I recall her name was Marguerite. She opened the book and read a couple of chapters from the New Testament. We were then allowed to eat. While we were eating, Nurse Marguerite read aloud from a newspaper, giving us the news of the day.

When we were finished, I returned to the dormitory, got undressed and fell asleep immediately.

There would be time in the morning to get acquainted with my roommates. Actually, I was awakened several times during the night, due to circumstances that, in the months to come, were to be routine and that I will relate in the coming chapters.

There was a staff doing the cooking, maintenance, etc. However, my contact with them was very limited. My immediate world was confined to just a handful of keepers. Berthe was the one who had given me my initial scrubbing bath. I remember her as a big, terrifying woman who looked like a military commander. We called her "*La Grosse Bertha*" Big Bertha, after the infamous German siege gun of The Great War. (In later years, Ruth would tell me that Berthe loved me very much and there is photograph of me, leaning into her body. She looks kind and pretty).

Juffrow Klazine was Berthe's assistant. She was a spinsterly looking skinny woman, with grey hair knotted in a bun. She wore very thick glasses, encased in thin golden frames. Juffrow Klazine was from Holland and the French that she spoke in a high fluted voice was very halting. She was much nicer to us than Berthe, but she was powerless to help much. She would play the piano and lead us into songs, mostly hymns. What fascinated me most about her was her ability to sing harmony. I would stare at her as we sang, marveling at the sounds she made in another key. However, while Berthe was in charge of the boys, Klazine was in charge of the girls and she was Ruth's tormentor. Klazine would submerge and "drown" Ruth in the bathtub whenever Ruth objected to something or was disruptive in any way.

Nurse Marguerite completed the trio. We went to her when we were in pain or ill. Each evening before the meal, we would sit still as she read us from the New Testament. She was also our contact with the outside world, with her news commentary each night. Nurse Marguerite was very fond of me; she would often draw me to her and run her fingers through my black curly hair.

Mme Kerremans, the directress and Pastor Van Gouthem rounded the group of adults I came in contact with, but they were seldom involved in our daily routines and I saw little of them. Pasteur Van Gouthem, who was the Protestant chaplain for the Belgian Army, having been mobilized, would show up now and then in his officer's uniform.

We woke up early, rushed through the rooms where the cold-water sinks hung on the walls. Our washing consisted mainly of scrubbing our hands and face with harsh brown laundry soap. I do not remember if we had toothpaste, or even toothbrushes.

After that, we would run to the smaller room next to the dining hall and had breakfast. Each of us had a soup plate into which was poured a ladleful of *pap*, oatmeal made with sour milk. In the middle of each table, sat a larger platter, with generous mounds of white or rye bread. Small containers of yellow butter and *confiture* were placed here and there. *Confiture* was the generic name for all kinds of spreads, preserves, jam, jelly and even marmalade. Large pitchers of milk stood on each table to be poured into bowls that required two hands for safe drinking.

I would not eat *pap;* its sour taste was foreign to me. I much preferred the white bread, which I carefully and evenly buttered until the spread covered each and every surface with a smooth, thin coat. The same procedure was repeated with the *confiture*. Meanwhile, the other kids had devoured everything in sight and by the time I had finished eating my first *tartine,* all the food had disappeared.

I slept in the dormitory mostly with the younger boys who were eight or less. I resented my early bedtime, because during the day, I was placed with the other, older boys who had to do chores. My primary job was shining shoes for all the boys. I had no personal contact with the older boys, except Léon, who was fourteen and my great friend. He was an orphan, having lost both his parents. He was in charge of cleaning the garbage and the offal pit, where one would collect the *purin*, the liquid manure. Léon had to remove the heavy steel lid, dip in a large bucket held by a rope, into the manure and pull out buckets of *purin*. This he had to carry to the vegetable garden to be used as fertilizer by the gardeners. When we had time, he would talk to me about his dead parents and I would tell him of my fears of never seeing my parents again. Once, Léon fell partially in the offal pit, his right leg went right down the opening. We pulled him out and he stank for a long time thereafter.

Gilbert and Jacobus were fraternal twins. Gilbert was heavy and round, Jacobus, skinny and long. They were eight-years old and the eldest of the young boys. We were not allowed to go to the fenced-off vegetable garden, but Jacobus, who was skinny, could squeeze between the bars. His head just about made it through if he wiggled hard enough. We would play loudly in front of the fence so that he could sneak unnoticed by the staff, and steal carrots for us.

I had a pet turtle named Sophie, after a character in French literature. Sophie actually came to me when I would call her, although she did not come very fast. I fed her little pieces of lettuce that Jacobus would bring from the garden. Sophie was about a foot long, had a beautiful shell and long sharp claws. One day someone threw Sophie up in the air, when she landed, her shell crushed her leg. After that, a cottage cheese like substance would ooze from her injury and she died shortly thereafter. We buried her in the back of the garden, with all due ceremony, marking her grave with a white cross and some stones.

Gunther about sixteen years old was from Germany and spoke French with a marked German accent. I did not know it then, but he must have been a German Jew, placed in the orphanage so he would be safe from the oppression in his native land. At sixteen, he was the monitor of our dormitory. Gunther had the brutal soul of the German military. He ruled our dormitory by beating up smaller children from time to time, especially if they made noise at bedtime.

At night, little Pierre, who was only seven, would moan softly "pipi, *pipi*". It was dark; Pierre had to go to the bathroom but was afraid of the dark. Receiving no reply from anyone, Pierre's moans would become louder and more persistent "*pipi, pipi!*" It could not be ignored.

"Silence" would yell Gunther, but the moans only grew louder and more frequent. Gunther would then order Gilbert to get up and take Pierre to the bathroom. Of course, Gilbert would ignore Gunther. There then developed a shouting match between Gunther, Gilbert and Jacobus. Gunther would become verbally more abusive and Gilbert would shout perfect imitation of Gunther's words and accent. Gunther would then get out of bed, jump on Gilbert's bed and start to hit and pummel Gilbert with his fists. Gilbert, cowering under his blanket, yelled, screamed and would beg for mercy. In the next bed, Jacobus was hollering bloody murder, begging Gunther to stop beating his twin. "*Pipi, pipi, pipi*" sang Pierre.

When exhausted, Gunther would retreat back to his bed. Gilbert, laughing, would emerge from under his blanket and start to mock Gunther again. Gunther would then repeat his assault all over again, with the same results. This would end only when Pierre would begin to cry, having pissed in his bed. This nightly occurrence would become routine after a while.

Gunther had a beautiful fountain pen, which I stole, probably because I disliked him so much. He was furious when he discovered his pen missing. He concluded that one of the younger boys was the thief. He conducted individual interrogations in the breakfast room. As the oldest of the younger boys, I advised them all that they had nothing to worry about.

"When he calls you in, just look him right in the eye and tell him you did not steal it. No matter how he yells at you, just stand your ground. Tell him you didn't take the pen".

Gunther never learned the truth and I don't remember what happened to the pen, which I couldn't use anyway.

With the coming of September, school had started again. Ruth and I had just a few weeks of schooling in Jette and now, we had to start all over again in our new environment. There were no classrooms in the Orphanage and we had to attend public schools in the neighborhood. Every morning, we left the orphanage and marched, two-by-two, to school. These were just a few streets away. Ruth and the other girls went to the *Ecole Communale, Rue Xavier De Bue* and I went with the other boys to the *Ecole Communale Rue du Doyenné*. Actually, the two groups left together to cross the large *Chaussée D'Alsemberg*, under the supervision of two adults and then the groups would split in two directions. Although two-by-two, we were really two-by-lonely, lost as we were in our individual world.

Most of the men who worked at the Orphanage had been mobilized and additional chores were assigned to the older children. After school, my new chore was to go and get the bread for the next day's meals, at a bakery on the *place Goossens*. This was not far from where I went to school, but it was a trip I took by myself, having to navigate across the wide *Chaussée d'Alsemberg* alone. For a nine-year-old, it was an adventure each day. I would bring a big red-checkered tablecloth, into which the baker would place eight or ten round loaves of fresh bread. The four corners would then be tied together and I'd sling the bundle over my right shoulder, and headed back to the orphanage. It weighed about ten kilos (22 lbs.). The odor of the fresh bread followed me as I walked back to the orphanage. I could reach with my left hand, between the folds of the tablecloth and tear off pieces of the hard crust. I'd munch on these all the way back to the orphanage, the weight of my burden forgotten in the pleasure of the tasty crust.

One day, we were all taken to a nearby movie theatre to see *Blanche Neige et les Septs Nains*. The Disney movie about Snow White was a beautiful revelation to me. It was even more marvelous than what I had seen in the windows of the *Bon Marché*, in Charleroi, a couple of years before. The whole thing was dubbed in French, songs and dialogue. The dwarfs: were *Grincheux, Prof, Dormeur, Atchoum, Joyeux, Timide and Simplet*. For weeks after that, we reenacted the story at the orphanage. Léonce, one of the older girls, played Snow White and I played Prince Charming. Mostly, it consisted of Léonce, pretending to bite into an apple, fainting and lying down. I would then pretend to get off my white horse, kneel near Léonce and kiss her. She would then get up, we would dance and everyone would be happy. I liked the casting.

In December, we heard that the Russians had invaded Finland. The Finns were very brave and the underdogs. They were fighting on skis and inflicted great losses on the Russians. At the time, the Russians and Germans were allies in some sort, having signed a non-aggression pact and having divided Poland between them. The Finns, under Marshall Mannerheim, were our heroes.

LA DROLE DE GUERRE (The Funny War)

With Poland fully occupied and divided between Germany and Russia, things returned to normalcy. Officially, there was a war between Germany and the Allies, France and England. The two sides settled in, The French behind the Maginot Line, which ran from the Swiss to the Belgian borders; the Germans behind their Siegfried Line, facing the French. Little was happening, most activities limited to reconnaissance patrols probing the territory between the two armies. The British were getting an expeditionary force (BEF) ready to support the French, but little was heard about them. Even the air force was restricted from harming anyone. Its activities were limited to dropping propaganda leaflets over the German border. Much care had to be taken to untie the bundles of leaflets, for fear that falling bundles might injure someone on the ground. This was referred to as La Drole de Guerre, The Funny War.

We were getting to be a restless bunch of kids. With the ever-present rumors of war, our games were turning more and more to fighting and battles. Mostly, no one wanted to be the Germans, it was either the French or the English. If you were picked to be a German, a *Boche,* Kraut, there followed an argument, which could escalate to a real fight. Berthe would then intervene severely and if peace did not follow real fast, punishment was swift and severe. The milder punishment was to be sent to bed without dinner. For more severe offenses, you would be plunged, struggling, into the bathtub filled with the pink liquid and brushed vigorously with the scrubbing brush for what seemed to be an eternity. Then, off to bed, without dinner. After that, the skin raw and swollen, you would walk funny for a couple of days.

If you persisted in misbehaving or went hysterical, as I sometime did, there was the water punishment. In this, you were dragged still screaming to the nearest sink filled with cold water and your head would be plunged and held under the water. You held your breath as long as you could, which was not long, as all control had been lost to anger. When your lungs begged for air, large gulps of water were aspirated, filling your lungs with cold water. The tormentor, usually Berthe, would then release her grip on your neck and let you stumble off, coughing and belching the water that had filled your lungs. It was painful, but it did have a sudden calming effect. After that, came confinement to your dorm, without food.

1940

Nous Irons Pendre Notre Linge Sur La Ligne Siegfried.
We're Gonna Hang Out The Washing On The Siegfried Line

On February 26th, 1940, my tenth birthday, Berthe gave me ten franc and said I could spend it on *spekuloos, a* spicy, traditional Belgian cookie, something like gingerbread. I went to the small store across from the orphanage and bought a whole brown paper bag full of spekuloos, then retreated to my bunk where I ate every one of the cookies. Later, Berthe asked me if I had shared my cookies with the other boys. It was my birthday, not theirs. I had never thought of "sharing"; a new concept to me. "That was not right" Berthe said, "You should have shared them with everybody else." I took her lesson to heart and would always remember the incident on my birthday.

Sixty years later, my friend Marie and I walked by Dandoy, the best spekuloos store in Brussels. We entered the store and I asked the young girl behind the counter how many spekuloos I could purchase for ten francs. She seemed puzzled and pointed to the signs that indicated that the spekuloos could be purchased in bags of 250 grams, pound, kilo, etc. I insisted "How many can I get for 10 francs?" She finally replied that I could have two spekuloos for ten francs. I gave her ten francs; she gave me two spekuloos cookies. I gave one to Marie and slowly ate the second one. It was not my birthday, but Berthe would have approved.

One day, I finally got tired of being in the orphanage. Berthe had just punished me for some offense now long forgotten. I was lonely for my parents and still homesick for Charleroi. I knew my Mother was living in Jette but there had been little contact. I didn't even know where my Father was. I hadn't seen him for nearly a year. We usually returned from school around two o'clock and did our homework and chores. Then, at about seven o'clock, dinner would be served in the big dining hall. On this day, late in the afternoon, I took my little school bag, filled it with my worldly possessions and headed towards the huge, black metal gate at the entrance of the institution. The gate had a big brass handle. It was my key to escape. As I passed the main house, Mme Kerremans appeared in her office window. She called out to me, "Rodolphe, is it at this hour that you come back from school?"

I was so relieved that she thought I was just now coming in late. I sheepishly replied, "Yes."

"Go straight to your room," she ordered, "And you will not have supper. Go immediately to bed."

Years later, I came to realize that she had known exactly what I was doing but had chosen not to make an issue of it.

When the war had started in 1939, it still wasn't our war. In April 1940, Germany invaded Norway and Denmark and while we didn't really understand fully the implications, we could see that the adults were growing increasingly concerned. Belgium was supposedly still neutral in the conflict and in January had refused to let the Allies pass through its territory. The German government had issued an ultimatum to the Belgian Government, asking for free passage through Belgium to France. As it had done in 1914, the Belgian Government refused. The French had fortified their border with Germany at the Maginot line, thought to be impregnable. However, the Belgian-French border was not protected. In 1914, the German troops of the Kaiser had then forced their way through the Belgian Ardennes forest. Now, once again, it was thought that the neutrality of Belgium would be respected by the Germans and besides, it was generally believed that the Ardennes forests were too dense to allow passage for the German motorized divisions.

MAY 10, 1940 THE WAR BEGINS

Our war started at about 5:00 a.m. on May 10, 1940. Asleep in the dormitory, we were awakened by thunder-like sounds. In the first light of dawn, we could see a blue cloudless sky on this pretty spring morning. The windows, big French windows, curving on top like those of a cathedral, were rattling with each noisy blast. We soon realized that this was not thunder, but the blasting of the *DCA (*Defense against aircraft*)*, the *ack-ack* of the Belgian ground forces. We quickly got dressed. Air raid sirens were wailing the beginning of the alarms, in other words, the wavy tone, rising and falling, filling us with frightened anguish.

We rushed outside. The blue sky was full of planes. There were German planes all over the place. We saw one Belgian plane, a biplane with an open cockpit, as it flew low overhead, over the orphanage. We could see the black, yellow and red Belgian colors of the *cocarde*, circular emblem painted on the underside of the wings and we cheered. It looked like a relic of the Great War and I could not even tell if it was outfitted for combat. All the kids cheered at this friendly plane. I seem to remember that the pilot banked slightly and waved at us kids. It then disappeared quickly over the trees.

There had never been such a magnificent, sunny, dry month of May as that of 1940. It seemed as if even the elements were in concert with the German invasion. The German planes were crisscrossing in the sky at different altitudes. Rounds of Belgian antiaircraft fire exploded in big puffs of black smoke. We had seen pictures in the newspapers and newsreel film of German Stukas dive-bombing during the invasion of Poland, so I easily recognized them in the air, that morning. I also saw some Messerschmidts, both single-engine planes and the twin-engine 110's.

We were rushed into the basement shelter. In the weeks preceding the German invasion, we had been issued gas masks. Everyone was mindful that Germany had used poison gas during the 1914-1918 war. There was no reason to believe that they wouldn't do it again this time, but to my knowledge, they never did, not for military purposes at least. The masks were in khaki canisters about the size of a large thermos, with corrugated metal sides. We had been practicing how to put on our gas masks, but on that morning, we slung them on our shoulders, sat on the floor and waited until the "All clear", when we went out and had breakfast. Now, we were having fun, it was all very exciting.

Monitoring the radio, we learned conclusively that Germany had invaded Belgium and that the German ambassador had tried to deliver an ultimatum to surrender to Paul Henri Spaak, the Belgian Foreign Minister. Spaak had stopped him in his tracks, uttering "Moi d'abord!" Me first!

He then read a declaration condemning Germany's undeclared invasion and violation of Belgium's neutrality. Belgium resisted and British troops of the BEF (British Expeditionary Forces) rushed to Belgium's aid. I had faith that the Belgian army would prevail. I knew the French would also be on our side, with the French *élan* and courageous ferocity they had demonstrated in the trenches of 1914-1918. We discussed at length the advantages the French had, with their longer bayonets, against the shorter ones in use in the German army.

"On the evening of May 9th, 1940 . . . . Colonel J.G. Sas, the Dutch military attaché in Berlin, ate a farewell dinner with his friend Major General Hans Oster, chief assistant to Admiral Canaris, the head of German Military Intelligence. Six days previously, Oster had warned Sas that the German attack through Holland and Belgium would begin on May 10, and after their farewell dinner together Sas confirmed the warning to his government in a dramatic message: "Tomorrow at dawn. Hold tight!" *"—From "1940" by Laurence Thompson.-*

It would seem hard to believe that if the Dutch military attaché had been given such stupendous news by Oster on May 3rd, 1940, he would not have warned both his Dutch government as well as his counterpart in the Belgian government

King Léopold had given the Belgian Air Force a couple of days off. It has never been determined why, in that tense period, just as Norway and Denmark had been invaded by the Germans. As it was, the Belgian planes, consisting mostly of vintage biplanes and some modern but inferior Hawker Hurricanes, purchased from England, were destroyed on the ground, that first day of the war. A single German plane bombed Brussels and dropped seven bombs on the open city. One incendiary bomb fell on a house in the Brussels suburb of St. Josse. The fire was quickly put out. There was a twelve-year-old girl living in that house, by the name of Rosa Wauters. She was later to become my wife.

While the German armies were bursting unchecked through the Belgian eastern provinces, the British, to live up to their commitments of helping Belgium and Holland if their neutrality had been violated were trying to come up from France.

"At one point, a unit of Major General B.L. Montgomery's* Third Division was refused permission to enter Belgium by a zealous (Belgian) frontier guard, on the grounds that it did not have the necessary permits. A fifteen-hundredweight truck charged the frontier barrier and the advance continued." From *"1940" by Laurence Thompson.*

*later famous as Bernard Law Lord Montgomery of El-Alamein, Commander in Chief of Britain's land forces.

Pastor Van Gouthem, the Orphanage supervisor, was also the Protestant Chaplain to the Belgian army. He left that day to rejoin the troops. He was a handsome man, a David Niven figure elegantly dressed in his jodhpur and the boots of a cavalryman. He drove away in a camouflaged Peugeot sedan. I don't believe I ever saw him again. I heard that after the war, he had left his wife and children and moved to the Belgian Congo with his mistress.

By the next day, May 11, 1940, our routine had pretty much returned to normal and I was even allowed to venture out to the bakery to get our bread supply. As I left the orphanage, I saw a large artillery piece, a huge, long cannon and the first I had ever seen, mounted on a carriage drawn by eight horses. The carriage was surrounded by Belgian artillerymen wearing their dark khaki uniforms and distinctive head caps with the artillery braid. A "*floche*" tassel of the same color swung back and forth as they walked. Hanging from their belt, a gas mask canister and the Belgian helmet, unchanged since the Great War. The soldiers had stopped in the grocery store where I had purchased my birthday spekuloos less than three months earlier. They were buying food and beer.

News from all over was tumbling in. The fortress of Eben Emael, on the canal Albert, reputed as the most modern and impregnable fortification was actually captured by German glider forces on the night of May 9th to 10th. The German armies were already outside of Liège and traveling fast and many people from that region were streaming south for the supposed safety of France that no one believed would be occupied by the Germans. The enormous wave of Belgian refugees, carting possessions on pushcarts, bicycles and cars stuffed to their roofs, was desperately trying to reach France. When gasoline ran out, cars were abandoned by the side of the roads. German warplanes bombed and strafed unimpeded by anyone. The narrow roads were clogged with refugees and debris, obstructing both the access of reinforcements to the front and the movement of the defeated Belgian and French troops trying to flee the German advance.

Those Belgian refugees lucky enough to reach and cross the French border, were to find themselves aggressed and insulted by French citizens, especially some weeks later, after the exhausted Belgian Army had surrendered to the invaders. The French population made brisk profits selling water and food at exorbitant prices to the refugees. They further compounded their misery by insulting them as *Les Boches* du Nord,* the *Boches* of the north.

*Boches, derogatory term for Germans (from d'Alboche, German demeaning word that became notorious during the First World War. Boches were supposed to live in Bochie.

I knew my Mother was in Brussels, but I did not know where my Father was and I panicked for him. I imagined him on the road someplace between Brussels and France, maybe being shot at by the German fighter planes. I was in tears, telling my friend Léon about my worries. He tried to console me by saying "Look, at least, your Father is alive. I don't have a Father, I don't have a Mother. So I'm worse off than you are." I tried to explain that in some ways, it was easier knowing that his Father was dead and buried, than worrying about the unknown. I was ill with fear, but Léon managed to calm me down.

During one of the nurse's nightly dinner reports, we learned that Neville Chamberlain had resigned as Prime Minister of England and had been replaced by Winston Churchill. We all knew of Chamberlain, he had been a figure of ridicule, with his black umbrella. Of Churchill, we knew nothing, but we were to become quite familiar with him in the years that were to follow. We learned that just forty-eight hours before the German attack, King Léopold III had granted leave from training to the entire mobilized Belgian air force. That, of course, resulted in great suspicion and rumors. The anti-royalists and those who believed in the conspiracy felt that Leopold's Father Albert I, who died in 1934, would have been less sympathetic to the German cause. Royalists, even those who disliked the Germans, saw nothing insidious in the coincidence.

Within three days of the air attack, on my daily trip to the bakery I saw my first British soldiers. The *Tommies* had arrived to help the Belgian armies and to cover the French flank. The *place Goossens* where the bakery was located was filled with men and military vehicles. I couldn't understand their English, but when the soldiers gave me the thumbs-up sign, I returned the gesture. They seemed to be a jovial lot, becoming serious only when asked if they were English. They seemed to be very intent about being called "Scots". They had set up a field kitchen in the square, made large amounts of tea and ate out of mess kits. The Scots seemed prepared and that made me feel good; if the English were here, then everything was going to be *okay*. They didn't seem worried, with their cocky caps and ready smiles. To me, they were the "English". I knew about Scots, Great Britain, perfidious Albion, the British Empire, but the general term in use was *Les Anglais,* the English and they came from *Angleterre*, England.

I don't remember seeing any Belgian troops at all during those days, except for the artillerymen of the first day. I guessed they were all at the front, fighting the advancing Germans.

On May 14, we learned that the German Luftwaffe had bombed Rotterdam heavily and I thought about *Tante* Rosa. I never did receive any information about her fate. The bombing was regarded as pure terrorism, to force Holland's quick surrender. The center of the city was virtually destroyed, the first time in warfare that an urban center had undergone such heavy bombing. We hoped that the Germans would not bomb Brussels. However, at about the same time, Hitler made a declaration: "If Brussels failed to surrender to his German troops, it would share the fate of Rotterdam and be heavily bombed."

When I was on my bread mission the day after Rotterdam was bombed, the English soldiers camped in the square seemed busier then they had been the earlier day. Mechanics were climbing all over their flat-nosed Lorries, preparing them for travel. The easy humor of the troops had evaporated.

Over the next two days, I watched the trucks leave the square, at a fast pace, one after the other. They were loaded with the Scots, now wearing the flat soup-plate helmet dating back to the trenches of 1914-1918. Rifles were slung over their shoulder or placed between their knees. They were still giving me the thumbs-up and smiling, but now they were yelling "good-bye" which I yelled back without quite knowing the meaning of the word. In fact, the English were retreating to the sea. There was nothing they could do, except try to save the British Expeditionary Force from certain annihilation by the vastly superior German forces sweeping through Belgium. The Belgian army was collapsing and the French army was being battered. Everywhere, soldiers were throwing away their rifles, discarding their uniforms and looking for the safety of civilian clothes, to escape the enemy. As the Scots fled, muffled explosions could be heard in the distance, as the English were blowing up the bridges around the city, as well as anything they felt could be of use to the advancing Germans. These Scots, with their smiling faces, had a rendezvous with *Dunkerque* (Dunkirk). Who knew how many would make it that far, as the Stukas and fighter planes of the Luftwaffe were strafing unimpeded everything that moved on the roads to the coast.

At dinner that night, we heard that more and more refugees were on the roads to France, traveling under terrible conditions, being strafed by gunfire from German planes and pushed off the roads by the advancing German tank columns. I could not sleep, having visions of my Father, body riddled with bullets, lying in a ditch, somewhere in France.

As it was, Bernard Horowitz, on May tenth, had decided to flee to France and had urged my Father to follow him. However, Bernard's parents, Feibisch and Bischka-Bischka, had resisted leaving. They felt too old for this new adventure and had preferred to await their fate in Jette. Unwilling to leave his aged parents behind, Horowitz reluctantly stayed put and so did Hilaire. Of course, neither Ruth nor I knew anything about this and we continued to worry about the fate of our Father.

When I arrived in the square on May 16, to pick up the bread, the *place* was strangely quiet. There was not a military truck or a soldier to be seen. There was also very little civilian traffic, even though the shops were open. I got the bread, slung the bag over my shoulder and walked back to the orphanage along largely deserted streets. At dinner, there was news that the Belgian government under Prime Minister Pierlot and Foreign Minister Paul Henri Spaak, had decided to evacuate to London, to set up a government in exile. Spaak was urging the King to follow them and to continue the fight from England. The grown-ups at the orphanage looked grim and unsmiling.

On May 17, after school, I went, as usual to pick up the bread. On my way back to the orphanage, just as I was about to cross the *Chaussée d'Alsemberg,* I became aware that people were looking at something in the distance. The street, paved with round Belgian cobblestones rose at a steep grade at that point and the crowd was looking south, down the hill. I heard the sound of horses' hooves ringing on the cobblestones. Then I saw two German soldiers on horseback coming up from the south. I recognized the German uniforms immediately, because of pictures I had seen in books and I had also seen German soldiers in Germany while visiting my grandMother in Cologne.

The highway was rounded along the center and the two horsemen rode along the lower outer edges near the curb. One was riding near the left sidewalk, the other along the right. They were scouts for the advancing German army, checking doorways and basement windows for *franc-tireurs,* snipers. When the Germans had entered Belgian towns in 1914, they had been fired upon by civilians sniping at them with hunting weapons and the German troops had taken stern reprisals against them. When caught, the Belgian civilians had been shot or hanged on the spot. In many cases, officials from the town had been marched to the main square and shot. All this, I had learned in history books. Lucky for us, no sniper was around as the scouts advanced up the *chaussée.*

As the right scout passed in front of me his brown horse looked huge to me. I noticed that his horse was slipping on the smooth cobblestones, making the distinctive sound one heard when horse-carts, such as beer wagons, passed by. The horse was chewing on its bit, white foam streaming from its mouth, nostrils flaring. Its eyes seemed gigantic to me and the animal looked more scared than the young soldier riding astride. I froze as the soldier passed by me. I had never been that near to a horse in my life. The scouts were in full battle uniform, with black boots and imposing steel helmets. A gasmask canister hung from a strap and each soldier held a pistol in the hand that gripped the reins. As I remember, their swords were drawn and glistened in the sun as the scouts leaned and peered around. They advanced slowly, one step at a time, each man carefully inspecting the windows and basements of every house on his side of the street. They continued on in the direction of the center of Brussels.

A little old lady, all dressed in black, with a white lace kerchief on her head, stood next to me. She looked like she was eighty or ninety. She turned my way and asked in French, "Are these French soldiers?" She must have been confused, because she remembered the German soldiers of the Great War, with their typical spiked helmets. These soldiers were coming up from the south, from the direction of France and she must have thought that they might have been French soldiers, coming to help us. I replied, "No, those are Germans" "Ah" she said. I never knew why I remembered her; maybe because she asked me that and was so innocent in her question.

Even after the two horsemen had moved on out of sight, everyone stood frozen, as if they were still watching a parade. Then, just a few minutes later, while we were all still standing there, pondering what we had just witnessed, the two scouts came back down the *chaussée* at a much faster pace, almost at a gallop. Soon, a line of six soldiers on horseback came up the road, followed by German squad cars filled with officers and soldiers and infantry behind that contingent. They were headed for the center of the city. They were coming up from the south, probably from Namur or Mons. There were no big tanks, just some armored cars. The German occupation of Brussels had begun.

When I got back to the orphanage, I told Mme Kerremans what I had seen. She softly placed one hand on my shoulder and touched me under the chin with the other hand. "Rodolphe, go and get ready for supper" is all she said. That was the only time Mme Kerremans had shown any tenderness towards me. She might have had a good idea of what were in store for Belgium, as well as for Ruth, Gunther and me, the Jewish children.

The advanced units of the German army had arrived in Brussels on the evening of May 17, 1940; most of the city was not occupied until the 18th. The German army had entered Brussels from three different directions and a special delegation had gone to see Mr Van de Meulebrook, the *Bourgemestre* the Mayor, to negotiate the surrender of the city without any fighting. Hitler, it was learned, was ready to bomb Brussels into ruins if any resistance was offered. On the 18th, The German commanders and German troops staged a parade in the historical Grand-Place, the heart of the city and of Belgium.

Hilaire in his memoirs related the events as follows:

"Then, it is the entrance of the German troops into Brussels on May 17, 1940, at 7.45 in the evening. The long nightmare of fifteen hundred and sixty-one days of occupation begins. It is lucky that the thousand years of Germanic peace that were promised by the Führer were brought back to more modest proportions.

From the sidewalk of the Rue Léopold Premier, I see passing, without realizing all of its implications, an endless parade of foot soldiers, dusty and tired. They were marching together with carriages drawn by horses. If it weren't for the color of the uniform and what these chariots contained, this would resemble more a return from the fields than a military parade. More than one of the onlookers makes the same naïve reflection as I do: Is this really this redoubtable army believed to be completely invincible?

The high command apparently did not judge useful to parade its elite troops and its most modern combat materiel in this particular place, just to impress the people. In a sense, what the spectacle lacks in grandeur, its improvised size seemed almost benevolent and it gave us a little bit of reassurance.

The next day, pushed by curiosity, I go down to the station of Tours Et Taxi, the huge bonded government warehouse area. The complex and its content have been seized by the Germans and it is now under the occupier's control. A benevolent soldier, an armed guard, invites me to enter. Fearing I don't know what trap it might conceal, I enter. This image of abundance belies for us the long period of deprivation which will now begin."

Frieda's recollection of the German entry in Brussels was more limited:

"And on May 18, later on that day, we saw the Germans coming in on horseback. They were good-looking men and they had a bag on their horse like a mailman's and that was filled with food supplies for them.

And I went to see my children (in the orphanage) *and they also explained to me what had happened on that particular day. And all the bridges had been blown up and a lot of people had no money and they all lined up at the borough hall of Jette and I went there too and I got a hundred francs and I had to sign a paper stating that when my personal situation got better, I would reimburse the borough for that money."*

MAY 18th, 1940, OCCUPATION

For Ruth and me, in the orphanage, the arrival of the German army did not create much change. We returned to school and I continued my daily trips to the bakery. Almost from the day the Germans occupied Brussels the color of the bread changed. The best flour was confiscated for food for the German occupiers and our white bread turned gray. It would get darker and more suspicious looking as the years went by.

At breakfast, instead of heaping the food in the middle of each table for a free-for-all, we were now allocated one soup-plate of pap, one slice of rye bread and one slice of "white" bread. After a few trades, I would wind up with three slices of the now gray bread, which I would butter carefully and cover with *confiture*.

At about this time, we were overjoyed to receive a visit from Mother. She had moved and was now living at the home of her old Cologne school friend, Bernard Horowitz, who was now living in Jette with his parents. They were Jews who had fled Germany a few years before. I cannot remember if Frieda even mentioned Hilaire. She told Ruth and me that she still couldn't afford to bring us home with her.

During the night of May 25th, the government of Belgium attempted once more to convince King Léopold III to follow them and to establish a government in exile in London. The king declined, stating that he wanted to share the fate of his armed forces and of his country. He retreated to his palace in Laeken, just northwest of Brussels.

Fierce fighting continued in the Western provinces of Belgium until May 27, 1940 when all resistance became futile and the Belgian army capitulated at midnight. The French and British armies were in full retreat. They had begun the evacuation from the continent at Dunkirk on the French coast. Over 330,000 British, French and Belgian troops would be successfully evacuated to England.

The reports, on June 15, that the Germans had entered Paris, came as terrible, confusing news to me. I had been sure that the French would stop the Germans advance in the trenches, just as they had done in 1914. I was crushed by France's defeat. Belgians and especially Walloons had an affinity for the French. As a schoolchild, I was taught that Napoléon was a hero, unaware that much of the rest of the world looked upon him as a tyrant. Waterloo, the scene of Napoléon's great defeat by Wellington, the English commander, is located in Belgium not far from Charleroi and Brussels.

On June 10th, Italy had declared war on France. We thought it was ironic, as the Italian army had not done too well in Ethiopia and we were sure that the French army would soon defeat Mussolini's troops. Meanwhile, the French were bitterly denouncing Belgians, *"Les Boches du Nord"* for having surrendered to the Germans in just eighteen days. However, under fierce attacks by the Germans and having been invaded from the south by the Italian army, France quickly capitulated to the Germans on June 22nd and to the Italians on June 24th. Thus on June 25th, 1940 fighting ended in France, just a short month after the surrender of Belgium.

A large numbers of Belgian soldiers were taken prisoner by the Germans and shipped to *Stalags* all over Germany and the newly conquered territories in Poland. The French-speaking Belgians were to remain there until the end of the war. Flemish-speaking Belgians would be released sooner as the Germans felt they had more of an affinity with them, as they did share an almost similar language. It was also a deliberate attempt at dividing the country between its Flemish and Walloon population.

Some soldiers, having succeeded in avoiding capture, had changed into civilian clothes and had made it back to their homes. The men who worked for the orphanage were among these and my bread duties soon came to an end.

CAFÉ RUBENS

Meanwhile, the path that had brought us this far, continued in the bizarre twists and turns of our lives. Hilaire, unable to find a job because, classified as a Stateless resident of the country, he did not have the proper work papers necessary to find employment. Shortly after the start of the occupation, he met, near the *Bourse,* the Stock Exchange, a Mr Beguin, whom he knew from Charleroi. Beguin confided that he planned to open an establishment, Rue *du Pont-Neuf* and asked

Hilaire to take care of the alterations and decorations. In reality, Beguin was broke and he would not be able to pay Hilaire until much later, when this *café dansant*, dancing, would be well under way.

Hilaire felt he could trust him and took care of putting the premises in condition to be used. Of course, Mr Beguin had to pay all the bills that Hilaire incurred. A few weeks later, the *Café Rubens* opened.

When the work was finished, Beguin mentioned that he needed to recruit waitresses. Since most of the clientele would consist of German soldiers and officers, those waitresses should be able to get along in German. Hilaire, when he got home to Horowitz's, talked about it with Frieda. Frieda, very courageously proposed to take such a job, while awaiting better days.

Rue du Pont-Neuf, where the Rubens opened, was on the fringes of Brussels' sprawling Red Light district around the *Gare du Nord,* the North Railroad station. The Rubens was a combination tavern, café and dancing. Some food was served, but that was not its primary attraction. The ladies working there were divided into three classes, waitresses, *entraineuses*, and prostitutes. Waitresses, took orders, looked pretty, smiled at the customers to make them feel special and delivered the food and drinks. *Entraineuses,* "dance hostesses", were there to entice the soldiers to drink and have them buy mostly champagne for the ladies. The champagne would arrive already poured, bubbling in the glasses or in bottles opened before these appeared at the tables. Mostly, the *entraineuses* were served ginger ale, which they dumped in the ice buckets when their customers were suitably distracted. The Larousse dictionary discreetly describes them as "Young women attached to a night establishment to engage the customers to dance". Frieda had befriended two of them, Edith and Helene, who were lovers. Edith was a tall dark Jewess, while Helene was a statuesque blonde Polish woman. Prostitutes made no pretense of being anything else and for an honest fee, took the soldiers upstairs, after they had been softened by the *entraineuses* and had little money left for anything else.

One evening, to cater to and please the German military clientele, the orchestra chose to play a selection from the popular Viennese Operetta," The White Horse's Inn" by Ralph Benatzky. And so, with gusto, they broke into the title song, a bouncy, lilting melody singing the praises of an inn in Tyrol.

Almost immediately, a German officer stood up and pounded on the table, hollering "Stop the music! *Das ist von einem Jude,* It is from a Jew! Stop the music!" But the band played on louder and louder, drowning out the chorus of German officers who, by then, had joined in the yelling and clamoring for the music to be stilled.

And Frieda worked very hard, waitressing. The soldiers liked her, she was pretty, engaging and had a good attitude. Naturally she spoke German fluently. All these years, she had been homesick for Germany and at the time she considered herself more German than Jewish. It is not known if the Germans were aware that she was Jewish, if they did, they did not seem to care. It was "Frieda here, Frieda there". The German customers would call on her to make change "Frieda, here, take the money, and pay for us". All the German officers seemed to have a lot of money and did not seem to care how much change she gave them back. Between her tips and what she kept for herself, she was making more money than she and Hilaire had seen in a long time.

63

Unfortunately, Mother had to work very late, past the 10 PM curfew and long after the last streetcar back to Jette had left. And she had to walk back to Jette and to get there, had to cross over a bridge, at least what was left of the bridge, after it had been blown up by the British during their retreat. And there was a German sentry and as Frieda passed, he said in German "Fraulein, if you come this way tomorrow, I'm going to have to shoot you in the ass." He was probably making a poor joke or trying to impress her. However, Frieda took the threat very seriously and the next night, she had to go on foot again and there was this big German staff car with officers in it. They called to her and asked "Fraulein, can you tell us where the King's palace is, in Laeken?"

"Sure, I can show you if you take me with you" she replied. They were officers, on the way to see King Léopold III, to bring him a special short wave radio as a present from Adolf Hitler. And Frieda had to lie down at the bottom of the big Mercedes-Benz convertible, because the officers were afraid that the *Feldgendarme,* the German Military Police, might see her. At that time, civilians were not allowed in German military vehicles.

Jette was on the way to Laeken and after she showed them the way, they brought her back to the house of Bernard Horowitz, where she now lived with Father. When Bernard saw Frieda arriving in this huge German staff car, he was furious and started to yell at her in French. Frieda knew that Bernard was right, but she had guided these officers to the King's palace because they had to see King Léopold III and then they took her back to where she was living. And Bernard yelled and the next day he said that she could no longer stay in his house and that she and Hilaire would have to leave.

Having to leave the Horowitz house, Hilaire found an apartment on the second floor of number thirty-seven, *Rue de Malines,* above the Café Cambridge, in the very center of the city. This also had the advantage of being just a few streets away from the Rubens. The lady in charge of the Cambridge took a liking to Hilaire and rented him the apartment at a very reasonable rent. He was a handsome man and she thought he was unattached. Much to her surprise, Hilaire moved in with Frieda, his wife. She was going to be even more miffed a few months later when Ruth and I were to rejoin our parents.

Hilaire, meanwhile, worked part-time at the Cambridge, as a *garçon de café*, a waiter, figuring that if Frieda could accept a job as a waitress, he could be a waiter. Together they could prevent their meager capital from melting away. At the Cambridge, Hilaire would meet a number of characters, Belgians and Germans, who would be instrumental in his ability to make money, which in the years that followed, would assure our eventual survival.

SUMMER 1940, BOOM (rhymes with Rome)

With the end of June 1940, I was finishing my fourth grade at the *Ecole Communale*. No recollection of the time spent in the classroom, no memory of friends or teachers have remained. I must have sailed on without any effort, relying on my ability to absorb without having to study or even open a book. It was likely that the combination of being separated from my parents and the advent of the German invasion and occupation obliterated all souvenirs of that time. There remained the mental pictures of walking to the school and of walking back to the orphanage, but not a single memory of the time actually spent inside the walls of the school.

Belgium had always been overwhelmingly Catholic. There was a small Protestant minority and an even smaller Jewish presence. The Methodist church administered the orphanage and it must have received funds from various allied organizations. There were Methodists around the country that supported the church in various ways. Near Antwerp, in Boom, lived a family of Methodists. The head of the family, Mr Van A. was the deputy-chief of police of Antwerp. He lived in Boom in a large house with a big garden. Each year, MrVan.A. would invite a few children from the orphanage to spend the summer vacation at his home. Together with a couple of girls, I was chosen to spend a few weeks there. Ruth, I guessed, had been sent somewhere else.

It almost felt like home, actually, it was more like home than any place I had ever known. The family had a little black cat that became my friend and slept near me every night curled up by my feet, under the blanket. The food was good and plentiful. The large garden had been changed from flower to vegetable growing and in these early months of the occupation, food was still available in the countryside. I tried to impress the girls by making rose water. I assured them that using petals from the flowers in the garden, I could make a nice perfume. Much to my dismay, days and weeks passed and the petals floating in water bowls never turned into scented liquid. Sundays, we went to services in a small Methodist church nearby.

Mr Van A. had a daughter, Anneke; she must have been thirteen or so. One Sunday, there was a get together party in the garden. The deputy-chief had invited a few policemen and their wives to share the afternoon in the garden. It was a hot day and the grown-ups were drinking beer in one area of the garden, near the house. A little ways off, a white camping tent had been erected and the daughter and two other young boys had taken residence in it. Curious, I lifted the flap and entered the tent. There was something going on. The boys and Anneke were embracing and kissing, I soon noticed that the boys had their pants buttons open and Anneke's blouse was undone. Hands had disappeared in the open clothing and there was a frozen moment as I poked in through the tent opening. The trio looked at each other and invited me to join them.

They were at least three years older than I was and my interest in this adventure had nothing to do with sex. However, the sight of Anneke, sitting on the ground, undone, fascinated me. I became obsessed with the need to see her naked behind. "I want to see her ass "I demanded.

There was a long silence. Outside, you could hear the grownups talking and laughing. A bit louder now I repeated my demand to see Anneke's *derriere*. Aware that my raised voice might attract the attention of the adults, Anneke complied, pulled down her panties and turned up her behind to me. Outside, it was bright sunlight and the light illuminated the inside of the white tent with a shadowless glow. The white skin of Anneke's behind dazzled me. I had never seen skin so white. Too soon, the panties were back on and the trio resumed the embraces I had interrupted. Satisfied, I left the tent. Mr Van A. and his friends were still joking and drinking, seemingly unaware of what was happening in the tent. I went looking for my friend, the little black cat.

One morning in August, a surprise visitor startled me. It was my Mother, riding in a German staff car and surrounded by German officers. She was radiant in her happiness to see me and I was thrilled to see her. It was the first time I had seen her since May 18th. Frieda had told her German officer admirers that she had a son in Boom and they had been only too glad to drive her there in their chauffeur driven Mercedes-Benz convertible. She assured me, that our family would soon be reunited. A kiss and she was gone!

In September, I returned to the orphanage, but in my impatience to leave this place, I became more and harder to control. I had daily arguments with Berthe and refused to obey work orders. I was really out of control. Punishment followed punishment. One day it was the severe horsehair brushing in the tub, the next day, it was immersion in the cold-water sink until I gasped and choked and water filled my lungs.

One evening, having been sent to bed without dinner, I began to scream. Berthe grabbed me and pulled me to the outside sink. There, she dunked my head under water until I was out of breath. Large gulps of water filled my lungs and Berthe threw me inside the dormitory and locked me inside. I was hysterical, yelling, kicking and throwing the beds around in the dorm. Ruth came to the door. I was not to be reasoned with. "I'm starving to death," I yelled. I banged against the door, trying to pry it open by wedging a big piece of wood under it and finally using a chair leg to force open the door, the bottom of which disintegrated under the force of my fury.

Not long after this incident, Mother arrived to take my sister and me home. Before I left, I cut off some of my black curls and gave them to nurse Marguerite as a souvenir. She had always been nice to me. She laughed when I told her that since she had always admired my hair, I was leaving her these locks, in memory of me. And so, in October 1940, after ten months in the orphanage, the Rosenberg family was reunited for the first time since early 1938. We settled in the apartment above the Café Cambridge in the *Rue de Malines*, in the center of Brussels.

At the very same time, Baron General Alexander von Falkenhausen, German military governor, decreed that Jews, in Belgium, be registered with all the members of their household.

RUE DE MALINES

Our apartment sat on the second floor of the building. The Café Cambridge occupied the *rez-de-chaussée*, the ground floor and we lived two floors above the café. The apartment had one large room, with two sets of French windows that opened onto two balconies overlooking the Rue De Malines. That room served as living, dining and main bedroom. In the back stood the kitchen, with a gas stove, a sink and a narrow counter along the wall. Washing was at the sink, with cold water and a washcloth. Soap was still available, but it did not lather very much. I have no recollection of where we slept or where the bathroom was situated. I guess it was a common toilet, on the landing between floors, as was usual at the time.

At the Café Rubens, Frieda had made the acquaintance of Hans, a fighter pilot of the Luftwaffe and had a brief affair with him. Hans flew the Messerschmitt Me-109 during the Battle of Britain and according to Frieda was to fall in 1941 in the Russian campaign. Hans was short and compact in his blue Luftwaffe uniform. Fighter pilots had to be short in order to fit in the confined space of the cockpits. The time was late August of 1940; the Battle of Britain was raging.

I saw Hans in the apartment once and Mother told me about him. I didn't find that unusual either that my Mother would talk about boyfriends or that this one was in the German military; there was a certain thrill to be in the presence of a fighter pilot, even a German. It must have been fun for Frieda to walk arm in arm with a fellow countryman with whom she could speak German again.

When the Germans had invaded Belgium and destroyed the Belgian Air Force on the ground, Giovanni Dieu, a young Belgian fighter pilot, had escaped to England and joined the Royal Air Force to continue the fight against the Germans. As it was, he was assigned to a Spitfire squadron and fought bravely in the Battle of Britain. He was shot down three times, but survived to become a much-decorated hero. He too, was short and compact in his blue RAF uniform. After the war, he was to have a long affair with Frieda.

It was one of the ironies of the war that both Hans and Giovanni may have met in the air and fought against each other, only to share an affair with the same woman.

In September 1940 Mussolini volunteered his Italian Air Force to Hitler, offering to support the German effort against the RAF. Italian airmen soon became visible in the streets of Brussels. They were walking around with lose-fitting uniforms, the belt askew pulled down by the pistol hanging at their right hip and a leather shoulder strap cutting across the chest. Somehow, they did not appear as martial as the Germans were. The reputation of the Italian fighting forces was the subject of derision and numerous jokes were circulating around. The Duce's army was about to suffer severe reversals in North Africa and in its campaigns in Greece and Albania. There was a joke about Hitler asking Mussolini for assistance with crossing the English Channel, *La Manche*, (the sleeve). Mussolini could not help, as "His hands were full of Greece". At the time, these were the only good news we could hang our hopes on in an otherwise somber period.

My favorite place was the balcony of our apartment. From that vantage point, it overlooked streets filled with crowds of soldiers, civilians and pushcart peddlers. It was an unending theatre of activities. To my left, Rue de Malines crossed the Boulevard Adolphe Max. At the corner, the Plaza Hotel served as the headquarters of General von Falkenhausen the German military governor of Belgium. Several times a day, I could watch the changing of the guard. Six soldiers, with rifle at right shoulder, would come down the boulevard, goose-stepping loudly on the pavement. Under the barked direction of a corporal they would change places with the soldiers guarding the hotel and the old guards formed ranks and goose-stepped away. As much as we hated the Germans; it was a ritual that fascinated me and the crowd of gaping onlookers.

To my right, I could see the *Rue Neuve,* the commercial center of Brussels, a mostly pedestrian street in which only local traffic and delivery trucks were allowed. There, a constant parade of pushcarts circulated, with their vendors peddling fruit and vegetables outside of the Innovation department store. The unlicensed pushcarts were in constant danger of being fined by the Police.

67

They would disappear quickly at the sight of an approaching policeman. In their haste to escape, they would rumble up the *Rue de la Blanchisserie,* under the arch and the clock of the *Innovation* and turn right into the *Rue du Cannon,* a dark, mysterious impasse, right out of Charles Dickens. I would sometime venture to the edge of it, but never had the courage to penetrate its area.

Shoppers bought from the pushcart vendors. It was quicker and perhaps cheaper than buying from more legitimate stores. However, from our balcony vantage point, we were able to see a constant cheating game perpetrated by the vendors. Each cart had a weighing scale at one end. This consisted of a deep metal basket and a flat tray on which rested a weight. There was always a weight on the flat tray, either a kilo or a *livre* (500 grams, a metric pound). Thus, when the deep basket was empty, the scale always tilted to the weight-bearing tray. There was no way one could check for the accuracy of the scale. However, from our balcony, we could see that there was always at least one piece of fruit or whatever in the deep basket. This was not visible to the customers. Thus, if you bought a kilo of apples, the merchant would pick the apples from the bottom of the pile, usually the worse fruit, make a large newspaper cone and fill it with the apples. The merchant, always a woman, would then slam the filled cone into the basket, forcing the scale away from the flat tray position. Before the scale could return to a balanced position, the bag was lifted, closed and the whole thing was thrust into the arms of the shopper. Since there was always a fruit in the basket and it never made its way into the paper cone, the shoppers were invariably cheated. And often, as a lookout spied a policeman arriving, the pushcart was wheeled into the impasse, the customer vainly trying to get the change that was due for the transaction.

The policemen strode very slowly, their duty being to disturb the whole set-up to please the legitimate merchants but not to interfere too much. Only occasionally did the white-helmeted *agent de police* issue a *contravention,* a summons. It was a game that was repeated endlessly and which I enjoyed very much observing.

Mr Fleugelhofer, a Cologne friend of Frieda, came to visit us one day. He was a German forced out of Germany because he had married a Jewess. However, he was very German in his comportment and enjoyed all the privileges of being a German citizen in occupied Belgium, like not having to pay when using public transportation. As he was in our apartment, Frieda, to amuse him, showed him the little "Pushcart" comedy that was being played under our balcony. Fleugelhofer became incensed and stormed down to the street below. He quickly found a policeman and in his heavy German accent, demanded that the peddlers be arrested immediately, for cheating the public.

The policeman, well aware of the games played, was not inclined to take any action. What was more, since he realized that he was dealing with a German national, he was not about to please him, no matter the legitimacy of his grievance. He smiled at Fleugelhofer, "Monsieur, he replied, people who buy *a la charrette* know they are being cheated" Fleugelhofer came back to our apartment, furious and complaining loudly that such things would never be tolerated in Germany.

Forty years later, while visiting Brussels, my friend Marie and I were walking in the Rue Neuve. The same pushcarts were still lined up at the corner of the Rue de Malines, not far from the Café Cambridge. As I had told the story many times, we approached one pushcart and I told Marie that I was going to show her something. As I stood on tiptoe, I strained to see inside the deep basket to see if one or more tomatoes already lined the bottom. The merchant, not amused, let go with an insult in Brussels slang.

"Espece de Crotter!" She hurled at me. That translated loosely as "Specie of shit-covered pauper". I almost fell to the ground with laughter. I felt so honored to have been able to provoke that woman to compliment me with such a rich Brussels insult. Nothing could have pleased me more.

School year 1940-1941 came along. Ruth and I were now able to resume our schooling. We were both registered in an *Ecole Communale,* public school, Ruth in an all girl school, me in an all boy school as was the custom at the time.

That's when the impact of anti-Semitism really began to strike us and was now painfully obvious to me. Every day we were exposed to German propaganda, about the Jews and how they were responsible for the war. Everywhere, on the radio, in posters, newspapers and magazine articles, a vicious campaign against Jews was launched. There were always caricatures of the Wall Street Jews, the fat, thick-lipped, cigar chomping, big-nosed, big-eared and pot-bellied Jew.

On my way to school, some of the meaner kids at the nearby *Institut St. Louis*, run by the Jesuits, would chase after me, threatening to beat me up and calling me names, usually *sale Juif*, dirty Jew. They accused my Father of having killed Jesus Christ. I was ten years old and the only defense I had was to start crying, which I did easily. They usually left me alone after that. At the time, Jacques Brel, also ten years old, was studying at that Jesuit school. As a song writer/singer/performer, he would become my idol some twenty-five years later. I have often wondered if Brel had been among my tormentors.

In school, I was now in the fifth grade. Some of the children called me names, mostly the usual *sale-Juif.* By now, I felt that these two words went together, as I did not ever recall hearing the word "Jew" without that prefix. Yet, I was still a bright student, well liked by my teachers.

On one occasion, we had been taken on a field trip to a nearby library. There were some of the latest books of Tintin & Milou. These stories by Herge were becoming very popular and I longed to read these large hardcover comic books. Tintin was my hero; I had seen his comic strips in *Le Soir,* the main Brussels newspaper. However, never had I been fortunate enough to read a whole book of his adventures. The teacher allowed the class to pounce on the Tintin volumes, while they suggested that Rosenberg, being so smart, should concentrate on History and Geography books.

And I sat there, at the library table, perusing through "The History of Gaul under Julius Cesar", while trying to steal a look or two at the Tintin books my classmates were devouring.

Every other month, the whole class was marched, two by two (Two by alone, as Jacques Brel would write years later), to the *Bain Royal,* the Royal Bath, where we were to take a shower, before venturing in the large public swimming pool. Still being water-shy, I managed to remain in the shallow part of the pool, not daring to venture any deeper. In the shower stalls, I was intrigued and uneasy in the presence of the many naked grown men taking showers. The sight of them, naked and hairy gave me a strange, embarrassed feeling. As for me, remembering my Father's admonitions, I did the best I could to hide the traces of my circumcision. After the bath, on the way back to the school, we would try to slip away into a store or two and after the class had passed by, we'd meander through Brussels, before finding our way home again. The teacher, at the head of the column, seemed completely unaware of the dwindling number of children that were left following him.

I had become fascinated by German toys that were now on sale in a number of stores. In the *Rue du Marché aux Herbes,* a toy store had a display of Marklin electric trains. The Marklin were 00 gauges and miniature marvels. Whenever I had free time, I would go and admire the intricate tracks, tunnels, train stations and little people of the display. That was what I wanted as a gift from St. Nicolas.

As December approached, I told Mother that what I wanted for my St. Nicolas was a Marklin double-0 train set. Bernard Horowitz happened to visit our apartment on that day. He quickly voiced the opinion that I would be better off with a *Mecano* erector set. Horowitz calmly explained that I would soon get tired of watching the train go round and round and that with the erector set, there would be endless hours of fun. I did not want an erector set; I wanted a Marklin train set! I was quite vocal about it, accusing Bernard Horowitz of wanting to spoil my feast of St. Nicolas.

On December 6th, I eagerly opened my present. Neither a train set, nor a *Mecano* awaited me. Instead, I received a small mechanical car, about four inches long, with a key-operated coil spring. It was blue and shiny and quite attractive. From the center of the roof, an umbilical cord extended upward for about a meter, (three feet). At the top end, a miniature steering wheel allowed you to control the direction the car would be headed for. I could wind the car up, place it on the floor or on a table, release the brake and guide the car forward or make it turn every which way with the steering wheel. I soon tired of that. Oh, how I hated Bernard Horowitz!

A little before Christmas of 1940, the Germans, in a surprising demonstration of generosity, decreed that each family would be issued a special ration coupon for one half goose. Since the goose is the traditional meal for Christmas, the news was received with much enthusiasm.

Mr Fleugelhofer showed up and offered to sell us his coupon for a half goose. At the time, Hilaire was starting to make a lot of money in the black market and we could well afford to purchase Fleugelhofer's half goose. We paid him and wound up with enough coupons to buy a full goose. A few days later, the geese arrived in specified stores and the populace went to purchase this unexpected windfall. Unfortunately, these had been wild geese, fed on fish. The birds, no matter how carefully cooked, reeked and tasted of fish. Our goose was inedible and had to be thrown away.

Frieda decided to prepare a carp, Jewish style, with raisins, onions and carrots in a clear jelly. She was very proud of her ability to make this exotic dish, unknown in Belgium, except among Jews of German and Eastern European origin. In the fish store, she had had to explain how she was going to prepare the fish. She had managed to buy the whole fish, still half-alive. On the counter of the kitchen, she pounded the beast into submission with repeated blows from a square, knuckled, wooden mallet. The carp would strike back with hard swipes of its tail. Mother insisted that the fish was dead and all we were seeing were nerve reflexes. It was quite a sight to see. However, the meal was a delight, finished off with a noodle pie, also of Jewish origin and made with noodles, raisins, almonds and lemon rind. Although I had not been raised in the Jewish faith, there were indeed parts of the Jewish culture, culinary, mannerisms and linguistic being infused in me and of that, I was totally unaware.

One evening, at the Café Rubens, Frieda was called upon to wait on a group of German soldiers. With these soldiers, Frieda recognized a woman who used to be our maid in Charleroi (not Léona). Unwilling to be demeaned by having to wait on her, she went to the Rubens manager and in tears, asked that she not be forced to wait at that table. The manager insisted that she did. With that an argument ensued and Frieda was fired. By then, we did not need the money any longer and Frieda stopped working.

At the Café Cambridge, Hilaire met a Gestapo colonel by the name of Eppstein. A button had come off his uniform (I never learned what button; this was in pre-zipper days.). Hilaire volunteered the services of Frieda to sew the button back on. Soon, Eppstein became a regular visitor to our apartment. Eppstein knew we were Jewish, but he liked Frieda. I believe they both came from the Cologne region. They became lovers. Eppstein delighted in telling Frieda stories about what the Germans were doing to the Jews in Poland. He took pleasure in describing the killings that were going on. Mother wondered how Eppstein could be a part of this, which a name like Eppstein. He replied that he spelled his name with two "P"s and that made him a non-Jew.

After a particularly vivid description of the atrocities against Jews in Poland, Mother said, referring to the Jews in Belgium, "That it will be very bad for us, if Germany wins the war "With that, Eppstein stood up so quickly that he knocked his chair over. He placed his hand on his pistol holster and said, "IF Germany wins the war? You mean WHEN Germany wins the war!"

It was the end of 1940, and the only dimly bright spots on the horizon were that England had not been invaded and was our only hope; that the Italians were being defeated by the British in North Africa and by the Greek army in Greece and Albania.

1941

Wenn wir fahren,
Wenn wir fahren,
Wenn wir fahren, gegen Engeland.
(When we embark against England) German military marching song.

BLACK MARKET

Father had no citizenship, he was Stateless. When Frieda married him, she became Stateless. Ruth, though born in Germany and I, born in Belgium were Stateless too. As foreigners in a small country, it was almost impossible to find work without working papers. Hilaire, working as a waiter at the Cambridge, met numerous characters and developed a network of Belgian and German contacts. Father would become very involved in several black marketing enterprises. These would bring us huge sums of money and soon, Hilaire would be able to stop working at the café and concentrate on his black market activities.

By then, except in official documents, the name Rosenberg was seldom used. Father's transactions would be strictly under the name of *Monsieur* Hilaire. No one would know his name was Rosenberg but it was hard to believe that the Gentiles, especially the German officers he was dealing with, didn't suspect he was a Jew. Not only did Hilaire have Jewish physical characteristics, but he also had a pronounced Jewish accent when he spoke French or German and showed distinct Polish-Jewish mannerisms and inflections.

At the Cambridge, Hilaire met a Mr Carlier, a musician, who asked Hilaire if he could denounce black marketteers and other persons of interest to the German police. Of course, he would be amply rewarded for such a service. Hilaire briefly toyed with the prospect of turning himself in, for the reward. However, he could see that there would be little sense in playing that game. However, another Cambridge customer, Mr Charles from Luxembourg, found that proposition to his liking. Mr Charles denounced Jews, members of the *Resistance*, refractors and black marketteers. The dangers of this particular trade had not been apparent to Mr Charles, until the Resistance shot him sometime later

Hilaire became more and more involved in his black market activities. Once he began his role as a middleman, his reputation spread by word of mouth and he became well known. If someone had something to sell, there was a *Monsieur* Hilaire who would know where to offer it. Hilaire never would invest his own money, but worked on a commission once the deal was consummated. He spent a lot of time at a Café, near *La Bourse,* "The Stock Exchange". That Café was mostly a meeting place for dozens of Jews, all in the same boat as Father and trying to make a living in an illegal trade; legal avenues having been closed to Jews by the occupying Germans. Everyone was involved, including the Belgian Resistance and the German military. Some of these, as well as a steady stream of Belgians also involved in Black Market activities, regularly showed up at the Cambridge and in our apartment. Among these, there was a Mr Sabot and his beautiful sister-in-law Marthe. I could not help but wonder if Marthe and Hilaire slept together. As I remember Sabot, he was a thin, blonde man, with darting eyes, smoking one cigarette after another and an air of not having slept for weeks. Hilaire claimed that Marthe had a German boyfriend and through her contacts, many good deals could be made with the German Army. After the war, Sabot would be declared an *Incivique,* unpatriotic. He would be convicted, fined and served time in prison for dealing with the occupier. At the time, there was talk of a Mr Hilaire, who was involved in those same transactions, but little had been known about him and Father was not inculpated.

Hilaire got involved with a Mr Gosselin to dispose of spoiled merchandise, mostly large tins of "Hard-tacks" biscuits salvaged from barges that had been sunk in the canals when the retreating British blew up the bridges. Some of the biscuits found their way into our diet and despite a slight musty smell, the taste was acceptable.

There was also a matter of cigarettes. A large lot of cigarettes originally destined for the British troops had been seized by the Germans in Antwerp. They were transferred to Brussels, in a warehouse run by the Germans. Little by little, these cigarettes were spirited away from the depot and Hilaire had to find a way to sell these on the black market. These "Gasparades" cigarettes had been salvaged from a sunken barge. They had been stored for a long time and the silver paper of the packs had become green with mold. So, for days and weeks, Ruth and I spent our evenings opening each pack, scraping off the mold with a flat blade and resealing each pack. Thus, this enormous lot of cigarettes was salvaged and sold on the black market for a very nice profit. All the while, none of us developed a need to smoke, although these "Gasparades" were of the finest tobacco.

Even Bernard Horowitz would surface and got Hilaire involved with a warehouse full of house linens from the Tank Company in Alost, in the Flemish area of Belgium. These were eventually sold to the German Quartermaster. All along, I would be sitting in the common room, Rue de Malines, doing my homework and being a witness to all that was going on.

Hilaire, in his memoirs, continues:

> At that time also a Viennese woman whose husband is in prison in Breendonck (a political prison//torture camp near to Antwerp) accused of money laundering, for having sold stamp collections in a foreign country, asks me if among the customers of the Cambridge, there couldn't be one who would be able to obtain the freedom for her husband. I talk about it to a female customer who seems to be very intimate with a German officer. She advises me to offer a chicken to this officer to obtain a friendly and useful intervention. I find a way to procure the poultry and I bring it to the requisitioned apartment where the officer is residing near the Place General Meiser. Unfortunately, he will not, or cannot do anything, and the enterprise is a total failure.
>
> I do remember, with Mr Gosselin, the shipment of a stock of string, in the (train) station of Vilvorde (just outside of Brussels), where I learned that it was supposed to be for the manufacture of anti-aircraft camouflage nets. Despite the intervention and the words of caution of a Belgian commandant, member of the (Belgian) Resistance, who collects part of the money and splits it with us, I find this kind of business dubious, and I declare that I no longer want to be involved in it.
>
> I will more than once have the occasion to be astonished by the part taken by the Resistance in this business of supplying to the German Army and the veritable racket of protection and extortion of which I became a victim or witness. I will get back to it later.

Several times, Father would invite me and Ruth to join him for lunch or dinner at *Chez Gino*, a small Italian restaurant in the *Rue du Marais*, a couple of streets away from our apartment. There, we would join him at the table, surrounded by German officers of all rank. Father would encourage us to order antipasto and pasta, however, the combination of unfamiliar foods and the presence of so many Germans made us very uneasy and we did not hide our displeasure at having to be there at all. At Gino's, more transactions were being undertaken, including minor ones that had to do with providing the German Officers with silks, perfumes and other items they needed for their romantic pursuits.

PROSPEROUS, BUT UNEASY NEW YEAR

With our newfound prosperity, Mother, maybe feeling remorse at having placed us in the orphanage, decided that Ruth and I should now be exposed to the finer cultural things.

We were enrolled in the *Jeunesses Musicales,* a group of youths going to classical concerts. Although we went to several concerts, the sole piece of music that was to stick in my memory was the Children's Symphony, which is geared to please little kids. Even at age eleven, I found it corny.

After that, it was piano lessons. Frieda found a piano teacher who would come to our apartment once a week for one half-hour classes each for Ruth and me. I did not get along with the teacher, I hated the way she would press on my fingers and force me to hit the keys. The more force she applied, the more I struggled back. She would turn to me and yell in my face, as she pounded on my hands, "Do,Re,Mi,Fa,Sol,La,Si,Do". The poor woman had the hands of the witch in "Snow White", with gnarled knuckles on all fingers that protruded from either very hard work or arthritis and very dirty nails. She had garlic breath and in those days, I was not used to that odor that I found repulsive. So, for a half-hour, we wrestled and struggled and little if anything was learned. Of course, there was no way I would practice during the week and she found me just as obtuse by the time she would return for the next lesson.

More than once, Ruth would find a pretext to skip her lesson and I would wind up having to suffer through both half-hours. I would then try to beg off and escape having to stay there. The poor woman was a Jewish refugee from Poland and obviously needed the money. So, even though both Ruth and I had run away from our lessons, Mother would pay the lady for the full hour and feed her to boot.

On one occasion, Ruth had been invited by a school friend of hers to go for a day trip in the country, just outside of Brussels. Rather than stay and face the garlic all by myself, I tagged along. We went to a field of berries and harvested baskets of ripe green gooseberries and red currants. Strings of red currants would file into my mouth and I'd pull the stem out between my closed lips and teeth, capturing the red berries as they exploded against my palate. That was a sensation so new to me and the memory returns whenever I eat red currants.

In these early months of the occupation, there was food available for those who could afford it. Ration cards had been issued, as well as ration stamps. Unfortunately, most of the food would disappear from the regular stores where prices were fixed and ration stamps required. The food would reappear on the black market where the prices continued to rise higher and higher with each passing month.

Hilaire had even found a Jewish bakery nearby where he could buy Jewish pastries and specialties he had not eaten since he had left his homeland nearly twenty-five years earlier. He would bring us some and we'd eat those strange cakes and cookies.

Once, Frieda managed to buy an entire Ardennes smoked ham and it hung in the kitchen without refrigeration. She would slice a piece or two for breakfast or lunch. As the weeks went by, the ham began to be attacked by maggots and entire living colonies swarmed with vermin. Mother would take a knife and scrape off and cut away the contaminated parts. We would then be served a pristine slice of delicious smoked Ardennes ham. Frieda would admonish Ruth and me not to tell Father about the maggots, as "It is already difficult enough to have your Father eat ham. If he knew it was full of maggots, he would never touch it."

In those days, Place de Brouckere was the heart of the Capital and the center of the Place was the Hotel Metropole. The hotel featured an extended terrace, with tables and seats, all oriented toward the center of the Square. If you sat there long enough, you were sure to be seen and to see all of Brussels parading in front of the Metropole. The German Army had requisitioned the hotel, but the Café Metropole and the terrace were open to all. Next to the hotel, stood a *Marchand de Primeurs,* a store that featured early, out of season or exotic fruit and vegetables at astronomical prices. It was a wonder that such food was available at all and the clientele was confined mostly to German officers and prosperous civilians. As by now, we had shifted into that last category; Frieda would often buy tangerines that came from Spain, figs, bananas and other delights heretofore unknown to me.

On the next corner, a very large café-restaurant prospered on the Boulevard Anspach. Once again, the patrons were mostly German officers consuming salads, sandwiches and wonderful Belgian pastries, all washed down with wines, champagnes and the finest coffee. Cigars and cigarettes were everywhere and the whole dining room would be hazy with the blue smoke rising from hundreds of German mouths and nostrils. On a few occasions, the Hilaire family would be invited to eat there, in the company of Hilaire's contacts. I would observe the distinct way the officers had of holding their cigarettes. These would be held straight up, between the thumb and the index finger, palm up, the other fingers fully extended. To puff, the head would tilt back, the palm would travel to the chin and the smoker would reach under the cigarette to take a deep drag. The smoke would then be exhaled with the head still tilted backward and expelled straight up. It seemed to me that the higher the rank, or if they were in the Gestapo uniform, the more pronounced the mannerism would be. Perhaps it was taught in military school, or it was a style that enabled them to recognize each other by the way they held their cigarettes.

While we ate there, we could see a steady stream of beggars, trolling from table to table. The older beggars would grab the ashtrays and empty the butts into paper bags. These butts would later be stripped and new cigarettes fashioned with the bits of tobacco left unburned. These salvaged butts would then find their way in the streets, to be sold at high prices to the general population. The younger beggars, some smaller than I was at the time, would go from table to table, begging to be given uneaten sandwiches, claiming that they had not eaten in days and were starving. Some of the patrons, feeling sorry for the poor creatures would give them a half sandwich, or an uneaten fruit. The beggars would never eat the food at the table, but, bowing low and professing great gratitude would then leave the restaurant with their bounty of food. Outside, an adult would collect the food and offer it for sale to the passer-by. It was early in the war and there was already quite a contrast between that which was available for the German Armed Forces and the penury for the general population of the occupied countries.

In North Africa, Marshal Rommel had come to the aid of the Italian army and was reversing the early defeats with constant and smashing victories against the British. A popular German marching song of the period told of the bounty flowing from Africa:

"Panzers are rolling over Africa
We are there now, we are there now
Coffee, cigarettes, chocolate,
All come from Africa,
We are there now, we are there now."

SALAMI SLICES

In later years, someone would always ask me why we had not left Belgium at that time and why other Jews had remained in the face of the danger that was facing them. Perhaps, if we had been told that on a given date, all of us would be killed, some measure of resistance or escape would have been taken. However, the German approach was slow and deliberate, like cutting a salami one thin slice at a time, with decrees that one could live with. After a while, the whole salami would be gone and so would most of the Jews of Europe.

Our parents talked to Ruth and me about the problems the Jews were facing across Europe. We knew what was happening in Poland. Father had met a Polish Jew who had fled Poland in 1939 when the Germans invaded. He told of how the Germans immediately began executing Polish Jews. He was one of a number of Jews who thought they would be safe in Holland, Belgium or France. When the Germans entered Brussels, he committed suicide by leaping off a building. He knew what was coming.

The advance of the German armies had been so swift that few Jews had been able to escape Europe. In most cases, Jews were unable to find sanctuary abroad and unless you were rich or famous, there was nowhere to go for safe haven.

In those days, very few non-Jews were circumcised and my Father taught me a trick he had learned in Poland where there were no public bathrooms and you had to urinate in ditches. To avoid being identified when I was in a public bathroom, he showed me how to hold my *zizi, Pierrot,* the French vernacular for penis, by cradling it on my thumb, while the other four fingers formed a protective "roof" so that my *zizi* could not be seen. I am sure that didn't do any good, since most people could tell just by looking at my face that I was a Jew. Still, this was important to my Father, who was deluding himself by thinking that our Jewishness could be so easily camouflaged.

In early 1941, the first slice of the salami was cut. All Jews were ordered to report to the local German authorities to have their identity cards stamped "Jew". Since Belgium is a bilingual country, the I.D. cards were stamped both in French and Flemish, a bold, bright red "*Juif*", above an equally visible "*Jode*". Since a large number of Jews were not Belgian citizens, they carried the infamous yellow I.D. card and the bright red stamping was very visible. Belgian Jews carried a green I.D card, and the stamp was not as contrasty, yet still very visible.

Why did the Jews go to the German authorities and meekly submitted their papers to be stamped? Perhaps, it was because it was the law and it had to be obeyed. Perhaps it was because the penalty for resisting the decree would have been more severe than the dimly perceived dangers of complying. Had a Jew been stopped by a German in the street or in any of the *raids* that were becoming more and more frequent and identified as a Jew, without the red stamp, the penalty would have been arrest and deportation. Did many Jews decide to avoid being stamped and simply took their chances? I never found out if some did, and if so, how many.

Frieda took her card to the German authority, smiled nicely at the soldier and he rewarded her with a very light imprint, barely visible. Hilaire had no such luck. Ruth and I were too young to have identity papers, and thus escaped that ignominy.

The I.D. card was not made of strong material and, being carried every day, they would tend to deteriorate quickly. So, most citizens carried them in a small celluloid sheath. Some clever Jew figured out that if you carried the card in pink celluloid holders, the red stamp would disappear. Almost overnight, every Jew had a pink holder sheathing his I.D card. This now made it easier to identify Jews, as all one had to see was the pink sheath and it was evident that its holder was Jewish.

In early 1941, the Germans made a raid, a sweep in Antwerp's Diamond district and arrested hundreds of Jews. They were carted off to a concentration point in Flanders for further disposition. However, the majority of these Jews were Belgian citizens. The Queen Mother Elizabeth*, having found out about these arrests, interceded with the German authorities, claiming that Belgian Jews were under her personal protection. Unbelievably, all were released. The protection of the Belgian Jews by Elizabeth was to last for a while, but eventually, Belgian Jews were to suffer the same fate as the large number of foreign Jews living in Belgium, who had no initial protection from the Queen. Being Stateless, the Rosenberg family had no protection at all and had to survive by its wits.

nee Elizabeth of Saxe-Coburg-Gotha in Possenhofen (Bavaria, Germany), wife of Albert the First, King of Belgium during World War One, Mother of King Leopold 111.

On Easter Monday 1941, there was a *Pogrom* in Antwerp. Two synagogues and all their books were burned. Over 200 windows of Jewish stores were smashed by a mob of Flemish SS, *Zwarte* Brigade and VNV. The police did not intervene.

A second decree followed shortly thereafter, Jews would be subject to a special curfew. From 8 in the evening, until 5 in the morning, Jews were restricted to their homes. Any Jew circulating between 8 PM and 5 AM would be arrested. Thus, the Germans now knew that if they wanted to arrest Jews, these would be home where they could be seized during the night. Many a night, as the clock of the Innovation Department Store would begin to toll the eighth hour I would find myself running wildly back, in order to safely be in our home before the dreaded hour.

The second slice of the salami had been cut.

<u>FRIENDS</u>

After school and before the curfew forced me off the streets, I would play with a few friends; mostly along the *Rue de la Blanchisserie* and the *Rue du Marais. The Rue du Marais* had a few private houses, but mostly it was a large construction area, boarded up and transformed into barracks occupied by German troops. It was halfway between our apartment over the Cambridge and the school I went to. The construction area was part of a project known as "the Junction", which was supposed to connect all of Brussels railroad stations through a Central Station. The project had been started well before the First World War and had become a national joke as an example of a work that would never be finished. It was finally completed in the Seventies. Meanwhile, it was an almost deserted area. This suited a few friends and me. We could use the street as our personal turf. There we could play and carouse without disturbing anyone. Although we were a group of six or seven, only two names have remained in my memory. There was Freddy McKenzie, who was supposed to be Canadian. That impressed me a lot and I had difficulty accepting the idea that he was a Canadian. It seemed much too romantic a notion to be true. Although he was about my age, he was much taller than I, had a toothy smile and a ready laughter. Somehow, he reminded me of Fernandel, the French movie comedian. Freddy lived above Gino's Italian restaurant with his Mother and sister. Both were very tall and good-looking in a flashy way and could often be found in the restaurant. I always felt that their way of making a living was not completely legal; however, being barely eleven, I never had the occasion to verify my hunches.

Lucien was quite a bit older than the rest of us, probably fifteen or so. He was experienced in the way of girls and would give the rest of us little sex lessons and advice on how to get under the skirts of any girl. Lucien would sit on a stoop and we would stand around him, listening and absorbing his lessons. Mostly, he would regale us with his tales of accomplishment and describe the pleasure of caressing and exploring a girl's private parts and to enjoy the heady odor of *crevette,* shrimp that would emanate from them. Sometimes, he would allow us to smell his fingers but I must admit that I mostly failed to detect anything remotely fishy about them. Since the rest of us did not come in contact with girls, either in school or on the street, we had no occasion to verify his stories or even to doubt these.

We had gone to see "The Three Musketeers" at the movies and we were all full of swashbuckling ideas. At home, Father still kept his tools and some supplies from his decorator trade, even if his occupation was now solely confined to his black-market activities. I found half a dozen curtain rods that I spirited away. I ran with these up to the *Rue du Marais* where my Musketeer friends were waiting for me. Our re-enactment of the movie was short lived as a dreaded policeman appeared out of nowhere and seized all of our "weapons". I tried to talk him into giving them back to us as these belonged to my Father. The policeman advised me that my Father could easily retrieve these by showing up at the police station. This was out of the question as Hilaire was not aware that I had borrowed these curtain rods and I was not too anxious to tell him.

One afternoon as we were playing as usual, a German soldier emerged from the barracks of the *Rue du Marais* and approached us. He stopped near us and unwrapped a package containing two sandwiches filled with thick slices of ham. The bread was of that special variety issued to the German troops, nutritious and full of grains. He offered these to us, extending his arms as far as he could stretch them. We stood there, our hands in the small of our back, refusing his offering. He was a German and we were not going to accept anything from him. Finally, he re-wrapped the sandwiches and placed them down on the curb and slowly walked away. We played a while with the package as if it were a football, finally guiding it to the gutter and into the sewer opening.

Occasionally, the soldier turned to look back at us. This was not a young man but an older soldier. He probably had children of his own in Germany. Later on I felt badly about the incident.

And always, as the dark of the winter evening descended over the city, the clock at the Innovation department store would warn me that it was time to return home before the eight o'clock curfew. I would then run as fast as I could to reach the entrance of the Café Cambridge before the bell's last strike.

One evening, as I was making my way toward our home in the *Rue de Malines,* I passed by two women who were standing near the entrance to the *Rue du Canon*, that dark, mysterious impasse, across from the Innovation. As I went past them, one reached out quickly and snatched my cap. Laughing, she began to tease me "If you want your cap, little man, you will have to come and take it back".

With that, she retreated to the entrance to the dark alley. I made a futile attempt at grabbing my cap back, but they were too fast for me. Now, both were teasing me and urging me to follow them into the impasse. "*Viens, petit gamin*! ".Come little kid! I was barely eleven and could not imagine what they wanted with me. All I knew was that my cap was gone and there was no way I was going to enter into the dark cul-de-sac. After a standoff of a few minutes, I realized that it would be foolhardy to follow them and I continued on my way home, sans cap. At home, I told Mother how I had lost my *casquette*, and Frieda laughed, but offered no explanation. She told me that it was good that I did not follow the two women and offered me another pearl of wisdom:

"By the way, she said, if a man wants you to feel his hernia, don't do it."

The impasse was a forbidding place, dark, dank and peopled by low-class inhabitants. That was where the pushcart vendors would retire for the night and where they took refuge when the cops were after them. Even the policemen did not venture in that street. Even today, I still am not sure what these two women wanted. Did they want to initiate a young boy to the pleasures of love? Did they want to have their fun with me? Would they release me afterward or have me killed? Was I to be kidnapped and sold to Gypsies in an Oliver Twist-like Dickensian nightmare? I never found out, I just lost my *casquette*.

TRIP TO KŐLN (COLOGNE) GERMANY

At the Cambridge, Hilaire met Franz Bauer, a German corporal, who was General von Falkenhausen chauffeur. Franz was also the lover of Madame Yvonne, Frieda's seamstress. Franz drove regularly to Cologne and from time to time, he accepted to take a small package for Frieda's

Mother and brother Richard. They had been dispossessed of their house and business and were now living in a tiny apartment. After a while, they let us know that they didn't really want to see this official German staff car, with a General's guidon, stopped in front of the building in Cologne, because the whole neighborhood talked about it, and it created some unfriendly commentaries.

Frieda was concerned for her Mother Emma and her Brother Richard's safety. Both Hilaire and Frieda counseled them to come and join us in Brussels as quickly as possible, before it was too late and to take advantage of the fact that Franz has made several offers to drive them into Belgium in von Falkenhausen's staff car. They were still not persuaded that they were running a real mortal danger and this indecision would be fatal for them.

In February 1941, Frieda decided that she would travel to Germany for her Mother's birthday. She had discussed this with Madame Lobet, her old friend from Charleroi. Madame Lobet, though married to a Belgian, had retained her German nationality and was a Christian to boot. She and her daughter Rita had been denied a visa to return to Germany for a visit and she scoffed at Frieda's chances for a similar visa. Frieda, brazen as usual, marched into the German embassy in Brussels and demanded that she be granted a visa to visit her Mother, not only for her, but also for Ruth and me. She apparently pressured the officials with the argument that her husband, Hilaire, holder of a Nansen passport, was a refugee, protected by the League of Nations. Furthermore, since Hilaire's birthplace was in Russia, he was a citizen of Russia and thus, at the time, an ally of the Third Reich. Whatever the reasoning or the guile used or the charms offered, Frieda did obtain a two-month visa to visit Germany, for her and her two children. Needless to say, Madame Lobet was incensed that Frieda, a Jew, had been granted a visa, while she, a good German Christian, had been denied the same.

So, in the first week of March 1941, Mother, Ruth and I boarded the train to Cologne. I was all excited about the prospect of seeing my uncle Richard again. I had asked Mother to teach me a phrase in German: "Please take me to the toy store." I wanted Uncle Richard to take me to a toy store and to buy me a pair of roller skates. I remembered the streets of Cologne all covered with Macadam, on which one could skate from one end of the city to the other.

When the train reached Herbestahl, on the Belgian/German border, the train halted for the better part of an hour while all the passengers had to get off and go into the station to have their passports controlled and checked. We did not have to; instead, we sat in our compartment and waited. After a short while, the door slid open and three officials appeared, one Belgian border guard and two German officials in uniform. They stayed in the hallway of the car, saluted and asked for our papers. Mother, sitting down, handed over her passport and visa, for which one of the Germans reached in, perused lightly and gave back to Frieda. He turned to his two companions and said "Ah, three of our Russian allies coming to visit our Reich." With that, he saluted us, withdrew and closed the door. We did not even have to show them our luggage or anything.

A mere seventy miles separate the border from Cologne; however, it took us nearly three hours to cover the distance. We kept getting sidetracked, while long freight trains slowly passed by. Mostly, these were flatbed railroad cars, with guns and tanks lashed to their platforms. Mother remarked that they were all going in the same direction we were, east. The German campaign in the West was over and Hitler was preparing for the invasion of Bulgaria, Yugoslavia and ultimately Russia, that was to come a little more than three months later. Of course, we had no inkling of this very near future, but we could not help noticing that all the military trains were headed eastward.

Arriving in Cologne was always very special. The large Rhine River, with its enormous Ludendorf bridge, the sight of the magnificent twin towers of the Dom, Cologne's eighth century cathedral, were enough to inspire awe in the eyes of an eleven year old. The train pulled in the huge central railway station covered by an immense vaulted arch of steel and glass. Steam, whistles, porters, filled the air with a hubbub never to be forgotten. I was to see it again a decade later, as Germany was clearing up the rubble left by the war and the Allied bombers.

Once in Cologne, we had a shock. My grandMother Emma, Uncle Richard and his wife were confined to a small apartment, in a large building, on 24 Kaesenstrasse. They lived in a room, or a room-and-a half. There was a common kitchen to be used with the other tenants of the building. Uncle Richard had married a woman who had been born in Germany, but had lived in Cleveland, where she had grown children. Anny had come to Germany to marry Richard, with the hope that both of them could emigrate to the USA if they could obtain an exit visa. This would have been the same exit route the younger brother Paul had followed in 1935.It was shocking for us to see our grandMother, who had always been a very proud, strong and wealthy woman. She would lie all day with her face turned to the wall. She wouldn't talk any more.

Richard had to get up very early each day and leave to perform menial physical labor in the far away suburbs of Cologne. He would return late at night, exhausted and in a poor state of mind. I remember that I did ask him, in German, to take me to the toy store to buy me a pair of roller-skates. There was an embarrassing silence and Mother insisted that she would go with Ruth and me to the large department store and buy a pair each for Ruth and for me. We could well afford it, while obviously, that was no longer within the means of Richard.

That first night, we were awakened several times by the sounds of the air raid sirens. We had to get up and run to the basement shelter. We cowered there, hearing the explosions of the anti-aircraft shells trying to bring down the British bombers that passed over the city. The humming of the RAF motors was punctuated by loud noises of exploding bombs, but these seemed too far away to cause us damages. Nevertheless, it was a terrifying first night.

The next morning, Ruth and I walked out of the building and were surprised to hear French being spoken. The city garbage trucks were collecting the refuse from each house. The garbage pails were canisters sunk in covered receptacles dug into the sidewalk. The garbage men would lift the full pails, place them in neat rows in the truck and replace the full pail with a washed, dried and sanitized one. Ruth and I were impressed by such Teutonic neatness.

The garbage men were French prisoners of war, still wearing the remnants of their army uniforms. On their backs, they bore the letters "KG", *Kriegsgefangener*, Prisoner of war. We spoke with them in French and they seemed very pleased to talk with us in their Mother-tongue, even if we were just a couple of children. To prevent them from escaping, the Frenchmen were supervised by an armed guard. The prisoners were contented to do this job, as it gave them an opportunity to get out each day from their prisoner-of-war camp. In addition, they would give long looks to the German *frauleins* passing by and some of the inhabitants would slip them a fruit or a piece of bread as they went about their chores. In the evening, they went back to their Stalags. For the Germans, it helped relieve a manpower shortage as the regular garbage men were serving in the military.

Frieda took us to a store to buy us each a pair of roller-skates. Ruth remembers that the store manager, or owner, at first absolutely refused to sell us the skates that were not on display. He inflated his chest when saying "Herr Marshall Goering needed the ball bearings for the Luftwaffe" and he insisted he did not have any roller-skates. Mother eventually got them, how? We were baffled and puzzled, but he caved in and we walked out of there with two pairs of skates.

These had rubber-coated metal wheels, leather straps for wrapping around the ankles, and adjustable front clips that could be tighten, with the help of a metal key, to fit the front of the sole. Cologne was an unusual city in that it had Macadam all over its streets, which to us, was very new. Brussels mostly had only big Belgian cobblestones. In Cologne, we could put on our roller skates and skate all over the city, just as my Mother and my uncles had done when they were young. They had skated all over Cologne to deliver poultry to the various hotels and restaurants.

So Ruth and I went skating through the streets of Cologne and we spoke French to each other. One day, all of a sudden, there descended upon us about half a dozen German kids with the swastika on their arm. They were Hitler Youth. Girls and boys with their *lederhosen*, short leather pants. They came running up to us and questioned "*Bist du English? Bist du English?*"-They knew we spoke a foreign language and wanted to know if we were English.

We said, "*Nein, Franzosen.*" No, French. We didn't think they would know where Belgium was, so we told them we were from France.

We spoke for a while and one boy said suddenly "*Verstehst du Jude?*" They obviously wanted to know if we understood Yiddish. My sister and I looked at each other and we thought we'd better get out of there. We excused ourselves and we skated back to my grandMother's apartment. When we told the story to Mother, she laughed, because in the patois of Cologne, the hard G isn't pronounced. Instead of saying *gut*, you say *yut*. They had been asking if we understood "well". We had thought they wanted to know if we were Jewish and that would have been unhealthy for us. So we got out of there.

Richard had managed to keep a small radio, even though Jews were no longer allowed to own one. One evening, we all listened to Adolf Hitler harangue the German people. Mostly he was ranting against Winston Churchill and the British Lords "They should take off their wigs". Hitler promised that the German Luftwaffe would "eradicate" the British cities and that the war would be won by the Axis that year.

There were air raids every night. The British RAF bombed Cologne almost every night, as it was one of the major German cities nearest to England and it was easy to bomb and harass Cologne. Ruth was especially terrified by these nightly bombardments. Although we had a visa for two months, we left after about two weeks. Very little would remain in my memory about the long train ride back to Brussels. Along the way, more freight trains with military materiel heading east forced us to be sidelined. At the border, the formalities were as brief for us as they had been on the way into Germany. Ruth and I were bringing back our roller-skates and these were not seized by the border guards, unlike our teddy bears which had been confiscated on our earlier trip in 1936.

That was the last time we ever saw Mother's family. Frieda tried to convince Richard and Emma to leave, if they could. She spoke about Franz Bauer, General von Falkenhausen's chauffeur and his offer to help them escape. It never came to pass, we never knew why. It just would not be done. Richard held on to the hope that they could still get a visa to the USA. Besides, the Führer had just announced that Germany would win the war by the end of the year and things should improve for the Jews by then. After all, the Friedemanns had been Germans for many generations and Philip had been a decorated soldier in the German Army in the First World War. And yet, Uncle Richard knew Jews were being killed, he knew that people had disappeared. Some had escaped from the wagon trains. Some people corresponded from the ghettoes. There was an underground; there was communication. Anyway, before they could leave Germany, the United States entered into war with Germany in December 1941. So, they were never able to leave.

Perhaps Richard did not understand the speed with which death came in the concentration camps. These were really extermination camps. Even Charlie Chaplin in "The Great Dictator", naively saw the concentration camps as places where the Jews were made to suffer somewhat, but not to be killed systematically. What I didn't know and I didn't find out until many years later when I watched the movie *Shoah*, was the swiftness with which death came. Most Jews were murdered and exterminated within three hours after they reached the extermination camps. I had thought they just died of malnutrition, beatings, forced labor, but that only happened to a minority of "privileged" ones. The majority was slaughtered right away.

On October 29th, 1941, Richard and his wife Anna were deported to the new Eastern German Territories that were once Poland. They were sent to the Ghetto of Lodz (Litzmanstadt) where they were murdered. Since the German Railroads were being paid for each trainload of Jews that were being deported to the death camps, they kept good records, including the numbers and dates of each transport. When we found out that Richard and his wife had been taken, we sent care packages to them through the Red Cross. One day, either the packages came back, or we were told not to send them anymore.

On May 30th, 1942, the RAF staged the first One Thousand Bombers Raid of the war. The target was Cologne. In a concentrated raid that lasted about two hours, more than one third of the city was destroyed. Immediately after that, we heard from Emma that she had escaped injuries and was still alive. By then she had been moved to an old folks home "Altenheimer on Cecilienstrasse".

My grandMother, Emma Wolff Friedemann was not deported until June 16th, 1942 when she was sent to Theresienstadt (now Terezin) near Prague. There was the old fortress of Terezin, where the Germans kept, tortured and murdered mostly political prisoners. Next to the fortress, stood the town of Theresienstadt. This was a "show" concentration camp where the Germans invited the Red Cross representatives to see for themselves how well the Jews were being treated. Elderly, middle-class German Jews were often sent there for a few months, until malnutrition made them unsightly for the Red Cross inspectors. They were then shipped off to the extermination camps. Emma would remain there for about three months. On September 19th, 1942, Emma was shipped to Auschwitz, where she would be murdered a short while later.

PROPAGANDA

All through the war, the Germans relied on movies, radio and magazines to carry on a concentrated propaganda, under the masterful leadership of Dr. Joseph Göbbels. While we hated Hitler, he was also the object of contempt and ridicule. Reichsmarschall Hermann Goring, was too much of an obese fop figure to be hated, he was simply too ridiculous. Göbbels, was hated mostly for the vitriolic assault on our senses. We knew the little club-footed *morpion*, (crab louse) was lying, but his lies were so blatantly clever that we simply hated him.

The magazine "SIGNAL" was published in German and also in all the languages of the occupied countries and English. It was patterned after "LIFE" and contained articles on a variety of subjects, art, sciences, geography, NAZI politics and mainly the ongoing conflict. It would often show how welcome the German troops were by the population of occupied countries. The promise of a greater Europe under the Third Reich's aegis was a constant recurring theme.

In April 1941, after the British had been forced to evacuate Greece, they retreated to the island of Crete. Hitler launched an aerial assault on Crete, with thousands of airborne troops. Although the German paratroopers suffered very severe losses they were able to rout the British once again. Except for Gibraltar and Malta, that was the end of any British presence on the continent.

SIGNAL, published an issue, with the cover showing a smiling Max Schmeling, in a paratrooper's uniform, leaping out of a Junker 52, supposedly over Crete. The caption: "A paratrooper the whole world knows". It was very impressive. Max Schmeling had defeated Joe Louis, one of my earliest American idols. (There was also Jesse Owens), but beside the Hollywood Stars, Joe Louis was my favorite American. I had once seen a poster of him in Charleroi and I resented the picture of Schmeling being used for German propaganda.

Went to see "Wűnschkoncert", an almost subtle German propaganda film. In it, numerous German cinema, operetta and radio stars held a weekly radio concert, made entirely of requests mailed in by German soldiers in the field. A young, handsome blond soldier made a request for a song. Meanwhile, while the troops are advancing, they come upon a magnificent French church. As the hero enters the church, he sees the large organ glittering in the dusk. Being a musician, he sits at the organ and begins to play. The French (the bad guys), hear the organ from their positions outside the town. They lob a few shells into the (French) church. The German soldier (the good guy), persists on finishing the religious piece he is playing on the organ and dies under the French shells. As his buddies decry the barbarism of the enemy (the French), they hear the radio giving the requested song for the now-dead German hero.

I felt manipulated, knowing that my sympathies should have been for the French and against the Germans and yet, in this movie, clearly it was the German soldiers who were portrayed as the good guys. I knew this and tried to reason my feelings. Even as I was only eleven at the time, the objective of this movie was very clear to me.

In May 1941, I went to see "*Panzerkruizer Sebastopol*" (Battleship Sebastopol). It had to do with the Bolshevik revolution. In it, the Bolsheviks had commandeered a Russian city and were in the process of liquidating all who they perceived to be aristocrats. There was sex, songs and mostly brutality. The *Kommissar* sat at a table, in a black leather outfit, two bandoliers criss-crossing his chest and would look at the papers of prisoners, or their hands. If the hands did not show calluses, the *Kommissar* would mock, "Too bad, liquidate" and the victim would be summarily shot by the Bolsheviks.

I found the movie puzzling. Why would the Germans portray the Russians, their allies, in such an unfavorable light? Little did I know at the time, that all the trains we had seen heading east in Germany were for the coming invasion of Russia. Less than a month after the movie, Hitler would unleash his might against the USSR. The film was just a way to prepare public opinion for the forthcoming conflict against Russia and Bolshevism

ARRESTED

It must have been mid-May, when the news came that Hilaire had been arrested by the Belgian police. Naturally, this was a great shock to Ruth and me. Mother, on the other hand, seemed to take it in stride and went about to try to get to see Father who had been taken to the prison of Forest, a suburb of Brussels. A couple of days later, we were allowed to go and visit Father in jail.

We entered through the imposing front gate of the fortress that was the prison of Forest. After a while, we were ushered into a large room where detainees were allowed to see their family for a short visit. Most of the detainees were Gypsies who were surrounded by wailing women and children in heteroclite clothing. We considered ourselves well above their status in life and Ruth and I were terribly embarrassed to have to mingle with such riff-raff. After a while, Father appeared, unkempt, without a tie, and with stubble grown during his days in the prison. To be there, with all those Gypsies, was so mortifying for us. We briefly hugged and kissed Hilaire, then could not wait until we would be allowed out in the fresh air again. Luckily, he was released after about one week. Hilaire has related the incidents that led to his arrest in his memoirs:

> *M. Deferre tells me about an unfortunate story of cigarettes that had been seized in Antwerp, which he feels are definitely lost. I want to get to the bottom of this and I go and find a toy manufacturer in Antwerp who I had met previously. In the meantime, we learned that the cigarettes had been transferred to Tours et Taxi (an enormous depot requisitioned by the German Army) in Brussels, where they are confiscated in customs. There my man from Antwerp knows a German employee, member of the Todt Organization (part of the German Quartermaster and Labor).*
>
> *They make him a proposition to release the confiscated merchandise, and to sell it with the understanding that there will be a four-way split 25% for the bank, 25% for the employee of Tours et Taxi, and 25% each for the fellow from Antwerp and me. M. Deferre, who considered this merchandise completely lost, is absolutely in agreement for the bank to receive only a quarter of the profits of the sale, if that can be done despite everything.*

A friend of Frieda's, Mr Fleugelhofer, who fought for Germany (in the war) from 1914-1918, married to a Jewess, chased from his printing business in Cologne by the Nazis and whose two daughters are safe in England, declares himself ready to be used as a go-between. Thanks to the complicity of the German working at Tour et Taxi, who naturally finds a substantial interest in this, the cigarettes are gotten out, little quantities by little quantities, until they are all out of the depot. They will be resold little by little. The cigarettes (Gasparades) were originally destined for the British troops and for some obscure reason I have to sign a paper by which I certify that I will not sell these cigarettes to anyone except the Germans. Even the damaged packets are recuperated and eventually the cigarettes are reconditioned with the help of a machine to roll cigarettes. There is an Austrian who helps us in this endeavor. Unfortunately, he will be deported later. At a certain time, even Rudy (and Ruth) takes care of this work and these revamped cigarettes will be sold in small quantities in a café in town . . .

. . . . A German noncommissioned officer, named Ernst from Eberfeld, who I also met at the Cambridge, brings me one day to the Residence Palace, a hotel requisitioned by the Germans. We climb to the roof, where we find two machine guns from which he removes essential pieces that he throws down into the back yard. After this astonishing demonstration, he thinks that he has given me convincing proof of his anti-Nazi sentiments and that he deserves my confidence. All he has been able to do so far is to give me cold sweats.

Ernst undertakes to sell to the Germans the coffee that M. Gosselin and I have bought from a torrefactor (coffee roaster) on the Rue de Laeken. A little while later, he confides in me his intention to desert and asks me to supply him civilian clothes so that he can join the Resistance, bringing with him some weapons. He will accompany them in some sabotage missions, of which the minor ones will consist of putting sugar in the gas tank of military trucks.

M. Deferre also has to get rid of an entire shipload of rice that is in Antwerp. He does not want this food to fall into German hands. I promise him to try and resolve this little problem as quickly as possible. M. Herman, manufacturer of soap on the Rue de France, asks me to find him a buyer for an important quantity of soap powder. I check with M. Blinkers, who is the German officer in charge of the buying services of Tours et Taxi. A seller of the Maison Carillon, who was there for another business, and who knew me from Charleroi, denounces me as a Jew. Blinkers signals me immediately to a German who follows me and motions me to go to the Rue de la Loi, under his surveillance. An ambulant photographer takes my picture while we are en route. On this picture, which I will retrieve the next day, one can easily recognize my guardian angel behind me.

At a certain moment, I propose to him that we take a taxi together, at my cost and we are driven in front of the Parc de Bruxelles. I am searched, but without success, interrogated to find out where this famous soap powder could be and I pretend to ignore everything about it. My papers are peeled, and finally they call Blinkers to advise him that they have nothing against me because I am a refugee protected by my Nansen passport. Thus, I really get away lucky this time and I decide, without hesitation that I will not continue on this soapy endeavor.

One story, which has a less-than-happy ending, has to do with my efforts to sell the shipload of rice of M. Deferre's. For that purpose I had asked Horowitz if he could find me a Belgian buyer.

He puts me in a relation with a Mr Dujardin of La Petite-Espinette (just outside of Brussels) and Mr Dujardin comes to Antwerp with two prospective buyers. The rice is offered at ten francs a kilo, eight francs for the bank and one franc each for M. Dujardin and me. We are promised an answer for the next day. Returning from Antwerp, at the north station, we exit at the Place Rogier and we are subjected to an identity control, which seems to us suspect at best.

The next day, at eight o'clock in the morning, on the Rue de Malines, two men, the same ones who had examined our papers the previous day asked me to follow them. At the police station, near the Gare du Midi (the South Station), I am joined by Mr Dujardin, who has been picked up the same way. At noon, we are still waiting. The commissar allows us to go for lunch, but we will have to come back at 2.00 PM. From the Bon Marché department store, I call Mr Deferre to make him aware of the intervention of these false buyers.

At two o'clock, we are hauled into the Panier a Salade, (Black Maria, paddy wagon), that takes us to the prison of Forest. We will stay there eight days without being charged with anything specific. Frieda and the children come to visit me, but of course, they cannot do very much for me. Mr Dedunne, a friend of Mr Dujardin, obtains our liberation. The things are done very quickly for Mr Dujardin, but as far as it concerns me, the fact that I am Jewish seems to be an obstacle. Mr Dedunne insists to obtain the liberation of both people and is finally able to it. It goes without saying that I was very, very much relieved.

After that, there was a lot of chamois leather that Fleugelhofer goes to deliver to the Gestapo. We were wondering what was the usage reserved for such a quantity of chamois. There was enough there for one million francs.

Without really being aware of it, I slide dangerously into the role of supplier to the enemy armies. That means in economic collaboration, terrain extremely dangerous, especially in my being Jewish. I have always avoided, in most cases, to take care of the transactions personally, to cash the due payments, or to have the merchandise in my possession, but despite all of that, the least indiscretion could be fatal and I don't even talk about the risk of being denounced.

After all the problems, Mr Dujardin has definitely pulled out of the rice affair. Despite a few hesitations, I manage to go and offer the merchandise to the Moulin de Marcinelle, a mill near Charleroi, planning to make semolina with it. When all is said and done, despite the unpleasant interlude in prison, the transaction is finished in an interesting way for me. I get ten francs to a kilo, as predicted, but the two francs of commission are for me.

It is at about that time that we move to the Boulevard Bischoffsheim, without notifying the authorities that we have changed our domicile.

BOULEVARD BISCHOFFSHEIM

Hilaire, for reasons of safety, decided to move to the Boulevard Bischoffsheim, still near to the center of Brussels and nearer to the school I was attending. The move was made without fanfare and without notifying the city authorities, as was required. As far as the City knew, we were still registered Rue de Malines and it knew not that we had moved or where our new domicile was located.

This was a beautiful house, of which we occupied the second floor. Our apartment had a large living room with a bay window. Separating the living area from the dining room, two sets of four wooden columns twirled to the high ceiling. I liked to squat among the columns in my peaceful little world where I didn't have to worry about anything. Deeper in the apartment, stretched a bedroom, a small kitchen and our own toilet and washroom. Whenever Father came home for the night, Mother invited me to share their bed. I slept between my parents, happy to be near them, unaware that Frieda was using me as a sex-prevention buffer.

About once or twice a week, a gentle Jew, refugee from Poland, would come to visit us. He was involved in the black market of food and would bring us eggs and butter, for which we paid handsomely. Sometimes, his wife would accompany him on his visits. Being a Polish Jew, he had difficulty pronouncing the letter "B", thus greeting us always with a "Ponjour ". To us they became *Monsieur et Madame Ponjour.* They spoke little French and most of the conversation, which centered on butter and eggs, was in Yiddish. One day, as Mr Ponjour had delivered our quota of dairies, Mother asked him if he would like a cup of coffee? "With a sandwich, yes, I would like that "he replied.

I never did learn their real name. His clothes were always tattered and he always seemed to be in need of a shave. They had little money and eked out a living selling their groceries. They were probably arrested, deported and killed. After the war we never heard from them again. They were to live on in my memory with the little anecdote that I would repeat whenever someone wanted a definition of the word "chutzpah".

On May 10th, 1941, just one year after the Germans invaded Belgium, we learned that Rudolf Hess, Hitler's trusted third in command, had flown to England in a bomber and parachuted in Scotland. To us, it was stunning news, as we felt that Hess had deserted Hitler and that perhaps there could be a revolution in Germany. This would have brought peace and an end to the occupation of Belgium. However, Hitler promptly declared that Hess was insane and nothing further came of this affair. In school, I took a bit more teasing, as my classmates made a lot of the name Rudolf we had in common. They would also tease me because Germany had a Minister named Rosenberg (Alfred), an anti-Semitic ideologue. Rosenberg would be arrested after the war, tried during the Nuremberg trials and hanged.

Prodded by the German authorities, intent on exploiting the linguistic division between the Flemish-speaking Flemings and the French-speaking Walloons of Belgium, the school boards of the capital had decided to force the children to attend either French or Flemish schools. There was no problem in Flanders or in Wallonia, where schools were in the local language only. However, it was a different problem in the Brussels region. Although most of the inhabitants spoke French, there were Flemish suburbs where French was seldom heard and there was also a substantial population that spoke "*Bruxellois*", a local patois made out of French with a liberal spicing of quasi-Flemish words and even a few remnants of Spanish and Hebrew words dating back to the Spanish occupation and Inquisition of the 16th century.

In an effort to determine the language that was spoken at home, the authorities would question the children, asking them what terms of endearments their parents used in addressing each other. If it was a word in Flemish, you went to a Flemish school. If it was a French term, i.e. *Mon Petit Chou*, my little cabbage (or cream-puff), you were assigned to a French school.

A large number of households that spoke mostly French or Bruxellois, would use the common and very popular Flemish word: *Crotje*, (Little turd) meaning love, girl friend, etc. Even people who spoke no Flemish at all, like Frieda, would refer to someone's paramour as a *Crotje*. So, if the student said that his Father called his Mother "Crotje", he was immediately labeled a Flemish speaking person and sent to a Flemish school, whether or not he or she spoke any.

Since my parents did not use terms of endearments and their insults were mostly in German, I was reassigned to a French speaking school where I would resume my studies after the end of the current school year. Ruth also, was assigned to a Francophonic school.

STEEL TIPS

Almost daily now, a Major Peters came to visit at our home. Peters was from the German Quartermaster and in charge of procuring goods for the German military. Peters and Hilaire had met at the café Cambridge and had developed a business relationship to channel black market goods. Peters was regular army and had fought in WWI, he was not a Nazi and was a very friendly fellow, albeit in a German officer's uniform. Almost nightly, Peters and I played checkers and I did not have the civility to let him win now and then. Always, he would marvel about how *kluge*, smart, the little boy was.

Somewhere along the way, Major Peters let Hilaire know that the Quartermaster was looking for millions of *stiehle*, steel tips for the soles of their boots. My Father, being a Polish Jew, never could tell the difference between U and I. Both sounded like E to him. So, when he heard *stiehle*, he thought it meant *stühle*, chairs and he couldn't figure out what the German army wanted with millions of chairs. Father did sell millions of steel tips to the German army and made a fortune. That large amount of money would soon allow us to hide and escape death in the years to follow.

There had always been a discrepancy between Hilaire's verbal recollection of the Steel Tips Affair and his written memoirs. Mostly, did he find steel tips for which he had to develop a market or did he have to find a supplier to fulfill the German's requirements? Whatever the sequence, it has always seemed ironic to me that Hitler's armies went to their fate on the Eastern Front wearing my Father's steel tips on the sole of their boots.

Hilaire's memoirs:

> *At our new address, on the Boulevard Bischoffsheim, a limping shoemaker recommended by Banda shows up one day. He is looking for a place to sell metal shoe tips. He tells me that three Belgian factories are producing this article in great quantity, and that he is looking for an important customer capable of absorbing the entire production. Mr Gosselin is looking for shoe polish, so I go the Franco-Belge (bank) where I tie up with two employees, Mr Edmond Sabot and his sister-in-law Marthe. The business of shoe polish is taken care of quickly, as well as the purchase of candles shortly thereafter.*

> *Having now built up her confidence in me, Marthe offers the help of her uncle, Mr Hase, who has his office in the Shell building at the Ravenstein, for all purchases in favor of the German army. In this case, would the shoe tips be of interest? Not only does the article interest him, but also we should be able to supply a very large quantity. I never see anyone but a single go-between on the Rue D'Assault who guarantees the entire production.*

> *In reality, it would appear that there are about twenty go-betweens for this business, but because of the large size of the market, this remains very lucrative for everyone. Mr Sabot delivers, cashes in and splits the profits half-and-half with me. As per my advice, he and his sister-in-law resign from the Franco-Belge so that they can spend all their time with similar businesses of the same kind.*

> *Some of the money will be paid to the Belgian Resistance, with which they will purchase weapons to fight against the Germans. The part of the Resistance, for which money apparently has no odor, is estimated by them to be one million francs, which they insist they want to receive in used bills of twenty and fifty francs. I go to fetch this sum at the bank and pay it to them at the Café Wellington.*

> *There is no sense to discuss the requirements of these people. A fellow named Mr Friture, if I remember well; who decided that he was going to refuse to pay the required contribution is shot in cold blood in the woods. A Luxemburger, who was a big supplier to the Germans, was executed in his office because he didn't think it was necessary to split the profits that he was getting. It was a curious mentality, that of the Resistance, that did not punish you for supplying the enemy, which might have seemed understandable, but punished instead those who refused to associate with it in some way, since the resistance expected to benefit from it as largely as possible*

> *One day, out of curiosity, I accompanyMr Sabot to where the merchandise goes. In a depot, I hear a German talk in a loud voice that he knows about the existence of a "straw man" called Hilaire. I promise myself to avoid this particular place in the future. After the Liberation, MrSabot will have to justify himself in front of the tribunals and will speak also without any other details of a small boss called Hilaire, but thanks to his discretion, I will never be bothered or questioned.*

While all the other black market activities of Father were very profitable, the "Steel Tips" business would become a veritable gold mine. Many of Hilaire's acquaintances were Jews who needed cash. They were anxious to try to leave the country and find refuge in Switzerland, Spain, Portugal and eventually the USA or South America. Father had more cash than he knew what to do with. Thus, Hilaire purchased the worldly goods of those Jews who needed cash. For the first time in his life, Hilaire actually began to purchase and own tangible items, such as antique furniture, valuable paintings, oriental carpets and of course, all forms of jewelry, from unset diamonds to bracelets, rings and diamond watches.

JUNE 22ⁿᵈ 1941, INVASION OF RUSSIA

On that morning, INR, the Belgian National Radio station announced that the armies of the Third Reich had declared war on Russia. The initial advance of the German armies was very swift and large portions of Poland that had been occupied by the Bolsheviks had already been "liberated". Italy and Rumania had also declared war on the Soviet Union. A couple of days later, Finland declared war on Russia.

A swift realignment of ideas and sympathy and allegiances was in order. Up to that time, Russia had been on the side of Germany, having shared a non-aggression pact (the Molotov-von Ribbentrop Russo-German Pact). Now, the Russians and Stalin were on our side and we had quick hopes that the might of Russia's population would swiftly bring Hitler to his knees. Memories of Napoléon's disastrous Russian campaign were vivid in every schoolboy. We were all familiar with Meissonier's painting "1814" depicting Napoléon's snowy retreat from Russia.

Finland was another matter. In 1939, Finland had been invaded by Russia. The Finish army under General Mannerheim had fought bravely and had inflicted surprising losses on the Russian armies. The "brave Finns" had become our heroes, and we were all surprised at the weakness of the Soviet Union's military. The sight of Russia's impotence against tiny Finland, probably emboldened Hitler to undertake his Russian adventure. Finland, after a heroic resistance, had finally capitulated to the Russians in March 1940. The Finns, under Mannerheim, probably joined with Hitler in the hope of recovering territories they had to cede to Russia in 1940. Nonetheless, Finns were now "our" enemies, Mannerheim a villain.

Major Peters came to visit us the day after the invasion of Russia. He was pale and distraught. "We have lost the war" He declared. He continued "If, when this war is over, I can put all my belongings in a pushcart and walk back to Germany, I will consider myself lucky". Such talk was of course treasonous. However, he trusted us and felt safe to confide in us.

For the first couple of weeks, there was not much news from the Russian front and we were hoping it meant that the Russian armies were resisting and perhaps defeating the Germans. However, by mid-July, German boasts of victories were confirmed by the BBC. We were to become too familiar with the names of Russian cities falling to the Germans one after the other. Minsk, Vitebsk, Smolensk, the Dnieper River were pinpointed on the world map we kept in the kitchen. In the cinema theaters, newsreels showed the dusty but victorious German troops marching east. Unending columns of dispirited, defeated Russian prisoners were filmed straggling to the rear. The news almost always ended with scenes of Hitler, Mussolini and von Ribbentrop, smugly shaking

91

hands and photos of Panzers, guns, and Nazi flags unfurling in the wind bathing the whole exercise in loud Wagner music. Our hopes for an eventual victory by the British and Russians were getting dimmer with each passing day.

I BECOME A CATHOLIC BOY-SCOUT

I do not recall whose idea it was that I join the Boy-Scouts. But join I did in the late spring of 1941. Was it an attempt by Mother to insulate me from the danger of being Jewish? Actually, this troupe was *Les Scouts de la Chapelle,* connected to the Brussels Roman Catholic Church of La Chapelle. In Belgium, the Scouts were under the administration of the Catholic Church and not directly related to the Baden Powell organization.

I was a sorry Scout, the smallest one in our *troupe* and the only one without a uniform. We did have to go to church and were designated to assist the priest in his Mass duties. I was given a red and white chasuble to wear and was expected to serve the priest on Sunday. I had never served in a Catholic Church in my life and I had no idea what I had to do. As an altar boy, I found myself with a glass of red wine in my hand, but the memory of what I did with it has gone from my mind. Whatever was to be done was probably done, as I cannot recall any traumatic experience connected with it.

The *troupe* left on a camping trip to the *Chateau de Beersel* a medieval castle located well south of Brussels. Although I was the smallest, my backpack was enormous and the mess kit and canteen were clanking with my every step. We walked a long distance until we could catch the *vicinal tramway* that connected Brussels with the surrounding localities. We camped in a large barn next to the castle, filling our sleeping bags with straw.

I was the only Jew in this catholic *troupe* and my brother scouts were not about to let me forget it. Insult followed insult. It was the same all over again: dirty Jew, why did your Father kill Jesus Christ, etc. I had no basis on which to rely, no strength of religion, no moral or mental support. At night, I would lie on my straw mattress and cry. The monitor in charge became aware of my distress and wanted to know the reason for my constant crying. Of course, I could not tell him about the harassment to which I was subjected. Instead, I told him that I was suffering from a terrible toothache. He then went to get some tincture of iodine that he broadly painted onto my gums and teeth. Of course, this did not solve my problem with the *troupe* that continued to lace into me with their insults. And so, the tears continued and so did the tincture of Iodine treatments. Each evening, as I cried, the scoutmaster would paint my gums again to dull my "tooth ache". By the end of our stay at Beersel, my gums and mouth were a swollen mess. By then, I had resolved to quit the Scouts as soon as we got back to Brussels and so I did.

WERPIN, LA PENSION SOVET

It was late June 1941, the end of the school year had finally arrived. Before the *Distribution des Prix,* graduation, I was told that I would be presented with a special award in mathematics for exceptional achievement. This was to be a citywide prize, based on a handicap calculation, without regard for the grade you were in. It made me very proud to have achieved this honor. However, my parents were told that the award had been withdrawn and given to someone else instead. I guess, in 1941, the authorities did not want the award going to a Jew. Although I resented that for many years, it did not hurt as much as the taunts of my boy-scout friends In Beersel.

As the summer of 1941 unfolded, hopes for the miracle of a Russian victory had faded; In the meantime, we went on with our daily lives, which seemed more and more restricted with each passing day. In the summer heat, Hilaire took Ruth and me to a "Solarium", a very large green area, surrounding a huge outdoor swimming pool. At the entrance of the facility, a big sign announced, "No dogs or Jews allowed". We went in anyway. Inside, such cares evaporated for me, an eleven-year-old-boy, fascinated by the sight of a young woman sitting on the grass nearby. She had long, straight blond hair, her seated body rested on her arms and hands propped behind her. Her long thin legs pointed toward the water in the pool. She wore a bathing suit and from the edge of her top, I could see the fullness of her breast. She seemed totally unaware of my presence as I stood there, above and slightly to the right rear of her. My eyes were glued to her bosom; I did not want to and was unable to move. I watched her breathe. With each breath, a trace amount of her areola's darker flesh would be revealed to my stare. I stood there for an eternity, hoping that a deeper breath would maybe reveal a peek of her nipples.

I had never been moved by anything so beautiful and fascinating. I guess I would have been there yet if Ruth had not called out to me and snapped me out of my trance. It was not yet sex, but an awakening of my youthful sensuality. Even though we would never return to the solarium, I would never forget her.

The Germans forbade the flying of Belgium's tricolor national flag, or any flag other than that of Germany's Nazi flag. On July 21, 1941, the national holiday commemorating the coronation of King Léopold the First following Belgium's 1830 revolution and its independence from the Netherlands, I was walking near the Brussels opera house. I saw three young women walking side by side, each wearing a different color dress. One was in black, another in yellow and the third in red, the national colors. They had formed a living Belgian flag. It was daring of them and dangerous. I and others thought the trio was a joyful sight.

In early August, we took the train for the Belgian Ardennes. It was so unusual to go anywhere with both our parents. We were actually going on vacation as a family, the first time since at least 1935. We took the train to Hotton, in the province of Luxembourg. From there, a vicinal tramway took us to the small village of Werpin. Werpin's claim to any fame was a twenty-five foot high statue of the Virgin Mary erected halfway up a hill.

In Werpin, there was a *pension de famille*, a family hotel/restaurant run by the Sovet family. It was a large farmhouse, partially converted into a hotel, where one could rent rooms for the season.

As soon as we were settled, Father returned to Brussels and would come in a couple of times for the weekend. Camile, the elder Sovet, was renowned as The Painter of the Ardennes. He roamed around the countryside, painting scenes of the area and offering these for sale to the guests. Hilaire bought a sober painting of a farm entrance and took it back to Brussels with him.

The son, Germain, and his wife Elise, ran the hotel with the help of their son Emile, who was a few years older than I. Ruth and I enjoyed the pension very much. We had never really been in the country before and we had the run of the place. Young animals roamed the courtyard and could be fed and petted. Emile took a liking to Ruth and me. He would show us the workings of the house and the farm. The atmosphere was informal and relaxed. The guests were very friendly.

Hilaire had found a folding Agfa camera at the North Station in Brussels. He gave it to me. It had belonged to a German soldier and the strap holding the carrying case had broken off. Hilaire had casually pushed it with his foot and found it was heavy, the camera still being inside. Now and then, we would all go to the statue of the Virgin to take some pictures. The tension was always palpable whenever Father joined us and that was reflected in the pictures we took of our family.

Among the guests was a couple on their honeymoon. He was Paul Brackman, the Belgian one hundred meter champion and record holder. He ran the 100-meter in around eleven seconds and although he was not in the class of Jesse Owens, I was impressed. There was a Champion of Belgium and he ate at the next table in the Pension Sovet.

When it came time for Paul Brackman and his bride to leave, they came down after packing their bags, two enormous black suitcases. They bade their farewell to all. The pension was high on the hill and the only road would wind down to the main highway. There the Vicinal would stop and travel on to Hotton's railroad station. The bridge in between had been blown up during the May 1940 fighting and replaced by a wooden walkway; the only way down was on foot or bicycle.

From far away, we heard the horn signaling that the Vicinal was approaching. Brackman waved a last goodbye, struggled to pick up the two heavy suitcases and his wife in tow, proceeded down the road. Surely, he was going to fly down the hill in record time. Much to my dismay, he could barely place one foot in front of the other, the bottom of the suitcases scraping the gravel as he slowly made his way down. I was so disappointed. Was he not the 100-meter record holder? Even his wife ran faster than he did. My idol was shattered.

As the summer ended, we returned to Brussels. I kept a warm feeling for the Sovet family and its friendly pension. For a brief few weeks, the war had seemed so far away. Now, the Germans were at the outskirts of Leningrad that would soon be cut off and under a siege that was destined to last for 890 days, until January 19, 1944, at a cost of nearly one million casualties among its civilian population. Hitler was making final preparations for the capture and destruction of Moscow. From the BBC, we learned of new Russian heroes with names that would become familiar as the war raged on, Voroshilov, Timoshenko and Budieny, preparing to defend Moscow, even as their armies were being clobbered left and right.

FALL 1941, BACK TO SCHOOL.
REXISTES AND V.N.V.

In September, I resumed my studies in the all-French *Athenée* Leon Lepage, near the *Bourse*, the stock exchange, in the heart of Brussels. I was entering the sixth grade. On the first morning, as we gathered outside the school entrance, awaiting the opening, an older boy approached me, and insulted me. "*Sale Juif!*" He spat. This time, I decided to fight. I dropped my briefcase and swung at him. I missed his head as he ducked under my blow. His right fist came up with a vengeance and struck me hard on the left temple and ear. I thought my head was going to explode. That was the end of the fight. We never became friends.

(On that September 3rd, 1941, gas chambers were first used in Auschwitz.)

Thinking back to that period, I am unable to remember the names of any of my classmates, teachers or casual friends I played with near our apartment on the Blvd. Bischoffsheim. No faces pierce the fog of my memory; even Freddy McKenzie disappeared from my life after we moved from the Rue de Malines. And yet, there were boys I played with, even the scouts of La Chapelle, ugly as they were to me, all swallowed into nothing, no souvenirs, blanks.

There were boys I hung around with. Often, we played around the *Place des Barricades,* a square just one block away from our apartment. I guess it had gotten its name from the barricades that were erected during the fight against the Dutch troops when Belgium fought for its independence from Holland in 1830. A large statue of Andre Vesale graced the middle of the square. Andre Vesale had been the greatest anatomist of the sixteenth century, challenging the views of the Greek anatomist Gaien. These views of the human body had been in vogue since the second century. Vesale and his students would dig up corpses at night and proceed to dissect them, writing treatises on the human organs, their functions and placements in the body of man. Since Vesale did his work in secret during the rigors of the Spanish Occupation and Inquisition of the Low Countries, he had always been a hero and symbol of the resistance and struggle for truth and against the foreign invaders of Belgium.

The afternoons and Sundays would find a bunch of us kids, running around the statue, ringing doorbells at random and making mild mischief. One favorite prank was to ring a doorbell, then retreat for a few steps and double back to the house, timing it so that we would pass in front of it just as the owner opened the front door. We would walk on by slowly, trying to look completely innocent, as our victim strained to see who had been there, at his door.

One afternoon, a huge firecracker materialized out of nowhere. One of us must have brought it there, but no one knew whom. Of course, we had to light it up. It exploded with an ear shattering "BANG". We scattered in all directions, as I ran towards the Blvd. Botanique. I had managed to reach the corner of the Blvd.Bischoffsheim and the Rue Van Orley, barely one block away, when a Rexiste, a Belgian Blackshirt brandishing a pistol stopped me. He grabbed me by the arm and demanded to know what I was running away from. He had emerged from the corner building, a massive *Maison de Maitre*, private hotel, where these Blackshirts were billeted. Hearing the explosion, he must have believed that a "Terrorist" member of the Belgian Resistance 'the F.I' had set off a bomb.

The Rexiste wore the black German uniform, the flat Gestapo-like peaked cap and an armband emblazoned with a Swastika. All I could see was the barrel of his gun, pointed in my face.

He shook me repeatedly, threatening me with his weapon and wanting to know where the "bomb" had been set off. When he stopped shaking me, I managed to tell him that I was running away from some kids who had exploded a firecracker. I swore that I had nothing to do with it. He let go of me and put his pistol back in its black holster. Muttering something about "stupid kids", he went back inside the building. I would not set off a firecracker again until May 1945 and another in the summer of 1952.

In Belgium, as in other occupied countries, Denmark, Holland, Norway, France, etc., local Nazi parties volunteered to form Legions to fight for the Reich and Europe against "atheistic Communism" in Russia. There were large rallies at sports stadiums, drumming up propaganda to join in the Crusade against Bolshevism. Young men, with extreme-right views were encouraged to join, however, mostly thugs blinded by the promise of glory and the prestige of the German Uniform enlisted in these Legions. Puppet governments from Bulgaria, Romania and Hungary, volunteered their own Legions. From Spain, General Franco sent in the Spanish Legion. By most accounts, these groups often placed in the front line of battle conducted themselves bravely and fought ferociously,

Naturally, Belgium was to have two Legions, the VNV from the Flemish regions and the Rexistes and their Walloon Legion, led by Léon Degrelle. I had seen Degrelle in the mid-thirties, in Charleroi. The rest of the population hated the VNV and the Rexistes. Even the German Military had a profound dislike and distrust for these soldiers-for-hire, who were essentially traitors in their own country. In 1943, the Légion Wallone was virtually annihilated in Cherkasy, on a muddy Ukrainian battlefield, as the German army was retreating behind the Dnieper River. Hitler personally ordered a plane dispatched to pluck Degrelle out of danger. Degrelle returned to Belgium to conduct more stadium rallies to recruit new candidates for the Legion. I heard Degrelle on a radio broadcast from the *Palais des Sports,* the Sports Palace. He explained that mud was so deep in shell holes, that if a soldier fell in them, he would disappear and drown. "I myself had fallen in one and was rescued just in time". At the time, I was hiding in a basement and I lamented that it had not been a hole deep enough to drown the hated bastard.

After the war, Degrelle would flee to Spain. He was tried "in absentia" by the Belgian Government and condemned to death. He was never extradited by Franco of Spain and died of natural causes at a ripe old age.

An apocryphal story:

Place Rogier, the large square in front of the North Station. A civilian, in hat and coat, carrying two heavy suitcases struggles to reach the North Station. By accident, one of his suitcases clips a uniformed Rexiste Blackshirt in the back of the knee. As the civilian trudges on, the Rexiste kicks him in the behind with his black boot. The civilian drops his suitcase, turns around and proceeds to beat up the Rexiste. The early crowd, massing around them, encourages and cheers the civilian. Flemish voices shout out: "Beat him dead, beat him dead". A couple of Brussels Policemen watch, but do not intervene. After a while, after the Rexiste has been beaten to a pulp and is lying on the pavement, a Policeman approaches the civilian and demands to see his papers.

The man hands over his papers. He is a German officer in civilian clothes. He picks up his suitcases and proceeds on, being saluted by the two policemen. The crowd cheers the German officer and disperses.

"V" FOR VICTORY. Who Sows the Wind, will Reap the Tempest (Winston Churchill)

About the only bright light in our occupied existence in the fall of 1941, was the constant reminder that the Royal Air Force (R.A.F) was bombing Germany on a regular basis. Each night, the air raid alert would sound, soon followed by the drone of the British Lancaster and Halifax bombers. These flew high above us on their way to drop bombs over the German cities of the Rhine and Ruhr regions.

It was with glee that we anticipated the bombing of the German cities. Too long had the Germans bombed the British Isles with impunity. London had been bombed on August 24th 1940, some say by mistake. However, Churchill had retaliated by sending RAF bombers to strike Berlin several nights in a row. This was the more vexing to Hitler since Air Marshall Goering had vowed that such bombing of the German capital would never happen. Enraged, Hitler ordered the Luftwaffe to concentrate on London. From early September 1940 until May 1941, London and other English cities were hit by the "Blitz" every night. Hitler boasted in a speech that "We will erase your cities from the map" He used the German term *Aussradieren,* meaning to rub out with an eraser. On November 14th, 1940, Coventry and its ancient cathedral were completely destroyed. Joseph Göbbels, in his radio broadcast, declared the coining of a new German word *"Koventrieren",* "to Coventry", to mean destroy utterly and completely. Every major city in the U.K. felt the fury of the Luftwaffe. It spared neither England, nor Scotland, nor Northern Ireland. The list of target cities read like a map of Great Britain: Liverpool, Birmingham, Belfast, Glasgow, etc. By May 1941, most of the bombings abated, as Hitler was turning his air force eastward, in preparation for the invasion of Russia that June.

Now, it was payback time.

Throughout occupied Europe, "Vs" began to appear. With chalk and paint, walls, doors, lampposts were adorned with the letter V. The V was bold, or furtive, but everywhere, even on the loading tailgates of German Army trucks. And to make sure the message was unmistakable; the inner V was filled up with the initials of the RAF. The most popular sign was that of the familiar British helmet (like an upside down soup plate) capping the V, with the letters R A F as two eyes and a nose. The Germans did not like it one bit and decreed severe punishment for those caught defacing any surface with this graffiti. Still, the Victory signs multiplied by leaps and bounds. I recall having drawn many a "V.RAF" all over downtown Brussels and even in our schoolyard, during recess.

Frustrated, the German authorities came up with a parry of Teutonic subtlety. Since they could not stop the proliferation of those pesky markings, they decreed that the "V" was a symbol of German victory and they proceeded to plaster the city with their own signs. Overnight, more "V"s began to appear, big, bold, as flags and banners strung all over the city. Over the entrance to the North Station, an immense V hung, as high as the building was tall, in Nazi colors of white, red and black. And with each German "V" came the added slogan "V is the sign of German Victory". It was an admission of defeat and the occupier's inability to halt the pro-British manifestations in the occupied lands. As a by-product, we were now free to go on carving "V" all over the place. If the Germans had seen us, we could always claim that our "V" was the sign of German victory.

Another apocryphal story:

A crowded streetcar in Brussels. On the packed rear platform, a German Gestapo, in civilian clothes, is trying to pass unnoticed. His garb gives him away. A shiny full length black leather coat, a green loden hat, adorned with a feather and a face to stop a tank at twenty paces, spell Gestapo even to the least observant rider. The ticket receiver, slowly making his way from the front of the car, stops a few feet away from the rear platform, unable to proceed any farther. He sings his little refrain "Tout le monde servi? Alleman gedient? Has every one paid?" in French and Flemish. Germans did not have to pay on public transportation and our Gestapiste simply ignored the streetcar man.

The receiver insists and repeats his little song. Still ignored. He now directs his attention squarely to the German in civilian clothes "Hey, Monsieur, are you served?" Annoyed, the German lifts his lapel, and points to a paper inside his suit's breast pocket.

"What is that? "Presses the receveur. "Let me see".

The civilian pulls out the paper and passes it on to the agent, who takes a careful look at it and then, to make sure everyone present overhears him, he exclaims "Ah, Gestapo! It is all right". With that, he hands the Gestapo back his paper. At the next stop, under the mocking stare of the other riders, the Gestapo gets off the streetcar.

NORMALCY OF A KIND

For the Rosenberg family, things were better and better economically with each passing month. Ruth asked for and received a magnificent pair of leather boots. We had discovered horse racing and we went several times to the racetrack at Boitsfort, south of the capital. At the beginning, Father would come with us, but he soon tired of a game where one had to wait nearly 30 minutes for the next race and the next occasion to bet. Ruth had a knack for picking the winning horses.

We would go in with Mother and sit in the upper stands. Frieda had recently twisted her ankle while stepping off a curb in the Rue Neuve. She had remained standing with her leg up, unable to bring down her foot. It was not broken, but a very bad sprain that left her with a swollen ankle that made it difficult for her to walk properly. Mother would then limp her way to the upper tiers, finds her favorite seat and dispatch Ruth and me to go and place bets for her. She had become fond of a jockey named Denaigre and would follow and bet his mount whenever he was riding. The choice was not bad, as he often rode the favorites.

Since Mother could not walk too well, she would give us the money to go and place her bets. Near the grounds of the track, bookies were lined up in rows, standing on small benches with a chalkboard upon which they would write the odds for each horse and each race. I was eleven, Ruth was twelve and we'd tell the bookies that our Mother was in the stands but could not walk down to place her own bets. We'd watch to see which bookie gave the best odds and would judge when was the best time to place our bets so that we would get the best odds.

Later on, neither Father nor Mother would go to the races, but Ruth and I continued to go. We'd take the streetcar to Boitsfort and walk the short distance to the track. Children, accompanied by adults, could go in for free. We would wait until we saw someone about the age of Hilaire passing through the turnstile and we'd run after him, yelling "Wait for us, Papa!" And we'd get in without paying. At the bookie stands, we'd say that our Mother was in the upper stands, etc. They never questioned us, and took our money willingly.

The best bet we ever made was on a horse named Spire that paid thirty-three to one. Ruth also picked winners with names like Kellyetre, Equinoxe, etc. They were almost always winners. It was ironic that I would remember these winning horses, while not being able to place a face or a name on any of my classmates or teachers in school.

Around the *Bourse*, which was at the center of Hilaire's life at the time, Father met a Mr Wolff, a Jew married to a Viennese. Hilaire had had a few business dealings with Wolff at the Rue de Malines. Wolff then lived above the restaurant Chez Gino. They decided to go and have dinner there. At the moment that they were to sit, he introduced Father to a fellow named M. Kruschinsky, the son of Wolff's ex-landlord in Vienna and this one, in turn presents Hilaire to his companion, who was no one else but Kurt Asche, the SS chief in Belgium. Asche, in civilian clothes, approached my Father and said; "You're MrHilaire, aren't you?" Father replied he was. Asche continued "I understand that you are a very resourceful person, and that you can get anything. Would you do me a favor? I would like a dozen silk stockings for my girlfriend. Could you get them for me?"

My Father replied that he could. "Good, Asche continued, when you have them, you can bring them to me in my office on the Avenue Louise "(The Gestapo Headquarters).

Father easily obtained the desired merchandise and delivered it to the Gestapo headquarters, a place one would prefer to avoid. He was escorted up a few flights to Asche's office where he delivered the package. "How much do I owe you?" Asche asked.

Rudy Rosenberg

"Nothing. It's a present "my Father said, backing out of the office as quickly as he could without arousing suspicion. He was terrified and he told me later that he could feel the hair on the back of his neck stiffen and he began to sweat.

The German campaign in Russia had stalled. After the capture of Smolensk and Minsk, the Germans had suffered a severe defeat at Rostov. The early onset of the Russian Winter made it unlikely that Moscow or Leningrad would fall to the Germans that year.

DECEMBER 7TH, 1941. PEARL HARBOR. AMERICA ENTERS THE WAR

On or about Tuesday December 9th, 1941 we heard the news that Japan had attacked the American base at Pearl Harbor, in Hawaii. It must have been of momentous importance, as all the papers, the Belgian radio and the BBC were reporting the news. We knew where the Hawaiian Islands were and I thought these were part of the United States. The attack was trumpeted as a great victory for Japan and the Axis powers.

Over the following days, we heard that the Japanese army had invaded Hong Kong, The Philippines, Malaysia and Singapore and that the British were reeling under the assault.

On December 11th, we learned that the USA had declared war on Germany, Italy and Japan. That was great news! Now, there would be the might of America weighing in the fight against Hitler. We all had learned how after the US entered the war in 1917, the balance of power had shifted and had brought about the final defeat of the Kaiser's army a year later. Talking it over with my school buddies, we were all optimistic that the end of the German occupation would come soon and the final Allied victory assured and quick. The grown-ups and that pesky Bernard Horowitz were of a different opinion. The war, they felt would last quite a few years longer and the victory was in no way assured.

As for me, I had a new hero to worship, Franklin D. Roosevelt, alongside of Winston Churchill.

Frieda was expressing the view that FDR, who she pronounced "Rosenfeld" was Jewish and would certainly come to our aid.

We waited with great expectations the news of American victories against the Japanese, but these failed to materialize. Instead, on Christmas Day came the news that Hong Kong had fallen to the Japanese. There was no goose for Christmas dinner that year. We had money, but nothing special was going on in our family life. Christmas and New Year 1942 left no imprint in my memory, except that the British were again victorious in North Africa and the Russian Winter offensive had thrown back the Germans hundreds of kilometers. Such news was a great morale booster and we had little inkling of the events that would make their entrance in 1942.

100

1942

Falderi, Faldera, Falderi, Ha-Ha, Ro-o-se-Marie! German marching song

On January 30 1942, we were all set to hear a major speech by Herman Goring from Berlin on the occasion of the 9th anniversary of Hitler's coming to power in Germany. I had wondered why Hitler was delegating the task to his Air Reichsmarschall, hoping that perhaps Hitler was sick, or even dead. Unfortunately, that was not the case.

At the appointed hour, the German announcer introduced Herman Goring. Instead of Goring, we heard many noises of chairs being moved about and of great rushing. We waited and waited and waited. The announcer spoke again; "The Reichsmarschall Goring would speak in a few minutes". Military music kept being broadcast interrupted occasionally by the announcer assuring us that Goring would soon speak. It took a full hour before Goring delivered a forgettable speech.

The next day, the BBC shed some light on the affair. At the exact time when Goring was scheduled to speak, RAF Mosquito light bombers swarmed over Berlin, setting off air raid alarms and sending Goring and the assembled German and foreign dignitaries scurrying to bomb shelters. The raid lasted a full hour. This was particularly vexing for Goring as he had often boasted that as long as he was head of the Luftwaffe, no enemy bomb would ever fall on German soil.

It was a great morale booster for us in the occupied countries, perhaps the only bright moment in a very dark year.

The war was going badly for the Americans and the British. On the Place de Brouckere, in the center of town, the Germans had erected an enormous poster board. It stretched next to the movie theatre and up the five or six stories of the façade. The poster depicted a rotund "John Bull" with the Union Jack encircling his toppling hat. John Bull, perched on the Globe, was struggling to keep his balance while juggling with a serie of large spheres. Each sphere was marked with a British colony that had been lost to the advancing Japanese or was about to be captured. Malaysia, Hong-Kong, and Singapore were falling to the "Rising Sun Empire".

In early 1942, on the Place de Brouckere, I went to see a movie, called *Jud Suss,* The Jew Suss. It was a German propaganda tract about a Jew in Germany in the middle Ages, who had been accused of raping a German girl. He was caught and condemned to die by hanging. At the end of the movie, he was hoisted in the Village Square in a cage, with a sign, "JEW". The bottom of the cage opened up and he was hanged. The people in the village were cheering wildly. A voice-over announced something to the effect that "so will perish all the Jewish enemies of the German nation" I recall vividly the spectators in the movie-theater standing up, applauding and cheering. I was chilled. I was petrified. I was frightened. I was afraid that they would find out that I was Jewish and that I was sitting there. Everybody around me was standing up and cheering. In the audience, there were Blackshirts, Belgian Blackshirts, with the REX Insigna on their arm. These *Rexistes* also stood in the aisle, feet apart, arms crossed against their chest, making sure that there would be no counter-demonstrations against the film.

I rushed out of the theater, onto the *Place de Brouckere* and felt the sun of the day and looked around. Everywhere around the square, which was one of the major squares in Brussels, there were huge panels of German propaganda, aimed mostly at Jews. I ran home. I got on my bed and I cried. I couldn't quite understand this, because I had never really considered myself different, or Jewish. I didn't ask my parents for an explanation of what was going on. They were busy. Father was making a living in his black market and Mother was making friends.

FALSE PAPERS

The Germans were beginning to conduct raids more frequently. Sometime, they would erupt in a café or restaurant and would check the papers of all the patrons. Folks coming out of movie theaters would be similarly searched. Now and then, they would seal off a street at both ends and would not allow anyone to pass until their papers had been checked. At the time, they were looking more for members of the underground forces (F.I), or for *refractaires*, workers who had been selected to go to Germany to work in the factories and had defaulted.

The Germans did not yet express their brutality to Jews in Belgium. Still Jews with foresight predicted that the day would come when the Germans would bear down on them harder than ever and many Jews tried to leave the country. But there were few places to go. Virtually all of continental Europe was occupied or allied with Germany. The nominally neutral countries of Portugal, Switzerland and Sweden, were buffered from us by occupied lands and getting to England was impossible. Border crossings were always dangerous, even if one had the money to pay for such a trip.

Close calls and events convinced Hilaire that it was dangerous to walk around with his I.D card stamped with the red Jode/Juif slogan that, if asked to produce it, would brand him as a Jew. Soon, with the help of a past relation in Charleroi, Hilaire was able to procure false Belgian Identity Papers. These papers were delivered to him in a Brussels phone booth against a sum of three thousand francs, a bargain at the time.

There were three false I.D. *triptyques*, with the coveted green color of Belgian citizens. Thus, officially, or if you want completely illegally, Hilaire was now Jean-Baptiste Tenasse, married to Bertine Wuilmart. Tenasse worked in a carton manufacture. Born in Brussels on September 18, 1897, (they aged him quickly) and living on the Rue de la Samaritaine, number fifty-two. His previous addresses also did not place him in very good neighborhoods; 26 Rue de la Plume and 10 Rue des Radis, street made very, very famous as the headquarters of the black market in Brussels.

Frieda was issued a false I.D. card under the name of Therese Daeleman, spouse of Francois De Moyer, born on April 10th, 1901 in Brussels. Daeleman worked as a newspaper seller and was domiciled 6 Rue Christine. All these addresses were within a couple of blocks from one another, right in the middle of the Marolles area, dating back to the 16th century Spanish occupation and the center of the black market, where anything could be obtained, for a price, even false papers.

Ruth's false papers would identify her as Marie Jeanne Reynders. No other details are known to me. However, four decades later in California, Ruth would meet a woman, about her age, named Marie Jeanne Reynders, whose identity Ruth had borrowed for the duration.

I was twelve and still too young to be required to carry any kind of identity papers.

Luckily, none of us ever had the occasion to use these false papers. Nevertheless, they gave the bearer a sense of security when compared with the yellow I.D. card foreigners had to carry. And these green Belgian papers did not carry the red-lettered "Jew" stamp. As it was, the security would have been tenuous at best. Both Hilaire and Frieda spoke a much accented French. When conducting raids, the Germans often had French-speaking civilians with them. The deception would have been discovered as soon as either of our parents had answered any question.

INVASION! (well, sort of)

"The British have landed in St. Nazaire!" The news was everywhere. On the night of March 27 to 28 1942, a British force had invaded the French port on the Atlantic. The Belgian radios, the BBC, Le Soir newspaper, all were reporting it. This was great news. Was this the opening of the liberation of Europe? Alas, after a couple of days, our hopes were dashed. It was only a raid by British commandos aimed at destroying some docks at this major German submarine base.

The operation was not well coordinated and most of the invaders were killed or captured. The Germans gloated over this "failed invasion" and reaffirmed the invincibility of the Third Reich.

On the BBC, we were told that the objectives of the raid had been achieved, mainly to prevent the U-Boats from using the harbor as a base from which to roam the Atlantic and threaten the vital shipping lanes between America and England.

For me and for my school buddies, it was a great disappointment and we spent much time during recess discussing future strategies on how to best organize the defeat of Germany and Hitler. As we were all about twelve-years old, everything seemed possible.

As spring 1942 came around, the German armies resumed their offensives. In Africa, the dreaded Marshal Rommel drove the British almost all the way to Egypt. Tobruk again fell to the Germans and it looked as if all of North Africa would fall to the Axis.

In Russia, the German troops punched their way through the Crimea, took Sebastopol and reached the shores of the Black Sea. The Caucasus and its oil reserves were within the grasp of Hitler.

On the bright side, we could hear the planes of the British Royal Air Force pass overhead every night on their way to bomb Germany. There was a constant drone of engine noise high in the sky. Sometimes, the Germans fired antiaircraft guns, but usually ammunition was reserved for planes over Germany.

Public demonstrations of German power were everywhere. German soldiers marched through the streets, their hobnailed boots loud on the pavement. Their marching bands played rousing martial music; sometimes the soldiers sang military songs. It must be difficult for those who have not experienced it to understand the psychological pressures of being occupied, of being downtrodden by hated people who are unjustly in power. The Germans tried to conquer not only physically but emotionally. Even as a Jew, while fearful of their tactics, they could impress me. The rhythm of their marching music captured me and the music lingered in my mind.

BROKEN ARM

I had been flung into the air. During recess in school, a boy grabbed me by the hand and sent me flying in the air like a slingshot. I landed on my left shoulder and heard a sharp cracking noise. Though not fully broken, my upper arm was badly cracked. Rushed to the clinic, it was decided not to place me in a cast but to wrap my arms tight to my torso with yards and yards of gauze. For the next six weeks, I resembled a mummy. In the years to follow, I would often use my "broken arm" defense whenever I got into a scrape with my sister Ruth. For the next six weeks, I could not wash my upper torso, or my underarms. Since we bathed very seldom and used no deodorants, I must have been a walking insult to the olfactory senses.

When the wrappings were finally removed, I had to go to the clinic once a week to get heat treatments to my shoulder. Each session was to last 30 minutes under a red heat light for the purpose of strengthening my bones. In the waiting room of the clinic of the avenue Brugmann, three very large books attracted my attention. These were books put out by the Shell Oil Company, dating from the 1920's. The books chronicled the establishment of fueling depots in Africa so that biplanes could explore uncharted territory and find places where gasoline had been stored in 55-gallon drums all through the unexplored jungles and deserts. Thus they would establish "Bidonvilles", literally "drum towns". These were numbered Bidonville 1, Bidonville 2, etc.

The books were full of marvelous illustrations of spear-carrying Africans, biplanes, Shell pumping stations, maps, etc. I could not have enough of these and could not part with the books when my sessions were done for the day. So, I proceeded to steal one book each week, until the whole set was safely in my home. Each book measured about 45cm x 30cm (18" x 12") and there was no way I could conceal it as I made my way out of the hospital. My pulse beating with excitement, I stole away each time, never being caught or stopped. We were soon to vacate our apartment at the Blvd Bischoffsheim. The books would be left behind and I never saw them again after that. The Germans confiscated our furniture and the books which had remained in the apartment. Hilaire would be indemnified for our furniture after the war.

Some fifty-five years later, I returned to the Clinic. In all the years, I had felt guilty at having stolen these three tomes and wanted to make amends. I walked up to the reception desk and asked if I could see the director. After briefly explaining the purpose of my visit, I was ushered in the office of the director, who turned out to be an attractive woman. We had a pleasant conversation during which I related the events described above. I also explained that although I could not return the long lost books, I was hoping to be able to make a donation to the clinic, in repayment for the theft. The director seemed amused and in a laughing tone explained that the clinic once privately held was now a government-operated institution. Any money I would donate would go to the state and would in no way benefit the clinic. She told me to go home and forget all about it and that my conscience could now rest in peace. And so it does.

BAPTIZED

There was more and more talk about Jews being arrested and sent away to Malines (Mechelen in Flemish), north of Brussels. There, it was understood that the Jews were gathered and assembled for train convoys going east towards Germany or Poland. Father talked about seeing at the North Station, convoys filled with Antwerp Jews who were taking the road to deportation. Our fears grew daily.

Frieda contacted Madame Kerremans at the Foyer des Enfants and pleaded with her to have the children baptized. After all, we had taken religious instruction regularly during the year we spent in the orphanage. Madame Kerremans, aware of our plight, did not hesitate and arranged for Ruth and me to come to the Foyer and be baptized Methodist.

On the appointed day, August 6th, 1942 Mother, Ruth and I took the *tram* to go to the Orphanage. There, a Methodist pastor read to us and had us kneel. After more incantations, he placed his hands over our head and declared that we were now good Protestant Christians. All during the "ceremony", Ruth and I were seized with an uncontrollable laughing fit. We were laughing so hard that tears ran down our cheeks. Although I was only twelve at the time, I was conscious that this was inappropriate, given that this should have been a solemn moment. However, there was no way I could repress this laughter and Ruth must have felt the same way. Madame Kerremans gave us a signed statement certifying that we were now good Methodists.

I do not believe that Mother had great difficulty with the decision for the children to become Christians. Frieda did not follow the tenets of Judaism and had a profound dislike of Orthodox Jews. She also felt that by having us baptized, it might save the children's lives and put an end to the persecutions Jews were subjected to throughout history.

However the baptism certificates would have been of no use anyway. The Germans had already decreed that only a family tree free of Jews for at least three generations was racially "pure". In the years to come, being nominally Protestant and having no foundation of the Jewish faith would contribute greatly to a crisis of identity that would plague me for decades to come.

There is a certificate of Baptism, dated and signed by Pastor William Thomas of the Eglise du Christ in Antwerp, that the baptismal ceremony took place in Brussels on August 6th, 1942. Also a letter from Madame Chr. Kerremans dated July 30th 1942, certifying that Ruth and I were living at the Foyer Des Enfants from December 1, 1939 to October 1, 1940. "During that time, they have followed our cults and classes of Protestante Evangelique. Before they left they continued to take classes in our Sunday school, in the Protestant Temple; 5 Rue du Champs de Mars, in Ixelles" This last part neither Ruth nor I remember and I suspect that Mme Kerremans added that phrase to give more weight to the baptism had the Germans questioned its validity.

YELLOW STAR OF DAVID

In June 1942, the last "slice of salami" was cut. The Germans decreed that all Jews would henceforth wear a large, visible, yellow star on the lapel of their outer clothing. The star, yellow and delineated with black lines was marked with a bold, black letter "J" for Jew. The intentions of the German authorities were, to us, very clear. Jews were now registered, had to be in their homes from 8 PM to 5 AM and could easily be spotted with the yellow Star of David on their outer clothing. It thus would become very simple for the Germans to pick up Jews whenever they chose to do so. Since we were still registered at the Rue de Malines, but had quietly moved to the Blvd Bischoffsheim, we felt a bit more secure. However, we made the smart decision not to wear the star. To our parents, it seemed to be an invitation to deportation and murder. My family did not wear the star, that demeaning patch of cloth with the word *Juif* embroidered on it. We felt it did not make sense to advertise. Who were we going to antagonize by not following orders, just the people who would kill us anyway if we wore the star. In school I had a friend, Salomon Rosenstock, who was a sickly child with a bad heart and a defiant attitude. He sewed his Jewish star on his behind and was soon picked up by the authorities. Surprisingly, I saw him again after the war, looking very healthy and built like an armoire. I never found out how he had survived.

There were many Jews who meekly obeyed the law and they could be seen in the streets, on streetcars, sitting with the Star of David plastered on their jackets or their coat, the women on their dresses, over the heart. They would stare at me and I'd avert their eyes, feeling as though I was betraying them.

WINTERTHUR INSURANCE

Two salesmen who represented Winterthur, the big Swiss insurance company, visited us at our apartment on the Boulevard Bischoffsheim. I had not gone out that day. It was probably early July 1942 and school must have been over for the summer holidays. The visit and the purpose of these two Winterthur men have remained vivid in my memory. We were seated at a small table in front of the large curved window that looked out on the boulevard. One of the two men sat to my left, he had dirty blond hair, a light brown suit and his legs were folded back under the chair. His worn, brown leather briefcase was leaning against the right front leg of his chair. The briefcase had a single clip closure and its flap had been folded back, revealing several sheaves of paper. Hilaire sat in front of me, with his back to the window. Frieda was seated to my right near the second salesman who has faded from my memory. My sister Ruth was absent.

On behalf of Winterthur, a renowned Swiss insurance company, the salesmen were offering a good deal on an insurance policy. By then we knew that Jews were in mortal danger. The mere idea that an insurance company would issue a policy on a Jew's life seemed very generous and more than we could hope for. The men explained that they had been given our name and address from other Jews who had bought this policy. They let us understand that it had been designed especially for Jews.

All we had to do was subscribe to the life policy, pay half the premium now and the second half on the anniversary of the policy, a year later. To me and to my Father, it must have seemed like manna from heaven. We did not understand the obvious swindle involved. The salesmen and Winterthur must have been aware that a year hence, there would have been no Jews left to pay the second half of the policy which would then become null and void.

I did not know at the time if Father had taken a policy or not. All I remembered was that, as they were leaving, the men asked us if we could give them names and addresses of other Jews to whom similar policies could be offered.

After the war, when I became aware of the enormity of the tragedy that had befallen our Jewish nation, I came to understand the duplicity of these salesmen and by extension, the dastardly conduct of Winterthur. For years, the very name of Winterthur would ring in my mind as the personification of evil sharks looking to reap a profit from the tragedy of the Jews.

Going through my Father's papers after his death, I found a copy of his "separation of wealth" decree with Mother. Among the meager possessions they had to share, was a Winterthur policy; the cash surrender value being ceded to Mother. That was the first evidence that Hilaire had indeed taken up that policy. He had probably paid the entire sum at the onset and thus the policy had remained in effect.

I could not help but wonder how many other policies these two men and other Winterthur agents in Belgium and other occupied countries of Europe had sold. The Jews who perished in extermination camps would never have been able to claim those policies. Most of them died together with their entire families. Those who did not die were not around to make the second payment by July 1943.

During the nineties, a commission was set up to look into the failure of European Insurance companies to honor the many policies that went unclaimed. The insurers were taken to task for having failed to search out if there were survivors or if policies were left and forgotten. All the while the insurance companies kept the considerable premiums and paid no benefits.

I was privileged and able to testify all that I knew about what I related above. At first, Winterthur denied that such life insurances, targeting Jews, were ever offered. When pressed, they confirmed that Hilaire Rosenberg had taken such a policy, but pointed out that the cash value had been paid to Frieda Rosenberg in 1946. That was correct, but it was proof that these two men had indeed sold such policies to Jews. I wanted to know how many more such policies had been sold. Surely, that was not the only policy these men had sold. I did testify, together with then New York Senator Alphonse D'Amato. Winterthur, as far as I know, has refused to reveal the existence of other such policies. One of the arguments presented by Winterthur was that no other similar claim had been made against them. The reason was simple. All other adult Jews had not been around to make the second payment, or did not return after the Holocaust. Their children, if they had survived, were probably not aware of the policies. I would not have been aware of this had I not been around on that July 1942 day to witness the visit of these two salesmen. I could have been in school, or out playing with my friends. But I was there and saw and heard.

Winterthur is now bigger and richer than ever.

DIEPPE

In the morning of August 19ᵗʰ, 1942, the Second Canadian Division invaded the French port of Dieppe, in the English Channel, about a hundred miles North-East of Paris. Although the action began at 4.50 AM, we only heard about it on the radio at about 8 AM. The Germans were cautious about the extent of the fighting and declared it an invasion by the British. This they billed as an attempt by London to open the "Second Front" that the Russians had been clamoring for in order to relieve the pressure on the Eastern Front.

We held our breath this time, remembering the failed "invasion" at St. Nazaire just five months earlier. This time, however, this seemed to be a major operation involving thousands of troops instead of the few commandos involved in the earlier raid. Could they succeed? Could they roll on to Paris, just 150 kilometers away? Could this be the beginning of the end for the Germans in the occupied countries?

By 1.30 PM of the same day, the "invasion" was over. It was a total disaster, of the 5,100 troops that landed, nearly 4,000 did not return. The Allies suffered nearly 2,000 dead, mostly Canadian. The Second Canadian Division was wiped out in their first action of the war. The total German dead numbered 297. For weeks, the German propaganda made much of the fact that the "English" had fought to the last Canadian and Scottish soldier. Pictures appeared in "Le Soir" and "Signal" showing the destroyed tanks, landing crafts and captured Canadian soldiers. This was billed as a failed invasion and warned of a similar fate, should the Allies try it again.

For the Allies, it was a costly lesson proving that attempting a landing in a port would be nearly impossible. This would bring decisive dividends nearly two years later when the Allies invaded in Normandy. However, on that bleak day in 1942, the German army seemed more invincible than ever. Rommel was victorious in Africa and the German 6ᵗʰ Army began its offensive against Stalingrad in Russia. There seemed to be no hope for an Allied victory in the future.

In the Dieppe debacle, Lieutenant Edwin Loustalot, 19, a US Ranger, was the first American soldier to be killed in the European Theater of War.

SWITZERLAND

Soon, Hilaire thought about leaving for Switzerland with the family. A hairdresser who lived in our building gave him an address where Hilaire could obtain four passports for the sum of one hundred thousand francs. Frieda immediately refused to let him spend such an exorbitant sum that she felt was grossly exaggerated. Without her knowledge, Hilaire obtained these passports anyway but was able to bargain down to seventy-five thousand francs.

In the summer of 1942, the first raids of Jews had occurred in Antwerp. Mostly those arrested were Jews who had not attained the Belgian citizenship, the foreign Jews. Belgian Jews, still under the protection of Queen Elizabeth (Saxe-Coburg-Gotha), were mostly left alone. Since the Rosenberg family was *apatride*, stateless, Hilaire's concern was well founded.

We had heard that the arrested Jews and their families were taken to the Caserne Dossin, in Malines (Mechelen), a few kilometers north of Brussels. "Malines" as the camp was referred to, was to serve as a gathering point for the Jews of Belgium, until enough Jews were assembled to fill a trainload for shipment to the death camps, mostly in Poland. A convoy would then be loaded into railroad cars for the final voyage.

On August 4ᵗʰ, 1942, the first convoy left Malines for Auschwitz followed the next day by a second convoy of nearly 1,000 Jews, including 140 children. Over the next two years, more than 25,000 Jews from Belgium, including 5,000 children would be deported to the killing camps. The vast majority would never return.

Dr. Samuels had been a reputed surgeon in Cologne. He was well known to Frieda, as he had been her family's physician. With his wife and daughter, he had been forced to flee Germany after the 1938 pogroms and had found a safe refuge in Brussels where he continued to practice at the renowned Hospital Brugmann. For a few months, he was our family doctor He was a tall, portly, impressive sort of a man, with a full graying beard. Despite his formidable appearance, he was a gentle, soft-spoken man.

Now, the safety he had sought for his family in Belgium was being threatened by the new policy of the Germans. Dr. Samuels told Father that he had plans to leave for Switzerland, with his wife and daughter. He would use false papers and travel south to France, then east to the Swiss border. There, a *passeur d'homme* would smuggle them across the Swiss border to the safe haven of Switzerland, a neutral country. A large amount of money would have to be paid to the men who would walk them through the woods to safety, but it would all be worth it in the face of the danger that his family was risking had they remained in Belgium. In Early August, Dr. Samuels bid us farewell and departed for Switzerland with his wife and daughter. Dr. Samuels advised us to follow his escape route. He would call us once he had safely arrived in Switzerland.

Meanwhile, Colonel Eppstein had warned Frieda that there was a timetable for the deportation of all Jews from Belgium to camps in the East, mostly Poland. He further explained that in a few weeks, in September, he would have to have us arrested if he ran into us. Mother advised Hilaire accordingly and we agonized over the best course of action to follow in order to survive. At the time, we had several choices, none too safe.

There was the flight through France, toward Switzerland or Spain and Portugal. Switzerland was the nearest and seemed to be the safest. There was the AJB, *Association Juive de Belgique,* who could be contacted. The AJB would place Jewish children in Christian religious orphanages or convents, while the parents tried to find a hiding place elsewhere. This did not appeal much to our parents, perhaps still feeling guilt for having placed Ruth and me in the Foyer Des Enfants just a couple of years before. It might also be possible to find families willing to hide us in their home, for a fee of course. Hiding four Jews would have been very difficult and we had to consider splitting the family. The penalty for hiding Jews was fine, arrest and deportation. Lastly, we could stay in our apartment Blvd. Bischoffsheim and hope for the best. However this was never a sensible option.

Hilaire decided that Switzerland would be the safest route to follow. Now that he had procured the false passports, we planned to follow Dr. Samuel a few weeks after his departure for Switzerland. Mother confided in Colonel Eppstein that we were making preparations to escape to Switzerland. Eppstein listened carefully and then told Frieda that we would probably make it there safely, "except for the boy, who would surely be picked up, because he has Jewish ears". He went on to explain that the SS had made studies of Jewish physical traits and that some ears were characteristic of Jews. Protruding ears and detached lobes were a sure indication of Semitic origins. He stated further that they could recognize Jews from the back of the head, just by the shape of their ears. Not all Jews had Jewish ears and not all people with Jewish ears were Jews. However, men with "Jewish ears" would get picked up in the streets. If they could prove they were not Jewish, they would be let go, if not, they were arrested and sent to deportation camps.

Since my ears were protruding and my lobes meaty and detached, that presented an immediate danger. In those days, except for my black curly hair and my dark eyes, I did not have too many Semitic features. My nose was still small and straight and had not yet taken the larger, aquiline shape that would come with maturity. Of course, I had the mark of my circumcision, but that was not outwardly visible. Had I been picked up because of my "Jewish ears", a simple inspection of my *Pierrot* would have doomed me.

It was evident that I had to be operated on and my Jewish ears reduced to more "Gentile" proportions. We found a Doctor Van Eyck, a member of the Resistance, who was willing to perform the required surgery. He had his office in his house, in a large apartment house on the Ave. De La Toison d'Or, not far from the Gestapo Headquarters, in a wealthy section of Brussels.

And so, a few days after Ruth and I had been baptized Protestant, I was taken to Dr. Van Eyck's office to have the required operation.

I was just twelve years old, and the thought of the operation filled me with apprehension and fear. There is no recollection of who took me there; it must have been Mother. In the operating room, I was alone with the doctor and a couple of nurses. They placed me on an operating table, under blinding bright lights. It was so bright that I could not see anything or anyone, just white lights. I might as well have closed my eyes. Dr. Van Eyck said something about giving me "a local" and I felt the sharp intrusions of needles on the back of my head into the gully behind my ears. I could hear the scraping against my bones as the needles were maneuvered into the several places where the anesthetic was injected. I was petrified with fear.

I could not feel anything, but the sounds of the surgery resonated in my head. Everything was happening about my ears and the anesthesia had in no way dulled my hearing. Dr. Van Eyck was now working on my right ear. I could hear the slicing noise of the instruments and it sounded as if my skin was being cut apart. Next came the cutting of the cartilage and what sounded as if my ears were being ripped apart. I felt panic. I began to scream in terror, it was uncontrollable. Everything in me wanted to escape. I wanted to flail my arms and my legs. Perhaps these were restrained, but it made no difference to me. I was wild with fear. A voice hollered "Put him under, get the ether". I felt a mask slam against my face; a heady odor of ether overcame me. I fell into a void of nothing.

When I awoke, I was in a strange bed, my ears throbbing, and my head splitting with pain. It was night. Sharp sounds of gunfire reverberated outside. I got up and stumbled to a large window and balcony. The night was alive with the noises of warplanes streaking overhead. Tracer shells from the German anti-aircraft guns pierced the darkness with long fingers of light aiming at the sky. I felt dizzy and fell back onto the bed and passed out. I slept the rest of the night. I awoke with the first morning light, in a strange room. I had no idea where I was.

THE HOUSE OF THE DEKNIBBERS

While I was having my Jewish ears fixed, Mother had received a last, urgent warning from Eppstein. "Leave now, or be arrested"

The first great *raids* round up of non-Belgian Jews had occurred in Brussels that September of 1942. And so, Frieda and Hilaire had abandoned most everything at the Blvd. Bischoffsheim and tried to find refuge elsewhere, until such time that the family could safely flee to Switzerland. Frieda had turned to her Casino acquaintances, Monsieur and Madame DeKnibber, who agreed to give her a temporary place to stay in their house, at 32 Avenue De La Cascade, in the borough of Ixelles. Hilaire, through his black market contacts would find a place to hide in Uccle, another borough of Brussels where he would find refuge for himself and Ruth. In these places, we were to wait for the propitious time to embark on our journey to Switzerland and safety.

Somehow, on the day I was operated on, the time had come to get out of our home. The plan had been for me to go directly to the hiding place after the operation, either by tramway or in a taxi. However, since I had been put out completely, I must have been taken there unconscious, in an ambulance. When I came to, in the middle of the night, I had absolutely no idea of my whereabouts.

The next morning, I was relieved to see Mother who explained that we had to leave the apartment at Blvd. Bischoffsheim. We would stay in this new house until we were ready to move on to Switzerland, as planned. A few days later, I would have to return to Dr. Van Eyck to have my earlobes grafted onto my cheeks to complete my transformation. I wanted none of it. I argued that I had suffered enough and that I did not want to go through another episode on the operating table. My argument won out.

While we were adjusting to our temporary quarters, alarming news was received. Doctor Samuel, his wife and daughter, had never arrived to the planned safe haven. We heard that they had been turned over to the Germans. We assumed that the *passeur d'homme*, after having collected the money, turned them over to the Germans and collected another reward. After the war, we came to realize that the Samuels might have made it all the way to the Swiss border, but might have been barred from entering the country and that the Swiss border guards may have pushed them back to the German border where the Samuels were arrested. Unfortunately that was not an uncommon occurrence. After the war, we were to learn that Mrs Samuel and her daughter were killed almost immediately. Dr. Samuel was assigned to the Auschwitz concentration camp where he was forced to work as a doctor and finally murdered. He was gassed when he became too old and feeble to go on.

There was no question now of fleeing to Switzerland, it would have been suicidal. We had to find permanent hiding places where we would be safe. Every day now, Germans would conduct *rafles* raids all over Belgium and Jews were being sent to Malines at an alarming rate. Mr Bernard, a friend of Hilaire, announced that he was leaving for Spain by train, in a sealed tank car. As it was, he never left Brussels, but had found a place to hide in the city where he survived the occupation. Mr Bernard would not trust anyone, not even my Father and had invented the ruse of the "tank car" for self-preservation.

What about the Pension Sovet? The family Sovet had shown kindness and fondness for the children during our stay there the year earlier, for our summer vacation. After a few phone calls, it was decided that we would be welcomed there and that the Sovet family would hide the children. Was there a price attached to the safety, I never knew, but they were willing to take Ruth and me, keep us, nourish us and save us. A few days later, my head still fully bandaged, Mother took us by train to Hotton, then by *vicinal* to Werpin, and delivered us to the Pension Sovet. We bid farewell to Mother, aware that we might never see her again. Frieda walked down the hill, over the temporary wooden bridge and was gone. For the second time in three years, Ruth and I were left to fend for ourselves.

In Brussels, on September 3rd, 1942 and again on the 11th, the Gestapo made sudden raids to arrest all the non-Belgian Jews who lived in the Capital. When the Jews had to register and have their identity cards stamped "Jew", their addresses had been noted on the general Gestapo records. Thus, the Gestapo knew where the registered Jews lived and where they would be between 8 PM and 5 AM. All they needed to do was to raid the homes, arrest the Jews and have them pack a few essentials before being loaded onto trucks destined for Malines (Mechelen). Malines was 20 kilometers north of Brussels and halfway to Antwerp. Thus, Malines was ideally suited for the roundup of Jews, between Brussels and Antwerp where the largest concentration of Jews could be found. There was a railroad siding immediately adjacent to the Caserne Dossin. That allowed the Germans to load the convoys of Jews without the need for trucks. Thus the Jews could be deported toward the East without negatively alarming the local Flemish population. The arrested Jews were mostly *Apatrides,* Stateless; the rest, Polish and German Jews who had sought a safe haven in Belgium. The Belgian Jews were still under the protection of Queen Elizabeth; their turn would come about one year later. When Frieda and Hilaire had their I.D. cards registered and stamped

"Jew", the address of record was Rue de Malines, in Brussels. In early 1942, Hilaire had decided to move to the Blvd. Bischoffsheim without notifying the authorities. Thus, we were still registered at our old address. Father had had the foresight to make the clandestine move. When the Germans came to the Café Cambridge on the Rue de Malines, we were gone and safe. Of course, by then we had also gone into hiding. However, had we stayed there, we would have been arrested and on our way to Malines and Auschwitz.

Malines' Caserne Dossin was just a holding camp where Jews were held under degrading and pitiful conditions When the Germans had assembled enough prisoners, about 1,500, these were loaded aboard trains destined for Auschwitz. The journey would take two days. Now and then, some inmates would try to escape while the trains were still traveling through Belgium. They could hope for the help of Belgians whilst such help would have been denied them once the train crossed into Germany or into Poland where the population was very hostile to Jews.

There were to be a total of twenty-six convoys from Belgium to Auschwitz. The early trains had regular third class cars; later on these were replaced with the cruel cattle cars. More than 25,000 Jews from Belgium were deported to Auschwitz, of which more than 5,000 were children. Of the Jews living in Belgium, about 40,000, nearly half, survived as they found refuge and hiding places with the local population. Belgians hated the Germans more than they disliked Jews. Hiding Jews was not only a humanitarian gesture but also a means to defeat the will of the occupiers.

After the war, a former acquaintance of Hilaire came back from Auschwitz. He related the following. He and his wife and daughter had been arrested, sent to Malines and loaded on one of the convoys destined for Poland. The train stopped shortly after leaving Malines. Inexplicably, the doors of their cattle car slid open and they decided to make a break for freedom. It was a trap. Apparently, the German guards were waiting for them and under the glare of searchlights, began to fire on the prisoners trying to escape. His wife and daughter were killed almost immediately. He took refuge under the train, sliding between the rails. After a while, the guards re-sealed the cars and the train resumed its way to Poland. When the train had disappeared, the man walked until he arrived at a farm. The farmer spoke only Flemish and the Jew only French. He explained with gestures and in Yiddish that he had escaped and needed a place to hide for a while. The farmer took him in, fed him and gave him a place to sleep. The next day, the farmer turned him in to the Germans. He was taken back to Malines and placed on the next convoy to Poland. He survived Auschwitz.

It was early September 1942. In the war news, besides the German General Rommel (The Desert Fox), we began to hear about the British General Montgomery "Monty". El Alamein crept into the news, as well as Stalingrad in Russia. Mostly, the news was bad as the German Summer offensives continued to roll forward on all fronts. Soon, the German war machine would reach its high tide, but in the early fall of 1942, neither Ruth nor I had any inkling that the tide was about to turn, even ever so slowly. The future did not appear bright.

I was 12, Ruth had just turned 14.

HIDING IN THE ARDENNES

We quickly settled into a routine at the pension. Ruth and I shared a small room to sleep in during the day; we had the run of the pension and made ourselves useful. Chores were assigned to us, mostly to keep us occupied. Nothing heavy or demeaning was ever asked of us. The Sovets were kind, cheerful and treated us as if we were family. It was the end of the summer and there were still many guests at the pension and two more children were hardly noticed.

Emile Sovet, a few years older than I, showed me how to operate a hand-powered pump drawing water from a well to a tank in the attic of the building. This I had to do about every other day to maintain water pressure in the pension. Another chore was to collect eggs from the chicken coop. The hens would protest my intrusion and scatter about while I reached for their freshly laid eggs. As a city boy, I marveled at the rough texture of the shell, contrasted with the soft warmth of the eggs in my hands. Once I had to help in the killing of a chicken. I didn't hold on properly and after I had cut off its head with an ax, the body kept on running all over the place like a balloon propelled by escaping air. The headless chicken was running in erratic circles, its open neck spraying blood on the gravel and dirt of the yard. After that, everyone thought it would be safer to teach me how to milk the cows. I never became comfortable with that either, as the warmth and feel of the teats remained strange to me. I did not have the boldness to pull and squeeze smartly in order to propel the milk into a tin bucket. Yet, when others did the chore, I'd marvel at the distinct music of the milk striking the bottom of the bucket. Whenever I could, I'd spend long hours in the kitchen watching Mme Elise Sovet prepare the day's meals. A large blue and white speckled coffeepot always steamed on the stove, and I'd love to watch Elise plunge what looked like an enormous sock filled with coffee grounds into the boiling water. On the farm, food was abundant still in that year of 1942. Except for not knowing the fate of our parents, those were the most carefree and happy days Ruth and I had ever known.

Usually I wandered through the countryside exploring with Emile. The Germans had prohibited Belgian civilians from keeping firearms, but the Sovets had hidden a beautiful single-shot hunting rifle under some hay in a trough in the barn. Emile took me hunting and I was horrified as I watched a little bird he shot struggle for life. When it was my turn to shoot, I rested the rifle butt against the wall of the barn so the powerful recoil wouldn't knock me over. After watching the bird die, my heart wasn't in shooting and I fired only once. Emile also took me fishing in the nearby Ourthe River where, I was told; beautiful trout were plentiful, although I never caught nor saw one.

We'd set out amid the boulders strewn about under the ruins of the bridge blown up in 1940. Balls of cooked oatmeal were used for bait at the end of heavy barbed hooks. Emile demonstrated how to toss the hooks away at the end of our fishing pole and to slowly draw back the bait toward us. When I suddenly felt a resistance, my heart pounded, but briefly. My hook had snagged between rocks and as I pulled violently, the line broke and the hook was lost. As the evening arrived, we drank the last of the coffee from the metal thermos bottle. Feet wet and with an empty bag, we scampered back up the hill to the Pension Sovet where a good soup and meal awaited us.

One guest bothered me, a man from Yugoslavia or Hungary I think. The man was always in need of a shave, wore a dirty gray cap, a torn sweater and baggy trousers over worn muddy shoes. He never spoke to my sister or me, but always seemed to leer menacingly at Ruth who was now fourteen years old. I felt protective of my sister and made sure that she was never alone when the man was nearby. He must have been a refugee himself, hiding from the Germans just as we did. The Sovets did manage to hide nearly 70 people during the war.

One day, my imagination created a frightening experience as I had wandered afar, alone. I had followed a path through the dense woods. Suddenly, I heard what sounded to me like the bloodcurdling howl of a vicious animal. I pictured wild boars attacking, a common action theme in certain paintings and sculptures. I had never seen a wild boar, except as a trophy, on walls in dining rooms. The head was large, with huge menacing white tusks protruding from an ugly snout. As the noise became louder and louder, the beast must surely have come nearer and nearer to my path. I was frightened that I was going to die right there in the woods and I clambered up a pine tree. When I was high enough for safety, I realized that my palms and fingers were covered with sticky pine tar. I heard that strange sound again, closer to me now. Then, I saw it was only a cow and watched her pass under the tree meandering harmlessly down the trail. Back at the Pension, Emile had to use kerosene to clean my hands, which on the climb down had also become soiled with cow dung left by my shoes on the branches when I climbed up.

In the meantime, the Germans, whose grand hope of invading England had evaporated, were consolidating their hold on the countryside, having long since taken charge of Belgium's cities. German guards were placed at every strategic location in the country; bridges, railroad crossing and the like. The underground had become skillful at sabotage and at every opportunity the Resistance was blowing up transportation lines. Along with soldiers came officers and more Gestapo agents, easily recognizable in their leather coats and feathered green hats. Whenever German officers came to the pension, Ruth and I had to hide in our rooms. That may well have been a useless exercise since it apparently was well known in the village that we were hiding there. I would not have been surprised if, when a stranger asked for directions, he was told to "make a left at the house where the Jewish kids are hidden". But the situation was, of course, not funny. We were in a dangerous predicament as many of the villagers were openly wondering about the two children living in the pension. Now that the school year had started anew, they could not understand why Ruth and I were not in attendance. The Sovet family was wonderful to us, but we did not know where our Mother and Father were at the time.

On September 26th, convoy No. 11, with 1,742 Jews, 523 children, left Malines and arrived in Auschwitz two days later.

One day, Ghislaine Fraiteur a woman we had never met showed up at the Sovet pension and explained that she had come to take Ruth and me back to Brussels. Hilaire hiding in her house had decided that we would be safer there, with him. Ghislaine's husband Jacques Fraiteur came from a prominent Belgian family. He had been an officer in the Belgian army and was taken prisoner of war by the Germans during the invasion. He would never come back. As a French-speaking Belgian, the Germans kept him in a prisoner camp in the Eastern territories (Poland or the Baltic States) and it was later learned that he had been shot by the Russian troops liberating his camp. After five years of captivity, his Belgian uniform may have been indistinct, and when the Russians came through the camp, they killed most everybody. Ghislaine was in her thirties and a beautiful woman. I guess that she must have had a document signed by Hilaire, or Hilaire may have called the Sovets to confirm that the children would leave. Otherwise, it is doubtful that we would have been released to the care of Ghislaine.

Mme Fraiteur had brought a pair of men's shoes that she hoped to exchange for butter from a local farmer. With German rationing, good butter was nearly impossible to find in the city. First, Ghislaine was told of a beekeeper that would be willing to trade some honey for the shoes. We were told to walk upstream along the Ourthe River to where we would find a boat to cross to the beekeeper. As I was going to make the journey with Ghislaine, I was warned to cross the river with the boat "straight" in the water. We found the little boat. The current was swift and a low-slung rope hung across the river, between two trees. The rowboat had no oars and someone wanting to cross the river could pull himself across hand-over-hand. Ghislaine sat at one end of the boat and I stood to pull on the rope. As instructed, I aimed the boat "straight" toward the other bank of the river. We had not gone far before the current made the boat spin under me.

As I hung on to the rope, I found myself lifted off the floor, while the boat began to drift downstream. I did no know how to swim and I was scared, having lost contact with the boat and hanging in mid-air over the water. As the boat circled on, Ghislaine grabbed me by the legs and I managed to regain my footing on the back seat while never letting go of the rope.

Apparently, when I was instructed to keep the boat "straight" in the river, it meant straight with the current, not straight across. As soon as the boat had left the bank, the current grabbed us broadside and spun us in the direction of the water flow. Now wiser, I managed to pull the boat safely to the other side and we set out once more to find the beekeeper.

Once we obtained the honey, we found another farmer willing to trade butter for it. We returned to the Sovet side of the river by walking across a small bridge unguarded by the Germans. We bid farewell to the Sovet family and made our way to Hotton to board the train back to Brussels. Now, the problem was getting the butter back to Brussels without being detected by inspectors; our little trading mission would have been classified as black-market activity. We had little luggage for the train trip to Brussels and thus, no good place to hide the butter. We divided the butter into two five-pound packages wrapped in oilpaper. Then we tied those packages to my legs at the calves so my knickers would cover them. The train was full and we had to ride on the platform between two cars.

The trip from Hotton to Brussels should have taken about two hours, however, due to special circumstances it took us nearly seven hours before we reached the *Gare Du Midi*, South Station, in the capital. A short time after we left Hotton, we became aware that the engineers on the train were shoveling coal over the side of the tender and onto the banks running along the tracks. There, a gang of acolytes was collecting the discarded coal, squirreling it into large jute sacks. The coal would find its way into their home or would be sold on the black market for a profit to be shared with the railway men. All this was done at a crawling pace, with the engine chugging along slowly. After a while, the coal supply being exhausted, the train came to a halt in the middle of nowhere. One of the engineers trotted out to the nearest village and telephoned for a fresh supply of coal. It took a couple of hours before another locomotive and tender sided over to our train. Laboriously, some fresh coal was shoveled to our tender, the locomotive was fired again and we waited some more for a full head of steam to be generated. We limped slowly into the South Station, just before the onset of the curfew, with little time to spare to catch the last streetcar to Uccle. The trainmen were doing double-duty, disrupting the train schedules so dear to the Germans and thus doing their bit of sabotage. Incidentally, they were also lining their pockets with the proceeds of the adventure.

In the meantime, in the seven hours we were in transit, much of the butter hidden in my knickers had melted and some had turned into a gooey, dripping mess that soaked my shoes.

Ghislaine Fraiteur, Ruth and I got on the streetcar to Uccle and we walked the last few blocks to her house on the Rue Copernic, a block away from the large Uccle Observatory. Uccle was the southernmost borough of Brussels and in a well-to-do section of private homes and villas. Nothing of that impressed me on that night, as I did not know what awaited us and we were sad to have to leave the friendly environment of the Pension Sovet. To our delight, we were reunited with Father who had been hiding in the Fraiteur house since mid-Summer. Of course, Mother was not there, as she was hiding at the house of Mr and Mme DeKnibber, in Ixelles, a suburb closer to the center of Brussels.

The Sovets had been wonderful. We did not have to pay them much, if anything, to hide there. I had no further contact with them until some thirty years later. I had been on business in Belgium and was driving near Liège, at the edge of the Ardennes. I found the river Ourthe, which is near to Melreux and Hotton and there is this tiny village, Werpin, near it, and I found it.

With a colleague, we drove across the bridge and it struck me how small everything was. In 1941, of course, I did not drive and we had to walk across the bridge, which at the time was a wooden passerelle, a footbridge. During the 1940 conflict, the retreating Belgian troops had blown up the bridge over the river. A bit past the bridge, the Pension looked the same as thirty years earlier, but I had doubts about being in the right place. With the rented car, the distances had been so shortened, unlike three decades ago when all had to be traversed on foot.

I walked to the pension and there was a younger Mme Sovet. I asked her, "Where can I find Mr Sovet?"

In the Ardennes, one is suspicious of strangers and she asked "What do you want with him?"

"I just want to speak with him."

"You'll find him in the sawmill."

There was another building near the pension, across the road. It had not existed when we were hiding in Werpin. I walked over to the sawmill and there were two men in there, an older one and a younger one. The younger seemed slightly older than I was. I walked in and he looked at me from afar, and said, "Qu'est ce que vous voulez? What do you want?"

It was difficult, thirty years later. What do you say? I started, "Je m'appelle Rudy Rosenberg"

He looked closer at me and exclaimed" Rodolphe! Ruth et Rodolphe!" "We were just wondering what had happened to you! We were talking about you the other day, because we had hidden many people during the war, but only two children. We were wondering if you had made it"

It was Emil. We embraced. "And how are the ears?" he inquired. Indeed, when we had arrived there in fall 1942, soon after my ear operation, I still had my head bandaged up. We had dinner and had a great time. The Sovets should really be called "Righteous Ones", to my knowledge they never took a penny for anything, but eventually we had to leave as our presence there had been compromised.

UCCLE, HIDING WITH FATHER

While Ruth and I had been spirited away to the Ardennes, Hilaire had dealings with Mr Wolff, a Viennese refugee, then living in Brussels and like Father, involved in black marketing activities, albeit with less monetary success than Hilaire. When Hilaire related the failure of our attempt to leave for Switzerland, Mr Wolff advised him to forget about trying to leave Belgium. Instead he suggested a possible hiding place near the Observatory of Uccle. If Hilaire promised to pay half his pension in this villa on the Rue Copernic, he would intercede with the landlord to accept Father and the two children. Frieda would find a separate place to hide.

Hilaire in his memoirs relates:

> *Thus I go find Mme Cuvelier, who lives at 8 Rue Copernic, with her daughter Ghislaine Fraiteur, whose husband is a war prisoner in Germany. We get together on the conditions of our hiding there. She demands six thousand (Belgian) francs per person, thus I will give three thousand francs each month for Mr Wolff, as far as he is concerned. These are enormous sums of money for the times, but luckily I'm able to pay it without any problem. Of course, one must remember that all of our nourishment will come exclusively from the black market and that we must pay a premium because of the danger involved.*

> *Make no mistake about it; we are not dealing with good souls ready to make important sacrifices to save Jews from deportation. Instead these are people who have made the decision to make a comfortable profit from the situation under the guise of patriotic conduct. Nevertheless I am very happy to have found this solution to safeguard the entire family and to put them in a safe place.*

> *I think that I made the same proposal and the same conditions to the DeKnibber. (Note by the author: DeKnibber charged only BF.1,500—per person). I do remember that at a certain time we required fifty thousand (Belgian) francs per month for our hiding expenses, but I don't remember to what this sum corresponded, unless of course, there were supplements or an increase in fees that were charged to us. There was also a little bit of money that was spending money for us, but we never had any occasion to spend that.*

> *Before going into hiding, I place all the money, the jewels, the paintings and other valuables with a supplier in whom I have full confidence, Mr Croisier on the Avenue Rogier, without any*

receipts or any form of acknowledgment. During all the time of our hidden life he will regularly bring the required sums, every month to one person in Uccle who will be the courier and at the liberation will give me back every item that was left in his depot without prevailing anything.

Thus, at the beginning, the two children are with me, but soon, Mme Cuvelier, who happens to have a terrible temper, declares that Rudy is much too noisy and he will have to go and join his Mother at the Etangs d'Ixelles. I then stay with Ruth to await, in relative security, the end of the war . . .

. . . . Mme Fraiteur (Ghislaine) also lets me understand, without doubt and with precise gestures, that sexual favors could also be provided. I now understand why the family of her husband was opposed to this marriage in its time as Mme Cuvelier (her Mother) would tell us very often with great indignation. But I have no intention to fall entirely under the influence of our hostesses, especially since I have noticed a young girl who lives further down the street. I have her contacted by Ruth to ask her to go each month get the necessary money from the Croisiers and to bring a part of it to Frieda. Not only does she declare herself ready to help us in this way, but she will also not take long to give me other services of a quite different nature when her Mother is not there. She must have found serious doubts with the forbidden fruit of her religion, because she was a very faithful Catholic and very practicing. She tells me that the only love advances she has had to refuse so far were from the priest at her local church.

Hilaire would remain very proud of having "deflowered" his young neighbor. After he died, I discovered that he had also "deflowered" Odette, the other part of the money connection. I guessed that he was thus assuring that the money trail would be more secure if it was paved with love and passion. It was Odette who later would reveal the liaison to me. At the time, she was still a very attractive woman. We resolved that someday we would make love, in memory of Hilaire.

Unfortunately, she was to die before we had a chance to firm up our plans.

Mme Fraiteur's house seemed like a mansion to me. It was the most beautiful house I had ever been in. It was surrounded by a big garden where, by this time, with food shortages throughout the country, flowers had been supplanted by more practical vegetables, cauliflower, Brussels sprouts, rutabagas, etc. A grand piano graced the living room and over the mantelpiece, there was a bigger than life full-length portrait of Ghislaine done by Jacques Maas, a well-known Belgian painter.

Fifty years later, in 1993, I would return to the house at 8 Rue Copernic, now inhabited only by Ghislaine Fraiteur and at least twenty cats. Ghislaine, though in her eighties, did recognize me, but showed signs of advanced senility. The house was neglected both outside and inside. I was allowed to walk about and to try to remember things and rooms as they had been. It seemed strange and oddly small. Ghislaine kept repeating: "How is your Father? It is your Mother who is dead?" and I'd say that my Mother was fine, at ninety-one and that my Father had died in 1988. Ghislaine would nod her comprehension and then ask me the same question over and over again.

In the living room, the Jacques Maas portrait still hung over the mantelpiece and Ghislaine, in her past beauty still commanded the room. I tried to find a little resemblance with the ravaged figure of MmeFraiteur standing next to me, but in vain. Depressed, I quickly left the cat-urine smelling house.

Ghislaine Fraiteur, her Mother, Mme Cuvelier and Ghislaine's grandMother inhabited the mansion at 8 Rue Copernic. The grandMother was completely senile and sometimes had nightmares at night. We only knew her as "*grand-mere*". Grand-mere's late husband, Gustav, had been dead for many years. Both were Germans and Gustav had probably fought during WWI in the same Kaiser's army where my GrandFather Philippe Friedemann had served. Grand-mere, who by then spoke only German, wandered through the house in her white nightgown at all hours of the day or night, opening doors, peering in rooms, asking where her husband Gustav was. She would question: "Gustav?" and receiving no answer would then utter a couple of "Ah. Ah!" and continue her quest to another floor, another room. Now and then, she would wander to the attic floor where there was no light and afraid to come down in the dark, would yell her head off for Gustav to come and help her until Mme Cuvelier, her daughter, or Ghislaine would clamber up to the attic landing and guide Grand-mere back to the living room.

Often, Grand-mere would stand by the enormous mantelpiece in the dining room and sing an old German military song, "*Ich hatte einem Kamarade*" "I had an old comrade"; she would command the room with her cracked voice and emaciated gestures and retell again the story of two soldiers, friends, standing side by side. One got shot and died, the other survived. She would shoot her finger to her breast, then raise the other hand to indicate that he had gone to heaven, while the other soldier wondered "why him?" and mourned his old comrade.

Besides Hilaire, Ruth and me, Mr Wolff, a Viennese Jew and his wife were also hidden at 8 Rue Copernic. Mr Wolff had had dealings with Father, but was nearly broke. He had found the place to hide and in return had bartered that Hilaire would pay half of his six thousand Belgian francs monthly hiding fee. This fee was per person and was an important sum of money even in those times. Luckily, Father had garnered enormous sums of money by then and we were in a position to sustain such expenses for the foreseeable future, provided the war did not go on too long. Incidentally, where Frieda was hiding, her monthly fee was BF 1,500 and she scorned that Hilaire had to pay 6,000 because he had boasted that he was such a wealthy big shot.

Mr Wolff was a huge man. He reminded me of Walter Slezak. It was from him that I learned the art of hand kissing and such Viennese expressions, as "*Kuss die Hand, gnadige Frau*", I kiss your hand, gracious woman. He was a very effusive and charming man. He survived the war but I never knew what happened to him afterwards. Strangely enough, his wife, MmeWolff, kept going in and out of our hiding place. She would be gone for days at a time. She was not hiding with us, but would come through the front garden, wearing a black coat with the yellow Star of David and a large crucifix dangling from her neck over her ample bosom. Her obvious comings and goings had us concerned that she might be followed and bring back the Gestapo to our hiding place.

And then, there was Kiki, Ghislaine's wire-haired fox terrier, active and high spirited and playful. Kiki reminded me of Tommy, the Pesch's fox terrier at Zeebrugge who had been so horribly burned six years earlier. Kiki and I became good friends and I'd be allowed to feed him now and then. When Father had learned that the dog was named "Kiki", he thought that this was a funny name for a dog. With his Polish/Jewish inability to distinguish an "I" from a "U", he thought the name was "Cu-cu" which would have meant "ass-hole" and would indeed have been a strange name for a dog.

Kiki was enamored of a huge square Belgian block in the yard outside of the dining room. For hours, Kiki would furiously mouth and mount that unresponsive piece of stone, snarling, panting and drooling, pushing and dragging it from one end of the yard to the other. It was obvious even to a twelve-year old that the dog was sexually aroused by this Belgian *"pavé"* paving stone. This was an almost daily occurrence and tough I tried to avoid the sight of it, it was almost impossible not to notice it. It gave me an uncomfortable feeling and a visual image that would come back to haunt me in years to come.

MmeCuvelier and Ghislaine did not hide us for purely altruistic reasons. They really charged us a lot. They also did not know where we had hidden the bulk of our money and the sum was considerable. Turning Jews over to the Germans was not unheard of and was done now and then for the reward money or to keep their possessions. Hilaire trusted very few people and made certain that Ghislaine and her Mother did not know where the bulk of our wealth was hidden.

In the early weeks of hiding, we might not have been completely conscious of the reality of the danger we were facing. At times, we took foolhardy chances by venturing outside for a while.On at least two occasions, Frieda came away from her hiding place to visit us at the Rue Copernic. Of course, unlike Mme Wolff, she was not wearing the infamous yellow star, but she had the luck that often accompanies "The ignorance of the danger".

Inexplicably, Ghislaine decided to take Ruth and me to a show near the Rue Neuve, in the middle of the city. The Gaité was a famed Variety Theatre (today it is a shopping center), next to it were two nightclubs, the Gaity and the Broadway. I had passed by these many times when we were living in the Rue de Malines but had never had a chance to go to that theatre. The show consisted mostly of imitators of Laurel and Hardy, Charlie Chaplin, Astaire & Rodgers, Maurice Chevalier and Marlene Dietrich. They did skits, sang parodies of songs and told jokes. I was very impressed and the memory of the performance was to stay with me during my hiding months. It was a good morale booster. However, it was not worth the chances we took by going there.

On another occasion, Ghislaine took us to see a movie in the same theatre. It was a broad, rollicking farce called "Bosseman & Coppenole", a Belgian movie about the rivalry between two Brussels football (soccer) teams, Daring and the Union St. Gilloise. There was a boy and a girl of course, with Fathers being fans of the competing teams. There was a song extolling the virtues of Leek, the king of vegetables. The boy, who is also the star center of the Union St. Gilloise team, is kidnapped so he won't be able to play in the championship match. On the day of the game, the boy escapes without clothes and runs through the streets of Brussels with just a towel wrapped around his midriff. The lovers reunite, the Fathers relent. Happy ending! It was so unusual to see a film made in Belgium, its film industry being non-existent at the time.

It must have made quite an impression on me as I can still recall the skits, the songs and most of the plots as I write these memoirs, more than sixty years later.

The first time Mother came to visit us at the Fraiteur's we had a late lunch in the dining room. Seated around the table, we engaged in idle banter. Mr Wolff, Ghislaine and Mme Cuvelier were seated with their back to the window. Ruth and Father had found seats at either end of the table and Mother and I sat across from Ghislaine. Hilaire told a joke about the different behavior of men and women when food was dropped in their lap. That was bad enough, but he went on with another riddle about why Jewish women had curly hair while gentile women had straight hair. The answer made it quite clear that the hair in question was the pubic hair. Obviously, until then, Hilaire had not realized the racy nature of the joke and he became embarrassed and blushed mightily.

During the meal, I had gotten up from the table and when I returned, Ghislaine remarked that I had circles under my eyes. It is unclear to me why my eyes were thus marked, as being months short of my thirteenth birthday I had not yet crossed the threshold of puberty. Ghislaine said "*Il est cerné*" which can be interpreted as having circles under the eyes or that I was surrounded. So, I looked around and in back of me and replied that I saw no one surrounding me. This made everyone laugh, except for Mr Wolff who did not understand that much French. For me, it was a revelation that I could be funny and was able to make people laugh. I felt good about it.

All the while, I noticed that Frieda was becoming more and more agitated over what she perceived to be a flirt between Ghislaine and Hilaire. The tone at the table soon changed noticeably from amiable to barely concealed hostility. Mother left shortly after that to return to her hiding place in Ixelles.

MOTHER, THE LOTTERY TICKET AND THE PUPPY

Frieda had maintained friendly relations with Edith and Helene, the lesbian *entraineuses* from her days as a waitress at the Café Rubens. Shortly before she went into hiding, Mother had pooled some money with the girls and together they had purchased a lottery ticket. The number of the ticket had been duly noted. A few weeks later, the drawing occurred and they had a winning ticket. It was not for the big prize, but the sum to be disbursed was considerable. So, Frieda called Edith and Helene (it was always *Edith et Helene,* never Edith or Helene, they were inseparable) and told them that she would take the risk of leaving her hiding place and come to visit them to collect her third of the winnings. Frieda traveled by tram to their apartment in Anderlecht; a suburb of Brussels with a large Jewish population.

When Mother arrived, Edith pointed to a little puppy dog and explained that the dog had eaten the lottery ticket and that there was thus no money to be shared. There was not much Frieda could do or say. However, she stayed and they had cookies and coffee and talked about the old Café Rubens days. All the while, the puppy was nipping at Mother's dress and peeing and pooping all over the carpet. It got to be late evening, way past the eight o'clock Jewish curfew time and Edith and Helene urged Mother to stay for the night so she could safely go home in the morning when the curfew would end.

Frieda had never been fond of dogs and the sight of the puppy doing its business all over the apartment was highly repugnant to her. So, even though it was by then close to the general curfew, she decided that she would take her chances outside and return to Avenue de la Cascade. Mother managed to catch the last streetcar and made it safely back to her basement in Ixelles.

The next morning, at five, the Gestapo made a raid in Anderlecht and arrested a large number of Jews. Among those arrested was Edith. Helene, though not a Jew, opted to stay with Edith and to share her destiny. They were sent to Malines and from there were shipped to Poland on a subsequent convoy to the extermination camps. Frieda would later say that they had been shipped to Theresienstadt, the "Showcase" Concentration camp. They never returned. No one knew what happened to the puppy that had been so instrumental in saving Frieda's life. If it had not been for the little dog, Frieda would have slept the night and been arrested together with *Edith et Helene*.

LE GROS JACQUES. (Icek Glogowski, born in Poland)

We had become aware of a notorious individual known to us only as *Le Gros Jacques*, Big Jake. He was a Polish born Jew living in Anderlecht, a suburb of Brussels, near the *Gare du Midi*. After Antwerp, Anderlecht had the largest concentration of Jews in Belgium. Le Gros Jacques was helping the Germans round up the Jews from all over Brussels.

Jacques would assist the Germans during the many raids being conducted to seize the Jewish population in the Capital. Often, he would appear, riding in a German car, leading trucks full of German soldiers. They would seal off a street and empty out the houses, looking for Jews. Le Gros Jacques would lead them and help them peruse the identity papers of the people rounded up in the streets. Since he was a Jew, he had a special affinity to recognize his co-religionists, gain their confidence and denounce them.

Until late in the occupation, Jacques would circulate in town, with the yellow Star of David sewn on his lapel or as an armband, trying to trick people into his confidence so as to ferret out more Jews. Often, he would ride the streetcars, brazenly displaying his Star of David. People would stare and eventually ask him if he was not afraid to circulate openly wearing the yellow star. He would then feign surprise and ask why he should be afraid. The riders would then explain that they had heard of Jews hiding in fear for their lives. Jacques would then try to inquire about the identity of those "hidden" Jews, wondering if perhaps they were acquaintances or friends of his. Further gaining the people's confidence, he would try to have them divulge where and by whom these Jews were hidden. Armed with that knowledge, he would inform the Germans and arrests would soon follow.

We had heard that the Gestapo was holding Jacques' wife and three children as hostages in return for his help in capturing Jews. Eventually, as Jews became scarcer to find, his usefulness to the Germans diminished to the point where the Gestapo no longer needed him. In September 1942, Jacques' wife, daughter and two sons were taken to Malines and then on to Auschwitz where they were murdered. Jacques continued his nefarious task until the end of the occupation when he fled

Belgium for Germany in the fall of 1944. He either was deported by the Germans he had served so well or went of his own free will with other SS or Gestapo members.

Members of the Jewish Resistance tried several times to have him assassinated but he was very wily and suspicious. He was reported to be wearing a metal bulletproof vest under his shirt and all attempts at executing him failed.

After that, the accounts of his fate are murky. There are rumors that he was sent to Auschwitz near the end of 1944 where he was beaten by other Jews who had recognized him. Jacques was subsequently gassed and killed. Another rumor had him escaping with stolen money to Switzerland and finding refuge in South America.

There was an instance where Le Gros Jacques seemed to have better intentions toward Jewish children. In late 1942 or early 1943, The Gestapo, led by Le Gros Jacques, raided a catholic Convent Avenue Clemenceau. There should have been twenty Jewish girls on the premises. By chance, they were away that day for catechism, as explained by the Mother Superior. The Gestapo told her that they would return the next day and that the girls had better be there, packed and ready to be taken away. They left but Le Gros Jacques returned shortly thereafter. Jacques reportedly told the Sister that she should make sure all the girls had left the orphanage before the night was over. If they were still there in the morning, they would all be killed "as they have killed my wife and my children". The girls would have been of about the same age as Jacques' own children.

The Mother Superior contacted the underground. That night, the twenty Jewish girls were spirited away and placed elsewhere. They all survived the war.

That was the only instance ever reported where Jacques actually risked his life to help Jews. It probably was influenced by the fact that his wife and three children had just been murdered by the Germans he was working for.

Although *Le Gros Jacques* was accursed by his victims and their survivors, one had to wonder what others would have done had they been in his shoes. True, he plunged into his task with the greatest of zeal, but turning informer in order to save his family must have been a horrific choice. Most of us were lucky that we were never faced with a similar dilemma. Who knows what path we might have chosen?

The three children of Icek Glogowski (Le Gros Jacques) Elka, Simon and Léon were of the age group of the girls in the Avenue Clemenceau Convent. They were registered in Malines together with their Mother Eva, on September 30th, 1942. They were ages 6 to 8. On October 12, 1942 they arrived in Auschwitz with the 12th convoy (from Malines). A Mother with three young children? They would not even be numbered or tattooed! (They must have been gassed within three hours of their arrival).

According to the testimony of Otto Siegburg at the Belgian inquest, Le Gros Jacques fled with him during the retreat to Germany in the fall of 1944. (From the book "La Traque des Juifs, The hunting down of the Jews) volume 2.

RUE COPERNIC, SETTLING IN

The Fraiteur home had a library with a good collection of books. The one that fascinated me most was a multi volume set on the human race. The illustrations were explicit as to the differences between humans and the continents they lived on. What I remembered most were charts and drawings of parallel lines to illustrate that ears and noses were always of the same length. Semitic types had long ears and noses; African tribes had small noses and small ears, etc. It may have been similar to whatever guided the Germans in their racial purity studies and it held my attention.

There was an automatic record changer/player and a selection of records. The selection was limited and I'd be playing records by Edith Piaf, Yves Montand and Maurice Chevalier that I'd soon know by heart. Between meals, there would be the constant distraction of Grand-Mere shuffling in and out, wondering where Gustav might have been. Kiki would bring me a ball to play with or concentrated on his Belgian paving block in the yard.

It was fall and Ghislaine would invite me to join her outside whenever she was walking Kiki in the evening darkness. There were not many streetlights and we felt safe in the dark streets where we would seldom run across anyone else. Following Kiki, I'd shuffle my feet deep in the dried leaves that had accumulated along the gutters of the sidewalks. It made a crisp noise unlike any other. I could enjoy seeing my breath exhale in moist ribbons as we walked in the cold, crisp night. Overhead, lost in the sky, the constant purring of high-flying RAF bombers was our nightly companion. No searchlights or ack-ack pierced the darkness as the Germans preferred to concentrate their air defenses over their homeland. On the ground, I could find thin aluminum strips dropped by the bombers to foil the German's RADAR defenses. I'd pick up these strips and squirreled them away as precious emanations from outside our occupied world. Now and then, I'd stop walking and fixed my gaze on a distant star or the moon, hoping that I'd be able to see the silhouette of a bomber, flying alone on its mission to bomb Germany. Of course, I never did.

At night, I'd sleep in Mme Cuvelier's room. We shared her large bed. Being around sixty, she seemed very old to me at the time. Mme Cuvelier was not a warm person, at least not towards me, but I do not recall any constant hostility. On the other hand, she would never miss a chance to deride my sister Ruth and to torment her for being a "dirty little Jew."

There was no heat in the bedroom we shared. In the evening, to remove the icy chill, a large heated stone was placed under the blankets shortly before we went to bed. The first time we shared the bed; Mme Cuvelier took me aside and told me that if I had to pass gas at night, it would be all right and that I should not hold it back. Actually, she was giving herself license to pass gas. All night long, she would fart loudly and continuously. I felt it was so funny that I had to bite the blanket in order not to burst out laughing. I did not want to chance waking her up as she had a terrible temper.

Hilaire had found a small recess in the basement that he decided would serve as an extra hideaway should the Gestapo search the house. With sheets of plywood, he constructed a wall that could be opened by lifting it and dropped for complete closure. Inside, we placed a blanket on the floor and stashed away bottles of water and some dry biscuits. A flashlight, a couple of candles and matches completed the inventory. It was only to serve us for a few hours, while the Gestapo searched the rest of the house. Actually, it would not have helped much had the Germans come. All through the house, there was evidence that at least four extra people slept there. The Gestapo usually came at dawn and wasted no time coming in. They would have searched with dogs that would have smelled our presence in the basement, plywood walls or not. However, at the time, it did give us some sense of security. We held drills at regular intervals, to see how fast we could abandon what we were doing and meet in the hiding room, with the wall dropped behind us.

At five one morning, we were awakened by screams of "Gestapo, Gestapo!" I scrambled out of bed and grabbing only my slippers I ran in the early darkness down the stairs, towards the hiding place. A loud crashing sound shook the house filling me with terror. I was sure that the Gestapo was breaking down the front door. In the hiding place, Ruth and Father were waiting for me. Mr Wolff was nowhere in sight. We waited a short while for him to join us and then decided that we would shut down the opening and hunker there as quietly as possible.

After what seemed an eternity, Ghislaine came to the basement and knocking on the plywood wall, urged us to come out. It was a false alarm. In the night, Grand-Mere had had a nightmare and awoke yelling for her dead husband: Gustav. She had yelled his name several times and to the rest of us, in the middle of our sleep, it had sounded like "Gestapo". Relieved, we returned upstairs. From the bedroom on the second floor, we heard muffled sounds that came from Mr Wolff's room. We rushed up to his room and found him pinned under his armoire. When he had heard "Gestapo", he had gotten up, had not bothered to put on his thick glasses and in his night shirt, stepped into the first door he could find. That was the door of his armoire that promptly fell on him with the crashing sound we had heard as we rushed to the hiding place. He had been unable to get out of there and decided to keep as quiet as a mouse for fear that the Gestapo would find him. When he heard us moving about, he started to yell for our help.

All in all, we were very relieved that this only had been a false alarm. After that night, we never had use for the hiding place again.

Ghislaine had a regular boyfriend, a bookmaker who worked at the racetracks. He was a tall, heavy-set man. He wore a gray fedora and this being late fall, a herringbone overcoat. I never knew his name, we just referred to him as "Le Bookmaker" He usually carried large sums of cash in his pockets, the proceeds of each day's betting. He delighted in showing me where pickpockets had slashed his coat with razor blades. It was always near a pocket where thieves felt he was carrying the money. They would usually cut him while he rode the streetcar. The coat showed many such slash cuts that had been sewn back after each attempt. He did not visit Ghislaine every day, but when he came, they would retreat to her room on the second floor.

Ruth decided that she would teach Father to read and write in French. That was not an easy task as Father, though very bright, had never attended school. There was also the constant problem of the "U" and "I". When told to spell a word with either of these two letters, Father always inquired if it was written with one leg or two. Ruth did not have the greatest patience in the world and after a few lessons, the project would be abandoned.

THE TIDE TURNS, NOVEMBER/DECEMBER 1942

In Africa, Rommel, the dreaded "Desert Fox" had finally met his match in General Montgomery (Monty). At the battle of El Alamein, the British Eighth Army under Montgomery inflicted a decisive defeat on Rommel's Afrika Korps. From the breakthrough on November 4th, 1942, Monty's forces drove the Germans out of Egypt and most of Libya by year's end. This was the first great victory for the British since the start of the war. Montgomery became our newest hero.

On November 8th, 1942 news came that an American invasion force had landed in North Africa under the command of a General Eisenhower, who went by the nickname of Ike. Quickly, French Morocco and Algeria were liberated from the forces of Vichy. By the end of the year, only Tunisia remained under the control of Germany. This was great news. Ike became the newest name in our roster of heroes.

Even though we were not French, anything that involved France was of special importance to Belgians and in particular to those living in the southern French-speaking half of Belgium. The Vichy Government, sanctioned by the Germans, was particularly repugnant to us as it collaborated openly with Hitler. Marshall Petain, the hero of WWI had turned traitor and headed the German supported government of unoccupied France. Although he became mostly a figurehead, his prestige was still great and millions of Frenchmen, especially schoolchildren, still worshiped him. To us he was a villain. Pierre Laval, the real head of the Vichy Government, was hated even more as he was a total lackey of the Germans. Admiral Darlan, head of the French Navy completed this trio of ignoble Frenchmen.

Meanwhile, the German propaganda machine mocked the Allies' invasion of North Africa. There had been talk of opening a Second Front to relieve the pressure on the Russian troops. That Second Front was always understood to be the invasion of France. The Germans laughed that the Americans could not count "1, 2, 3" but "1, 3, 2" instead.

On November 11th 1942, German troops occupied the rest of France despite the agreement made earlier with the Vichy government of Petain and Laval. This was bad news for the many Jews who had taken refuge in Southern France where Vichy had previously let them alone by and large or placed in "benevolent" concentration camps.

Admiral Darlan, after defecting to the Allied side was assassinated on Christmas Eve, a great way to finish a year that had started so badly.

STALINGRAD

Deep into Russia, nearly eight hundred miles southeast of Moscow, the large industrial city of Stalingrad straddled the Don and Volga Rivers. In 1925 its ancient name of Tsaritzyn had been changed in honor of Joseph Stalin. We first became aware of Stalingrad in August 1942, when the German High Command trumpeted that the next objective for the 6th Army was to capture the city and invade the Caucasus Mountains, rich in petrol. Over the next five months, Stalingrad would appear prominently in all war news. It would become the symbol of Russian resistance and eventually of Germany and Hitler's ultimate defeat. Despite stiff resistance by the Soviet Armies, by mid-September the first units of the German army had penetrated the suburbs of Stalingrad. It soon became apparent that Hitler wanted Stalingrad taken because it was Stalin's City. In speech after speech, Hitler and Göbbels barked "Stalingrad would be taken, when and how we chose to do it". Each day, glued to the radio, we would tune in to the BBC. Its opening line would be:

"It is the 90th day of the battle for Stalingrad and Stalingrad still holds, it is the 120th day of the battle for Stalingrad, and Stalingrad still holds." It became our opiate each day, to know that Hitler had not won, that the Russians still held, that the Führer could be denied.

By the end of December 1942, the Russians had launched a wide offensive that drove the Germans armies from the Caucasus, surrounded and trapped the 6th Army in Stalingrad and forever ended the myth of German invincibility on the battlefield. Hitler ordered General von Paulus, the commander of the 6th Army to dig in and fight to the last. About January 29th 1943, Hitler promoted von Paulus to the rank of Field Marshall for his gallant fight in Stalingrad. Two days later, on the 31st of January 1943, von Paulus surrendered what was left of his army to the Russians and by February 2nd, all German resistance in Stalingrad had ended.

On January 30th, 1943, the anniversary of Hitler's coming to power; Hitler did not speak but left it to Dr. Göbbels to spew more lies and calls for German sacrifices towards the final victory against Bolshevism.

Of the more than 300,000 soldiers of the 6th Army, only about 90,000 had survived and were marched to prison camps in Siberia. Only 5,000 ever returned to Germany. Most of the others perished in a city 1,500 miles from Berlin.

For the writer, who lived each tense moment for nearly 150 days hoping against hope that the Russians would hold, that the Germans would be defeated, Stalingrad remains the turning point of the conflict against Hitler. Without the enormous sacrifices of the Red Army (300,000 dead), we would not have survived. It was the most titanic battle of the war. Yet, today, Stalingrad no longer exists, having been renamed Volgograd in 1961. France named a Metro station in Paris "Stalingrad". Most Parisians think it was named after one of Napoléon's victories.

1943

I remember sky,
It was blue as ink.
Or at least I think
I remember sky . . . .
And at times I think

I would gladly die
For a day of sky. "I remember" Music and lyrics by Stephen Sondheim

APPENDICITIS

Ruth had developed terrible pains in her right abdomen. A doctor was summoned to the house on the Rue Copernic. Ruth's temperature was elevated and a quick "bounce" check confirmed that this was a case of appendicitis. If left untreated, the appendix would surely burst and peritonitis and death would follow. Such medical emergencies were feared, as it was nearly impossible to obtain medical treatment in a hospital without the danger of being unmasked as a Jew. Yet, this was a matter of life or death for Ruth.

Frieda had maintained a special relationship with a Professor Delporte*, one of Brussels' top surgeons. We were able to reach him by phone. It did not take long for Delporte to understand the gravity of the situation. An ambulance was sent and Ruth was admitted to the Clinic Edith Cavell under her false name of Marie-Jeanne Reynders so as to hide her Jewish identity. Even so, the nurses had wondered that Ruth was extremely pale. They were not aware that we had not been in the sun for several months.

Professor of Gynecology at the University of Brussels and physician to the Belgian Royal Family. He was Frieda's gynecologist and had employed Dr. Samuels on the sly when he had taken refuge in Belgium from Germany.

Professor Delporte successfully performed the appendectomy, and Ruth was soon out of danger and resting in a private hospital room. Incredibly, I was taken to the hospital to pay her a visit. I cannot recall who took me there, but it must have been terribly dangerous and chancy. I was shocked to see Ruth, looking very thin and pale, smiling at me wanly from her hospital bed. The nurses suggested Ruth might be suffering from anemia. "They are letting me die of hunger" she complained softly.

After a few days, Ruth left the hospital and was taken to the house on the Avenue de la Cascade where Mother was hiding It was felt that Ruth would be better taken care of by Mother than by Father and a house full of strangers. There she would stay with Frieda while recuperating from the operation. After a week or so, Ruth would return to Uccle to continue hiding with Father and me.

On the morning of January 19th, 1943, Jean de Selys-Longchamps took off from an airfield in England. A pilot in the Belgian air force, Longchamps had escaped to England during the May 1940 debacle and had joined the RAF. That morning, he flew his Hawker Typhoon fighter/bomber across the Channel and headed straight for Brussels. The plane, reaching optimum performance at low altitude, flew undetected over the treetops. Once over the Capital, Longchamp's path took him alongside the Etangs D'Ixelles where Mother and Ruth were hiding. At the end of the avenue, he guided his Typhoon up the Rue de L'Aurore, a short block from the Avenue Louise intersection. There, the imposing Gestapo Headquarters building towered over the neighborhood. As he neared the building Longchamps opened fire with his machine guns, rockets and cannons, strafing and riddling the Gestapo Headquarters with bullets and exploding shells. Although the Typhoon was able to carry two thousand-pound bombs, there is no record that such bombs were dropped. The Germans were completely taken by surprise and suffered large numbers of dead and wounded. The pilot then turned his plane around and headed back to his base in England.

Local people immediately flocked to the scene, curious to see the damages and to savor the casualties inflicted upon the hated Gestapo. The Gestapo Headquarters was a brutal symbol of the occupation. Jews and members of the Resistance were routinely taken there for interrogation and worse. Germans, incensed by the carnage, were seizing the passersby and beating them up as they walked in front of the Gestapo building. People were pulled into the damaged building, beaten and then thrown back into the street, dazed and bloodied.

Mr DeKnibber took a chance and ventured to the nearby Avenue Louise to survey the scene. He stayed on the opposite sidewalk and avoided being snatched and beaten. He returned safely to his house and related all he had seen to Mother and Ruth. There were so few Belgian heroes to look up to. We learned Jean de Selys-Longchamps's name from the BBC and he became an instant hero. We thought it was a wonderful moment.

Inexplicably, foolishly, Frieda decided that she had to go and see for herself. With Ruth in tow, Mother brazenly left the safety of the DeKnibber house and walked to the Avenue Louise. There, ambulances and wrecking crews were still hovering about, looking for more victims and trying to restore some sense of order to the structure. After observing the confusion for a while, Mother and Ruth finally returned to their hiding place. Luck had been with them and they were neither beaten nor uncovered as Jews.

Frieda had always been fearless and took chances. Our 1941 trip to Germany had taken a great amount of courage and so did this excursion to see the damages inflicted upon the Gestapo. Some might call it foolhardy. However, Frieda had a sense that she was indestructible and she was to be proven so again and again in her life.

After a few more days resting and recuperating, Ruth was ready to return to Uccle. Ghislaine Fraiteur came to pick her up and they returned to Rue Copernic by streetcar without incident.

Mother was left alone at the DeKnibber home. Father, Ruth and I were together again at the house of Mme Fraiteur.

Jean de Selys-Longchamps, son of a noble family, returned safely to his aerodrome in England. There, he was reprimanded for taking off on an unauthorized mission. Shortly thereafter, the Belgian Government in Exile decorated him for his act of bravery. Seven months later, he was shot down and killed as he was coming back from a mission. A German fighter plane jumped him as his Typhoon slowly came in on its final landing approach. A quick burst of fire and Jean de Selys-Longchamps crashed and died. He was 31.

ANONYMOUS LETTER

In Uccle, life once again settled to our daily routines. From the BBC we heard new words, Guadalcanal, where the U.S. forces were engaged in a fierce battle with the Japanese; Burma, Papua. However, these were far away places, with strange sounding names and not relevant to what concerned us on a daily basis.

In Russia, a general advance of the Russians along the whole front followed the German defeat at Stalingrad and we knew that the Axis forces were reeling under the attacks of the Red Army.

In Africa, the Afrika Korps was being pounded by the Allies and it was just a matter of weeks, days perhaps and the German armies would cease to exist there as a fighting force. We had a last visit of Bernard Horowitz and we engaged in an assessment of the war situation. In my enthusiasm over the victories in Russia and Africa, I was convinced that the war would now be over within a few months. We would soon be able to resume our normal daily lives. To my dismay, Bernard dashed my hopes by opining that the war would last at least another two years. We had a short but heated argument, but I could not get him to join my more optimistic point of view. Oh, how I hated Bernard Horowitz!

Despite Ghislaine's preoccupation with her "Bookie", I could not help noticing a current of interest flowing between her and Father. After all, she was a beautiful woman and Hilaire was a very attractive and charming man. At 42, he was in his prime and Ghislaine was his junior by five or seven years. When Hilaire turned 85, I asked him if he had ever made love with Ghislaine. He blushed and admitted that once, in the shower, *"Elle m'a {sicé}"* (she had "sicked me"). It was so cute. The correct word should have been *"sucer"* or "sucked" but with his inability to say the letter "U", he had pronounced it *"sicé"*, or "sicked". He then insisted that it was the only time it happened. I seriously doubted that, but did not press him further.

Although my recollection is vague, we regularly had visits from a woman by the name of Mme Limbosch, wife of a writer from around the Avenue Louise. Mme Limbosch was a well-intentioned Catholic and she did her humanitarian and religious duty by going to visit numerous Jews hidden in different places. She never realized the danger that she put us under with these visits. All we would have needed was an indiscretion and she could have been followed by Le Gros Jacques and the Germans. Mme Wolff's constant comings and goings, parading with her Yellow Star of David, was also a source of worry for us for the same reason. We never found out how she could move around so brazenly without being bothered by the Germans.

Mme Cuvelier, who had a terrible temper, complained a lot that I was often too noisy. I guess that at the age of twelve, I may have been somewhat mischievous and the confines of the house left little room for my energies to dissipate. At one time, there was talk about getting a live pig and killing it in the garage. Since there were German troops billeted in an adjacent property, it seemed a dangerous endeavor, certainly noisier than I was supposed to be. Despite the strong objections of Father and Mr Wolff (for religious reasons) the pig would be slaughtered. By then, I had already left the Fraiteur house.

Having had Ruth with her for those few days had given Frieda a different perspective regarding her hiding. It had been nice not to be alone and apprehensive about being found, discovered or denounced. The relationship between Frieda and Hilaire was as bad as it had ever been. Frieda must have realized that while Ruth was hidden with her, she had felt more secure. Mother began to want me with her, to be less lonely but also to be more secure where she was hiding. Hilaire had the two children and she had nothing. Frieda became more and more worried that Hilaire could denounce her to the Germans.

Hilaire could have denounced Frieda to the Germans and she would have been deported. Naturally, she would not have revealed where Hilaire was hiding because it would have put Ruth and me in danger. Father, on the other hand, felt secure since he held the two children. In later years, Father was always upset when I would remind him that I went to hide with Frieda because I was her insurance policy. He assured me that he would never have done anything like that. I was sure that he would never have denounced Mother, but Mother could never be sure. However, Father kept Ruth because he was afraid that Mother might denounce him if she had both children. When reminded of this, he had this justification:

"Oh, yes" he replied "she would have done it, but I never would have done it".

They both had shared the same anguish. Neither of them would ever have denounced the other, but they could not be sure. These were strange times and there was so much poison between them. In those days, for Jews, it was so easy to get rid of a bad partner; you simply had to denounce your spouse to the Germans. There were instances where spouses denounced spouses who were never seen again. "What fools these mortals be "Shakespeare."

One afternoon, Ghislaine Fraiteur retreated to her bedroom with her bookie boyfriend. I stole up to the landing and stood in front of the door. I had just turned thirteen. My curiosity got the better of me and I leaned over so my eye could peek through the large keyhole. Either they heard me or saw my shadow under the door. While I was straining in vain to see anything, the door swung open. There I was, bending over, my face where the keyhole had been a fraction of a second before. Ghislaine was furious and accused me of listening at the door. This I denied, because technically, it was not correct. I had been looking, not listening. My legalistic explanation did not help matters. Ghislaine ran downstairs yelling that this lying boy could not stay in her house anymore. It was then decided that I would soon rejoin Mother in Ixelles. Of course, that meant a reduction of BF 6,000—each month in what we were paying for our room and board.

This was end of February 1943 and soon a typed letter appeared in the DeKnibber mailbox. The anonymous writer stated that he (or she) knew that a Jew was hiding in the DeKnibber house. The letter further threatened that Mr & Mme DeKnibber would be denounced to the Germans for harboring a Jew unless that Jew left their premises immediately. Ghyslaine knew where Frieda was hiding since she had gone to the DeKnibber house when Ruth had been well enough to return to Uccle after her appendicitis.

There was panic. Obviously Mother could not stay there, as it would endanger not only Frieda but the DeKnibbers also. This was an enormous crisis for us. The only logical place Frieda could turn to was where Father, Ruth and I were hiding. For the Fraiteurs, it would have meant another six thousand francs more each month. We became suspicious that the typewritten letter might not have been genuine. Why would not the writer simply denounce Frieda instead of sending a threatening letter? What could be gained by scaring Mother away from the house, forcing her to go elsewhere? Father had the feeling that the letter had come from the Fraiteurs because Guislaine's bookie boyfriend had a portable typewriter. Ruth compared the paper that was used in the letter and the characters on the typewriter with those on the machine in the Fraiteur house. She believed that she could judge these to be identical. Our suspicions were confirmed after the liberation when Father somehow got a hold of the bookie's typewriter and was able to compare the typeface. Mme Cuvelier later accused Hilaire of having stolen the typewriter. That was probably true. We would never find out the true story.

Apparently Ghislaine, Mme Cuvelier and the bookie thought that the letter would be enough to force Mother to move in with us in Uccle. In this way, they could charge us even more money. What's more, they did not know where the bulk of our money was hidden. Indeed, Marie-Josée D. brought in money at regular intervals, but in small increments, enough to tide us over another month or so. Perhaps Fraiteur hoped that we would now have to bring all the money to the house. Perhaps they felt that they could then denounce us and keep all of our money. The motives of Mme Cuvelier and her daughter were not altruistic. Hiding us was a very lucrative, albeit risky business. They could not be considered decent people. We had to come up with a different plan for survival.

THE "LIÈGE" DECOY

It was decided that we would employ a clever ruse. Mother would pretend that she had found a hiding place in Liège, about 180 Km. east of Brussels and that she was immediately leaving the DeKnibber house where she had been hiding. Pointedly, this "move to Liège" was made known only to Ghislaine Fraiteur and her Mother Mme Cuvelier. Since they and the mysterious writer of the anonymous letter were the only ones who knew a Jew was hiding at the Avenue de la Cascade, there was no need to notify anyone else. In reality, Frieda never moved from the DeKnibber house.

Father announced to the Fraiteur household that Frieda now wanted Rudy to join her in the safety of her new hideaway in Liège. And so, in the first week of March 1943, Hilaire, disguised as a gardener, took me away from Rue Copernic. Ruth and I embraced. We would not be reunited again for nearly two years. I had turned thirteen a few days earlier, but nothing special had marked my birthday. I was not aware that according to the Jewish religion, I had just become a man.

Hilaire pretended that we would take the train for Liège where I would rejoin my Mother. No address was given, as we wanted to make the move in the greatest secrecy. There would be danger involved but, with Father's disguise, and traveling with a little boy, we should be able to reach Liège without incident. We left the Fraiteur house in the late afternoon. Hilaire was carrying a bag of tools; I carried a small brown cardboard suitcase filled with my meager possessions.

We got on the streetcar going to the train station but once in the city, we changed for the tram that would take us to Place Flagey, a few blocks away from the house of DeKnibber. It was late and because of the blackout, very dark when we reached the house on the Avenue de la Cascade.

We had decided to arrive in the darkness so as not to be noticed by the Germans who occupied the adjacent house. Actually, we were still within the general curfew, but well passed the 8PM Jewish curfew. Luck was with us and we rejoined Frieda without incidents. I have no recollection of my reunion with Mother. It must have been very emotional. However, the coming together of Father and Mother must have been full of tension and surely put a damper on the occasion.

The next morning, I was surprised to discover that Father's toolbox contained tools, but also three lead pipes, several candles and a fortune of diamonds, precious stones and gold and platinum jewelry of all sorts. For the next few days, Father carefully buried this treasure under the stairs that lead from the hallway entrance to the basement where Frieda and I would remain hidden in the months to follow. I helped as much as I could.

Under the stairs, Hilaire carefully lifted one tile and dug deep into the ground. We then filled the three lead pipes with the jewelry. We melted the candles in a cooking pot and poured the molted wax in each of the pipes filling the gaps between the precious jewels. I guessed it was to keep the diamonds from rattling and making noise. We then pinched each pipe shut and buried them straight up into the ground. The dirt was replaced back in the hole and the tile carefully reset so that the secret place would not be revealed. Hilaire scratched a large "X" to mark the tile. The job was done. Only Hilaire, Frieda and I knew of the existence of this buried treasure. If we did not survive, the three lead pipes and their precious contents would be lost forever.

On the second day, Mme DeKnibber called the Fraiteur house and pretending to be a long distance operator, declared "*On vous demande de Liège*", you have a call from Liège. Father got on the phone and asked to speak with Ruth. Mother and I spoke with her in turn and talked about how fine we were and that the house in Liège was a pleasant and safe place to be.

After a few days, time came for Hilaire to venture out and travel back to Uccle. That last evening, a ferocious fight broke out between Hilaire and Frieda. Everything from Léona Kohlen *"La servante"* to Ghislaine Fraiteur came out. The heavy artillery of insults flew in the air. *Sale Boche* & Dirty Pollack sullied the basement. These two were apparently unmindful of the Germans who were in the next house. I tried in vain to calm them down, appealing to their good sense, expressing my fears that they would be overheard next door. Crying, I tried to separate them, pleading that this might be the last time we would ever be together and that we might never see each other again. The logic of a 13 year-old had no effect on the two grownups. The fight continued until exhaustion and Hilaire finally left to return to the Fraiteur house. Mother cried late into the night, calling for her dead Father,—*Mein Papa, mein Papa*-.

Every other week for the next couple of months, Mme DeKnibber called the Fraiteur home, pretending to be the long distance operator announcing a call from Liège. We would then talk a few moments with Ruth and Hilaire. It was to reinforce the impression that we had indeed left the house in Ixelles and were hiding in Liège. After two months, we decided to end the calls. The

Germans were tapping phones. It would have seemed suspicious to them if local calls had been made stating that the calls were coming from another city.

We never received another threatening anonymous letter. This confirmed our suspicions that the letter had indeed originated from Ghislaine Fraiteur, Mme Cuvelier and the Bookie.

32 AVENUE DE LA CASCADE, IXELLES
(renamed Ave. General de Gaulle after the war)

Ixelles, one of the 19 boroughs of Brussels, stretched a few kilometers southeast of the center of the Capital. It was just an extension of the inner city without any discernable separation from borough to borough. Uccle, where Ruth and Hilaire were hidden lay a few kilometers farther out due south of Brussels's center. The farther out one traveled, the more there was space for greenery and the sizes of the housing plots would increase with the distances from the Center.

From the *Porte De Namur,* the Namur Gate, the *Chaussée* d'Ixelles descended to the Place Eugene Flagey, a large square that housed the INR, the Belgian National Radio Station, in a large imposing building. Facing it, a church with a high steeple dominated the square. Over a thousand years earlier, swamps filled the area. Now, all that remained were two ponds sitting from the Place Flagey to the base of the next hill that led to the Avenue Louise. Along the West side the Avenue de la Cascade followed the curve of the two ponds. Three-story houses lined the avenue. These had been built at the onset of the Twentieth Century, either just before or after World War One. Although all stood side-by-side, wall-to-wall, and fronted with a small garden enclosure, each house was individually designed and different from its neighbor.

The DeKnibbers owned and lived at No.32 Avenue de la Cascade. The house adjacent to No 32 was occupied by units of the German military. The occupiers had requisitioned it after the rightful owners had fled in the early days of the German invasion. Had the owners anticipated the hardship of the occupation? Were they Jews who foresaw the coming dangers? We never knew and Mr DeKnibber never spoke of them. DeKnibber used to refer to the Germans next door as "Gestapo", however they wore the field-gray uniform of the Wehrmacht. They might have been members of the SS, but I never got close enough to them to get a good view of their insignias.

The DeKnibbers were in their mid seventies. To me, they were *Monsieur et Madame DeKnibber.* I am sure they had a first name but it was never known to me or I have forgotten it. They had emigrated to Philadelphia probably before WWI and had become US Citizens. When time came for them to retire, they returned to Belgium, bought a house and lived comfortably with the pension they received from the USA. They were gamblers who used to frequent the casinos of Namur and Ostende where Mme DeKnibber had become a friend of Frieda's. Of course, they were not good friends, but part of the circle of people who frequented the same gambling haunts.

After Pearl Harbor, when the USA declared war on the Axis, DeKnibbers had become enemies of the Third Reich. However, because of their advanced age, they were left alone except for having to report to the German Kommandantur every two weeks just to show that they were still around and accounted for. With the entrance of the US into the war, their funds and been blocked and they could no longer collect their money from the United States. They were now without any financial means.

When the Germans occupied Belgium, they restricted access to the gambling casinos to members of the Nazi Party, Blackshirts, or the German military elite, i.e. officers. Clandestine casinos had sprung up here and there. It was in such a clandestine casino that Frieda and Mme DeKnibber had renewed acquaintance. They got to talk. Mother needed a place to hide, the DeKnibbers needed money. They made an arrangement whereby Mother paid them a monthly fee for rent and food. In exchange, Frieda would have a place to hide in the house on the Avenue de la Cascade. The fee would be fifteen hundred Belgian Francs which was reasonable. After all, we had simply disappeared. We had no ration card, no food stamps so the DeKnibbers would have to buy food for Mother on the black market.

Gambling had provided us with food when we were stranded in Namur, now it would be instrumental in finding us a place to hide. Had it not been for gambling, we would probably not have survived and I would not have been around to tell the tale.

The hiding place was commonly known as a *cuisine/cave,* a kitchen/cellar. In truth, it was more cellar than kitchen. Instead of being completely under ground level, it was two thirds underground with a small window just at ground level. To access the basement there were about seven steps to descend from the *rez-de chaussée,* the ground floor. This basement ran the whole length of the house. It was comprised of two rooms separated by a wall and a door. The front room had a three foot by four foot window; a throw rug covered some of the stone floor. A plain lighting fixture hung from the low, white ceiling. A round table with three chairs occupied the center. There was a bed and a chest of drawers. A small coffee table completed the décor.

The second room was longer and ran to the back courtyard. There, a set of windows and a glass door gave to the inner walled yard that separated the house from the three neighboring houses that were hunched together. The back room had no furniture but a black-stone cold-water sink and a gas stove on opposite walls. The floor was covered with black slate flagstones of uneven shapes and sizes. At the far left the toilet sat in a small room, behind a wooden door with a large brown frosted window. A single light bulb hung from the ceiling.

Squeezed behind the left wall, a crawl space followed the shape of the underside of the stairs leading to the upstairs apartments of the DeKnibbers. In this crawl space our hosts kept dry food supplies and a large stoneware butter-keeper.

There was also a small bedroom on the third floor, with a balcony overlooking the avenue and the ponds. It had a larger bed and an armoire. It was in that room that I had come to after my ear operation a few months earlier.

These confined spaces were to be our entire world for the unforeseeable future, until such time as we were liberated or captured.

Monsieur DeKnibber was of medium height, very, very skinny, with thinning *Brilliantine* hair slicked back like converging railroad tracks. A thin black mustache accentuated his upper lip and hollowed cheeks gave him a mortician's appearance. A pince-nez and his perpetual black and silver cigarette holder completed the picture. He was always fully dressed with vest and bow tie. He looked like Clifton Webb, but more severe.

Madame DeKnibber was a bit taller yet thinner that her husband. An ankle-length dress covered her stingy body and she wore high-heeled black shoes with a single button strap around the ankles. Like her husband, she smoked endlessly, one cigarette after the other, stuck in a silver holder double the size of his. Mother would only refer to her as "*La Cheminée*" The Smoke-Stack. Together, they seemed like a couple frozen in the time of 1920 and plucked right out of a New Yorker cartoon.

Cigarettes were scarce and expensive, yet the DeKnibbers somehow managed to find enough to chain-smoke endlessly. However, as the occupation lingered on, they increasingly resorted to crumpling dried chestnut-tree leaves into make-do tobacco. This they would roll onto cigarette paper, carefully licking the sides before inserting these in their cigarette holders.

Fluffy, their black and white Papillion dog, and a red cat completed the cast of characters at 32 Avenue de la Cascade.

SETTLING IN

We were hiding in the house at number 32; the house next to ours was number 31. Since we faced the ponds, there was only one side to the street and it used all the odd and even numbers for the addresses. Number 31 was occupied by German troops. In back, there were two other houses that backed to a little yard at the back of our basement. On the left side, women of the German Women's army corps occupied the house. German Labor forces of the Todt Organization occupied the house straight in back of ours. And so, German military personnel on three sides surrounded us. Because there were only supposed to be two old people living in the house, I was not allowed to make noise, play loudly, yell or run. I wore slippers, as shoes would have been too noisy.

Most of our time was spent in the front of the basement. The small window would become my favorite place. It was at ground level and faced a very small entrance yard that led to the street. A metal fence surrounded the yard, with a wrought iron gate near the side that abutted the house occupied by the Germans next door. The window was covered with Hindu blinds, made of very tiny slats the thickness of toothpicks. With the lights out inside, one could not be seen from the outside. When I placed my eyes against the slats, I could see outside without being seen. Mr DeKnibber had given me a pair of binoculars, that, when placed against the slats threw these out of focus and made them disappears as if by magic.

I would turn off the light in the basement, climb on a chair and press my face against the blinds. Then, I could survey the outside world, the small yard, the fence, the street and a section of the pond between two tree trunks. On the other side of the pond, another street and a row of houses were visible. To see clearly, I had to use the binoculars. It was like being at the movies and having a living screen before me. There were ducks, a pair of swans and moor-hens that would float by in the space of my "screen". If I looked to the right, I could see into the yard at number 31 and observe the coming and going of the Germans next door. When I looked up between the two trees, I could see a patch of sky.

At night, we would cover the window with a blanket for an effective blackout. We could then turn on the light safely and go about our other activities until it was time to go to bed. For a while, we would go upstairs to the third floor and sleep in the bedroom. However, we soon abandoned that idea. A couple of times, we were still upstairs when visitors came to see the DeKnibbers. We found ourselves trapped, afraid to chance being on the stairs back to our basement and be seen by the visitors.

We had a small Phillips radio that rested on the table. It was our contact with the outside world for music and variety programs. Mostly it was for news from the war. With the radio, we could tune in on the BBC broadcasting from London. It was our one link to hope. We would listen with our ears glued to the radio as we could not play it loud for fear of being overheard by the Germans next door. A cloth covered the back of the radio so that the glow of the tubes would not be visible from the outside.

Besides the radio, Mr DeKnibber would bring us magazines and a newspaper, Le Soir. As the war went on, Le Soir got thinner and thinner until it eventually consisted only of four pages. I did not keep a diary, did not make notes of important events. My recollection of happenings would be accentuated by battles, victories and defeats. These would be the markers of my time in hiding.

Mother did not confide in me. We talked, hugged, cried sometime, but she never shared her feelings regarding her hopes or beliefs that we would be liberated or captured. I was aware that we were hiding for our lives, but I did not think we would actually survive. We lived from day to day, meal to meal. In the spring of 1943, there was not much hope. Things were still going badly.

After their defeat in Stalingrad, the German armies had launched new offensives on the Russian front. There was a lull after the British victory in Africa. The Allies were preparing to land in Sicily and later Italy, but that was unknown to us. It appeared that the war would go on for a long time. Liberation was a dimly perceived hope.

DAY TO DAY

There was not much to do in our basement. We lived from day to day and the desire to see another day probably sustained us. We had no idea of when we might eventually be allowed to walk out again without the fear, the certainty that we would be sent to a concentration camp. The vivid descriptions Colonel Eppstein had told Frieda left no doubt in our mind that death was waiting for us outside the confinements of our hiding place. I did worry about it, but never talked about it with Mother or DeKnibber. It was unspoken. My concern was about my survival and the hope that I might see Ruth and Father again someday. I was sure that Frieda shared my fears, but I did not realize that she feared not only for her own safety but also for mine, her beloved son. The concern I had must have been of a totally different nature than Mother's.

As the weeks and the months followed in the same slow motion, Mother would often let me take refuge in her arms and she would rock me slowly as if I was still her little baby. I could have stayed there forever but as I was now thirteen, light and skinny as I was, ten to fifteen minutes was all Mother could tolerate. Invariably she would repeat "*On n'l'avait pas voulu*" "we had not wanted him" a reference to the abortion she had tried to have almost fourteen years before. Yet, despite all the tribulations, troubles, disappointments and vexations of my childhood, I was never in doubt that I was loved, not only by Mother, but also by Father and my sister Ruth. And I felt that my parents loved me best, a sentiment that Ruth would often echo and complain about.

Another phrase that kept recurring when I was in Frieda's arms was "When he was small, he was so good-looking. Look at him now!" I had now turned thirteen and my features were changing from those of a boy to an adolescent and then to a man. I was neither fish nor fowl and I guess I had lost all that was attractive in the boy and was gaining all that was ugly in the grown-up. The perception that stayed with me was that I was ugly and that my later life would be marked by that sad fact, if there was a later life.

We were always conscious of the Germans who were next to us. Since there were supposed to be only two old people living in our house, I could not run or make noises. Our talks were in whispers, our movements calculated so as not to make undue noises that could be overheard by our German neighbors.

In later years, an amateur theatre group on Long Island asked that I sit in on their rehearsals of "The Diary of Anne Frank". What struck me most was the abandon and loudness of the dialogues being spoken by the actors. I remarked that they did not project any feeling that danger was lurking just outside of their walls, nor that they seemed aware of the constant danger of being discovered by the Germans

I did not get dressed. Brown plaid woolen slippers were all I wore on my feet over woolen socks. Since the slippers were a couple of sizes too small, the heel part was bent inward and what I wore were really slip-ons. I wore a nightshirt during the day and night and a multicolored terry cloth robe that was badly frayed. Sometimes, when I had nothing to do or if I was absorbed in something, I'd pull at the threads and the robe became thinner and thinner as the months went by. I am sure I must have had some sort of *caleçon,* shorts, but I do not recall any. Surely, Mother must have collected my meager clothing now and then and passed these under water, but I cannot remember. Of course, we had no washing machine and minimal laundry soap and I cannot imagine what she would have used for washing our clothes. We surely could not go outside and hang these to dry in the sun.

I was once lecturing to young school children about remembrance of my months in the basement and one asked me if we could take showers while we were hiding. I then realized how much I had forgotten.

No, we had no shower, we had no hot water. We had the black-stone sink in the back basement with a cold-water faucet. We would wash with a terry cloth glove trying to coax a bit of suds from a bar of soap that was like pumice, hard, porous and would not foam. Now and then, we'd get the remnant of a bar of brown "Sunlight" soap from DeKnibber but that would be reserved for washing the few clothes we used daily. I had a toothbrush but no toothpaste and we used baking soda for a brushing agent. And of course, the concept of under arm deodorant did not exist in those years, at least not in Europe.

Another child marveled—You mean to say that for three years you did not HAVE to go to school and you could stay home and watch television!"-

Mother and I would listen to the daily broadcast of the British Broadcasting Corporation (BBC) from London, and after the end of the last segment, at midnight, we would go to sleep. We would stay in bed until noon of the next day, killing half a day.

I read the *Nouveau Petit Larousse Illustré,* the ever-present French dictionary. I could spend hours flitting from page to page, pursuing one word after another. It had wonderful illustrated charts, from armor to skeletons, automobiles to ships. I wish I had applied myself more to learn all there was to know about the deaf-mute alphabet and from many other topics of these illustrations.

There were dozens of plates illustrating classic paintings. These were in black and white, but I could imagine the colors based on the subjects portrayed. The paintings were mostly by French artists depicting classic scenes and France's heroes like Louis XIV and of course, Napoléon (including the Retreat from Russia). The Last Supper by Da Vinci and some Rubens were among the foreign painters also represented. With these, I formed a nucleus of culture that made me long to see the originals in museums and in color. Colorful maps of all the continents and countries also gave me knowledge of the world and helped me follow the development of battles and the war.

With the inability to go to school, the Larousse was to become a great tutor, letting me glimpse at the outside world that lay beyond the small window of my basement.

I invented games, improvised others. From some cardboard, I cut out a set of dominos and sometimes was able to coax Mother in joining me in a few games, but her heart was not in it and she soon tired of it. Mr DeKnibber had brought me a small coping saw and a few pieces of plywood. On these, I glued some illustrations and cut them up into puzzles. DeKnibber found a few puzzles that depicted some adventures of Tintin et Milou. These puzzles were very simple and made up of perhaps 40 to 50 pieces. I spent hours taking them apart and back together again. After a while, I could almost assemble them blindfolded. To give it a bit of drama, the puzzles came to represent islands in the Pacific being invaded by American troops. The invasions would start from different places on each island and from different cardinal points. Marines invading from the North would join up with soldiers from the South and cut off the Japanese garrisons. All that would be left to do was a mop-up operation to conquer the Island. I would work at these operations feverishly to complete the conquest in record time before the enemy had time to send in reinforcements.

Hours were spent with a deck of cards, playing solitaire. I played the Tour de France in 21 stages. Since there were only four suits, I could only have four cyclists. It never occurred to me to have a rider from four different nations. All four were Belgians, two each from Flanders and Wallonia.

The Flemings were Romain and Sylvaire Maes, cycling heroes of the Tour. Romain had won the Tour in 1935 (having held the Yellow Jersey from the first stage to the last, an unprecedented feat). Sylvaire had won it in 1936 and again in 1938. Although they were both named Maes, they were not related. In 1939, Sylvaire Maes was defeated in his attempt to win it for a third time by the great Italian champion Gino Bartali.

I needed two Walloon riders to honor my place of birth. Unfortunately, all the best cyclists came from Flanders. So, I picked a less famous Walloon rider named Francois Neuville as the representative of my region. For the fourth rider, I chose Marcel Kint, the "Black Eagle", former World champion. Kint had never won the Tour de France and was not even a Walloon. I do believe he was a Fleming, but he was a hero of mine and I enlisted him in my Walloon team. Besides, I could not think of any other except Neuville. Marcel Kint would be the Spade suit; Neuville the Heart and the Maes "brothers" would share the minor suits of Club and Diamond.

I kept elaborate charts of each race, keeping a system of points allocated by the finishing places of each stage and adding points as if these were minutes behind the leader. Subconsciously I found myself favoring the Walloon riders as my eyes tended to ignore the suits of the Maes and key in on Neuville and especially Kint. I guess I was still homesick for Charleroi and not at all comfortable with the Flemings I had encountered when we moved to Brussels.

In the crawl space of the basement, I had found an old leather armchair. It had lead piping sheathed in leather all around the back and the arms. I easily popped the brass nails that held the piping together and rolled the lead ribbons into balls. These, I placed in a deep cooking pot and melted the lead over the stove. I wound up with a huge wad of melted lead. With the leftover plywood, I cut out moulds that I nailed together in the shape of soldiers, leaving the upper part hollow. In these, I poured the molted lead, holding the mould with a pair of pliers so as not to burn myself. I did manage to extract a few lead soldiers from the moulds, but they were very crude and full of barbs as the hot lead found its way between the layers of plywood. I soon abandoned the whole idea especially when the only blade on the coping saw soon broke and could not be replaced.

Soon, I found a more exciting use for the molted lead. I would stand at one end of the basement and sling the entire pot of lead against the floor all the way to the other end. It rippled in a long sheet along the flagstones, making bubbles as it cooled and caught the air. Then, I turned it around and it made beautiful patterns on the inside where the bubbles were and espousing the shapes and texture of the flagstones. Rainbows of colors decorated the thin lead sheet in ever expanding deltas of patterns. I would then roll it up, melt it again in the pot and started the process all over again.

It was extremely dangerous and a dumb thing to do. Had I burned myself, we would not have been able to get a doctor or go to the hospital without the danger of exposure. Yet, Mother never said anything. After a few weeks, I tired of the game and never resumed it.

Mother and I shared the only bed. It was wider than a twin, but not much. We each had our own pillow but we shared the *plumeau,* the large eider-down comforter in vogue in Europe. In the winter, it gave wonderful cozy warmth. In the summer, you sweated profusely and wound up sticking arms and legs from under it so as to get away from the oppressive heat. We went to bed at midnight and tried to sleep. We had no way of telling the time at night. The only telltale sign of time was the clock of the church on the Place Flagey. It would toll once for the half hour and once each for the hours. Often I'd wake up and wait for the clock to chime the time. Almost invariably it would chime just once. That could mean that it was 12.30 AM, or 1, or 1.30 or any half hour after 2 to 7 AM when the daylight would begin to infiltrate our basement. I would then try to stay awake until I heard the next chime that could again be a single bell. I might also doze off and awake again to a single bell. It was all very frustrating. I could not explain why I had to know the time as we did not have to wake up until late morning and had no place to go or things to do.

NIGHTMARES

Nightly dreams, exciting dreams would come to visit my sleep. I could fly! I'd be standing in place with both feet firmly anchored on the ground. I'd start to oscillate from side to side, then gradually swing around on the axis of my feet, never losing my anchor. The spinning went faster and faster until my feet eventually left the ground and I had become a huge, swirling propeller. I'd then spread my arms and glide in a blue sky looking down on the pretty green landscape laid out under me. At times, the whole exercise would start as a slow walk. I'd take longer and longer steps until I traversed the air between steps. First, for a few moments, then several seconds and soon I was flying in long strides up in the air, gliding and flying. The sensation was so real that even now, before falling asleep or in the fog of waking up, I am often still convinced that I can indeed fly.

Invariably, as I was flying about in my dreams, I would reach a great height, a mountaintop or just the top of a large armoire. These would suddenly turn to soft rubber and bend forward. Desperately I would cling to the place I had reached and everything that was around me would slip off the top and fall into a bottomless precipice below. My fingers would try to get a grip on any asperity to prevent my falling. When I found one, it would become smooth, slippery and I'd find myself plunging into the dark void below. I'd wake up in my bed, the shock of the fall deeply marking the mattress, my body drenched with sweat and my heart pounding in my chest. I'd lie there, afraid to fall back to sleep for fear that I'd plunge right back into a similar tumultuous nightmare.

Sometimes, the nightmare would start as a distant bright pinwheel deep in space, like a faraway galaxy. It would swirl and swirl, coming closer and closer in ever-greater circles towards me. As it finally swallowed me, it exploded. I'd awake in terror, drenched in perspiration and with a pounding heart.

These nightmares terrorized me several times each night for nearly a year. One night, as I was falling into the black void, I reassured myself "It is all right, it is only a dream, you will awake in your bed, next to Mother" And I woke up, still perspiring but without the usual shock, my heart beating normally. Gradually, I managed to allay those fears and although I continued to have those same nightmares, they diminished in intensity and frequency. After a while, the nightmares disappeared altogether and never did return. I still miss the flying.

ASSASSINATIONS-EXECUTIONS

In mid-March 1943, we heard through the BBC and the Brussels INR that there had been an assassination attempt on Hitler's life. We never found out any details about it but it was soon apparent that it was a bungled affair and that the Führer continued his hold on the German people and his mastery over the conquered territories. For a moment, for only a tiny moment, we had hoped that the monster was dead. This was dashed within the first couple of hours as declarations came over the airwaves that Hitler was unhurt.

Paul Colin was the editor of two news magazines collaborating with the German authorities, *Cassandre* and *Le Nouveau Journal*. In his editorials, Colin espoused the full propaganda line of the occupiers. Four young men, members of the Resistance were assigned to execute him. On April 14th, 1943 the planned assassination was put in motion. The assigned killer failed to show up at the newspapers' addresses. The other three conspirators decided to carry on with the execution despite that defection. They were Arnaud Fraiteur, a month short of his 19th birthday, Maurice Raskin and Andre Bertulot who were just a bit older.

With a revolver, Arnaud Fraiteur shot the traitor Paul Colin and Gaston Beekeman, his collaborator. As they were trying to make good their escape, Raskin and Bertulot were arrested by the Belgian police and taken to the prison of St.Gilles (near the prison of Forest where Father had been incarcerated). Arnaud Fraiteur managed to escape but had to leave his bicycle behind. With the bike's license plate, the authorities were able to identify the killer and a dragnet was immediately deployed by the German and the Belgian police to arrest Fraiteur. In the early morning, the police invaded the home of the Fraiteur family but failed to flush out Arnaud. Just a few hours earlier, he had warned his parents that he was a member of the Resistance and that he would have to go into hiding. The Germans arrested his family and brought them to the Gestapo Headquarters Avenue Louise for interrogation. A reward of BF 500,000 (enormous for the times) was offered for the denunciation of the killers.

Ruth, Father, Mother and I were full of anxiety. Where else would Arnaud Fraiteur seek refuge but in the home of friends or relatives. We feared that the Germans and the Belgian police would search close relatives' houses and that included the house of Jacques Fraiteur, Rue Copernic, where Ruth, Father and Mr Wolff were hidden. We all spent some anxious days. They had no place to go and had Hilaire and Ruth been discovered, would Mother and I be next on the list?

Ruth, now nearly 15, had fantasies that young, handsome Arnaud would find refuge Rue Copernic and she entertained romantic thoughts of his sharing the Fraiteur home with her. It was not to be.

Barely a week after the killings, the Resistance would try to smuggle Arnaud into France in a small van. At the border, the driver would panic and reveal his cargo to the Germans. Arnaud was arrested and sent to St.Gilles prison. In the German controlled press, the three patriots were vilified and branded "murderous assassins."

On May 7th, the three heroes were transferred to the prison fortress of Breendonk near Antwerp where they were tortured, placed in chains and hanged on May 10th 1943; exactly three years after the German invasion of Belgium began. For us, we were able to return to the relative calm of our hiding places since the Germans had found and executed their victims.

After the war, three thoroughfares in Brussels were renamed to honor the three young patriots, Rue Andre Bertulot, Rue Maurice Raskin and Avenue Arnaud Fraiteur. Today, their significance has been lost to most that walk or drive there. Avenue Arnaud Fraiteur, in Ixelles, had been named Avenue Marechal Petain after the First World War. The name of the French WWII traitor was removed to be renamed for Arnaud Fraiteur. Sic Transit Gloria!

KATYN AND THE WARSAW GHETTO

Radio Berlin announced that, near the Russian town of Smolensk, in the Katyn Forest, the German army had uncovered mass graves with thousands of executed Polish officers. Apparently all had been shot with a bullet in the neck and buried in their uniforms. The Germans claimed that the Polish officers had been murdered by the Russians after having been captured in 1939 when the Germans and the Russians had invaded and divided Poland. The German propaganda claimed that this demonstrated the ruthless behavior of the Bolsheviks and of Stalin. "Signal" and "Le Soir" published picture after picture of the mass graves with the skeletal remains of the Polish officers.

For me, and I guess for many others, it was pure German propaganda. I could not believe that my hero Stalin would have been guilty of such a heinous crime. We had no difficulty believing that these were indeed slain Polish officers, but we were convinced that the Germans had murdered them. I could not understand why the Germans had waited until the spring of 1943 to bring up the Katyn massacre. The propaganda machine was using Katyn to drum up support against the USSR and trying to convince more young men in the occupied countries to enlist in the Legions Against Bolshevism. Germany needed fresh blood, non-German blood to contain and defeat the Russians now threatening on the Eastern Front. Months after months, in "Signal" the Germans would return to the Katyn theme. On the radio, rallies in the Brussels and Antwerp Sport Palace were broadcast, urging young Belgians to join the Walloon Legion or the Flemish VNV to go and fight on the Russian Front.

It was only long after the war that I came to understand and believe that it was indeed Stalin who had ordered the massacre of the Elite of the Polish Army in the Katyn Forests. But at the time, the Russians were our allies and were dying for our liberation and I could not conceive or admit this unpleasant truth.

On April 19th, 1943, the BBC informed us that there was an uprising by the Jews in the Warsaw Ghetto. I knew that Father had relatives in Poland but the news seemed of little importance to me. I could not associate with what was happening there, a world away from our basement. A month later, the revolt had ended and the Ghetto was destroyed. Again, the BBC announced this. I do not recall the German News and the collaborating press mentioning it.

It was now spring 1943 and outside our basement, the bushes and the trees were turning green. On the pond, between the tree trunks, ducks would make a brief appearance and sometimes I could glimpse a few ducklings trying to keep up with their parents. The pair of swans would glide by followed by some cygnets. I could spend hours with my face pressed against the bamboo curtain waiting for a showing. Ever since the baby swans had hatched, the male had been keeping a firm vigil on the brood and I'd see it swimming at full speed, wings raised in anger, chasing away the ducks that dared to come too close. It was a fleeting image, observed mostly through my binoculars.

In mid-May, what was left of the Axis forces in Africa surrendered to the Allies. On the BBC, Winston Churchill, in his beautiful measured baritone declared that this was not yet the beginning of the end, but surely it was the end of the beginning. The commentator dutifully translated this during the French segment of the news. Mother and I were elated yet my hopes were tempered as I remembered the words of Bernard Horowitz that the war would go on for at least another two years. I was growing impatient even as it had barely been a year since we had gone into hiding.

Almost nightly, the air raid sirens would wail in the middle of the night as the RAF planes were lumbering overhead on their way to bomb Germany. It was a comforting sound, a reminder that somewhere, out there, the Allies were working hard for our liberation. The map of Germany was full of towns that were being devastated night after night. We had heard that the US Army Air Force was now bombing Germany during the days and was having much success with "Precision bombing". However, the pages of "Signal" were now full of pictures of US bombers that had been shot down over Germany. The flyers taken prisoner were described as being drunk, doped up and generally afraid of flying their missions against the "splendid German air defenses". Special attention was given to pictures of Negro flyers that "had been coerced into the service."

With the coming of the warmer weather, flies and mosquitoes became our constant companions. In Belgium as in other parts of Europe windows were not covered with screens and any small opening would permit bugs to enter indoors. This was particularly true into our basement. The proximity of the two ponds left us vulnerable to flies and mosquitoes. It soon became a sport and a pastime for me to kill each and everyone of them. After a while, I rigged up a fly-killing gun. It was a length of wood, about a meter long and a couple of centimeters across. At one end, I had affixed a clothespin. In the front, a small v-dent was shaped with a knife. Several rubber bands were strung together and one end locked into the clothespin. The other end of the rubber band stretched to the front V-notch. With this secret weapon, I could sneak up to any fly; bring the front end to within a whisper of the bug. I'd then press the clothespin, sending the rubber band smashing into the fly with deadly results. It was sometimes a bit messy, but I'd seldom miss. Mosquitoes, being much slower than flies could be dispatched with a rolled newspaper or even with a swat of the hand. I also became very skilled at approaching flies with my right middle finger cocked and held by my thumb. I'd then flick the fly. It would not always kill it but it would stun it long enough for me to finish it off, usually by stepping on it as it lay on the floor.

One summer night, just as we were going to go to bed, the ceiling of our basement became covered with mosquitoes. More than one hundred of these bloodsuckers hung there, waiting for us to go to bed and to keep us awake with their constant buzzing and biting. I took the bolster from the bed and began to tamp it against the ceiling crushing large numbers of the mosquitoes with each thrust. The basement ceiling was rather low and I did not have any difficulties reaching it. More than a hundred fell to my anger that night; not one survived.

It was strange that I never kept a diary. However, I did keep a list of my "kills" that were to number over two thousand by the time we finally emerged from our hiding place.

When Ruth arrived in the USA in the hot summer of 1952 she found it impossible to breathe behind our screens. She always felt that fresh air did not come in, she had been used to fully opened windows in summer!

SEXUALITY

When did it start? Surely something of this great importance should have left a first impression on this young adolescent. All I know is that after I moved to the house on the Avenue de la Cascade, I discovered the pleasure and the addiction of sex. I was thirteen, of that I am sure. Did I wake up in the middle of the night with an erection and did I discover that it felt good to touch myself? All I remember is that it felt good and that the more I rubbed my excited member the better it felt. Yet, I knew that I had to do this in a furtive manner as Mother was asleep next to me. Something told me that it was not nice and that I should keep this action hidden and to myself.

There was no one I could focus my desires on since I had no contact with girls. Yet, in my delirium the image of Ghislaine Fraiteur would fill my imagination and I'd be thinking about touching her without knowing too well what the thoughts were about. We had a copy of the magazine "*Mon Copain*" My Buddy. It was a precursor to "Playboy". In it there were *risqué* cartoons and stories of sexual encounters with racy descriptive passages. Reading these brought me to a feverish pitch and I would feel the curse of the dreaded erection and of this need that I had to satisfy.

There was a full-page cartoon of a delectable young lady in a flowing dress that espoused her body so closely that it left nothing to the imagination. She stood there, legs slightly apart, her white teeth separating the cherry red of her lips. Facing her, a man in a bowler hat, cane held behind his back asks:

"Where are you spending the summer this year?"

"Oh, here and there, I'll probably have a foot in Paris and one in Amsterdam."

"In that case, I think I will go to Brussels" replies the man, looking skyward. (Brussels was halfway between Paris and Amsterdam).

Another story told about an electrician who had been hired by a church to place a microphone in the pulpit and to connect it to the loudspeakers. Unfortunately, the worker had never been in a church and placed the microphone in the confessional. When a lady came to confess her sins to the priest, she broadcast all the explicit details all over the church and of course in the pages of "Mon Copain" that I was avidly reading. At night, I'd relive what I had read during the day and I would caress myself until I came.

The whole exercise and "cuming" presented a number of problems. First, there was Mother sleeping next to me. I had to do the caressing slowly so as not to wake her up. I was aware in my frenzy that I had to control my breathing so that it would not be overheard. And there was the problem of what to do with the milky substance that would squirt at the moment of climax. *We had not yet heard of Kleenex or paper towels.* So, I'd pinch my penis very hard when I had to ejaculate so that nothing would come out. It was painful and terribly difficult to achieve. When the whole thing was over, I'd release my hold and would try to cup in my hand whatever would still ooze out.

This went on once or twice nightly. After a while (weeks, months?) I developed an infection. It became more and more painful to urinate. I became convinced that I had gotten a *"chaude pisse"* a hot piss as a result of gonorrhea or syphilis. What was more, I had begun to grow hair, thick, black hair about my pelvis and testicles. This was terrible. I could not tell Mother about all this, yet, it was just too painful to urinate. I finally had to tell Frieda that I had great difficulty to urinate and that when I did, it was very painful. I do not remember the remedy that she applied except that she washed me and applied Vaseline with some cotton swabs. After several days, the pain went away and I was able to urinate again without discomfort.

"Mais, plus frotter" No more rubbing! That was what Frieda said. No more rubbing. Apparently, she had known all the while despite all my efforts to conceal my masturbation. I was so embarrassed, humiliated, ashamed that she had been aware all along. I resolved that I would not *branler* any more, ever. That firm resolution lasted about one day. However, I could no longer do it in the comfort and secrecy of the bed. Instead, I would seek refuge in the back of the basement and do it either in the toilet room or by the black stone sink. This had the advantage that the ejaculation could be disposed of cleanly either in the toilet bowl or in the sink and could then be promptly rinsed away.

From the back of the basement, when I carefully lifted the blanket that protected us from onlookers, I could see one window above the brick wall encircling the backyard. That window was from the bathroom of the house that was occupied by the German Women Auxiliary corps, the *Souris Grises*, Grey Mice, as we would call them. When the weather was nice, the frosted window would be open and I could see the women as they made use of the bathroom. I seldom saw a face but the narrow window allowed me to see their torso and the brassiere. These chance appearances would feed my fantasies.

Being so young, and having no other outlet for my energy, I would continue unabated but never again developed the painful infection. Thinking back, I realize that Mother continued to be aware of my doings but chose to ignore it. Frieda must have had her own physical needs to satisfy and perhaps the space I put between us when I would take refuge in the back of the basement was also beneficial for her.

GAMBLING

The DeKnibbers still had the need to feed their gamblers' addiction. Every so often, they would leave the house in the evening to go and gamble in a clandestine establishment where a few Roulette tables had been set up. On a few occasions, they returned quite upset. While they were gambling, masked members of the Belgian Resistance had barged in the gambling joint and at gunpoint had confiscated all the money, watches and jewelry of the hapless gamblers. They were then given a slip of paper assuring them that all this would be returned to them at the end of the war, after the inevitable defeat of the Germans.

It was debatable if these bandits were indeed of the Resistance, or just freelance hold-up men. They might even have been in cahoots with those who ran the clandestine casino. Whatever the case, the victims could not even go and complain to the police as the whole thing was illegal to start with. Had the bandits been with the Resistance, reporting them to the police could also have been very unhealthy.

And yet, even after those repeated misadventures, the DeKnibbers, when some money was available, would return to the gambling places and face the same dangers again.

When the Germans had entered Brussels, one of the first decrees had been that all Belgians had to turn in their weapons. I had asked Mr DeKnibber if he had a gun. If he had, in my thirteen-year-old logic, he could have stood up to the hold-up men. Mr DeKnibber assured me that before the war, he had had a gun, a Browning Automatic, but that he had thrown it in the Ixelles Pond rather than to surrender it to the occupiers. I was not sure he was telling me the truth and was intrigued at the thought that there might be a Browning in the house or lurking right under the surface of the pond.

When he wasn't out gambling, Mr DeKnibber would come down to our basement and play cards with me. Although we did not play for money, it seemed to provide him with some satisfaction and an outlet for his need to gamble. We played five hundred points Russian Rummy, but not for money. I was very good at the game, especially that I would "salt"* the discards with minor cards. I would then be able to collect the whole stack and put together large numbers of sets for valuable points. I had the knack for remembering the cards DeKnibber had in his hand and when I'd skunk him, he'd be left with a lot of points in his hand. However, he'd never show me his hand and would fold his cards, announcing a sum much smaller than he actually had. He was cheating!

*"salt" To place away minor cards (2s and 3s) in the common discards so you could sweep the entire pile of discards thus being able to form many lucrative sets and increasing the value of the total that you could tally at the end of each hand, whether you won the hand or not. Also method used during the gold or silver rush when shooting worthless ore powders into a mine's walls to convince would be buyers that the mine was worthy of purchases.

We did not play for money and still DeKnibber was cheating! It was so frustrating and yet I dared not say anything. The man was saving our lives! Night after night, he would come to play and night after night he cheated. After he'd go back upstairs to his apartments I'd complain bitterly to Mother and would often cry because this man was cheating and we could not say anything about it.

There were visitors who came to see the DeKnibbers and whenever they came, we had to make sure that the door leading to the basement was locked so that no one could walk in on us as that door was just right off the main entrance to the house. And of course, we would have to be extra quiet and seal the bottom of the door so no light would filter under and into the hallway. Any light would have revealed that something might be going on in the basement.

One constant visitor was an old lady who came so often that Mother called her "*La Drogue*" The Drug. She would visit and stay and stay. When it was time for her to leave, La Drogue and La Cheminée would come down the stairs and talk interminably next to the basement door before they would finally bid goodbye. All the while, we had to hold our breath and stay quiet as a mouse for fear to be overheard.

Nieces and nephews would visit regularly but not too often. Mother figured that they were coming to make sure that their inheritance was in good stead as surely uncle and aunt were wealthy and worth courting. DeKnibber would save their meager ration of butter that was allocated monthly and stored the minuscule patties in the brine-filled earthenware crock they kept in the sub-basement. When the family came, out came the butter patties to convince all that the DeKnibbers were still wealthy and could afford to buy butter on the black market.

Our hosts would bring us food on a regular basis. Since we had gone underground, we did not have any ration cards or food stamps and all that could be brought us had to be purchased on the black market. We were never really hungry. Mother would do some cooking on the basement stove. We had watery soup and very dark bread. Sometime we had margarine to "butter" the bread. Mostly we covered our *tartines* with apple butter that was available. Herring, fresh, smoked or pickled was plentiful and became our staple. For vegetables, we had *rutabagas*, turnips and beets. These were now grown all over the city wherever a plot of land could be found. In the fall, we'd get an apple or a pear now and then. We drank water from the faucet and prepared *ersatz* coffee made from malt grain as real coffee had completely disappeared. Of course, there was no milk and no sugar to be had. I resolved that I'd never eat herring again after the war.

When the Germans invaded Belgium, bread changed color almost overnight. White bread just vanished. Grey bread became the norm. As the occupation continued, the bread became darker and darker, wetter and wetter. By the end of the war, the bread was so gooey that one could have thrown it against the wall and it would have stuck there. Of course, we never did try as we did not have much of it to spare. All that was being produced in the occupied countries was requisitioned by the Germans for their own use or for shipment to Germany. Some food products were still available, having been stealthily withdrawn from what was supposed to be requisitioned by the Germans. This purloined food would find its way to the Rue Des Radis in the capital and elsewhere and would be sold at the highest price to those who could still afford it.

Frieda has salvaged one glass tube full of real coffee beans. There might have been two dozen or so of the beautiful roasted bean. She kept these jealously, determined that when we would be liberated, she would prepare one cup of real coffee and offer it to our liberators. I would sometime hold the tube in my hands admiring the oily dark brown beans. On special occasions, Frieda would let me open the red rubber stopper and allowed me to breathe in the faint odor of the coffee. *Eventually, we were liberated by the British and they were resolutely tea drinkers!*

We had spirited away one small can of Nestle's sweet condensed milk. We eventually opened it and over several weeks' time, I ate the whole can one teaspoonful at a time. I'd heap the thick golden milk on the spoon and slide it back and forth between my lips, each time skimming a tiny bit off the top until my upper lip scraped the bottom of the spoon. It was a delight never to be forgotten.

Mother had beautiful hands and was proud of her long, painted nails. She decided that she would not cut her nails ever again until we were liberated. Over days and weeks, the nails grew longer and then began to curl downward. After a while, there were curls spiraling at the end of each finger and Frieda found it difficult to get a hold of anything and to go about her daily chores. So, since there was no sign that we would soon be liberated, she had to cut her nails and abandon that resolve.

As the month of July 1943 came around, the German armies in Russia began a new powerful offensive. They trumpeted it as the largest tank battle of the war. For a few days, much to our despair, it was announced that the Germans had made a deep penetration of the Russian lines along the Kursk/Orel salient. The Axis forces had been retreating since the defeat at Stalingrad and now, they seemed poised to take back all that they had lost since the winter. "Signal" described in glowing terms the renewed offensive and the new weapons that the German scientists had designed to ensure the final victory. It was to be the biggest tank battle ever, but it was the Russians who emerged victorious. It was to be the last major offensive the German army launched on the Eastern Front. From then on, it would be the Russians who would strike the blows and Germany began a long retreat that would eventually see the Russian Army in the streets of Berlin.

The German propaganda tried to make every retreat into a victory. This was the Elastic Defensive Movement that was meant to shorten the length of the frontlines. The BBC began to mock the German Army with songs about the *"Defense Elastique"*.

In mid-July, the Allies landed in Sicily. It was not yet Continental Europe, but it was a move forward. We heard about the exploits of the US Army under General Patton. Sicily fell in a month. In Italy, Mussolini was forced to resign and was arrested. The Fascist Party was abolished and a new government was formed under Marshall Badoglio. Shortly the Italian Army would surrender. Things were looking up at long last.

One warm night, we were awakened by a loud commotion in the ponds across the avenue. We could hear voices yelling and ducks frantically screaming and there was wild flapping of wings. When morning came, Mr DeKnibber went to see what all the noises had been about. Apparently, a group of men had waded into the ponds and snared all the ducks they could find. The female swan and the few cygnets had also been stolen. We could only surmise that these had been captured for food although, remembering our Christmas goose of 1940, I had great doubt that this wild fowl would be palatable.

After that, the male swan, now alone and robbed of its offspring, became even more angry and vicious. Time and again, he would pursue and try to harm the few remaining ducks that had escaped the *razzia*.

RELATING WITH OUR HOSTS

Mr DeKnibber asked me if I wanted to read books that he could obtain from the library. Since my only lecture was the Larousse dictionary and whatever newspaper and magazine were available, I thought it was a grand idea. I was particularly interested in *"Policiers"* mystery murder novels. Wanting to communicate this preference to Mr DeKnibber, I told him that I'd love for him to bring me "salty" novels. He swallowed hard, gave me a puzzled look and asked if I really wanted those types of books. I was not aware that "salty" meant sexy. I quickly corrected my request by explaining that I wanted murder mysteries. Actually, it would have been very nice to get a few sexy novels as the dog-eared copy of "Mon Copain" was wearing thin. Of course, I could not convey that to him. Mostly, he brought me mystery books by the Belgian novelist George Simenon. Among these there was one called *"Touriste de Bananes"*, "Banana Tourist". It was about a man who goes to Tahiti to find himself. That turned out to be a very salty book indeed. Mr DeKnibber must have chosen it because it was Simenon but had not bothered to research its contents. He did bring me a few other books, but there were not many of these and they were to fade from my memory.

As Mr DeKnibber had lived in the US, he must have been aware of many American songs. Just before the German invasion, I had heard a song that to my ear went: La, laaa Lomance, La, laaa Lomance etc. It had a lilting melody and great rhythm. I asked him if he knew the song about "Lomance". He was puzzled, wrinkled his brow and then confessed that he did not know any such song and that Lomance was not even an English word. *La Cheminée* was similarly ignorant.

It would be years later until I'd be able to hear the song again; sung by Fred Astaire, "A Fine Romance". I was not used to soft "R" of the American idiom that, to my French ear sounded like an "L".

The DeKnibbers did their laundry upstairs in their apartments. However, they would bring the laundry to be dried in the sub-basement that was accessed through our hideaway. One day, Mother noticed a pair of man's boxer shorts, white with four metal snaps for closures. Even after washing, the shorts were badly soiled with dark brown stains about the front area. Mother was very curious about the stained *brayette*, fly and was wondering what could possibly have caused it. In those days of recalcitrant soap, it was not easy to get things clean and obviously those stains could not be removed. Mother asked me if I knew where these could have come from. I confessed that I had no idea. Mother decided to keep those stains in mind and resolved to ask her Zeebrugge friend Mme Pesch when we were free again. "Mme Pesch knows about things like that" she muttered. I guess that Mr DeKnibber might have been suffering from an enlarged prostate or maybe some sort of urinary disorder, maybe cancer, but he never let on that he might have been in ill health while we were hiding there. It pleased me to know that Frieda was thinking ahead to a time we might walk out of our hiding place and that there was a glimmer of hope in her thinking.

LE SOIR AND "SIGNAL"

Every day, we received a copy of *Le Soir,* Brussels' main newspaper. As the war dragged on and shortages multiplied, the paper became thinner and thinner as the pages dwindled from 24 pages to 16, 8, and eventually there would only be four sides. Yet, starved as we were for news from the outside, we devoured *Le Soir* each day. We knew that the occupiers dictated most of the news but there was always something useful we could glean. Besides the obvious war and political news, there were movie and book reviews. Although we could not see any of the movies or read the books, it did give us a tiny window to the outer world. Daily, there was a comic strip of *Tintin et Milou,* by Hergé and these had always been my favorites. At the time, the strips were about "The Seven Crystal Balls" and each day I could view and read 4 or five tiny panels of the story. When I was finished, I would cut up the day's comic strip and glue it on a roll of brown strapping tape. All I had to do was to moisten the tape and the comic strip would adhere to it. I'd leave an extra 4 centimeters so I could glue each length on to the previous ones, thus making a booklet that I could flip through whenever I wanted to reread the story. Since the story was in black and white, I used colored pencils to color each panel. This was a daily routine until the pencils ran out of lead.

Almost daily, I would draw a cartoon in a lined Composition Notebook. The inspiration would come from the News or spring out of my head. Mostly these were funny cartoons, jokes on various subjects that I would think up. At least, I thought they were funny enough to be made into cartoons. As the months went by, the drawings became more and more skillful and funnier. There were days when I was not up to thinking of anything clever or funny, but that did not last long. I would draw 4 or 6 cartoons to a page, either in blue ink or in pencil. I fully intended to bring them to *Le Soir*'s editors when the war would be over and have these published daily in their "humor" pages.

"Signal" the German propaganda magazine continued its biased articles against all things American, Jewish or Bolshevik. There was not too much directed at the British. Curiously, the Hitler regime and Göbbels in particular felt that both nations had a lot in common. Göbbels would even discourse that Germany and England should have been allies in the formation of a new Europe and that it was a pity that Germany had to ally itself with inferior races like the Japanese and the Italians. He once wrote" Mussolini is a great man; too bad he has to rule over Italians.

During my months of hiding, Signal continued to be a great source of learning for me. It had articles on photography, notably on the "Robot" a semi automatic 35 mm camera that one could wind and it would take a whole roll of film at the press of a button. Or it would devote many pages to Maxi Herber and Ernst Baier Germany's 1936 Olympic champions in Garmisch-Partenkirchen.

From Signal I learned to identify all the Allied airplanes. This would help identify the ones I could see from my basement window when they flew over my vantage point.

Fortress Europe was a recurring theme, depicting Europe of tomorrow, after the final German victory. A Europe surrounded by a battlement to keep out the Judeo/American interests on the one side and the Bolshevik/Asiatic hordes on the other side. Germany, under the leadership of Adolph Hitler would bring this "New Order" to all of Europe whether we wanted it or not.

One issue devoted several pages to a plot concocted by the Jews of America to build a gigantic wall running from the Carolina coast due East into the Atlantic Ocean. This deep wall was supposed to impede the flow of the Gulf Stream, prevent it from reaching Europe and thus bringing back the Ice Ages to all of Europe. This would destroy Europe's industrial capabilities and eventually render Europe barren of population. Such was the dastardly cunning of the Americans under the Zionist influence.

I would read all of this avidly but with enough of a critical mind so that, even in my early teen years, I could discern the blatant propaganda and not be affected by it.

Today, at the Brussels Flea Market, on the Place Du Jeu De Balle, hundreds of old Signal issues languish on stalls or on the cobblestones, begging for the onlookers to pick up a copy or two for less than a Euro each. Sometimes I feel tempted.

FLUFFY

We developed a deep resentment for Mr & Mme DeKnibber. It was a strange relationship, almost like between jailer and prisoner; a sort of inter-dependence where they needed us as much as we needed them. We grew to dislike them and they probably disliked us also after a while. It was not hatred but certainly a feeling of unease at being tied so closely together. Psychoanalysts surely must have books on that phenomenon; I only know that there was often a palpable unease. Every night, Mr DeKnibber would come down our basement to play cards with me and of course he cheated. Now and then, Frieda would question the value of the cards he declared after I'd have skunked him. She'd reach over, turn his cards over and quickly would count the value of his hand. Most of the time, the count was wrong. Of course, it had to be done with a bit of tact (Frieda did not have much of that commodity) and not too often. After all, we could not afford to antagonize DeKnibber as he was saving our lives.

DeKnibber would join us each evening to play Rummy with me. Was it an occasion for him to get away from his wife for an hour or so? They never went any place separately. Was he also looking for a chance to be in the company of Mother, still a very attractive woman of forty? There was never anything that I could have observed or noticed. However, he did not seem to mind when Frieda would lean over the card table and rummage through his cards.

Sometimes, *La Cheminée* would join her husband in our basement. They would smoke foul-smelling ersatz cigarettes all the while they were with us. Whenever Mrs DeKnibber would join us, she would bring along Fluffy, the small black and white Papillion dog with a graceful fluffy tail. Fluffy had round bulging eyes and when he barked, the force of the air he displaced made him leap off the ground. He would bark until Mme DeKnibber picked him up in her arms. The dog was pampered; he got a lump of sugar when they had sugar, candy when they had candy. We came to resent Fluffy. We felt that this dog was better off than we were. He went out two or three times a day, prancing along the bank of the Etangs d'Ixelles as Mr DeKnibber would take him for a walk. Stuck inside our confined space, I could only watch Fluffy from my basement window. Mother would refer to Fluffy as "*Le leche-cul à Madame*" "Madame's ass licker". As vulgar as the expression was, it was not an original. Tiny dogs were often referred to in that way.

One day, when the DeKnibbers had gone for their bi-monthly visit to the Kommandantur, Mother and I crept up to the upstairs living quarters. I recall that we went up the stairs on all fours, like thieves, slinking like snakes avoiding making noise, like evildoers. We entered in the dark salon and cornered Fluffy. We hit him, again and again. Poor Fluffy cringed against the red plush velvet armchair, his bulging eyes looking at us, not understanding what we were doing to him. When our rage was spent, we retreated in silence and returned to our basement.

It was a foolish thing to do. Had the DeKnibbers suspected that we had beaten their precious Fluffy they surely would have turned us over to the Germans. I have had dogs since then and I would not have blamed them for denouncing us. I do not know why we did it. I was following Frieda. Why she did it, I do not know. Perhaps we just wanted to make one creature more miserable than we were.

After that, whenever Fluffy would come to the basement, safe in the arms of Mme DeKnibber, I would worry that he would show signs of being afraid of us. However, Fluffy never did betray us.

As I recall, it was the only time we ever ventured upstairs to beat Fluffy. That was one of the worst things I had ever done in my life, mean, ugly and foolish.

RADIO

Our little Phillips table radio was our link to the outside world. During the day, we would listen mostly to I.N.R. the *Institut National de Radiodiffusion*, the Belgian francophone station. It gave me a special feeling to know that it was broadcasting from the Place Flagey, just a few blocks away. It made it personal, almost intimate.

There were news, music and situation comedies. The news was badly slanted, being dictated by the German propaganda ministry. Sometimes we would listen to the speeches by Adolf Hitler or Josef Göbbels, although we would hear those mostly on Radio Berlin that we could catch on the short wave bands. I was fascinated by the vile of these people, by the meanness directed at us. Hitler was so charismatic that he had all of Germany following him. I understood that all he was saying about the Jews was propaganda. Göbbels followed suit but if he did not have the appeal of Hitler, his bile and clever lies were even more insidious than the ranting of the Führer. What had me confused was that all the hatred directed at the Jews should not really have affected me. After all, did not Ruth and I get baptized Protestant in August 1941?

Most of the music we could hear came from German stars like Marika Rock, Willy Forst or Sarah Leander, a statuesque Swedish dish, an actress who had caught the fancy of the Führer and the German public. Of the French singers, Maurice Chevalier, Charles Trenet, Edith Piaf and Yves

Montant were regular fare. Chevalier and Leander were briefly blacklisted after the war under accusations of having collaborated with the Nazis.

Weekly, I'd listen to two comedies. Adolf and Adolphine was a Brussels couple that mostly related minor problems that had happened to them or (mostly) to their friend Fromageol. Fromageol was always off-stage and you would never hear him. When the half-hour broadcast came to the ending, a doorbell would ring and Adolf would exclaim: "*Ah, voila Fromageol*". Thus he was about to appear, but he never did.

The other comedy was about a tribunal where the judge, lawyers and prosecutors were introduced with clever little ditties and proceeded to behave in asinine ways that brought discredit to the institution of justice. How this program could pass under the nose of the German censorship was a mystery, as the *Boches* did not take kindly to any disrespect for authority.

And then, there was the B.B.C., the news broadcast from London, our lifeline with the Free World, our opiate, our hope.

THE B.B.C.—Da Da Da Dahm

Da Da Da Dahm, DaDaDa Dahm. Here is London, Ic*i Londres, Hier ist London*. Every fifteen minutes, of every day, of every night, the BBC would broadcast to occupied Europe and to the Axis. The programs started with the first four notes of Beethoven's Fifth Symphony. The three short notes followed by the long one also signaled the "V" for victory (dot, dot, dot, dash . . . _). We would mostly listen to the broadcast in French, but the BBC had programs in German, French, Italian, Dutch, Danish, Norwegian, Polish, etc. Every fifteen minutes the language would change. The news was followed avidly throughout occupied Europe and even in Germany and Italy. Everywhere, listening to the BBC (British Broadcasting Company) was a serious offense instantly punishable by fines, imprisonment or worse. Yet, everyone tuned in and listened daily for any news that might bring a bit of hope for the eventual defeat of the Axis forces. The Germans had special squads circulating in motor vans that would attempt to triangulate the provenance of radio signals. However, their primary purpose was to detect clandestine radio transmitters used by the Resistance to communicate with London. There would not have been enough room in all of the prisons of Europe had they arrested all those who were listening to the BBC every night.

All over occupied Europe, people would huddle near the radio, straining to hear the news while keeping the volume low enough so the Germans, the police or any traitor that might be nearby could not overhear it. In our basement, we had to be doubly careful, as we feared that the Germans in the adjacent house would hear us tuning in to the forbidden BBC. The vacuum tubes in our little Phillips table-radio would emit a warm reddish glow that could be visible from the outside, even during the day. For concealment, during daylight, a dark cloth was draped over the back of the radio, thus shutting out the light of the tubes. During the day, we could move about in the semi-darkness of our cellar without being seen from the street as the bright outdoors would effectively mask our activities. At night, because there was a "black-out", our little window was always covered with a blanket so that we could turn on the lights in the basement. We could then move around without fear of being observed from outside. The large window and the glass door at the end of the basement were permanently blacked-out with dark blankets.

While the back of the radio was covered with its cloth, the face of the Phillips was turned to the inside of the room. The radio had a large lit yellow face where world-wide stations had been printed: Paris, London, Berlin, Rome, Moscow, Copenhagen, New York, and other far away places; enough to make me dream of another world outside the four walls of our prison.

The radio had several wavelengths, long, medium and short. The long and medium would give you leeway as to the exact position of the station you were aiming for. The short waves, on the other hand, required exact positioning of the wand to capture any signal. It was a tedious and demanding exercise to zero in to a specific broadcast station.

Invariably, we would tune in to the BBC French segment on the long wavelengths that would give the easiest and clearer reception. First would come the "Dah dah dah Dahm" repeated several times, then "*Ici Londres*, here are the latest news, but first a few personal messages."

There followed several obscure messages for the benefit of the Resistance. "*Les carrotes sont cuites*" "The carrots are cooked" was a popular one and the only one that I have been able to remember. The Germans never interfered with these personal messages that could be heard clearly. It was crucial for the occupiers to hear these secret phrases and to try to figure out the actual meaning. After that, a barrage of high-pitched noises would hit the airways making it nearly impossible to continue to listen. Yet, we knew that the Germans would keep an open channel somewhere so they could go on listening to the BBC broadcast. We would then frantically search from station to station, from band to band until we found another place where we could hear the BBC without interference. After a few minutes, that station would be jammed and off we went turning the dial to locate the next undisturbed one. We soon developed quite a skill at this so we would lose only a minimum amount of news. Those were rare nights when we could listen to a broadcast from beginning to end without any jamming.

While Brussels INR and Radio Paris were broadcasting lies and propaganda for the Germans, we felt that the BBC gave honest accounts of what was happening, good and bad. From the BBC, we followed defeats and victories (at the beginning, mostly defeats) and news of the Allies that kept up our morale and hopes. By the later part of 1943, the BBC would rail with a ditty about "The elastic defense" that the Germans were using to explain away their constant retreats before the surging Russian Army.

"*Radio Paris ment, Radio Paris ment, Radio Paris est Allemand*" "Radio Paris Lies, Radio Paris Lies, Radio Paris is German" would sing the BBC to the tune of "La Cucaracha". Then we waited for the last line: "*On les aura, les Boches!*" "We will get them, the Boches!" Thus armed with a little more hope and resilience, Mother and I would retire to bed and wish for a better tomorrow.

One day, the little Phillips refused to work. Try as we might, there was no way we could coax life, light or sound from the radio. This was terrible as this was our only link to the outside world. I grabbed a screwdriver and took the whole radio completely apart. Soon, the table was littered with tubes, wires, resistances and screws. That was when I noticed that the little cardboard tubes of the resistances were empty. The waxy substance they had contained had melted down and now covered the base of the radio cabinet. The heat generated by the tubes and concentrated under the blackout cloth had melted the tar-like wax. With a knife, I scraped off the wax from the cabinet and stuffed it with my fingers back in the empty cardboard tubes. I then re-inserted the tubes to where I though they belonged, connected wires here and there and screwed the whole thing back together. When I was finished, there were a couple of odds and ends left on the table but I had no idea as to where these might fit. With apprehension, under the quizzical look of Mother, I plugged the radio back into the socket and *voila*! It worked! After that, the little Phillips never failed us again and continued to serve us faithfully until the end of the war.

A DAY IN HIDING, SEPTEMBER 1943

This would be our second fall of hiding. Although only seven months had passed since I went to hide with Mother at 32 Avenue de la Cascade, the monotony of each passing day had made it seem much longer. Actually, it had been sixteen months since I had been compelled to leave school and that we had been on the run hiding first in the Ardennes, then in Uccle and now in Ixelles. In the Ardennes, except for the occasional alert that forced Ruth and me to take refuge in the attic of the Pension Sovet, we had pretty much the run of the place. In Uccle, there were times when we ventured out albeit only at night, with Ghislaine while walking Kiki. In Ixelles, with the immediate proximity of the Germans in the next house, there was no question of venturing outside. Furthermore, we had finally become convinced that the penalty for going outside our hiding place would be instant arrest, deportation and death.

We'd get up at noon and took off the blanket that covered our small window. I'd get up on the chair and peer out to the outside world. I guess I wanted to be sure that we had been given another day. Pressing my face to the slats of the Hindu curtain, I'd survey my domain checking for any change in the scenery. The front yard, the fence and gate, the street, grassy border, couple of trees and the pond greeted me. Above, my small piece of sky was the only variable, going from gray to white to blue. Since this was Belgium, blue sky was rarely to be seen.

While I'd satisfy myself that my universe was intact, Frieda would quickly use the toilet and was up at the sink in the back half of the basement. It would then be my turn to go and take care of my body functions. Strangely, despite our minimal diet, I never did get constipated or if I did, there is no recollection of it. Now and then, we did get a roll of coarse toilet paper. Most of the time, there were only cut-up pieces of newspaper or magazines to do the task.

It was my turn to do my ablutions in front of the stone sink. Dipping my toothbrush in a can of baking soda, I'd brush without much vigor or enthusiasm as the cold water and the powder was unpleasant to the mouth. I'd then try to make the pumice "soap" give up a few bubbles to the *gant de toilette*, washcloth. I'd pass the washcloth over my face, my neck, my chest, under arms, crotch, behind and finally between my toes. That was it for the day.

By then, Mother had prepared breakfast, a palm-sized slice of black gummy bread covered with apple-butter spread and a bowl of *ersatz* malt coffee without milk or sugar. It did not take me long to finish my meal despite the tendency of the bread to stick between my gums and my cheeks.

At about one in the afternoon, Mr DeKnibber would knock at our basement door and hand us that day's Soir newspaper. In 1943, it was still full size and retained 24 pages. I would quickly devour its pages, reading from page one to the end, hungry for any news from the outside. The few jokes and cartoons always attracted my attention, especially the propaganda cartoons by Paul Jamin, a collaborator who had a special talent for mean but telling political satire. But by far, it was the daily strip of "Tintin et Milou" that I yearned to read each day.

I'd then pass the newspaper to Frieda who would mostly glance at the headlines. French was not her Mother tongue and it was too tiring for her to try to read and understand all that was printed. Once Mother was finished with the paper, I'd cut the "Tintin et Milou" strip and pasted it on a piece of glue paper cut from a large roll of strapping tape. With color pencils I'd color each panel. It would then be affixed to the previous strips that I had been saving since the story had begun. The rest of the *Soir* would then be cut up into small squares to join the stack of paper in the toilet. I guess that it was a suitable end for that vile paper.

Inspired by the cartoons or the news, I'd then sit at the table and I'd draw one or more cartoons that I felt were humorous. This I did with a pen and blue ink dipped from a small square Waterman bottle. When I was satisfied with my day's output or when I had run out of imagination, I'd place my notebook in a drawer and got ready for a next task.

A lot of my daylight hours would be spent standing on the chair by the front basement window, looking out at my reduced world. Few cars or trucks passed by as there was by now a shortage of fuel. The Germans had gasoline while the Belgian trucks or automobiles had stove-like contraptions affixed to the trunk. These I think would burn coal or wood and somehow manage to develop some kind of energy to propel the vehicle. I never did find out the scientific reason behind it. Traffic and parked cars were minimal and I usually had an unobstructed view of the pond. Twice a day or so, Mr DeKnibber took Fluffy for a walk and I'd see Fluffy stepping out smartly, its tail flagging high. If the weather were suitable it would take at least twenty minutes before they would return. Now and then, DeKnibber would return with groceries in a green mesh net. Since paper was scarce, it was the custom to carry a small mesh bag rolled into a ball. This could then be opened and filled with the day's purchases. Mr DeKnibber, would then come down the steps of our basement and give Mother our daily ration, usually some herring and rutabagas together with half a loaf of the dreaded black bread.

At times, I'd see the German soldiers go in and out of the house next to ours. I'd make myself a bit smaller and was careful not to press too hard against the viewing curtain for fear that they might notice a movement or a shadow. In the late afternoon, a company of German soldiers would march by on the avenue singing marching songs in cadence to their steps. Mostly it was "Ro-o-se-Marie" or a song about marching to conquer England. It was actually nice to hear, the voices being perfect for the guttural nature of the language. They would also march by in the evening when the curtains were closed. I could hear them approaching as the company got closer, the voices booming louder and the crump-crump-crump of the hob-nailed boots reverberating against the pavement. It was weird to hear them pass in front of our basement and then to listen as they faded away. There was always a mix of terror and thrill at the sounds and the fear that they might stop and decide to search the houses. It never did happen.

When the Germans did not march by, there might be a company of Flemish VNV, in their black uniforms, arm adorned with a swastika, emulating their German masters. Even at night, I could tell the difference. The VNV would sing the same marching songs as the Germans but being Flemish speaking, the voices and accents were much softer and the songs lost all martial tonality. I was always struck by the difference, the lack of cohesion, the missing force of the Dutch sounds as compared to German. The VNV did not instill the same fear in me.

With my binoculars, I'd concentrate on the portion of the pond that was laid out in front of me. Water birds swam to and fro through my "theatre" as if they had been waiting in the wings to make an entrance. The trees may have been filled with smaller birds but I did not notice any. Even common sparrows were scarce, perhaps because there was little food that could be spared by passers by. It rained often and the rainy days gave me the most pleasure. Everything would become shiny, droplets would pockmark the pond and water would roll off the bushes in the front yard. Even the sound of the window being pelted by the rain was music to my ears. The patch of sky I could see from my window was almost always cloudy, sunny days being very rare in Brussels.

With the evening, I'd cover the window with a blanket and we would then be able to turn on the lights in the basement. This was the time I would play with the puzzles and assemble them over and over again. After that, it was time to play solitaire "Tour de France" and to keep track of that night's results to tally the race, to be continued the next day. At intervals, depending on the season, I'd take time off to hunt and kill whatever fly or mosquito had dared to venture in our hideaway.

Supper was around seven. Herring and rutabaga, rutabaga and herring, now and again, a piece of fruit. Water was readily available from the faucet and we could drink a cup of ersatz coffee. I soon gave up the coffee as it made me get up in the middle of the night. I resolved that I would never eat herring again if we ever made it back to the outside.

Strangely, even though we ate each and every day, I have not a single recollection of sitting at the table and actually eating, tasting, putting food in my mouth. As well as I can recall so many details of our daily life and the events of those times; I cannot remember that simple act. All memory of it is absent. I can summon the taste of the herring, the crunch of the rutabaga, the slush of the dark bread, the grit of the apple butter, but not the act of eating it. It is as if we had never eaten for all these months. The only exception is the tasting and the savoring of the Nestle's sweet condensed milk that I can recall as vividly as if I had stepped away from my own self and had watched me as I slipped each spoonful between my lips.

We would turn to the radio, mostly INR, and listen to music, mainly classical, plays, comedy and news until about 8 when Mr DeKnibber would join us for our nightly game of Russian rummy. It was always the two of us as Frieda had never gotten the hang of cards, although in later years she would discover the joys of playing Black Jack in Vegas and Lake Tahoe. Of course, as usual, each night, I would trounce DeKnibber and as usual, he would cheat continuously. While we were playing, Frieda would study old monthly reviews from the Casino of Namur that detailed charts of

Rudy Rosenberg

every turn of the roulette wheel. Mother would then study new schemes and combinations, refining her "system" for the day when she would be free to return to her beloved *Roulette*.

There were nights when Mme DeKnibber, with Fluffy in her arms, would join her husband in our basement. Both of them would be smoking foul smelling crushed horse chestnut leaves that they had rolled into cigarettes. The basement soon was filled with gray billows of smoke that penetrated everywhere. Since there was no ventilation, there was much wheezing and coughing but the couple seemed unaware of our discomfort and kept on sucking the end of their cigarette holders.

Between 9.30 and 10, the DeKnibbers would bid their farewell and retreat to their upstairs apartment. I'd be left to complain bitterly to Mother about the brazen cheating I had been subjected to by Mr DeKnibber.

By ten o'clock, it was time to listen to the BBC's French program to glean some hope for a liberation that in 1943 was only a distant glow in our long night. After the French program, Frieda would tune in to the BBC's broadcast in German, hearing again the same news but perhaps being able to catch a few nuances she might have missed in the French version. Meanwhile, I'd leaf through the Larousse dictionary looking up names and places that had been mentioned in the broadcast and flitting from word to word, page to page, enthralled by the unending treasure of words beckoning on every page.

And of course, once or twice each evening, while Mother huddled near the radio, I would find refuge in the back room of the basement or in the bathroom and feverishly masturbated quickly to satisfy this need of my body and senses. Furtively, quietly, I'd ejaculate in the toilet or in the large black stone sink in the back. This took care of the problem of disposing of the milky substance of which, in my thirteenth year I seemed to have an abundant supply. I knew it was not to be done, but it was so good! I would rejoin Mother only after my fever had cooled down and my breathing and heartbeat had returned to a normal state.

At midnight, after stalking for a few more flies, we'd go to bed, sharing the same bed. Mother slept to my left and I'd go to sleep turning my back to her and facing the wall of the basement. We'd have no conversation, just a *"Bonne nuit, a demain"* Goodnight, until tomorrow. Briefly, I'd worry about the nightmares that were sure to visit and torment me during the night, but I had no difficulty in falling into a deep sleep. I did not know if Mother stayed awake for long or if she was able to find a few hours of peace through sleep. We'd sleep until the next noon. The cycle would then repeat for another day.

ITALY, THE INVASION, SEPTEMBER 1943

In the first week of September 43, the BBC announced that the Allied Forces had landed at several places in Italy. With the arrest of Mussolini in July and the capitulation of Italy in mid-September it looked as if all of Italy would soon be occupied and this would hasten the end of the war. Rome was declared an Open City. That meant that there would be no fighting for its possession. My hopes were rekindled and the prospect of an early end to the war loomed large again in my mind. This time it was Mr DeKnibber who was to dash my hopes. He felt, rightly so, that the Italian campaign would not have any effect on the ability of the Germans to keep their grip on the rest of Europe. We would be liberated only if the Allies ever decided to cross the *Pas de Calais* (the Channel) and undertook a costly and devastating campaign through Northern France. Remembering the slaughter of the First World War, it was not a pleasant prospect.

That was not my only disagreement with Mr DeKnibber. Earlier, in April he had expressed his concern that American troops were suffering heavy casualties in the Pacific and in North Africa. After all, he was an American citizen, albeit a naturalized one and he took their losses very personally. With the insensitive logic of a thirteen-year old, I replied that these soldiers were all volunteers and that they expected to be killed when they enlisted. That argument did not go over big with DeKnibber. We argued back and forth and he had the good sense to end the discussion before it degenerated into a brainless fight. Although I did not know it at the time, the US, as well as England had long ago instituted the draft and the majority of the troops were draftees.

As it turned out, the hope for a quick end to the Italian campaign was short lived. After the Italians surrendered to the Allies, the German armies under Field Marshal Kesselring quickly occupied all of Italy. The Italian campaign would become a succession of slow and bloody battles that would not cease until the end of the war. In mid September, the Italian government made an about face and declared war on Germany. Thus, the Italians, in the space of a few weeks had turned from a hated enemy to an ally. I thought that in total, it did not amount to much as the Italian Army had never demonstrated the ability or willingness to put up a good fight. Although Italians had become an object of derision, I came to appreciate in later years that they felt it was often preferable to live than to die, no matter how gloriously.

Mussolini had been placed under house arrest in the Italian Apennine Mountains. On September 12, on the direct order of Hitler, a rescue party of German SS troops landed at the mountain resort where Il Duce was being held and liberated him. The rescue party was under the command of Major Otto Scorzeni, a dare-devil who had a long history of doing special tasks for the Führer. In "Signal" several illustrated pages were devoted to the daring rescue. These depicted the German paratroopers having secured the house where Mussolini had been held captive. The article gloated over how Major Scorzeni had landed his Fieseler Storch (Fil56 Stork) on a narrow mountain shelf and taken off again, but this time with Il Duce as cargo. From there he was flown to a meeting with Adolf Hitler who embraced him. In the pictures, the Duce had seemed dazed, gaunt and ill. "Signal" went on to rhapsodize about the superior German technology that had created the "Stork" that could land and take off on a minimal site and get away at a top speed of about 100 mph. I was furious that the Italian government had once again been found lacking and had allowed Mussolini to escape.

Mussolini would survive until April 28ᵗʰ, 1945 when Italian partisans caught up with him near the Swiss border. They brought him back to Milan where he was shot and hanged by his feet, half-naked, in a public square. His mistress, Clara Petacci and several other fascists suffered the same fate. He was 62. Two days later, on April 30ᵗʰ, 1945, Adolf Hitler committed suicide together with Eva Braun, his mistress (He had married her the day before). He was 56.

SNOW IN BRUSSELS

In late December 1943, it snowed on Brussels, not a heavy snow, just a few centimeters. From my basement window I could see my universe shrouded with a white covering. Only the water in the pond had retained its dark complexion. This was very rare; it just did not snow in the capital. Rain, cold rain, yes! Snow was to be found further east, near Liège or in the Ardennes due to the higher elevation. I did not recall having ever seen snow! I wanted to touch it, feel it. I begged Frieda to let me go out in the back courtyard and steal a handful of snow. Mother agreed.

We waited until after midnight when we knew the Germans occupying the three houses in back of us would be asleep. We turned off all the lights in our basement and carefully removed the blanket that covered the window on the back door. That door had not been opened since Mother had moved in the basement a year and a half earlier. Slowly we opened the back door hoping that the hinges would not betray us. A blast of cold fresh air greeted us. The moon must have been shining somewhere as the snow glistened blue-white on the ground surrounded by three brick walls. There was no light streaking from the three other houses. They also had to follow the blackout rules and could not let light shine into the night. Five or six steps led to the ground and beyond, snow! Carefully, furtively, I climbed up the first two steps. Leaning forward I was able to gather and scoop a ball of wet cold snow between my two hands. The snow made a strange sound as it crunched into a snowball under my fingers.

Quickly I retreated to the safety of the basement while Mother closed the door and replaced the covering over the window. It was now safe to turn on the light. The snow I held in my hands had started to turn a shade of gray and it was cold to my palms. I placed the snowball in the black stone sink and watched it melt very slowly. It was dissolving into a trickle of water meandering to the drain. I stared on for maybe 30 minutes. By then, it was past one in the night and it was time to go to bed. By morning, there was no trace left in the sink. Outside, most of the snow had gone and dirty gray soot covered what was left.

That was the only time I went out.

CHRISTMAS 1943

Nothing happened on that Christmas, the second one occurring during our captivity. No memory remains of candlelight, tree, chocolate or sweets. If the DeKnibbers celebrated, it was upstairs with a few nephews and nieces. Because of the frequent visits, we had to be extra cautious not to make noises. Frieda sang "*Oh Tannenbaum*" very quietly and softly cried out for her dead Father "*Mein Papa, mein Papa*". A few days before, the feast of St. Nicolas had come and gone the same quiet way. No toys, no *spekuloos*. A snowball had been my winter present to be remembered always.

In Italy, the Allies were bogged down and unable to inch forward toward Rome and the German mainland. On the Eastern Front, the news was much better. The Red Army had thrown the Axis troops out of almost all of the territories that had been conquered and the Russians were rolling into Poland on their way to Germany. However, that was so far away from us and there seemed to be no sign of a coming second front that might someday liberate us.

I kept a map on the basement wall. Pins and ribbons were moving in the east, but nothing was moving in Italy and there was not even a single pin along the North Sea and the Atlantic. Rommel was building the Atlantic Wall meant to repulse the Allies and throw them back into the sea were they ever bold enough to attempt a landing. *(The Germans had conscripted Bernard Horowitz for forced labor. His task was to pour concrete to build the Atlantic Wall on the Belgian coast.)*

The prospects for 1944 were not brilliant.

1944

Over there, over there! Send the word, send the word over there!
That the Yanks are coming, the Yanks are coming . . . .

MONTE CASSINO

In the early months of 1944, most of the news we were receiving from the BBC, the occupied press and "Signal" was preoccupied with the Italian campaign. Sure, there was much action in the Pacific but it was too far removed from our problems to receive much of our attention. We had not learned to hate the Japanese. Aside from being allied with Germany, Japan had done nothing to us. Our concern was now Germany, Hitler and his henchmen.

Daily, reports came of huge bombardments over German cities: Hamburg, Berlin, Cologne, Essen, Frankfurt and Düsseldorf. It seemed as if no German city was out of reach of the Allied bombers. The Romanian city of Ploesti with its extensive oil fields and refineries began to get its share of notoriety as news of repeated bombings by the USAAF became more numerous. The German High Command kept talking about the high losses that the Luftwaffe was inflicting on the Allied Air Forces but I felt that all of it was propaganda. "Signal" devoted several pages to General Adolf Galland and how in his Me110 he was finishing off damaged American planes struggling to make it back to England. Other "Propaganda" talked about "secret" weapons the Reich was developing that would soon turn the war around and bring Germany to its final victory. Mostly, the secret weapons illustrated would turn out to be mini-tanks, individual anti-tank weapons and other minor equipment.

But in those early weeks of 1944, it was Monte Cassino that took front stage. The Allies were mired down on the Gustav Line and in front of Monte Casino, a mountain capped by a sixth-century Benedictine Monastery at its summit. Anzio, Salerno, Cassino saw ferocious battles between the well entrenched Germans and a collection of Allied troops. All this was reported daily, captured my imagination and fueled my despair. There were high discussions as to whether the Allies should bomb the monastery that was supposedly used by the German Army as an observation post, directing all the action in the valley below. The Pope intervened, pleading for the preservation of the artistic and cultural value of the abbey.

In February '44 the abbey was completely destroyed by combined air and field bombardments. I cheered the news, hoping that this would hasten the victory in Italy. German propaganda made a big thing of this "Barbarian" act by the Allies. After the monastery was reduced to rubble, the Germans reoccupied it and it became even more difficult to dislodge them from the ruins. The task of taking Monte Casino fell to the British 8th Army; however the actual fighting was being done by a heteroclite group of soldiers from all nationalities. There were the Commonwealth soldiers of Australia, New Zealand, Canada and India. Fighting groups from Poland, France, etc. were involved in the fiercest battles. And again, the Germans made propaganda of the fact that the English were letting others do their fighting.

"Monte Cassino and the ruins of the Monastery would not be captured until May 18, 1944, when the Abbey was finally conquered by members of the Free Polish Brigade. The battle had lasted 6 bloody months."

THE YANKS ARE COMING!

One March night, we were listening to a BBC program. It talked about the American troops who were massing and training in England. Suddenly, a song broke on the radio, a song I had never heard before. It was sung by a marching chorus. It swelled as it was passing by the microphone.

"Over There, Over There,

Send the word; send the word over there,

That the Yanks are coming, the Yanks are coming . . ."

I was stunned. The song was new to me and I did not understand a word of English. Yet, I knew what the song represented, I understood it and so did Mother.

The commentator came back on the air and said (in French): "Do you hear them? They are millions in England waiting to come and liberate you."

I was speechless. My heart was jumping in my throat. Hope for our liberation swelled in my whole being at the thought that we might indeed, some day, come out of our basement and be free to walk out again. And yet, it was impossible to believe, to conceive, could it be?

Mother and I fell in each other's arms and we cried, uncontrollably, softly, quietly. On that night, I had simultaneously reached the depth of my despair and the height of my hope.

AIR RAIDS AND BOMBARDMENTS

Almost nightly now, the sirens would wail. It meant that the Allies were flying overhead on their way to bomb German cities. "Signal" devoted pages showing the "terror" bombings over Germany and how great treasures of art and religion were being obliterated by the "propaganda attacks of the British Air Force on *Military objectives* like the Lübeck Cathedral, one of the most venerable monument of European culture". Signal seemed to forget that barely two years earlier; its pages had been filled with pictures of London and Coventry burning under the incendiary bombing of the Luftwaffe.

"Do you see London burning underneath us? I should hardly think the Englishmen are now singing their soldier song [The bells of hell go tingelingeling, for you and not for me] Do you think they are singing that now?"—Signal

It was now payback time and we enjoyed the sounds of the RAF plowing the skies over us on their way to Berlin et al.

Sure, the Allies had bombed Le Creusot, a suburb of Paris where France had a large automobile factory and according to the German news, hundreds of French civilians had died in this "terrorist" attack by the USAAF. In my mind, it was justified as the cars were for the German forces. The French casualties would have had to be exaggerated by German propaganda.

One March afternoon, as I perched at my usual observation place, the sounds of exploding shells filled the air. From the left, a twin-engine bomber lumbered into view, its bright white stars evident on the wings. Something in my brain announced "A20, US Attack Bomber". It seemed suspended for a moment right in front of me. I could see the airmen in the cockpit. Shells were exploding all around it. "Karoomft, karoomft, karoomft" puffing black smoke with each blast. The pilot was banking the wings left and right and then, they were gone, plane and crew. They had flown so low they had barely cleared the trees around the ponds. I was amazed at the *sang-froid*, the coolness and courage of those airmen I had glimpsed. I had no idea where the Ack-ack shells had come from. I guessed that perhaps, since the earlier raid by Jean de Selys Longchamps, some German battery had been placed in the vicinity of the Avenue Louise Gestapo Headquarters. Later, I wondered why the Germans had fired so close to the ground in the middle of a city. To my knowledge, no one had been injured by the shrapnel darting from the exploding shells.

There had been no sirens, no warning. The whole episode may have lasted three seconds or so. However, it stayed forever embossed in my memory. How brave were those men! Nothing could touch them. Where were they going? These two in the cockpit were the first Americans I had ever seen and the first Allied soldiers since the British had evacuated Uccle on that fateful day in May

1940. Somehow, it filled me with excitement and a renewed feeling that the war, the fighting, was getting closer. Perhaps we had not been completely abandoned. Something was at hand.

April 10th, 1944, it was Easter Monday, mid morning or early afternoon, I cannot recall. In Belgium, there is Easter Sunday followed by Easter Monday, which is also a holiday. Banks, schools, businesses were closed. To us, it did not make any difference, as we did not have daily agendas. However, the DeKnibbers had somewhere to go to and would be gone for most of the day. They had taken Fluffy along and would not return until the evening.

Since the day was so beautiful, I decided to take a risk and to venture to the third floor of the house, to the room where I had come to after my ear operation. As the DeKnibbers were gone, there was no chance that their relatives or "La Drogue" could trap me upstairs with a sudden visit. I had not told Mother that I was venturing upstairs. She must have been in the back of the basement and unaware that I had gone to the third floor.

The upstairs bedroom had a balcony. A Hindu curtain covered its windows. There, I would be able to have a much wider view than that visible from the basement. Unexpectedly, the little cat had followed me to the room and jumped on my lap as I sat on the large bed. I started to caress its soft body and was rewarded with a deep purring. All at once, the cat became agitated and struggled to get away from me. Fearing being scratched, I had to let it go. Simultaneously, the air raid sirens began to wail and the cat bolted through the door and down the stairs. Excited, I pressed myself against the Hindu curtains and strained to see what the alert was about. In the distance, I could hear the rumble of a large number of aircrafts. Planes began to appear to the left, high above the Etangs D'Ixelles. I studied the planes with the binoculars I had brought along on my foray. Clearly delineated against the blue sky, three squadrons of USAAF bombers flew in perfect tight formations traveling from West to East. There was no "flak". This apparition was very exciting as I counted the number of planes and tried to identify the type and model. There were three squadrons of twelve four-engine bombers each. I knew these were Americans as I could plainly see the Allied Star. My initial thoughts were "B-25 Mitchells"! However, they all did not have the distinctive twin tail and I could plainly see the four engines. No, these were B17 Flying Fortresses, the most famous of the Allied bombers. The fat ones with twin tails were B24 Liberators. I gave no thought to the fact that I should have been scared out of my wits.

The bomb bays were wide open.

Suddenly, from the middle of the second squadron, a rocket zigzagged down to earth, leaving a jagged white trail as it cut trough the air. I heard the whistling as if a white lightning had struck down. All at once, all the planes released their bombs in the same split second. The bombs screamed on their way down to the city. I watched in disbelief as time seemed suspended for a fraction of eternity. Then, explosions ripped through the air and flames, smoke and debris darkened my view of the city. A dark swirling shape (probably a pigeon as scared as I was) shot across my line of sight, shooting over the roof of our house. A single thought seared through my mind "Terrorist bombings, terrorists bombings!" My first instinct was to dive under the bed to find shelter. The bed was too low. I ran downstairs where Frieda was as frightened as I was. Soon, the steady wail of the sirens let us know that the raid had ended. The whole thing had lasted less than ten minutes.

The bombs had fallen on the borough of Schaerbeek, near the center of the capital and all around the North Station. The aim of the Allies was to cripple the German's railroad network so as to isolate the entire French coast in preparation for the planned invasion. Schaerbeek had important marshalling yards and the Americans had slammed it with "precision carpet bombing". This meant that instead of each bombardier aiming its bombs at the target, the entire group had dropped their bombs at the moment the middle plane was judged to be on target. The bombs had generally been on target but they fell among the rails and missed the bridges. Railways were difficult targets and little slow-down was achieved. However, damages to the Belgian civilian population and their homes were considerable. The Allies had seldom before bombed Brussels and the warnings of the air-raid sirens had been completely ignored by the population. Since it was Easter Monday, the children and most of the population were home. Hundreds perished. They died in the streets and in the rubble of their houses. After that raid, alerts were taken seriously and people would seek refuge in the many air-raid shelters that had been provided throughout the city. Although there would now be almost daily and nightly alerts, this was to be the only Allied bombing of Brussels that I would remember.

> *Yet, according to the records of the Eight AAF (Army Air Force) brought to my attention by John V. Nichols of the UK Brussels and its surroundings were bombed extensively seventeen times by the 8th USAAF between September 7th 1943 and August 3rd.1944. During those months the 8th Air Force also dropped tons of leaflets over Brussels on eighteen separate occasions. There were three additional bombing missions over Brussels that were recalled because of bad weather or low cloud cover. The August 3rd 1944 was the last raid over Brussels by the 8th Air Force. There would be five additional sweeps by fighter-bombers of the 8th in the last two weeks before the liberation.*

> *During the same perios, there would be light-bomber activity by the 9th USAAF over Brusels, mostly A20 Havocs and B26 Marauders flying very low that I chanced to see from my basement window.*

> *I am indebted to John V. Nicholls (john@nicholls-online.com. for the above data on the USAAF bombings of Brussels.*

As for Mother and me, we now took the air-raid alarms very seriously. Each time the sirens would wail, whether day or night, we would take refuge in the corners of the basement nearest to the street, Frieda in the west corner and me under the stairs leading to the entrance. We had observed that when a building was hit, its four main corners would often remain standing and thus offered the best chance of survival. To help our chances, we had fashioned crude helmets made of cooking pots, lined with small pillows and fastened to our heads with leather belts running through the pot handles. At every alert, we would huddle in our corner, with our cooking pots over our head and we'd stay until the "all clear" was sounded.

We weren't worried so much about getting injured or killed. At least I wasn't. What worried us was what would happen if the house was bombed and we would be uncovered. We would be there for all to see, especially our German neighbors. I'd be sitting there in my thinning terry robe and worn slippers. What would we be doing there? What were those Jews doing there, hiding? That was our real worry.

As April turned into May, raids became ever more frequent as more Belgian cities were bombed heavily. Charleroi, Courtrai, Ghent, Liège, Louvain and others suffered heavy damages. The Germans tried to make propaganda points by claiming that these were terrorist bombings of civilian targets. In some photos of dead civilians, they stressed that these victims had been "liberated" by the Allies. Most of the population understood that if the Germans had not occupied the country, there would have been no need for all these bombardments.

On June 5th, 1944, a short two months after the bombing of Brussels, we learned that Rome had been declared "an open city" and that it had been conquered (liberated?) by Mark Clark's Fifth Army on June 4th. While it was 1,500 km. from Brussels, it was still good news and we went to bed with a lighter heart.

JUNE 6TH, 1944 D-DAY

As usual, Mother and I were still asleep when Mr DeKnibber came bursting through our doorway at a few minutes before 8 AM on that June 6th, 1944. Holding on to the doorjamb, he was leaning into our basement and his voice was full of excitement. "I think something has happened. The Allies have landed, I heard the news on the Italian segment of the BBC, I could not understand it all, but I think the invasion has begun!"

The next segment, at 8 AM was going to be in German. Since Mother understood that language he wanted us to listen to the BBC to confirm that the invasion had indeed begun. We turned on our little Phillips radio and listened avidly. The preliminaries sharpened our appetite, first the announcements that this was the BBC "Hier ist London" and the ritual special messages albeit in German. After what seemed an eternity came the news. From the Headquarters of Supreme Allied Commander General Eisenhower, a special announcement: "This morning the Allied forces under my command have landed on the coast of France and the liberation of Europe has begun". Despite our initial disbelief, we fell in each other's arms, overjoyed at the prospect that we might be liberated at last. Fifteen minutes later, the BBC's broadcast in French confirmed the same news.

Whereas the BBC broadcast in German had referred to "D-Day", the French version was talking about "*Le Jour J*". Being a student of the First World War, I was familiar with the terms *Jour-J* and *Heure-H*, H-Hour that were always used for the time and the day when an attack had been started.

We tuned in to the Belgian INR to hear if the Germans would confirm the invasion but nothing was mentioned until much later in the day. There was a laconic message that an invasion had been attempted but that the forces of Third Reich were attacking the "invaders" and would soon push them back into the sea. Remembering the fiascoes of Saint Nazaire and Dieppe in 1942, I held my breath and hoped that this was the real thing at last.

As the day wore on, we strained to listen to each subsequent broadcast from the BBC. Ste. Mere Eglise had been liberated and the British and Canadians were advancing towards Caen, the first major city in Normandy. Despite the German's denials of Allied advances on that first day, it sounded as if the Allies had landed to stay. There were now new names to be learned and new pins to stab onto our map of Europe. I had trouble going to sleep that evening and could not wait until the next morning in anticipation of good news. From that day on, we no longer slept until noon. By eight each morning, it was BBC time and we hungered for the slightest encouraging news we could glean from the radio. On our maps, we followed the progress of the Russians on the Eastern front and that of the Allies in Normandy. At first, the advance in Normandy was slow and difficult but the front was soon consolidated. German propaganda gave glowing news on how the Allies were being thrown back into the sea with very high casualties. However, after a few days, even INR could no longer pretend that things were going well for the Axis. The official word was that the Wehrmacht was now containing the invading armies and that the Luftwaffe was inflicting huge losses on the invasion fleet. We now believed that there was a light at the end of the tunnel.

German propaganda made a few announcements about new and devastating secret weapons and on June 13th, the first V-1's were launched against England causing heavy damages and casualties mostly on the civilian population.

ENGLISH LESSONS

Now that there was more than a glimmer of hope that we would someday be liberated, I began to imagine how my first encounter with our liberators would happen. Somehow, I should be able to greet them and to express my gratitude. Since DeKnibber was fluent in English (actually in American), having lived and worked in Philadelphia for decades, I asked him to teach me a welcoming sentence. *Je suis tres heureux de vous voir* was my choice. DeKnibber translated it as "I am very glad to see you". Like a parrot, I pounced on the phrase and repeated it flawlessly. He was impressed at the ease with which I had picked up the sentence and suggested that I learn a bit more. A few days later, he brought me a small booklet of "Conversational English". Daily, I'd learn a few lines and some vocabulary. In a short while, I could remember and say nearly forty short sentences and perhaps one hundred words in addition to being able to count up to one hundred.

"Yes, no, willingly, good morning, please indicate how to get to the train station." "I apologize for troubling you" was one of my favorite phrases that I often use to this day. It does tend to get me in trouble whenever I approach a policeman and intone: "Pardon me officer; I apologize for troubling you but . . ." They tend to look upon me as if I was a wise guy, especially in *tough* cities like New York, Chicago or Los Angeles.

As it was, I was very proud of my budding ability to speak English and could not wait until I'd be able to put it to use. Each day I'd rehearse my initial greeting for our expected liberators: "Good morning, I am very glad to see you" I guessed that Frieda would break open that glass tube filled with coffee beans and brew a cup of coffee for the soldiers, be they English, Canadian or American.

Meanwhile, we continued to monitor the news and kept up our daily routine, hoping that each day's news would bring us closer and closer to our liberation. With the renewed hope, my daily anxieties had been slowly replaced with anticipation and impatience.

Although I did not know it then, somewhere in Amsterdam, Anne Frank, in her attic, must have been following the same news and anticipating her liberation. However, by August 4ᵗʰ, she would be arrested and deported with the rest of her family.

NORMANDY

After the euphoria of the first days, the fighting on the French coast began to bog down. Montgomery and Eisenhower were now in France but the Germans had apparently recovered from their initial surprise and the Allied advance appeared stopped. Mostly we heard of the fierce fighting for Caen and I began to worry that it might be months, perhaps years before we could be liberated. The Germans gloated that as long as they held the harbors of Cherbourg and Le Havre, the Allies could not bring in heavy reinforcements and that they would be contained near the beaches. I could not always reconcile the details given on the BBC and those being transmitted by the INR, Le Soir and Signal.

There was a joke making the rounds on the radio. American and British when asked where they'd prefer to fight, Italy or France, would chose Italy because: "I'd prefer to die at Milan (Milano) than at Carantan (in Normandy). The pun being that they'd rather die at the age of one thousand instead of forty.

For DeKnibber, it became harder and harder to obtain food rations as the supply lines all over western Europe were being cut off by daily Allied bombings. We were still able to get our herring and rutabagas but any other provisions had become extremely scarce. For us it did not make much difference except that the occasional fruit or sugar was now completely unavailable.

At the end of June, the port of Cherbourg was taken by the US troops but the harbor had been so completely destroyed by the Allied bombers and the Germans that it was of little use.

On July 9ᵗʰ, Caen was finally taken by the Canadians after more than a month of bloody fighting. It did not look good for the prospect of a swift liberation.

On July 20ᵗʰ, we heard the news that Hitler had been assassinated with a bomb placed in his headquarters. At last the monster was dead! The war would now end very soon, regardless of the outcome of the fighting in Normandy. Just a few hours later, the word came that the plot to kill Hitler had failed and that the Führer had survived. Another hope had been dashed as many had before. The prospect for freedom had been dashed once more.

By the end of July a General George S. Patton, at the head of his armored divisions was blasting his way through the German lines. At long last there was movement and a titanic battle was developing around Avromanche and St. Lo. A number of German divisions had been cut off and trapped in the Falaise-Argentan pocket. I followed each day's news with utter fascination. It would take another two weeks for the Germans to finally pull out and try to escape from the trap. On August 13ᵗʰ

Patton, more than two months after D-Day was now on the march. His advance would be swift and each day brought news of more and more French towns that had been liberated. On August 20th, Patton's Third Army crossed the Seine. The Seine, it meant Paris! I could not contain my enthusiasm at the prospect that the war had taken a turn for the better. Each day, new anticipation lifted my spirits and the pins on the map danced from day to day getting ever closer to Brussels.

On August 15th came the news that the Americans had landed in Southern France with little or no resistance. Familiar places like Marseilles, Toulon, Grenoble were liberated but it had little impact on my perception of the war. It did show that the German army was collapsing and that the Allies were on the march. These were incredible days of anticipation for us, still cooped up in our basement and still in fear for our lives. We hoped that our hopes would not again be dashed as they had been so often in the past.

In Paris, heavy fighting between the FFI and the retreating Germans had broken out on August 20th. The Parisians had erected barricades in the streets of Paris and were fiercely battling the Germans while the American army was advancing on Paris. Only a few rumors were reaching us as the BBC did not make much of the event and the German news was completely silent about it.

On August 25th, the Allies entered Paris and liberated it after more than four years of German occupation!

PARIS IS LIBERATED

The confirmed news that Paris had been liberated filled us with exhilarating anticipation. Paris, the premier city in Europe was free! Victory would soon be at hand. Paris was about three hundred kilometers from Brussels. I'd fantasize that if the Allies were to advance one kilometer each day, we would be freed in 300 days, ten months. With luck, we would be liberated by the end of June 1945, barely one year after D-Day. It was hard to conceive, a mere 300 days. One kilometer a day, that was not asking too much. And then I'd think that if the Allies could advance ten kilometer a day, we could be free in thirty days, one month. My head would spin, thirty days, how could it be? Of course, the nagging fear of a stalemate would soon curb my enthusiasm. In the First World War, fighting went on over four years over the same strip of territory that now separated Paris from Brussels. A few kilometers had been won and then lost over weeks of bloody fighting. Sure, Patton and Monty were devouring distances but what if the resistance stiffened?

The 300 days seemed so much more plausible. And even that seemed hard to conceive. Hunger, fear, danger had been relegated to the back of my mind. What mattered now was the news coming out of our radio, morning, noon and night, ever changing, Air raid alerts blared constantly and the Allies seemed to be in complete control of the skies over Brussels.

GERMAN INTRUDERS

A couple of days after Paris was liberated; I was looking out to the outside world from my little window. Suddenly, I saw four German soldiers come out of next door and enter our gate. A civilian was leading them to our front door. I ran over to Mother and warned, "The *Boches* are coming".

We never called them Nazis. They were either Germans or Boches. I didn't really hear the term Nazi until I arrived in the United States. For us they were all Germans regardless of the color of their uniform. By the time I landed in the USA, there was an effort to rehabilitate the German nation and to blame the whole misery on the Nazis. That distinction did not exist as far as Japan was concerned, the Japanese were "barbarians" and there was no effort made to separate the military from the general population. But, we never said "The Nazis are coming", it was the Germans or the Boches.

So, on that summer morning, I warned Mother that the Germans were coming and we both ran to the back of the basement and took refuge in the bathroom just as the Germans rang the bell. The small six by three-foot bathroom had no window, only a toilet. The bottom of the door was solid wood, but most of it was frosted amber glass. We closed the door behind us, did not turn on the ceiling light and waited, holding our breath.

When the bell rang, Mr DeKnibber came down the stairs, unaware of who the visitors might be. It must have been a great shock to see these five men, four in German uniforms, demanding to be taken to the basement. DeKnibber did not know that I had seen the Germans and that Mother and I had fled to the bathroom. He opened the door to the basement and to his great relief, we were nowhere in sight. From the darkness of our bathroom, we heard the voices in German and that of the civilian speaking French. We could not tell what they were saying. Through the frosted glass, we saw shadows passing and returning. They were on the other side of our glass door. We could hear their voices. They were maybe four feet away from us. My heart was beating so hard that it was painful. It was like a bass drum beating in my chest. I thought it was going to burst. I was sure they could hear my heart beating. I was scared. I pressed my body against Mother. I guessed that her heart was beating as loud as mine.

After a few minutes, the intruders were gone. I never understood how they did not hear the beating of my heart. It was so loud!

Mr DeKnibber called out to us that it was all right, that the danger had passed. We came out of the bathroom, still shaken. Mr DeKnibber was quite cool. He had kept his composure even though he knew we were in the basement and about to be discovered by the Germans. Had they looked around, they would have seen that the basement was occupied but they had not come looking for Jews. Because Paris had fallen, they had come in our house to see if they could tie a telephone line to ours thus doubling their ability to make and receive phone calls.

Just a few days later, the Germans came again. As before, I saw them leaving their small garden and enter through our gate. I warned Mother that they were coming and we hurried to the bathroom again. Mr DeKnibber, who had not been aware of the visitors, must have thought he was reliving a nightmare as he answered the bell and found himself face to face again with a half-dozen Germans.

They wanted to see the basement. DeKnibber held his breath as he opened the door. Relieved that we were again out of sight, he guided them through the basement. If the Germans had not heard my heart beating the first time, there was no excuse for them not to hear me now. I thought I was going to faint as I saw the silhouettes passing in front of the frosted door pane. The sound of my heart and the pressure on my temples made me retch. I could not throw up. I would not throw up. I kept my silence and tried to control my panic.

After a while, they left again. The Allies were moving very quickly and were approaching the Belgian border. In a few days they might be entering Brussels. The Germans had come to see if they could pierce the basement wall between our house and theirs and on to the next house. They expected that there would be house-to-house fighting and with the pierced walls, the Germans would be able to run and fight from block to block without having to venture out in the street. The prospect of having armed German soldiers passing back and forth through our basement was not reassuring. Even as they were being defeated and on the run, the Germans had not lost sight of their mission to rid Europe of Jews and despite the lack of time and arms, they still pursued Jews and tried to make sure that trains left Malines for Auschwitz to the end.

Luckily, the Allies were now advancing very fast. Brussels was declared an "Open City" where no organized fighting would occur. The Germans never had time to implement the extra phone line or the piercing of the walls. It was now time for them to get out as quickly as they could. Their time was getting short. I could not help but think that had one of these Germans had weak kidneys or a full bladder and had to use the bathroom, we would not be here to tell the tale.

LIBERATION

In the early morning of September 2nd, the Germans next door brought in three trucks and began to loot the house they had been occupying. Under the direction of an officer, the soldiers carried out files, boxes, furniture, silverware, paintings, light fixtures and everything they could carry out. Everything was then loaded on the trucks. Within hailing distance, on the sides of the ponds, a group of Belgian men was hanging around and observing the looting that was going on. Little by little they were coming closer and closer to the trucks in a narrowing circle.

A couple of soldiers appeared carrying three *Jerry Cans* of gasoline, a precious commodity at this stage of the war. I watched as a heavy German Corporal poured gas into one of the trucks. He had not been using a funnel and as much spilled on the ground as went into the tank. The officer in charge began to loudly berate the corporal calling him a *dumkopf* and a damned *schweinehund*. With the window open and feeling safe behind my curtain screen, I was not missing a word and enjoying the spectacle with total disregard for my safety.

By late afternoon, they got two trucks going, but the third one would not budge. The officer and all the soldiers left in the two trucks and an assortment of cars and motorcycles, leaving one lone soldier behind, ostensibly to guard the truck that would not start. The Belgians who had patiently watched the proceedings were now encircling the wounded truck, less and less concerned with the lone private left to protect the vehicle and its contents. The soldier found himself completely surrounded by the mob and wedged against the tailgate. He drew his pistol and fired twice in the air. The mob quickly pulled away and the soldier found his way out of the circle. The Belgians returned to the truck like flies to a piece of carrion. As they started to loot the truck, the guard prudently slipped away. In the space of a few minutes, the truck was emptied, even the tarp had been ripped away. The mob now ransacked the house that had been vacated. There was not much left after the Germans had looted it. However, the mob managed to rip out mantelpieces, doors, curtains and anything else that could be ripped off the walls. I could not help but wonder at the mentality of the mob. The house belonged to a Belgian family that had fled the invading Germans in May 1940. After the war the family would return to find just a shell of their former home. The Belgian civilians would have caused most of the damage.

As the evening fell, the mob had gone. The lone German soldier came back to the truck and placed a hand-grenade under the hood. He pulled the cord and hurried away. I watched as the truck blew up and started to burn. There must have been little gasoline in the tank as the truck burned for just a few minutes and did not explode. The house next to us was now empty and the Grey Mice as well as the German labor group in the adjacent houses had vanished.

We awaited the next day and went to bed.

There was nothing salient on the morning of September 3rd, 1944. We surely were up early and listened to the BBC. However, nothing special comes to mind about that morning. I guess we were waiting, just anticipating the momentous events that were sure to follow that day. From the city came vague reports of gunshots as the Belgian Resistance *(F.I., Forces Interieures)* was harassing the retreating Germans with small arms fire. Brussels was an "open city" but so many of the occupiers had stayed too long and were now trying to get out of the city ahead of the advancing Allies. The F.I. was taking potshots at everything German that moved, whether on foot or by car.

In late afternoon, one could hear vague noises far away, a bit like distant surf. The Allies were entering the capital from the South, from the direction of France. We knew that our liberation was at hand. Mother and I went upstairs to the DeKnibber's apartment. They had opened the french doors of the balcony and we lay down on the floor. The evening was mild and there was electricity in the air. We wanted to witness what was happening.

A man drove down the Avenue De La Cascade on a motorcycle. He had on a F.I. armband. We recognized him as Dr. Van Eyck, the same doctor who had operated on my ears two years earlier. As he rode by, he was yelling, "Put out the flags! Put out the flags! The British are coming! Put out the flags!

From every house around the avenue, flags came out from windows and balconies. There were Belgian flags, French flags, English flags and Red flags waving in the soft afternoon breeze. American flags were visible but were few in numbers as it was a complicated flag to sew together. Until that day, all those flags had been banned, as it was forbidden and dangerous to own, let alone display an Allied banner. Now, everybody was putting them out.

In the distance, the noises were getting stronger and stronger. It was now like a distant rumor, a vague chorus in the wings, off-stage. Suddenly, another man rode by on a bicycle, and he was yelling, "Pull in the flags! Pull in the flags! The Germans are coming!" Everybody started to pull in the flags from the windows and the balconies. A company of German soldiers came running down the Avenue de la Cascade. They were coming from the direction of the Gestapo Headquarters on the Avenue Louise and heading left towards the Place Flagey. They were running at half time with their rifles at port-arms. There must have been several platoons of them. This time, they were not singing as they used to during the occupation. All one could hear was the sound of their hobnailed boots going *cha-rump, cha-rump, cha-rump* on the pavement. They did not look left or right, they did not look up, they were just running as fast as they could. They were not looking at the people who were frantically trying to pull back the flags from the windows. As the soldiers disappeared down the avenue, the flags were re-appearing from the houses.

It was dusk now. The rumor had turned into joyful yelling and shouting. It was like a sudden flush rising from the streets and spilling over the roofs. We did not see any troops that night. We just knew we were free. Mother and I got up from the floor and we embraced. We hugged the DeKnibbers. We had survived. We were free. I was fourteen.

MORTE LA BETE, MORT LE VENIN.
(When the beast dies, so does the venom)

On that September 3rd, we did not venture out; it would have been too dangerous. It was the British 2nd Army that liberated Brussels but on that day, I did not see any English soldier. We could hear a lot of shooting echoing from the streets all over the city. There was furious though unorganized fighting all over Brussels as retreating Germans tried desperately to escape towards Germany. Artillery shells exploded when a German tank was caught and destroyed in the Rue Royale. We did not know the nature of the commotion but we could hear the explosions. The Germans were retreating on foot, with pushcarts loaded with personal or looted possessions. They were trying to make it back to Germany on bicycles, horse drawn wagons and cars. Along their escape route, the partisans and whoever had a gun were taking potshots at these remnants of the once mighty Wehrmacht. For days after the liberation, German cadavers remained in the streets where they had been slain. Some hung grotesquely out of private cars they had commandeered to try to flee. Germany had occupied and ruled us nearly four years and four months since I had witnessed their entry in Brussels on May 17, 1940. Now they were leaving. How sweet it was.

The F.I. partisans were settling private scores. They were rounding up collaborators, beating them up and shooting some in place. Mobs were seeking revenge. Poor Madame Yvonne, Mother's seamstress, who had been the lover of Franz Bauer, von Falkenhausen's chauffeur, had her hair and eyebrows shaved after being beaten by a crowd

My sister Ruth and Father, being hidden further south were liberated a couple of hours before us. They had left the safety of their hiding place to witness and cheer the Tommies as they were advancing up the Chaussée de Waterloo. Ruth and a young man had taken place on the steps of a house for a better vantage point. Shots rang out as the Germans were fighting a rear-guard action and the young man collapsed with a bullet in his chest. Although I was not aware of this, I wasn't about to go out in the street and pick up a stray bullet, not after having survived over fifty months of war.

That night, Mother and I went to bed with the window open. As we were trying to sleep, we heard a man's voice outside yelling "Move!" Another voice replied plaintively "I can't, my leg hurts" Then, there was a pistol shot and the first voice was heard again "Now, your leg hurts! Move!"

The following day, September 4th, Father and Ruth appeared at our hiding place. Because there was no regular municipal service in the bedlam of the liberation, they had taken a few trams and walked to the Etangs d'Ixelles and arrived in the late morning. I remember little of our first reunion except for one thing. When I had last seen Ruth, I had just turned twelve, now I was nearly fifteen. My voice was changing and had turned into a painful adolescent croak. When I greeted Ruth, she looked at me severely and admonished—"What have you done to your voice? You are going to change that immediately!"

In the afternoon, I decided that I would go downtown and join the festivities and the crowds that would surely gather about the *Bourse* and the *Place de Brouckere.* I put on my knickers and suit jacket. I had not gotten dressed in eighteen months and I guess my clothes and shoes must have been very tight. I went out of the house. The warmth of the sun and the gust of fresh air made me dizzy. I had to steady myself against the doorjamb. I could feel the sun on my face on that warm September afternoon. I was very conscious of the multitude of sounds that greeted me as I ventured into the street.

I got on a streetcar that was going to the *Bourse.* As I stepped onto the platform, a man, with a black bowler hat, looked at me and yelled "Hey *Youpin* (Kike) how come they did not get you?"

I felt my blood rush to my forehead. I was angry. I was ashamed and filled with anger and frustration. I looked at him and said, "What would you say if I called you a dirty Catholic?" I swung at him and tried to punch him in the face. He was much bigger than I was and my punch went wild, missing him. I did knock his hat off. I did not know who he was, never knew his name, never saw him again but that man crippled me emotionally for the next twenty years.

More than anger, there was shame. There was a man who, just by looking at me could tell that I was a Jew, and he insulted me "Youpin" for all to hear. It was not written on my face, I thought. And no one had come to my help even though the platform had been full of people. I never got to the *Bourse* but returned to my basement, my heart in pain and my spirit badly bruised.

Before the war, I had not been much aware that I was a Jew and "different". In Charleroi and Namur, we passed mostly unnoticed and being Jewish held no special stigma for me. With the advent of the war and the German propaganda, I had become painfully aware of the dangers and the penalties for being a Jew. The word alone had become an insult especially that it was always preceded by "dirty". What was more; I was no longer a Jew. Had I not been baptized Protestant?

In my *naivete*, my innocence, I had thought that this anti-Semitism that had been brought in by the Germans would be gone with them. The French have a saying, *"Morte la bete, mort le venin"* "When the beast dies, so does the venom" I thought this monstrous venom would be gone with the Germans. It was not to be. The virulence of the hatred for Jews had been there before and would remain. The Germans had simply made it respectable while they were occupying the whole of Europe. The beast was dead but the poison was still very much alive.

On that very same September 4th, although I would not find out about it until decades later, the same thing happened to Mother, Ruth and Solly Turin, Mother's childhood friend. Elated that they had all survived, they went to a restaurant near the Bourse. As they walked into the restaurant, some loudmouth yelled," Hey! Look at the *Youpins*! Look at the Kikes! They are coming out of the woodwork again" Solly turned around and ran out of the restaurant. Ruth, scared, looked for a place where she could hide. Frieda stared at the guy and pointing her finger at him said, "Look you! You are too late, or too soon! Now, you have to keep your mouth shut!" She had been right. It was then too late to be hunting Jews and too soon for the next wave to come along.

From that day on, I became ashamed of being a Jew. I denied that I was Jewish. I refused to be Jewish. I would spend the next decades trying to hide that I was a Jew, running away from it. All I wanted to do was change my name, not to be a Jew anymore. To me, being Jewish was a disease. I had it and I did not like it.

From that day on, I went back into hiding, a different kind of hiding, a denial of who and what I was.

END OF VOLUME ONE
PART ONE

Edited and revised : July 4th, 2011

Final revision and corrections. July 22, 2012

VOLUME ONE
PART TWO

(MEMOIRS OF RUDY ROSENBERG),

Rudy and Ruth (3 and 4)
Loverval, Belgium 1933.

Rudy and Ruth (3
and 4) Blankenberge,
Belgium, 1933

RETURN TO "NORMALCY"

While Antwerp had been liberated on the 4th of September, it would take another week for the eastern part of Belgium to be liberated by the Americans who would cross the German border near Aachen on the 12th. Clearly it was time to rejoice and on the 5th, I decided to go and join the festivities downtown. I do not remember how I wound up in the city, in the area of the North Station and the Rue Neuve just a couple of blocks from the Rue de Malines where we had lived in 1940. I must have taken the tram but because of my unhappy experience the preceding day it must have been erased from my memory.

The streets were teeming with people wanting to greet, embrace and kiss our liberators. Grapes of young girls and women of all ages surrounded the Tommies eager to smother them with kisses and more. Mothers were pushing their daughters to rush into the arms of the British soldiers. Brussels was theirs to enjoy. British trucks, though not running, seemed to be vibrating with agitation from within. There was happy insanity. With the British troops came a contingent of ATS's, British Army Technical Service. These young women, similar to the German "Gray Mice" and the American WACS, drove trucks, ran special services and generally performed duties that did not require exposure to the front. They were pretty in their dark blue uniforms, smart hairdos and emblemed caps. The ATS's took part in the celebrations. A young man I had never met planted himself in front of me and leering, gave me some tips on how best to approach them. Whether they wore a skirt or a pair of trousers, they had a pair of pockets over their belly. These front pockets had no bottom and if you were fortunate to drive your hands in them, you could go all the way and feel their "pussy". With that, he disappeared, probably to go and spread around his momentous revelations. Since it had not been part of my English book's content and having never heard the word before, I was left to imagine the meaning of my newfound vocabulary.

A Belgian Brigade had been part of the troops that liberated Brussels. Colonel Piron had formed his "Piron Brigade" among Belgian soldiers who had fled to England after the 1940 debacle. Eager to fight and to help liberate their Mother country, they had fought bravely in several theatres of the war. Colonel Piron had requested that his brigade be permitted to enter Brussels together with the British Second Army. That had been granted. The men of the Piron Brigade wore the same uniform as the British except that their insignia on the cap and shoulder patches represented the Belgian Lion. This made them recognizable from the British. There was a strange phenomenon, whenever someone would reach a "Piron" soldier, the interest would cool immediately upon discovering that he was a Belgian and the soldier would be dropped like a cold fish. It seemed that if you were not British or foreign, there was little interest in you. It was embarrassing and I felt bad for the Belgian soldiers. Some family and friends of the Brigade soldiers had rejoined them in Brussels and the relatives would complain bitterly at the crowd's rejection.

Nothing ever came of the coffee beans that Frieda had saved for the liberating armies. Mostly, the Allies lacked for nothing and the British were tea drinkers anyway. The coffee beans were forgotten. These would have made a nice souvenir from our days of deprivation.

The British High Command had requisitioned the suite in the Plaza Hotel that had once been headquarters for General von Falkenhausen. Somehow, the toilet had been booby-trapped by the

Germans prior to their retreat. As a British officer pulled the chain to release the water from the tank, a bomb exploded with a tremendous noise and blasted the side of the building. History did not record the final word of the unfortunate officer.

In the euphoria that followed the liberation, we slowly tried to regain some sense of normalcy and to resume a semblance of life as a family. Hilaire and Ruth had left the Fraiteur home hastily. There had been accusations (well founded) by Mme Cuvelier that Hilaire had carried on an affair with the daughter of the neighboring house. Father would have wanted to continue life with Marie-Jose D. but he found himself persona non-grata and forbidden ever to visit her again. The only place opened to him and Ruth at this point was with Frieda and me at the DeKnibber house

For a short while, we occupied both basement and the bedroom on the top floor of the house. I do not remember the sleeping arrangements but it is certain that Hilaire and Frieda did not share a conjugal bed.

As soon as Hilaire entered our basement, he dug up the three lead pipes we had buried eighteen months earlier. I helped as much as I could especially in the cleanup of the jewelry. Everything had to be placed in warm water so that the wax that had been poured in the pipes could wash away from the jewels. It was tedious work and I wondered what the wax had accomplished since no rattle would have been heard from where the jewelry had been hidden.

The value of the recovered pieces must have been considerable, worth several millions in Belgian currency. It would have been sufficient to enable us to buy a house, set up a new furniture business and rebuild our lives. As it was, Hilaire gambled it all away in less than three months. There was also the fortune in antique furniture, paintings, Oriental carpets and *objets d'art* that had been entrusted to the Croisiers. Over the next three months, Hilaire retrieved them all under the guise that he needed to sell them to finance new business ventures. They were all sold and the proceeds found their way to Namur and Ostende casinos where they were swallowed up in a variety of Baccarat and *Chemin de Fer* games. Later, Hilaire would try to explain this madness. He had done his duty and had managed to save our family. He had felt liberated, free of any guilt and had abandoned himself fully to his gambling demons.

Even with the zeal with which Hilaire plunged into his gambling addiction, it took a few months before we were completely broke. Fights broke out again and Mother would continually accuse Father of pretending to be *Un Grand Seigneur*, a big shot, dining with his cronies and women in restaurants where they served real butter while we had to be content with margarine at home. For Frieda, Ruth and me, we would soon again be left destitute and in need to scrounge for our daily existence.

Ruth and I were not fully aware of the melting down of our fortune and we enjoyed our newly found freedom. Somehow, the roller skates we had bought in Germany during our 1941 visit had turned up and we would spend wonderful September afternoons skating on the Avenue de la Cascade's asphalt, speeding from the heights near the Avenue Louise to the banks of the Etangs d'Ixelles. I discovered that although I was a right handed, it was more natural for me to take sharp turns to the left than to the right. This propensity would carry through in my life, whether walking, running, biking or driving a vehicle.

With the liberation of Brussels, "Le Soir" ceased to be a "collaborating newspaper" and resumed publication under a new direction and editors. In the last days of the occupation, my main interest in the paper had been the *Tintin et Milou* comic strip. We had been deep into "The Mystery of the Seven Crystal Balls "and the action had become very tense and animated. I eagerly awaited the resumption of the story when "Le Soir" was printed again. Much to my chagrin and dismay, my beloved Tintin & Milou had been banished from its pages together with Hergé its creator. Because he had collaborated with the occupiers and had his work published in the "stolen" Soir, Hergé was to be banned from publication for at least two years. Hergé had always displayed a bias against Jews, Americans and Communists and he now had to be cleansed before he could rejoin the ranks of honorable citizens. I would have to wait two years before I'd find out what happened to all the archeologists who had fallen in a coma after being exposed to a mysterious gas emanating from broken crystal balls.

Shortly after the liberation, I went to "Le Soir" with my notebook filled with the cartoons I had labored on during my time in hiding. I was ushered into the office of the artistic editor of the newspaper and presented him with the fruit of my humor and drawing skills.

The editor seemed interested but flipped through the pages without as much as a smile.

"Some of these are very good, but they cannot be used as submitted. The cartoons would have to be in "*Encre de Chine*", India ink, to be acceptable for publication"

With those words, he handed my work back to me and walked me out of his office. I could not be certain if the cartoons had any merit and might be acceptable when redone in India ink, or was he just being kind. Perhaps he had wanted to spare the feelings of a fourteen-year old boy who might have had no talent.

I never touched the notebook again, nor do I know what happened to it.

As September came to an end, it was time to resume school. We had been forced to abandon our studies in June 1942 and the Board of Education had to decide where Ruth and I had to be placed. For me I was assigned to the seventh grade in the *Athénée* Léon Lepage, Rue des Riches Claires, near the *Bourse*. This would provide three years of Middle school, in descending order, 6th, 5th and 4th, to be followed by College and later the University. As it was, I would be over two years older than my new schoolmates.

Right after the liberation and to satisfy the appetite of the population for American movies, a cinema was showing "The Adventures of Marco Polo" a 1938 movie starring Gary Cooper as Marco Polo and Basil Rathbone as the arch villain. Since this was the first Hollywood movie to be shown in four years, the cinema on the Rue Neuve was mobbed. It was a two-reeler and the first fifty minutes were dubbed in French. Once the projectionist switched to the second reel, it was in English but without French sub-titles. A near riot ensued, as the large majority of the patrons had absolutely no comprehension for the dialogue that these foreigners would gabble. Most wanted their money back. I was delighted to have a chance to practice my English but it was hard to understand anything among the general brouhaha in the theatre.

A week after D-Day, the Germans had begun to launch V-1 bombs against England and mostly London. On September 8th, just five days after the liberation of Brussels, the first V-2's were lobbed against London. Given that the Allies controlled the skies and that the Germans had lost all of their airfields in France and Belgium, the V-bombs were now the only way they could still terrorize England. The bombs had primitive and inaccurate aiming systems and would fall at random over the City of London.

The Allies had captured the Port of Antwerp, one of the largest in Europe and crucial to the supply route for the British and American armies. Antwerp had been liberated almost intact due to the rapid advance of Montgomery's Second Army. The Germans still occupied the Island of Walcheren that controlled the Schelde estuary and completely shut off the access to the sea. Until Walcheren was retaken in very bloody fighting, the use of the harbor would be denied to the Allies for many weeks; the Germans were determined to obliterate the Port of Antwerp with a shower of V-1's and V-2's.

From bases in Germany, The V-Bombs now aimed at London, Antwerp and Liège. Liège, close to the German border and with its converging roads and rail lines was a natural staging area for the Americans. Brussels, though not a direct target, was just in the way.

The V-2, an early ballistic missile (courtesy of Dr. von Braun) did not have the "terror" factor of the V-1. One could not hear or see the V-2 unless it happened to strike down right in front of your eyes. Also, it would strike with such velocity that it dug a deep crater with most of the force of the explosion going up in a deep "V".

The V-1, on the other hand, was audible, visible and gave notice that it was about to strike. The sound was unmistakable, a series of deep explosions, cough, cough, cough. It flew across the sky like an avenging black cross. When the engine cut off, it would nose down and fall to earth a few seconds later. As it had wings, its descend was slower than the V-2 and it would explode on contact leaving a larger radius of destruction.

As we had returned to school, our classes were constantly interrupted by the air raid alarms. A first alarm would sound as the V-1 was spotted crossing the border from Germany. A second alarm would sound if the V-1 passed Liège and we would then have about 10 minutes to get in the shelter. Liège and Antwerp were hit time and time again. The most notorious incident was the V-1 that hit a movie theatre in Antwerp and killed hundreds of civilians. Brussels suffered just a few hits in the capital area. Flak did not seem to be effective.

The RAF was trying to intercept and shoot down the V-1's over Belgium so that the "buzz bombs" would fail to reach London. Shooting down the V-1 was risky business as the flying bomb would explode and spray dangerous shrapnel at the attacking planes. A favorite ploy of the British fighter planes was to slide a wing under the V-1's wing and to tip it over. This would activate the switch that stopped the engine and the V-1 would plunge to the ground and explode. There did not seem to be much consideration given as to where the buzz bomb would fall and explode as long as it did not get over the Channel and strike England.

We soon became jaded as alert followed alert and few of the flying bombs came down on Brussels. Sometimes, when we were given a surprise test in class, we'd look at each other and openly wished that a V-1 had been launched so we'd have an excuse to leave the room and take refuge in the shelter where we'd be able to discuss the test among us. Our teacher would warn us not to take the test sheets with us but there were always one or two copies that made it to the shelter.

As the Allies pushed deeper and deeper into Germany, the frequency of raids greatly diminished and we wound up having to study more diligently.

THE ENGLISH

Along the various *chaussèes,* highways, a steady stream of Allied vehicles convoyed day and night through the city. They'd press north and east, five abreast, in the direction of Germany and Holland. I had never seen such an abundance of war materiel. The roads had been turned into one-way avenues with truck, jeeps, loaded tank-carriers and amphibious DUKWs, nicknamed Duck by the soldiers. There would be three lanes of traffic in the road and two more lines of vehicles on the sidewalks. We'd stare in amazement, how could anyone have ever doubted the inevitability of the Allied victory in the face of such overwhelming superiority of supplies. The convoys went on, five abreast, day and night. The Ducks and the amphibious armored vehicles had a rendezvous with the Rhine and Meuse rivers that were the last obstacles to the final invasion of Germany.

I had fallen into a lulling mood. The war was doing fine and except for the V-1 raids my mind was no longer following the developments with the same keenness that motivated me while in hiding. We felt that the balance of the year would see the Germans pushed back towards Berlin and it would be a matter of weeks before Hitler surrendered or was killed. The end was in sight.

Reality came down on me on September 21st when news came of the disastrous foray into Holland at Arnhem where the British, Canadian and American paratroopers suffered one of the worst defeats of the war. It showed that, although severely wounded, Germany was still a force to be reckoned with.

Meanwhile, the English soldiers stationed in Brussels had pretty much the run of the place. These were mostly service troops and they never carried any weapons. By and large, they were a jolly bunch. Ads had been placed in the newspapers and on the radio, asking anyone who spoke English to wear the Allied Star (five pointed white star in a white circle) so they could be identified. The English would then be able to know who to address themselves to should they need an interpreter. With the knowledge of my forty phrases and words, I felt confident enough to wear the white star on my lapel. It was certainly more fun than the yellow star Jews had been forced to wear during the occupation. The soldiers would take a look at this young boy and jokingly question if indeed I did speak English. With the daring of ignorance, I'd reply affirmatively and dive right into translations.

- Little boy to English soldier "Vous avez du chocolat?"
- English soldier to me "What is he saying?"
- Rudy "He want (sic) chocolate"

It worked like a charm and in the space of a few weeks; I could defend myself quite well in any situation, even negotiating prices for the English when they wanted to hire the service of prostitutes near the *Gare du Nord*.

It did bother me to hear the English constantly using "Ja" instead of "Yes". Once, on the tram, I complained to a soldier that we did not like to hear the word "Ja" as we had had to listen to it long enough when the Germans were the masters. The soldier seemed surprised and explained that the "Ja" was very common as an abbreviation of "yes". Somehow, I never became quite comfortable with it.

One day, Hilaire and I were waiting for the tram on the Boulevard du Botanique. When the streetcar came to a stop, an English soldier came off the tram and landed squarely on my Father's foot, crushing his toes with a heavy boot.—"Sorry" he tossed as he sped away. "Sorry" shot back my Father angrily. "What do they want from me with their "herring?" (*Sauret* being another word for herring) Hilaire was in pain but also very angry with the soldier. I could not help but remark the changes that we had witnessed. Had this been done by a German soldier during the occupation, not a whisper of reproach would have been dared.

German propaganda had accustomed us to "facts" about Americans. All Americans were cowboys, gangsters or drunks, or a combination of all three. When the British came, they told us that all Americans were cowboys, gangsters or drunks, or a combination of all three. When the Germans had told us that, we took it for just propaganda, however, when an ally told us the same, it must have been true. I was so disenchanted by Americans that I resolved never to meet any.

Frieda, who definitively had a weakness for uniforms, did her best to make the Tommies welcomed. One day she announced proudly that she had learned a new English word: Forever! That she explained meant 24 hours. With the arrival of the English came English cigarettes. At first, Mother would smoke one cigarette each day, at four 'o clock with a cup of coffee and a cookie. Pretty soon, she was smoking a pack a day and would eventually graduate to three packs a day. Ruth would take up the habit at about the same time with the same addictive results. Hilaire and I never took up smoking. Father once had a cigar and a cognac and got very sick.

THE BATTLE OF THE BULGE, THEY ARE COMING BACK

December 16th 1944, news came that the Germans, under General von Rundstedt had punched through the American lines in the Belgian Ardennes and were marching towards Liège. Several towns had been taken by two Panzer Armies and the American First Army was in a panic retreat.

After Liège, the next objective was to be Antwerp, thus cutting the Allies supply route. This would become known as "*La Bataille des Ardennes*" The Battle in the Ardennes, "The Battle of the Bulge". Once more, someone had been caught napping. The Germans had followed that invasion route in 1914 and again in 1940, now four years later, the Germans were again sprinting through the "impregnable" Ardennes. Von Rundstedt had led the invasion in 1940 and was doing it again. In a few days, the German armies had been nearing the Meuse River crossings and battlegrounds included the area where the Pension Sovet had been located and where we had been hiding for a few months. It was good that we had not remained there.

Hilaire and Frieda, worried that we might have to go back into hiding, decided to remove Ruth and me a bit farther away from the danger zone. They got in contact with Madame Pesch in Bruges and asked if they would take the children near the coast. It was felt that if the German advance could not be stopped, perhaps there would be a chance that Bruges would offer a safer haven than Brussels that seemed about to be overrun by the German onslaught.

Ruth and I were put on a train to Bruges with a small suitcase containing just the minimum needed for a few weeks. The future would determine what course to follow. It had been just three months since the liberation of Brussels.

In Bruges, Mr and Mme Pesch were waiting for us. They did not seem to have changed since we had last seen them in Zeebrugge before the war. Mme Pesch still wore a turban and smoked. She still "chipmunked" her lips and was constantly struggling to spit out tobacco particles from her mouth.

My friends Jean and Colette picked up our friendship as if we had never left them. There is a photo of Ruth, Colette and me walking through the streets of Bruges on that cold December day. On my lapel, one can see the Allied Star of the Interpreter. I look absolutely horrible and it is easy to understand why Mother used to complain that "When he was a boy, he was so good looking, but look at him now". I am also wearing dark rimmed round glasses. When I had returned to school, I had taken a math test and although I had all my answers correct, the problems I had copied were not the same as those that appeared on the blackboard. The teacher suggested that I should wear glasses. Since we were short of money again, we had gone to the Flea Market and had found a cheap pair that seemed to help somewhat.

Only Claudie Pesch, the eldest daughter was not in Bruges. She had fallen in love with a German soldier during the occupation much to the displeasure of her parents. When her lover had to return to Germany, she entered a convent and became a nun.

Jean took me around Bruges and showed me the road the Canadians had followed when they liberated the city on September 4th. Since the streets of the old city of Bruges were very narrow, the Allied tanks often had been caught in crossfire as they had been unable to turn their gun turrets and aim their guns. The Germans had been directing fire from the tower of the famed Belfry and the Canadians had not wanted to destroy this medieval relic.

One night, as we were walking along the canals of the city, we heard the roar of a low-flying plane. It was a German Heinkel 115 seaplane lumbering low at treetop level. Much to my amazement, I saw a V-1 attached between its pontoons and as Jean and I watched, the V-1's engine ignited with its characteristic "cough, cough, cough". The plane veered to the right and the buzz bomb flew off in the general direction of England. The Heinkel seaplanes had been designed to carry and drop torpedoes. This one must have been modified as a launching pad for V-1's. As their launch sites in Germany had been pushed back by the Allied advance, it had become harder and harder to reach London. What we had witnessed was a desperate attempt at bombing England. I never saw such an incident again. Years later I read that the Heinkel 111 had been used to launch V-1's, but the 111 was a land-based aircraft. The one Jean and I saw was indeed a seaplane, the He 115.

The heroic action of the American First Army, the Third Army under General Patton and the steadfast resistance of the encircled 101st Airborne Division in Bastogne had prevented the German armies from reaching the Meuse River, their first objective. By December 23rd, the German advance had been stopped and the danger of another invasion of Belgium had evaporated. Brigadier General Anthony McAuliffe, commander at Bastogne became an instant hero when he replied "Nuts" to the Germans' ultimatum to surrender. By coincidence, Bastogne has a yearly "Nut" festival in honor of the local walnut crops. Each year now, the added flavor of the McAuliffe reply gives a deeper meaning to the feast. Later, McAuliffe would be promoted to Major General and I was to briefly serve under him while with the US Army of Occupation in Germany, but that will be for a later chapter.

It was nearing Christmas and it was deemed safe to return to Brussels and rejoin our parents. We bade farewell to the Peschs. If my heart skipped a beat when I left Colette again, I cannot recall. She was as beautiful as she had ever been and her energy and charm had only increased tenfold since we had first met in 1937. Alas, she was two or three years my senior and ugly as I knew I was, I felt that I should keep my passions well hidden. I was never to see her or any other Pesch again.

As we got off the streetcar at the Place Flagey, on our way back to the DeKnibber house, we were greeted by a weird spectacle. A German soldier, in full uniform, carrying his rifle like a yoke on his shoulders was walking up the Chaussée d'Ixelles, apparently intent on surrendering to anyone who would take him into custody. He was wearing the soft garrison cap and the hated helmet hung over his gas mask canister. I guessed that he had been left behind when the Germans retreated on September 3rd. someone, probably female, must have hidden him pending the return of the Wehrmacht. Now that the attack in the Ardennes had fizzled, he must have realized that the jig was up and had decided to surrender. Had he tried to escape in civilian clothes, he could have been shot as a spy. In full uniform, he would simply be captured, placed in a POW camp and with a little luck, sent to Canada or the USA for the rest of the war. The incredible thing was that not a single person paid any attention to him. The last I saw of him, he was disappearing around the bend in the direction of the Porte de Namur, still carrying his rifle.

Upon rejoining Hilaire and Frieda, we were told that Father had found a suitable home for us all and that we would be moving out of Ixelles after the first of the year 1945. There was no recollection of bidding goodbye to the DeKnibbers. I was never to see them again.

This had been one of the coldest winters in recent Belgian history. The plight of the soldiers fighting in the Ardennes had been made worse by the cold and the snow they had to endure. When the battle began to ease up and the Germans gradually retreated towards Germany, Brussels became a rest and recreation area for the exhausted GIs. Until then, I had never seen an American soldier. One cold day, right after Christmas 1944, I had descended near the North Station to see if I could eat a waffle and perhaps a *cornet de frites,* a paper cone of French fries.

As I turned into the Rue Neuve, I came face to face with two Americans soldiers. They had apparently been plucked right out from the front lines and were still wearing their battle uniforms, boots and leggings, fatigues and combat jackets. Topping it all, the battered helmet liner was anchored to their heads with a leather strap. They were haggard and sported several days' growth of beard. To fight the cold, their hands were tucked deep in the chest pockets of the combat jacket and they walked along hunched against the December north winds. So, those were Americans!? The admonitions of the British (and of the Germans) came back to my mind and I resolved to steer clear of these men and to stay away from Americans in the future.

1945

You are my sunshine, my only sunshine,
You make me happy when skies are grey . . . .

AVENUE ZAMAN, FOREST

The First of January dawned and with it the promise that school would soon start again and all the vexations of the prior years would be left behind.

On that day, the Luftwaffe made a last desperate raid against Allied airfields and other targets of opportunity over liberated Europe. Eight hundred German planes attacked airfields in Belgium, France and Holland. Some pilots had petrol enough for one-way trips only and were forced to crash-land or bail out as their engines petered out. In mid-afternoon, I saw an RAF Bristol Blenheim being pursued by a German fighter plane. The Luftwaffe pilot floundering from left to right was lazily harassing the British plane, riddling the Blenheim with short bursts of machine gun fire.

The rear gunner must have been killed as his gun turret hung lifeless, pointing to the ground. It was a dreamlike scene, as if in slow motion, like a slow elephant being pursued by a persistent yapping mongrel. Yet, it was deadly. I watched the two planes disappear behind the rooftops and I wondered about this continued need to kill and destroy even as the war was winding down. The sights and sounds were to leave an impression of sadness in my mind that still persists to this day.

Avenue Zaman ran downhill towards the center of Brussels. It was in the borough of Forest about two or three miles from the center of the capital. We rented the full three-story house. In the back, a long narrow garden flanked the other houses and high-whitewashed brick walls separated the properties. It reminded me of the house on the Blvd. de L'Yser in Charleroi but more austere.

Hilaire was now dabbling in currencies and there was some money coming in. We had two semi-permanent guests who stayed with us for a while, both were members of the Allied Armies, both were Jewish. There was Mr Davis, a roly-poly Englishman from London. I guess that he was involved in a little black-market with Hilaire. He seemed forever in wonderment and exuded a refreshing *naïveté*. Whenever he would ask for something and that had been granted, he would squeal, "I may?" "May I have a slice of bread?" "I may?"

Harvey Fishman was a Canadian Jew from Toronto, very serious, handsome, with a dense mustache. Both Fishman and Davis wore the thick rough British uniform and they reeked of wintergreen, a mint that pervaded all they wore. We were convinced that the soldiers had been fed a special wintergreen and saltpeter diet that was designed to reduce their sexual desires. This would have minimized the usual problems that arose from having too many soldiers and too few willing women. Even the chewing gum they were issued reportedly contained the same calming mint. Fishman would get up in the morning and go to the kitchen and prepare his breakfast. Frieda would marvel that he did not have to go to the bathroom first and urinate. He was young still and apparently did not have to worry about an enlarged prostate.

Father had received a check from a Mme Kraus, a Viennese Jew who had paid Hilaire $20,000 in exchange for something I was not privy to. Unfortunately, the check was drawn on a Canadian bank and could not be cashed in Belgium. Hilaire entrusted the check to Harvey Fishman to go and cash when he would return to Toronto. I questioned Hilaire's trust of a complete stranger. Father replied that Fishman could be trusted "because he was Jewish". After a few days, both Davis and Fishman left Belgium. I never heard from them again. I never did find out if Fishman had been able to cash the check when he got to Canada and if Hilaire ever got the $20,000.

MY PEUGEOT BICYCLE

Although I do not recall asking for it, one day a beautiful bicycle materialized at Avenue Zaman. What a gorgeous piece of machinery it was, silvery blue with "Peugeot" stenciled in black letters on the main frame. With a five-speed *derailleur*, light and made of "*duraluminium*" it had all the lines of a racing bike except that it had slim fenders and regular cruising handles instead of curved racing ones. Dual hand brakes, an attached drinking flask, a pump and a leather tool pouch completed the picture. There was only one problem, the tubes in the tires were porous and every few kilometers I had to get off the bike and pump new air in the tires. The Peugeot and I would become inseparable. The bike gave me a freedom to roam that I had never known before.

Ruth had also received a bike, but more stodgy. Black, heavy and with a three-speed gear system in the back wheel, it was reminiscent of the Dutch bikes suited to the flat terrain of Holland. It also had a "Torpedo" brake that you activated by reversing the pedals to the rear. In a panic stop, you had to stand up and stomp backwards on the pedals while the bike slithered and slipped sideways.

The bike did have one right hand brake that worked on the front wheel. Ruth never did get the hang of the "Torpedo" and would rely on the single front brake. The porous tire was the only thing Ruth's bike had in common with my sleek machine.

In Belgium, bikes had to be registered and were issued a yearly, numbered license plate that had to be affixed near the front wheel axle. Each year, the color changed so the police could see if the license had expired and they would issue a "*contravention*", ticket payable at City Hall. At first, we did not have a registration. When we would see a policeman or gendarme ahead, we would dismount and walk our bikes right to them. We would then ask them for directions and continued on foot, pushing our bikes along. Since bikes required a license only when being ridden, we would thus escape the dreaded ticket. Some "*agents*" would look at us and tell us that we probably knew where we were supposed to go but that we were very clever indeed. We'd then proceed on foot until the law officer had vanished and we'd mount our bikes again.

Ruth and I had seen American war movies with dive-bombers. The pilots would yell out "Going down!", then bank their planes into a steep dive. Whenever Ruth and I got to a steep descend, we'd yell "Going down!" And went hell bent down the hill. One day, diving down the steep Chaussée D'Ixelles, Ruth's front wheel got caught deep in the streetcar track, a dangerous ever present trap. Panicked, Ruth squeezed the right-hand brake. The front wheel locked. Ruth and the rear wheel made a complete summersault in the air. Ruth landed on the pavement, unhurt but badly shaken. Ruth, by then nearing seventeen, decided that it would be more lady-like to abandon the bike riding and that was the end of our joint outings.

Ruth did not completely abandon the bike rides and would sometimes ride into the countryside with her friend Georgette. She related that on one occasion, as they were riding by some vegetable fields, they stopped and filched a couple of carrots. The irate farmer yelled at them and made a couple of disparaging remarks about very private parts of their anatomies to which Georgette yelled back "Perhaps, but you'd still like to dip in your cookie if you had the chance!".

It had been snowing in that unusually cold January 1945. As I rode down the Avenue Zaman hill, I heard a short cry, sharp, quick, like a wounded bird. A little girl had been sledding down the avenue's embankment over the fresh snow. She had overshot the sidewalk and slid under the wheel of a passing truck. For a moment, there was no more sound, all was silent in the pure Winter cold air. A spreading bright red stain marked the spot under the truck's wheel. The small body was barely visible. It was like a still life. Was it the first time I ever saw a corpse? I got back on my bike, standing and pedaling furiously, watching my breath float in the cold air. It felt good to be alive.

THE AMERICANS

Increasingly, the walls I had built against all things American were being eroded. Hollywood, with Gary Cooper, James Cagney, Errol Flynn, Gene Kelly, James Stewart, Cary Grant, brought us images of America and Americans that made us dream of that far away land. These movie heroes transformed my vision of America. I wanted to emulate them, be like them. It did not matter that

Grant and Flynn were English and Australian. To us, they were AMERICAN. The newly discovered music of Glen Miller and Jazz electrified me. There was no way my thirst for these and Coca-Cola could be slaked. Frieda would say—*Tu mangerais de la merde si c'etait Americain*—You would eat shit if it were American.

A few blocks from our house on Avenue Zaman, the U.S. Army had established an enormous depot where damaged war materiel was stored. It was a giant junkyard for everything from jeeps to tanks, all wrecked. Of course, it had to be guarded day and night as everything had value on the flourishing black market. The materiel was stored until a reclamation unit could salvage tires, seats, tarps, batteries and the myriad of usable remnants of war. When the war would end, most of it would be abandoned. However in the early part of 1945 this junk needed to be protected. A wire fence enclosed the field and there was just a single gate with a small shack for the guards.

There were usually two guards who pulled three-hour duty. Another team would relieve them for the next three hours. The quantity and types of trucks and tanks fascinated me and I began to hang around the depot. The GI's took a liking to me and I became a mascot and "gofer" to them. After school, I'd join them and I'd pull guard duty with them until past midnight. They'd give me money to go and buy sandwiches and coffee. Since meat was still scarce, the best I could get for them were sandwiches slightly buttered, with onions and tomato slices. There was always some extra for me and I'd delight in the crunchy feeling of the raw onion slices as I'd devour my onion-tomato sandwich. They would talk to me and tell me all about America. Day after day, my vocabulary and ease with English would grow. They would pass me "Yank", "Stars and Stripes" and marvelous pocket books. "Yanks" was filled with photos and cartoons. I'd translate the captions into French and it seemed that overnight, I became fluent in English.

When I wanted to, I had the free run of the depot. Often, I'd climb in the cab of a wrecked truck and imagined driving along a highway. The steering wheel and the on-the-floor gearshift held a special attraction for my imagination. As the tires were flat or non-existent, steering was impossible. The batteries had also been removed and nothing moved inside the truck. Now and then I'd find a truck that still had a live battery. The dashboard would light up as I turned the switch. The fluorescent fuel gauge needle would tremble and hypnotize me with its greenish glow. Wanting to possess such treasure, I'd smash the glass cover with a stone and would rip out the needle. Much to my chagrin, it would immediately become lifeless and dull. Dozens of dashboards were thus smashed before I came to realize that what was bright and alive in its glass enclosure became dull and inanimate once I possessed it in my eager hands. I was sure there was a life lesson to be learned somewhere.

Jim McLain was tall, lanky, long-jawed; he reminded me of Jimmy Stewart. He and another soldier would forever throw a baseball into a catcher's mitt. It was a strange ritual with arm movements like windmills, high leg kicks and mysterious incantations. "Coom baby, coom baby". The exercise seemed futile. One threw the ball into a glove and the guy who held the glove would throw it back to the first guy. We were not used to throwing a ball. When we had a ball, we kicked it.

There was Carl DelVecchio, he said he was Italian. Broader than McLain, olive-skinned, always seeming in need of a shave and with a thin mustache, he said he lived in Newark. I thought he did not know how to pronounce New York. He was usually the catcher to McLain's throws.

They smoked continuously, mostly Camels. They seemed to feel that smoking made the cold nights more bearable. They'd give me a lit cigarette to hold. I would not smoke it but would cup it in my hands trying to extract some warmth from it. It only provided warmth if I held it close enough to burn my skin.

One night, McLain used the word "a lot" while talking with me. I had never heard the expression and asked him to explain what it meant. He said it meant *"many" "beaucoup"* he said in French. Suddenly he fired his carbine three times in the air. Within minutes, eight MPs arrived in a couple of jeeps to investigate why shots had been fired. McLain explained that he had seen shadows running around among the vehicles in the depot. He had fired warning shots to drive intruders away. The MPs looked around the depot, flashlights piercing the night. They found nothing and after a while, they left. When they were gone, McLain gave me a wry smile. "That was *a lot of* MPs" he explained.

My favorite was Bruce, Bruce Flansburgh from Philadelphia. His real name was Arthur J. Flansburgh but all the others called him "Bruce". Always, as they called him Bruce, it was with a tinge of irony in the voice. It was not mockingly nor sarcastic, just as if there was an inside joke I was not privy to. Bruce would always walk forcefully, swinging his arms in unison, like windshield wipers across his body, a la John Wayne but with more energy. His garrison cap (they would refer to it as "Cunt cap") at a rakish angle, gave Bruce a jaunty air. The Philadelphia A's were his team even though they were perennially in last place in their baseball league. Each issue of Stars and Stripes had the latest baseball scores and standings and Bruce would moan at the news of the A's foundering in last place. He'd tell me about Hoffstetter who was supposed to be a great pitcher although I did not quite know what a pitcher's duties consisted of. And then, there was Joe Di Maggio, "Joe D" "The Yankee Clipper", even though he played for the New York Yankees, Bruce ranked him among the greatest player of all times.

Bruce had a relation with Lisette, a young Brussel's girl of the neighborhood who would come and join us during our talks. She'd bring him more tomato/onion sandwiches and Bruce would sometimes leave with her at the end of his guard duty time. I never knew how serious the relationship was as they were not very demonstrative in my presence. Lisette would give Bruce a peck on the cheek when they would greet and that was that. Bruce was married and had a wife in Philadelphia named Jane.

Each night, I was told how he had met Jane, when they were engaged and all about the wedding. His description of the church ceremony was always well detailed and he'd relate every facet of the wedding. I soon came to know all about it and so did Lisette. Poor Lisette, though she was sweet on Bruce she was aware that there could be no future in their relationship. I guessed that Bruce had to keep some distance between them as he was bound to return to the conjugal life that awaited him back in Philadelphia.

In the years that followed, when it seemed possible that I might make it to the USA, I wrote Bruce a letter telling him that I was looking forward to visiting him in Philadelphia and to meet Jane whom I knew so well thanks to his descriptions. I was shocked to receive a reply from Arthur ("Bruce" had been dropped) telling me the sad news that Jane had died after a short but fatal illness. I replied with a letter of condolences expressing my chagrin at the loss of such a young bride. Another letter arrived, this time from Arthur's Father. In it he explained that Arthur had never been married and that he had invented Jane so that he would not have to get too serious with Lisette. Upon hearing the news of my imminent visit, he had to get rid of Jane and thus "killed" her.

The remarkable thing about my American apprenticeship was that my collective teachers never cursed or used foul language or four-letter words in front of me, with the possible exception of the aforementioned "cunt-cap" that was more descriptive than rude.

It was a sunny afternoon in February and we had opened a few windows in the house at Avenue Zaman. Suddenly, bright, loud Glenn Miller music flooded the house. The sound came from a neighboring house. In quick succession, "In The Mood, Stardust, American Patrol" and other Miller tunes came blaring in my ears. What radio station might be broadcasting such great music? Frantically, I turned the radio on and flipped from station to station to be able to receive the program. There was nothing there. After a while, I realized that someone in the next house was playing Glen Miller records on a Victrola. How hungry I was to hear more. The window on the third landing was open and I climbed out on the sill and leaned as far as I could better to hear the music that charmed me so. As I strained to see and hear, I lost my balance and began to fall forward. I was going to fall three stories to the courtyard below. Desperately I reached back and was able to grab on to the edge of the window and I regained my balance. I never told anyone.

A few days later, Frieda and Hilaire, all monies gone, separated for good this time. Renting the entire house at Avenue Zaman was no longer possible and Mother rented a small apartment on the Place Madou and Hilaire moved to a furnished room on the Rue Hydraulique. For me, it meant saying goodbye to my American friends and Lisette.

PLACE MADOU

Boulevards ringed the heart-shaped center of Brussels. Place Madou, at the edge of the borough of Saint Josse stood at the head of the Chaussée de Louvain that headed east in the direction of Louvain. The four-story building at 5 Place Madou had previously been the site of the Cinéma Madou but had been converted in the late 1930's into an apartment building with the Maison Dunesme, a beauty salon on the ground floor. A wide staircase led to a door that opened onto the first floor where Madame Dunesme had some rooms; from there, another staircase snailed to the second landing where Frieda had her apartment. The landing was part of the rented space as it had a sink and a gas stove for Mother's use. A door opened onto Mother's apartment, a large room with two balconies opening over the Chaussée de Louvain.

A Madame Sarto occupied the apartment on the third floor. Ruth and I each had a room in the converted space on the fourth floor. Our rooms were minimal with a cold-water sink and no toilet facility. The rest of the fourth floor was an unfinished attic that had previously served as the projection room for the cinéma. There was a hole in the brick wall that I would squeeze through. There, among broken bricks, the floor was littered with snippets of 35-mm movie film, remnants of the days when movies were projected to the theatre below. I'd spend time holding these to the light to try and see what movie they had been cut from. Although I could not see anything or recognize anyone, they filled my head with dreams of Hollywood where I yearned to go some day soon and where Mother always said that I'd become a famous director.

My room had a high attic window. A bed, small desk and chair completed the inventory. On the desk, the guts of a radio provided music and news. It had no cabinet and glowed with an eerie glaucous greenish light. From the ceiling, a single bulb provided light. A chamber pot waited under the bed in the event I did not make it to the toilet on one of the landings. Ruth's room was basically the same with her own sink and radio. One day, as Ruth was doing acrobatics trying to wash her feet one at the time in the sink, it collapsed and crashed to the floor. I do not recall if Frieda was upset but it was soon replaced with a new one.

From our "residences" we could see the Rue de la Charité and one block into that street, turning left stretched the Rue Hydraulique where Hilaire had rented a furnished room. Thus, Father lived about one hundred meters from our apartment but we seldom saw him.

The Rue de la Charitĕ, Street of Charity, housed a *bordello* with prostitutes that catered strictly to the clergy. It was fun to watch from Mother's balcony, as Catholic priests, in full habit, would regularly enter the Charity whorehouse ostensibly to minister to the poor creatures.

Place Madou was much closer to the school I was now attending than Avenue Zaman. There was a taxi stand and a streetcar stop on the Place and it was a short ride to the Bourse where a quick four-block walk would get me to the school. Being a schoolboy, I was granted a special reduced pass to use on the streetcar. Such a pass could only be used to travel to school on schooldays and never on Sundays or holidays or in the evenings when school was not in session. On one occasion, there was no school and I decided that I was going to take the tram to go fishing in the country. It did not take long for the controller to figure out I was not going to school, especially since I was carrying a fishing pole. No amount of pleading would dissuade the tram employee and my pass was confiscated.

Ruth also had gone back to school. Nearing seventeen, she had developed into a very attractive young lady. Her charms combined with a keen intelligence enabled her to capture many a heart especially among our American liberators. In March 1945, Ruth brought home a young GI by the name of George Metalik. He was dashing, polite and personable. Mother and I took a liking to him even though we only saw him briefly. George was a combat engineer and on a short furlough in Brussels. He soon had to rejoin his unit in Germany.

On March 5th, the Allies captured Cologne, the city of Frieda's birth. A few days later, the American First Army crossed the Rhine at Remagen after the Germans failed to blow up the bridge. However, the bridge had been seriously damaged by German artillery and the Combat Engineers were sent to try and repair it. It eventually collapsed killing a great number of the soldiers desperately trying to salvage it. We heard that George Metalik was among those who died at Remagen. He was all of nineteen.

BACK TO SCHOOL

There was a choice to be made as I started school again after a three-year interruption. I had been designated to attend the Athénée Léon Lepage. It had two sections: the *Modernes* and the *Greco-Latines*. The *Greco-Latines* guided you to higher spheres of learning and was a prerequisite if a career in Medicine or Law was planned. In the sixth and fifth grades, Latin would be taught, with the addition of Greek in the fourth. The *Modernes* would teach "useless" things like German, English and Spanish. Dutch, the second language in Belgium was taught in both sections. Somehow, the *Latines* students looked down on the *Modernes* and it seemed the place to go for me as I fancied that I might like to become a medical doctor or maybe an astronomer.

We were a varied bunch when we started our 6th Latine in that fall of 1944. Most of my Christian classmates were twelve or thirteen, while I, together with five other Jewish survivors was nearing my fifteenth birthday. Our class must have been comprised of two-dozen students, only a fraction of these made a lasting impression. As is the custom in Belgium, most were known to me by their last names only; the brothers Petitjean who may have been fraternal twins, kept pretty much to themselves. They reminded me of Gilbert and Jacobus at the orphanage as one was heavy, the other thin as a necktie. I do not believe that we spoke more than fifty words in the two years we wore out our pants in the 6th and 5th Latin. Maggi's distinction was that his Father owned an Italian restaurant three blocks away from the school and that made him special as there was an aroma of wealth that came from owning a restaurant. Maggi's face was round with sunken eyes and he always looked as if he was about to burst out of his too-small jacket and knickers. When Maggi smiled, his eyebrows would narrow and take on a downward slant that gave him a look of cruelty that mirrored his demeanor. Gilbert was about the tallest in the class and ran around blushing with a perpetual erection, especially during gym classes. All the other fellows made fun of him and called him *une tapette*, queer, behind his back.

Only three of my classmates were known to me by their first names, Maurice Goldman, Robert (Bob) Van Meckeren and Roger Somme Maurice and Bob became close friends of mine although the same cannot be said about them, as they cordially disliked each other. They felt that the other was a rival in their affection for me. Although I was to share the same desk with Roger Somme for the next two years, we never got to be on first-name basis, he remained "Somme" and I, "Rosenberg". Somme had a mean laughter and a disconcerting way of snickering at the slightest incident. If I were to ask him to lend me an eraser or any other class item, he'd snicker and say "Yes that will be two francs" Often, as I prepared to write on a fresh page in my notebook, Somme would slash a line with a pencil across the page. I'd take my eraser and try to rub out the line. Somme would then place his pencil against my hand and the more I erased, the more his pencil would mark my notebook following the pattern of my hand as I tried to erase the subsequent lines. It was a losing battle and I'd wind up having to tear off the page and start again, hoping that Somme would not repeat his action. I did learn a valuable lesson: It takes less time to soil something than to clean up afterwards.

Besides Goldman and me, there were four other Jews in our class. They were ultra Orthodox Jews who followed their religious rules to the extreme. With my lack of knowledge of Judaism I could not figure out what motivated them and what tenets they were following. I could not understand why these four would go out of their way to proclaim that they were Jews when I wanted so much not to be taken for a Jew. They had been seized by the Germans in one of the last raids and had been shipped to Malines to await the formation of a convoy to Auschwitz. They had been part of the last deportation train that had been blocked when the British troops liberated Malines on September 4th 1944. They had been saved in extremis. For them this was a sign of divine intervention by Jehovah who had personally reached down from the heavens and had saved them from certain death. Maurice and I had continuous arguments with them. Although we did not yet know the monstrous proportions of the disaster that had befell the Jewish Nation, reports of camps being liberated in the East were flooding in more and more with each passing week. Maurice had lost his mother and his brother in the camps and it galled him that this quartet could give credit to a "non-existent god" for having saved their lives. Why had their god not lifted a finger to save the millions of Jews who went to their horrible death in the killing camps?

Kruman, Herentreu, Hansbacher and Friedman were referred to as *The Orthodox*. All of us six Jews were at the head of the class. Kruman, small and puny was the brainiest by far. Like the others he dressed only in black with a white shirt. His hair was closely cropped and there was no indication that any facial hair would dare to grow on him. We'd call him Truman or Einstein.

Herentreu, dirty blond, tiny and sickly looking was a paler version of Kruman. There was something unhealthy in his appearance. While Kruman was able to explain his many theories, Herentreu would get lost in his own explanations and would soon lose the attention of his listeners.

Hansbacher and Friedman, although they were already bearded, sporting payesses and wearing a *tallitt* were the most likeable of the Orthodox. Hansbacher was witty and glib; Friedman had a sense of humor and was an adroit debater. He was unable to exhale as he was talking and instead aspired when he spoke. This meant that he could only speak in very short sentences. He had memorized many Latin phrases but could only manage to say the short ones and inhaling at the same time. It was funny to hear him declaim *"Aquila non-caput musca"* in a cavernous tone that sounded as if the Frankenstein monster was about to croak. We liked each other but lived in completely different worlds.

The *Orthodox* had only one dream, to go to Palestine and help form a Jewish State. Maurice Goldman, the glibbest of us all was a professed Communist and could talk for hours about the proletariat and the oppression of the masses by the evil of capitalism. There was always a glint in his eyes and an air of jest that made his arguments palatable. The *Orthodox* were Jews, Zionists of various political leanings, Maurice was a Communist and he always wanted to know what I was. Invariable I'd reply "An American". He'd scoff that "American" was not a political philosophy. Stubbornly I'd repeat that I was an American. That was the only thing I wanted to be. I wanted to leave this old Europe and go to the United States. America was my dream!

The Orthodox would not come to school on Friday afternoons or on the Saturday mornings. I had no idea that it was because it was the Sabbath. However, when the quartet would return on Monday mornings, they were subjected to verbal abuse by some of the teachers. Monsieur Narcisse, our art teacher, was particularly vicious, yelling and insulting them. As they would not respond Narcisse would become more and more violent and would grab them by the nape of the neck and throw them to the floor and pummel them with his fists. When I tried to intercede on their behalf, he'd curse me and would knock me to the floor. No one, teacher or principal came to our rescue or tried to put an end to this brutality.

APRIL 1945 DEATH OF PRESIDENT ROOSEVELT

There was still a war out there and in the Pacific. For us, it all seemed far away now. The conflict in the Pacific was remote at best. On the European front, the British and Canadians were pushing into Holland and would finally take Arnhem. The Russians had entered into Austria and Vienna was theirs. All over Germany, city after city fell to the Allies. All that was left was to capture Hitler and force the Germans to capitulate. It was now just a matter of time.

On the twelfth of April, we were shocked by the news that President Roosevelt had died. There now remained only two of the giants that had been so instrumental in defeating the Axis, Churchill and Stalin. I felt a deep sense of loss; one of my heroes had suddenly died. For a moment I feared that the whole Allied edifice would now collapse and that Hitler would be reborn. In his lair in Germany, the Fuehrer had felt the same way. He regarded Roosevelt's death as a sign that providence would smile on him again and that, with the help of his "secret weapons" the tide would turn and Germany would again emerge victorious. The radio informed us that there was now a new US president, a Harry Truman. He did not inspire me confidence as I had never heard of him before.

By the end of April, the British and Americans liberated the concentration camps of Bergen-Belsen, Buchenwald and Dachau. Tales of horror and photos filled the airwaves and the newspapers. Almost immediately, the Red Cross and military services began to repatriate the camp survivors. Near *the Gare du Midi*, the South Station, crowds of people gathered to see if any of their missing relatives had survived. I joined the onlookers as I felt that I wanted to witness that part of history, the returning of the deportees from the death camps.

The Place de la Constitution, near the South Station was crowded with the pitiful survivors of the labor and death camps. These wrecks still clad in their striped camp garbs and round caps were barely human, gaunt, emaciated, just skeletons draped in shiny skin,. To add to their humiliation, they were instructed to drop their trousers and open their shirts so that the health officials might spray them with disinfectants. After that, bowls of steaming soup were distributed and eagerly grabbed by bony fingers. How strange it was to see walking cadavers with toothless grins slowly sipping a cup of broth. Fascinated, I looked on forcing myself to observe and remember all that I witnessed, never to forget it.

A story went around of a survivor standing naked, awaiting his disinfectant dousing and modestly holding on to his striped cap to cover his privates. The pretty Red-Cross nurse encouraged him to drop the cap so that she could spray every part of him. He let go of the cap, but it did not fall, it just hung there defying gravity.

As April 1945 came to an end, US and Russian soldiers met near Torgau. The West and the East were now joined. On the 28th, Italian partisans killed Mussolini and two days later Hitler committed suicide in his Berlin bunker. Although the end of Mussolini was well documented, that of Hitler left me with a nagging doubt. Was the monster really dead or had he escaped justice?

FIRST OF MAY 1945

The first of May had always been very special to me. It was *Le jour du travail*, Labor Day in Europe that brought me back to the workers' parades in Charleroi. Although perceived as a communist and socialist holiday it was observed by virtually everyone regardless of their political affiliation. The first of May would signal the return of spring even if it came six weeks after the official date for it. May first was also the day when the *muguet des bois*, Lilly of the valley, made its first apparition on the stalls of flower shops. In streets and public squares, peddlers walked about with large baskets full of *muguet* hanging in the crook of their elbows. Depending on the location, the flowers sold in small bunches tied with rubber bands for 5, 10 or 25 francs.

During the German occupation, all May Day demonstrations had been strictly forbidden since it was a "Communist holiday". In the late 1950's, at the height of the Cold War, President Eisenhower, concerned that the US labor movement continued to celebrate May Day, decreed that henceforth May first would be known and celebrated in the USA as Law Day. Henceforth, Labor Day would be celebrated on the first weekend of September.Does anyone still remember "Law Day"?

This May Day was going to be the first to be celebrated since 1940 and I decided that I would bike to the woods of the *Forĕt de Soignes* for a glorious day in the country and to pick fresh *muguet* in the forest. I could feel the weight of my faithful Peugeot bicycle digging in my right shoulder as I carried the bike down from my room in the attic. Once on the street, I rode the 8 miles to the forest in the early morning. I felt so free and elated, listening to the hum of the *derailleur* as I sped along the Avenue Louise and through the Bois de la Cambre, the lovely woods near Uccle. From the woods, it was a short ride to the heart of the forest. As my lungs filled with the cool fresh air of the morning, I felt a sense of freedom and independence I had never experienced before. I felt light-headed, happy, serene and free.

The forest yielded no *muguet.* The woods were too dense, wet and cold. Here and there, I could see the plants huddled around the base of the large oaks but it would take weeks of sunshine before any flowers would bloom. All I managed to do was to get sopping wet from my shoes to my head. I had not realized that the *muguet* that was sold in the shops and on the streets of Brussels came from greenhouses. "Another lesson?"(El Gallo in The Fantasticks).

As I entered deeper and deeper in the forest, I made another discovery. In every clearing and on both sides of every path, tons of ammunition had been laid out in large mounds. Mostly these were stacks of British artillery shells tightly hidden from German observation planes with the complicity of the forest. As far as I could see, rows upon rows of thousands of live shells had been stashed away pending transportation to the front. Now that the war was nearly over, these would remain hidden in the woods possibly until they were needed for another conflict. I could not see how all these explosives could be safely removed and shipped back to England or the USA.

By then, all thought of *muguet* had left my mind. The bright brass casings fascinated me. At one end, a large brass cap was clamped to the shell and showed target-like circular rings. It was obvious to me that these caps could be removed, revealing the explosive propellant hidden inside. After several unsuccessful attempts at prying open the shells with my bare hands, I remembered that I had a tool kit on my Peugeot. I soon produced a metal screwdriver from the leather satchel hanging under the seat. I wedged the blade of the screwdriver between the cap and the body of the shell and with the help of a large rock I hammered away to pry the detonator cap loose. The shells were stuffed with rope-like lengths of cordite explosive. Each shell looked as it had been filled with thick spaghetti but of a deadly nature. I pulled out several fistfuls of the cordite and stuffed these in my shirt to take home. As I biked home in the afternoon, I began to sweat profusely with the realization that I could have blown the entire forest and myself to smithereens.

Back in my room and for several days after this adventure, I spent much time making paper airplanes and strapping a string of cordite between the wings. I'd then light up the cordite with matches and watched as the airplane became a jet-propelled buzz bomb flying erratically around in the attic of Madame Dunesme's house.

The First of May had indeed been a lucky day for me.

MAY 8ᵀᴴ, 1945 THE WAR ENDS IN EUROPE

During the first week of May 1945, we were flooded with reports that the German armed forces were surrendering in all theatres of operation. Hundreds of thousand of German soldiers, sailors and airmen streamed to the West to be captured by the Americans and the British rather than surrender to the Russians. Russia having been devastated by four years of German occupation, its troops were to be much less lenient towards the war prisoners. On the 4ᵗʰ, the German troops still occupying Holland and Denmark laid down their arms thus finally ending their five years of occupation.

On May 7ᵗʰ, 1945, German General Alfred Jodl signed the unconditional surrender document at General Eisenhower's French headquarters in Reims. The war in Europe was officially ended; three days short of five years after the German troops invaded Belgium and Holland, eleven months after D-Day and at the cost of over thirty million lives.

General Jodl would be tried in Nuremberg, found guilty of war crimes and hanged in 1946.

May 8ᵗʰ, 1945 was proclaimed as V-E Day by Churchill, Truman and Stalin. Victory had come to Europe at long last. Spontaneous celebrations were held all over the world. In Brussels, delirious throngs gathered in all the public squares but the major celebrations were centered at La Bourse and the Place de Brouckere in the center of the capital. I soon found myself on the upper steps of

La Bourse, the Stock Exchange. From that vantage point, I could see a mass of humanity, an ocean of faces swaying, dancing and yelling. Hundreds of people crowded the streetcars and dozens more rode on their roofs. It was pandemonium. Someone next to me had a case of firecrackers and would lob them into the crowd below us or onto the crowded roofs of the streetcars. People screamed as the dangerous projectiles exploded among them. Since the streetcars could not move freely because of the mass of people surrounding them, the hapless passengers had no place to run or hide to escape the exploding firecrackers.

The man handed me a stick and lit the wick. I lifted my right hand behind my head to get in a better throwing position and the firecracker exploded in my hand. My fingers were badly burned and I thought I was going to lose my hand. The man laughed and told me that I had to scrape the wick with my nails to slow the burning process and that I would have to underhand the sticks so they could be thrown before they exploded. I threw maybe a half dozen firecrackers into the crowd on top of the streetcars but soon desisted as I could see the horrified looks on the faces of our victims. Besides, my hand was hurting too much for me to continue to find pleasure in that sport.

A British three-quarter-ton vehicle was leaving the *Bourse* and I jumped in the back together with two other fellows. We just wanted to be with our allies and to ride in a British truck was thrilling. The Tommies soon told us that we should get off as they were driving to Mons, near the French border and a full 100 kilometers away (65 miles). We did not believe them and felt that they just wanted to get rid of us. One of my companions did jump out when the truck slowed down for a turn. It soon became obvious that the British soldiers were indeed on the road to Mons and as the evening fell, we realized that we were getting farther and farther away from Brussels. As the truck reached Waterloo, we begged the driver to stop and let us off. It was late; there was no transportation back to Brussels now 40 kilometers away. We spent the major part of the night walking back to Brussels. Exhausted, I arrived home in the early morning and explained my misadventure to Mother who had a good laugh. Probably concerned that I had been away with four strangers in a truck and far away from home, she repeated her bit of advice: "If a man wants you to feel his hernia, don't do it".

BOB

While Maurice Goldman was my intellectual friend, Bob (Robert) Van Meckeren was my poetic friend. Where Maurice and I discussed politics, ideologies and sporting events, Bob would talk artists and music, especially the songs and the poetry of Charles Trenet.

Mr Van Meckeren, Bob's Father still had the trappings of wealth although he no longer seemed to be working at anything very profitable. He had a scruffy mustache and seemed to miss part of his lower nose so that from any angle you would always look up his nostrils. That made him ugly, at bit like MrMitsuhirato in Tintin's Lotus Bleu. I had seen Bob's Mother a few times as well as his older brother Raymond, but they did not leave a descriptive memory in my mind. I understood that when the Van Meckerens lived in Ostende, on the coast, Bob's Father had been a noted journalist but that he had collaborated with the German occupiers. After the war, he had been declared an *incivique*, unpatriotic and had been barred from ever working again in the news media. Still, they lived in a big, three story beautiful house on the Rue Fraikin, in Schaerbeek not far from Brussels' bustling North Station.

In late 1940, the family still lived in Ostende. The Germans, fearing raids or invasion by the English, had mined most of the beaches along the North Sea. A British fighter plane had been shot down by the German defenses and its wreckage lay on the beach, beyond the dunes, behind barbed wire fences. The wing's RAF's circular red white and blue emblem was flapping in the early wind. Nine years old Bob wanted the emblem for a trophy. Gingerly he slithered under the barbed wire and walked towards the plane. As he was about to reach the wing, a landmine blew up. When Bob came to, he was bleeding profusely from a huge gap in his left thigh and his right leg was almost completely severed above the knee. A woman on the other side of the barbed wire was calling to him and encouraging him to crawl on the sand to the edge where he could be rescued.

By the time Bob had crawled to the barbed wire fence, an ambulance had arrived and he was rushed to the Ostende hospital where they were able to save his left leg. The right leg had to be amputated and the force of the explosion had knocked off most of his front teeth. After months of rehabilitation, a heavy, artificial leg was fitted and a curve of false teeth would replace the missing ones. After this tragedy, the family moved to Brussels as the souvenir of the beaches of Ostende was too much to bear.

When I first met Bob, in the fall of 1944, he seemed quite normal except that he had the disconcerting habit of pulling out his false teeth to tease you with his gaping mouth. Of course, he had a terrible dancing limp, as he would drag his heavy prosthesis behind him. Like us, he wore knickers over white socks and brown shoes and if he did not move it was not possible to discern that he had an artificial leg. When he walked, he'd sometimes have to help bring his leg along with his right hand. He had a very pronounced limp that made him very self-conscious and he'd glare angrily at whoever stared at him. He had become extremely mobile and could hop about as fast as anyone. In a streetcar, sitting was a problem as the artificial leg never folded under the seat but had to be grabbed at the ankle and pulled into position. When people would stare as he passed by, he'd often hum or whistle the little ditty made famous in the films of Laurel and Hardy.

We became the best of friends. In the back of his garden, there was a large greenhouse with a Ping-Pong table and he'd play a mean game. Now and then, if frustrated that he had not been able to beat me, he'd jump me and we'd wrestle. He had an unfair advantage as he would clunk me on the head with his artificial leg. In the years that would follow we became inseparable.

BLACK MARKET

Just like Paris, with the war now over, Brussels became a center for rest and recreation for the allied soldiers waiting to be shipped back home or to the Pacific theatre of war. There were also the troops who would now occupy conquered Germany where the possibilities for recreation were non-existent after the destruction of entire cities.

The red-light district near the *Gare du Nord*, the North Station became a magnet for the multitude of soldiers wanting to spend some "quality" time with the prostitutes that lived in one of the oldest section of the capital. Street after street of small houses with bedroom windows filled the neighborhood. Women wearing more make-up than clothing sitting on love seats or sofas in red lit windows would suggestively beckon passersby, enticing them to come and sample their wares. Some would take special delight in fondling a breast or mockingly offering a naked breast to the young curious boys who'd wander in the area. For myself, I would have been scared out of my wits if one of these ladies had grabbed me and pulled me into the dank doorways.

For soldiers who wanted to partake of this luxuriant booty, there was a need for money. The British but especially the Canadians and the Americans had a seemingly inexhaustible supply of trade material that they could sell for money. The Rue du Pélican, across from the red-light district soon became the focus for the sale of anything that could be purchased. So soon after the war, there were shortages of everything and the soldiers had a wealth of goodies to sell. Everything from socks to stolen Jeeps was available for immediate cash. Chewing gum, chocolate, K-rations, the famed L-shaped flashlight, batteries, soap, army boots, "long johns", blankets, etc., everything was for sale. But by far, the most popular item were "CIGARETTES". Apparently, one could exist without all the other necessities but cigarettes were needed, desired, irresistible and indispensable.

I had staked a spot in the Rue du Pélican where I could be found almost every night, buying all I could from the GI's and Tommies. I would buy just about everything I could carry home but drew the line at Jeeps. These were always stolen vehicles and could be traced easily if one attempted to sell them. Now and then, the Military Police would make a raid in the Rue du Pélican and one had to be swift to escape through some of the nearby little streets. Some of the streets were impasses and cul-de-sac and there was no issue. You could be trapped like a rat.

Although I was only fifteen, I was doing very well and even had a steady and repeat clientele. American and English cigarettes were the stock in trade. I would buy these at one franc apiece and resell them the next day for two francs, a 100% profit with no overhead. Camels, Craven A and Players in their fancy cardboard boxes were preferred. The GI's especially seemed to have an inexhaustible supply of cartons of Camels that they would get for nothing or very cheap at the PX or distributed free by the Red Cross. Of course, the big tobacco companies were giving these away thus ensuring that the addicted GI's would become hooked customers once they returned to civilian life. Somehow, I never took up smoking. I guess I could not see much sense in lighting up and seeing my profit go up in smoke.

The British had metal tins of Woodbine cigarettes (about the size of condensed milk cans). Each round tin held 50 cigarettes slightly smaller than the standard Camel. Woodbines would only fetch 75 centimes each and would resell for 1.50 franc (or 75 francs a tin). If the tin was still sealed, it was fine. However, now and then a tin had been open and one would have to pull out a sample cigarette to be sure that the tin contained 50 full cigarettes instead of fifty halves on a bed of sawdust.

The next morning, I would go to school with a bulky stash of cigarettes hidden in my shirt and jacket and also in my *cartable*, school bag. As I came in through the school lobby, dozens of customers descended on me like bees on honey; the principal, the teachers and most of the students. In less than 10 minutes all my supply had been sold and I was richer by 100%. Once home, I'd give my sister Ruth half of my profits, it made me feel good.

One evening, a Canadian soldier offered to sell me brand new long johns. When I asked him to show them to me, he said that we'd have to go around the corner as he was wearing them and would have to get undressed. I felt that these were no longer new and I had to decline. However, one night, an older British soldier did fool me. He was carrying a duffel bag and wanted to sell me the bag and its contents. He explained that he had a variety of goods to offer me but that we would have to go to a darker corner of the street as he did not want the other soldiers and dealers to see what he had brought. As we were walking, he began to tell me he had been a football player *(soccer)* and that he had been severely kicked in the belly. "Here, he said, feel it" with that he took my hand and guided it to his body. Apparently he had opened his pants as we were walking and I felt myself holding his bloated penis. I instantly recoiled as I realized that I was holding his warm but flacid member and I ran away. In back of me, I could hear him plead with me to come back but I could not run away fast enough. Mother' admonition was ringing in my head: "If a man wants you to feel his hernia, don't do it!".

On a summer evening, I had wandered to the Rue du Pélican just to see what the action was. I had no money on me and was not on a buying mission. Suddenly, from several corners of the streets jeeploads of American and English MPs sealed off the area and proceeded to seize and confiscate all the goods and monies of the traders caught in the raid. I understood that these occasional raids were really "protection" money from the dealers and that the seized goods and the money were always distributed among the Military Police. They would then leave the dealers alone for a few weeks. No one was ever arrested. I felt that I had been lucky and from that time on I always made sure that I did not carry too much capital on me, should I be caught in a raid. I never was.

By mid 1946, the majority of the allied soldiers would be demobilized and gone. With the return of a normal economy the need for smuggled goods would wane rapidly and my adventures in black market soon came to an end.

MORE AMERICANS

Ruth had many acquaintances among the GI's who visited Brussels. They were fun, special, with a certain child-like quality that endeared them to us and to the population in general. Americans seemed more relaxed, less conformist than the bourgeois population of Belgium. I got to meet most of the boyfriends that Ruth would know or bring home and I became more and more enamored of Americans with each passing day.

Gene from Portland Oregon had a date with Ruth. Gene was a really nice guy; honest, not too cultivated (he had never heard of Chopin and kept pronouncing it Chopp-inn). Just before he showed up, who should turn up but Billy Batson. Now, Billy Batson was a good-looking guy, suave, smooth as he could be. He had a slightly soft face and heavy sensual lips. He looked a bit like Louis Hayward, the actor. We felt that he must have had some distant American Indian ancestry although we were not sure why. He had dated Ruth a couple of times and had gone off the radar for several weeks.

Well, anyway, this Billy Batson showed up unannounced and wanted to take Ruth on a date that afternoon. And here came Gene, who had the date with Ruth. Ruth wanted to go with Billy, but Gene would have none of this. The situation was getting tense in our apartment and the two GI's were not in a good mood.

"Wait a minute" intervened Mother; "who had the date with whom?".

Gene affirmed that it was he who had made the date with Ruth. Ruth had to admit that much.

"Well," retorted Mother "then Ruth, you go out with Gene and I will go out with Billy"!.

Although Frieda was a good twenty years his senior, Batson did not seem to mind too much. Mother was still a very attractive woman and Billy must have felt he was betting on a sure thing.

Gene and Ruth went out on their date and I could only assume that a good time was had by all.

Near the *Gare du Nord* at the bottom of the *Blvd. du Botanique*, the US Army had rented a storefront to house a Military Police station. The MPs manning it were particularly sharp in their dress codes with polished boots and helmet liners, white leggings and MP brassards. On their collars a blue and white enamel emblem stated "We Control" that they jokingly referred to as "V.D.Control". It was really Ruth who had befriended them but I was only too glad to partake of the residuals that came with knowing more "wonderful" Americans.

Marion Otstott came from a small town in Texas. He was tall and slim, good looking with a great smile. I was happy he called me a friend. One day, as he came to our apartment he mentioned "Popcorn". I had never heard of popcorn, had no idea what it was. A few days later, he brought a cardboard can of corn to pop. It was a revelation; what sounds as the hot kernels exploded against the lid of the pan! A marvelous aroma of butter and corn filled the landing where Mother's kitchen was perched. We ate it all up, even to the kernels that had failed to explode.

Ruth had a fling with Ray Hostettler, another MP whose origin I never knew. He was a handsome redhead looking a bit like Donald Sutherland. After a while, the fling cooled off and Ray stopped seeing Ruth who was very distraught. She came crying to me unhappy that her affair with him had ended. This called for action from her younger brother. So I went to Ray and with fifteen years old logic I insisted that he must marry her now. Hostettler smiled and said—She knew the score-. This I could not understand. What score? I had never heard the expression before. She knew the score? Was it 3 to 1 or what? I insisted and Ray explained that Ruth knew what the story was going to be and that this was the way it was. I guessed that both Ruth and I learned something from that.

Bill Kennedy lived in Blytheville, Arkansas. He looked like, well, a Bill Kennedy. I guess that he must have been of Irish origin, just as Hostettler was of German extraction and Otstott was from Scandinavia, but in those days, all those names sounded completely American to me just like Los Angeles, San Diego or New Orleans. I liked Bill a lot. He had a lively manner and was always very friendly with me. He wore a large indianhead silver ring on his right hand that I much admired. When it came time for Kennedy to return to the US, he gave me his ring and a pair of dice that I prized enormously.

Ruth and I were very much immersed in things American. It always surprised us that the GIs could not give us the name of the 48 states and their capitals, while we could rattle them off without hesitation. It was their turn to be impressed.

NEW CURRENCY

When Belgium was liberated, King Leopold III left his palace in Laeken and followed the retreating Germans to Germany. With him went his new wife, Princess de Rethy and his retinue. There were discussions as to whether the King fled of his own accord or if the Germans coerced him to come along.

However, when the war ended on May 8th, 1945, Leopold elected to seek asylum in Switzerland rather than to return to Brussels. Years later he forced a return and a referendum was held. Leopold won by a minuscule majority with the bulk of his support coming from the Flemish provinces. Thus, a King who was supposed to unify the country became a divisive factor. There were public demonstrations and the King was finally forced to abdicate in favor of his son Baudouin

With the King out of the country, the Government that had been in exile in England during the occupation returned to govern. Its Finance Minister was Camille Gutt. Gutt, a Jew, was a brilliant economist and had helped the British war effort by transferring all of Belgium's gold reserves to the English Treasury, thus preventing Hitler from putting his hands on it. Now, with the ravages of the war threatening uncontrolled inflation, Gutt had come up with a daring plan, "The Gutt Plan." This consisted in freezing the old currency and replacing it with new paper money. Each household would be allowed to exchange six thousand Belgian Francs in old bills for a like amount of new currency. This meant that those who had hoarded currency, especially illegally during the war would be left holding mattresses full of cash that would become worthless, at least for the foreseeable future. For Hilaire, it should have presented no problem as by then he had lost all the money he had accumulated during the war thanks to his black market activities. For the majority of Belgians, it meant that they had to turn in the money they had squirreled away in their mattresses but only to the maximum of BF 6,000-. Although it was hinted that more money might eventually be exchanged at a later date, it would not be until the danger of inflation had passed. There were rumblings about the plot by "The Jew Gutt" to make everyone a pauper. This in turn gave fodder to the anti-Semitism that was once again rising in Belgium. France and other countries that would later adopt the "Gutt Plan" would soon see the reawakening of the hatred for the Jews. There were a few instances when strangers approached me in the street and had shouted "Dirty Jew, give us back the money you stole". This was particularly painful for me as indeed had I not been baptized Protestant back in 1941? Somehow, the general population had not gotten the message and despite the flattening of my ears and the baptism certificate, they were still able to see and recognize me as a Jew.

One afternoon, as I was riding my beloved bike in the *Bois de la Cambre*, a man hailed me and offered to purchase my Peugeot for ten thousand francs. It had cost six thousand when purchased new. I was not even tempted, what meant money when I could have the bike? Besides, this man wanted to give me 10,000 francs, a considerable amount, in old currency that would not be negotiable anymore. Later that day, I told Hilaire about the incident. Father was upset. He felt that I should have taken the money as he had ways to have that old currency exchanged for the new bills. Apparently one could negotiate with people who did not have the 6,000 to exchange. For a fee (usually 10%) they would officially exchange your old currency. The foxy ones (i.e. Hilaire) would wind up with an additional 5,400 New Francs. This could be repeated as often as old currency and a new "poor" person could be found, thus insuring a tidy profit. Had I known that, I still would have refused to part with my Peugeot.

Later, Hilaire would make money by buying large, winning lottery tickets from winners who were in a high tax bracket. Whereas they would have had to pay the State up to 60% of their winnings, they could sell the winning ticket at 15 or 20% discounts. It was then a simple thing to find low-income people in lower tax brackets. They would then go and cash it for a small fee. A few personal ads in the newspapers did the trick.

Soon, this would become an organized business run mostly from a few cafes near the *Bourse*. Presumably, it included strict accounting and probably strong-armed enforcers who made sure that no one but the government was short-changed.

THE COUSIN FROM AMERICA

I had a taste for America and I came to feel that if I were ever to achieve anything, I would have to go to the States. I went to the American Embassy a couple of time to inquire about the papers required to emigrate to America. The personnel was invariably friendly but words like quotas and affidavits kept cropping up. Also, it seemed that since I was still stateless, it would be extremely difficult to obtain a visa for America. Apparently, when someone left his country to permanently reside in the USA, the government of the country of origin would guarantee that it would accept the return of the individual for criminal behavior etc. I had no country of origin and the Belgian government would not vouch to take me back once I was out of Belgium. Effectively, the United States would be stuck with me. I could not pin anyone down about this, but it seemed to be the general attitude. Had the USA accepted me, it would have been stuck with me should I have misbehaved. To complicate matters, having been born in Belgium, I fell under the Belgian quota, which was not very good. Ironically, since Ruth had been born in Cologne, she would come under the German quota, which was very good at the time. However, she would have faced the same obstacles I faced since she was stateless just like me.

On one of my visits to the American Embassy, I had the thrill of coming face to face with General George Patton, all resplendent in his olive dress uniform, shiny cavalry boots, polished helmet liner and twin pearl-handled revolvers at his sides. It was an occasion to be remembered but of no help whatsoever in my quest for a visa to America. *General Patton would be killed in a car accident in Mannheim, Germany later that December of 1945.*

Although I cannot recall the exact date, whether late 1945 or early 1946, I did come home from school one afternoon and walked in Mother's apartment, place Madou. There, Frieda introduced me to a Leo Wolleman, a distant cousin from Cologne. This was not an "uncle" like so many of her lovers, but a genuine albeit distant relative. Frieda had mentioned him several times before, never in very flattering terms. It seemed that Leo had worked as a diamond cutter in the Cologne diamond district. The story went that while cutting the stones, he would swallow small chips of diamond and leave work with bits of diamonds in his stomach. Later, at home, he would have a BM in a chamber pot and sift through it until he'd recover the diamonds he had previously swallowed. After a few years he had accumulated enough money to buy a passage to New York where he had established himself in the Diamond business. Money indeed had no odor.

Mr Wolleman had done very well in the U.S.A., he was a 32nd degree mason (just like President Harry Truman) and had been elected as vice-president of the American Jeweler's association. Frieda had explained all this to me in reverend tones. It seemed odd to me that so soon after the end of the conflict Leo Wolleman was able to circulate all over Europe. Apparently, he was on a mission to rescue large numbers of Jewish children who had been orphaned in the war and to try to find them homes in the United States under the auspices of various Jewish organizations. For that work, he had been written about in several newspapers that Leo proudly showed me during his visit.

"Uncle" Leo and I had animated conversations that afternoon and he seemed to take a serious interest in me. I impressed upon him my enthusiasm about America and how much I wanted to go to the States. My lack of a sponsor was my major handicap. After a while, he declared that he wanted to take me to America with him. Not only would he bring me to America, but he had a son, Walter, who was about my age and he would put me through college and take me in his business when I graduated. I was in seventh heaven. I did not want the extras, just an affidavit that would enable me to go to America. It was wonderful that Uncle Leo would do all the other things he promised but my ticket to the USA was my dream.

As he was ready to leave, Leo stated that he was going to Paris for a week and that Frieda "Should have the boy packed and ready to go in one week". Well, we cautioned that it could not be done quite that way. There was a need for a passport, a visa, all the necessary documents, medical certificates etc. Leo agreed and declared that he would take care of all the details once he returned to New York.—The boy will be in America in six months-, he proclaimed as he left our apartment. On one of the scrolls of the balcony at 5 Place Madou, I wrote the date and the caption:"6 months to USA" I could not sleep that night. The next day, I hurried to school where I excitedly announced to all my classmates that I would be in America within six months.

I never heard from Leo Wolleman again.

V-J DAY

August 7th 1945 brought the news that the United States of America had dropped an "Atomic" bomb over Japan. I could hear the voice of President Truman speaking over the American Forces Network (AFN) in Munich. He spoke in clipped tones and declared that "This morning, the American Air Forces have dropped an atomic bomb over Hiroshima, a military target". There was something funny about the way Truman pronounced the name of the city, with the emphasis on the second syllable. I remembered thinking that I would have placed the accent on the third syllable. Later that day, the radio and the newspapers were full of details about a terrible weapon of destruction that had completely obliterated the Japanese City in a matter of seconds. I felt elated, happy that those little yellow people had been so completely crushed. There was no second thoughts, no pity, no real understanding of that which had just happened. The GIs we knew and who were preparing to ship out to the Pacific were celebrating. On that same day, Russia finally declared war on Japan and invaded Manchuria. Russia wanted to be there for the kill. I could not help but think about Chaim Rozenberg, my Father's eldest brother who had fought the Japanese in Port Arthur, Manchuria, barely 40 years earlier.

A second Atomic bomb destroyed Nagasaki on August 9th and Japan surrendered a few days later. There was not much celebration among us. By then, we were just a bit numb. For the American and British soldiers, it was a time to rejoice. The cigarette business would be booming in the days to follow.

"Camp Top Hat" had been established near Antwerp and countless thousands of GIs were being processed each day to be shipped back to the States. Ruth and I were losing our American friends at an alarming rate. One afternoon, we went to look for some Americans at a building on the newly renamed Avenue Winston Churchill. There were new American faces there and they told us that our buddies had left for the States. Seeing that we were sad, the soldiers showered us with handfuls of chewing gum, chocolate and condoms.

The days when friendly Americans were crowding the streetcars and tossing out change from the platforms were coming to an end. The Belgian franc was worth two cents and the pocket change in 1,5,10 or 25 centimes were worth fractions of a penny. The GIs would toss them out into the street much to the delight of little boys who'd pick them up. For them, it was money. One night, I went with Ruth to a compound that had been vacated by the Americans. We searched all over for some souvenirs. We wandered the vacant rooms in the empty buildings but could find little to take except a few paperback books, including a "Sad Sack" pocket book that we avidly seized for our own. From a long-forgotten GI I inherited a gorgeous officer's half dress coat and the softest full-length muffler. Both were in the strictest regulation khaki and were it not for my horn-rimmed glasses, I could have passed for an American soldier. Soon, there would be nothing left except a thirst for Coca-Cola.

FLAGRANTE DELICTO

Getting a divorce in catholic Belgium was extremely difficult. Hilaire and Frieda, not wanting to cohabit any longer but unable to obtain a divorce sued for a *"separation de corps et de biens"*, a Judicial separation of body and wealth, a sort of post-nuptial. Although there was by then no wealth to speak of, there was the Winterthur life policy that Hilaire had purchased in the summer of 1942. There was a small cash value that was surrendered to Mother.

I only discovered those records some forty years later after the death of Hilaire. Winterthur had long denied that those "Jewish policies" had ever existed.

In 1942, MmeKraus, from Vienna, in order to save herself from deportation had married a Catholic Belgian *"en-blanc"* a non-consummated marriage. For a sum of 10,000 Belgian francs, a laborer had agreed to marry Mme Kraus without ever meeting her. Now that the war was over and with the threat of the concentration camps behind her, Mme Kraus wanted a divorce. Not only did she not want to stay married to a gentile, but she had a considerable fortune in Canada. She wanted to be free to resume her life without being shackled to a Belgian husband she had never met.

It was determined that the only way she could obtain a divorce was to be caught in *Flagrante Delicto*, in the very act of adultery. That would be grounds for divorce in Belgium. Mme Kraus, Hilaire and Frieda hatched a plot to have Hilaire and Mme Kraus caught in the act of adultery. In this way, MmeKraus could get a divorce from her "husband" and Father and Mother would also get a divorce, thus killing two birds with one stone.

Mother had a boyfriend, René Van Langendonck who was Deputy Chief of Police of the borough of St.Josse where Frieda and Hilaire both resided. It was a simple matter to enlist René's help in serving a process of adultery.

On the appointed day, Hilaire (43) and Mme Kraus (late 70's) met in his furnished room in the Rue Hydraulique. They got undressed and climbed into bed. After a while that must have seemed an eternity to both of them, René Van Langendonck, in uniform, flanked by another policeman, burst in the apartment and made a *constat* of *Flagrante Delicto*.

In the space of a few weeks the matter was presented in court and the judge granted the divorce to Mme Kraus's husband. However, when it came to Hilaire and Frieda, the judge inquired as to how long they had been married and how old were their two children. Well, they had been married over twenty years and the children were seventeen and fifteen respectively. Upon hearing that, the judge leaned over and smiled. "After twenty years of marriage and two grown children, do you really think I will grant a divorce for such a minor thing as this? Divorce denied!".

And so, Mme Kraus got her divorce but Hilaire and Frieda remained married albeit legally separated.

SCHOOL DAYS

It had been nearly three years since I had been in school and it took a bit of adjusting before I could feel completely comfortable in the strange surroundings of a Middle School. In my former years, I could absorb everything like a sponge. Now, what we were given in class was rudimentary, the rest you had to study on your own at home or from books borrowed from the library. I was totally unprepared for that. What was more, I had no one at home to prod me or to assist me with my studies. Father did not live with us and Mother was busy with her own life and certainly unable to help me given the paucity of her French education. I did manage because I was bright but my inclination to daydream about America was not conducive to perfect marks.

Though not mean, I was mischievous and had a quick retort. Soon, I discovered that I had a smile that would baffle my teachers. I was told once that I had *"une gueule a vous foutre du monde"* literally "a mug that tells the world to fuck-off". There was something in my smile that seemed to say that I was amused by something, like a private joke, like the whole world was walking around with an unbuttoned fly, or later, an open zipper. This trait, this affliction seemed to be more prevalent with Europeans than with Americans who seem to regard a smile as a friendly indication.

We did not run from class to class between periods. We had one assigned classroom and the teachers rotated. We could do bedlam for a very short time while awaiting our next teacher, but we did not have the whirlwind of activity and running that exists in the US. We had one class and we hung our coats and caps on hooks in the hallway. Lockers were unknown. All our books and notebooks, pens, pencils and erasers were carried in one *cartable*, satchel usually made of leather with a center clip or two locking straps. It was always carried by the handle or if that was broken, it would be cradled under the arm. I had seen American movies where the students carried their books loose under their arms or strapped with a leather belt. This seemed very quaint. Certainly, the books would get wet whenever it rained. Since it rained an average of seventeen days each month in Belgium, I could not imagine sunny Southern California where the majority of the Hollywood films seemed to be taking place.

Monsieur Barbier, who taught Latin, was our main class teacher. This meant that he was in charge of the 6th Latin and all personal matters, schedules and school details were administered by Barbier. Barbier also thought Greek but we would not get to Greek until the 4th Greco-Latin two years hence. He was a fair man, big of stature, given to wearing brown sports coats and green trousers. The most memorable thing about him was that he would write on the blackboard with his right hand while still turning his body to the class thus never losing sight of the students. Thus, he could keep tight control of the students even as he was writing. Mr Barbier would end each class with a listing of the homework and lessons that were scheduled for the next day. There were always 4 or 5 chapters to be studied. As he wrote the numbers on the board, the students would moan and protest at the number to be studied. Barbier would then furiously write a few more additional listings on the board until the grumbling subsided. We soon learned to keep quiet as he gave us the initial set of homework. I got along fine with Barbier and cannot recall any friction. He did not seem to mind my smile.

The last time I had a woman teacher was in kindergarten and now we had Mlle Truffaut as our math teacher. I and I guess none of the other boys were ready for her. She was very pretty and slim and looked just like the Hollywood star Joan Leslie we had admired in "Hollywood Canteen". Like Joan Leslie, Truffaut was very flat chested but that did not seem to bother us. As it was, we hung on her every word and devoured her eyes, her lips and her hair. I was still too young to concentrate on any other part of her anatomy. Of course, when we spoke about her among us, we would denigrate her, claiming that she was not at all attractive and that she did not appeal to any of us. The Athenaeum was strictly a boy's school and we would not come in contact with girls in school for another four years once we got to our "superior study classes". Thus, the daily contact with Mlle Truffaut was fuel for our dreams and fantasies.

In between periods, while awaiting our next teacher, we had taken to opening the windows overlooking the Rue Des Riches Claires and we'd launch paper airplanes that would zoom and glide down to the street below. During the classes we'd furiously fold new ones into shape so we could have a new squadron to toss out the window at the end of the period. We had become so skilled and adept at our paper plane production that we could tear a sheet off our notebooks, fold the nose and wings and introduce the tail assembly in the hollow of our desks without having to look at what we were doing. We could have done it blind-folded.

So, while we were attentively listening to Mlle Truffaut, fixing our eyes to her eyes and lips, our hands were going a mile a minute under the surface of our desks. After a while, Mlle Truffaut became aware of our movements under the desk, but she could not figure out what we were doing, only that our hands seemed to be very busy under our desks. She knew that we were doing something between our desks and our laps but could not figure out what we were doing. Since we were all full of passion for her and kept staring at her face, she could only surmise that we might have been thinking about her in a most amorous way and that we might be gratifying ourselves. All that while she was trying to enlighten us in the mysteries of mathematics. She kept muttering "But what are they doing under their desks". Yet, she did not dare to come and look and would often start to blush, which made her prettier still.

Of course, once she had left the room, up would go the windows and the paper airplanes would rain out to the street below.

Mlle Truffaut seemed to like me and did not mind my smile.

Monsieur Beernart thought us History and Geography. Of medium build and wiry, he had black hair and a tight, slim mustache that seemed to accentuate his bright black eyes. He did not have a good grip on the class but he made learning fun. On his first day, he had us open our notebooks and insisted that we covered the first page with the word "Prehistory" Then on page two, "in letters half the size of "Prehistory" "Cro-Magnon Man". His courses were full of grand-titles, titles and subtitles. We ran through notebooks like an express train through small local stations. From Beernart, I learned a method for studying that I would always use in later years. He taught me to organize my work and mind and although I would recall very little of his teachings, he might have had the most influence of all my teachers. He did teach History and Geography but most of all he taught me how to learn.

In Belgian schools (except for religious institutions) there were hours regularly set aside for religious instructions. However, those who did not wish to take the religious courses could opt for *"Morales Laiques"*, Secular Ethics. Most of our class chose the later. The course, which was given by Mr Beernart consisted of his telling stories with a moral and was very sought after. I liked Mr Beernart and he did not have a problem with my smile.

Flemish, or rather *Nederlands* Dutch was the domain of Mr Thielemans, or *Menheer* Thielemans, as he preferred to be called. We were all francophone and took all of our studies in French. Dutch was a foreign language for us and although we had a smattering of Flemish, most of it was *Brusseleer*, the *patois* of Brussels. With what we knew of Flemish, we would not have been able to venture more than twenty kilometers north of the capital and still be understood.

We resisted Thielemans' teachings, arguing logically (we thought) that to ask, *"Hoe laat is het?"* "How late is it?" in Brussels would get us nowhere fast. The local expression being, "Wat d'heure is het". Thielemans went on undeterred, not seeming to care whether we learned Dutch or not. He was tall and good-looking but in a gaunt way. His eyes, cheeks and nose were sunk-in as if he was on a permanent drug binge or never got enough sleep. He always wore a double-breasted light gray suit. When he did not have both hands deep in his pockets, he would pull the back of his chair to his lower belly and rock back and forth, his gaze far away, seemingly unaware that we were there at all. Some were suggesting that he was gratifying himself while in the class and there might have been more than an iota of truth in that.

For Gym, we had Van De Perre, Monsieur Van De Perre. A one-word description would be "vulgar", better yet, extremely vulgar. Van De Perre might have come from the "Marolles" the oldest section of Brussels where the purest patois was still spoken and French was spoken with the purest Brussels accent heard anywhere. *Brusselleer* was a rich and colorful language, but when Van De Perre spoke it in a thick gravelly voice it lost any beauty it might have had. Besides, any sentence he spoke was accompanied by body histrionics that saw him contorting like a boa constrictor and constant grabbing of his crotch. Add to that curly black hair dripping with brilliantine and you would get an accurate picture of the man.

Actually, being the foremost basketball referee in the country he was quite a celebrity. We had the impression that the teaching job was just a paid cover-up for his activity as a referee. He never seemed too interested in what we did in his gym class. As it was, we were a sorry bunch without any collective or individual athletic talent. We really unexcelled.

When my wife (the then Rosa Wauters) was in her late teens, Van De Perre walked by her on the Place de la Monnaie. As he passed her by he said, "How is your little sister?" This surprised her, as she did not have a little sister. It was only much later that she realized he had made a gross reference to the most private part of her anatomy.

Art and History of Art were taught by Monsieur Narcisse who, though possessor of a most poetic name, did not show any predisposition to anything artful or beautiful. Narcisse was violently anti-Semitic and devoted an enormous amount of his classes berating and abusing the *Four Orthodox*. When he wasn't verbally abusing them and thrashing them and throwing them to the floor, he'd direct his anger towards Goldman and me even though we had little in common with

Kruman and Co. since we showed up for Friday and Saturday morning classes. The fact that we were Jews was reason enough to detest us. Narcisse would also ignore us completely during his classes, never checking or commenting on the work we were doing. The six of us would routinely receive low marks for our homework.

Monsieur Narcisse was a sartorial mess in baggy pants and worn jacket. His shoes were forever splattered with multicolored oil paint and he used the lining of his coat to wipe the tip of his paintbrushes. His hair was a curtain of wet gray noodles that fell to his collar and never showed signs that it had been washed.

Monsieur Narcisse had a terrible skin condition. All visible parts of his body, hands, wrists, face and neck were covered with a thick layer of pustulous scabs. It was hard to think of anything else when he came near you and touched you to redirect a pencil or brush. Rumor had it that during the First World War, he had been at the front and had bathed in stagnant water where poisonous gas shells had exploded. The water had become contaminated and his skin had begun to rot away. Thus afflicted he had been removed from the frontlines and sent to finish the war in a hospital. Rather than remain at the front, he had chosen the coward's way by washing himself with the gas-contaminated waters. Now, he had to spend the rest of his life looking like a monster in a cheap Hollywood movie. Of course, we had no basis for these rumors, we did not even know if he had been in the Great War. It simply suited our thinking that Narcisse was not only repulsive but also a coward. He probably suffered from an extreme case of psoriasis. Monsieur Narcisse did not like to see me smile but he never threw me out of the class. He probably had more fun berating me and throwing me to the floor whenever I came to the defense of the *"Orthodox"*.

On the occasion of a joint art class with students of the 6th *Moderne,* we had an assignment to paint a white vase that Monsieur Narcisse had deposited on a table. It was a common bulbous vase with a constricted neck and a flared top and I quickly drew its outline. It was a white vase and I drew a white vase. Narcisse passed by my desk, took a look at my work of art and said nothing. At the desk next to mine sat a student from the *Modernes* whose name I would soon forget. I would remember his Flemish flaxen straight hair. He had only a left arm and from his right shoulder a single finger protruded. During *recreation,* recess, he had once gotten a hold of me with the grip of that right finger. It was as if all the strength of his missing right arm had been concentrated in this one single digit and I had been held as if in a vise.

Now, he pointed to my drawing, then to the vase on the table. "Rudy" he said, "you are not looking *in* the vase. You see a white surface because that is all your brain is getting from your eyes. Look into it, observe! You will soon see that it is not a white surface but that all that surrounds the vase is reflected on it. See the walls, the desks, and the reflections of the windows and beyond, the surrounding gray houses, the white clouds and the blue sky. They are all there for you to see and paint! You look but you must learn to see! ".

In the two years that I would study at the Athenaeum, Monsieur Narcisse would teach me absolutely nothing, not even how to sharpen a pencil. This young boy, in one sentence, had opened my eyes, taught me how to see, and forever changed my perception of the world around me.

And then, there was Monsieur Moyson, our French teacher, he heartily hated my smile. Moyson must have been in his thirties, slight of build and forever wearing a light gray double-breasted suit. With a white handkerchief neatly folded in his breast pocket, he looked quite dapper. Moyson had a high forehead and wavy dark blond hair combed backward and parted to the left. He looked a lot like King Leopold III. Now and then he would tell us about his war exploits when he was a member of the Resistance but we did not believe a word of it and felt that he was just trying to make himself appear important.

He had a neat appearance; however whenever he entered our class, Moyson would take out a comb and proceed to repeatedly comb his blond hair back making sure that his part was well delineated. He would then carefully examine the teeth of his comb before replacing it back in the inside pocket of his jacket. Then, he would take out the handkerchief from his breast pocket, blow his nose, deeply clear his throat and spit an "oyster" in the handkerchief. This, he would also examine with care and would then fold it and replace it in his breast pocket. Monsieur Moyson would then survey the class and start his lessons. If his eyes came to rest on me and he detected what he thought was a smile on my face, he'd admonish me to stop smiling at once. He thought that something was amusing me and that I was making fun of him. If I was unable to wipe that smile off my face, he'd throw me out *"Rosenberg, sortez"* Rosenberg, get out! And being our French teacher, he'd pronounce my name the French way "Ro san bear". After a while, I felt that my name was hyphenated "Ro san bear-sortez".

During the course of that first school year, someone had the bright idea to ask that each student in our class write an essay describing a teacher of our choice. It was such a thoughtless or cruel thing to do. It was possible that they felt that the students would chose a favorite teacher and write about all the reasons that teacher was liked. As it was, most of the class picked on Monsieur Narcisse as he was such an easy and tempting target. They wrote with all the cruelty of youth describing how revolting he looked and smelled and how repulsed they were whenever he came near them.

For my part, as much as I disliked Narcisse, I could not join in attacking so easy a target. I took on Monsieur Moyson. In a lengthy essay, I wrote about his "phony heroics" and described in full how, for such a neat person, in a daily ritual, he had those terrible, uncouth habits of combing his hair, blowing his nose and spitting in front of the class.

We never thought that the teachers would share the essays and that the "victims" would get to read each composition.

Inexplicably, the next time Moyson came in our class, he went through his ritual exactly as I had described it in my essay; comb, blow, "oyster" and spit. His eyes fixed on my face. I was mightily trying not to smile. With both hands, I was pulling down on my cheeks to bring my mouth in a downward position so my smile would not show.

"Ro san bear" Moyson intoned, "stop smiling! It is unnerving!"

Despite all my efforts and trying in vain to pull down my cheeks I burst out in a loud, uncontrollable laughter.

215

"Ro san bear, sortez!" Yelled Moyson. Laughing, I ran out of the class into the hallway, on my way to the principal's office. It felt good. I had bested Moyson. I knew he'd remember me now.

Despite my lack of application and without ever opening a school book at home, I breezed through and finished the school year somewhere near the top of the class, the "Orthodox" sharing the first four places with Goldman and me not far behind. Bob Van Meckeren, even though he had done his homework and studied assiduously, failed to pass and had to redo his 6ᵗʰ *Latine* the following year while the rest of us would enter the 5ᵗʰ. Bob was very upset and I tried to console him as best I could and promising him that our friendship would continue unabated.

SUMMER 1945

Once school had been over, the summer months seemed to flow peacefully. With the ending of the War in the Pacific peace had returned, at least in my life. There might have been firefights and smaller conflicts in other parts of the world, but for me, it was a time to enjoy my newfound freedom and my Peugeot bicycle. Since Mother and Father had gotten a separation, that source of tension had evaporated even though Hilaire had set up his domicile just a couple of blocks away. I'd spend some afternoons with Bob and the evenings with Maurice. With Bob, we talked about movies, especially about Kathryn Grayson. We had both been smitten by her charm and singing in "Thousands Cheer". It had also introduced us to Gene Kelly, Red Skelton and a stable of MGM stars. With Maurice, it was all about sports and politics. Maurice had a dazzling array of knowledge and he spoke with a *bagou*, an impudent gab that always delighted me.

I had become quite skilled at Ping-Pong to the point that we had taken to call it "Table Tennis" My matches were against Bob and against Maurice, but never at the same time or in the same locale. With Maurice, we'd play in a few Café Establishments where they had a Ping-Pong and billiard tables. All the matches were accompanied by generous helpings of Coca-Cola and *cervelas*, a dense, solid and tasty Belgian sausage.

With Bob, Ping-Pong was confined to the back garden of his house where a greenhouse had been converted into a playroom; its only furniture was a regulation-size Ping-Pong table. Both Bob and Maurice had strong attacking games while I enjoyed playing several feet behind the table, returning almost everything they hit my way with deep cuts from the paddle that would send the ball back with the most deadly *"English"*.

I had to keep my two friends apart and would never see them at the same time except in school. Maurice, who had lost his Mother and a brother in the Holocaust, disliked Bob probably because Mr Van Meckeren had collaborated with the Germans. He also felt that Bob was a "tapette", queer, but since he was also accusing Gilbert of the same thing, I did not place much credence in it. Years later, Maurice would confide in me that he thought that I was also a queer because of my closeness to Bob. For his part, Bob did not like Maurice because Maurice was brash and the opposite of Bob's sensitive and poetic nature. Bob was also jealous of my sharing my time with Maurice when he would have wanted to keep me all to himself.

Escapades with my Peugeot were my greatest pleasure. I would spend hours careening in town or taking refuge in the Bois de la Cambre, the beautiful woods around Brussels. Often, I'd explore the many small towns that encircled the capital. Waterloo was a couple of hours away and there was always a friendly *Coca* awaiting me somewhere. Somehow, there were always a few francs in the bottom of my pocket for a Coke and a *sachet of frites*

The town of Spa, in the Ardennes had been famous since Roman times for its sparkling waters that were renowned for their curative powers, especially for liver ailments caused by heavy drinking and too much eating. It gave its name to a multitude of springs where ailing people would go to seek a cure for what ailed them. Spa also had a gambling casino where Hilaire had left his skin a few times, but that was another story. Spa also had a thriving industry producing SPA Monopole, the most popular sparkling water in Belgium.

With the advent of Coca-Cola, it began rapidly to lose sales to the American import. So, in the summer of 1945, SPA decided to come out with *"SPA-Cola, The American Drink with a Belgian twist"* or words to that effect. It did not take long for mighty Coca-Cola to slap a suit against Spa Monopole and the reign of SPA-Cola was short lived. Perhaps SPA should have called it simply SPA-Cola without the reference that it was an American drink. After all, there were already Pepsi-Cola and Royal Crown Cola in the USA. and SPA-Cola would have seemed a safe bet.

Maurice who at the time fancied himself to be a Communist explained the whole thing to me, over a Coca-Cola. "After all, after having spent huge amounts of dollars and countless lives for the greater glory of Coca-Cola and General Motors, you do not think that the USA would allow an upstart like SPA Monopole to infringe on a trademark?"

In the early 2000's, after the collapse of Perrier on the US market, SPA tried to capture the sparkling water business in New York with a vigorous advertising campaign. It was not successful. At this writing, the writer owns stock in Coca-Cola and Pepsi Cola, but none in Perrier or SPA.

There had been a movie on some natives in South America using blowguns to shoot poisoned darts at preys and enemies. Inspired by their skills, several boys in school had gotten lengths of copper tubing and fashioned blowguns. I had become very skilled with a *sarbacane*, pea-shooter. Armed with a two-foot length of copper tubing and a pocketful of whole dry peas, I became a terror. My favorite sport was to ride on the platform of the streetcars and hit any target that came in sight. I'd clang the peas against metal street signs, startling passers-by. I'd also target people as they walked in the street, from the safety of my moving tramway. I could have taken out an eye or dangerously hurt innocent pedestrians. I seemed totally unaware of the harm I was causing.

From the perch of the window of my third floor room, I'd spray the street below, hitting passing cars and pedestrians. One day, a crowd gathered on the other side of the street and started to point at me hollering that they were going to get the police after me. That was the end of that career.

FOOTBALL GAME (OR WAS IT SOCCER?)

Mother had gotten in her head that somehow she had flat feet. After a few visits to a podiatrist, it had been decided that she needed to have inserts placed in her shoes to correct that situation. Thus, her shoes had been fitted with Dr. Scholl inserts. These were curved, heavy metal plates that filled the shoes from the heel to under the ball of the foot. A width of brown leather was screwed on to the forward edge of the plate to prevent it from slipping forward when one walked. Somehow, Frieda felt a great sense of relief when she was wearing her "Dr. Scholl" and she would not rest until she had convinced Ruth and me that we were also afflicted with flat feet and that we would be greatly helped by wearing similar inserts in our shoes. So, willy-nilly, we were fitted with the heavy Scholl plates and forced to wear these always, under penalty of death or worse. I believe that Mother even tried to make it a family affair by trying to convince Father that he too would benefit from wearing Scholl inserts. Since he was no longer living with us, he did not have to share our misfortune and escaped the footwear pillory.

One day, I had run into René Van Langendonck, Mother's boyfriend who was Deputy Police Chief of St. Josse, and he had offered me a cigarette. When I declined, he laughed and asked if I was saving my "wind" so that I could play football without losing my breath. Van Langendonck, a strapping six footer, used to play soccer but being in his forties had given up the sport. Although here and there I had read that smoking was bad for health, this was the first time it had been brought to my attention by someone I liked and respected that smoking was nefarious. Somehow, that lesson would remain with me always and I never did take up the *"herbe à Nicot"* tobacco. *This familiar French word came from Jean Nicot, a French diplomat who introduced tobacco in France in the latter part of the sixteenth century (hence "nicotine").*

Somehow, the chance meeting with Van Langendonck had made me yearn for a game of football *(soccer)*. Thus, I contacted Maurice and together we enlisted a few of our school comrades to join us for a match. We were able only to gather a total of five warm bodies for a team that normally required eleven players. We were Maurice, Maggi, Gilbert, Eekhoudt and I. Only Eekhoudt had the rudiments of the game. Maurice and I had never played it, Maggi was too heavy and Gilbert had an aversion to anything physical. We had not invited Bob Van Meckeren as we felt that he would not have been much help with only one leg. Actually, he would have made a passable goalkeeper.

Somehow, we had rustled up a football and in our street clothes, we set out to find a place where we could play and hoped that we would find a team of boys as eager as we were to play a match on that hot August afternoon. We took the *Vicinal* an inter-city streetcar in the northerly direction until we arrived at a football field where we could see half-a-dozen boys kicking a football around. A sign at the vicinal stop told us we were in BelAir, just north of the capital. As it was, we were now in the Flemish area of Brussels and the six kids we encountered spoke no French and, except for Eekhoudt, we could speak no Flemish. The terrain was in the middle of cultivated fields and our adversaries were peasant children who were not even wearing shoes.

We divided into two teams, the kids from the capital and the farmboys. Since we were only five and they were six, one of them was volunteered as the referee. We were to play two 45-minute halftimes and since I had the only working watch, I also became the timekeeper.

We soon found out that although they had no shoes, they could outrun and outkick us. We gave up trying to keep score and played on just for the fun of the game. However, I soon discovered that I had a problem with my Scholl inserts. Whenever I managed to get near the ball and gave it a kick, the plate would shoot to the front of my shoe and I could not take another step so great was the pain caused by the pressure of the insert on my toes and the ball of my foot. I'd have to stop and repeatedly stomp my heel against the ground until my insert slid back to its appointed place. I could then resume my running after the football. And so I played on, running, kicking, hobbling and stomping my heel each time I got near the ball. It never entered my mind that I could, that I should remove my Dr. Scholl's from my shoes.

We played nearly four hours. Instead of playing 90 minutes, we played until the evening fell. Only then did I discover that my watch had a broken spring and the hands moved only when I ran. We had run all over the field, the eleven of us without as much as a drink of water. By the time we hauled ourselves on the vicinal to return to the city, we were exhausted and aggrieved that we had been thoroughly beaten by a bunch of shoeless bumpkins. When I returned to my room Place Madou, I threw away my shoddy watch. A few days later, quietly and without notifying Mother, I discarded my Dr. Scholl's forever.

After August 15th, the Ascension holiday, traditionally the only warm day in Belgium's short summer, it was time to think about September and the return to school.

MOTHER'S FRIENDS

There was a man who lived in an apartment house. A very sexy woman had the apartment across from his and he pined for her night and day. However, he had noticed that each evening, a different pair of men's shoes was placed outside the woman's door to be shined by the building's porter. Well, there was never a pair of shoes on Wednesdays. One day, the man summoned up his courage and he asked the woman if she would take him on as a regular customer. The lady replied that she regretted, but that she was fully booked.

"Wednesday" he uttered "How about Wednesdays?"

"What about Wednesdays? "She replied."

"On Wednesdays there are never any shoes outside your door"

"Oh" she replied with a smile. "On Wednesdays I have my cripple".

Mother was not fully booked, but she had a rotation of steady boyfriends that kept her social calendar occupied. Frieda had found a full time occupation with the firm Simmons, the makers of mattresses but I never found out what her duties consisted of. She still found time to go to Namur or Ostende on a semi regular basis to find her pleasures at the casinos. Frieda would continue to play her little system until the day she left for the United States.

Frieda was now an attractive woman of 43 and she knew her powers. The fact that she spoke French with a special German accent added to her charm. There were five regular suitors she entertained and they all seemed unaware of the others or they chose not to notice them:

René Van Langendonck, the police chief, looked like Gary Cooper, but more muscular. Mother loved him a lot.—He is so beautiful!—She would exclaim, but in the same breath she would bemoan that he was impotent. René was friendly and easygoing. We had a good rapport and he seemed to genuinely like me. In later years, when Frieda would speak of Van Langendonck, the remarks were always exactly the same, beautiful but impotent. I never knew if he was married or not.

On Wednesdays, the Brussels stock exchange would be open and there was always an influx of businessmen on that day. Often, a greenhorn would wander into a nightclub or bar after the end of the day. There, an *entraineuse,* hostess would sidle up to him and become very friendly. Making him feel important, the "mark" would be plied with drinks and hors-d'oeuvres while the hostess downed glass after glass of ginger ale. At the end of the evening, the patsy would be told that since he was so nice, there would be no bill to pay and that everything was on the house.

Delighted with the free experience and special treatment, the patsy would come again the following Wednesday and the whole treatment would be repeated but to a much higher level of expenses. The visitor was encouraged to order rounds of champagne for everyone.

Late in the evening he would be invited to one of the upstairs bedrooms with a willing female companion. Much to his surprise, when it was time to leave, a stiff bill was presented for him to pay. If he refused to pay, threats were made that the police would be summoned and that word of his escapade would be relayed to his wife.

Monsieur Lemaitre, our former landlord at the *Quai de Sambre* in Charleroi was a regular visitor. Wednesdays were his days to visit Frieda. I would see him now and then looking like a little functionary, all dressed in a black suit, white shirt and long black tie, a dark mustache underscoring his black bowler hat. Mostly we'd cross paths in the staircase when he was either on his way in to Mother's apartment or on his way out. He'd turn his head away from me, avoiding my glance as if he was embarrassed that I might recognize who he was. I'd greet him—Bonjour, Monsieur Lemaitre-but he would never greet me back.

Ostensibly, he must have told his wife in Charleroi that he took the train to Brussels to go to the *Bourse*, the Stock Exchange. While in Brussels, he would also go to the barber and get a haircut and shave. He'd also get a shampoo and a manicure. In that way, he could go back to Charleroi with the evening train smelling like a French whorehouse, without having to explain to Madame Lemaitre why he was all perfumy. It must be said to Frieda's credit that, out of discretion, she did not douse herself with perfume.

Monsieur Genard, our Charleroi accountant and great friend of Frieda's was a sometime visitor. He had been instrumental in helping Father and Mother survive the numerous bankruptcies we had been plagued with. After the war, Mr Genard had also helped in negotiating a fair separation of wealth between Hilaire and Frieda. Whenever he came to see Mother, he always made it a point to spend a little time with me. He was a brilliant man and the depth and the breadth of his knowledge always impressed me. Mother always had some cookies and coffee set for him and he would invite me to sit with them and share in the cookies.

The last time I saw Monsieur Genard, he was on his way to Antwerp. The weather had turned colder and he asked me if I could lend him a sweater. I felt flattered that he should call on me and I gave him my finest blue cardigan. I would never see him or my cardigan again but I was pleased to know that I had kept him warm.

The most regular and constant of Frieda's friends was Major Frère. I did not keep track of his schedule, but he was there a lot. Mostly he was in his civilian clothes and I do not recall if I ever saw him in his Belgian Army uniform. The major was in charge of the financial branch of the military and it was his duty to see to it that all the military personnel were paid on time. He gave Mother fifteen hundred francs each month. That went a long way in keeping her solvent.

We would talk quite often even if most of our conversations were somewhat confrontational. He never seemed to take offense. Major Frère had very conservative views and was not overly fond of Americans. Of course, I would talk at length about my desire to leave for the USA and he'd argue and question my reasons for wanting to go there. He considered the US to be short on civilization and social graces, probably as a result of his contacts with the GI's after the liberation. Knowing that he was financially important to Mother, I refrained from getting into too many heated arguments with him.

Frère cautioned me that if I went to the United States I should learn to speak Spanish as "it was the prevailing language of the country". We had a short argument about that. His words would prove strangely prophetic in view of the later influx of Latinos in the USA. Even decades later, I would often recall that conversation.

Mother's stormiest relationship revolved around Major Giovanni Dieu, a much-decorated hero of the Battle of Britain. He was reputed to have been shot down three times in the English Channel and had been rescued by the British Navy. Dieu had been part of the famed 69th Squadron that was composed of volunteers from several nations and had fought under the banner of the Royal Air Force. He would eventually become the Commandant in charge of the Fighter Pilot School in Gosselies, a suburb of Charleroi. His brother Robert would become director of SABENA Airlines, the National Belgian Airline. This prompted the newspapers to claim that, since "Dieu" meant "God", the Belgian aviation was polytheistic.

Giovanni, as Mother always referred to him, was short and compact. Having been a fighter pilot, he had to fit in the cramped cockpit of a Hurricane or Spitfire. I only remember seeing him in his blue uniform and officer's flat cap but once or twice. Mother did not want to have him confront Major Frère and Dieu was not anxious to be seen at the Place Madou. There was an ongoing feud between Frieda and our landlady, Mme Dunesme over their respective boyfriends and Giovanni did not want to be caught in the crossfire. Giovanni knew about Frieda's other friends. Of Van Langendonck, he would opine that René "could not get it up" as he had seen many men in the military and the big ones were always dismal in bed. Frieda, knowing that Van Langendonck was impotent, would never confirm it to Giovanni.

When she first met Giovanni, he had assured her that he was not married. However, he had indeed married an English woman during the war. Giovanni had rented a small garret in an apartment house where he and Frieda spent many happy hours. Often, when Giovanni would be away, Mother would go to the apartment and spend the night there, cozy in the memory of their time together. If Giovanni was to occupy the garret with his wife (or with another woman), he would leave a note on the bed so that Frieda would not spend the night there. Thus he hoped to avoid an embarrassing encounter. One night, as Mother was preparing to go to sleep in the garret, Giovanni came in. As he was a gentleman, he effaced himself in the doorway and let his wife come in first. She found herself face to face with Frieda. There was a short exchange in French between Giovanni and Frieda that Dieu's wife did not understand as she only spoke English. The major quickly pushed his wife out of the room and went back in to ask Frieda why she was there and why she had not seen the note he had left. Frieda professed that she had found no note and that she would not leave the room as she intended to spend the night there.

Giovanni, always quick on his feet, told his wife that the woman was the sister of the landlord and that he sometimes let her use the room when the tenant was away. I never knew if MrsDieu bought the story, however, years later, when Giovanni died, the condolence card that Frieda sent was returned unopened.

Mother always felt that Giovanni was a cheapskate. Many colorful and salacious stories were told about their relationship. Most can be found among Frieda's Memoirs *(See: And Somehow We Survive).* When Mother left for the USA in 1952, she stood on the rear deck of the SS Rijndam and threw all the correspondence and photos about Giovanni into the Atlantic Ocean.

There were other boyfriends and lovers during Mother's stay in Belgium. However, I once asked her about whom she had liked best. Of course, René De Lange was "hors concours" with no possible rivals. Of the three other major ones; Van Langendonck was for love, Major Frère was for the money and Giovanni, for the prestige.

THE GIRL WITH THE CURLY RED HAIR

The Café Cambrinus stood at the base of a multiple story building making the corner of the Place Madou and the Chaussée de Louvain. It faced 5 Place Madou where we lived. Just above the café, a long balcony ran the length of the building. Only the width of the Chaussée separated that balcony from the one that graced Mother's apartment. A few times, I had noticed a tall young girl appearing at the balcony over the Cambrinus. With my poor eyesight, I could only guess at her beauty but she seemed very attractive. When the early sun would glance at her, it was easy to discern that her hair had a reddish glow to it and it made a large halo around her pretty face. Her hair was not just curly; it was frizzy, very frizzy. In the 1960's it would have been described as an "Afro" or as a cluster of "Brillo" pads and would have been very fashionable. In 1945, it was just very unusual. Whenever I fancied that I might start a romance with her, I could not help but wonder if I would have the nerve to walk down the street with her.

In any case, there was no question of romancing her as she seemed very beautiful and my Mother's "Ugly" comments still reverberated in my head. Be that as it may, I came to notice that whenever I'd go out to the balcony of Mother's apartment, *"La Rousse"* "Redhead" as I came to name her would appear at her balcony and lean languorously against the railing. After a while, there seemed to be a blurring of the intentions. Did she appear when I chanced to be on the balcony or did I spy her being there and then made my appearance? This sterile flirting would go on for the better part of the next four years without as much as a greeting or a word and yet, there was a union there, a meeting of the eyes, a private and very silent longing.

Thinking back, given the shade of her hair and the mysterious texture of her hair, I could not but wonder if she too had been a Jew, a survivor of the Holocaust although at the time, I was not conscious of the narrow escape I had gone through. My sole preoccupation was to fit in school and in a world that seemed very alien to me. "La Rousse" must have thought that I was either shy or very dumb, or perhaps both.

BACK TO SCHOOL, SEPTEMBER 1945

With the coming of September, it was time to return to school. For me, it meant entering the Fifth *Latine* with all my usual buddies except for Bob Van Meckeren who had to remain behind and repeat the 6th. Although the *Modernes* had been learning German and English for a year, the *Latine* would now add English to the curriculum. Greek and German would come the next year, in the 4th. After the 4th, we would be leaving the Middle School and go on to the *Ecole Superieure* for another three years and then move on to the University. All this was very nebulous to me, as there was no history of higher schooling in our family. For me there was only a vague perception of my future as I was fixed on leaving for America as soon as I could get my affidavit from "Uncle" Leo Wolleman whose promises to bring me to the USA still rang in my ears.

In the early days of the new class year, I had been befriended by Guy Cordemans. Cordemans studied in the *Moderne* classes but we had connected in school anyway. Guy was tall, handsome and from an upper-class family. He looked like Louis Jourdan and was always well dressed and impeccably groomed. Except for the fact that the schools did not have a "Sports" program, he would be described as an "All-American" if we had been in America. Guy had taken me under his wing and would often bring me home for dinner, as he knew that there was no such thing as a regular meal at the Rosenberg home. Guy's Father was an *Agent de Change,* a stockbroker but I had no idea what that meant. All I knew was that his Father had played and speculated with other people's money and was no longer allowed to practice that profession. Guy had an older brother, (Jacques if I remember well) who was enamored with the military and dreamed of going to the Belgian Congo with the Belgian Armed Forces.

Mostly, when I had dinner at the Cordemans home, it was Guy and his Mother, Madame Cordemans. She was as tall as Guy and a very good-looking woman. Aware of my unfortunate situation at home, they would invite me for dinner at least once a week. Invariably Mme Cordemans would inquire if I minded eating pork. To me, it was always a bit surprising. I knew that Jews were not supposed to eat pork, but I thought that these were rules set up hundreds of years ago and no longer enforced. Throughout my fifteen years, we had never eaten Kosher. I did not even know the word or, for that matter, its meaning. The only time there had been a reference to pork being objectionable was in the early days of the war when Frieda had cut away maggot-infected ham "Because it was difficult enough to get Hilaire to eat pork".

Now that I was going to have English as a taught language that year, Guy had told me about our new English teacher, Monsieur De La Province. For some unknown reason, De La Province had been nicknamed "Bedel". That must have been an English word as it did not exist in French. It would be years before I found out that a "bedel" is an usher. Anyway, we had been cautioned never to use the word in front of him as Mr De La Province was well aware of his nickname and that he loathed it.

On our first day in school, De La Province entered our packed class and introduced himself.

"I am Monsieur De La Province" he began; "I am your English professor!"

This was too great an opening for me and I could not resist it. With what I tried to show as innocent a face as I could muster, I held my hand up to be recognized. With a quizzical look, De La Province beckoned to me.

"Isn't Monsieur Bedel teaching this course anymore?—" I asked.

A mortal silence fell upon the room. I did not have enough sense to know that teachers compared notes on the students before venturing into the Coliseum to face the lions. Surely I had been signaled as a troublemaker. "Watch that Rosenberg and his smile"

Bedel's eyes got rounder, his face red as a beet, pointing to the door he yelled *"Rosenberg, sortez!* "And off I went to the principal's office. It was not the best of beginnings, but there would be more to come.

It must be remembered that by then, I spoke fluent "American" albeit not always grammatically correct. However, no amount of modesty could have convinced me that my command of the language could have been less than perfect. I had had a few minor skirmishes with Bedel but we had managed to co-exist in peace since our first conflagration. I was also deep in my Anglophobia and my love for all things American.

De La Province asked me to translate a sentence into English. I did this without trouble except that I used a wrong pronoun. Was it a "That" instead of a "With" or vice-versa? I would not recall. However, when Bedel corrected me, I would not accept the correction. It was too humiliating to be told in front of the whole class that the *"Americain"* had made a mistake in English. I defended my use of the wrong pronoun by boldly stating that it was the way Americans spoke. De La Province retorted that I was in his class to learn English and not American. I could have dropped the matter, but I did not.

"English disgusts me! "I spitted out. "When I hear people speaking English in the streets, I step to the other sidewalk so as not to have to hear them!"

The next thing I heard was *"Rosenberg, Sortez!* "And I was on my familiar trot to see the principal.

There was no more conflict with Bedel after that. He never called on me again and we were content to circle each other with knives drawn for the remainder of my time at the Athénée Léon Lepage.

MONSIEUR DUBOIS, THE MATH AND SCIENCE TEACHER

The cast of characters in the 5th *Latine* remained mostly that of the 6th with the addition of our English teacher Mr De La Province and sadly the replacement of Mlle Truffaut by Monsieur Dubois. Dubois would now be our main teacher, replacing Mr Barbier as our home-rule teacher.

Monsieur Dubois, of average height, straddled the floor like a wrestler. With powerful limbs and a bald head he always looked as if he were ready to take on all comers. There was a problem with his eyes as one would stare in one direction and the other at a completely different angle. However, his voice and accent were his most unusual features. Dubois rolled his "R's" as if he had come from Flanders, in thick rolling succession with his tongue scraping his palate from the back to the front. This made it sound as if there were an endless *"rrrrow"* of "R's" in a *worrrrd.* When he spoke, he seemed to empty his lungs with each syllable and that forced him to gasp for air in the middle of his words. His sentences made the air and the desks tremble. Dubois was impressive.

We had run into him the previous year when he had come in as a temporary replacement for a teacher who had taken ill. It had been pretty uneventful except that Dubois was generous with his "Zeros" that he flung around whenever an answer was not entirely to his liking. It did not matter to us as he was just a replacement for one day and the bad marks would not appear in our totals at the end of the year.

However, on that special day, the previous year, Dubois had sprung a special question to the class.

"Who can give me the definition of "*Interrrrest*"?"

Everyone gave it a try.

"Interest is the percentage paid when you borrow money"

"No! Sit down, you will have a zerrro! "He bellowed, the desks trembling under his voice.

One after the other, the students ventured a definition of interest and one after the other; they were shot down with a fusillade of zeros. After a while, no one dared to venture an opinion. Then,

225

Dubois, obviously relishing the moment, granted us his own definition. Spitting, bellowing, rolling his "R's", gasping for air between each syllable, making the desks tremble, he declaimed:

"L'intérrrêt est la rrrétrribution accorrrdée au prrrêteur parrr l'emprrrunteurrhhh!"

"The interest is the reward granted to the lender by the borrower" That was it, the Dubois definition of interest. I would never forget it and for months, whenever I wanted to give an imitation of Dubois' bellowing, that was the phrase I would parody including the rolling "R's" the spitting, the gasping for air and with enough force to make the desks tremble.

Dubois did not like me, he did not like my smile, he did not like the fact that I had good marks and that I could always come up with the correct answer thus depriving him of the pleasure to grant me his favorite zeros. He'd throw me out of his class as least once a week. He once even gave me a "zerrro" in Algebra during a science class after a classmate Maggi's guffaw that Dubois chose to blame on me.

There was another problem with Dubois. When he pointed to a student, his left eye aimed in another direction. Thus he would point to Friedman sitting near the window and ask him a question. Hanspacher, from the middle row would give him the answer. Dubois would now turn to him and bellow: "I did not ask you anything!" And Kruman, from his seat near the door would complain that he had not said anything. This would bring about a general laughter and "Rrrosenberrgghh" would get a zerrro".

It was about mid-term in our 5th *Latine* and Dubois (now our 5th grade teacher) was giving our class his regular course when, without warning and who knows for what fateful purpose, he again sprang the "Interest" question on us. By then, all had forgotten the definition of the interest he had given us the previous year. All, that is, except "Rrrosenberrgghh".

For a while, the comedy of the last year repeated itself with everyone venturing a definition that was unacceptable to Monsieur Dubois. He began to distribute "zerrros" all around until no one dared to put up a hand. I had my hand up from the start as I knew the answer, boy, did I ever know it! Of course, Dubois would not call on me. Finally, there was only my right hand, as high as my arm could raise it, with my left hand pressed to my armpit, propping up my tired right arm until Dubois would recognize me. He looked at me and quizzed "Rrrosenberrgghh?"

It seemed as if I had been training my whole life for that moment. Spitting, bellowing, rolling my "R's", gasping for air between each syllable, making the desks tremble, I began:

"L'intérrrêt est la rrrétrribution accorrrdée au prrrêteur parrr l'emprrreunteurrhh!"

Thunderstruck, flabbergasted, his mouth wide open, Dubois seemed made of granite. He should have given me a "ten" as the answer was accurate indeed. After a long while, lucidity seemed to return to his eyes and he pointed to the door.

"Rrrosenberrrgghh, sorrrtez!" Dubois croaked, his voice weak and trembling. And off I went for another encounter with the principal. How sweet it was. How sweet it still is after all these years.

JUNKERS JU52, FIRST FLIGHT

There had been a minor celebration planned for the end of the war and the re-opening of the Brussels aerodrome of Melsbroek, just northeast of the capital (near the present airport of Zaventem). The school children were offered the opportunity for a maiden flight in a captured German Junkers 52, the box-like tri-motor transport workhorse of the German Luftwaffe. To relieve the schools of any liability, each student willing to participate had to buy a ticket for the minimal sum of 2 francs that most paid willingly. The Ju52 with its corrugated metal construction and the three cowlings that shrouded its engines made quite an impression on us. It had been the workhorse of the German Air Force and had been used as a transport and to drop paratroopers during the war. Standing under its wings, waiting to board, it looked enormous yet sturdy. When we boarded, we sat on small wicker seats. I was lucky to have a seat next to one of the right windows. As the plane gathered speed on the runway, I noticed that the wings were swaying up and down, almost touching the ground. I thought that this thing would never get off the ground; it was too heavy and too ungainly to fly. Suddenly, we were alight and the wings were straight and steady, tilted upward. I was aloft, on a plane, for the very first time. The Ju52 made a couple of turns and headed for the capital that we viewed from above for a short while. A few more turns and we landed back in Melsbroek. As we taxied to the crowd of children waiting their turn, the wings were drooping and swaying again, but this time I trusted them more. It would take nine years before I'd fly in a plane again.

As part of the festivities, it had been announced that Henri Garat, the French Music Hall and movie idol of the thirties would be flying in and arrive from Paris. The press and newsreel reporters were on hand to see him come off the plane. Actually, Garat had fallen on hard times and had boarded a small plane at the end of the runway and the plane had then taxied to the hangar where the reporters were waiting. Nevertheless, the next day, the papers were highlighting Henri Garat's arrival direct from Paris.

FIRE

Out of nowhere, Lucien, my old *sex instructor* from the Rue du Marais materialized. How had he connected with us was a mystery. All I knew was that we were sitting in Mother's apartment, Ruth, Lucien and I. We talked, drank coffee and Ruth and Lucien were smoking cigarettes. Lucien did most of the smoking. Although I did not know it then, Frieda as she would often do was probably spending the night in the garret that she shared with Major Dieu.

Thinking back, it was probable that Lucien wanted to make it with Ruth but I was in the way. Ruth made no attempt at having me leave the apartment and go to my room, giving me the impression that she had no interest in Lucien's advances. As it was, Lucien hung around until nearly three in the morning smoking and smoking until the room was filled with blue and white acrid smoke. When he finally left, Ruth and I went up to our rooms in the third-floor attic.

Later that morning, Madame Sarto, *La Buchenwald,* rushed into our rooms, yelling that the apartment was on fire. We rushed downstairs to Frieda's apartment. The room was filled with smoke and flames were jumping out of the chimney. The curtains over the French windows to the balcony were now aflame and the furniture was smoldering with smoke and flames. Ruth and I opened the windows and pulled down the burning curtains that we flung out in the street. The curtains spiraled below in lazy burning circles. Under the balcony, we could see dozens of onlookers. They were yelling "Put out the fire, put out the fire!" As if it had been within our control. Shortly after, the fire brigade showed up and they were able to douse the flames with much water. The fire had also done much damage to the downstairs apartment of Mme Dunesme. It had started in the chimney and what we thought were all the cigarettes that Ruth and Lucien had been smoking, was instead the smoldering chimney that ran up and down the back of the living quarters.

When Mother came home late that morning, she was greeted by a nasty surprise, what had not been burned was covered with soot. All of our clothing would reek of wet smoke for months and months. We did not have money to buy new clothes and we would dress in smoke day after day. It was an odor I would forever remember, burned in some mysterious corner of my mind.

Ruth had a different recollection of the incident. Ruth also has *"absolutely no memory of the evening with Lucien except we had been out and came home and said that Mother must have once again smoked like a chimney . . . but I don't remember Lucien being with us"* That shows that different people recall differently. I do stand by my version but feel that Ruth's comments should be inserted here.

"Here, Rudy, I must absolutely disagree with you—you said "I'm not going in there"-you didn't. I went in—opened the French doors to the balcony and pulled the drapes that were burning and threw them out on the street with people screaming "don't throw fire on us". You didn't go in—I was intent on getting to the "armoire" in the far corner of the room to retrieve all the important papers that were there . . . later, I realized that the fire had been coming from just the left of that and it had left a large hole in the floor I really could have fallen in. I also remember dragging a box full of photos and negatives outside . . . Honestly; I don't recall that you went in.

Later, I don't think you were around, several hours after Mother came home and the next day, she and I scrubbed the floor to remove ashes and blackened stuff to make the place livable;-we had nowhere else to go. Also, we were given some clothes. I know I always undressed downstairs and left the clothes in the armoire overnight and the clothing all burned.

As far as I know, we never heard from Lucien again.

SAINT NICOLAS, DECEMBER 1945

I was so hungry for America. The rest of the year had gone by without news from Leo Wolleman. I knew that I would be an American some day. Presently I wanted everyone to think, to know that I was a Yankee. From the platform of the streetcars, on my way to school, I'd sing at the top of my lungs the only American song for which I knew the words. "You are my sunshine, my only sunshine . . ." And I wanted everyone to hear me, to know that I was not a stateless Jew, but an American.

At night, hours would be spent listening to the AFN, the American Forces Network that broadcast nightly from Munich, Germany. At midnight, there would be a little skit lasting perhaps a minute or two and would turn into a question as to what was happening. What was happening was that it was "Midnight in Munich". Then, the Skyliner tune by Charlie Barnett would fill the airwaves and I'd listen, transfixed, to the best of the big bands and songs until one or two in the morning or until I fell asleep or turned off my radio.

There was nothing that would mark the end of that year of 1945. I did meet Bob Van Meckeren and we took the tram to go to a movie. We were standing on the platform and he asked me what I had received for St. Nicolas, the traditional day when children receive presents. Well, I had received nothing. I had to invent a gift; a football, I said. Bob wanted to know what else I had received. I made up another one and Bob wanted to know what else I had received. I kept coming up with one gift after the other and Bob kept pressing me for more. The platform of the tram was filled with people who were listening to our discussion and they soon became aware that I was fibbing, that I really had received nothing. It took me a long time to realize that Bob was leading me on, that he and the rest of the listeners knew I had received nothing at all. I felt myself blushing and had to get off the streetcar at the next stop with Bob limping after me, telling me that he had just been kidding.

1946

Give Me Five Minutes More, Only Five Minutes More
Let Me Stay, Let Me Stay In Your Arms
Here Am I Begging For, Only Five Minutes More,
Only Five Minutes More Of Your Charms. (Frank Sinatra)
(Or as the GIs would sing: Give Me Five Inches More . . .)

WINTERTIME IN BRUSSELS

"The Orthodox" at school talked a lot about Zionism and the need to establish a Jewish home in Palestine. We were hearing rumors about Jewish terrorism against the Arabs and the British. Monsieur Narcisse was becoming more violent and abusive in his hatred of our four Jews and by extension of Maurice and me. My shame of being Jewish grew daily and so did my determination not to be a Jew. Ruth and I could not even bring ourselves to say the word "Jew". It had a bad connotation. We would refer to being "Israelites" that was passable, easier to swallow It did not have the understood prefix "Sale" dirty in front of it.

Public transports went on a general strike in Brussels. No buses, taxis or streetcars were circulating. I found myself near the North Station. I would have to walk home to Place Madou. A woman with a suitcase and a large wicker trunk had just arrived by train and she was now contemplating her next move with great apprehension. I offered my help that she gratefully accepted. The wicker basket was loaded with silverware and was almost as heavy as I was. The lady said that she lived near the Place St. Josse, which was perhaps one kilometer down the Chaussée de Louvain from Place Madou. With great effort, I lifted the trunk and placed it on my left shoulder and proceeded up the steep long Boulevard Du Botanique. The woman followed me, dragging and lifting her suitcase (no one had yet thought of putting wheels on luggage). After about two hours of lugging, walking and shifting the load from my left to my right shoulder and back we arrived to her apartment. She lived on the second floor and I brought it up there.

She thanked me sincerely and asked if she could give me money for my efforts. I would not take money. Rather I looked at her and said "It was done as a service, Madame. But please remember one thing, I am a Jew and I have helped you!" With that, I turned away and went home. I had mixed feelings about it. I just wanted to tell her, to tell the whole world that Jews were not all bad, that here was a Jew who selflessly helped a Christian in her moment of need. Maybe I was striking a blow against this hatred we were victims of. Looking back on it, maybe I should have taken the money.

The winter had not been as severe as during 44-45 when the Allies were struggling during the Battle of the Bulge. However we did get one snow fall in Brussels, not a big one, but enough so that the streets were covered with a couple of centimeters of the white stuff. This was great news to us school children. The schools were closed and we roamed the streets looking for good snow to make snowballs and find suitable targets for our aim. Some of us found our way to the *Place Des Martyrs*, a large public square close to the *Rue Neuve* and we began to pelt the façades of the surrounding buildings. Much to our distress, a flatbed truck appeared loaded with granulated salt. On the truck, a few men were spraying the snow with shovelful of salt. They were destroying our snow, killing our pleasure. As one, we began to pelt them with dozens of snowballs and they responded by peppering us with the salt. It stung and hurt and we soon had to retreat. The snow quickly turned to slush and a couple of hours later, all was gone except some dangerous black-ice that forced pedestrians to walk about carrying a couple of burlap bags so they could step on them and walk about without falling.

G.I. JOE

Movies made in Hollywood during the war were now flooding the local theatres. Avidly I went to see as many as I could afford to. Many of these were war stories that would go a long way to reinforce my love for America and its soldiers despite their obvious propaganda content. "Air Force" introduced me to John Garfield; it pleased me to learn that he was Jewish. "Thirty Seconds over Tokyo" featured Robert Walker and Van Johnson. There was a tentative softness about Johnson that made me a longtime fan of his. "Laura" a detective story and "The Purple Heart" and "A Walk in the Sun" brought me Dana Andrews and I had to see all the films he had ever made. I became so disappointed in him when I found out that he was an alcoholic and would throw away his career in later years. For now, he was my favorite actor and I was thrilled to receive a "signed" copy of his picture.

There had been a documentary about the aircraft carrier USS Enterprise. I came out of the theatre convinced that I wanted to become a carrier pilot in the US Navy. Much to my chagrin, it became apparent that my eyes were not going to get any better and that my dreams of becoming a carrier pilot were sinking rapidly. I was full of despair about it.

"The Story of G.I. Joe" made the deepest impression on me. Perhaps it was that the leading character in the movie, Robert Mitchum was so believable and was killed in the end. There was also an archetypal set of American GI's that reminded me so much of the ones I had come to know and love. Most of all, there was the journalist and writer Ernie Pyle portrayed superbly by Burgess Meredith. Pyle had been killed in the waning days of the war in the Pacific and I could not wait to get my hands on his book "G.I. Joe". I was able to buy a paperback issue in English that I began to read avidly. Since it was in English, it was a laborious task that would take me a few weeks to complete. The book went everywhere with me and I'd read it whenever the time was available.

I would not recall which of our teachers did not show up in school on that fateful morning in 1946 but we were told that for our last morning period we would have to go and mingle with the *Moderne* class of Monsieur Grillard. Monsieur Grillard taught French to the *Modernes*. Grillard was a spare fellow, very properly dressed, with a pencil-thin mustache and slicked black air. He looked like a thinner, miniature version of Hercule Poirot. He was also a writer of songs, albeit not a very successful one. Under the nom de plume of Jean Reveu, one of his songs had been published *"Je me Moque de la Pluie"* "I Laugh at the Rain". Like so many of the teachers of the *Modernes*, it was believed that he felt that his tenure was considered inferior to that of the *Latines* teachers.

Well, at about eleven that morning, we entered his class and he motioned to us to take a seat wherever there was space in the room. I found a free desk in the second row, about four seats from the front. Grillard, totally ignoring us, told his students to open their books at a certain page.—*Les Modernes*—He spoke.—Open your book on page 45.—

Thus, he left us to fend for ourselves. In my *cartable,* Ernie Pyle's book was awaiting my eager hands. I pulled out my copy of G.I.Joe and was immediately fully absorbed in my lecture. When I read, it was not some word on a sheet of paper. For me, it was a plunge deep in the world of the story. All around me would become foggy and I was lost in my reading. Somehow, I became aware that Monsieur Grillard had been circling around, going down one row of desks and coming up the second row until he was behind me and slightly to my right. Suddenly, Grillard's right hand reached for my book and pulled it from under my eyes. For me, it was as if my world had been snatched away and I was falling into an abyss.

Grillard, without a word, was leafing and browsing through my copy of G.I. Joe. I could see his face getting redder and redder with anger. Then, in a fury, he attempted to rip my book apart, his hands trembling, his face contorted with rage. Ernie Pyle was resisting and Grillard had to resort to ripping the book a few pages at a time. When the book had finally been torn and shredded, Grillard threw the remnants in a wastebasket. He was yelling that I was never to bring such trash in class again. Monsieur Grillard then took a while to compose himself. All the other students held their noses close to their desks, not daring to make a peep.

I was not pleased, not in the least. Grillard had ignored us and had not given us any instructions. "G.I.Joe" was not trash, it was English literature and since I was studying English it was a legitimate matter to bring to school. However, that could have been a subject for discussion at a later time.

Again, I reached in my *cartable* and opened my school notebook. There, pasted under the cover, the school rules were laid out in plain sight. It read:

"If a student brings an unauthorized item to school or class, it will be confiscated and returned to him at the end of the school year".

That was plain and easy to understand. If my book was not authorized, it could have been confiscated but to be returned at the end of the year. Of course, it would have been difficult to return it as it was now in shreds and lodged at the bottom of the wastebasket. I had paid twenty five francs for that book and I wanted my money back.

The morning session ended and we all headed for the hallway and the stairs. Grillard was at the end of the column, making sure that we all vacated the premises. I walked slowly, letting the class go by until I found myself at the height of Mr Grillard. I then turned to him and said "I am sorry Monsieur Grillard". With that, his face showed the outline of a mean smile. I continued "But you owe me twenty-five francs! ".

He threw me down the flight of stairs. Luckily, my friend Guy Cordemans was at the bottom of the stairs and caught me before I slammed into the wall.

I GET ALONG SWIMMINGLY

Somebody's elbow cracked me in the nose, sideways. We were in the hallway of the school, struggling to enter the recreation yard and out of nowhere I got hit. It was unintentional of course and one of the penalties of being short among taller people. Anyway, I saw stars. I was sure my nose was broken. As soon as I got home, I stood in front of the mirror with another hand-mirror to assess the damages.

What I saw shocked me. I had a hooked nose, a Jewish nose. Some kind soul would later refer to it as a "Roman" nose. For a while, I fancied that it had been caused by the blow from the elbow but no, it was genetic, passed on to me from generation to generation. Until then, I had only seen myself from the front and what I had seen was just fine. Now I knew why I looked Jewish and that I would have to go through life advertising it. The ear operation had been for nothing. The mark of Moses was on my face.

Of course, when the class went to the Royal Baths for our irregular swimming sessions, there was the circumcision scar for all to see. The baths was not my favorite place to visit. I did not like the cold water, I did not know how to swim and the water made me wince. Certainly I would not plunge into the pool. I had to remove my glasses to dive and without my glasses I had no sense of where and how far the surface might be.

We had to enter the pool by the middle ladder. From there, I'd hang on to the bar that circled the entire pool and went hand over hand until I arrived at the *petite profondeur* the shallow end where I would have safe footing. Trying not to get splashed or dunked, I'd hang around there until it was time to vacate the pool, which could never be too early for me.

On that day, the whistle blew for the end of the swimming session and I began to follow the safety bar to reach the middle ladder. I was just about to reach the ladder when a sudden rush occurred. I felt myself pushed away from the safety of the wall. Unfortunately, Fanesse, another student had also been pushed away and he was thrashing about in a wild panic. He grabbed the nearest object and that happened to be me. We were now both drifting to the middle of the pool and neither of us knew how to swim. Fanesse, being taller and stronger than I climbed over me and we both went under. As my feet felt the bottom of the pool, I sprung up as hard as I could and we rose up until Fanesse's head was above the surface. He took a great lungful of air and I swallowed a great gulp of water. I hit the bottom again and once more, Fanesse got to breathe while I swallowed more water.

I was going down for the third time when someone managed to pull Fanesse from me and get him out of the water. Someone's arm reached under me and dragged me to the safety of the ladder. I stayed on all fours, draining the water from my lungs and my stomach until I felt strong enough to get up, shower and get dressed. It would take a long while before I went near a pool again.

WINDING DOWN MY SCHOOL YEARS

By then, it was becoming obvious that I would not survive the year in school. Clearly, I had a problem with discipline no matter how I felt about my rights.

We were being marched to class and climbing a set of stairs when someone let out with a great big "whoop!" The teacher who was supervising us asked to know who had made the offending noise. When no one came forward, he announced that the whole class would now be punished until the culprit came forward. In the Hollywood movies I had become familiar with, there was always a young man who took the blame and he would become an instant hero. At least, that is how I had seen it in some of Mickey Rooney's Andy Hardy movies.

Well, for whatever reason, I heard my voice say "I did it, it was me who had yelled". Bad idea, very bad idea! The roof fell in on me and no one came to support me. Certainly the culprit was never going to admit that it was he who had done it. There was punishment after punishment, no time out for recess, no participation in any games and confinement to the classroom week after week.

When I finally went to the principal to explain that I was not the one who had yelled, I was even more reprimanded for having lied about the whole affair. I had a bone to pick with Andy Hardy.

MAY 1946, ALLIED VICTORY DAY

A celebration was planned to commemorate the first anniversary of the end of the war in Europe. There were to be speeches by all sorts of bigwigs, bands and a parade of the flags of all the Allied nations. All this was to take place at the Place des Martyrs, the enormous square where the Belgian heroes who had died during the 1830 revolution against the Dutch are buried. The children of the city's schools would assemble there and sing the national anthems of the various nations.

And so, we laboriously learned "The Star Spangled Banner" for our American Allies, "God Save the Queen" for the British and "Oh Canada, . . . thou land of noble name" for the Canadians. For the Canadians, we had to learn it in English only as the French movement in Canada was not yet as pervasive as it would become in later years.

"Willhelmus van Nassau" was the Dutch anthem and we had to learn that one in Dutch. I felt it was an ironic anthem to sing at the Place des Martyrs and fancied that the heroes buried beneath our feet would be turning around in their graves. The Dutch anthem ended with the statement that Willhelmus van Nassau, the Dutch king in the 16th century, had always shown respect for the King of Spain. The entire hymn seemed to me to be so anachronistic as to worry about offending a Spanish monarch who had died four hundred years before.

For the French, we had to learn "La Marseillaise" that most of us knew by heart anyway since it had always been a stirring and popular anthem. Of course, we all knew "La Brabançonne", the Belgian national anthem and we only had to sing it in French. In 1946, the Flemish separatist movement was not yet as virulent as it would become later. All we had to remember was to sing the real version, not the well-known parody that had the Belgian people emerging from a beer-keg after centuries of drunkenness.

For Poland, there was a tame French translation that "Poland would never die as long as we were living". Also that Dombrowsy, whoever he was, should march on and on, chasing away Poland's enemies.

During the war, Russia had abandoned its famous *"Internationale"* in favor of a tamer song. The beautiful *"Internationale"* had always been distasteful to the governments of the United States and England and, in order to appear gentler and to receive aid from the "Capitalists", Stalin had opted for an inoffensive new anthem. It was a dull and stodgy melody with words duller yet. *"Lasting is the union of the Soviet people". It is still in use today even though the "Soviet Union" is now a thing of the past.*

Thus we learned to mumble and blunder through nearly a dozen national hymns to be sung on the appointed day. I felt lucky that we did not have to learn a few more honoring Australia, New

Zealand, Scotland, India, etc. At the time these were still part of the Commonwealth of Great Britain and were covered under the blanket of "God Save the Queen".

Tens of thousands of school children covered the square on that May Day (including Rosa Wauters whom I would later marry). I would not remember the names of the speakers or their speeches. What I would remember was the ambiance of sullen hostility that emanated from the ranks of the school children. Somehow, they all seemed to resent being there at all and to have to participate in a glorification of nationalism. After five bloody years of suffering because of the excesses of nationalist doctrines, the youth had a sense that this demonstration was wrong. A mild wind of revolt circulated through our ranks and I felt myself engulfed in it without quite knowing why. I was willing to sing the American anthem but resented having to sing the Belgian one. I had suffered too many heartaches and disappointments in Belgium. There and then, I resolved to renew my efforts to escape to America as soon as possible.

This strange wind of unease that blew among the youth gathered there would culminate in full-blown revolts in Europe and America in the decades to come.

A PARENT'S NOTE TO THE PRINCIPAL

The principal needed a letter from one of my parents. The reason has long escaped my memory. Was it as a consequence of my "Andy Hardy" episode? It might have been as simple as having failed to turn in some homework and I would have needed a letter from home explaining the reason I had been delinquent. Whatever the reason, I had to come up with a letter from Father or Mother. Father was out of the question, as even if he had known how to write, he was not living with us. Mother was out a lot and spending most of her evenings at the *mansarde* she shared with Giovanni Dieu, whether he was there or not. Frieda's ability to write in French was negligible and she would not have been able to compose a suitable letter.

Ruth decided to solve the dilemma by writing the letter of excuse for me and she signed it with Mother's name. The next day relieved and armed with "Mother's" letter, I turned it in to the principal's office and went to attend my first class of the day. About twenty minutes into the class, I saw a face peer through the window of the class door. The door opened and a woman entered. She was the principal's assistant and she went directly to the teacher's pulpit. She spoke a few words while pointing an accusing finger in my direction. I knew I was in trouble. The teacher nodded in agreement and the lady came and grabbed me by my shirt collar and showed me out the door. We walked fast through the corridor and down the steps and I found myself sitting just outside the principal's office.

"Come in" a voice growled. I was facing an angry principal. He pointed to a piece of paper on his desk and asked "Who wrote this letter?"

My mind was racing. I did not know if I should lie or blurt out the truth. All the while, I was trying to figure out how he had found out that Mother had not written the note. I insisted that it was indeed my Mother who was the author of that missive. The principal would not accept that and threatened that my continued denials would only make matters worse. I finally had to admit that it was my sister Ruth who had penned it. I explained that neither of my parents were around or able to redact such a letter in French. This seemed to soften him a bit. The principal then gave me a letter to give to Mother and told me that he wanted to have a conference with her.

That evening, I explained the whole thing to Mother. Incredibly, she did not get mad at Ruth or me. I cried a bit and told Mother that I knew I was failing in school, that none of my teachers liked me and that I was sure to have to repeat the 5th next year.

The next day, Mother went to see the principal and relayed my fears to him. "*Celui-la!* That one! "He laughed. "He would like nothing better that to be left alone at his desk and to repeat this class over and over again. But that is not going to happen. He is too smart a boy to fail. He just has to apply himself a little more"

So, the episode ended without dire consequences. However, I just could not go on. I could barely get to school in time. I was burned out. At night, I'd have repeated dreams. In those dreams, I'd arrive very late for class. I'd take off my cap and hung it on the hooks lining the hallways. Then I'd take off my coat and would find myself completely naked or just with a short T-shirt on. Obviously I could not enter the class in that condition. I'd try to leave and run back home but my coat and cap had disappeared from the wall. Crying, I'd run naked through the school's corridors, the laughter of my schoolmates ringing in my ears.

I'd awake in my bed, drenched with sweat and trying to reason out where I could have left my clothes. It became harder and harder for me to get up and ready myself for school. Soon, I stopped trying altogether and in late spring 1946 I quit school. There was no sudden decision, no planned defection. I just stopped going.

FIRST JOB, LEVER BROTHERS

Five hundred meters down the Rue du Congres from our apartment, the Monument to the Belgian Unknown Soldier spiraled high in the sky with the statue of King Leopold the First gazing down on the city of Brussels. Flanking the square and the Eternal Flame, two imposing edifices occupied the Rue Royale. The one on the right held the Headquarters of *Lever Freres SA*. Lever Brothers Belgium also known as Unilever of soap and "Sunlight" fame. I would not remember how I found myself on the fifth floor of this impressive building, in the office of Monsieur Van Hamme, the personnel manager. Obviously I had gone there to apply for a job and I would recall nothing of the interview.

In England, Unilever, founded by Lord Samuel Lever, a Jew, probably hired quite a number of Jewish personnel. In Belgium, there was gentlemen's agreement that made it difficult, if not impossible for Jews to find a position in the firm. After my interview there, I had been told that my chances of being hired were nil. However, Mr Egget, one of the directors had married his former secretary, known as Miss Hart and she was Jewish. She was then the secretary to MrLapage, the director of SEDEC, one of the many societies that formed the Lever Group in Belgium. Apparently, Miss Hart had heard of my application for a job and interceded in my favor. I was hired as an office boy for SEDEC. I was elated and in the summer of 1946, at the age of 16, I started to work almost immediately.

Several hundred people worked in the five-story building. When one entered the main lobby it was as if one had entered in a bank or a government ministry. Grand marble staircases flanked both sides and continued on to the top floor. An iron-gated elevator invited important people to the upper floors. There was always a doorman, an elevator man and several men scurrying about polishing the brass and keeping the lobby impeccable. SEDEC occupied the second floor in Kafkaesque-like offices. It was all very impressive to me.

Lever Brothers owned vast palm plantations in the Belgian Congo where the palm oil was being converted into raw material for soap. The *Huileries du Congo Belge* oversaw the production. A huge number of Congolese worked and were housed in the African plantations. Under conditions that might have resembled indenture, the *Noirs,* Blacks worked for the Company, were paid by the Company and purchased most of their food and essential goods from the Company Store. SEDEC (roughly Society for the Exploitation of the Congo) was in charge of running the Company Stores. SEDEC supplied food and trade goods where the Blacks were obliged to spend the money they had earned with their labor.

All that was of no importance to me; I had a job albeit just as an office boy. Once a month I would receive a paycheck and would be given time off to go and cash it at one of the banks a kilometer away, near the Place Royale under the proud equestrian statue of Godefroy de Bouillon, the Belgian Crusader. Godefroy, leader of the First Crusade, had himself crowned King of Jerusalem after the first conquest of that city in 1100. He died shortly thereafter, was succeeded by his son Baudouin who promptly died of the plague. Godefroy de Bouillon remains a great Belgian hero for having "brought Christianity to the heathen Arabs".

I had never had a bank account and that was the only way I could cash my Lever check. Apparently I was not the only one in that position as there was always a crowd at the bank for the similar purpose. Getting paid once a month created a hardship; having spent most of my meager salary in the early part of the month, it was "sucking" time during the waning days of the month until we got paid again.

I shared my "office boy" duties with Henri Guérin, a friendly young fellow with a very slight harelip. Guérin would make his entire career at Lever Brothers and would even marry one of his colleagues. Together we occupied a space between the stairs and the enormous SEDEC office. Huge oak doors separated the two. Pretty girls flitted to and fro from stairs to landings. I was not used to girls and my curiosity about them grew daily. Once, I heard the clacking of heels rapidly descending the stairs. Wanting to discover if I knew the girl, I bent over and peeked through the large keyhole. Bang! The door opened with great force and crashed into my face sending my glasses flying. My nose was bruised and bloody. I had a hard time explaining that I had been near the door to retrieve something that had fallen on the floor. It would have been impossible to admit that I had been peeking. I resolved that I'd now have to stay far away from keyholes.

Lever Bros. was unlike anything I had ever known. At noon, we would get our meals in a large dining hall where we'd be served a substantial *diner*, lunch. It was sumptuous enough to last you the whole afternoon and night. There were two sittings, the noon one and the one at 13 hour (1 PM). We had a two-hour lunch period that enabled you to get some errands done. We'd also work until noon on Saturdays and of course, there would be no lunch served on that half-day.

After a lifetime of food on the fly, it was a most welcome change for me. In the morning, I'd come rushing down the steps from my attic room, always in a hurry, as I could never get up early enough for a leisurely stroll down the street that led to my place of work. Mother would be waiting on her landing and I'd snatch a piece of bread from her extended hand. That was my breakfast. I'd never manage to get to work on time even though it was only a ten minutes brisk walk away from my house. I would always wonder how some of my co-workers who commuted from Namur, Louvain, Charleroi and other far away towns would be sitting at their desks long before I arrived at mine. Of course, they had their trains to catch and once they were in the train, they were assured to arrive well on time. By contrast, I'd wait until the last minute and always left too late. If I had to be there at 8.30h, I did not consider that I was late until it was 8.30 and I was still at home. Actually, I was late at 8.15 but it would not enter my mind. *"Rien ne sert de courir, il faut partir à temps"* "It is useless to run if you do not leave on time" The Tortoise and the Hare, La Fontaine. It would take me decades until that bit of wisdom was able to penetrate my mind.

When my sister Ruth graduated from her school, I went to see Mr Van Hamme, the head of personnel and suggested that perhaps Lever Brothers should hire her. I pleaded her case with all the arguments I could muster. Mr Van Hamme was not receptive. He seemed to take delight in teasing me and wanting to know why I felt that Ruth would want to work at Lever. By then, the thought of having two Rosenbergs working for the company must have been more than he was willing to bear. One of my arguments was that the lunches were of great importance to me and would be to my sister. Van Hamme laughed in my face. How could he have understood that those lunches represented stability and the chance for a daily decent meal? I felt humiliated. I could have punched him. Ruth did not even get an interview.

In the middle of the afternoon, the "Tea Ladies" would come around pushing a cart with coffee, tea and cookies. There were three or four of them, happy, friendly and mostly overweight. Everyone, from the directors to the office boys was entitled to a cup of brew.

For routine health problems, there was a dispensary supervised by Madame Stouf, the nurse. She was in her early thirties, very pleasant looking and with a friendly yet distant demeanor. I had started to grow a mustache, more in the nature of a fuzzy growth. Mme Stouf would tease me about it. "Is it to tickle the ladies? "She'd inquire teasingly. I'd demur a little, blushing but thinking that she meant that it would tickle them when I'd kiss them on the mouth. Later, I would come to realize that she meant to tickle them on another, more private pair of lips. Perhaps, it was her way of flirting with me. I'd never imagine that, being so convinced that I could never be attractive to any girl or woman.

THE PATEK PHILIPPE WATCH

In the fall, Father showed up at the apartment of the Place Madou. Apparently he had made a killing at the Baccarat tables of the casino. A beautiful gold Patek Philippe watch with a gold band adorned his wrist. I commented that the watch was a beauty. With a quick movement, he slipped it off his wrist and offered it to me. "Do you want it? It's yours!" He smiled at me. I was sixteen. Who had a watch at 16? Who had a Patek Philippe? Who had a gold Patek Philippe with a gold wristband?

I told Hilaire that I would be seventeen in a few months and that he should keep it for me and gift it to me for my birthday in February. Hilaire placed the watch back on his wrist. A couple of days later, I saw him shove a big wad of Belgian francs in the pocket of his tan raincoat. Two weeks later, when I saw him again, he had lost everything at the casino and he no longer had the Patek Philippe watch.

I strongly resolved that, in the future, if he ever offered me anything again, I'd grab it and run. Unfortunately, the occasion was not to present itself again. I would never forget "my Patek Philippe".

Over forty years later, my friend Marie and I were at the Armory Antique Show in Manhattan. In a jewelry glass case, three antique ladies' Patek Philippe caught my eye. Suddenly, I was overtaken by a desire to own a Patek Philippe and I resolved that I'd actively look for one. On my next trip to San Diego, I went to a pawnshop near Horton Plaza. There, sitting under a glass counter, a gorgeous gold Patek Philippe was staring at me. It was probably a few years newer than the one Hilaire had almost given me. However, the size, the heft, the gold of the watch and its band were a match. When I inquired about it, the price was $7,500-, a large sum indeed. I decided that I would wait until I was in Europe again where I would search one out.

In 1988, in Brussels, I went to an antique watch shop near the Grand-Place. The sales lady showed me the only Patek she had in the store, a beautiful ancient gold pocket watch. She wanted sixty thousand francs (about twelve hundred dollars at the time). It was nice, but not "my Patek Philippe". That evening, I was visiting my 86 year old Father and mentioned that I was thinking of buying a Patek in town. "Ah!-Said Hilaire pensively; I once had a Patek Philippe". With that, he went on to tell me that he had won it from a lady in Ostende at the Baccarat tables. As he was recalling the play, his face was flushed with excitement as he recalled each card he had been dealt. "I yelled "Banco" and she turned up an eight, I turned up a nine. The entire pot was mine. The lady did not have enough money to cover and she handed me the Patek Philippe".

When he got over his excitement, he said that he did not remember whatever happened to the watch. I could not help but to tell him what had happened forty-two years earlier. Again, he blushed, but this time it was from embarrassment. I felt bad.

Hilaire told me that he knew the Patek Philippe representative who lived in Ostende and that he would try to get a nice watch from him at a later date. The next day, he went with me to the antique watch store and talked the price down from sixty to fifty thousand francs. I bought the pocket watch. Father

239

then bought me a beautiful antique gold chain for the watch. We were both happy. However, it wasn't the wristwatch that I had really wanted. We talked it over and Hilaire said that when he would be in San Diego to visit my sister Ruth later that year, he would go and get the watch at the pawnshop.

In June 1988, Father spent a few weeks with me in New York. He was to travel to San Diego to see Ruth and talked again about arranging to buy the Patek Philippe when he'd be there. Hilaire died in my house that June and never did make it to Ruth's. When he died, he had very little money on him.

The next time I went to San Diego, I visited the pawnshop and offered $5,000—for the Patek Philippe. The owner accepted and I purchased it in honor of Hilaire. We had made our peace long before that and the Patek Philippe sealed it.

Today, I own a couple of Patek Philippe watches and each one is a souvenir of Hillel, my Father.

THE ARGUMENT, THE FIGHT AND THE FINIAL

Who would recall what had brought out this nastiest of arguments? All that I would remember was that Mother was out of her mind with rage against Ruth and me. It may have been that since we were now both working, Frieda had wanted that we pay her a monthly rental to help with the expenses of running the household. Mother was seldom home and did not cook for us. We could not see it her way. The base argument soon developed into a violent confrontation with Mother completely losing her composure. Frieda was yelling, shrieking and saliva was drooling from her twisted mouth. It was horrible.

Ruth and I, fearing for our lives barricaded ourselves in Mother's apartment with Frieda locked out on the landing outside the door. Mother, screaming and banging on the door wanted in. We were afraid she would kill us if we were to let her in. Incensed, Mother filled a tub with water and repeatedly slammed its contents under the door, trying to flood the apartment where we had taken refuge. The water covered the linoleum and began to leak to the downstairs floors. After a while, Madame Dunesme and one of her employees came up and managed to calm Frieda and to persuade her to go downstairs.

The next day, Father showed up at the house. Unable to control us, Mother had called him pleading that he should try to talk some sense into us, as she was no longer able to handle us.

Father met Ruth and me at the base of the stairs that led upstairs. Immediately, the discussion got off to a wrong start as Hilaire attempted to insert himself in the previous day's discussion. Ruth would have none of it. She immediately accused him of having deserted us and thus forever surrendering any right to come and lecture us. She had touched a raw nerve as Hilaire was probably carrying a heavy guilt burden. When told that he did not have any right to talk about our behavior, he got real angry. The discussion exploded into a shouting match between Ruth and Father. Soon, they were pushing and shoving each other and I could see that it would come to blows. Hilaire

240

grabbed a hold of Ruth and was about to strike her when I intervened. I was not about to let him strike my sister.

It was so unusual to see Hilaire in such anger. He had always been a patient man and slow to lose his temper. Ruth's words must have touched a raw nerve and he was now as mad as Frieda had been the day before. I pushed him away from Ruth and he now turned on me. I saw his fist fly in the air and knew that my face was now his target. I ducked and his blow struck the solid wood finial at the end of the banister. Father let out a loud howl and left the battlefield, cradling his right hand in his left arm.

Hilaire would come back a couple of days later in a more conciliatory mood. We were all calmer by then and he pleaded that we should not let ourselves be drawn into such terrible altercations. "Look what you've done to my hand!" He wailed to me. Indeed, his right hand was badly swollen and resembled a squashed grapefruit. I had to remark that if his fist had connected with my face instead of the finial, it would be my head that would now look like a pumpkin. Somehow, that remark had a salutary effect and we started to laugh and embrace.

Mother's financial situation remained precarious and I cannot recall if we ever did contribute money to the household. Bill collectors would often ring the bell at the folding iron gate entrance and Frieda would greet them with the dumbest face she could muster. *"Mevrouw is niet t'huis"* She would say in Flemish, pretending to be the maid. Madame is not home! The bill collectors, figuring that Frieda was only a slow-witted servant, would shake their heads and leave.

GILBERTE DOMS

I had noticed a pretty young girl who worked for the "cable" services. Her duties consisted of sending and receiving telegrams and telexes and making sure that these were distributed promptly to the various services at Lever Brothers. Blond soft hair framed her pretty face. A pair of light gray eyes, nice straight nose and lovely lips parted in a smile, completed the picture. Her teeth were well formed but serrated at the end, like a file. This somehow gave her a slightly hungry look that made her even more desirable. Of slight build, she'd come flying through my office with her batch of cables to be distributed to the purchasing department. I would anticipate her visits and she always had a friendly "Hello" for me.

On several occasions, Mme Stouf, the nurse, would tell me that Gilberte liked me and that she might be interested in being tickled with my mustache. I did not need much encouragement to be interested in Gilberte; however, the news that she actually liked me was a revelation. There was a girl, a pretty girl who thought I could be attractive. It did not take much for me to reason that if a girl could care for me, I'd better latch on to her as she might have been the only chance I'd have at romance.

I made shy advances at Gilberte and indeed she was not adverse to them. In a matter of days, we had become deeply involved. We shared the same early lunch shift and we arranged to sit next to each other at the lunch table. Lever had a benevolent and tolerant attitude regarding office romances. The company did not care if you were single or married, if the romance was straightforward or if one or both of the couple were married to someone else. Lever's sole concern was that lovers' spats or quarrels remained as discreet as possible so as not to disturb the smooth running of the office.

If a couple carried on a romance to the point of marriage, there was a fast rule. One of the two would have to leave the department and find work in another division of the company. Obviously they felt that there was a difference between lovers' and married relationships.

Gilberte and I met every day, by chance or design. We were inseparable. However, I had made up a stupid rule. We were both sixteen but Gilberte was nearly three months older than I was and I had decreed that I would not kiss her until she became seventeen on December 5th 1946. I would not be seventeen until February 26th 1947. Was I being ultra cautious, not wanting to be accused of statutory rape if she had not achieved the legal age of consent? Actually, I would still have been only sixteen and the onus would have rested on her lovely shoulders. Actually, Gilberte was fifteen months my senior but I would not find that out until a lifetime later.

As it was, for a few weeks, the need and desire to kiss grew daily. We had to be content with a touch of hands, a furtive brush of her dress against my suit, longing looks and deep sighs. On December 5th, 1946, I got up extra early as I had decided to surprise her in her office as she came in. The cable office occupied a room almost adjacent to the Personnel Office on the fifth floor. At ten minutes before opening, I let myself in the cable office and hid under Gilberte's desk so I could surprise her and share our much anticipated kiss.

As I was hunched under Gilberte's desk, the door opened and I heard steps coming in. These were not the tap-tap steps of a woman. This was a man. Not only was it a man but it was Monsieur Van Hamme, the chief of personnel. "What are you doing there under the desk?" he inquired. Embarrassed and blushing I explained that I wanted to surprise Mlle Doms to wish her a happy birthday. Monsieur Van Hamme laughed and seemed satisfied with my explanation. He did not hang around and returned to his office leaving me to wait for Gilberte.

As I edit these memoirs, I now wonder about Mr Van Hamme's sudden visit to the cable office. After all, as Chief of Personnel, Van Hamme was well placed to know the birthdate of all the employees. Gilberte was an attractive young lady and he may have wanted to sample a kiss or two. Perhaps I was not the only surprised visitor that morning. His precipitous retreat might explain his enmity and some gratuitous remarks made in later years!

When Gilberte came in, she did not seem surprised that I had been waiting for her under the desk. It was a bit awkward as we tried to find the best position to exchange our first kiss. We both must have been aware that this was going to be the only first kiss we'd ever exchange. My left arm went around her shoulder, my right arm found her waist. Our lips met and I could feel her hands against the small of my back. My chest could guess at her breasts pressing me. My penis swelled against her soft belly and I was embarrassed that she might detect my sudden emotions. If she noticed it, she said nothing. Our lips insisted for a moment and we parted. "Happy birthday!" I blurted. We were both blushing and I hurried out of her office. I wanted to go back in and kiss her again, but people were filing in and it would have to wait for another time.

After that first kiss, our hunger grew daily. Kisses were chanced frequently and caresses became bolder. We'd walk together to the Rue de Moerkerke in Schaerbeek where Gilberte lived with her parents and a little Pekinese dog that I loathed. The walk should have taken a half-hour but we'd make frequent stops in doorways to hug, kiss and pet. I had to be careful not to press her body against the doorbells lest we aroused the tenants who lived in the building. It was winter and cold. I'd kiss Gilberte with an open mouth now, our tongues invading our senses. I'd unbutton her coat and Gilberte would lift her left leg inviting my fingers to come and search her hot body. I was not wearing gloves and my fingers were icy. I could not understand how she did not jump in the air when my cold fingers found her melted burning pussy and penetrated deep in her like an insistent icicle. Gilberte never seemed to mind.

I did not dare let Gilberte touch me or handle my penis as we were petting in doorways. I would kiss her and caress her and get so excited that I would soon cum in my underwear. Did Gilberte have an orgasm? I could not tell nor did I worry much about it. I knew I was giving her much pleasure within the limits of our confined space and she made no secret that I was pleasing her.

We did get dirty looks from the "honest" passersby but we did not mind.

For Christmas 1946, Lever Bros. had a special luncheon for its employees. There was the traditional stuffed goose and sweets. There was also a lot of wine, both red and white. Port was also being dispensed and I managed to drink more than my share of red wine and port. The white did not appeal to me. So, I drank a number of glasses of red wine and drank many glasses of port as a chaser. By the time the Christmas lunch was over, I was quite light-headed. I left the lunchroom without Gilberte and walked back in the direction of my home at Place Madou. As I waited for the light to change at the Boulevard Bischoffsheim I noticed that my shoes were shining with unusual brilliance. My shoes were actually winking at me as they pulsated with the light. I could not focus on them. I had been holding on to the spindly trunk of newly planted saplings at the edge of the sidewalk. Suddenly, the boulevard was swirling all about me and I threw up my lunch, the wine and the port all around the base of the tree. It was about three in the afternoon and I had gotten sick in front of all the people waiting to cross the street. Ten years earlier, at the age of six, I had gotten drunk with Chassard in the basement of Monsieur Lemaitre. This time, I was sixteen and it did not bode well for the future. I was never to get drunk again.

1947

Que reste-t-il de nos amours,
Que reste-t-il de ces beaux jours?
Une photo, vieille photo de ma jeunesse . . .
. . . Et dans un nuage, le cher visage de mon passé.

What is left of our loves?
What is left of those happy days?
A photo, faded photo from my youth . . .
. . . And in a cloud, the dear face from my past

Charles Trenet "I Wish You Love".

THE THREE OF US

We were two friends, Bob Van Meckeren and I, and Gilberte loved me. We formed a strange trio. Everywhere we went Bob came with us. We went to the movies together, drank Coca-Cola together, went to the woods near Brussels together. I was convinced that Bob was in love with Gilberte and that he just tagged along to be near her. In late evenings or on weekends, the three of us would go to Bob's house and listen to records on his gramophone. He had a collection of records by Frank Sinatra, Benny Goodman, and others. Mostly, with Gilberte around, we would play "In The Mood" by Glen Miller and "Que reste t'il de nos Amours" by Trenet. "Near you" and "Besame Mucho" could always be counted on to put Gilberte in an amorous mood, which was not difficult to do.

I did not mind having Bob along all the time, he was a good friend and we had a lot in common. I did not realize how much Gilberte resented him as she felt that his affection for me was not natural and that he was very jealous of our love. Later, she would blame Bob's jealousy and possessiveness for the eventual destruction of our love affair.

Bob's Father had a 1938 coupe with a rumble seat. It was perhaps a Buick or a DeSoto but definitely an American car. Mr Van Meckeren would drive around the center of Brussels with Bob, Gilberte and I crammed inside the rumble seat, deliriously happy to be seen with our hair windblown and our arms around each other. We had the feeling that the whole world was gaping at us with envy. It was grand.

One afternoon, as I was visiting Bob's house, he came out of a room carrying a heavy package wrapped in a small sheet. When we were safely outside, Bob lifted one side of the sheet and revealed a big black Underwood typewriter. He had stolen it from the house and we were on our way to find a fence that would buy it from us. Apparently Bob had planned the whole thing, as he knew immediately where to go and sell it. He got about 400 francs for it. Bob probably needed the money to buy cigarettes and there was no evidence that his Father ever found out about his missing typewriter.

Twelve years later, French film director Francois Truffaut, in his 1959 autobiographical movie, The Four Hundred Blows, had his protagonist Antoine Doinel steal and sell his Father's typewriter. I could not help but smile.

There had been rumors and newspaper articles that our idol, Charles Trenet, was a pederast, a child abuser and a homosexual. Nothing had ever come of this but it was disturbing to me. I did not want to believe it. Bob and I were having a drink in a café when he looked at me very seriously and asked "Do you think it is true that Trenet is a *"Pédé"* and how would you feel about it if it were so?" At the time, with all the wisdom of my seventeen years I found the thought very repugnant to me. However, I simply replied that I did not think so and that I was certain that Charles Trenet would never do anything like that.

That was the end of the discussion. In the light of later events, I came to understand that Bob had been testing me. Had I said that I had no problem with Trenet being a "homo", it is probable that Bob might have declared his passion for me and revealed that he too, was a homosexual. My negative reaction forced him to remain silent about his own tendencies and he continued to profess his affection for Gilberte and his devoted friendship for me. Neither Gilberte nor Maurice was fooled by Bob. Only I remained blissfully unaware of his deeper feelings for me.

At Lever, Gilberte and I had found an ally in a young man named Léon. After the lunch period, the three of us would walk away from the building and ten minutes later we were at my house. There, we would go up to the door that separated the stairs from the first landing. We'd park Léon on the stairs and Gilberte and I would enter the landing, closing the door in back of us. While Léon sat and waited; we fooled around. We'd kiss, caress, pet and carried on until we ran out of sighs. We still had not made love nor had Gilberte actually touched my member. I did not have trouble cuming, but it was all done without actually getting caresses from Gilberte. After that, we'd tidy up and rejoined Léon. Ten minutes later, we would be in the Lever building again ready to work the rest of the afternoon. In this way, the people at Lever saw the three of us leaving for a walk and then returning an hour later. No one ever made a remark and we guessed that our ruse was successful. What did Léon get out of this? I felt that he had a desire to be loved by Gilberte and that he was content to be close to her even if she was in the arm of another man. We never discussed it. Léon was very loyal and never betrayed us.

All the while that I was caressing and petting Gilberte, I would talk to her about how wonderful it would be if she could hold me and feel me penetrating her. I had no idea how much she was aware of a man's anatomy. After I had finished penetrating her with my long fingers, I'd show her the thickness of my thumb and I'd ask her to imagine something twice the breadth and length.

It did not take long for Gilberte to be driven crazy with the desire to hold me and to have me take her with all my strength. The problem was to find a place where we could make love. I did not want to take Gilberte up to my attic room where the bare surroundings might have cooled her ardor. I should not have worried! However, Mother offered a solution. She would consent to have us use her cozy apartment and bed if in exchange I paid her enough to go to the movies for a couple of hours. She would even provide us with coffee and cookies to have after we made love. That seemed a workable solution and we made use of her offer many times. We were both passionate and learned many of the secrets of lovemaking through mutual exploration and curiosity.

Once, I was sick with a fever and Mother had me sleep in her room, as it was more comfortable and warmer than in my attic. Gilberte came to visit me and was insisting on making love. I protested that I was really sick and weak with a fever. There was no stopping her. She got undressed and sidled up to me in the narrow bed. She insisted that a good sweat would cure me and we made love with all the passion I could muster on that day. A day later, I was cured.

As time went on, Gilberte did not want to make love in Mother's apartment. She preferred the abandon of my attic room. It was more spontaneous and natural. We had fun, we laughed and we made love. Once, I had made her laugh so hard that she had to squat on the wooden floor of my room and she peed until she stopped laughing. It was wonderful. We did not have or use any contraceptive. We did not even use the rhythm method. We did not know what it was. I'd pull out when I knew I was about to cume and she never got pregnant. I did not want Gilberte to have a child, as that would have curtailed my chances of going to America. We were very lucky, or at least, I was.

Lever Brothers had made an alliance with Solvay, the chemical giant. It meant nothing to me except that Solvay had a property and sports center on the outskirts of the city. Now, all Lever employees could partake of the club and sports facilities. We were even allowed to bring a guest. There were tennis courts, Ping-Pong and pool tables. Tennis did not smile on me as I got hit on the bridge of the nose on my first attempt at that sport. The ball smashed my glasses that went flying in two directions.

I'd bring Bob or Maurice for the Ping-Pong and the billiard tables. Jean César, one of my Lever friends would come with his girlfriend and I'd be there with Gilberte. Although César was a fine Ping-Pong player, he much preferred to lay his girlfriend on the billiard table while I was on the lookout. When he was finished, he'd keep an eye out for trouble while Gilberte and I made love on the same billiard table. As it had a high border, it may not have been the most comfortable of beds. However, Gilberte would not complain and the extra angle seemed to increase the sensation when we'd do it with her legs hanging down off the table. We must have been out of our minds but we never got caught.

DANNY KAYE

"Wonder Man" was playing at the Metropole cinema in the Rue Neuve. Gilberte and I went to see it. It was a revelation. From that day onward, I was Danny Kaye. Gilberte would call me "Wonder Man". In quick succession, we saw "Up In Arms" and "The Kid from Brooklyn". I could imitate every routine performed by Kaye, but also do imitations of S.Z. Sakall and later, the routines of Red Skelton in "Bathing Beauty" and other movies.

I had been promoted to the "Buying Department" at SEDEC and at the drop of a hat; I'd stand on my desk and do gratuitous impersonations of Danny Kaye. My dreams were now not only of America but Hollywood where fame and fortune would surely await me if and when I'd finally make it there. A couple of times, Mr Lapage, the big boss at SEDEC, had walked in the department as I was in the middle of a routine. As was his wont, he had continued to glide through the room, like an ocean liner, neither looking right nor left. Fred, who occupied the desk next to mine, would comment now and then that Monsieur Lapage was a great admirer of my Danny Kaye routines. Of course, I'd swallow that as a compliment, not aware that Fred was pulling my leg.

Fred, who spoke with a British accent, would sometime have long discussions with me, mostly about girls. We both had the same problem, that of having an erection when we were in the vicinity of a pretty woman. "Up the Flag" he would call it. At the time, we felt that it was some kind of infirmity and a damn nuisance. We never considered it a privilege and one of the gifts of youth.

I felt that my talent at mimicry would carry me far in life. It focused interest on me, made me special. After years of perceived mediocrity it gave me confidence. Gilberte loved her "Wonder Man" and at the time, not much else seemed to matter.

LE COQ D'OR, OSTENDE

It was July 1947 and Father materialized again. Apparently he was flush with money, having probably made a killing at the gambling tables. Father invited Ruth and me to go and spend a week's vacation in Ostende, on the coast. He even invited Mother who immediately declined the invitation. *"Je connais ça!"* She exclaimed.—I know that one!—. Ruth and I accepted. The prospect of spending a week at the beach was inviting.

It was vacation time at Lever and also where Ruth was working. We had each been paid our July salary and in addition we had received the *pécule de vacances*, an extra month's pay due when you took your vacation.

I confided to Hilaire that I was in need of a new pair of glasses and we went to the local optician to have my eyes checked and make the purchase. I settled on a pair of rimless "Glen Miller" glasses similar to those worn by the American Army Air Force "boys". I was resplendent in those and with my new American style jacket, I was sure that I would pass for a Yankee. This was styled like an "Eisenhower jacket", made of three different textured cloths with leather piping. A front zipper completed the look. A few weeks earlier, I had purchased a new Agfa-Karat camera with a F3.5 lens and an "ever-ready" case. I'd sling it or draped it nonchalantly on my right shoulder. Now, no one would doubt that I was indeed an American.

On Sunday morning, we went to the South Station and Father bought three first class roundtrip train tickets. An hour later, we were in Ostende. Father wanted to rent rooms at the Hotel Wellington, on the promenade along the *Digue*, the dike, the most expensive hotel in town. Ruth and I would not go along with that. We were not dressed for the Wellington and we pleaded with Hilaire to go to a more modest place where we could relax and not feel completely out of place. We settled on the *Coq d'Or*, The Golden Rooster, a notch below the Wellington and situated one street away from the beach.

As we were seated for lunch in the hotel, we admired a very attractive young lady at the nearby table. She was very tanned, tall and thin, with limbs that seemed to go on forever. Attractive long hair framed her angular face. She did have a very prominent angular thin nose and "English teeth" but the whole effect was extremely sexy and pleasing. Father, who had the misfortune of sitting with his back to her, kept turning around time after time and feasting his eyes on her charms. After a while, the girl could not help but notice Father's ogling and began to look back at him. "She's looking at me! "He whispered to Ruth and me. We laughed because he had been so obvious in his attempts at getting her attention. She did join us at our table. Her name was Miss Margaret MacMillan and she was indeed British. Margaret stayed with us that afternoon and we never found out how far Father had been able to charm her.

In the afternoon, we put on our bathing trunks and we all went to the beach. Miss MacMillan's skimpy bathing suit made her even more fetching and I could not help but envy Hilaire's ease when he was flirting with her. Father and I went running along the surf where the sand was packed and hard. After a while, I put on some speed and left Father in my dust. He gave me a surprised look as I sped by him. I was seventeen and Hilaire was now forty-five. I would never forget his look.

Years later, I would vividly recall the incident as I went biking with my son Rudy. He suddenly pressed on his pedals and left me behind. I must have given him the same look that Hilaire gave me in Ostende. "La main passe", "The torch is being passed".

There were small, collapsible paratrooper's motorbikes that one could rent. The wheels had a diameter of less than a foot and you sat about two feet from the ground. We each rented one and we went cruising about Ostende and along the dike. It was fun and I dearly wanted one to take back to Brussels with me. The cost was just a few thousand francs and with the money Father had, it was a mere pittance. Hilaire did have a mishap. He took a turn too sharply and went sliding along the pavement. Only his pride was hurt. I wanted to take a bike back to Brussels with us at the end of our vacation and Father promised that we would buy one before returning home.

It was Sunday and the stores were closed. We went window-shopping. Ruth saw a pair of magnificent alligator shoes. She begged Father to buy her a pair the next day when the shops would open. Father promised that we would go and buy the shoes the next day.

As night fell, Father, Ruth and I were sitting at the terrace of the Coq d'Or enjoying some pastries and coffee. I was sharing a room with Father and at about 11 PM, it was time to turn in. At the hotel entrance, Hilaire kept temporizing. He asked me if he should first go to the casino. I got angry. I told him that he should not lay that responsibility on me. If he wanted to go, then he should go. If I told him not to go, he would still go. He did go.

At three in the morning, Hilaire crept into our room and quietly began to undress. He did not turn on the lights. I was awake. "How much did you lose? "I inquired. He replied "I broke even ". To him, breaking even meant that he was broke, that he had as much as when he came into the world. He was at point zero.

The next day, after breakfast, we asked that he buy us the paratrooper bike and Ruth's alligator shoes. Well, the motorbikes were too dangerous; after all he had fallen off one. As for Ruth's shoes, there would be much nicer ones in Brussels. We began to press him to try to find out how much he had lost at the casino. He would not tell us. That evening, he went back to the gambling tables and borrowed money from someone he knew. He promptly lost that too.

That Monday evening, there was no question of staying in the hotel for the rest of our vacation. The vacation was over. Now, the problem was how to pay the bill. Father did not have a centime left. Ruth and I pooled all our money; we each had two months' salary with us. It still left us short. Hilaire took my 3.5 Agfa-Karat camera and sold it. We had just enough to pay for our two nights at the Coq d'Or. We did not even have enough to tip anyone. At least we had not stayed at the expensive Wellington Hotel where we could have landed in jail. Ruth remembered our leaving the hotel like thieves, slinking between the chairs and tables on our way out hoping no one would see us leave.

The walk to the Ostende train station was in complete silence. We still had the first class tickets for the return trip and we rode back to Brussels in our first-class compartment, without a *sou* to our name. When we reached Brussels, it was late and the last streetcars had checked out for the night. We did not have money for a taxi and we walked home, dragging our suitcases behind us.

In the morning, Mother had a good laugh when we told her our vexations. "I told you so!" She crowed. Ruth and I never did get our money back from Father. I kept pestering him about my Agfa-Karat and I finally shamed him into buying me a new one. However, it was with an F 6.3 lens, an optic very inferior to the F 3.5 he had "borrowed".

PAN AMERICAN AIRWAYS

PanAm had established a base in Brussels. Ruth had become acquainted with Ed Young, its chief engineer in charge of the Brussels PanAm operation. Ed was extremely smart and "William Holden" handsome. It had not taken long for Ruth to become deeply involved with Young. Almost every evening, Ruth, Young and a few other PanAm flight personnel could be found at "Mom's" a well frequented bar near the center of town. Ed had taken a liking to me and Gilberte and I tagged along on Ruth's coattails. There were always pretty girls to entertain the PanAm crowd at "Mom's". Although Gilberte and I stuck to Coca-Cola, I was astounded at the amount of drinking that was going on at the bar; especially that some of the personnel was often scheduled to fly on the following day. Young was never scheduled to pilot and anyway he did not drink as much as the others. Tulio was the loudest and hardest drinking one of them all. I never knew if he was a flight engineer or a pilot but he loved his cognac and his girls. Sometimes, heavily engaged with his girlfriend of the moment, one could hear him bellow in the back room "Oh, take-off". He'd then roar like a plane taking off the runway. At the bar, he'd like to joke and yell out "Kansas City, here I come". He'd then jab the air with his extended index finger and slowly let it droop, limp, as if spent. That always brought much laughter from the other patrons.

Gilberte and I were there as often as we could, like groupies, happy to be able to rub shoulders with the glamour boys of Pan American Airways.

I once visited the hangars of PAA at the Evere Airport just outside of Brussels. Ed and a few mechanics were struggling with an engine. They had taken it apart and were in the process of reassembling it. They were having difficulties replacing the propeller on its shaft without having pieces drop out of the assembly. With great care, they'd lower the propeller placing their hands and fingers so as to keep the loose parts in place. As they got close, the hands were quickly removed in an attempt to prevent the small parts from sliding off to the ground. It was of no avail and they had been at it for a frustrating hour. Seeing this with fresh eyes, I suggested that they substitute some thin wire for their fingers to hold the pieces in place. They could then pull out the wire just as the shaft made contact with the rest of the motor. Young agreed and in a few moments, a new technique had been developed. Impressed, Ed Young suggested that I should become an engineer and that I should one day present myself at PanAm headquarters in the States. I was elated and it further reinforced my determination to go to America.

1948

There's just one place for me,
Near you.
It's like heaven to be,
Near you.

NEAR YOU

Gilberte and I went crazy over "Near You". Of course, we were fond of Trenet and Glenn Miller, but "Near You" was so simple and special. It had a throbbing boogie rhythm and basic lyrics easy to remember and sing. Each night, the AFN in Munich would feature it with GIs clamoring to have it played or offering to pay to have it banned and the record destroyed.

The relationship with Gilberte was getting bumpy. We fought over minutiae. I would not remember specific instances but there was a lot of jealousy going around. Bob wanted to see more of me even though we hung around all together most of the time. Gilberte wanted me to stop talking about America even as she knew I would not rest until I could leave for the USA and those plans never made room for her. And then, there was the incessant desire Gilberte had to go dancing. I would not, could not and resolutely refused to go dancing. Naturally, for Bob, the thought of dancing was unpleasant, as he would have had to drag his artificial leg along the dance floor and of course we would not dream of going dancing without him. For me, it was the fear of being ridiculous that held me back. I was not much different from other boys my age in those times. Dancing was for girls and the apprehension of being dragged into a dance made my brain turn to mush. My funds were also severely limited and Gilberte insisted on going to the movies, to dinner, dancing etc. We would wind up at Bob's home, listening to some records and tearful arguments would ensue. On occasion, Gilberte would fly into a rage and she'd bang our favorite records against the table or do a fair imitation of a flamenco dancer while trying to destroy "In the Mood" or "Que Reste-t-il de nos Amours" that proved more resilient than her heels. When all else failed, Gilberte would let out the dreaded "sale Juif" dirty Jew. Of course, that was a mortal blow for me and it did hurt terribly.

Poor Gilberte was at her wits end and wanted to hurt me as deeply as she could. Sale Juif, she knew, would always pierce my heart.

At Unilever, we sat together in the large lunchroom and we sometimes carried our quarrels with us. Our affair was now common knowledge and it did not sit too well with the management, especially when we were openly feuding. However, we would always make up and the passionate lovemaking that would follow almost made the quarrels worthwhile.

One Saturday night, I let my guard down and agreed to go dancing with Gilberte. She had picked the place, "Het Toekomst", "The Future" on the Rue Godefroid de Bouillon, near the Botanical Gardens. Gilberte, Bob and I took the tram, paid our admission fee and entered a sort of immense hangar painted black and with just a few tables. An enormous sphere covered with small mirrors provided the only lighting. As it rotated, the shimmering mirrors reflected the light of a couple of projectors and illuminated the public. The place was filled with smoke and loud music. We made our way to a large bar that ran the length of the hall and ordered our share of Cocas. I was not in a good mood. This was not at all where I wanted to spend an evening. Gilberte was tapping her feet and swaying to the music. She kept looking my way, silently begging me to go and dance with her. This was not my thing. Even if I had wanted to dance, I knew that my feet, both of them, would be permanently anchored to the wood floor and any attempt at dancing would result in a disaster.

As we stood there, a sleazy blond fellow, with a big mole on his right cheek advanced on Gilberte with a sailor's roll. "Wanna dance, girlie?"

Gilberte lowered her eyes and followed him to the dance floor. They danced on and on. I was jealous, hurt and furious. I guess we stayed there less than an hour. After that, I made it clear that I wanted to leave. We took the streetcar back to Gilberte's home on the Rue de Moerkerke. Her parents wanted to know if we had had a good time. The stinking Pekinese was yapping and snarling at me. No, I had not had a good time but I did not let on to her parents but Gilberte knew how I felt. I would not remember kissing her that night.

We had a few more painful arguments and I decided that our romance should end. On the weekend, there was a track meet at the Heysel stadium. Bob would wait for me at the streetcar stop near the North Station and we would go on from there to attend the meet. Bob seemed pleased that I had broken up with Gilberte. I was broken-hearted.

On Saturday morning, Gilberte showed up at my house. She was full of tears and begging me to take her back. She was so pretty with her blond head and her eyes full of tears. Even her little serrated teeth were pretty. She was wearing a gray tailored suit with white pin stripes over a white blouse with a frilly collar. She was pleading, imploring me to take her back again. We were standing on the landing in front of my Mother's apartment. Frieda came out and wanted to know what the discussion was about. Gilberte thought she had found an ally and began to beg Mother to make me change my mind.

Mother chided her. "I am flattered that you should want my son so much, but to run like that after a man is terrible. You should never run after a man or a streetcar. There is always another one that will follow." Obviously, Frieda was suffering from amnesia, having apparently forgotten how she used to run after René DeLange

Gilberte would not relent. "Please take me back" She continued. "I'll wash your clothes, I'll iron your shirts, I'll do anything for you ".

I was weakening. She did look so pretty and I still loved her so. I did not have the heart to watch her cry. I hugged her and told her that I would take her back and that we could go to the Heysel track meet together. She was so happy, she dried her eyes and her small hand took my arm as we walked down the stairs and went to the tram stop. As we were waiting, she stayed very close to me, happy, her eyes so pretty and moist with love.

We stayed on the tram platform and as the streetcar approached the North Station we were at least an hour late. I leaned out to hail Bob who was still waiting for me. When he climbed onto the platform, he saw Gilberte and made a face. He had thought that we would have the afternoon all to ourselves and he was not pleased that I had relented and gotten back together with Gilberte.

We did manage to have a good, albeit tense, afternoon at the track meet.

However, the underpinnings of our relationship were beyond repair and we soon resumed our quarrellings to the point that we broke up again. This time it was almost by mutual consent. We still had love to share but the emotional price we had to pay was too steep.

After our break-up we continued to eat lunch next to one another. We were unable or unwilling to uncouple. We tried to find ways to injure one another. Nasty was the order of the day. There was still mutual bondage and we simply could not unhook. It was very hurtful.

One evening, as Maurice and I were walking down the Rue Neuve, someone tapped me on the shoulder. I wheeled about and found myself face to face with a man. I thought I recognized the mole I had noticed on the dance floor at "Het Toekomst". He pointed in back of him and said that if I did not leave this young girl alone, he would knock my block off. And there, a few feet away, stood Gilberte. Apparently she had told him about us and must have complained that I would not leave her be.

After her new lover saw me, he beat up Gilberte because he had just realized that she had been sleeping with a Jew.

ALONG THE WAY

It was lucky I still had my faithful Peugeot bike. It enabled me to escape again and again to the country around Brussels. I'd go riding for hours at a time, alone with my thoughts, listening to the soft sound of the chain meeting the sprockets and shifting the *dérailleur*. On one occasion there was news that General Eisenhower would be visiting Brussels. That was nice but what really had me interested was that he would be landing in Melsbroek (the military airport north of Brussels) in a Lockheed Constellation. The "Connie" was the latest four-engine passenger airplane, graceful with a body undulating to its triple vertical rudders. I had seen photos of it and the thought that I could actually see it fly and land fired my imagination. Seeing Ike was nice, but the "Connie" would be very special. I got there just in time to see it fly in and land. It was like a giant porpoise. I caught a glimpse of General Eisenhower as he left the plane.

After that, I rode around the airport just in time to see a Hurricane or Typhoon of the Belgian Air Force come in for a landing over one corner of the airfield. It passed so low over me that I could have counted the hair on the pilot's head if he had not worn his flying helmet. Oil was dripping from the engine and one drop splashed on the shoulder of my jacket. It was thrilling. I wanted so much to go to America and join the naval air arm of the Navy.

As I rode back to Brussels on my silver blue bicycle, I pondered again about my poor eyesight and wondered if I would ever be accepted in the U.S.Navy. At the moment, I did not even know if I would ever make it to America and I promised myself that I would renew my efforts to leave for the New World.

POST GILBERTE

Although the wounds of first love had been deep, I had to turn to newer endeavors. While the romance was still going strong, Marie-Therese V. had once made a snide and cutting remark about "Madame Gilberte Rosenberg". Marie-Therese had flung that at me as she was walking up the stairs leading to the Unilever first floor. Now that I had had time to reflect upon that, it struck me that Marie-Therese was jealous and that she might have had personal designs on me. I began to look upon her in a different and interested light.

Marie-Therese, or MTV as she was known, was a very handsome young girl. Taller than Gilberte or me, she had a svelte figure and long dark hair. Her eyes were very dark and her skin was perpetually bronzed. Dense but soft hair covered her arms. Looking at her, you could readily believe that the Spanish occupation of the Low Countries in the 16th century had left genes circulating about. Under normal circumstances, I would never have had the nerve to approach her. Now, given her peevish remark, I would take my chances. When the occasion presented itself I made it my business to intercept her in the hallway. It took just a few words and MTV agreed to accidentally run into me after lunch. We met at the base of the "Colonne Du Congrès" on the Place of the Unknown Soldier, just adjacent to Lever House. I invited her to join me in a climb to the top of the tower. The stairs were steep and narrow and Marie-Therese preceded me. I could glimpse at the fine ankle and calf that her long flowing skirt would reveal with every step. On the way up, she would pause during the arduous climb and rest against the inner wall of the staircase. I'd take advantage to get real close to her and to hold her up by placing my hand under her arm and my arm around her waist. She did not seem to mind and her breathing was becoming more labored. I was not sure if it was due to the long climb or the excitement of the nearness of our bodies. It was delicious. Her long hair was draping over my shoulders and being one step behind her, my face would come in contact with the nape of her neck. A few strands of softer hair draped over her ears and down her temples and cheeks. That hair was moist with perspiration and I longed to slake my senses with my tongue.

When we reached the top, exhilarated but out of breath, we surveyed Brussels from our vantagepoint. Hip to hip, I'd point to the city's points of interest and she'd strain to look in the direction of my pointing finger while pressing her cheek to mine. I could inhale the warmth of her body. Too soon, we'd have to go down to earth again as the lunch period was now just one hour. She was mine for the kissing but I could not dare. I was still "ugly".

In 1948, there had been a referendum submitted to the employees to determine if we should now work only 5 days a week instead of the extra Saturday. In exchange, the lunch periods would be cut from two hours to one. Surprisingly there had been a lot of opposition to this. Some would go home for lunch but would not be able to do so with only a single hour. Others had used the hour to do shopping or to repair to a *pied-a-terre* for the occasional tryst. Despite the opposition, the measure was passed, probably pre-ordained by the management. I liked it as it now gave me a real weekend to enjoy.

One day, I found the nerve to ask Marie-Therese to meet me after work and we made a rendezvous at the entrance of a nearby park. It was really not a park, but an enclosure where a statue of the Virgin Mary had been erected behind a metal fence. It was almost dark by then but MTV's eyes burned brightly. She leaned back against the fence and I pressed my body against hers. Darn, she was tall! Our lips met in a warm, wanting kiss. The feel of the fuzz on her upper lip surprised me but I did not care. I poured all I had learned with Gilberte in that kiss. My hand searched for the hollow of her long woolen skirt. The wool felt warm and friendly. Marie-Therese, her eyes closing, did not stop me nor did she encourage me to go farther. After a few kisses, we stopped and went our separate ways. I guess I did not want her that much. We never kissed again but remained friends.

Maurice and I were now spending much time together, going to the Solvay Club every chance we got. Often we would take the tramway with a couple of Simones from Lever. They were well endowed and beautiful. Simone Sacrée was gorgeous if a little on the plump side but she was a delight to the eyes, dark-curly haired and with eyes that would damn a priest. Simone No. 2 was fairer and blander than Sacrée but not someone one would throw out of bed. I had no idea why these two beautiful girls hung around with us. Apparently there was nothing sacred about Simone Sacrée (sacred in French). Everyone would call her "Sacrée Simone" that would translate more or less into "Darn Simone". I never did find out how far her teasing would go. However, Maurice would flirt very heavily with her in the streetcar, asking her how her boobs were doing. He'd then lean over and grab her breast and give it a pinch. Simone would laugh with an open throat as I sat there wondering about Maurice's daring nerve.

Once at the club, it was all Ping-Pong business for Maurice and me. We would play for hours until closing time. Maurice would attack and I'd defend from far away from the table, returning everything he would smash my way. I'd usually win the first three matches and Maurice the last three. By then, I'd be tired by my constant running and jumping and would slow down enough so that he could beat me.

Then, the two Simones would reappear and we'd take the train back to Brussels while Maurice ogled and fondled Simone Sacrée who would laugh and squeal while the other Simone would go to sleep in her seat. And I'd sit there, my body full of desire but unable to make a move for fear of rejection.

Maurice and I would finish the day with a newspaper, a couple of hot sausages and a Coca-Cola. We'd sit on the ledge in the entrance of a store that had closed for the night and we'd talk politics and sports and I'd talk about America where I was sure to go some day. The depth of insight and knowledge Maurice had crammed in his head always astounded me. He had an impudent loquacity that would leave me smiling with an open mouth, like an idiot. We had dubbed our little refuge "The Hacienda" and we made sure to clean up after our passage so that we would not be chased away on our next visit.

Guy Loscau, a colleague in the SEDEC buying department belonged to a Table Tennis club where he was a top player. Since he knew that Maurice and I were assiduous players he invited us to enter a tournament that matched a few teams, notably Maccabi, a group made out entirely of religious Jews. The name had surprised me as I knew it only as "Maccabée" that in a student song referred to a corpse, often a drowned stiff.

Anyway, my first opponent was from Maccabi and I promised myself that I'd give him a tough match. However, I was nervous. Hands shaking, I tried the wicked serves I knew. Time after time, I hit the ball with the edge of my paddle, sending the ball straight up to the ceiling. It was nothing and five by the time I finished my serves. That was the good part. The guy, without even a sweat, trounced and eliminated me in straight sets, both 21 to 3 if I recall. Maurice, with his attacking game, fared a bit better but could not salvage a set either. In less than 20 minutes, we were out of the tournament. There was indeed a difference between Ping-Pong and Table Tennis.

With all that, I still found time for Bob. We'd go to the movies and Jazz concerts in small cafes. There we would listen to Belgian bands like Stan Reynders that were busy imitating the "Big Band" sound with passable success. There were also pretentious seminars where Carlos de Radzinsky would project snips of musical movies featuring Count Basie, Harry James, Benny Goodman and the likes. We could not get enough of it.

At these concerts, now and then, I'd meet Rosa Wauters who worked in another department at Lever. She was beautiful and vivacious. I'd call her "Rosette". There was also a skinny kid who played the guitar and harmonica. He went by the name of Jean-Baptiste Thielemans and liked to be called "Toots".

MORE ROMANTIC ADVENTURES

I finally had the nerve to nod to "La Rousse", the attractive redhead who lived across from our apartment. One morning, I went out on Mother's balcony and after a short while "LaRousse" came out on her balcony above the Cambrinus Café. Our eyes met and boldly I gestured to her that I'd like to meet her downstairs. She nodded 'Yes" and I started out. With a hand gesture, she advised me to wait a while, as she had to get ready. It had been almost four years since her first appearance. I quickly ran down the stairs and across the Chaussée de Louvain and waited at her door with controlled anticipation. She finally appeared. She was beautiful even with her Brillo hair. We walked for a while in silence. She was tall, much taller than I. We exchanged names but I was so intent on being at ease that I never heard her name or forgot it as quickly as she said it. We walked the length of the Rue du Congrès. We were both at a loss for words. I could only wonder what she must have been thinking of. Glimpses of clever phrases kept lighting my brain but the words would not come out. When we arrived at the Colonne du Congrès, I had to bid her adieu, as I had to get to work at Lever. There is a vague memory of a quick kiss on tiptoe. We would never meet again.

I was now nearing my nineteen birthday and had a gaunt look about me. Mother would say that I looked like Jean-Louis Barrault, the French actor. I weight all of 54 kilos (119 lbs.) with a prominent nose and black curly hair. Although I was totally unaware of it, I had become sexy-looking in an arresting way.

One day, as I walked to work, I stopped in a chocolate store. I had a yearning for a bar of Cotes-d'Or milk chocolate with hazelnuts. I ordered a bar from the lady behind the counter. She must have been in her late thirties, plain but nice. I gave her a twenty-franc bill to pay the five francs for the chocolate. She gave me back ninety-five francs change. I protested that she had given me the wrong change that should have been fifteen francs. She smiled and insisted that I had given her a hundred-franc bill. I argued with her that I did not even possess a hundred-franc bill. She gently insisted and pressed the change back in my hand. I took it, thanked her and left. I was dumbfounded. Of course, there had been a man in the next room of the shop. He might have been her husband or her boss. Perhaps she did not want him to know that she had made a mistake and thus would not admit to it. On the other hand, perhaps she had seen me so skinny and not well dressed and had wanted to make me a present of eighty francs. Perhaps she had taken a liking to me. I would never know but it set my mind to wonder.

At Lever, there were a few tentative tender moments with Rosemary Barchy, a sweet young girl who worked in bookkeeping. No words, no kisses, no flirting. Only now and then, a grazing as we passed each other, a look, a smile. Rosemary lived in Wavre, a good distance from Brussels on the way to Waterloo and Charleroi. I could not envision starting something with her. But oh, her eyes were soft and smiling.

THE SAMPLE ROOM

SEDEC with all of its company stores in Africa had to keep a fresh supply of trade goods to sell to its African workers. New goods were constantly being offered to the company for sale to the natives. Offers arrived daily accompanied by samples of the latest offerings. I was put in charge of the sample room. One of my duties in the purchasing department was to sort, classify, tag and store all the samples.

The scope and variety of those samples were enough to boggle the imagination. Nothing was fancy or expensive. It had to be the cheapest trade goods available. Boxes and boxes of glass jars filled several shelves. Hair pomades, skin creams, soaps etc. were displayed in rows with lot numbers and suppliers' names. There was really only one fragrance, clove. Clove, it seemed was the only scent the Congolese would respond to. Bolts and swatches of multicolor cloth spewed out of cartons littering the floor. *Pacotille*, shoddy goods vied for attention from every shelf and wall. Worn tuxedos, especially white ones would please the Africans especially after cutting half the sleeves and legs. Those would be for evening and Sunday wear.

There were also samples of guns and machetes but the machetes would not cut. The guns were blunderbusses that at very close range could have disintegrated an elephant. However, at more than 20 feet, the charge would have dispersed so badly that it could not be used for a revolt against the white man. There was no sense in arming the natives with weapons that might have been used against agents of the company.

Although I was not in charge of the food lines, there was a branch of Lever that purchased tons upon tons of herring to be sold in the company store. It was specified that the herring were to be small rather than large. There would be more pieces per ton. In the Congo, these were sold by the piece and more would have to be purchased for a meal if they were small.

Whenever I spent time in the sample room, I was sure to be visited by one or more girls working at Lever. They were always coming to try to get samples. The brocades and gaudy cloths were especially prized and wanted. The girls would make eyes at me for a few yards of cheap merchandise. Rosa Wauters was an assiduous visitor to the sample room. Rosette as I called her had a beautiful singing voice and belonged to a group that performed in small theatres and cabarets at night or on weekends. Rosette would make her own clothes and the medley of fabrics and colors would be transformed into gypsy or regional outfits.

The sample room was on the landing between the fourth and the fifth floor. The fifth floor housed the cable office (where Gilberte still worked) and also the personnel department of Monsieur Van Hamme. Invariably, when Mr Van Hamme saw the lights on in the sample room, he guessed that I'd be there, entertaining the girls in search of presents. And there I'd be, like a bee after honey, with one or more girls. Since Rosette came to the room quite often, she was the one he surprised most often. There was never anything improper going on but it was embarrassing.

1949

There was a boy,
A very strange enchanted boy
They said he wandered very far, very far over land and sea . . . (Nature Boy).

MÈTÈQUE. (ALIEN, RESIDENT FOREIGNER)

With each passing year, the reality that I was a foreigner in the country of my birth and a Jew, or rather a "dirty Jew" was weighing more and more on my self-consciousness. Gilberte's frequent insults had deepened my awareness of the alienation I felt each day that I lived in Belgium. Of course, I knew full well that her insults had always been out of frustration and ultimate efforts to hurt me. However the effect of these insults always had the desired effect and hurt deeply; just as *"Boche and Polack"* hurt Frieda and Hilaire each time they had fought.

In later years, I would often hear arguments that there was no such thing as "looking Jewish" but I was bearing too many scars to accept those denials. Perhaps the Europeans, living in mostly closed societies were more aware of *mètèques* living in their midst than Americans who lived in a more integrated society. In 1947 Jews desperately struggling to establish a Jewish state in Palestine were at war with the British. The King David Hotel in Jerusalem had been blown-up by Jewish "terrorists". As I was walking up the Chaussée de Louvain, a man coming from the other direction planted his face before me and screamed "Dirty Jew, why don't you go to Palestine!" and he shook his fist at me.

There was no doubt about it. I was a Jew. I looked Jewish. My name was Jewish. However, Ruth and I had been baptized Protestant in 1941. How could we still be Jews? Yet, I had the map of Jerusalem on my face. To me being Jewish was a disease and I had it. I hated it. I wanted so much to leave this Jew-hating Europe behind and to become an American. Once in America, I would change my name to Rosemount or Montrose. Lord Battenberg had changed his name to Mountbatten so he could be closer to the British crown. If Battenberg could do it, why couldn't I change my name and leave all that behind me?

Somewhere along the way, Paul Friedemann, Mother's brother in Brooklyn had found out that we were still alive and had survived the war and Hitler's repression. Paul had divorced his first wife and later had married a German Jewish nurse, Lilli Meyer who had fled Nazi Germany in 1935. At first he had sent us a few "Care" packages. After that, our contacts had become scarce consisting of rare exchanges of postcards or brief letters between Frieda and Paul. Since we had not heard anymore from "Uncle Leo Wolleman" Paul was now my only hope for an affidavit that would open the door to America for me. I began to pester Mother to contact Paul and to plead with him to become my sponsor in America. We assured him that I would not become a burden, that he would have no obligation to put me through school. All I wanted was the chance to go to the USA. I'd stay with him and Lilli for a few weeks and then be on my own. There were no firm replies or even acknowledgments of my desperate petitions.

MOTORCYCLE

It was a monster, a beast, an old German motorcycle had caught my eye, "For Sale" the sign read, 2,800—francs. It was a large sum but I could manage it over a period of a few months if I deprived myself of most extras like chocolate and Coca-Cola. Since I no longer had Gilberte to entertain, it did not seem completely out of reach. I would not remember the brand of bike but it was German, pre-war, much pre-war, possibly a BMW. The beast was completely black, had a long tubular body that encased a metal gas tank. Enormous wheels and a long chain with angry sprockets gave the monster the appearance that it was ready to pounce down the pavement once you touched the controls that stood out like antlers on the handlebars.

I could taste the beast. Visions of zooming along the flat roads of Belgium towards Waterloo or the North Sea coast danced before my eyes. There was a debate between my mad desire to possess the brute and my timorous and prudent side. I was sweating and felt myself getting sick with the need to buy the motorcycle. Everything in me said "Yes, yes!" And yet, I knew that the beast was sure to kill me.

I made one of the wisest decisions of my life and walked away from it. I would often think about the bike, especially in later years when a brief desire to own an Indian or Harley would flare up in my head. I never regretted it.

I AM FIRED

I had gone to the men's room at Lever Bros. It was a large, bright room completely covered with white tiles. There were no urinals. About a dozen cubicles lined each sides of the room. It was the middle of the morning and the place seemed empty. I chose a far away stall as I had noticed that people would usually rush to the toilets closest to the door. The toilets farther from the door had the least traffic and were generally much cleaner. I opened the door of the stall and there sat Monsieur Egget, the Director of the SEDEC, the husband of Miss Hart. We were both embarrassed in the brief moment of surprised recognition. I blurted that I was sorry and quickly closed the door. The jerk should have locked the door. I do not believe that it endeared me to him.

A few days later, just after 5 PM, the office had emptied out. As I walked out through the cavernous lobby of Lever House, I saw Mr Higgins, a visiting Director from the London Unilever Headquarters standing in front of the elevator. It was after five and the elevator was idle with its iron gate closed. The lift operator had gone home. Mister Higgins, an enormous walrus of a man was sweating at the thought of having to climb five sets of stairs to join a meeting on the fifth floor. I rushed to the rescue.

"Would you like me to take you up?" I offered.

His large mustache curved up to follow the smile on his lips. "Could you do that?" His voice was imploring.

It was easy for me to open the gate, flip on the light and operate the handle control that took us up to the fifth floor. Higgins marveled that I was able to operate the elevator even though it was not my job. As we reached the top and I opened the gate to let him out, he thanked me and said "Thank you, young man. You will go far in this organization!"

Two weeks later, I was fired.

As I understood it, there had been a routine audit of the employees. Since I had been born in Charleroi, it had been assumed that I was a Belgian national and I had been working for three years without alien working papers. Lever could have been fined heavily for employing an illegal alien. Of course, had I been a valued employee, they might have interceded on my behalf and helped me obtain the necessary papers. However, there had been too many escapades, too many girls and too many Danny Kaye imitations on top of my desk. Perhaps Mister Egget had a hand in it. As it was, I was fired in the spring of 1949. I was 19 and the loss of my job was such a severe blow that I would not remember the actual action of dismissal.

HEBREW-CHRISTIAN ASSOCIATION

There was a meeting of a Hebrew-Christian Association in Baarn, Holland thirty miles from Amsterdam. The HCA was searching for likely Jewish candidates to be converted into good Christians who would be allowed to emigrate to the USA when the quotas permitted. Since I had been baptized protestant I felt that this would be a golden opportunity to hitch a ride to America. I would have embraced the devil or his wife for the chance to go to the States.

I got in touch with the group and took the train to Antwerp. There we all got on busses. It would be easy to cross into Holland on a charter bus. I did not have a passport and would not have been able to cross by train or traveling alone. We traveled to Baarn for a religious jamboree near the grounds of Queen Juliana's summer palace. We could see the palace from the river where we would go boating. The palace was bland like a white handkerchief. Christian girls would surround the few Jews who had joined the adventure. Their purpose seemed to be to entice them to convert to Christianity. I did not have to convert as I had already been baptized but I welcomed the special attention of two pretty Dutch girls assigned to me.

"Pastor' Jotz was in charge of the Hebrew-Christian group. However, nothing concrete came out for me or probably for the other young Jews who had been roped in the adventure. However, "Pastor" Jotz eventually made it to the States where he changed his name to Yates and became a protestant pastor. That was probably the only purpose of that entire exercise.

For me, it was a total failure. I did not get my chance to go to America and the two guides assigned to me turned out to be completely untouchable.

THE AFFIDAVIT

Summer was fast approaching and I found myself without a job. Even though I was stateless and not a Belgian citizen, I became eligible to collect unemployment. It was not "the Peru" as Frieda would say but it kept me in Coca-Cola with a bit to spare. Going to the unemployment office once a month was somewhat humiliating, especially as I found myself immersed in the world of the "professional unemployed".

And one day, the American consulate in Brussels notified us that there had been an affidavit given in my name by Uncle Paul in Brooklyn, N.Y. It was incredible. It had been more than four years since I first began to dream of America. There were still many hurdles to jump, as I was stateless.

There began an endless round of examinations, tests and X-ray. A passport would also be needed. I now had an identity card, the yellow one assigned to foreigners. At the age of eighteen I could have opted for the "small" Belgian Nationality at a cost of 10,000 Belgian francs. That would have given me the opportunity of serving in the Belgian Army and at the end of my service I would be granted the full Belgian citizenship. Frankly, by then, I was not really keen on being a Belgian national especially that I was certain that I would soon leave for America.

The U.S. was requesting an endless number of papers that all had to be notarized. This meant that each time another paper was required, I had to make an appointment with a Notary Public at a great expense of time and money. When I arrived in America, I realized that any candy store owner can be a notary public and all he does is certify that your signature is genuine and that you are the person you claim to be. That can be done anywhere and for a couple of dollars. That was why the embassy could so casually ask for notarized papers without realizing that a Notary in Europe sat to the left of a judge and to the right of God.

Meanwhile I was looking for temporary employment. I could not take something permanent, as that would cause me to lose my unemployment benefits. My hopes that I'd finally make it to America also precluded the idea of a long time job. In the papers, an announcement that there was a need for extras in a theatre production caught my eye. The auditions were being held at the Chateau de Beersel, southwest of the capital and the scene of my 1941 debacle when I was a Catholic Boy Scout. The play was about The Crusades and the director needed extras to play Crusaders. Since my Danny Kaye days, I had nurtured a not-so-secret ambition to be in the theatre; this was my chance. I joined the long line of candidates. A tall young man, a clipboard in his hands was walking up and down the line, pulling people out at random. When he got to me, he stopped for a fraction of time and motioned that I step out of the line. My heart stopped in anticipation. "Too short! Get out "He said. My heart sank. It was the end of my acting career in Europe. I rode my Peugeot back to Brussels, my heart on my saddle.

A few days later, I rode to Wavre, a small town southeast of Brussels, not far from Waterloo to pay a visit to Rose Marie Barchy. I had missed her gentleness since I had left Lever Bros. Her Mother greeted me graciously. Rose Marie and I spent about an hour together, talking of the rain and the sun. As I rode back to Brussels, I felt a bit better and promised myself that I would soon return. I would not see her again for thirty years.

My sister Ruth was spending the summer months in Ostende where she and her friend Georgette had rented a room near the beach. I decided that I'd ride my bicycle all the way to Ostende just to pay them a visit. This was a journey of 120 kilometers, *(roughly 80 miles)* about four times as far as I had ever ridden in my life. Undaunted, I set out in the early morning without provisions or extra water in the warm summer weather. It became quite an endeavor worthy of an epic poem that I would never get around to write.

En route, I would try to catch a ride in the slipstream of stronger riders who would overtake me on the highways or in the bicycle paths. Mostly, the roads were made of Belgian paving stones and that made for a rough, jolting ride. I'd hang on as long as I could to the riders who would pull me in their slipstream. Of course, they were always much stronger than I and would do all they could to shake me off. Once I let go, the headwinds and the loneliness of the trip would slow me down and discouragement would set in. I'd then look back to see if another rider would soon come along and I'd hop his stream again for a few kilometers. Many times I felt that I would quit but I could not admit to failure. In the evening, after about nine hours on the road, I limped into Ostende and found the room Ruth was renting. Her surprise at seeing me must have matched my surprise at having been able to complete the journey. Georgette, Ruth and I talked late into the night about subjects of which there remains not a single recollection.

The next day, we spent a little time on the beach. I did not realize that having her little brother there was a hindrance to Ruth and Georgette's abilities to pick up guys. In the afternoon I returned to Brussels. This time I placed my bicycle with me on the train and rode the rail back home in a little less than two hours. However, I had succeeded in my goal of riding all the way to the littoral and I felt elated as if I had completed a Marathon. This euphoria was to remain for several weeks and is with me still when my thoughts turn to the few things I did achieve in my life.

Even though I had been fired from Lever and no longer had the right to partake of their sporting facilities at Solvay, or even to be on the premises, Maurice and I continued to visit the club very frequently. Our passion was still Ping-Pong and we'd spend many hours contesting matches and playing billiard. No one had told the caretaker that I was now a persona non-grata and as long as we were not disruptive or destructive, he raised no objections to our assiduous attendance.

The caretaker had two children, a thirteen-year-old daughter and a little boy of about two who was just beginning to talk. Paulette had short blonde hair and was developing a charming pair of breasts. She would come and join us each time we would be in the facilities, her eyes as wide as if she had been a kid in front of a candy shop window. Maurice would ogle her precociously nubile boobs and inquire: *"Poulette, comment vont les nichons?"* Little chick, how are your tits? And Paulette would blush and smile timidly. She was not beautiful but her shyness gave her a very special charm. Apparently, she could not get enough of Maurice's words, as she could not stay away from us.

Paulette and her little brother would come and watch us play Ping-Pong or billiard on every occasion. When I'd make a particularly lucky shot, Maurice would exclaim *"Cocu"* "cuckold", after the French custom that ascribes great luck to anyone who has been cuckolded. After a few such outbursts, the young boy who was just learning to talk decided that this easy word should become part of his vocabulary. He began to repeat "cocu" whenever Maurice would yell it loudly. The last time we saw him, he was running through Solvay yelling "cocu" to all that would hear it and even to those, like his Mother, who did not wish to hear it.

The caretaker complained to Solvay that there were these two members who caused consternation in his family by using improper language. Solvay inquired with Lever and learned that this

Rodolphe Rosenberg had been fired and no longer had the privilege of using the Solvay Club facilities. The next time we showed up, the caretaker threw us out without much ceremony. Thus ended our forays into the club and the pleasure of observing the soft "nichons" of Paulette.

MY NIGHTS AT BOB'S

I did not have a job anymore. I had little money and no home life. Often, for dinner, I ate a sausage with Maurice at our "Hacienda". Then I'd go visit Bob and we'd play Ping-Pong in the greenhouse at the end of the garden of his home on the Rue Fraikin, not too far from where Gilberte lived. In the heat of the match, when frustrated by my lucky shots, Bob would come hobbling to my side of the table and would jump me and pummel me good-naturedly. This was all in fun and I saw nothing wrong in his actions.

After we had our fill of Ping-Pong, we'd wind our way to the kitchen where Bob would prepare a few sandwiches for us while I made a deep saucepan of hot chocolate. We'd then talk and eat and drink the chocolate into the wee hours of the morning. Sometimes, we'd place the saucepan and sandwiches in the dumb-waiter and sent the whole thing to the salon where we'd have our feast and played some of the records we were so fond of. We'd talk about America and Kathryn Grayson and music and movies. At times, we'd talk about sex and masturbation and Bob would make quite a thing about the fact that, even with his amputated leg, he enjoyed riding the side of the bathtub while doing it. It gave him a thrill to press his thighs against the enamel of the tub. He was a bit uneasy about it but I told him that anything that fired his imagination while having sex was acceptable and nothing to worry about.

Once, we sent the food upstairs but the handle of the saucepan was sticking out of the dumbwaiter. It got caught as it passed the ceiling line. The saucepan tilted and the entire content of hot chocolate spilled all over the dumbwaiter, the walls and the kitchen floor and counter. We spent the next few hours cleaning up the mess so Bob's parents would not notice anything the next morning. When we were finished with the clean up, it was too late for me to go home and Bob suggested that I spend the night with him.

Of course, this had to be done in complete secrecy so that his parents and his older brother Raymond did not hear us going up the stairs. On the way to his room we had to pass the room where his parents slept. Bob could not climb the stairs but had to jump one step at a time while dragging his artificial leg behind him. As I was following him, I had to mimic his actions so that it would sound as if only one person was climbing the stairs. It must have been comical to see both of us, like Siamese twins, hopping up the stairs in unison so that it sounded as if only Bob was going upstairs. Once upstairs, we'd go to his bathroom and wash up in tandem and flush only once so that no one would find out that I was still there.

We shared his bed. There was barely enough room for the two of us. In view of later developments, I must say that our bodies never did come in contact and that Bob never made any attempt at touching me improperly. It never entered my mind at the time that there could be something wrong or untoward as my mind and inclinations were strictly in the direction of girls, girls, girls.

In the morning, we got up early and did our morning ablutions in Bob's bathroom. Again we had to do everything as if there was only one person in the room. To Bob' horror, I blew my nose quite noisily. "Hush! "He warned, "I never blow my nose in the morning!" Of course, I always did. It might have been ethnic. When we were finished, we'd go down the stairs thumping our way to the lower floors as if we were one. On the ground floor, Bob opened the window and eased me onto the sidewalk. Once outside, I'd come up to the front door and rang the bell. Bob would open the door and feign surprise. "Diddy, good morning, how nice to see you this early. Have you had breakfast yet?" Of course I had not and Bob would invite me in to have breakfast with him. We once did this for three weeks straight without me going home.

It was now certain that I'd soon be leaving for America and Bob began to get morose about that certain separation. We promised to stay in touch and that we would surely see each other again. Bob who would always eat his nails and cuticles was telling me that he wanted to become a musician but that he did not know what instrument to choose. Tactlessly, I dashed his hopes by remarking that his fingers were too short and stubby for him to excel with any instrument. This had a devastating effect on Bob and I regretted it as soon as I had spoken.

LAST TRIBULATIONS

A series of incidents marked the weeks that preceded my departure, some trite, some that could have been serious. Looking back on these I wondered what I could have been thinking of.

I had met an extremely pretty Parisian girl. We could call her Madeleine for the sake of this anecdote. That was not her name, which I have long forgotten but I still remember her well. The only marring feature she had was a terribly bloodshot eye. Her entire right eye was covered with blood. She said that one of her blood vessels had burst and that she'd soon be perfect again. We made a date for the next afternoon to meet in a café a good distance from the center of town.

I did not want to be late for our date so I took the streetcar and arrived early. The place was almost deserted. I waited and waited. There was another guy who was nursing a beer while I sipped on my Coca-Cola. We made eye contact and after a while began to share our mounting frustrations at waiting for our mutual dates. Well, anyway, mine was worth waiting for. The other fellow readily acknowledged that his date was equally worth the wait. He described how pretty she was and I found myself lucky to be waiting for a girl that was as pretty as his. He said that this one was from France. I asked him if she was from Paris. What a coincidence, she was indeed a Parisian. "Don't tell me" I said. "She has a bloodshot eye?" Indeed she had. She had made the same date with him and me, at the same place and time. She never did show up and must have gone out with a third guy.

The guy and I stayed a while in the café playing a few games of billiard until the night fell. We then parted and I returned home *bredouille* like a hunter with an empty bag and my cock slung under my arm.

"I'm waiting for Madeleine, Madeleine who never came." (Jacques Brel).

There were two weapons in my room. I never knew how they got there. They just appeared one day or I have forgotten where they came from. One was an old five-shot revolver. There were a dozen bullets with it. The unusual bullets were not percussion type. Each bullet had a small pin over the end and it was placed in the chamber so that the pin slipped in a slot and stuck out a couple of millimeters. When the hammer was cocked and released, it drove the pin into the bullet causing it to fire. The bullets and the gun were so old and corroded that I feared having to fire the weapon as it would probably have exploded in my hand.

The knife had been purchased at the Flea Market. A sharp, deadly looking seven-inch blade nestled firmly in its leather scabbard. A loop enabled the wearer to carry the weapon on his belt. It was a grand knife and I delighted in how well it felt in the palm of my hand. I fancied that I might have been James Bowie even though it might have been of a different type. Both the gun and the knife always remained confined to my room on the Place Madou.

Late on an August evening, I strapped the knife in my belt and placed the gun in my pants pocket. I was wearing a shirt outside over my belt and the knife and pistol were not visible. At about midnight, I left my home and walked along the Belt Boulevard that encircled the center of Brussels. For the next three hours, I walked around Brussels. It gave me a strange feeling. I was almost daring anyone to make a move against me. I was ready. Now and then, I'd feel in my pocket to make sure that the loaded gun was still there, loaded and ready to fire. My left hand would lift the knife from its scabbard making sure that it would slip out rapidly if I found the need to flash its seven-inch blade.

I dared anyone, who or for what I was not sure but I was ready to shoot or cut anyone who would not get out of my way or who'd have the misguided idea to call me a Jew. The gun could have been more of a menace to me than to any possible victim. It was so old that it might have blown in my hand had I fired it. However, the knife felt great, friendly to me, terrifying for an opponent. The night ended without any incident and I got home feeling a bit cheated and disappointed. I also felt relieved that I had gotten home untouched as it began to dawn on me that I could have been arrested for carrying two deadly weapons in the middle of the night. Such an arrest would have scuttled my chances of going to the States. I must have been insane. It was a dumb stunt. That three-hour walk could have ruined my life. I never touched the gun or the knife again. There is no recollection of whatever happened to the weapons. These were not part of my luggage when I left for New York.

FAREWELL TO EUROPE

Everything was falling in place. I had garnered my visa, passport, boat ticket and a large, sealed manila envelope protecting a life-size x-ray of my lungs, testifying that I did not have tuberculosis. All was set for me to leave for Rotterdam and board the SS Tabinta of the Holland-America Line. After a ten day crossing, I would arrive at long last in the Port of New York.

In mid-August, I rode my bicycle a few miles to Koekelberg, a borough just northeast of the center, where Rosette Wauters lived, not far from the imposing Basilica of the Sacred Heart, better known as the Basilica of Koekelberg. I had trouble finding the Wauters Apartment. I asked a few people and finally found the house. It was a typical redbrick house with red geraniums blooming in window flower boxes. Geraniums made me uneasy. Perhaps it was the eerie red of the flowers that had an artificial look. Perhaps it was the strange odor that emanated from geraniums. Perhaps it was that geraniums were ubiquitous all over Belgium and that they represented all that I needed to get away from.

I rang the bell and someone let me in. I met Rosette's Mother, Christine Veulemans Wauters and her Father Armand. It was the typical small bourgeois apartment. Rosette invited me to her tiny bedroom. She was really beautiful with her luxuriant hair and her eyes shining brilliantly. On a shelf over her bed, I noticed a well-thumbed copy of "The Memoirs of Fanny Hill". It had been read so often that none of the pages talked to one another anymore. The size of the book must have been twice or triple its original thickness. Fanny Hill was the most infamous sex book of our generation. "Oh, you read Fanny Hill?" I half inquired. Much to my surprise, Rosette formally denied It. "Oh, I have the book but I have not read it." And that was that. I did not believe her but at the time I did not make any inference from it.

I told Rosette that I had at last gotten my visa and that I would be leaving by train from the North Station on the morning of August 31st. She assured me that she would come to the station to wish me good luck.

The day before I left, I was taking a last ride through Brussels on my faithful Peugeot and was pedaling at a fast clip alongside of parked cars when someone opened the door of his car. I had no time to react and drove the front wheel of the bicycle into the open door. I went flying over it. As I was hurtling through the air, one thought flashed in my mind. I was going to get hurt badly and would wind up in the hospital. The Tabinta would sail without me and my dreams of America would be squashed as I smashed against the cobblestones of Brussels. Luckily, I managed to roll a landing and except for a few minor bruises I was fine. I thought myself lucky even as fate seemed to want to prevent my departure.

On the morning of Wednesday, August 31st I found myself on a platform of the *Gare Du Nord,* the North Station alongside of the train that was scheduled to leave for Rotterdam. My suitcase must have been sent ahead to the ship, as I do not recall that I had one to carry. Mother was there, together with Ruth and René Van Langendonck. Rosette was there too. I do not recall if either Maurice or Bob showed up. I do not believe they did. Van Langendonck embraced me and wished me luck. Mother took me in her arms and kissed me. Ruth was crying as she kissed her *"petit frère"*, little brother. Rosette got real close to me and gave me a kiss on the lips, the first ever from her. She quickly turned around and was gone.

I could not see my Father and worried that I might leave Belgium without his goodbye. Then, I saw him getting in at the other end of the train. Apparently he was going to ride with me part of the way and did not want to share the platform with Frieda as they might have had another altercation.

With a blast of its whistle and much slippage of the wheels, the train spewed white smoke and I was on my way to America. Those who had come to see me leave quickly became a blur of waving figures left behind on the platform. I did not know if I would ever see them again but my eyes were on the future and I was dry-eyed. America was waiting at the end of the line. I was embarking on a great adventure.

Shortly after the train left the station, Father worked his way to my compartment. It must have reminded him of the time, nearly fifty years earlier, when his Father accompanied him to the train that was to take him to Krakow. He never saw his Father or his family again. Hilaire was grim. We did not have much to say to each other. Twenty minutes later, when the train got to Vilvorde he got off the train. It was summer and Hilaire wore a gray suit with an unbuttoned white shirt and the collar split over that of his suit. I was surprised that he was not wearing a tie. He looked sad and suddenly older than his forty-seven years. He closed the door of the compartment, the train sped away, and he was gone.

After leaving the train station, on that Wednesday morning, Rosette went back to Lever Bros. and began a long affair with Gustave Bauters, a married man who worked for Lever but was mainly employed there because he played soccer and was on the team that played for Lever and Solvay. Of course, I was to find this out quite a while later.

SS.TABINTA

After leaving Brussels, the train stopped briefly in Antwerp and then it was the Dutch border. I was really on my way. In the early afternoon we arrived in Rotterdam where I had the instructions to get to the harbor where I would board the SS Tabinta of the Holland America Lines. I got on the streetcar in Rotterdam but did not get in the platform It was very crowded and I stood on the step holding on to the ramp with my left hand. As we crossed a square, the conductor applied the brakes and my body continued to travel. As I held on, my left hand was not powerful enough to stop my forward motion and I began to pivot until I found myself ahead of the streetcar. I slid further, my right leg slipping under the tram. The right front wheel was still turning and moving forward and for a moment I thought that my right leg was going to get amputated by the wheel. The conductor applied full force to the brakes and the streetcar finally came to stop just inches from my right leg. I was safe again but this had been a really close one. All I could think about was America and the ship that was waiting for me. Really, there was something there that wanted to prevent me from ever leaving Europe. I became very cautious. Nothing should happen to me now, not after having waited so long.

As the SS Tabinta loomed before me on the wharf, it impressed me by its size. In reality, it was rather small. The Tabinta was a ten thousand-ton Liberty ship that had been used as a troop transport by the US.Navy. After the war, it had been sold to the Dutch Government and used to ferry troops to the Dutch colony of Indonesia. It had retained its original ABCD bunks and was the latest style in non-comfort. I did not care. It was romantic and exciting. The ship was crowded with young American college students who had spent the summer of '49 in Europe, mostly in France. They were now returning to the US to resume their schooling. There must have been 300 passengers, half of them young American girls. I had never seen so many attractive women all in one spot. Too bad I had to be so ugly and unattractive. We sailed off with the tide on the evening of August 31st.

We ate all together in a gigantic mess hall. The food was plentiful but forgettable. I had managed to get a B. bunk. That meant that I did not have to climb too high to go to sleep and the roll of the ship was less noticeable than in the upper bunks. There were separate washrooms and toilets for the boys and the girls.

As the weather was warm we spent most of the days lying on the deck or leaning against the lifeboats. Some of the students were quite talented and they'd play guitars and sang popular tunes. There was one girl who looked to me just like Ava Gardner. I could not keep my eyes off her. Another girl was introduced to me as Betty Krasner. Her claim to fame was her grandMother Emma Lazarus who had written the poem that graces the Statue of Liberty. I was duly impressed.

There were also a number of emigrants who were going to America just as I was. On the first day, a man came to me and said that he knew me. I did not remember ever seeing him before. He explained that in Brussels, he drove a taxi that was always stationed on the Place Madou. For the better part of five years, he had seen me leave each morning for school, then to go to work. Now, he was on his way to Canada where he was hoping to make a new life for himself. We had both smiled at the coincidence.

Two young Americans had befriended me and were giving me a crash course on America, giving me insights on things I did not already know. Andy Siff was very tall and had the build of a fullback. He lived in New York City. Roy Silver was almost as tall but had a much slender figure. Both were about to complete their college years and I had the feeling that they were both from prosperous Jewish families.

At the time I was still sporting a slender mustache but neither Roy nor Andy liked it. They urged me to shave it off. I politely declined. I ran into a problem in the washroom. I had an electric razor that had to be plugged in to work. This was well before battery powered razor had been invented. There were no outlets that would fit the cylindrical prongs of my razor. As far as I could see, there were no outlets. Andy showed me that in the US, the outlets had flat openings that would only fit flat plugs. Thus, as there were no adapters or converters, my razor was useless. This presented a real problem, as I would not be able to shave.

Roy and Andy offered to help and they combined their efforts to shave me daily with their Gillette blades. So, they set out to shave me, Roy on one side and Andy on the other. Roy trimmed my mustache but when he had finished, he noticed that he had cut a bit too much and that it no longer was symmetrical. Now it was Andy's turn to try to even his side. He trimmed a bit, a bit too much and his side was now too short. Roy clipped some more to match Andy's side. With each trim, the discrepancy persisted and by the time they were finished, my mustache was completely gone, vanished. Roy and Andy seemed quite pleased with their handiwork. They recruited Ava Gardner to give her opinion about my new clean-shaved look. She pronounced it a great improvement and gave me a kiss on the cheek. I was convinced and satisfied.

However, I now had a new mystery to ponder. I had not known that my European plug did not fit the US receptacle since mine was round and the US was flat. What about the girls? I had never known an American girl. Would my round penis . . . ? I must confess that I did not dwell too much on this question except that I promised myself that sooner or later I would have to find out.

In the middle of the Atlantic Ocean, the P.A system came to life. It was the Captain alerting us that we were passing the Queen Mary on its way to Southampton. He cautioned that we should not all go to the port side for a full view of the Queen for fear that our tub might tilt over. There were now three hundred passengers on the Tabinta straining to catch a glimpse of the QM. It was fun to think that on the QM, three thousand passengers were straining for a view of our tiny SS.Tabinta.

About eight days out of Rotterdam, we were hit by a ferocious hurricane. For over one day and night, our little ship was buffeted and slammed by waves that towered over it. The view was awesome. As the ship plunged into the deep hollow of the waves, the next wave loomed higher than our masts and smokestack. The decks were off limits to the passengers as we would have been swept off the ship. It was all so exciting that I did not even think about getting seasick. I kept remembering my Mother's favorite joke about two Jewish immigrants, travelling steerage to America and caught in a fierce hurricane. Frightened, one calls to his friend: "Moishe, the ship is gonna sink!" "Why worry?" Replies Moishe. "Is it your ship?"

The next day, the sea was still very rough and it was like being on a roller coaster even though the threat of disaster had passed. Looking at the heaving of the waves I suddenly felt queasy and found myself having to heave. I rushed to my bunk and lay down quickly. My stomach made a few deep turns around but I did not throw up or get sick.

Because of the storm at sea, we had been delayed one full day and would not be able to land on the Saturday and ships could not unload on Sundays. On Saturday September 10th, we stopped by the Ambrose Light ship to pick up a pilot and some customs and immigration officers. I had been told that new immigrants would no longer have to be processed in Ellis Island unless their papers were not in order. I had been in fear of having to stay for months on the dreaded Ellis Island if I were afflicted with a contagious disease.

As I was standing in the long line that waited outside the dining hall where the immigration officers were checking all papers, I was clutching my large envelope containing my x-ray. This was my most prized possession on board, my key to New York. When it was my turn to enter, I was directed to a center table where a burly customs officer grabbed my envelope. He popped the seal that had kept it shut and extracted the big x-ray negative. He held it to the light for a moment then in a single motion; he ripped it apart and threw it in a garbage can. I wanted to lunge forward and save my x-ray. What was he thinking? This was my entrance paper to America. He could see my anxiety. With a quick smile, he shook my hand and said: "Welcome to America, Mister Rosenberg! ".

Because we had been delayed at sea, the Captain had received special permission to proceed and dock on the Sunday morning, September 11th, 1949. With the new pilot on board, we eased into the Hudson River. Someone said that Brooklyn was to our right and the island on the left was Staten Island. As we stood on the port side above the prow, the isle of Manhattan glistened in the distance under the early sun. Passengers began to point and shout. There, in the middle of the harbor, stood the Statue of Liberty, her lamp held high.

I had arrived in America.

Tears welled in my eyes.

I was home.

END OF VOLUME ONE
PART TWO

Completed November 26th, 2005.

Edited August 5th, 2012

Brussels, Belgium 1939. Just arrived in Brussels. Last photo taken before Ruth and Rudy are placed in orphanage. We are broke. Rudy, 9; Hilaire, 37; Ruth, 11; Frieda, 37. Photo taken by street photographer, Blvd. Adolphe Max, Brussels.

June 1942 – Brussels Belgium. Last photo prior to going into hiding. We are prosperous. Frieda, 40; Ruth, almost 14; Hilaire, 40; Rudy, 12. (note : broken arm in cast). Photo taken by street photographer, Blvd Adolphe Max, Brussels.

VOLUME ONE
PART THREE

MEMOIRS OF RUDY ROSENBERG,

Hilaire, 40; 1942,
shortly before his arrest.
Note: German Airman.
Photo taken by street
photographer, Blvd
Anspach, Brussels.

Rudy, 15; taken
in school, Brussels
1945.

AMERICA

I'm dreaming of a white Christmas,
Just like the ones I used to know . . .

September 11th, 1949

ARRIVAL IN AMERICA

I hurried downstairs to my bunk as our ship, the SS Tabinta of the Holland-America Line steamed up the Hudson River towards its mooring pier in Hoboken NJ. There was little time to waste and my suitcase was quickly packed. It would be great to tell all the details of going up the Hudson and seeing the Empire State Building and all the skyscrapers. However, after the vivid view of the Statue of Liberty, everything else went into a fog. It must have been early afternoon as we maneuvered into the slip. Was there a tugboat or did the captain ease the ten-thousand ton Liberty ship alongside the pier in Hoboken?

My dream had been to land on US soil and to kiss the ground. However, we landed on immense steel plates and these did not seem so appealing to me. What's more, the docks in Hoboken were rusty, dirty and the noise and cacophony drowned everything. I did not know what I had expected but it certainly was not kissing a steel plate. Perhaps there should have been a plot of grassy ground where the immigrants could have knelt and kiss the American soil. In later years, the peripatetic Pope John-Paul the 2nd would lie prostrate and kiss the tarmac at every airport he chanced to land. It was just cement, oil stained concrete and had no connection with the land he was visiting!

There were no formalities at the harbor as we had gone through customs and immigration by the Ambrose Light ship as we had entered the US waters. Uncle Paul and his wife Lilli were waiting at the pier to welcome me to America. I recognized Paul as he had changed very little since I had last seen him in Charleroi in 1935. Lilli though a strangers for me immediately made me feel welcomed.

We must have taken the Tubes that connected New Jersey to the lower tip of Manhattan and from there the IRT subway to reach Brooklyn where my uncle lived. It was Sunday and the subway was deserted. The train entered a station and I could see blue tiles spelling "Wall Street". Wall Street, the center of the universe! The doors opened and I expected to see opulent millionaires flooding our subway car. Instead, one unkempt, dirty, smelly bum came in. He sat across from me and quickly went to sleep. What a letdown that was!

It was dark when we got off at the Utica Ave. station and Eastern Parkway. Paul and Lilli lived a block away at 1733 Union Street. After we deposited my luggage they insisted on taking me for ice cream an American treat. We walked up to Dubrow's Cafeteria on the corner of Utica and Eastern

Parkway. The place was brightly lit and filled with late evening diners. A pervasive aroma of coffee, steaming meat and pickles filled my senses with a friendly assault never to be forgotten.

We sat at the counter on round leather covered stools and Lilli ordered an ice cream sundae for me. In short order I was confronted by the largest boat-dish I had ever seen, filled with three enormous scoops of ice cream, red, green and white. The whole thing was covered with clouds of whipped cream, sprinkled with nuts, multicolored sprinkles and daubed with dark chocolate sauce. A maraschino cherry sat above this incredible structure. I had tasted ice cream in Belgium; mostly it had consisted of a small, single flavor scoop with a pie-wedge wafer. I had never developed a great taste for ice cream perhaps out of self-defense, as I was not supposed to desire something that was not often available.

Perhaps I was tired and stressed by my arrival in America but this sundae was beyond my capacity. I made a feeble, half-hearted attempt at tasting this monstrous offering but soon had to beg-off the feast. Paul and Lilli were very disappointed. We retired to the apartment where Lilli had prepared a bed for me out of the living room sofa.

The next morning I joined Paul in the kitchen where Aunt Lilli had prepared a light breakfast. Lilli worked at the Hospital for Incurable Diseases. Her day started at five AM and she had left by the time I awoke. I had finished unpacking and was eager to show Uncle Paul the few treasures I had brought with me from Belgium. Of course, there was the Indian-head silver ring that Bill Kennedy had given me. Next I brought out the pair of dice that had also been Kennedy's gift and placed them on the breakfast table. Instantly, Uncle Paul exploded with uncontrollable rage. He grabbed the dice and tried to throw them out the window into the inner courtyard below. Frantically he strained to open the window so he could heave out the dice. Unfortunately, this was Brooklyn and there were at least seventeen coats of white paint all around the frame. The window was not going to open even if King Kong had tried to pry it open. Frustrated, Paul kept slapping the dice against the window with his palm.

I was taken aback by this extreme behavior. I realized that Paul was not a gambler and had always had a deep resentment for the gambling addictions of his brother Richard, Hilaire and Frieda. I was not a gambler but the dice had been a gift from my "G.I". There was no evil attached to it. Paul would not relent and threw the dice in the garbage. I was to retrieve them later and have them still.

On the second or third day of my arrival, Andy Siff, my shipboard friend came to pick me up at my uncle's apartment. There were a few things he wanted to show me. We took the subway to Manhattan and walked over to his parent's home, a vast apartment on Riverside Drive. I remembered a phrase from a notorious French book *"J'irez cracher sur vos tombes"* "I will go spit on your graves" supposedly written by an American Negro who seduced white women because he hated whites so much. Actually it had been written by a Frenchman under a pseudonym and had caused quite a scandal in France. Oh, yes, the phrase: "Why is Riverside Drive like the leg of a woman? Because the higher you go, the nicer it gets". And mister Siff senior lived way up on Riverside Drive.

There was a television set in the Siff apartment, with a huge screen, at least twelve inches. It was the first TV set I had ever seen, black and white of course, no one even thought that there was no color, the mind made the adjustment. I was very impressed.

From there, we went to Yankee Stadium where the Siffs had front seats in a box just opposite the "On-Deck" circle, although I did not know what that was at the time. The Yankees were playing the St. Louis Browns. There was a player from St. Louis who was throwing a baseball to a Yankee "pitcher". This was the batter but to me he was pitching with a stick and must have been the pitcher. For a while, I felt that the fellow throwing the ball was pretty good as he hit the bat almost every time and the crowd would cheer each time he did. Andy was trying to explain the game to me but it seemed to be quite complicated.

A Yankee player stepped onto the on-deck circle. A large number "5" decorated his uniform. It was Joe DiMaggio! I knew who he was; the G.Is had told me all about this superstar. He was so near. I felt that I could reach out from my seat and touch him. I had never been so close to a celebrity, a legend. I was thrilled. I knew I'd never forget that moment, I had arrived in America! I became a life-long Yankee fan. The Yankees were in the American League. Any country could have a "National League", but only America could have an "American League". And could there be a more American team that "The Yankees"?

We had a couple of hotdogs and Cokes but all that was an anticlimax after seeing and being so near to Joe DiMaggio.

That evening and the next day, Andy Siff took me around and introduced me to a number of friends. I felt like a celebrity. He would introduce me and say that I had just arrived from Europe. Later, he told me that he had to tell his friends that I had just arrived to America. "Your English is so good" He told me "But now and then, you will make a mistake and I don't want them to think that you are ignorant" I was flattered.

In the days that followed, I immersed myself in everything that was at hand, Times Square, the Empire State Building, Macys and Gimbels on Herald Square. In Gimbels, as I entered, a young Vic Damone was singing, introducing his latest hit "You're Breaking My Heart For You're Leaving". I was living a dream, another star to be seen and heard live, in person!

In Brussels, one of my favorites had been Vaughn Monroe. I knew all his songs, from "Dance Ballerina, Dance" to "Ghosts Riders in the Sky". He was appearing live, on stage at the Brooklyn Paramount on Flatbush Ave. I spent most of the performance in the isle, in front of Vaughn Monroe, taking picture after picture with my faithful Agfa-Karat 6.3 loaded with black and white TriX, without flash. It did not take long for Monroe to become aware of me and to give me pained looks each time I tripped the shutter.

TIME TO GO TO WORK

By now, the eighty dollars I had landed with had dwindled down to a precious few and it was time for me to find a job. Aunt Lilli was telling me that there was a recession on that summer of 1949 and that I would do well to learn a trade. Since I had not completed my education, a trade seemed like the wise thing to learn. I found a job in a French pastry shop in Manhattan on 82nd street between Second and Third Ave. It did not take me long to realize that I was not going to learn much about pastries with the job I had been given. My duties were to scoop out by hand the remnants of dough from the deep vats that served as mixers. These were like deep kettledrums, deeper than I was tall and into which I'd slip with annoying regularity. By the end of the day, I'd be white with flour and encrusted with dry dough. Being rather fastidious by nature, this was not to my liking. I quit on the fourth day not even bothering to collect the sixteen dollars I had earned. Thus ended my "promising" career as a French pastry chef.

Lilli suggested that since Hilaire had been an interior decorator it might be wise to gravitate to that trade. I had seen a shop near Eastern Parkway, Roman's Decorators. I went in and asked Mr Roman if I could work for him and learn the decorator's trade as my Father was in that business. Mr Roman, a kindly man, regretted that he did not need anyone. Actually, he was not a decorator but only sold cloth and accessories for home decoration. However, Mr Roman knew of someone who was looking for a helper. He made a phone call and gave me an address where I should go and apply for a job with a Mister Sirota.

Philip Sirota was a Russian Jew who lived in Brooklyn in a large apartment building on Empire Boulevard at the bottom of Utica Ave. We had a short conversation and I explained that I had been working in the offices of Unilever in Belgium prior to my departure for the United States. Sirota wanted me to type a business letter. I wrote a long letter in English about a claim by a customer who was not happy with the merchandise he had purchased and where we offered to make a fair exchange.

When the letter was finished, Sirota took it in the next room and after a while he returned. He pointed to a spelling error; I had spelled "marchandise" (the French spelling) instead of merchandise. Aside from that, he was satisfied and hired me on the spot for the "munificent" sum of twenty-seven dollars a week.

At the time I had not realized that Mr Sirota had only a rudimentary knowledge of English spelling and had to take my letter to the next room where Mrs Sirota, a schoolteacher, could peruse the letter for possible errors. When I suggested that I would start on Monday, Mr Sirota told me that he would prefer I start at once, the following day, a Sunday. This seemed strange to me but I decided to keep mum, leaving to the next day to question the odd nature of starting to work on a Sunday.

ELDRIDGE STREET, NEW YORK

The store occupied by Mr Philip Sirota stood on the ground floor at 89 Eldridge Street near the corner of Grand Street in the middle of the Lower East Side. This was the area of New York where the Jewish immigrants first were established at the end of the 19th century and the early part of the 20th Century. The Gershwin brothers were born there and Israel Isidore Baline (Izzy Baline) settled there when he and his parents arrived in New York from Russia. He went on to achieve fame and fortune as Irving Berlin.

Now, almost all of the tenements sheltered Italian immigrants and only the ground floor stores were still occupied by the dry-goods businesses that lined both sides of Eldridge Street. The stores spilled out onto Grand Street. One would have to go on to Worth Street and Lower Broadway to find the rest of the wholesale dry-goods community quite a notch above that of Eldridge Street.

Sirota's store measured about 25 x 25 feet with a front window where golden letters advised "P.Sirota, Dry Goods, Wholesale" On the side, a black painted door with a clear window pane served as the entrance. Inside, in the corner away from the door, a small office was separated by a glass and wood combination almost like a bank teller's partition. At the end, to the far left a minimal bathroom and sink completed the furnishings. The walls had been lined with wooden shelves completely filled with bolts upon bolts of percales, broadcloth, dotted Swiss and boxes of Dan River Mills pillow cases and bedsheets (mostly "mill seconds"). A packing table was laid out in the middle of the store amid a few cartons and cases containing yet-unpacked merchandise.

After I got oriented by Philip Sirota, I inquired about the unfortunate practice of working on a Sunday. Sirota advised me that Saturdays were "Shabbat" days and not to be worked on. "In the old days" He continued "We would work until sundown on Friday and come back to work after sundown on Saturday. The work would go on until late in the night of Saturday and would resume all day Sunday". This did not please me at all as I had been used to having my Sundays off. However, I was glad to have a job and I kept my displeasure to myself. Later, I was to find out that, at least during the last four months of the year, a variety of Jewish Holidays would be observed (Rosh Hashanah, Yom Kippur, Sukkoth and Chanukah) and that I would be getting quite a few days off. I began to feel that it was not such a bad deal after all. The working hours were from 8.30 AM until 6 PM except on winter's Fridays when we closed early as sundown would approach. All this was quite new to me.

This was a strictly wholesale business and only customers who had a resale number could purchase goods at Sirota's as Mister Sirota was adamant about not selling to the general public. Now and then, a woman would come in and attempt to purchase a few yards of a percale pattern or even a short bolt of this or that cloth. Sirota would politely but firmly show her the door and always refused to entertain even the thought of a sale. He made sure that I followed the same policy.

When there was a lull in the business, which was often, I'd spend my time rearranging the order of the bolts of cloth on the shelves. The percales had to be sorted out by shades, colors and patterns. New bolts waited behind the front rows of cloths or had to be lifted from the crates that were strewn in the middle of the floor. In a very short time, I had become quite proficient with the different types of cloth and the wonderful array of colors from "Sunrise Gold" to "American Beauty Rose" and the sizes and thread counts of the sheets and pillow cases held no mystery for me. Often, as I'd go about climbing up and down the ladder to shuffle around the merchandise, Mr Sirota would beg me to sit down and rest and take it easy. "You make me dizzy" He would complain good-naturedly.

I did not need to be coaxed. I could then stand in the doorway. Now and then, I'd see middleweight Rocky Grazziano, dressed in a long herringbone coat visiting his old neighborhood with his entourage. What I'd come to see were the gorgeous Italian girls passing in front of the store in an alluring parade of charm and beauty. In the warm autumnal weather of Manhattan, the girls would walk by, eyes ablaze with come-hither looks as they glided past the store entrance in their flat black slip-ons. This was the era of Dior's "New Look" and the slim girls seemed to be from the same attractive mold with striped cloth wrapped as a turban covering their black hair, a white shirt with a deep neckline hinting at treasures I could only dream of and a wrapped skirt that descended all the way to the ankle; they beckoned to me. They did not seem to walk but rather float by as if they were ocean liners going on a cruise and inviting me to sail away with them. I would stand there, cursing my ugliness and unable to take the bait and say something, anything. Now and then, the girls, when in groups of three or four, would giggle and dart a look my way. I was petrified and unable to smile, say a word or even look their way.

Pushcart vendors plied their trade in front of the store, selling yams and knishes. I was particularly fond of yams, sweet potatoes cooked in square flat metal stoves. The odor of the roasting yams would come to taunt me in the shop. When ready, the yams, once the peel had burst would reveal a dark red flesh. For thirty-five cents one could crush the soft warm fruit in the mouth. It was a delight that I'd repeat at least twice a day. At the corner of Eldridge and Grant stood a newspaper stand that also sold candy bars and king-sized pretzels at 8 cents a piece. The saleslady would hawk the pretzels. "Eight cents apiece" She'd yell. "Three for a quarter!" Most people would plunk down a quarter to take advantage of this obvious "bargain".

The Bowery with its many flophouses that rented a bed for a quarter a night ran just a few blocks from Eldridge Street. One rainy fall day, I noticed two derelicts having an animated argument. Their clothes were in tatters. Unshaven and unwashed, with gaping soles on their shoes, they were certainly down on their luck and one of them wanted to leave his buddy to go down to the Bowery. The other kept pleading with him to stay around Grant Street. "Don't go to the Bowery" He argued. "Do you want to become a bum?" It was such a sad spectacle, these two bums arguing about going to the Bowery as if there was a hierarchy among derelicts that made Grant Street a class above the Bowery.

We had steady customers who would come to restock their retail stores. They would pick several patterns and colors mostly of percale that outsold all other available cloths. Most of the time, they would not take the order with them and we would have to pack the merchandise and send it to them. Mr Sirota quickly taught me how to best cram the bolts in cardboard boxes, how to cut the boxes to fit the contents and how to secure the packages with brown tape, metal straps or cords. Those simple basic skills would remain with me always and even much later in life, whenever I'd cut a carton to size, it would be the voice of Philip Sirota that I would hear in my head.

It was early fall of 1949 and when Mr Roman, Mr Feuerstein, Mr Cohen and others would leave the store they would say "Goodbye and happy New Year!" I had never heard of saying "Happy New Year!" in October and since they were wishing me a New Year's greeting, I felt that it would be polite to shake their hand and to reply "Thank you very much, and merry Christmas to you ". This went on for a few days until Mister Sirota came to me and in his heavily accented English remonstrated "Rudolph, it is not nice to say merry Christmas when they say happy New Year". I was taken aback as I had no idea that there existed a separate New Year, a Jewish New Year.

Mr Cohen was a most orthodox Jew. He wore black clothes; black stockings showed from under his calf-length black caftan and a large fur-brimmed black hat covered his full-bearded head. Tall and broad, Mr Cohen towered over everybody else. With his black *payes* sidelocks tumbling from under his hat he cut a formidable and imposing figure.

I had been working at Sirota's for a good while when Mr Sirota told me "Mr Cohen likes you. He has a daughter. He would like you to marry her. If you marry her, he will give you ten thousand dollars and take you in his business. But, you have to be a little more religious!"

In 1949, ten thousand dollars was a lot on money, a large sum indeed. In those days, a "five thousand dollar a year man" was considered a success. At my rate of salary of $27—per week, it would take me over seven years to make that amount of money. It was tempting. The prospect of being taken into Mr Cohen's business made it even more attractive. However, I had never met the daughter he wanted me to marry. I remembered my Father telling me about when Mme Cousin in Charleroi wanted Hilaire to marry her daughter and inherit the business. He had called that "To fall with your ass in butter". At the time he felt he was not attracted to the young girl. What was more; the thought of marrying outside of the Jewish faith was anathema to him. So, he had declined the offer.

Now it was my turn to ponder the offer. I had never met the girl, had not even known that she existed. The irony was that, unlike my Father, I did not want to marry into the Jewish faith and certainly not into Mr Cohen's ultra orthodox community. I would have to be a little more religious! Me who did not want to be Jewish at all! I told Mr Sirota that Mr Cohen's offer flattered me, but that I would have to decline.

MISSING PIECES

I had now been in the States for about three weeks. My relations with Uncle Paul were tenuous at best while Aunt Lilli, his wife, was always gracious and warm towards me. She took delight in introducing me to her friends and relatives and on one occasion took me to her place of work. This was at the Hospital for Incurables and I must confess that this was one of the most distressing visits I ever made anywhere. It is impossible for me to describe the horror I felt when immersed in room after room of patients completely deficient in physical or mental abilities. All the patients were Jewish and I could not help but wonder if severe inbreeding had been the cause of so much deformities and deficiences. I found it impossible to go there again and I had to admire Lilli and her obvious compassion for the miserable creatures she cared for. In Hitler's Germany these patients would have been exterminated at once. In New York, they were being given the best of care even as their situation and future seemed without any hope. Eventually, the hospital would be renamed Hospital for Chronic Diseases, a kinder name than "Incurables" for such an institution.

One day, Lilli asked me if there was something special I might want her to cook for me. I realized that in the few weeks I had been at 1733 Union Street, I had not eaten an omelet. I replied that indeed it would please me if Lilli could prepare a ham omelet. "I don't cook ham" Replied Lilli. It seemed odd to me and I told her that I would go and buy some ham and that I would cook it myself. Lilli replied that I would have to buy my own skillet, as she would not permit me to use her pots and pans and dishes to come in contact with ham. With my gap in things Jewish, I did not think that ham was such a big deal. I thought that such dietary restrictions dated back to the Middle Ages and that no one paid any attention in our modern age. I went to Katz's Delicatessen on our block and asked Mister Katz if I could buy a few slices of ham. "In this neighborhood? I can't sell ham; it is not Kosher" He replied. "However, I have some for my personal use in the refrigerator and I will gladly give you a slice or two". So, I ate my ham with a slice of bread but never did get around to making my omelet. It did make me realize that I had moved into a Jewish neighborhood and that most if not all the people I would come in contact with would be Jews. It was quite a revelation for me.

Sirota's was closed for several days for Rosh Hashanah and Yom Kippur "And I saw that that was good". Uncle Paul, like his brother Richard and my Mother had been raised in a secular atmosphere. As I was finding out, that had not been the case for aunt Lilli who came from a religious background albeit not an orthodox one.

Paul wanted me to come to temple for the High Holidays. I declined, telling him that I was not only a non-believer but that I had no desire to learn or delve into Jewish lore. I just did not want to be a Jew. To me, it was bad news to be Jewish and I wanted to run away from all that. Paul insisted; he wanted me to come just to please Lilli. It took quite a bit of convincing and I reluctantly agreed that I would join them for the services.

Except for the vague memory of the services I witnessed at the age of five at the Cinema Eden in Charleroi, this would be the first time I would be attending a service in a Synagogue. I was less than thrilled and I found myself in the temple in a belligerent state of mind. Carl Meyer, Lilli's brother was standing next to me in the temple. I was surprised that the women had been separated from the men and were watching the services from the balcony on the second floor. A voice began to singsong in Yiddish calling names in alphabetical order.

- -Abraham?—
- -Twanzig doolah—Replied Abraham.
- -Cohen?—
- -Tzeen doolah—Replied Cohen.

And so on until they reached Friedemann and Paul pledged a sum of money. By then I had figured out that they were selling seats for the services. I would not remember if we had to go to the synagogue just once or on several nights. I would recall the uneasiness I felt and how much I resented being there at all. In my mind and attitude I had reverted to that of a five-year old.

As the services started, I stayed close to Carl and was careful to ape all that was going on around me. I sat and stood up with all the others. When the singing started, I grabbed a prayer book from the benches. I knew enough to open the book from the back, not from the front and pretended to hum along. Carl soon realized that I was out of my element and told me that there was an English translation in the back (front?) of the book. Belligerently I replied that I did not know the tune either. What was I doing there anyway, I was not Jewish, I had been baptized Protestant in 1942. I felt completely out of place in that synagogue.

Carl, now that he knew I could not read Hebrew asked me if I had ever been bar mitzvahed. That was the first time in my life I had ever heard the word. I asked if that was a cocktail.

"No, bar mitzvah" Repeated Carl.

I made scissors with my fingers in the direction of my crotch and asked Carl if he meant "when they cut a piece."?

"No, no" Said Carl, "When you are thirteen".

"Oh, when I was thirteen I was hiding".

"You can have it done now" volunteered Carl.

I had been circumcised but I feared that they might want to cut off another piece.

"No thank you. There is no rush" I said, ending the discussion.

Determined to complete my education, I enrolled in Thomas Jefferson High School for evening courses that would give me a High School Equivalency Certificate. I would take the bus to and from school. The odor of diesel fuel would instantly bring me back to a couple of past sensations. The smell of diesel and the motion of the bus would make me slightly nauseous as it reminded me of the hurricane on board of the SS Tabinta and how I had almost thrown up due to the heavy swells. The other sensation, the instant recall was of a much more pleasant nature. It reminded me of Rachelle in Charleroi and her long legs and her goose-shit colored stockings that always reeked of kerosene. The recall would feed my fever at night.

In School, I had befriended a pretty dark-haired girl. Her name might have been Sarah or Rachel. She was obviously Jewish and we would take the bus together and talk of many things about the future. However, on Friday night, after school, there was no question of taking the bus. I could not understand why. Sarah could not take the bus because it was the Sabbath. It made absolutely no sense to me. Thus, on Friday night we had to walk a great distance to her house. A couple of times, she invited me in the apartment she shared with her parents. Since it was "*Shabbath*", we could not take the elevator and had to trudge the five floors to the apartment. There, she would bang on the door, as for some unknown reason it was not permitted to press a little button to activate the bell. Pressing the button was forbidden, banging on the door was fine. Inside, her parents would scrutinize me by the dim light of a couple of candles. At first I had thought that they had not paid their electric bill but I was informed that turning on the light by lifting a switch was also not allowed on the Sabbath. My budding relationship with Sarah/Rachel did not survive very long. I had no desire to immerse myself into her family rituals.

Back in the apartment, my relations with Uncle Paul were getting very taut. In the evening, I'd write letters to Mother and Ruth and the friends I had left behind in Belgium and I also began to carry on a steady correspondence with Rosette Wauters. I'd sit by a small coffee table under the light of a single lamp and wrote away. The programs of Martin Block would play softly on the WNEW radio station and I'd salve my heart with the latest pop songs. In their bedroom I could hear Paul and Lilli having strong arguments about me. Mostly it was Paul blurting out in German *"Ich kann es nicht vertragen!"* I can't stand it! Aunt Lilli would calm him down. Around eleven PM, Paul would stomp into the living room and without as much as a "beg your pardon" would turn off both the radio and the light leaving me in the dark with my unfinished correspondence. I never did find out what exactly was bugging him. He never spoke about it. I finally decided that I would go and do my writing at Dubrow's Cafeteria where the owners and the waiters left me alone and allowed me to have a small table in the rear of the restaurant where I could write to my heart's content.

The best feature in my uncle's apartment was the bathroom. It had a large tub and a wonderful soaking hot shower. I got in the habit of taking long showers, a new luxury for me. My body was responding to the new sensations of soft soap, warm lather and the feel of my hands all over my body. It was only a small step to masturbation that developed into a daily compulsive obsession. After a while, Lilli asked if I could stop spitting in the shower as she did not relish wiping and cleaning hair and scum from the drain. I did not shower with my glasses on and had been unable to see the slimy mix of hair and semen I was leaving behind whenever I showered. Embarrassed, I took the habit of cleaning all traces of my passage in the shower and was able to allay Aunt Lilli's concerns.

Paul and Lilli's second floor apartment did not hold much appeal to me. I could always feel the tension of my uncle's disapproval or dislike and Lilli's obvious affection for me did not compensate enough for Paul's hostility. I cannot recall if I contributed to the household finances out of my meager salary or not. I spent little time there, choosing instead to become friendly with other tenants and other denizens of Union Street and its surroundings.

Doctor Henry Ritterman lived on the ground floor apartment. He and his wife had a young fifteen-year old daughter, Diane Paula. They adopted me almost immediately. Diane was pretty, with very long very black hair that flowed past her waistline. Although she was only fifteen, she could have given lessons to Vivien Leigh on how to play Scarlett O'Hara in Gone with the Wind. Doctor Ritterman was a retired Army doctor who had spent a great deal of his Army career in Alabama. There, being Jewish, he and Diane had accumulated a vast repertoire of anecdotes relating to being Jewish in the Deep South during the forties.

Diane immediately fell head over heels in love with this "Frenchman" and made it quite obvious. In my mind, there was no doubt that Diane had every intention to press the budding relationship to its farthest conclusion and her parents seemed to be completely comfortable with all of its implications. However, I had the feeling that being nineteen and having a love affair with a fifteen-year-old was not to be done. I did not yet know of the puritanical taboos that infused the laws of my adopted country but my instinct told me to stay away from sex with Diane. She'd offer me her hand that I would kiss as it was my continental obligation. Diane would then teasingly inquire if that were the limit of my ambitions. At the time, it had to be.

Anita Yesowitz, a friend of Diane, lived a few apartment houses down Union Street. With a luminous face and a myriad of freckles punctuated with light-blue eyes, Anita was fresher and more natural than Diane. They had both graduated from Erasmus High on Flatbush Avenue and I was made to believe that it was a prestigious institution to have attended. I readily believed it as both Diane and Anita showed an above average intelligence. There was something very comfortable about Anita. She did not put on airs and did not seem annoyed that she had generous curves. I did not mind either. Often I would come up to her apartment and we would watch The Fred Waring Show on television. All the while, we would kiss and I'd caress Anita's arms. Those were the limits she would allow me to go to although these limits would be tested but never breached as we'd struggle and wrestle during the commercials. Anita would muse about marrying a rich man and how we would meet again in later years and we'd be free to consummate our passion for each other.

With my arrival in America a new personality had blossomed and there was now a confidence in my outlook. The ugly duckling had not turned into a swan but I was discovering that there were girls who found this strange European duck to their liking even though I could not quite understand the attraction.

I had introduced Maurice and Bob to Diane and Anita and they would carry on a sustained correspondence in the years to come. Bob, with his romantic demeanor should have been an ideal pen pal for Diane while Maurice, with his gruff and more direct sexual approach should have been better suited for Anita. As it was they interchanged freely and although I was never privy to the contents of the letters, I felt that, at least where Maurice was concerned, flaming missives were exchanged long before the internet made that practice commonplace.

The Dubin family lived on the ground floor at 1733 Union. The four kids, Bob, Michael, Howie and Sandy were a wild, unruly bunch and Gwen their Mother lived in a perpetual disheveled and harried state. Their Father, Jack, was a gruff long-haul trucker and was away from home most of the time. Given to drink and an often-mean temper, he brought tension whenever he was home. Somehow I found a refuge from Uncle Paul's unfriendly demeanor in the maelstrom of the Dubin household. Often, I'd visit Gwen and the children and they would listen to me talk. I'd tell them stories of my experiences during the war except that I could not bring myself to talk about the real thing. Instead of the Germans being the villains, I'd tell them stories about the invasions by the Mongols. The Mongols became the villains. Unconsciously I was relegating my recent experiences to earlier times, centuries removed as if I had been unable to really face the memory of those recent times I had left behind me and could not or would not face. The scars were still too fresh.

Gwen would leave the four children in my charge. While I baby-sat, she would take a few hours off and found solace somewhere else. Except for the fact that she had been pummeled by married life, Gwen was attractive albeit a bit frumpy and slightly overweight. I believe that she was very fond of me but I could not then envision any kind of romantic attachment with a woman nearly twice my age.

The children idolized me and would sit, transfixed and quiet while I spun tales of the Mongols and introduced them to Gulliver, Robinson Crusoe and others.

By chance, I would meet them again nearly fifty years later. Bob had risen to be President of the California Chiropractic Association; Michael was a high-ranking official of the New York Educational system and little Sandy had become a successful real estate agent in Beverly Hills. Only half-brother Howie had met an untimely death under unhappy circumstances. Bob attributed his own survival and success to my influence in showing him that one could be a man without being a blusterer or resorting to violence.

One wintry evening, Jack Dubin offered that I accompany him on a trip to Providence, RI where he had a delivery to make. I had not yet been out of New York and I jumped at the chance. At midnight, we climbed in his eighteen-wheeler rig and drove away north to New England. The sound of the engine and the shifting into the many gears brought me back to the night Mother, Ruth and I had left Charleroi for Namur eleven years earlier. I would not remember the route we took. There was no interstate road system at the time and we must have followed Route 1. I do remember the smell of steaming coffee as Jack and I shared a cup from the thermos wedged near the gearshift, the steam climbing and clinging to the windshield where it met the cold of the winter night. There was a rag I used to wipe away the fog, happy to make myself useful on that long trip.

At dawn, we reached the hills where Connecticut meets Rhode Island. The rays of the sun rising from the East filtered through the stone walls lining both sides of the road. These were magic moments as the light fanned out from the crevices and spaces between the irregular shaped rocks. The air was dry and clear and for a few minutes there was nothing else that mattered to me except the beauty of the early New England morning. In Providence, we unhitched the trailer and drove back to New York in the cab. I would not remember anything of the return trip.

In November 1949, a hurricane hit New York dead-on. Except for the hurricane that hit the SS Tabinta I had never experienced that phenomenon of nature. With the ignorance of danger, I decided that I would test myself against the wind and the rain that had been announced. After work, instead of taking the subway back to Brooklyn, I walked to the Williamsburg Bridge and began to go across the river. The wind was pelting me with the cold November rain. I struggled on, holding firm so my coat would not fly away. By the time I reached the first tower, I had all I could do just to keep my glasses from being stripped from my face. A few more steps and I would be inching my way over the waters of the East River and I could see the bridge's lights swinging under the blows of the hurricane. I stopped. Surely this was insane. Although I felt defeated, I did not dwell upon it and turned around, running, pushed by the wind until I reached the shelter of the nearest subway station. I would never try that again.

The next day I went to the Bronx to visit *Tante Frieda*. Aunt Frieda had long been a favorite of my Mother. Aunt Frieda must have been a sister to Emma Wolff Friedemann, my maternal grandMother, I never did find out for sure. She had married a man called Wolleman and she was the Mother of Leo Wolleman who I had never heard from again after his visit to our apartment in Brussels six years earlier. She lived in a large development in the Riverdale section of The Bronx that had been built by the Metropolitan Insurance Company. As I walked out of the subway station, I was amazed at the amount of destruction that the hurricane had caused. All around, the force of the winds had blown out windows. Walking was made hazardous by all the broken glass that littered the wet ground. *Tante Frieda,* frail and thatched with thin wispy white hair was kind and appreciative of my coming to visit her despite the horrendous weather. We had tea and cookies and talked for a while. I was to see her again a few times in the years that followed. After that we lost touch and she must have died, alone in the Bronx.

As I was not completely happy working for Philip Sirota and the dry goods business I kept dabbling around with photography. In the evening and on some Saturdays I'd find myself in the camera store of Arty Greenstein on Utica Avenue. There, I would sell cameras and film to the customers and give them advice on how best to use their equipment. I had learned to make minor repairs and after a while Arty let me use the darkroom to develop film and make prints for the customers. Arty was married to an attractive woman and they had two children, an older retarded boy about sixteen; the girl was younger and you could tell that she would grow up to be as pretty as her Mother. I could tell that the condition of the son was weighing heavily on Arty as he must have been worried about the future when the parents would no longer be around. It was hopeless to dream about leaving the business to his handicapped son and there was no thought of leaving the business to a daughter. Perhaps he entertained the thought that I might sometime step in, take over the store, marry the young daughter and take care of the son. I was vaguely aware of all that but it did not figure in my plans, as a matter of fact, I had no plans at the time. I was just floating around, happy to be in the USA and vaguely confidant that something good would turn up.

On Union Street, I had met a young boy, Michael Kaye about two or three years younger than I was and we had become fast friends. Michael had taken a liking to this "Frenchman" and used to laugh when I would mispronounce an English word. We had our biggest laugh when I was talking about a prostitute and referred to a "hare" instead of a "whore". Michael had a sister that he was dying for me to meet but he insisted that I should have a pronounced French accent when I'd meet her. I promised him that this would be no problem as I could switch one on or off with ease.

Michael would take me along to see Nathalie, a skinny young blonde girl that he was flirting with. We were both charmed by her lithe person and she had a bright smile that fitted the halo of her hair. Michael was talking about getting serious with her and would entertain thoughts of marriage in a near future. However there was a problem. The Mother of Nathalie was obscenely obese and we would never see her except draped in what seemed to be a bed sheet, engulfing an armchair that would vanish under her. She looked as if you had let out half the air out of a blimp and let it fall over the armchair. We did not know if it was from overeating or the result of a malady. Michael would look at skinny, pretty Nathalie and then at her Mother. He'd then turn to me and we would shrug our shoulders in despair. That would certainly be the way Nathalie would be in a few years and any thought of romance would fly out the window.

All the while I was regularly writing to Rosette in Brussels. I was declaring my fondness, my love, my desires and passion for her on a rotating basis. I'd become emboldened by a word found in her reply, then when she'd slap me down in another letter, I'd go all the way down the ladder again and I'd profess nothing but friendship. I kept reading more in her words than what she had written and I'd get depressed whenever for a moment I'd become lucid and realistic.

Without meaning to and probably without being aware of it, I had slipped into a completely alien world. There was not a single person that I now knew or associated with who was not Jewish. I had plunged into a Jewish world when I landed in Brooklyn. This was so new to me and I found that I was missing the carefree, non-kosher world that I had left behind. It was hard to define. I was now amongst my people but I still did not feel comfortable in my skin. It was indefinable, a sort of malaise as if I felt clean among the unclean and yet aware that I too was unclean.

As December marched on towards the end of the year 1949, New York became engulfed in an orgy of Christmas. In the city, Salvation Army men dressed in Santa Claus costumes lined every corner, ringing bells and asking for contributions to be dropped in their hanging kettles. Department stores were festooned in red and green decorations and mechanical dolls awkwardly paraded in the windows. I felt assaulted. I did not belong in either world.

I was having breakfast in a diner just off Canal Street. I was early and would not have to be at the Sirota store for a while. As I was having a toasted English muffin with butter and jelly and staring at the steam swirling from my cup of black coffee, someone put a nickel in the record machine. "I'm dreaming of a white Christmas" It was Bing Crosby. "Just like the ones I used to know". Suddenly I missed my Peugeot bicycle, I had not thought about it in four months and now I missed it terribly. I was missing my friends and my family. And I started to cry, sitting at the counter in a diner. It was ironic. I had never known a White Christmas! The only Christmas I recalled was the one in 1939 when Ruth and I were in the orphanage! So, why was I sobbing on my toasted English muffin?

Here I sat, in the middle of the biggest candy store in the world and I was homesick! Homesick for what? I should have laughed but I could only cry. I finally calmed down after the song had ended. I wiped my tears, ate my muffin, drank my coffee and paid the bill to the cashier. She was wondering why my eyes were red. I shrugged and went outside. In the street, the noises of the East Side of New York surrounded me again and it made me smile. I was in New York, in America and it felt good.

It was now Christmas Eve 1949. Bernard, a friend that Andy Siff had introduced me to, called and asked if I would like to join him in Times Square for an afternoon of fun. He knew of a department store where, after hours, one could pick up all the unsold toys and gifts for a song or even for free. We agreed to meet at a Ping-Pong emporium in the basement of a building in the middle of Times Square. When I got there, Bernard was in the company of another young man sporting a cap. I was introduced to Marty Reisman. I had followed Ping-Pong in Europe. Earlier, that same year, Marty Reisman had won the British Table Tennis Open. Reisman was among the top five players in the world along with Bergman and Dick Miles (who would win fame with his 1971 trip to China with President Nixon). Reisman was a legend in the sport. Bernard told Reisman that I played table tennis. Actually, I replied that I played Ping-Pong only and that I was not very good at it, certainly not of the class of Marty Reisman. The only thing we had in common was that we were both Jewish and 19 at the time.

We were slapping a few balls in a friendly exchange while Bernard was sipping a Coke. A bystander was watching us. There was nothing to indicate that Marty was indeed Reisman, one of the top players in the world, a man who could beat you using his cap as a paddle.

"Do you want to hit a few?" Inquired Reisman to the patsy.

"Don't mind if I do" replied the mark.

I left the table and ordered a Coke. It was possible that the man, watching Reisman and me hit a few figured he could beat us both and that he was going to sucker us to play for money. It was also likely that Reisman had gone so easy on me because he wanted to sucker in the onlooker.

They started a friendly non-competitive exchange that remained inconclusive. After a while, the patsy said that he was ready to play a game and that he would wager a five-dollar bet, just to make it interesting. Making it look close, Marty won 21-19. The patsy, who probably had lost on purpose, now wanted to make it double or nothing. Reisman obliged and beat the guy again 21-19. Bernard now held the $20-.

Marty wanted to entice the patsy to play again, double or nothing. The guy hesitated.

"I'll spot you 15 points" volunteered Marty.

Reisman, making incredibly "lucky" shots won again 21-19. Bernard held the $40-.

The patsy had had enough and would not go for one more until Marty offered him double or nothing, spotting him 19 points. Reisman won 21-19. The poor guy did not even make a single point. Bernard held the eighty dollars. It was 1949 and eighty dollars was a goodly sum of money. The three of us went out for a good Christmas dinner.

Later, just before midnight, Bernard and I went to B. Altman to scrounge what was left of the season's gifts and toys but it was to no avail. All that was left were broken items and for the ones that were still viable the store wanted too much money. We really had no need for anything anyway and so we left and parted company.

I never saw Bernard or Marty Reisman again. Over the years I kept reading about Marty in the papers and magazines. Periodically he would get in trouble with the US Table Tennis Association for questionable practices but his legend continued to grow. In 1981 he was inducted in the USTT Hall of fame. I understand that he has a Table Tennis emporium somewhere in the Bronx and that he continues to dazzle onlookers and beating them using his cap as a paddle.

New Year's Eve found me in the middle of the action in Times Square among the throng of people celebrating the coming of 1950. Although it was crowded and noisy it had not yet reached the enormity it would become in later years. I enjoyed the noise and the crowds. All was well, I was in America, I had a job and I believed in a bright future. Truman was president and the entire world was at peace. I took the IRT subway back to Union Street and went to sleep.

1950

The evening breeze,
Caressed the trees
Tenderly . . . .

HELENE

Helene and I fell in love. We were both nineteen and it was sudden, at first sight. Of course, Helene only knew me with a French accent but I did not feel that I was being deceitful. Michael had introduced me to his sister with the specific request that I would speak with a heavy accent. It would create a few problems as most people I had met knew me without an accent and I had to juggle who I was with in order not to blow my cover whenever I was with Helene.

There was a slight problem. Helene was engaged to marry a Paul Ziefer. They had been courting for a long time, well before I ever arrived in America. Michael had introduced me to the rest of his family and I was welcomed in their Union Street apartment. Helene and I had very little occasion to be alone, yet we shared a yearning to be near one another, to hold hands, to let our bodies touch lightly, in passing. As I was still going to night school, Helene decided that she would also take evening courses at Thomas Jefferson High School so we could have an excuse and the opportunity to be together at least once a week.

Of course, being together in class presented a few problems in that I had to keep up the phony French accent I faked every time Helene and I met. There was an instance when the English teacher was going through the vocabulary and gave us the definition of the word "abate". After she had explained its meaning, I could not resist making fun. I rose and asked if "a bait was someteeng you use for feesheeng?" It got a lot of laughter and a look of pained disapproval from the teacher.

Now and then I'd go visit Helene when she was alone in her parent's apartment. Well, almost alone, there was always her uncle Harold but he was suffering of the sleeping sickness, a result of being bitten by tsetse flies when he had worked in Africa, or so I had been told. The uncle was always asleep and Helene and I would take refuge in her bedroom. Helene would put on Debussy's *Claire de Lune* on the record player and she'd lie down on her bed looking unbelievably desirable. I, like the idiot I was would sit on a chair, next to her bed and hold her hand. In my mind, I could not conceive that this beautiful girl would want me. I knew that she loved me but desire me, no! For me, there was this image of a wedding cake with the bride and groom dolls planted on top, the whole thing wrapped in cellophane. And Helene, for me, was wrapped in cellophane, desirable but untouchable. How could I have been so dumb?

Helene soon gave up the evening classes. The time for her marriage to Paul was getting nearer and there were a lot of preparations to be done to which I was not a party. One Saturday, Michael invited me to join him at a party in The Bronx where there would be a lot of girls. We took the subway to a station near to Yankee Stadium and found the apartment. It was full of girls and boys, Coca-Cola, smoke and loud music. One girl caught my eye; she was about my height, a bit plump with a beautiful face. Her cheeks were like ripe peaches and soft blond curly hair encircled her pretty eyes. "Nancy with the laughing face" I thought as she smiled at me. I moved towards her and asked her if she would dance with me. I could not believe it myself, that I would actually go up to a girl and ask her to dance. I remembered Gilberte and how unhappy I had made her by my stubborn refusal to dance. The girl advanced to me and trust her entire being against me

"The evening breeze, caressed the trees, tenderly,
I can't forget how two hearts met breathlessly . . ."

We were dancing; I was dancing with a girl! Our bodies melted into one. I was no longer an awkward geek but Fred Astaire sweeping Ginger around the room. Her cheek pressed against mine, I could hear her breathing faster and deeper. She was mine, all mine. I had never experienced such a thrill. The music seemed to go on forever. After it did stop it left me dizzy and unaware of the rest of the people in the room. She stayed pressed against me for a long while, and then we parted. We were both stirred by unspoken passions. We each turned and went our separate ways. We never danced together again, I never knew her name. She had changed my life.

Michael and I stayed a while longer trying to make passes at other girls at the party. After a while the food and drinks ran out and we took the subway back to Brooklyn. Michael said that we had been shot down, a new expression for me. I remember thinking that you did not have to go all the way to The Bronx to get shot down. It made more sense to get shot down in your own neighborhood.

Still, I would never forget that young girl and that certain wonderful moment when we had melted in a dance.

Helene's Mother worked at The Concord Hotel in the Catskills and Michael and I would go visit her at times. Because Mrs Kaye was a member of the staff, we could go in without having to register or pay. To me it was a New World to be explored and some weekends I'd find myself in the hotel with Helene, her fiancé Paul and Michael. It was all very cozy but harmless. When we did not go to the Catskills, Michael and I would visit his Father's luncheonette in Jamaica, Queens where the Long Island Expressway was being built. It was a grandiose project that impressed me each time I visited. In the luncheonette, I'd be initiated to egg-creams and the like and if I were lucky, Helene would appear but not really by chance.

I had taken many pictures of Helene and I'd spend much time in the darkroom of Arty Greenstein's photo shop printing black and white wallet sized portraits of the girl I was pining for. Arty thought I was touched in the head for I would forever print and reprint the same images.

In early 1950, Helene and Paul were hastily married. Helene's parents were concerned that she might become pregnant and they did not want a child to be born out of wedlock. The formal marriage would come a few weeks later in April. For me, it did not change my feelings for Helene as she had been promised to another when I had first met her. The formal wedding was held in April and I was an usher complete with a tuxedo and top hat. A movie of the affair caught

Rudy Rosenberg

me approaching the seated Helene and planting a deep kiss on her lips. The newlyweds went to Atlantic City on their honeymoon.

Mr Ziefer had given Paul a new white Buick as a wedding present and we went around together, Paul, Helene and me as a fifth wheel. Once, we were driving and a song came on the car's radio:

"As you desire me, so will I come to you".

Helene, seated in front, next to Paul, turned around with her left arm over the back of the bench seat and gave me a long look. It felt good and I knew then that someday, somehow, Helene would come to me.

As Michael and I continued to see each other, it gave me many occasions to be a member of the family and to continue to be with Helene as often as we could. My passion for her did not abate nor that which I perceived as her deep affection for me. We kept looking for those precious moments when we could brush furtively by one another and caress a hand, steal a look. However, I kept writing to Rosette in Belgium and continued my harmless flirting with Diane and Anita. I had to keep on seeing other girls if only to keep my sanity.

Back at the store on Eldridge Street, I had become more and more comfortable with my job and Mr Sirota would often leave me in charge of the place. He treated me as one of the family and I had much respect for the knowledge he had accumulated in all of his years. I would learn a lot from him, from how to tie a string around a parcel to how to deal with subordinates so they would do his bidding without feeling belittled.

One day, Mr Sirota noticed a full lipstick imprint on the left sleeve of my raincoat. "Rrrudolph" he exclaimed "You've been out with gorrls!" He seemed mildly horrified. I had no explanation. Wished that a girl had indeed smashed me with a kiss but not on my sleeve. All I could surmise was that Diane Ritterman had planted her lips on my sleeve to leave her mark on me. Diane was the only girl I knew who was short enough to make an imprint just above my elbow. I never did find out.

A gypsy woman and her daughter surprised me in the store. I had been working in the small glass enclosed office. I heard a noise and turned around and found myself facing a gypsy woman and her young, very pretty daughter. "Give me a twenty-dollar bill that I will hold in hand for a while and I will tell you your fortune-. I would have none of it and pleaded for her to leave before my boss returned. After a few more tries she wanted me to give her a five-dollar bill and "my daughter will do something nice to you". I had visions of being robbed by these two and I finally pushed them out of the store shortly before Mr Sirota returned.

The store catered only to dealers and we did not sell retail. Some days we would only see one sole customer. When we had nothing to do, we'd listen to the radio that would transmit the Kefauver hearings on the New York mobster Frank Costello. It was all fascinating.

A woman came in while I was alone. She wanted to buy a single bolt of percale. I told her that we only sold wholesale. She insisted. Normally, percale sold at 27 or 30 cents per yard; I sold her a thirty-yard bolt at 45 cents. She paid the $13.50 in cash. I wrote up the sale in the invoice book and gave her a copy. When Sirota found out about the sale, he was not at all happy. As we sold wholesale only, we did not collect any sales tax. On this one retail sale, he could have been in violation of New York tax law and he was most upset.

A few days later, we received a large wooden crate filled with "mill-seconds", mostly voile, dotted swiss, organdie and muslin. All the pieces were short-bolts and the organdie was badly stained with ink or grease marks from the mills. Sirota had purchased the lot for 15 cents a yard. While he was away, a customer came in and expressed an interest in the contents of the crate. Figuring that I was a "greener" and did not know the score he tried to put one over on me. "How much for the whole crate?" He inquired. I told him that I could let him have the whole thing at 75 cents a yard. He did not argue, took the whole thing and put it in his car.

When Sirota returned he was flabbergasted. "He will return it all!" He exclaimed. "That is too much money; we will have to give him back his money!" The man did come back a few weeks later wanting to know if we had any more of the mill-seconds. Mr Sirota never admitted that I had made a great sale.

I began to feel that I was not appreciated. The thought that I would spend the rest of my life in that little store did not appeal to me any longer. I was ready for better things. We used to get our sheets and pillowcases from Dan River Mills and their salesman would visit our store every couple of months. The salesman had taken a liking to me and had suggested that there might be a position for me with his company. When I mentioned that to Philip Sirota, he told me that Dan River was a restricted company and that they would never hire Jews. The next time the salesman came; I informed him that I was not really Jewish as I had been baptized Protestant in 1942. A few weeks later, he returned and told me that I could start working at Dan River Mills in a couple weeks at a starting salary of $35 per week. I was making twenty-seven at Sirota's and that represented a large increase. It also meant that I would be joining a large organization located on Broadway and with room for advancement. I accepted. When I told Sirota that I was leaving him, he was very upset. "Rrrudolph" He said. "Don't I trreat you like you arre my own son?" I replied that he was also paying me as if I was his own son. He pleaded with me to stay citing his weak heart condition and that he depended so much on me. He also offered me a raise to thirty dollars. He made me feel so guilty that I relented and had to tell the Dan River salesman that I would not be joining his firm. I would still make less money but I just could not leave Sirota.

Leo Wolleman was still very much on my mind. I wanted to confront him and find out why, after all the promises he had made, I had never heard from him again. I went to see him either at his White Plains home or at his office in the Diamond District in Manhattan. I was introduced into his office, an enormous dark room all decorated in mahogany. Leo sat behind an imposing desk, ensconced and engulfed in a huge leather sofa, like a replete Buddha. He did not bother to get up to greet me but made a vague gesture with his right hand as if to let me know he was ready to hear me. It had been over five years since Leo had entered our apartment and my hopes in Brussels.

Without anger I asked him why he had filled me with so many hopes back in 1945. He had promised that he would take all the necessary steps to bring me to America, put me through college and take me into his business together with his son Walter. I reminded him that all I had really wanted was an affidavit. He had filled me with hope and I had never heard from him again after he had left Brussels.

"I did not want to aggrieve your Mother" Was his terse reply. "The important thing now is that you are here." With that, he gestured again with his right hand to let me know that the interview was over. As I reached the door to leave his office he let out a whisper "If you are ever in White Plains, come and visit, don't be a stranger".

On the way back to Brooklyn I felt elated and cheap; elated because I had confronted him and exposed his callousness, cheap because he had made me feel insignificant. When I told Aunt Lilli that I had gone to see Leo Wolleman, she was very upset and made no secret of the extreme contempt in which she held him and his entire family. She would react the same way whenever the Wolleman subject would surface.

It was becoming increasingly difficult to stay in Uncle Paul's apartment. I would work late and continued my evening classes. It was getting near to my final exams and I would study in Dubrow's luncheonette. As I came home, Paul would pursue me and turn off the lights making it impossible for me to read, write or listen to some music. Every night I could hear Lilli and Paul in violent disputes. It was always the same subject; something about what I was or was not doing.

"Ich kann es nicht vertragen! "Paul would yell over and over again. "I can't stand it!" And Aunt Lilli would try to reason with him. Obviously my presence in their apartment was bugging him greatly.

I decided that I'd be better off leaving the apartment on Union Street. I found a furnished room at 1387 St. John's Place, just a few blocks away, on the west side of Eastern Parkway, I was now able to listen to Martin Bloch's Milkman's Matinee until all hours. I would play the radio very low so as not to disrupt my landlady. I was in music heaven; free to gorge myself with all the popular music I had hungered for since the end of the war. After 2 AM, there was another program called: "LonesomeGal", a sexy, sensual collection of talk and music to dream by.

> "If you've got dreams to share,
> Lips to spare, why don't you be a pal
> Share them with your Lonesome Gal"

I had to write to the "Lonesome Gal" and request that she mail me a signed photo. After a few weeks, I received the requested photo. To my great surprise it was a photo of a black woman, very attractive but still a Negro girl. It was still too soon after my arrival in America and I was not yet ready for the transition.

Shortly after I moved, I met a young woman at Dubrow's. Her name was Helen. This was close to "Helene "and knowing her was a balm on my bruised feelings. We talked and flirted. Helen had a great body with all the curves in the right places. Straight shoulder length black hair complimented her figure. There was only one drawback, her mouth. She had lips like *"un cul de poule"* the asshole of a chicken. Her lips were constantly puckered up as if she had sucked on a bitter lemon or swallowed alum as in a Marx Brother's comedy. A heavy down encircled her mouth.

Nevertheless, she was sweet and I wanted to make love with her. After a few days, I managed to bring her to my rented room. She did not talk much and let me undress her on my bed, garment by garment. I was kissing her softly as she helped me unfasten her bra. All that was left between us were her panties. I placed my hand between her thighs and watched her eyes get wider and wider. Then, she began to cry, first quietly then in louder and louder sobs. She was bawling uncontrollably, her entire body convulsed in tears. It was so embarrassing. People must have heard her across the street. I tried to calm Helen but it was to no avail. My landlady came banging on the door wanting to know what the problem was. I told her that all was well while I helped Helen get dressed as well as I could.

When Helen managed to get dressed, I walked her downstairs and she fled the house still in tears. My landlady told me that if I ever brought a girl in my room again, she would throw me out. I could not see what the fuss was all about. After all, in Europe, no one would see anything wrong with having a girl in one's bed. America would turn out to be more puritanical than I expected. I never saw Helen again.

Maurice Goldman had written that he was leaving for Israel and that he had been sent to a camp in southern France, near Toulouse where he would be indoctrinated in the mysteries of Judaism. He would also learn how to survive on a Kibbutz. Maurice was a city boy just as I was and there was much he had to be familiar with, such as reclaim, clear land and plant new growths. In the camp, boys and girls were very sexually active but Maurice complained that he had only shot blanks since he had been there. After a few weeks, he wrote me that he was returning to Brussels for a while and would resume his emigration to Israel at a later date. Of course, I realized that Maurice would never leave for Israel and would have to find a career in Belgium.

As far as Bob van Meckeren was concerned, our correspondence became more and more spaced. I had the feeling that he had never forgiven me for leaving for America and he would withdraw more and more within himself.

Rosette and I kept up our correspondence. I would profess my love for her and she would slap me down, talking to me as if I was a little boy with naughty thoughts. We did manage to make some plans for the distant future in the event that we should both be free. I did not know at the time that she was having an affair with a married man. She did become involved with still another fellow named Jos V. who she was seriously thinking of marrying. They did break up eventually and we resumed a vague flirt. I felt that we had wasted much time having kissed only three times in the four years we had known each other. I was encouraging Rosette to keep in touch with my Mother as I felt that Frieda liked her a lot. I never mentioned my love affair with Helene

My sister Ruth had left Mother's apartment and now lived on her own. Nevertheless I was trying very hard to convince both of them to follow me to America. I felt that there was a future here and nothing but a dead-end in Europe especially since they were both stateless and Jewish. Ruth was involved with a couple of lovers and very involved with "Le President" a sometime wealthy fellow of volatile reputation. Mother would say that "Le President" was very wealthy, as he was millions in debt and that only rich people could afford to have huge debts. It did make some sense.

WAR IN KOREA

It was June 25th 1950 when North Korea invaded South Korea. It all had been in the news for weeks but I had not paid any attention to these events. I had other cats to flog and girls to pursue. In a matter of days, the North had invaded Seoul the capital and most of the south. President Truman acted swiftly and a "Police Action" was started under the auspices of the United Nations even though the USA would do most of the fighting and the dying. The police action turned out to be the first of many euphemisms for war. Although I did not know it then, the entire course of my life would change once again

When the war started prices rose almost immediately and there was fear of inflation. President Truman appointed Michael DeSalle, the former mayor of Toledo, Ohio as head of OPA in charge of rolling back prices to pre-June 1950 levels. For Mr Sirota it meant that the percales (our main product), which were now selling around 40 cents a yard would have to be rolled back to 35 cents. Except, wait a minute! There was a single sale of one bolt of percale to a certain woman who had paid 45 cents a few months before the war. Sirota feverishly turned the pages of the sales book searching for that one sale. He found it and triumphantly showed it to me. There was the one sale, at 45 cents a yard. This meant that we did not have to roll back the prices to 35 cents but could use 45 as our base price. He never did give me credit for that one sale.

Heinz Franke lived on the ground floor of Aunt Lilli's building on Union Street. Heinz and his parents were refugee German Jews who had arrived in Brooklyn in the mid-1930s when Hitler had come to power in Germany. Heinz had taken a liking to me and wanted to show me his trade. He was a custom-peddler. Just as custom-peddlers would ply their trade in the Old West, Heinz would exercise his trade around Brooklyn, Queens and Long Island. Instead of a horse and wagon, he had a large Nash Ambassador filled to the roof with dresses, underwear, blouses and aprons.

We drove to Hicksville, Long Island, along Broadway where there was a farmer's market. There, Heinz would rent a stand for a few dollars and display all of his wares. Housewives would come and purchase dresses etc and place orders for the next week's visit. They did not have to pay the full price. Credit was a good part of the selling technique. Heinz would sell them an item for $20, take a $5 deposit and return every other week to collect an additional $5 until the dress was paid for. Of course, with each visit, he would offer more goods against which he took a small deposit and in this way he was assured of a constant market and clientele. This would create a never-ending cycle based on trust. Cars were few in those days, the population of Long Island was growing and stores had not yet caught up with the growth.

After Hicksville, we drove to Canarsie where the army had set up a row of Quonset Huts for military dependents. These huts were erected of corrugated metal and looked like elongated Eskimo igloos with a stove and a chimney sticking out of the roof. There, I met Margot Mc Barnette a war bride married to Curtis Mc Barnette, a black soldier who had been shipped to Korea when the war broke out. Margot had lived in the Eastern territories when Germany invaded Russia and the Baltic States. When the Russians beat back the Germans she was evacuated back to Germany and wound up in the American sector of Germany. There she met Curtis and they got married. At the time they had a young son, Curtis Junior who went by the nickname of Gigi (pronounced Guigui).

Margot was just a few years older than I was and we hit it off right away. Tall, blonde with a generous smile and a wonderful spirit, she was the most beautiful woman I had ever met. I did not fall in love with her. I fell in awe. Margot exuded life and happiness, even though the living conditions in the huts were somewhat rudimentary. However, Margot had managed to turn her corrugated home into a friendly little palace, well decorated and cheerful. Since her husband was away, I began to spend a lot of time with her and Gigi. Shortly after we met, the Army found an apartment for her in a new project in Brooklyn. There, I would use my newly learned photographic skills to take photo after photo of Margot so she could send them to Curtis. It was fun, Margot would lie on the bed and I'd climb on top of furniture just to get an extra angle. We were good friends, never lovers, never kissed either.

One day the three of us went to the Statue of Liberty and I carried Gigi on my shoulders all the way up to the top of the statue and all the way down again. It was something never to be forgotten. Later on, Gigi would grow up to be a commercial pilot and the size of Mohammed Ali, but bigger. There was never an occasion when we did not remind each other that I had carried him all the way up and all the way down again.

Somehow we struck a friendship that was to endure always. Curtis, her husband was still in the military and although Margot spoke at length about him, I didn't get to meet him until several years later. Perhaps we were both a little lost in America and with a small touch of homesickness for the people we had left behind. Margot, Gigi and I spent many happy moments together. Margot introduced me to the Café Geiger on East 86th Street in Manhattan where we had a few dinners. At the time, the Café Geiger had a violinist and a piano player. The program consisted mostly of Old World music that was like warm honey on our hearts.

The Café Geiger still exists, but has been renovated many times. The musicians are no longer there but the memory of the early years with Margot is still fresh in my mind. Together we had also discovered the little marzipan shop on the same block where you could buy the best marzipan in New York. It would also fall victim to the effect of changing neighborhoods.

Heinz also drove us to the Borscht Belt in the Catskills and we went from nightclub to nightclub. All the entertainers were Jewish and the entire program was in Yiddish. I could not understand any of the jokes. I spoke English and my knowledge of Yiddish was limited to the few expressions I had heard my Mother use when I was a child. Here I had arrived in the USA and I was confronted by an entire new idiom and culture.

As the year 1950 ended, the US military was short of men, as it could not draft those who had served in World War Two unless they were still in the reserves. The war was not going well and it became clear that a new crop of men would have to be drafted to fight in Korea.

1951

Because of you
There's a song in my heart.
Because of you
My romance had its start . . . . Tony Bennett.

I had been assigned a Social Security number when I first began to work in the US. Together with that came a green card that made it legal for me to work. In January 1951 I received a questionnaire from the US Army that I duly filled out. The thought of serving in the military did not faze me. As a matter of fact, it gave me a thrill to think that I might soon be wearing an American uniform, that in turn I'd be a GI! I was aware that the singer Dick Haymes, an Argentine, had refused to serve in the military during World War Two. At the time, Haymes was making a very lucrative career as a crooner and in Hollywood. Not being a US citizen he felt no obligation to give it all up to serve in the US Army. However, after the war was over, he took a trip abroad. When it came time for Dick Haymes to return to the States, the immigration service barred him from reentry. It took quite a while and much travail before he was admitted again. I was not going to take a chance on suffering the same fate and I was more than ready and eager to serve.

In the spring, I received a notice from the draft board that I should report to the US Army recruiting office on Flatbush Avenue in Brooklyn. That upset Philip Sirota. He did not want to lose his star (and only) employee. We went together to the recruiting office and Mr Sirota pleaded eloquently that his was a one-man business and that I was absolutely essential to the survival of his store. Convincingly out of breath and his right hand clutching his heart he maintained that he had a weak heart and that he surely would die if I were drafted away from him.

That did not please me at all as I was really looking forward to getting out from under Mr Sirota's tutelage. In addition, my relationship with Helene was getting quite sticky and it seemed a good idea to put some space between us. As we sat in front of the recruiting sergeant I sank in my chair and was making discreet eye, face and hand signals at him hoping that he would disregard whatever arguments Sirota was advancing. Unfortunately, the recruiter bought it and a few days later I received a notice that I was being deferred from the service.

I had made up my mind that I would volunteer and enlist in the Army. I had contemplated the Air Force and the Navy but four years was their minimum enlistment period. Sure, I felt the need to distance myself from Helene, but not for that long. In the Army, there was a minimum two years enlistment and that seemed much more reasonable for me to forget all about her. There was no need to join the French Foreign Legion or the Marines and two years in the Army was just what the doctor ordered. However, the recruiting sergeant had other ideas. He must have been getting a bigger bonus if he enticed the recruits to enlist for three years.

"With your education" He began (I had barely finished High School!) "You are sure to go to Officer Candidate School (OCS) and become a Second Lieutenant. And with your knowledge of foreign languages, you are a cinch for the C.I.D. (Counter-Intelligence). Unfortunately, the training for OCS and C.I.D. requires a minimum of eighteen months, plus your basic training. On a two-year enlistment, there would only be one or two months of service left when you did graduate. So you see, the only way you can get to those two schools would be to enlist for three years."

I was drooling at the prospect of being an officer and to wear the flat hat, pink trousers and O.D jacket. What a dream! I could not sign fast enough for the required three years. And so, on July 13, 1951 I enlisted for three years. I had to report to the Federal Building on Whitehall Street, downtown Manhattan where I was given a battery of tests and scored an impressive 93 points out of a possible 96. That made me eligible for Group One, whatever that meant.

After signing up for three years, I was eventually informed that since I was not a US citizen there was no question of going to OCS. Furthermore, since I still had family in Europe, Counter-Intelligence was impossible, as there was the possibility that I could be blackmailed into revealing secret. No one offered to reduce my time to the original two years I had wanted but now I was in for three years.

There were only a few weeks left to put my affairs in order. I wrote to my Mother and my sister Ruth that I had enlisted in the Army. A note was also sent to my Father. In a letter to Rosette I mused that there might be an opportunity to be sent to Europe. In that case, I would make sure that I'd come to see her in Brussels and that we'd go on a date if she were still single.

Philip Sirota had to be informed that I was leaving him. I could tell that he was not pleased but he took the news graciously and wished me good luck. I said goodbye to Uncle Paul and Aunt Lilli. Lilli was concerned and begged me to take good care and not do anything that would put me in harm's way. Paul did not seem concerned at all. I cleaned up my room, took leave of my landlady and brought all my clothing and personal affairs to Margot's apartment asking her to store these until my return. Saying farewell to Margot and her son Gigi was emotional, as we had become very good friends.

When I got discharged from the army, I went to the apartment to reclaim my clothing. I rang the bell and found myself face to face with Curtis for the first time. He must have been wondering who this fellow was who had come to his apartment to reclaim his clothing.

On my last weekend in Brooklyn, Dr. and Mrs Ritterman drove Diane and me to Coney Island. It was a beautiful summer's day and the car sped smoothly along the Belt Parkway that snaked around the belly of Brooklyn, past Floyd Bennett Airfield and alongside the bay. In those days, traffic was still light and one could really enjoy the short twenty minute drive to Coney Island and the George Tilyou Steeplechase Park. We parked for free in a parking lot owned by Dr. Ritterman's brother. I was impressed. We had some kosher hot dogs at Nathan's and Diane and I finished the evening riding the notorious Cyclone roller coaster. Strapped in our seats, Diane cozied up to me and as we neared the top of the initial climb she yelled "If we should die, remember that I love you!" And she kissed me firmly on the lips. With that, the little cars plunged into the dark abyss of the Cyclone ride and we mingled our cries of joyous terror.

And then it was time to say goodbye to Helene. We had never spent more than a few furtive moments together and we were determined to be together one whole day. Paul liked to sleep and Helene helped him along by giving him a couple of sleeping pills so he would be out for most of the day. We met in late morning and Helene could be with me until five when she would have

Rudy Rosenberg

to be home. The only thing we managed to do was to spend three hours on the Circle Line boat that went around Manhattan. I would not remember where we met and how we got to the pier in Manhattan. Helene was lovelier than ever. She wore a dark blue strapless dress with embroidered white flowers. Her shoulders were bare and only the roundness of her breasts held up the dress. In the glare of the hot July sun, her skin shone so white, so inviting. The boat was full of noisy visiting fez-wearing Shriners. We managed to find a bench seat near the stern of the boat where we could find a bit of privacy and sit arm in arm, stealing kisses. I took quite a few pictures of Helene and every time I stepped away from her to focus my camera, she would pucker her lips and blow me a kiss.

We may have been interested in the scenery as the Circle Liner sailed down the lower Hudson. There stood the Empire State Building, the bottom of Manhattan, the Statue of Liberty and all the bridges as we continued up the East River. After that, the route would become a monotonous two hours of drab, dull scenery. Of course, we were looking at each other and would not have cared if Paris were in view. I had never been so happy with Helene and she must have felt the same way. At the same time, there was a bittersweet feeling, as we both knew that I would be leaving for the army the following day.

I would often think back to what we did not do during those six or seven hours that were ours to grasp and the chances we had wasted. Again, the cellophane-wrapped wedding dolls had inhibited my desires. I had feared making an unfortunate move that would have made Helene vanish. And yet, it was so clear that Helene wanted me as much as I wanted her or she would not have given Paul the sleeping pills. We should have pooled our money and rented a hotel room. Making love would have been so marvelous. As it was, I stayed on my hunger and all Helene had to show for the four hours on the river was very deep sunburn on all the exposed skin of her willing body. I never found out how she explained the sunburn to her husband when she finally got home.

I'M IN THE ARMY NOW. RA12387469

The next morning, July 16th 1951, I had to report to Whitehall Street in Manhattan. I got there early, filled out more forms and received two sets of uniforms and a helmet liner. As we lined up to receive our first battery of shots we were ordered to wear our helmets. It did not make sense to most of us until we saw a couple of recruits pass out and keel over after being jabbed by one needle too many. We had to run a gauntlet of male nurses who gave us shots after shots in unison in both our left and right arms. Whatever we did not wear, we stuffed in an army-issue duffel bag.

As I had been baptized Protestant in 1942 and since I did not want to have anything to do with my Jewish origins, I had checked "Protestant" on my army questionnaire. Thus, when my dog tags were issued they were stamped with a "P" to denote my religion. When she found out, Aunt Lilli was not pleased, she felt it was horrible. Of course, she was right but I was not ready to accept being a Jew. Ironically, the "P" would fool no one in the Army or anywhere else for that matter, during the three years the dog tags hung around my neck. Since I had enlisted, the army issued my serial number prefixed "RA", (Regular Army as opposed to the US prefix issued to those who had been drafted). When I wrote Rosette that my serial number was 12387469, Rosette quickly replied that the ending number, 69, made it very interesting. All my articles of clothing, from helmet to shoes were now stamped: R7469.

In the afternoon, we piled into several busses and were driven to Camp Kilmer, near New Brunswick, NJ where we would be undergoing orientation to determine what we were best suited for. Camp Kilmer was a sprawling army base that had been reactivated at the start of the Korean War. Being thirty miles south of New York, it served as a staging area for the troops scheduled to sail away through the ports of New York and New Jersey. It did not matter that we were practically within sight of New York City, for us we were ten weeks away at best. Luckily we had been issued summer khaki uniforms and "fatigues" as the heat of that summer was brutal. Some recruits who had arrived from the New England area had been issued winter garb and were suffering greatly from the Summer heat.

I slept on the third bunk from the door in an immense dormitory. Exhausted, we'd collapse on our bunk at eleven. The first morning, someone shook me awake at three AM and ordered me to get dressed and report to the main mess hall "on the double". I had been honored to work the first KP shift that morning. The mess served several thousand recruits and it was backbreaking work. When I was finished, I had to take a quick shave and shower and double-time to the various buildings where I'd be evaluated.

That same evening, it was KP for me again. This time, there were four of us sitting around an enormous vat of potatoes. These had been machine-peeled but it was our duty to eye them all. I sat there, digging in with a sharp kitchen knife, removing eye after eye and tossing the finished potato into huge cooking pots. A slip of the knife and I had sliced a small cut in my left index. It was not a deep cut but it began to bleed steadily. Of course, I could not go on handling the potatoes as I was bleeding all over them. I asked the cooks, our masters, if I could get a Band-Aid. I might as well have asked for the moon. I would have to go to the dispensary to have my cut taken care of. This being my second day in Camp Kilmer, I had to get directions on how to get there. Armed with sketchy information and my finger wrapped in my handkerchief I walked about the camp trying to locate the dispensary. It was now near midnight and most of the streetlights had been doused. I found a barrack that still had its lights on and clambered up the steps hoping to ask for directions. A shriek greeted me. "Eek, a man!" I had wandered into the WACS area of the camp and the barrack was filled with women in various stage of undress. When they recovered from the surprise, some wanted to invite me in while the others were yelling for me to get out. I just wanted to get a Band-Aid.

It was way past midnight when I finally stumbled into the dispensary. Of course, they would not give me a Band-Aid but insisted that my "wound" be cleansed. They then wrapped my finger hand and wrist with yards of gauze. It was two AM when I got back to the kitchen where there were still mounds of potatoes to be eyed. The moment I plunged my hand in the vat and it came in contact with the water, my bandage unraveled and I bled again all over the spuds. From that day on, I resolved always to carry several Band-Aids in my pocket.

I fell on my bed after two and at three AM, they woke me again to get on KP. We had no nametag and nobody knew who we were. I noticed that shortly after midnight, someone would enter the barracks and tie a towel to the foot of several beds. At three, the non-com on duty would simply find the beds that had been marked with a towel and those were the designated victims that would go on KP. After a few days, I got smart. I waited until a towel had been attached to my bunk and then I'd untie it and placed it on a bed further into the room. After that, I was able to sleep until four and avoided KP in Camp Kilmer.

After a couple of weeks of tests and medical examinations, the army decided that, because of my weak eyesight, I would not be fit for fighting duty and I'd be assigned to the Quartermaster Corps. The Quartermaster training center was located in Fort Lee, just outside of Petersburg, Virginia. The next day, about a dozen of us boarded a train to Washington DC, Richmond and Petersburg. The heat was oppressive even though we had been told that the cars were air-conditioned. There was little air in the cars and when we pulled into Richmond we could not wait to pile out and get some fresh air. What a surprise! The moment we stepped out of the car, a wall of heat hit us. It must have been near a hundred. Never had I experienced such a high temperature. We retreated to the "cool" of the railroad car that when compared to the furnace of Richmond was now almost refreshing.

In Richmond, we picked up a contingent of recruits from Alabama, Georgia, Mississippi, Texas and other Southern states. We were a pretty large group by the time the train rolled into Petersburg, VA. There is no recollection of arriving in Fort Lee. Some of the recruits had arrived by bus directly into the camp. Did we disembark in the Petersburg train station and then bussed into the camp? Did the train make a special stop just outside the camp and did we march the final mile to our barracks, trudging with our heavy duffel bags? No memory remains. The next morning, we were assigned to Company "O" that would be our home for the next 16 weeks.

Situated 25 miles south of Richmond, the site had been named Camp Lee during the Civil War, after General Robert E. Lee. It had been linked to "the Battle of the Crater" a disastrous episode for the Union Army on July 30th, 1864. The camp had been used as a training center during WWI and WWII. With the start of the Korean "Police action" it had been reactivated and renamed "Fort Lee". It served as the Quartermaster Replacement Training Center (QMRTC). It was also the training center for the Women Army Corps (WACS). Because of the presence of the WACS, we would never be permitted to walk to "Jody" cadences and were restricted to "cadence counts" of "Up, *two, three, four*" for fear that "*You had a good home that you left*" and the like lyrics might offend the sensitive ears of the female recruits. As we soon would find out, the WACS cadre and their recruits could out-curse any of us any day or night.

Two hundred of us made up Company "O" under the command of 1st Lieutenant W.T. Hall. The number was divided alphabetically into four platoons of 50 men each. Recruits from R to Z were placed in the fourth platoon. We ran the gamut from Rifkin, Alex to Wright, Thomas H. Somehow the US Army had not been able to include any X, Y or Z into our group. Within each platoon we had been sorted out by height. Only Thomas Wright, Edward Souza and Piscatello (a late addition to the fourth platoon) were shorter than I and spared me the embarrassment of bring up the rear.

President Truman had just integrated the US Armed Forces and the officer in charge of the 4th Platoon was a black officer, 2nd LT. Ira Moore Jr. Seven recruits in the 4th Platoon were Blacks or Negroes. The term "African-American" had not yet entered our vocabulary. I could not help but wonder how the black recruits would be received by the many Southern fellows that were part of our unit.

By far, the most colorful of our "Cadre", Staff Sergeant Earl T. Booker, ran the platoon with a friendly, sarcastic humor that would tolerate no nonsense. A sharp, black soldier, he would flash a continuous smile that showed every one of his gold-capped teeth. Forever clasping a clipboard under his arm he would be remembered mostly for his peculiar syntax "Who are the mens with the sore feets?"

A few more corporals and privates rounded out the "cadre" charged with making soldiers out of us but except for PVT Lawrence Foote and PVT Frank Juliano, most have faded from memory. The general in charge of Fort Lee, General Arkin, soon to be replaced by Maj. Gen. Graham, was a shadowy figure visible only during the Saturday Post parade.

His motto was reported to be:

"If it moves, salute it; if it doesn't, pick it up; if you can't, paint it green (The color of the quartermaster corps)!

BASIC TRAINING

It was the army's task to take the two hundred of us and mold us into a cohesive unit. However, as we were to be part of the Quartermaster, our training was to be rudimentary and not to the same level as fighting units such as the Infantry, Artillery, Tank Corps etc. Our ritual commenced with a 3.45 AM reveille to the tune of a recorded bugle, quick but substantial breakfast, calisthenics and marching to various training fields or classrooms for practical or theoretical instructions. The training day continued until 6.30 PM, a fourteen hour routine. Until 10 PM we had free time that we filled with cleaning and oiling our rifle, hand-wash our laundry, shave, shower and shine our boots and brass. By 10 PM we struggled into bed to sleep until the bugle roused us at quarter to four again.

As the US Army was short of recruits the quality of the inductees varied widely. Most of us were not perfect specimen and were deemed unsuited for combat duty. Among our groups a number of recruits could only handle "light basic training" and had to be driven by trucks from training field to training field. My handicap was poor eyesight that did not make me suited for combat although glasses corrected it to nearly 20/20. My glasses tended to fog up badly making me very vulnerable for crucial minutes as I could see nothing when entering from a cold environment into a warm room. In contrast, the "light duty" guys suffered from a variety of ailments ranging from missing digits to poor balance and inability to walk any distance.

The boots I had been issued began to torment me. I had never been aware that short as I was, I needed size 12 AA or AAA footwear. To aggravate the matter, my big toes were nearly an inch longer than the next toe and my heels were extremely narrow. Now that we were marching long distances every day, my feet soon developed painful blisters and raw sores. My complaints were totally ignored and I was told to suffer with the footwear I had been issued in New Jersey. After a week of bleeding feet, I decided to take the leather by the laces and hailed First Lt. Hall, our C.O., to complain that I could not go on marching with the boots I had been issued. Much to my surprise, Lt. Hall approached our formation and knelt in front of me, feeling my boots. He turned to Sgt. Booker and stated that it was obvious that these boots did not fit and that I should be issued better fitting boots immediately.

Apparently, the officers and cadre seemed to be aware of my past even more than I was and must have been impressed by my high initial test scores. They looked upon me as a sort of phenomenon and although it did not bring me any special privileges they knew who I was. Sometimes it had weird effects as if I was the only name they could recall. "The man next to Rosenberg, straighten your rifle"; "The man in back of Rosenberg, get in step" It did not endear me to the rest of the platoon.

Although it was evident that most of us would be shipped to Korea after we had completed our basic training, I had hopes that somehow I could be sent to Germany for duty. The thought of prancing in "Deutschland" in my American uniform so soon after the end of the war was very appealing. Of course, I'd be able to go to Belgium as an American soldier and I dreamed of seeing Father, Mother and Ruth. Surely I'd impress Rosette. Gilberte would be mortified that she had let this handsome Yankee slip through her fingers. I'd be proud to see Maurice and Bob again. There was also all those who I had worked with at Lever Brothers and had seen me leave in disgrace; how I'd now be able to show-off!

So, while we were in informal formation, I called out to Sgt. Booker who was lecturing us on several subjects that had little to do with soldiering. "Sgt. Booker, what are the chances of being sent to Germany?" Booker twisted around and slapped his ever-present clipboard under his arm. All his gold-capped teeth shining under the Virginia sun he smiled "Rosie, do you really think that we are going to send you back to Germany with a loaded *rafle*?" That was the end of that. Next destination: Korea!

There was another Jew in our platoon by the name of Rosenthal. It had been rumored that he came from a wealthy family and that he was trying to be discharged for medical reason. While I tried to be a "soldier" Rosenthal, by his attitude and sloppy dress, made it plain that he was not pleased to be there and that his tenure in Fort Lee was only temporary. One day, as we were lined up in formation, Sgt. Booker stopped in front of Rosenthal, looked him over and declared loudly "Rosenberg, you are a sloppy soldier!". Was Rosenberg the only name they knew?

Later on, it dawned on me that the Rosenbergs, Ethel and Julius, the convicted Atomic spies, were in the news almost daily and had rendered the Rosenberg name infamous at the time. There was a lot of news about the numerous appeals, the possible pardons and the seemingly inexorable march toward their eventual execution on the electric chair.

Kenneth Rosenthal was now the Fourth Platoon's guidon. He carried the platoon's colors whenever we were in formation. It was considered an honor. A few weeks into basic training, his medical discharge came in. Apparently Rosenthal was allergic to wool and since socks and most of our winter uniforms were a blend of wool the Army sent him home to Milwaukee.

Each of us was issued an M-1, semi-automatic rifle. This Garand rifle had been standard issue for the US Army since 1941. With it, we soon learned the manual of arms and discovered how neatly it carved a space in our shoulders. We had to learn to take it apart and put it back together even in very dim light. It was rumored that we'd have to put it together while blindfolded but since we were service troops we were spared the embarrassment. Bullets, on the other hand, were a different matter, we never were issued any. When we were on the rifle range, the instructors would dole out an exact number of bullets that were counted as we fired at the targets. Any left-over rounds had to be religiously returned to the instructor after the exercise was over.

The army had just been integrated and there was friction between the black and white members of the army. I guess that the high command was more concerned with fighting between the races than with the possible danger of having to fight off the Russians. As it turned out, when most of the service units were shipped out to Korea, they were completely unprepared and ill equipped to fight against the North Koreans. There were constant incursions behind the lines and cooks, drivers and other service personnel suffered disproportionate casualties resulting from lack of proper training back in the USA.

POST PARADE

It seemed that Lt. Hall was more interested in having Company O do well in the Saturday post parade than whipping us into a fine fighting machine. From the first day we came to the unit, he seemed consumed with capturing the weekly trophy for his company. It was a big order as we were as green as we could be. Guy Sillay was the exception in our platoon. Sillay was a Georgia boy and had gone to Georgia Tech. where he had joined the R.O.T.C. He knew the Manual of Arms front and back and the weapons held no secret for him. He was the sharpest soldier in our company. Guy was friendly to everyone and especially to me. He had taken a liking to this recent immigrant and I admired him a lot. It was comforting to hear a Cadre call out "Silly? "At roll call. Invariably Guy's southern drawl baritone would reply "That's "Sill Lay", sir! "Guy was number one in our platoon; I tried very hard to be number two.

And then, there was Patrick Woods from Detroit. Woods should not have been drafted. Woods and the Army were not made for each other. He was the anti-soldier, not willfully; he was just completely out of his element, lost in an environment not of his making or choosing. Woods did not have a mean bone in his body, he was a victim.

In formation, Patrick marched to my immediate right. "Rosie" He'd say endlessly. "Am I in step?" A fast look confirmed what I knew; he was not! "No, Woods, you are not" We had been shown how to hop and skip once to get back in step. Woods would hop and skip about eight times, somewhat like a springbok and invariably wound up on the wrong step again. It was funny but oh so sad. And even when Woods was in step, he would still be a quarter-step off the pace. He had a bounce.

When the company marched by, you could see a helmet and a rifle pop up above the formation; that was Patrick Woods!

One of the Cadres had a brainstorm; keep Woods out of the parade; send him to the kitchen! We had been in Co.O just two weeks and we marched without Patrick. When we got back to our barracks, Lt. Hall, red with excitement, was waiting for us. He was practically three feet off the ground and hollering: "We won the parade, we won the Post parade!" Incredibly, we had, after just two weeks in Fort Lee. Even though Patrick Woods remained confined to the kitchen for the next fourteen Saturdays, we never won the post parade again.

On Saturday mornings, when we were waiting on our bunks for the call to form ranks and march to the parade grounds, it was easy to fall asleep all dressed up in our *Khakis* while the warm Virginia sun filtered through the barrack windows and kissed our young prone bodies. More than once, I'd wake up feeling the incredibly warm oozing of a "wet dream", an ejaculation so smooth, triggered by the sun. Then would come the realization that a big stain, like an oasis in the desert, was soiling your perfectly clean summer uniform. Quickly, a change of pants had to be made in time for the parade while your buddies laughed and yelled "Wet dream! Wet dream!"

The Saturday parades in the broiling Virginia summer sun inflicted casualties each week. It was not so much the marching but the standing in formation while some inane officer talked at length in a microphone while we stood at attention. Some of the recruits would pass out and keel over like empty sacks of potatoes However; it was mostly the cadre who suffered in the largest number. While the recruits were tired and went to bed in the evening, the cadre had gone partying and drinking in town on Friday nights. It was weird to see them suddenly slide and fall as they fainted. I was cautioned never to lock my knees as it was a sure way to restrict the flow of blood and lose consciousness.

Friday night was G.I night. The whole barrack had to be swept, scrubbed with soap and washed and rinsed in preparation for Saturday inspection. There were butt-cans strategically nailed to the center wooden post that supported each of the two floors. Despite the cans, someone always found it easier to toss the cigarette butts in the urinal that lined the wall in the latrine despite the prominent signs that asked that the butts be placed in the butt-cans. No matter how much or how recently the urinals had been cleaned, new butts would appear as if by magic. I never did find out who the culprits were.

There were usually enough buckets for the soapy water but the brooms, brushes and mops were always in short supply. Several of us would fan out to neighboring barracks, preferably occupied by greener recruits and grabbed broom or mop from the hands of the soldier wielding it. "Let me give you a hand" We'd say. Then, we'd pretend to work on the wet floor while working in the direction of the exit door. From there it was a short run to our own barrack where eager hands were waiting. At the same time, we would be watchful that our booty was not stolen by the other barracks.

Decades later, in the restroom of a diner in Westbury, NY I actually saw a man flick a cigarette butt in one of the urinals. "It was you!" I exclaimed. "You're the guy who has been leaving the butts in the urinals!" He gave me a quizzical look as he obviously had no idea what I was talking about.

MORE TRAINING

Donald Wingerberg had left his sweetheart in Ohio; apparently they had a love song that meant a lot to them, or at least to Wingerberg. Every time we stepped in the Mess-hall for a meal he'd put a nickel in the Wurlitzer and Tony Bennett's big hit would fill the air "*Because of you, there's a love in my heart*". It never failed. It was a standing but good-natured joke. Still today, whenever the first four notes resonate, there is an immediate transport back to Fort Lee Va., Wingerberg, the Mess-hall and the oppressive heat of that summer of 1951.

Spaghetti and meatballs turned up on the menu quite regularly. It was not a favorite of mine. However our Italian/American recruits adored it. It must have reminded them of home cooking. One dinner, I sat across from Dominic Trocchio, an Italian from Pittsburgh. Trocchio was forking his food with extreme delight. A full colonel was walking between the rows of tables to make sure that the men were happy with the quality of the food. He planted himself behind Trocchio and asked "How do you like the food, soldier?" Trocchio, his mouth full of pasta and tomato sauce and unaware that the question had been asked by a "full bird" spit out "Man, I eat this shit up!" Then, he turned around; saw this full colonel standing there, swallowed hard and added "Sir!"

The time spent preparing for the rifle range seemed endless. Days and weeks spent learning the various positions to be used firing the weapon. The army had a fetish about the proper body posture when aiming the weapon, the heels in the prone stance had to be completely flat, flush against the ground. The cadre took a maniacal pleasure to stomp on our heels if there was the slightest daylight showing between our boots and the ground. For me, that position was so unnatural and painful that it distracted from the act of aiming and pulling the trigger. Jay Wilson, a tall and gangly Irish Jew, was the most pigeon-toed person I had ever seen, his heels aimed away from his body and the toes of his left foot seemed forever attempting to kiss his right foot. Wilson, having endured the ignominious crush of the cadre's boot, had finally found peace by turning his heels outward. It made him look like a grotesque dummy with two broken ankles.

The Wilson family had originated in Ireland and Jay looked more Irish than Jewish. He had a ruddy complexion and widely detached ears that glowed pink and translucent whenever the sun shined around his head. Wilson was kosher and would not eat any pork products. Jews had special dispensation that allowed them to eat non-kosher foods while in the army under the principle that the preservation of life takes precedence over dietary laws. However, Jay would not eat ham, shrimp and any other questionable foods. I had taken the habit of following him through the chow line and what he did not want on his plate would find its way to mine. It was a good arrangement. Jay had refused to sign a statement of "loyalty to the USA" when he was drafted and would spend his two years without ever being assigned to any unit. He spent the remainder of his service working for the post chaplain, carving exotic musical instruments and helping with the religious services. Wilson was a remarkable fellow but totally unfit for the military. He made the most of it and was pretty much left alone.

There was always plenty of food whether in the field or in the mess-hall. "Take all you want, eat all you take" Lt. Moore would admonish. To be sure that no food was wasted, Lt. Moore stationed himself at the exit of the mess-hall near the garbage cans and would inspect every tray. "Look at

Rosenberg" He'd say" He knows what it means to be hungry, he does not waste food". That did not sit well with my fellow recruits and I'd make sure that I took just enough so I could eat it all. To me, it was further proof that my background had been a subject of discussion among the officers and cadre.

During a ten minute break on a long march in the field, Sgt. Booker pulled me out of rank and yelled "Rosie, you are going to give a lecture on sex education to the entire company" So, I summoned the little I knew about and talked. I relied on the little I had learned in the streets of Brussels and my experiences with Gilberte. It must have been pitiful but I persevered. I recall that I explained about "sixty-nine" that I called a "sandwich" position because both partners got to eat. This brought out some embarrassed laughter. Some of the recruits were married men; others must have had girlfriends and were certainly more experienced than I about sexual matters. When we resumed the march, Sgt.Booker came to me and his gold teeth glistening in the sun smiled at me and said "You did well, Rosie; you did well." I remember feeling that I had made an ass of myself.

There was a commotion in the doorway of our barrack as I was trying to enter. The subject of the slight altercation has been long forgotten but Shire, from Boston planted himself squarely in front of me and yelled "Fuck you!" I was shocked. Up to then, no one had ever said such a thing to me, not my GI's in Belgium, not my friends in Brooklyn, no one. Sure I had heard the word and knew its meaning but it had never been thrown in my face. It shook me for a while. I would learn to toss it off even though it would seldom enter my vocabulary.

The time finally came when we would be going to the rifle range and be allowed to fire our weapons with live rounds. At last, we would be real soldiers! Under the guidance of a cadre, we took the prone position and were issued five cartridges that we would be allowed to fire one at a time under strict supervision. A boot pressed on my heels; "You don't want the enemy to shoot off your heels while you try to kill him, soldier!" "Lock and load!". I inserted the live round in the chamber. "Ready, aim, fire!".

In front of me, the target had been raised; I squeezed the trigger, the rifle belched the bullet forward, an unexpected kick bruised my right shoulder. I fired again and again, five times. Each time, the target was lowered while the shots were marked. It would then come back up while a round disk danced at the end of a pole to indicate where the bullet had struck. A red flag would be waved (Maggie's drawers) if you missed the target altogether. I hit near or on the bulls-eye on all my shots. We were issued another five rounds and repeated the process. By then, my right shoulder was well sore and with each subsequent shot I winced and anticipated the recoil. The pattern of my shots was now scattered all over the target but I did not get any Maggie's drawer. I shot well enough to qualify as an Expert, one step above Marksman. It was rumored that if you could not hit the target, the cadre in the pit would punch the target with a round pencil giving you a "lead qualification". Nobody was going to flunk. That was the extent of our rifle training.

Our next training would be the machine gun. Several hours were spent on the theory. We were then moved to the firing range and one by one, we lay alongside a .30 caliber machine gun. The cadre lifted the gun cover and pulled the cartridge belt in place. Load and rapid fire in the general direction of the target, five shots. The sixth round had been removed from the belt, every sixth round. There was no way you could fire more than five shots. After the fifth shot you were pulled off the firing line and made way for the next recruit. That was machine gun qualification!

It was now time to qualify on the hand grenade. Once again, a few hours of theory; the explanation that the pin that holds the spoon in place must be removed prior to throwing the grenade. It was impressed upon us that the spoon must be held against the palm of the hand until the throw. The pin must be kept to be reinserted if the grenade is not to be thrown. The grenade would be lobbed in a high arc rather than be thrown like a baseball. It struck me that Americans were so good at throwing a baseball yet had to learn to lob a grenade in an unnatural and inaccurate fashion.

We were herded in an earthen enclosure with a cadre and lobbed two grenades in a general direction away from the pit. I pulled the pin, reared my right hand and gave a high lob. I had thrown a few dummy grenades in training and was prepared to see the spoon fly high upon release. On the live grenade, there was a "paff" that startled me as the grenade armed itself on release. I had no idea where the grenade landed. I was now qualified for the hand grenade.

The rifle-grenade was all that was left for us to learn. Like all the other qualifications, there were a few hours of theory to be followed by the actual firing. We marched to an open field where silhouettes of truck and tanks stood dispersed at various distances. I knelt next to my rifle and removed the bolt from the chamber. The rifle-grenade was now inserted over the barrel of the rifle. I inserted a large blank cartridge in the chamber that remained open. The elevation was checked, the rifle-butt firmly planted in the ground. I pulled the trigger and the blank went off propelling the grenade in the general direction of the target that was hit a few moments later. Unfortunately, when I fired, I had been leaning over the open chamber of my rifle. My helmet acted as an amplifier and the thunder of the shot reverberated violently inside of my right ear. It would not stop ringing and the next morning I went on sick-call to see what could be done. I was sure that I had caused permanent damage to my hearing. The medic gave me a perfunctory examination and assured me that the ringing would subside in a few days. I could assure myself and have additional tests done but I would have to go to the hospital for a couple of days.

We were now in our seventh week of basic training. In another week we would start the second eight-week phase. If you missed more than one day's training, you would be transferred to company "N" to wait until another training company had reached the level of training you had achieved. You would then be transferred to that unit. I had formed a bond with my fellow trainees and had no desire to resume my training among a group of strangers. Besides, most of the recruits who were waiting in Company "N" were soldiers who had gone AWOL or had been confined for a few weeks in the stockade. Anybody who came from "N" was immediately considered an "Eight Ball" and subjected to the worse kind of discipline. So, I decided to forego the hospital and to prudently stay in Company "O". After about a week, the ringing in my right ear stopped.

The Quartermaster Corps was responsible for supplying the army. Another duty was Graves Registration. I was hoping that I would not be assigned to that section. The thought of having to go collect dead bodies on the battlefield, tagging them and locking them in body bags held no attraction for me. Graves Registration had to chart each soldier's dental map. Often dead bodies could only be identified by dental records. One morning, a dental team arrived in our barracks, set up a chair and proceeded to examine and record everyone's teeth. When my turn came, I sat in the chair, the dentist peered into my mouth and said "One in a million; next!". Despite my years of malnutrition I did not even have a single cavity. Perhaps it was the herring diet and the lack of sweets. One in a million!

On the other hand, I was tempted to apply for the Air Supply branch. These were the boys who loaded supplies onto cargo planes for delivery to the forward lines. They would also supply from the air with parachuted pallets. For this hazardous duty, a bonus of fifty dollars a month was granted. Since Mother was getting part of my monthly pay, there was little left for me. The extra money seemed very attractive. All that I'd have to do were two parachute jumps each year to remain qualified. One afternoon the whole platoon was ordered to jump off the second floor overhang of the barracks, about fifteen feet. I could not do it. I tried again and again almost leaping each time but panic held me back. The ground seemed so far away and the fear of breaking my legs paralyzed me. After a long agonizing delay, I climbed back through the window and retreated in the second floor of the barrack. There was no punishment for failing to jump but it confirmed that I had a fear of heights. I abandoned all thought of joining the parachute branch of the Quartermaster.

We were nearing the end of September and the last days of our basic training. Soon we would begin our M.O.S (Military Occupation Specialty). Even though our combat training had been so shabby, we had developed into a cohesive unit and most of us, thanks to a rigorous schedule and daily calisthenics, were trimmer and more muscular than two months earlier. As for me, my mind was clearer and I felt confident in my abilities. Sometimes, when in rank or on a march, it seemed that we were still a bunch of schoolboys. Yet, we felt ready to fight and looked forward to being shipped to Korea. Secretly I was hoping to be assigned to Germany but the possibility was very remote.

I still maintained some contact with Helene hoping to see her again during the very first pass that would enable me to travel to Brooklyn. I kept a running correspondence with Rosette but her replies were becoming more spaced. Rosette was meeting other fellows and had little time to answer my "Love" letters.

MOS TRAINING

We were now entering the second phase of our training. Mostly it consisted of being marched to various classes where we would learn about the many paper forms that a Supply Records Specialist would come across in the service. Since most forms were to be typed, the primary training we receive was how to type. I had joined the army and would wind up as a typing clerk. I still had hopes to go the Leadership School for another 8 weeks. After that, OCS and perhaps CID as had been promised by the recruiting sergeant in Brooklyn. We now had the luxury of sleeping until 5AM, a full seventy-five minutes later than during basic training. It was now October and the early mornings had turned much cooler. We spent the first few minutes of class loosening our hands and making finger exercise to unlock our freezing digits.

I had been pecking at the keys for years but now I had to learn touch-typing. I did but never really felt brave enough to take my eyes off the keyboard.

USO

At least now, we were issued passes from after the Saturday parade until ten PM that same night. Whole day passes were available for Sundays provided you did not screw up during the week. If you passed the Saturday inspection and had no KP duty, Richmond and the USO were only an hour away by train or bus. I'd go as often as I could. Once we went as a group and tried our hand at bowling. I had never seen a bowling alley. It was a far cry from the single bowling lane of Solvay in Brussels where you'd have to go and reset the pins yourself. These were well-lit multiple lanes where several pin boys would nimbly reset the pins after you knocked them down. They'd then drop the ball into an elevated ramp and the ball would be returned to you. I was amazed and enthralled at such luxurious automated progress.

This was my first attempt at bowling. I chose a ball that felt comfortable in my right hand. Since my knuckles were a bit thick especially on my thumb, it did not fit too well. I threw four strikes with my first four balls. I was expecting to be tapped on the shoulder and to hear a cavernous voice telling me that he now owned my soul. I needed not worry. After the initial four strikes my thumb began to rub raw and my ball found the gutter with amazing regularity. I wound up with a very low score slightly above one hundred.

The USO offered a very pleasant atmosphere with donuts, coffee, pretty girls and dancing. I concentrated on the first two but felt confident enough to try mingling and dancing. One of the head hostesses had taken a liking to me and we spent a while talking. As I was ready to leave she asked me if I could take time to talk to her teen-age son. She'd bring him in the next week. I met the young boy and we spoke for maybe twenty minutes. The following week, his delighted Mother came to me, hugged me and thanked me for talking with her son. "He is a changed person. You have performed a miracle!" I never learned what I could have said to effect such a beneficial change or what the problem might have been in the first place. It did give me a different outlook on things, a feeling that perhaps I was special and that I could influence young people.

Olivia served the donuts. One of the youngest hostesses, she radiated pretty. We struck up a conversation. Whatever we spoke about made very little impression on me. What impressed and attracted me were her breasts. Olivia had the prettiest, pointiest tits I had ever seen. She wore soft, fluffy angora sweaters in pastel hues. Her breasts cried out, begged to be touched, handled, kissed. I was fascinated. Olivia was not altogether unreceptive to my obvious attention. We danced a few times and she was not shy. Our bodies were very close and she did not mind when I pressed myself against her breasts. Reluctantly I left her with a warm kiss when time came to go back to Fort Lee. Before we parted Olivia's eyes and touch let me know that she'd love to see me again the following week.

I made sure that I did not have KP that following week and found my way to the USO. I had been dreaming of her lovely tits the entire week. Olivia was waiting for me and we plotted a way for her to leave early. We met a couple of blocks from the USO and she took me to her apartment. The delightful points of her breasts had been dancing in my mind the entire week, distracting me to an unbearable degree. Now, she lay on her bed as I covered her with tentative kisses. Olivia sat up and helped me remove her soft sweater. Only her rose-colored brassiere stood between me

311

and the objects of my desire. Still sitting up, both her hands reached the catch in her back and with a flourish Olivia removed her bra and her breasts! "Now you know my secret!" She flung the phrase at me with daring and also a pleading look. I understood that she wanted me to keep it in confidence. She was completely flat-chested, nothing, zip! At that moment I did not care. Olivia was sweet, loving and very passionate. I would remember nothing of the rest of the night. I guess I returned to Fort Lee in time for 'reveille' the next morning. I don't believe I ever saw her again but she has remained in my memory especially when the subject of Grace Kelly comes up.

There was another pretty blonde girl. I seem to remember that her name was Betty-Lou. Betty-Lou was your typical college cheerleader, the kind you see leading the band in the Rose Bowl parade on TV.

A dazzling Pepsodent smile, perfect of body yet exuding a healthy attitude, she was friendly and could not wait until I agreed to go out with her. We walked and talked a lot in the streets of Richmond. We held hands and touched hips as we looked in the windows of the downtown stores. Kissing was another matter. Betty-Lou was in a "brushing mood" Her lips would brush my cheek and she would permit me to do the same to her. After we had "dated" a few Sundays I asked her if she ever petted. I was getting anxious to know her much better. Yes, Betty-Lou did pet but not past the neckline. I wanted to know if it was past the neckline going down or coming up. Obviously she meant going down, not an encouraging development.

The following Saturday, she insisted that I follow her to her Church. There, she introduced me to her pastor who warmly shook my hands, held me in a warm embrace and insisted that he wanted to see me and Betty-Lou in church the following Sunday. Suddenly a light went on in my brain. Betty-Lou was not interested in me at all. The church she belonged to was one of those that wanted to save Jews and convert them to Christianity. She loved me only to the point where it would bring me salvation and accumulate a few brownie points for her own after-life. I did not bother to tell her that I had already been baptized Protestant once, that being Jewish was still deplorable and that I wanted to be left alone religiously. That was the end of my adventure with Betty-Lou.

A VISIT FROM HELENE

The Jewish holidays of Rosh Hashanah and Yom Kippur came around that October as we were in the middle of our MOS training. I had been trying very hard to arrange for Mother and Ruth to come to America but it was extremely slow going. I felt that I should appeal to the JOINT in New York. The JOINT was a Jewish organization that had been set up to help Jews migrate to the USA back in the days of Hitler's Germany. I had appealed to them when I had tried to leave Europe. Fort Lee had decided that Jewish soldiers should be allowed leave so they could attend services and even be able to go home to be with their family during these High Holidays. I was advised that I would be given leave for a few days and that meant that I could go to New York and arrange something so Frieda and Ruth could at long last make it to the States. Of course, I did not really want to be Jewish (I was registered as a protestant and even had a "P" on my dog tags) but the Army seemed to be just as confused as I was at the time. I also felt that for once, being Jewish would be beneficial to me and I went along gladly. On the way to New York, I stopped in Newport

News, VA where I went aboard an aircraft carrier as a visitor. The Navy welcomed me and showed me around. They allowed me to have several meals on board and I was duly impressed at the variety and the quality of the chow they were serving. The Army lagged way behind in accommodations. However the Navy would have required a 4 year enlistment and I recalled how queasy I had felt during the crossing on the SS Tabinta.

I finally arrived in New York and hurried to the Joint office in Manhattan. Much to my surprise, they were closed. It was Rosh Hashanah! Who knew?

Somehow I found my way to the Wolleman house in White Plains where there was a small party going on. There I met Leo's son Walter and daughter Anna. I looked real sharp in my uniform with the bright shiny brass buckle and mirror-polished shoes. I sang "Blue Moon" in a mixture of French and English and Anna fancied that I sounded just like Eddie Fisher who was the hottest singer at the time. Anna and I seemed to hit it off quite well at the time and when I left to return I had to promise the Wolleman family that I'd pay them a visit when I'd be in New York again.

It is possible that I tried to get in touch with Helene in the short time that I stayed in Brooklyn. I have no recollection of my visit on that occasion. Did I call Helene, Diane, Anita? Where did I stay overnight, at Lilli and Paul's? There is a gaping hole in my memory.

I had my first taste of guard duty in the early part of October. About six of us were picked up in a truck and dropped off at night at several deserted locations in the far reaches of Fort Lee. The sergeant of the guard did a last check of my uniform, inspected my rifle and made certain that there was no bullet in the chamber. How could there have been bullets since we had never been issued any except for the ones that had been parceled out to us at the rifle range? The sergeant then counted out three bullets and placed these in the breast pocket of my uniform. "Keep them there" He instructed. "Under no circumstance should these be loaded in your rifle".

The truck drove off leaving me cold and in the dark, guarding what I could not see in the middle of nowhere. I stood there with a rifle I was not allowed to load and three bullets I was prohibited from using. The night was cold and we had not yet been issued overcoats. I was reduced to blowing in my hands and stomping my feet to keep the blood circulating. Walking up and down was out of the question as it was pitch dark and we had not been issued a flashlight. Ninety minutes later, the sergeant drove by in a jeep and demanded to inspect my rifle. I opened the bolt and showed him the empty chamber in the glare of the jeep's headlights. He then asked that I produce the three bullets from my pocket. He seemed satisfied and drove away. At the end of three hours the truck returned and a new recruit relieved me. We exchanged the three bullets under the watchful eye of the sergeant. I got back to the barracks just in time for reveille.

We had finally graduated from basic training and in Mid-December 1951 those of us who had shown special aptitude were chosen to attend eight more weeks in Company "S" for the Leadership Training Course. We were about two dozen that would be reduced to nineteen who'd survive the rigorous training and would finally graduate. I felt lucky that I had been selected as I considered it a stepping stone for an officer's commission and the eventual transfer to the CID. That impression was short-lived as I was once again informed that since I was not a US citizen, there would be no chance that I could become an officer or join the CID. Those who had not been selected for

Leadership Course were swiftly shipped to various places in the USA but most found themselves Korea-bound as the army was in dire need of replacements. There was no way anyone would remain state-side. Recruits who had plausible reasons not to be shipped to Korea were refused reassignment to the US. Several soldiers whose wife had difficult pregnancies were ordered to Korea. There was no deferment from shipping overseas.

At about that time, I received news that Mother and my sister Ruth had finally obtained their visa to come to America in July 1952. This presented me with a dilemma. I wanted very much to be there to welcome them. On the other hand, I had been together with my training buddies for four months and I was loath to see them leave for Korea without me. Finally, I decided that I should be in New York for Mother and Ruth's arrival from Europe. Asking for a deferment seemed hopeless; nevertheless I wrote a letter to Frank Pace, the Secretary of the Army. In it, I laid out the fact that I would like to be here when my Mother and my sister would arrive to the US. I wanted to help them get settled and become good US. Citizens. As far as the Army was concerned, since I had enlisted for three years, it would still have ample time to deploy me overseas. Much to my surprise, a positive answer was received and I was notified that I would be assigned to Fort Lee until Frieda and Ruth's arrival.

Guy Sillay and Charlie Wommack had rented a small apartment outside the post in Petersburg. Guy had brought up his wife Martha from Atlanta and Wommack's wife Julie had joined him from Oakland. Robert Bennett from Richmond had rented a separate apartment and had also been rejoined by his wife.

One day, Helene appeared out of nowhere. She had taken the train from New York and had come for a visit. I was overjoyed at seeing her although she was still very married. I never did find out what she had told her husband Paul to justify her absence from Brooklyn. Her first remark to me was wondering what had happened to my French accent. I told her that I had given it up while in the military. Later that evening, we went to Sillay's home where we all shared in a dinner that Martha had prepared. Helene took me aside and remarked that Martha had a funny accent. A bit later, Martha whispered in my ear that Helene "talked funny". I guessed that the clash of Georgia and Brooklyn was something neither was prepared for.

Later that night, Helene told me that she had come to Virginia to tell me that our "affair" was over and that she would now concentrate on her husband. I felt that it was perhaps the dropping of the French accent that had changed her heart. My chagrin was somewhat mitigated by the fact that Rosette and I had resumed our correspondence. I did not fall from so high although for a long, long time, I would continue to regret and miss Helene and the chances we had wasted.

LEADERSHIP COURSE. COMPANY "S"

We soon found out that Leadership School was basic training all over again albeit without weapons and with an extra helping of chicken-shit. The training's purpose was to make leaders out of us, ostensibly as squad leaders or Cadres. Where previously we simply had to hang our clothes by the head of our bunks, now the jackets and shirts had to be hanging "at attention", all the sleeves perfectly lined up. Our footlockers had to be arranged according to regulations; socks rolled up and laid in order. There was no room for anything extra, candy bars, potato chips etc. As the weeks went by, all of us had started to accumulate goodies we had purchased at the PX or during our forays into Richmond. Some of the fellows having wives off-post had civilian clothing that they would change into on Saturday afternoons. There were several hiding places in the rafters among the ventilating system above the false ceiling. Week after week all of us had squirreled our stash of pirated items above our living spaces. Each time the instructors pulled an inspection, we felt secure in the knowledge that we were putting one over on them.

One morning, the instructors came in the barracks for a "routine inspection". All went well, the footlockers properly filled and orderly, the tautness of the blankets was satisfactory, all our uniforms hung in perfect rows against the wall and the shelving had survived the "white glove" ordeal. Then, the instructors borrowed a chair from the barrack sergeant's room and stepping on it proceeded to open every single ceiling tile revealing the treasures we had carefully accumulated over several weeks. As we stood at attention in front of our bunks the instructors confiscated and carted off all our booty. Nothing would ever be seen again.

It was evident that the instructors had been wise to us from the start. After all, they had been recruits before us and had also been robbed by their instructors. Instead of raiding our secret places in the first days, they had waited until our hiding places were brimming with contraband. Then they struck. It was a lesson we would remember should we become cadres to subsequent recruits.

The Leadership School ranks got thinner as the weeks went by. You would get gigged for the slightest infraction. Many would flunk out and get transferred to other outfits, mostly in far away cities or overseas.

We would take turn leading the Company on our daily marches through the camp. It was not a great honor but something we had to do as part of our training to become Cadres in our subsequent assignments. Most of us were proud of being in Company S and its accomplishments. We considered ourselves an elite group. Naturally we did our best to march our group smartly and would call out the "cadence march" sharply. "Up, two, three four. Up, two, three, four" Since the camp had a large share of WACS we were proscribed from any "Jody" on the immediate post. However once we had reached the outer, wilder areas, we could "Jody" with abandon as long as there were no *risqué* lyrics."-*You had a good home that you left*"

> "*You're right*"
> "*You had a good home that you left*"
> "*You're right*"
> "*Sound off!*"
> "*Up, two, three, four*"
> "*Up, two (pause) three-four*"

Was all we were allowed to do.

James Wetzel from Pittsburgh made no bones about his profound dislike for the Leadership School and his contempt for being in the military in the first place. Whenever his name was called to lead our group, he'd step outside the column and holler "Road step!" This meant that we were allowed to walk at our own pace, without being in step and could converse with one another. To the rest of us it was somewhat funny but the instructors were not amused. After a few minutes, Wetzel would be called back in the ranks and a more pliant soldier would be called upon to march the group.

It seemed to us that Wetzel was angling to flunk out of Leadership School but the instructors would not grant him the favor. Wetzel was smart, had a good education and looked the part of an officer; he just did not want to earn a "stripe" while he was in the service.

Guy Sillay was someone I looked up to and I was glad that he considered me his friend. Guy was a sharp soldier, tall, athletic and speaking with an easygoing Georgia drawl. He was close to others, Bennett, Wommack, Welsh and "Red" McLaughlin. They would ship out to Korea as a group after graduation and continue to cultivate their friendship. He did reserve a special place for me and as a recent immigrant, I was very sensitive to his attention. I looked up to him. Each Friday, someone from the Leadership School would be selected as Colonel's Orderly. Guy, who had several years of ROTC before being drafted, was always a shoe-in for the selection. Spit and polish, mirror shoes, polished buckles and every rivet of his helmet liner stripped of paint and bright with "Brasso", Guy was a Poster-Boy for the army. I was quite sharp myself but I would be selected after a second or third inspection.—Rosenberg looks sharp too—was the usual remark and the both of us would be selected as Orderlies. The duties we were to perform were nebulous at best but is was an honor that I strived very much to earn.

At the end of our training day and before dinner, Guy and I would walk over to the small PX and share a pitcher of beer, the only time in my life where I actually sat down and had a beer, albeit very weak, on a daily basis. There was a Belgian girl working at the PX. I got to call her "Liège" as that was the town she came from. I came from Charleroi and that made us both Walloons (from the French part of Belgium) and if felt good to talk. Our occasions to meet were few and only a friendly kinship would exist.

We were not allowed to carry books in formation. Comic books were particularly forbidden. I had been a TIME reader since 1945 and would never miss an issue. It had been my habit to place my copy under the blouse of my *fatigues* and to read a page or two whenever we had a break in our training schedule. One afternoon, one of our instructors noticing a bulge under my blouse asked me what I had under there. I guess he was fully expecting a comic book to be produced. "Time magazine, Sir!" Was my reply. He asked to see it. It was TIME, indeed. A bit mollified, he gave it back to me and admonished me not to bring it in the field again. I did not.

Strangely, although I would remember most of the cadre in basic training, none of the names of our Leadership School instructors has stuck in my memory even though I can still see the silhouettes and faces in my mind.

We had been taught the special lingo of the *cadres,* the special inflections of words meant to convey a command, how to project across a marching field so you could be understood and obeyed. It was as if a command that could be deciphered was not what was wanted. "Company, Halt!" became

"Humpanee Hoat!". "To the rear, March!" became "To the rip, Ho!" and so on. We'd stand at opposite ends of the field and holler commands aimed at the other side. It was fun and made us feel secure that we would not sound like amateurs whenever we would have to bellow out commands.

Classes in public speaking gave us tips on how to present varied subjects and we had to prepare talks in front of groups; for us it was in front of our classmates and the instructors. We'd have to give fifteen minutes lectures so that we could be understood and clearly heard in open areas and large rooms. To fill the time, we'd spend the first five minutes telling the audience what we were going to tell them. In the next five minutes we'd tell them what we wanted to say. The last five minutes were a recapitulation of what they had just heard. There was usually enough time for a few questions from the audience. We were instructed to ask: "Are there any questions?" We'd then repeat the question loudly so that it would not be lost on the listeners and then answered the question. All that took a measured time and assured that a talk could be given without painful silences. I soon discovered that I had a talent for public speaking. The few guidelines that I learned in Fort Lee are still used by me today.

The topics we had to chose from could be on any subject. On one occasion, I had been given "Belgium" to talk about. "The sex life of a light bulb" had been Charlie Wommack's lot. Wommack did not have a good feeling for his subject and we decided to swap.

Although I had given Wommack some pointers on Belgium, his lecture was a disaster. He wrote the name of his lecture on the blackboard with a glaring spelling error. The instructor asked him if the title was correct. Wommack stared at the board and the title and could see nothing wrong. We could not say anything. Charlie had become completely unhinged. He started the lecture, uttered a few words and fell completely silent. In what seemed like an eternity, Wommack stood there frozen in place, a look of panic on his face. The instructor did not offer a single word to get him started again. I breezed through my talk on "The sex life of a light bulb".

As our training was coming to an end, all the theories and class learning had to be tested in practical applications. And so, one day we went on a day-long exercise to determine how good we would be as leaders of men. The object was to go on patrol in an area occupied by the "enemy". We were faced with sudden encounters and we had to react. As we approached one area, we heard cries for help and loud moaning. Cautiously, we got nearer to where the noises came from. In a ditch, we located a badly "wounded enemy soldier". He was covered with fake blood. When he saw us, he pleaded for help and mercy. It took us a few moments to discuss what we should do. It was decided that we would carefully retreat and leave him alone. This turned out to be the wrong decision. The cadre who was supervising the exercise let us know that we had taken a deadly course of action. Apparently, we should have kept away from the area where the cries were coming from; now that we had revealed our presence to the "wounded enemy soldier" the only course of action we should have taken was to kill him right there so as not to have him warn others that our patrol was in the area. The whole idea was repulsive to me even if the logic was inescapable.

Further on, we came to a moat filled with dirty, muddy water. A single narrow wooden board connected one side to the other. The point was to go across to the other side. I was picked to cross the moat. This was not to my liking. After all, though we were in our combat *fatigues,* these were clean, starched and pressed with razor sharp creases. Our boots were polished and my pockets were filled with stuff. Later that evening, we were supposed to stand "Retreat" and eat in the mess-hall. I studied the lengthy obstacle to be crossed, gauged the narrow board that I'd have to conquer. It was just wide enough for one foot at a time. Perhaps if I leapt to the middle and took a mighty bounce I might have landed safely on the other bank. However, that seemed like a very long shot. I had visions of my landing squarely in the middle of the muck and ruining my uniform. After all, it was just an exercise and I decided to skip the whole thing, stating that we would just have to stay on this side of the moat. That did not endear me to the rest of our group. Somewhere in the back of my head, I could not help but feel that they picked me for the crossing for one single reason "Let the Jew see if he can swim in the mud". Paranoia perhaps, but a thought that seemed quite real to me at the time.

When we got back to the barracks, each of us was given a last written test. It consisted of a map of an island with a harbor at one end and three roads leading to it. The object was to get a detail of men to drive to the ships in order to be safely evacuated. The "enemy" controlled one road; the shortest road had blown bridges and was not passable, the third was clear. The ships had to be reached within one hour; unfortunately it was 60 miles to the harbor and there was a 35 mph speed limit on the only free road. What to do? Obviously the answer would have been the third road and damn the speed restriction. At least that would have been General Patton's choice. However, the army had not approved of Patton's headlong dashes in France in 1944-45. Were we to disregard the posted speed limit or respect regulation? Such was the conundrum that faced us; the daring logical way or the Army way? I chose the "Patton" way and was rewarded with a "well done".

The head Cadre picked me for the next exercise "Sniper and Ambush" where I would be concealed in a reinforced position in the middle of an intersection in a clearing in the woods. There I should wait until a squad of recruits appeared, "fire" at them and be killed or captured as they swarmed over my post. That did not sit well with me. I had no intention of getting "killed" even as a pretend exercise.

I remembered one of the first training films we had been shown in basic training; a soldier wearing a khaki T-shirt had a better chance of surviving during an attack than one wearing a white shirt. So, off came my fatigue top and my white T-shirt. With these and my helmet liner I quickly fashioned a dummy that I half-concealed at the forefront of my position. I then scampered up the side of the gully and lay in waiting among the trees and bushes of the woods.

When the squad appeared at the edge of the clearing, I fired a "blank" shot. Immediately, the group of recruits began to fire blanks at the dummy I had fashioned. At the same time, prompted by their instructors, they swarmed forward and poured into "my position". There was consternation when all they found were a couple of shirts, a stick and a helmet liner. This did not go well with the cadre who had expected to find me there, "dead" or alive. "All right, Rosenberg, where the hell are you?" bellowed the sergeant. Bare-chested I stood up, smiling and waving my rifle. "You're out of uniform, Rosenberg. Get the hell down here." The cadre was not amused but I was still "alive".

As Christmas 1951 neared, most of the non-essential personnel on Post were given leave so they could go home for a few days. Mostly, Jewish recruits were left and would have to spend the Holiday in Fort Lee. Some well-meaning citizens of Richmond called the Post Services to invite some soldiers to join them for Christmas dinner. All Fort Lee could muster were about 6 Jewish recruits who rang the bell at the entrance of a distinguished old mansion in an exclusive part of Richmond. The enormous dining room with dark wood paneling was lit up with silver candelabras and upholstered seats surrounded the large table. The main course was ham as was the tradition in that part of Virginia; not just a ham but the biggest clove-encrusted, glazed ham any of us had ever seen. For me, it had no significance that we would be eating pork but for the other Jews who had also been invited, it presented a religious conflict of major proportions. We did our best not to seem ingrates to our hosts but the evening was far less than a success.

All the while, Rosette and I continued to exchange sporadic letters. Long intervals between these letters were hard to bear. It seemed as if Rosette was lonely and I was yearning. Between answers I would agonize that perhaps I had been too bold in expressing my "respectful" passion and Rosette was always quick to scold me. This did not help matters. I did detect that there had been two or three serious disappointments in Rosette's love life and I kept on wishing that I might be shipped out to Europe upon graduation and would use my leave for visits to Brussels. After all, we had kissed a total of three times in the four years we had known each other, at Lever, at the Solvay sport club and on the day I had left for New York. That last kiss had been the only passionate one much to the surprise of my Mother, Rosette and mostly me! And of course, later that day Rosette had started a three year illicit affair with a Gustave Bauters, a married man who had a job at Lever Bros. thanks to his talent to play football (soccer) for the corporate team.

1952

Again, this couldn't happen again
This is that once in a lifetime
This is the thrill divine . . . .

"CORPORAL" ROSENBERG

In early March 1952, I ranked second in the graduating Leadership School (Guy Sillay came in first). The entire graduating class was promoted to Private First Class (PFC) and after a few days, shipped directly to Korea. I was to be the only exception, being reassigned as a cadre to train new recruits in Company "D". The Army promoted me to Platoon Sergeant of the Fourth Platoon. Since I was a fresh PFC, they quickly gave me the temporary grade of Corporal, better to impress the recruits I would be training. My pay would remain that of a PFC but the double stripes of a Corporal did look good on my uniform!

As new "Cadres" (rhymes with Padres" we were urged to sew sergeant's stripes on our fatigue sleeves and wash these in strong bleach, leaving them soaking for long hours. The uniform would be thoroughly bleached except for the portion that had been covered with the sergeant's stripes. After that, it was a simple matter of detaching the stripes that had been sewn and to sew the twin corporal stripes back on. The sleeves now showed only two stripes but one could see the marks of the five stripes that had not been bleached by the extreme washing. When new recruits would see me, they'd think that I had been a sergeant, misbehaved and been busted in grade from an SFC down to a Cpl. That would be the mark of a "bad ass" not to mess around with.

The Fourth Platoon, Company "D" consisted of a heteroclite mixture of recruits; mostly white. Germans, Italians, English and two or three Jews. There were also a few African-Americans (we called them "Blacks") and a couple of Puerto-Ricans. They were neither better nor worse than our group had been the previous summer of 1951. It was up to us to mold them into a cohesive group and prepare them to go and fight in Korea. With a few exceptions this was a good bunch of recruits, eager to please me and giving me the least trouble.

Now and then, the discipline would slacken, especially when it was time to fall in formation from the barracks. The time allotted was 30 seconds. From time to time, the 30 seconds would stretch into several minutes before the last stragglers would deign to join the rest of the platoon. I would then send everyone back to the barracks and command to get back in formation with a specific object: a can of foot powder, a toothbrush or a hand towel. This ensured that they would not simply huddle next to the door but had to get to their bunk to retrieve the specific item. Only the stragglers were exempt from having to get back to their bunk; they would stay by me. This would not endear them to the rest of the platoon. After three or four round-trips at breakneck speed, they got the idea and the problem would be solved for a few days when the entire exercise would have to be repeated. Little by little I found myself being more of a disciplinarian, albeit not a "prick".

After a couple of weeks, some of the men complained that one of the recruits did not have any inkling of personal hygiene. As a matter of fact he had not taken a shower since he had arrived in Company D. It was probable that he had not had a shower since he first got inducted in the Army. This was a gentle giant of a man, peaceful, shy, and silent. But he had absolutely no knowledge of cleanliness. His name has been lost to me but he was a hillbilly from Appalachia. I guess he was deeply religious and could not bring himself to get undressed in front of other men.

One night, near midnight, I summoned him to me. I marched him to the showers. I was in my shorts and ordered him to get completely undressed. Not only had he not showered in weeks but he seemed to have no notion on how to use toilet paper after relieving himself. I commanded him to grab a bar of soap and to use it as I did on every part of his body. Then I grabbed a long-handled toilet scouring brush and proceeded to wash his ass as he bent down. I threatened that I would repeat the entire procedure if I ever got another complaint but this time it would be in the presence of the entire platoon. He got dressed and went back to his bunk. He never uttered a word. There never was another incident but it disturbed me to have violated the privacy of this "poor soul".

And then, there was private Colon, from Porto Rico. He was the complete 8-Ball. Always in trouble, late, without a complete uniform, unkempt, unwilling or unable to understand an English command. Colon delighted in trying to make me look like an idiot in front of the platoon. I remembered the sergeant in "All Quiet on the Western Front" who sadistically drilled his entire squad in the mud, over and over again. So I thought that a little extra training would do some good. Late one evening I ordered Colon to put on his helmet liner, full uniform and grab his M1 rifle. I marched him out to the field and drilled him until he could barely stand. Forward march, to the rear, by the left flank, by the right flank, to the rear, forward march, time and time again. For variety, there was the manual of arms: right shoulder, left shoulder, port arms, inspection arms! Colon took it all, all that I could dish out. There was a portion of the field that had been flooded and was now covered with dark mud. I maneuvered Colon to the muddiest section of the field and ordered him to march through it: forward, to the rear, to the rear, to the rear and so ad infinitum. The more he turned about, the deeper he sank in the mud. By now I was taking a sadistic delight in the punishment I was inflicting on Colon.

Suddenly, he made a last turn and stopped, facing me, boots deep in the muck with his rifle on his right shoulder at a funny angle. He looked at me and said:

"Wait a minute, Corporal Rosenberg. Am I not a man, a human being? Why do you treat me like this? Am I not a man?"

It took me by surprise. I was stunned.

There, in front of him stood the sadistic German Sergeant of the book and movie of "All Quiet on the Western Front"! And that German had taken the sadistic pleasure of abusing and torturing this "Man" simply because it was allowed by the authority of a couple of stripes on the sleeves of the uniform. And as we stood there, just a few feet apart, it struck me that I had become that German cadre and had allowed the stripes and the uniform to morph me into a mindless martinet.

The night had become very still and quiet. I heard my voice say "Private Colon, you are right. You are a man and a human being. Tell you what we are going to do. I will apologize to you and you will apologize to me. From this day on, I will treat you with all the respect you deserve as a man and you will straighten out and become a good soldier. Now go in the barracks and clean up".

There never arose another incident with Colon and he became a good recruit. I guess I taught him to be responsible. By resetting my priorities he taught me a greater lesson to carry through the balance of my life. On the last day of basic training for the men of Company D, one of my recruits gave me his photo dedicated "*To Corporal Rosenberg, the best Cadre the Army has to offer*". I really never knew if he was being honest or sarcastic.

How does one explain the sudden attraction between two strangers? The pretty wife of one of my recruits found Corporal Rosenberg much to her liking and Rudy fell in love with Gloria-Anne with what the French call "*Un coup de foudre*" love at first sight. I remember how attractive she was with auburn curly hair and her flowing summer dress that espoused the shapes of her lovely, young body. There was such mutual hunger between us and yet the entire affair was to be brief and unconsummated. Gloria-Anne was staying off post but she would drive to Fort Lee to be closer to her husband, my recruit. As far as I can remember, we met several times in the parking lot where she'd leave her car. We had so much to talk about; it was intoxicating. I was lonely without news from Rosette and after the loss of Helene. Gloria might have been in the first letdown after a hasty marriage. We needed each other. One afternoon, we share a lovely, tender kiss next to her car.

Two days later I was summoned to the Battalion Headquarters where I was confronted by my Commanding Officer, Captain Jacoby and the battalion commander whose name I never knew.

Apparently Gloria-Anne's husband had become aware of the "affair" and had lodged a complaint with Jacoby. To me, a product of a loose childhood, it was a tempest in a teapot over a single kiss in a parking area. To the US Army it was a serious offense by a superior in a position of command over a subordinate i.e. a recruit under my charge. Since the recruit was a private and I was really only a private first class, I could not see what the fuss was all about. I was read the riot-act and told without subtlety that any continuation of our liaison would be punishable by a Court-Martial. I never saw Gloria-Anne again and the incident was dropped.

I must say that I was not fond of Capt. Fred Jacoby. The Cadre mostly marched along with the recruits whenever we'd have field exercises that involved long treks along miles of dry roads in the Virginia summer heat. Mostly the difference was that the recruits marched under the weight of the M1 rifle while the Cadre carried a swagger stick. Captain Jacoby drove a big Packard automobile along the road, goading the sweating recruits and urging them on from the open window of the car. He'd admonish the Cadre to prod the recruits to better performance and stricter discipline. He'd then speed to the front of the column spraying dust over the weary foot soldiers. At the scheduled rest areas, when it was chow time, Capt. Jacoby and officers would regularly buck the line and ate before all the recruits had been fed, a violation of accepted practice in the field.

Sergeant First Class SFC Beasley would regularly comment on my size 12 boots: "Three feet make a yard, Rosie but three of them feet make a railroad yard!" He and SFC Keator were very close and teased me continually. Keator was blond, tall and muscular. With a ready smile and laughing eyes he looked like a Nazi officer in an American uniform. The trouble was that he behaved like one also, at least towards me. Somehow he had figured out that I was a Jew and that I had spent some rough years under the German occupation of Belgium. He would greet me with the Hitler salute, say "Heil" and called me Adolf. There was not a day when he did not make some anti-Semitic remark aimed in my direction. I did not think he was a Jew hater but simply that he was unaware of how hurtful and objectionable his remarks were to me. Keator's girlfriend was a WAC cadre and they had accepted me in their circle. One of our pastimes was to stand at the four corners of the parade field and hurl commands at each other to test who could shout the loudest and still be understood. As I wrote earlier, we were not allowed to "Jody" because of the presence of so many women on post (Fort Lee was also the WAC training center). Yet these WACs and their female instructors could and did out-curse us with ease. There were rumors that most of the WAC's were lesbians at best but I never had the opportunity to confirm or debunk that theory.

With the end of May 1952 came the news that Mother and Ruth had finally gotten their visa for the USA and I prepared for their arrival. Frieda, 50, was ready to turn a new page and looked upon her arrival to the States with cautious anticipation. Ruth, almost 24, had less optimism at finding a new life in America. In Belgium she had many friends and had always found employment easy to find. Now she looked upon this new adventure with some trepidation and was uncertain of what would welcome her in New York. It had taken a lot of persuasion by me to have her take the big leap across the Atlantic. Father, of course was not coming. He had gotten himself entangled with Gerty* and felt duty bound to support her now that she was in ill health. Frieda had also mocked him by suggesting that the only job open to him would be as a truck driver. At 50, he felt unsure at contemplating learning a new trade, a new language and to seek a new life in America.

Gerty (Gertrude) Bauer had been Hilaire's girlfriend since shortly after the end of the war. A woman of great beauty, she had become an alcoholic. They made a pact that if Gerty gave up drinking, Hilaire would give up gambling. To the best of my knowledge they both succeeded.

FRIEDA AND RUTH IN AMERICA

[What follows in italics was related to me both verbally and in writing by my sister Ruth when I asked her to fill in some blanks in my memoirs. It was checked for accuracy and permission to use]

{Mother and Ruth were supposed to leave Europe on the 12th of June 1952 but the departure of the ship was delayed till the 14th. They took the train from Brussels to Rotterdam on the morning of June 14th. In the afternoon they boarded the SS Rijndam of the Holland-America Line. Ruth cried all the way to Rotterdam, having left her boyfriend François that morning in Brussels. Ruth did not really want to go to America but when she had asked him if they would marry, he said "No!" and that she would never leave him. Ruth finally gave in to Mother and agreed to leave for America.

The ship took 10 sailing days to reach Hoboken, NJ. It stopped at LeHavre, France, Southampton UK and then Halifax, Nova Scotia. Although many passengers went ashore in Halifax, Mother and Ruth were not allowed to disembark as they only had a visa for the U.S. and were "stateless". On the ship they only had an indoor cabin without any porthole or daylight and Ruth hated it. It was small but acceptable.

Ruth made some friends on board including Jaap, the ship's Fourth Officer. Very intellectual, Jewish, from Holland, good photographer who took that one picture of her with her hair tied back (it appeared in And Somehow We Survive, page 104). He fell "in love". Jaap would see Ruth every time the SS Rijndam docked in the U.S. He wanted to marry Ruth but the thought of living in Holland turned her off.

Eric F., Swiss, was on his way to Puerto Rico together with several other Swiss friends on board. They were all going to open a "Swiss Chalet" hotel/restaurant. He also fell "in love". Ruth could not warm up to him because she had to speak with him in German and that went "against the grain". Eric was very handsome-and very blond. He also wanted to marry her.

It was strange that Ruth had left behind the man who did not want to marry her and on the ship she had received two proposals of marriage that she did not want and had turned down. "Of course, it did a lot for her ego"!

On the early morning of June 24th, 1952 Frieda and Ruth arrived in the port of New York. They had hoped to see the Statue of Liberty but by the time they woke up (early) the ship was already in Hoboken. Ruth would have to wait till she took the Staten Island ferry with Jaap to see the statue.

When Mother and Ruth arrived in Hoboken, the stevedores were on strike and no one was allowed to get near the ship to unload the luggage. However, I had arrived from Virginia and was wearing my uniform and we were allowed to back up our taxi all the way to the ship. Mother felt that there was palpable resentment from the other passengers that these immigrants were given special privileges to unload their belongings right into a taxi ahead of everybody else.

Mother had packed her meager possessions into a very large wooden crate and the customs officer wanted to know what the crate contained. As the crate was pried open, Mother carried on a constant conversation with the officer—she in German—he, obviously Jewish, in Yiddish. From the crate emerged Mother's large white eiderdown comforter. The officer searched among the assorted junk Frieda had brought along and exclaimed "All you have is *shmattes*!" (The Yiddish word for rags). "*Ya, replied Frieda, besser ein Stein zu haben!*" Better to have one diamond! With that word, the customs officer interest was revived. You have diamonds? He then proceeded to search and inspect the wooden crate all over again but for naught. I had to remind Mother, in French, that she should cool it.

As we finally got underway, driving along the waterfront towards the Holland Tunnel, we passed by the depressed area around Hoboken. Gutted and burned buildings lined up the road the taxi was following. Sitting in the back of the car, Frieda eyed the destruction, turned to me and with an understanding nod, she opined "Bombardments!" I did not bother to correct her as I did not want to tell her that what she was seeing was only the dilapidated area around the New Jersey waterfront.

Paul and Lilli had arranged for Frieda and Ruth to stay in an apartment on Union Street in Brooklyn owned by "Hilda" a big Jewish woman who could not understand that Ruth spoke no Yiddish. Hilda used to dance by herself in the middle of her living room, to a tune that was very popular at the time. All that fat jiggling! It was extremely hot, probably near 100 degrees in those days and Mother and Ruth weren't used to that. At night they would lie on the bed and eventually, the heat and humidity would knock them out.

The day after she arrived, Ruth called Ed Young, one of Pan American Airways' top engineers, who had returned to the US and he took her somewhere in Queens to have Southern Fried Chicken; she remembered it well, it was very good. Ed said he got her a job with Pan American to start two days later in Long Island City. So Ruth got Lilli and Paul to explain the subway system and off she went to work two days later.

Ruth was wearing a yellow dress, pretty and neatly pressed and at one of the subway stations (Grand Central," the shuttle") people came streaming out of the train and more went in and she was pushed between train and platform, one leg dangling down, her dress ruined. Of course, she was not used to that kind of pushing and shoving. It left Ruth very weary and leery of the spaces between the trains and platforms and very, very careful.

The new job consisted of reading invoices and making annotations. A few days later, Ruth called Ed Young and told him that was not a job for her. She hated it. Ed asked her to be patient and that he would find her something else, but then either he did not pursue it or he had to leave for Europe. Ed and Ruth were always good friends although he tried to have sex but in those days there was no Viagra and so they remained friends. So Ruth quit the job at Pan Am.

Then Ruth went to an employment agency and they got her a job with Gallard—Schlesinger, on Liberty Street around Wall Street, a company that specialized in Chemicals and Wool grease. Ruth was hired as Schlesinger's French/German/English secretary. Ruth had no problem taking dictation in all three languages and transcribed without any difficulty (even the German). Ruth's English was pretty good when she emigrated, thanks to all the G.I.'s we had known in Belgium and Ruth's innate facility for languages. She started there at $60—per week. Ruth remembered Aunt Lilli being kind of upset because, after all the years of working as a top nurse, she still made less than that.

In the meantime, after a couple of weeks at Hilda's, Mother and Ruth looked for an other apartment. Mother found one at 269 Prospect Place in Brooklyn, not too far from the subway. It was a one room apartment on the third floor with a bathroom and tiny kitchen with the usual fire escape outside overlooking a bunch of small backyards. They had a bed, a "trundle" bed that folded into a sofa and opened up into two beds at night. Not much privacy but acceptable.

One of the first thing they did was buy a TV, watched a lot of "I Love Lucy" and news. Thus, Mother learned English from watching the "tube".

Ruth worked at Gallard-Schlesinger for almost three years. All five girls in the office made the same money and one day Mr Hans Schlesinger told Ruth that because she was doing such a good job, he was going to give her $5 more a week but could not tell the other girls. So, every Friday, he would slip her the $5 bill "under the table". Sometimes he would forget and Ruth couldn't ask.

One of the other girls had a big (typical) Jewish wedding and would not invite Ruth because "Ruth didn't have a boyfriend and wouldn't want to attend the reception alone, would she?" Her friend Penny R., the Spanish/English secretary told her that "They just did not want this French girl to be at the wedding and take away everyone's boyfriend". "Can you imagine?" as Mother would have said. Ruth was really hurt.

After G.S. moved to Long Island City, Ruth continued to work for them even though the subway trip was long and convoluted. Ruth read a lot. Sometimes there were problems with the employees and Ruth would always speak up on their behalf. "Just off the boat and already difficult!" Schlesinger would say or something like that. Then one day, Ed Gallard wanted to drive to the city and insisted that Ruth go with him because "he did not want to have to park the car in the City". Hans Schlesinger got upset and told Ed to take his own secretary but Gallard won the argument. On the way Gallard told Ruth that they were very similar and then made advances that Ruth resisted. They had a ferocious argument. A few days later, Hans and Ed decided that it would be better for all if Ruth were to leave the company. So, Ruth did. Today, Ruth would sue the hell out of them, but then times were very different.

Meanwhile, Mother had found a job as a sewing machine operator, union, and making about $40 a week. She had met some guy who became her boyfriend. His name has been forgotten. We think he was a truck driver. He used to come to their one room apartment and sometimes spend the night. Ruth would then have to sleep in the tub. It was not the most comfortable bedding! Mother took a few trips with him. Then, Ruth would have the run of the apartment and it was a blessing.

Mother used to tell me about that boyfriend. They would drive to New Jersey and south towards Florida and he seldom had money on him. He would then hit on Frieda. She balked and told him that she had had one pimp in her life (René DeLange) and that one was enough. She used to say that he was "a nice little Italian fellow" but he never had any money. One day he brought her a small snapshot of himself and he hoped she would find a suitable frame to save his picture. "You go into the shoebox with all the others" she replied.

The time had come for me to be re-assigned for overseas duty and with the graduation of the recruits of Company D; I was sent packing to my new assignment. Losing my "Acting Corporal" double stripes was a blow to my ego and self esteem. At least the demotion was not all the way down to Private (PVT) but to Private First Class (PFC) rank that I had been granted upon graduation from Leadership School. Since I had been parading around Fort Lee with my Corporal stripes for six months, I still kept the double stripes for a couple of weeks but was finally persuaded to take them off and sew on the single stripe of my new lower rank.

Co. N, the dreaded "eight ball" holding company would be my new home for a few weeks until the powers in Washington would decide where it would be best to place me. My morale in this company of misfits dropped markedly and so did my attention to my appearance. Haircut, shoe shine and fit of my uniform left something to be desired. I managed to get a few days leave during which I took a trip to New York. When I told Aunt Lilli that I would probably be shipped overseas, she cautioned me not to get married while I'd be abroad.

A visit to the White Plains home of Leo Wolleman yielded about the same results. Much to the dismay of Aunt Lilli, I had been invited to join a small garden party on the Wolleman estate. Daughter Anna had friendly words for me and we hit it off but without any sentimentality. It was very friendly. Walter, the son, remarked that my appearance was somewhat less sharp than during my previous visit. I remember explaining that I was presently in a holding unit where I would stay until I was reassigned to my next outfit for duty overseas. When I left that evening, the entire Wolleman clan cautioned me against getting involved with a girl overseas and that I still should be single upon my return.

On my way home I mulled over their advice. Obviously they wanted me to return as a likely suitor for Anna. My Father would have called that "falling with your ass in butter". At the time I still had serious qualms about being a Jew and for me the Wolleman family was much too religious. In retrospect, Hilaire had refused to marry Liliane in Charleroi because she had not been Jewish and he did not want to break the tradition. Now it was my turn and I did not want to marry Anna because her family was a return to the Jewish faith. Besides, even as Anna was quite attractive, the fear that an eventual baby might turn out to look like Leo Wolleman was enough to dissuade me from matrimony. So, in the final analysis, both my Father Hilaire and I had decided to forego money and security for future romance. We had both been in our early twenties and still unwise. We both chose "the birds in the bush instead of the sure one in the hand" although for completely opposite reasons.

627ᵗʰ QM REFRIGERATION COMPANY

In late July 1952, I was finally assigned to the 627ᵗʰ QM Refrig. Co, a newly formed army unit now scheduled for service in Europe. Actually, the 627ᵗʰ had been commissioned in the early months of WWII and had served in the Pacific campaigns until the end of the war. After the war, as the army got back to a peacetime mode, the 627ᵗʰ had been disbanded. Now, with the double threat of the Cold War and the "Korean Police Action" it was being re-commissioned. The C.O, Captain Petersen and First Lt. Smith had culled through the files of available MOS in search for a suitable soldier to complement the roster of the 627ᵗʰ. It would have made sense for them to pick me for my knowledge of French, German and Dutch that appeared on my initial form when I had first enlisted. After all, the outfit was due to be stationed in Germany. However, the Army did not reason in that logical way. I had described that I knew how to draw and to paint. I had remembered that I had drawn cartoons while I had been hidden and had written that down as "Special talent". From there to a talent as a painter was a small step that I leaped boldly. And so, Capt. Petersen had selected me to join his 627ᵗʰ because they needed a painter.

The 627ᵗʰ had only one opening in their roster and that was for the C.O.'s driver. Thus I joined the roster as Capt. Petersen's driver. I had never driven a car, let alone an army Jeep. I had no civilian driver's license and thus could not obtain the required U.S Army license. It was simple army logic. Since I could not drive, I was placed in the orderly room as a clerk typist. Sanchez, the real company clerk was usually too hung-over to type the morning report and would beg me to type the report for him. His face was craggy, eyes hollow from lack of sleep and ugly teeth misaligned in his mouth made it look like the Siegfried Line after an Allied bombing. "Rosie" He would plead with his Mexican accent "Can you type the Morning Report, I can't see the keyboard!" Thus I settled in the position of Company Clerk and everyone was happy except Capt Petersen who still needed a driver.

The 627ᵗʰ had an assortment of regular army men (R.A's) that had been culled from other outfits around Fort Lee Va. Most were auto and truck mechanics who lived off-post with an array of wives or girlfriends. At least, they were sure to show up for pay-day once a month. The rest of the time, they were missing or nursing hangovers. The 627ᵗʰ, newly formed, had to pass a Proficiency Test to demonstrate its capability for overseas service. Every other week, the outfit was scheduled for a 36 hour maneuver to A.P.Hill, an army wooded area some distance from Fort Lee. This was over two days and one night of driving, setting up tents and headquarters in the woods and making certain that our refrigerated tractor and trailers would function properly under war conditions. It soon became apparent that most of our R.A.'s had no interest in passing the test. They much preferred living the good life in and around Fort Lee and routinely sabotaged the maneuvers. There were always several trailers that drove on the road with locked emergency brakes that caught on fire somewhere on the highway. The Umpires made notes of these deficiencies and would routinely "gig" the outfit, causing it to flunk its proficiency test once again.

I soon discovered the reason the C.O. had requested that I'd be assigned to the 627ᵗʰ. We'd always spend one full night in the unlit woods of A.P.Hill. During the day, long, narrow latrines had to be dug into the moist, dark and slippery soil of the woods. It was my job to prepare slabs of wooden boards and using fluorescent paint, write "LATRINES" boldly with a very visible arrow so it could be found in the middle of the night. Next, I had to dip about 20 sticks in a bucket of fluorescent white paint and plant these in strategic places to mark the path to the newly dug latrines so the GI's and the officers could find their way in the middle of the night. After all, an army does not only travel on its stomach! And that was why Capt. Petersen needed an artist-painter and the reason I was plucked from Company N to an outfit on its way to Europe instead of being sent on the next ship sailing for Korea. That simple action was to have an enormous effect on my life and change it forever.

In September 1952, about a dozen new drivers and refrigeration mechanics were assigned to the 627ᵗʰ. These were draftees in their early 20's. To get them into the trucks, they needed driving licenses. Of course, they all had civilian licenses but were not allowed to get behind the wheel without valid military permits. Captain Petersen made an urgent call to Battalion HQ. It was Friday afternoon and the new men needed to be available for Monday so the full company could field its complete roster of trucks for the next A.P.Hill exercise.

Too bad, the Battalion clerk was away on a three day pass and would not return until late Monday! There was no one else at Battalion HQ who could perform the required duty. Petersen turned a pained look my way "Rosie, can you go to Battalion and type out Army licenses for these guys?" With that he handed me a fistful of civilian licenses and I got a lift to Headquarters.

And so, I typed out army licenses for Testa, Xides, Sotelo and another dozen newly arrived draftees and while I was at it, I typed myself a license to drive every vehicle from Jeep to two-and-a-half ton truck.

Then, I learned to drive a Jeep. From that day onward, I was officially the Captain's driver although I kept up with my duties as "substitute" company clerk as Sanchez continued to be "high" most of the time. My Jeep did not have a working speedometer and Captain Petersen asked me if I could tell when I was driving at 25 mph and at 35 mph. I did not have a clue. I had never driven and my mind was still working in terms of kilometers per hour. Petersen told me to never mind "Just gauge your speed and never, but never go slower than the speed limit!" He began to call me "Barney Oldfield" and when he felt I was going too slow he'd ask me if I wanted him to get off and walk.

I idolized Petersen. His demeanor was calm and he exuded strength. He was for me the Father figure that had always been lacking in my life. Over the coming months we came to appreciate each other, the Lutheran Norwegian and the little Jewish survivor. He would often ask my opinion on matters that would normally not concern the enlisted men. Petersen seemed genuinely impressed by what he perceived as my intelligence. He was a fine man and I considered it a privilege when he'd call me "Rosie" and when he'd tease me about driving too slow.

As I was driving my Jeep along Fort Lee, I spotted my friend "Liège" jauntily walking near the PX where she was working. I had not seen her in a few months and I greeted her with a toot of my horn and I yelled out to her "Hey Liège!" She turned, recognized me and waved back at me. Unfortunately, some officer had seen and heard the encounter. I was again called on the carpet for having "insulted" a female civilian on post.

Once again, I found myself in a large room filled with officers and had to defend myself. My only defense was that I came from Belgium, the Walloon part of Belgium and that I considered the young lady as a friend and that we shared a bit of homesickness. It had been a friendly gesture, nothing more.

I do not recall that "Liège" was at that inquiry. She might have given some earlier testimony. Captain Petersen put in a good word for me, speaking in glowing terms about my character and honesty. There was a brief discussion during which I was excused from the room. All charges were dropped. I never saw Liège again. It made me wonder again about the "Puritanism" of the U.S.Army; but my belief in Captain Petersen got another boost.

"Landsman" rang in my ears and I felt a hand slapping me in the back. It was one of the new "reefer" mechanics, Mayo Sotelo from El Paso Texas. He had found me, the Jew with the "P" on my dog tags. How could he have guessed that I was a Jew? I did not want to be a Jew. Mayo repeated "Landsman!"

I refused his extended hand. I did not want to be a Jew, my dog tags showed me to be a Protestant. Mayo seemed puzzled. You're my Landsman; I am a Jew, so are you! I snarled back at him, defensibly, "I am not a Jew, you are a Jew!" For a long time I did not want to talk to Mayo, I would run away from him. He would later become one of my best friends. His real name was Ishmael Sotel. When he got drafted they thought he was Hispanic and had placed an extra "o" at the end of his name. He was now Mayo Sotelo and it would have been too much trouble for the Army to correct the error. And so, Mayo Sotel would serve his two years duty as Mayo Sotelo.

Cpl James J.Haley had been absent without leave for over a week when he showed up in the orderly room. A tall, heavy Irishman he stopped in front of me at my desk and announced that he was reporting for duty. I had been carrying him AWOL for over a week and I expressed my surprise to see him. That was the first time I had seen him since joining the 627th. "Oh, you are James Haley!" I exclaimed with a smile. Apparently he did not like my smile, judging it to be sarcastic. "I wanted to smash your face!" He was to tell me much later after we had become fast friends.

Private McNamara was absent three months in a row. He would come back on the last day of each month to report for pay. Had he failed to do so, he could have been charged with desertion but he was very careful to show up on the thirtieth day so that the worst offense he could be charged with was being AWOL. I had gotten so that I could type his name on the morning report with my eyes closed. On pay day, Capt. Petersen would dole out each man's pay. McNamara would appear and salute "Pvt. McNamara reporting for pay, Sir!" Petersen would give him a quizzical look, hand him his pay envelope and McNamara would turn around and vanish for another 30 days. As far as I knew, no disciplinary action was ever taken against him. Like so many of the other RA's both his uniform and sobriety were questionable.

The evening before payday and on payday, poker games would break out in the recreation room and the dormitories. Since most of my money was allocated for direct payment to my Mother, my actual cash allowance was very shabby. It became essential for me to recapture some funds and twice a month I'd sit at one of the tables and play poker, mostly 7 card draw. Actually, it wasn't really gambling, more like a regular income. Somehow, even though I had never gambled before

I was able to take away a good amount of winnings each time. Haley would lose regularly and I'd win back most of his losses. Since Haley smoked and loved to drink beer and whiskey I'd have to win enough to rescue him for the month that would follow. I guess the secret of my winnings was to fold very early when the cards in my hands did not look as if they had come from the same deck. However, whenever Corporals Parendo and Smalley appeared at our poker table, I had to be extremely cautious as I believed they were playing in concert, raising the bids in turn and eventually chasing everyone else from the biddings. I had the feeling that later on, they'd share the winnings between the two of them. I would stay in only if the cards I had were very solid.

One of the draftees from Ohio had a Ford Four-door and on Saturdays after noon, he would organize a trip to New York City for a reasonable fee. If one of us had KP duty on that week-end, we'd pay a fee to Julio Colon from Puerto Rico to pull our KP duty. Everett, the chief cook did not mind as Colon worked his tail off in the kitchen while the rest of us would have been goof-offs at best. Six of us would then pile in the Ford and drive to New York. In those days there were no tunnels and highways to cut through Baltimore and it took three hours just to navigate the big horseshoe of streets that circled the harbor. It was my task to sit near "Ohio" and to keep him awake with my tales and stories during the eleven hours that it took us to get to Times Square where we'd spread out to various parts of the city. For my part, I'd jump on the IRT subway to Brooklyn to visit my Mother and Ruth and to crash on one of their beds.

Early the following Sunday, it was goodbye time and I had to rush back to Times Square where the Ford was awaiting its cargo to return to Fort Lee before Sunday night. Mother would insist that I should have some breakfast and I'd regularly refuse as I did not have the time. On one occasion, she trust a full glass of tomato juice at me, it fell and the entire glass spilled all over my khaki uniform. I was angry and mortified and Mother was so embarrassed as she tried to wipe off the tomato juice with a wet towel.

We lost one of our draftees to a car crash as he was trying to spend one more weekend home in Pennsylvania. To my knowledge, he would be the only death our unit would suffer while I was associated with the 627th.

As for me, despite my denials, despite the "P" stamped on my dog tags, I continued to be tormented by a few members of my unit. It was not subtle. Threats of violence and daily insults pursued me constantly. There were mostly three guys who were openly anti-Semitic and who followed me with verbal slights and gestures that left no doubt that they'd do me harm if they had the chance. Morley was the most persistent; the other two had to be high on beer before they became truly abusive. As we were now ready to leave Fort Lee, Va. and to board a ship for Germany, I cornered Morley in the barracks and let him know that if he ever came close enough to me so I could reach him, I would kick him so hard he would not be able to walk again for months. I told him that this was the only warning he would ever receive. If he ever came close to me, I'd strike him viciously, in ranks, latrines, chow line or if he ever came close to me again even in the street. I told him that even on shipboard he would not be safe and that I'd throw him overboard if he came close enough for me to reach him. He began to avoid me. I had cowed him!

In late November 1952, the 627th moved as a unit to Camp Kilmer, N.J. with all its materiel, trucks, trailers, weapons, mobile kitchen etc. We had even been issued the new olive overcoats that were now replacing the "horse blanket" that had been the staple of the Doughboys and GI's since the First World War. Since we shipped out as a unit, we were allowed to keep our new coats and would be the first company to wear it in Germany.

Time was granted to those soldiers who lived in the Metropolitan New York area to say goodbye to their loved ones. Thanksgiving 1952, a new tradition for us, was spent with Mother and Ruth and we separated again having been together for a mere six months. In early August Rosette had written *"With the departure of Mother and Ruth from Belgium, our last chance to ever see each other ever again had vanished"*. I was able to post a short note to Rosette just before the ship left the dock; in it I explained that we should arrive in Bremerhaven during the first half of December and that we might have leave for Christmas or New Year and that it might be possible to travel to Brussels. I would try to see her during those holidays. I would be so proud to have her at my arm as we'd walk in the streets of Brussels. Would she allow herself to be seen with me in my American uniform? It would be Lever Bros. who would be flabbergasted!

On November 28th, we made the final preparations to board the USNS General Sturgis to Bremerhaven. Morley approached me with an apprehensive smile and extended a hand to me. "Rosenberg, why not let bygones be bygones? Can we not be friends?" We shook hands. Friendship never did develop between us but Morley never threatened me again nor did he hurl any more slurs at me.

The Sturgis had been moored next to the USNS General Patch a large ship that dwarfed our Liberty ship. The weather was spoiling as we slid out of our pier and I regretted that we were not on the Patch. Slightly more than three years after my arrival in the USA I was returning to Europe, going to Germany in an American uniform. A new adventure was beginning.

RETURN TO EUROPE

Just a couple of days out of the Port of New York, we hit the fringes of a huge weather disturbance in the Atlantic that soon developed into a full fledged Hurricane. Soon there were many soldiers throwing up and lining up to use the "Heads" (navy terms for bathrooms or latrines). The sea was so rough that nobody wanted to risk going on deck, near the edge railings, to throw up. Everybody was converging to the head to vomit.

Eating became a problem. Long lines would form in the hallway leading to the mess hall and people got sick just waiting to inch forward in the chow line. I would join the long queue, my head empty and dizzy. The floor was bringing you up and then down again as the ship was tossed by the power of the hurricane. Holding on to the railings was of little use as the roll of the vessel would rip the rails from your hands. By the time I got near to the galley's opening, I was so sick that I could not go forward another step and I had to run down to the nearest head to throw up.

It had been a few days since I had been able to swallow any solid food and I was desperate for sustenance. I decided to skip the chow line and to enter by way of the galley thus avoiding the long wait outside of the mess. I ran smack into an Army Captain who wanted to know where I was headed for. I explained that I could not wait in line as my stomach wanted to heave and I would never make it. I pleaded, argued and tried to mollify the Captain. He lost patience with me and we got into a heated argument. Finally he broke up the discussion and told me he was going to press charges against me for failing to follow his orders. "What is your name, Soldier? I thought quickly, realizing that my name would be mud if he knew who I was. Quickly, I gave him the first name that came to my reeling mind. "Coakley!" I replied. This was a ship crowded with nearly two thousand men. The chances of running into him again on this crossing were very remote. Perhaps he might have remembered Coakley but if he did find him "again" Coakley would not look anything like me and the matter would have stayed there. I never did see him again during the crossing. In those days, military personnel did not have to carry a name tag over the chest pocket of their garments and I took advantage of that loophole to throw the Captain off my scent. Today, with every member of the Armed Forces tagged and branded, I cannot help but think that I may have been instrumental in spreading the need for these name tags. I still do not like the practice. With the prejudices that abound especially in the military, it invites problems to be branded Ramirez, Piscatelli, Rosenberg, or any name that can give an immediate clue to your ethnic background.

I would not remember the ship's arrival in Bremerhaven or getting off on German soil or our trip to Hanau about 10 miles east of Frankfurt. I had lost 20 pounds on board the Sturgis and had become completely dehydrated. Somehow, in the cold wet weather of northern Germany I had caught a cold that developed into a full bronchitis. When I opened my eyes, it was to the loveliest blond apparition I had ever seen. The light in back of her shone like a halo and for a moment I thought I had died and been transported directly to heaven. I would stay in the hospital for several days, recouping and regaining my strength. I just had time to write to Rosette to let her know that I had landed in Germany and was now about 200 miles from Brussels. I felt confident that I'd be able to get a three day pass around Christmas that would enable me to spend a couple of days in Brussels and that I hoped to see her to wish her a happy holiday. The rest of my time would be spent seeing my Father, Bob and Maurice as well as friends of Frieda and Ruth as promised. I also wrote Rosette that if she had other plans I would understand and might see her 6 months later when I might have a full two weeks furlough.

Meanwhile, the hurricane that had plagued us at sea had slammed into Holland, breeched many dikes and flooded entire regions with ocean salt water threatening the future crops of The Netherlands. There were requests for US Army volunteers to go and provide assistance to the Dutch government. Payment in the guise of furloughs would be their reward. I was miffed that I could not join in their efforts as I was confined to my hospital bed. Holland was very close to Brussels and I would have loved to go AWOL for a few days and go visit Rosette.

Then, Captain Petersen came to see me in the hospital. "Rosie, how would you like to have 10 days' furlough so you can spend Christmas and New Year at home in Brussels?" Would I? Yes! 'Well, get well, get out of this hospital and we will arrange it'

A couple of days later, I was out of the hospital and getting ready to take the train to Brussels. I had managed to notify Rosette, Father, Bob and Maurice. Rosette was willing to see me but it could only be on the day after Christmas as she was committed on Christmas Eve and Christmas day.

There would be little recollection of my meetings with Father, Bob or Maurice. All my focus was on the meeting with Rosette.

By then, I had been to bed with only two women, Gilberte and flat-chested Olivia in Richmond Va. Helene and I had had much passion but our affair had never been consummated as I kept seeing her as the wedding doll that one finds wrapped in cellophane on top of a wedding cake. I thought that women only reacted to the desires of men, not aware that women had their own sexual needs and drives. And so, I worried about "Up the flag", when a young man got aroused and had a hard-on. That was something to be embarrassed by and should never be discovered by his date. How foolish I was! Anyway, it was crucial that Rosette should never discover that I would be sexually aroused the next time I'd be with her and certainly not when we'd kiss with any degree of passion. So, I decided that I would disarm my penis with a judicious unloading just prior to my trip to Brussels. I took the train to Frankfurt and found myself a prostitute. She must have been 50, was nice and not at all a hardened professional, the type you'd see portrayed in movies and books. We agreed on a price and she guided me to a room with a cold water sink and a high table with a straw mattress on it. She undressed me and washed me with soap and her hands. It was pleasurable. She dried me with a hand towel, and then she got undressed. She had a condom that she draped over my cock that had become hard just from her gentle soaping. I was lying on the mattress and she climbed on the table and proceeded to get on top of me. Carefully she spread the lips of her vagina and descended on my hard member. I watched as my cock disappeared inside her and I came! Just like that, no passion, not even a rubbing, no stroking, nothing! I guess I was primed and young and healthy. She began to cry softly. "Now you are going to beat me up" She wailed.

I put my hand on her cheeks, gave her a small kiss and reassured her that there would be nothing brutal. I paid her and tried again to console her. I felt so bad for her. All the while I could not help but think of my Mother and all the boyfriends she must have known in her life

Anyway, I was now unloaded and relieved that I'd now be able to be near Rosette and not to have to worry about her finding out that "The flag was up". I was not yet 23 and there was plenty more where that came from, but I did delude myself.

Around the 20th of December, the train took me from Hanau to Frankfurt where I changed for the train that would take me to Brussels. Every turn of the wheel along the Rhine River took me closer to Brussels, through Cologne where the twin tower Dom still stood among the ruins of the city. I had last been there in 1941. From there, Aachen, Herbestahl and Verviers and I was back in Belgium.

In Brussels I cannot remember where I stayed, perhaps at Father's apartment where I met Gerty, his girlfriend. She had been suffering from diabetes and had undergone several amputations. It seems to me that I was out more often than in and that I probably got to his apartment to sleep. I got in touch with Rosette but we could not see each other until the 26th as planned. On that day, we met in the city and had a light lunch. So many jumbled thoughts were going through my mind. Rosette was as beautiful as she had been when I had left Brussels over three years before. Her luxurious hair flowed over her shoulders. She was still two years my senior but now the difference did not have the same weight as when I had been 17 and she 19.

In the afternoon, we went to see "Luxury Liner" a 1948 minor MGM musical with George Brent and Jane Powell. It featured "Again" a song that was one of our favorites back in 1949.

> "Again, this couldn't happen again
> Though I have prayed for a lifetime
> That such as you would suddenly be mine . . . .
> . . . We'll have this moment forever
> But never, never again."

It had left us dreamy. A short while later, as we were walking in the city I told Rosette "*J'ai envie de toi*" I lust for you. Rosette immediately replied "*J'ai besoin de toi*" I have a need for you. With that, we embraced on the sidewalk. It was a kiss without any restraint, full of pent up passion where lips and tongues explored each other's mouth and my hands were finding her long forbidden breasts. Rosette was holding my head in her hands.

She took me by the hand and we walked over to the Porte de Namur. She knew where to take us, down one block along the Chaussée D'Ixelles and then right to the Rue du Berger. There we entered a cozy small hotel "Au Berger" a discreet hotel where only two people at a time could enter and use the elevator that took us directly to our room. Later, as we would leave the room, we'd take a different elevator, also for two, that would drop us off in the back of the hotel. It was obviously made to assure privacy so that couples leaving would never risk meeting new couple arriving. In the room I was surprised to find Lever Bros house literature. Obviously the Berger was used extensively for affairs of the Lever personnel and Rosette must have made good use of the discreet hotel in the years that she had been having an affair with Gustave Bauters that she had begun on the very day I had left Belgium in 1949. Rosette and Gustave had broken up shortly before my return to Europe and it might have been a factor in her need for me this Christmas time. Whatever, I did not mind, I loved her and nothing was going to come between us now. We were both hungry for love, it felt good to be in love and we followed our passions, at least I did and I believed she did.

I would not remember very much of our first evening of love. Rosette was very willing and I was very able. Not much thought was given to her satisfaction. Several times I came in her and Rosette moaned and thrilled giving me the impression that I was a great lover. Rosette would not let me use any protection claiming that she had an inverted, tipped uterus and that it was pinched in such a way that no sperm would ever travel past the blocked passage. For me that was so much the better as nothing would interfere with the extreme pleasure she was giving me. Later on it was time to get up, get dressed and experience the closeness of the small elevator that discreetly returned us to the outside world of Brussels. I would recall walking arm in arm through the streets of Brussels, Rosette holding on tight to my arm, her long hair brushing against my face giving me short bursts of chills as we rushed in the cold winter air.

We must have spoken about the following days and tried to explore the need for other encounters, I cannot recall. Rosette could not spare any more time for me as she had obligations of the season. I would recall that she had plans to meet with "Roger" but she would not elaborate on which Roger she was referring to. There were at least two Rogers but the most likely was a seemingly boneless heavyset giant with a cherubic face. In those days we did not refer to "gays" but effeminate men, more asexual than homosexual. I had known that Roger would often travel with Rosette, going to

Spain and elsewhere together. I vaguely understood that it was permissible for Rosette's parents to allow the relation as they felt that Roger did not present any threat for Rosette as he seemed very inoffensive from a sexual point of view. Yet, I felt pangs of uneasiness at this intruder who would spend the coming New Year celebration with my beloved while I had to return to Germany without any certainty that I'd ever see her again.

We did spend some time at Rosette's home and both Monsieur and Madame Wauters were very friendly to me. I would recall a delicious mushroom omelet that Christine, her Mother, prepared for me.

Three days after our thrilling encounter, I took the train back to Hanau. I was filled with a wild mix of hopes, fears and apprehensions as to what the future held for me and unsure that Rosette had any place for me in those plans that I dared dream. Both Rosette and my Father were at the station when my train left for Germany at 11 PM. They had urged me to hurry to my compartment and secure a seat, however I wanted to spend the last moment with Rosette and I climbed in the train as the trainman's whistle blew out the final warning. In my letter to Rosette on the day before New Year's Eve I called her "My Darling" realizing that we had fallen in love, yet so unsure of Rosette's acceptance of our liaison. The letter was written in English for fear that Rosette's parents, especially her Mother would find out about our love affair if I had written in French.

The army had given me a flu shot while I was recovering from my bronchitis but they had neglected to immunize me against the virus of love and that virus was now developing into a full blown infection from which there did not seem to be any cure for me.

1953

When I fall in love
It will be forever
Or I'll never fall in love . . .

IN GERMANY AND IN LOVE

Hardly a day went by that I did not couch my thoughts to Rosette in 6 to 8 pages filled with expressions of my love for her and yet complaining about my perceived inadequacies. I felt so unworthy yet I dared hope. After a while I left no doubt that I wanted to marry Rosette. Her objections were many including that she felt she had no right to hurt Roger. She also expressed fears that I might be with her for the time I'd spend in Germany and then I'd leave her again as I had done nearly four years earlier when I had left for the USA. I would argue my case, assuring her of my love and she'd reply with letters that were alternately warm and loving and again colder and questioning.

Of course, my romance had become the talk of the 627ᵗʰ and my buddies would counsel me with opposite views. Sergeant Carton and Byron D. Xides "X" and I were planning a car trip to Brussels toward the end of January and I was pleading again and again for Rosette to be available at that time so that I could see her again. I would not tell anyone else that I'd be in Brussels so I could spend all my time with her.

Meanwhile, the 627ᵗʰ was getting settled in its first winter in Germany. On a weekend, some of us took a train to the big city of Frankfurt. As we came out of the station an old beggar approached me for a handout. I wasn't in the mood for German beggars and I brushed him away with an angry answer "I would not give you anything, not after what you did to my grandMother!" The beggar was puzzled "I did nothing to your grandmother" He replied in German. Then he took a closer look at me and continued "Ach, perhaps you are Jewish! Yes, it was bad what we did; we took away all the furniture, threw it out the windows and set fire to it. (Obviously he was referring to 1938 and Kristallnacht when countless synagogues and thousands of Jewish businesses were sacked by German troopers)". He then stopped for a moment then continued "It was good furniture" I walked away, disgusted.

Besides the beggars we were besieged by black market dealers wanting to purchase American cigarettes, chewing gum, soap and coffee tins; Lyons Coffee was the brand of choice. On one occasion, Tony Testa of Belleville NJ. wanted to see the Zoo in Frankfurt and he inquired about it's whereabouts. Since he spoke no German, his attempts were futile (the German word for Zoo being Tiergarten). He tried another tack; "tigers, lions and bears" he shouted. "Ah!" Answered a local. "Lyons! You have coffee? You want to sell coffee!"!

I did not smoke but we were able to buy cartons of Camels and Lucky Strike at the PX and whenever I'd go to town, I'd carry a few cartons that were easily converted into hard currency. I'd appreciate the irony of it all, remembering that a scant 6 years ago I was buying Camels and Lucky Strike from the American G.I's in Brussels. I also remembered that a generation earlier, nearly a decade after the end of the Great War, my Father and Mother had met thanks to a gift of a tin of coffee he had brought from Altena to Cologne. Life, if you survived it, could be funny!

Our lined, olive colored overcoats were very prized, not only by the German black marketers but also by the American soldiers who had been in Germany prior to our arrival. We had arrived as one unit with all of our equipment and that had included the newly issued overcoats. Soldiers who had been in Europe prior to our arrival still had the old style khaki horse blanket that had been standard issue since prior to 1917. Also, when you shipped overseas as a replacement you had to turn in the new coats for an old one. One evening, we were enjoying some drinks in a Frankfurt restaurant when I noticed an American non-com deftly lifting one of our new coats from the coat rack on the wall. I turned to SFC Gilbert and told him that his coat was about to be stolen. Gilbert jumped from his seat and placed his hand on the arm of the non-com and intimating that he was grabbing the wrong coat. The man feigned surprise "You think so?" Then he looked the coat over, turned out the inside lapel and read Sgt. Gilbert's name. "Hum, you are right!". He sheepishly replied and he then took his own coat off the hook, a "horse blanket!"

SFC Gilbert was one of our top NCOs. He had a perpetual frozen smile on his face, possibly from an injury suffered during the war. It was unsettling. No matter what he had to say, it was always with that permanent smile. "Men". He would say. "I have bad news!" And the smile would be there, infectious, intimidating.

HANAU, HESSE

On the River Main, maybe 25 miles east of Frankfurt also on the Main and near Offenbach, Hanau before the war was an important silver center. With the silver trade it had a sizeable Jewish population among its 35,000 inhabitants. When we entered our *"Kasernes"* on Lamboystrasse the only traces of a Jewish population was the important walled Jewish cemetery. Having been bombed heavily by the allies during the war, only the statue of the Brothers Grimm seemed untouched in the middle of the main square. Everything else had been demolished with the exception of several *kasernes* that had been hastily rebuilt to accommodate the US Troops. A small inn on the outskirts of town displayed a plaque to celebrate that Napoleon had slept there when the French troops had defeated Austro-Bavarian troops back in 1813 (He would meet his Waterloo two short years later in 1815).

I would return to Hanau around year 2,000 with Marie, my companion. The town now completely rebuilt still centered around the Brothers Grimm statue but everything around the statue was modern and prosperous. The population had tripled with most of the merchants being Turkish or Arab. I could not help but think that Hanau had eliminated the thousands of its prosperous Jewish bourgeoisie and had it replaced by a triple number of "undesirables". Perhaps there was some justice after all. We looked for traces of Germans who might have been alive during the Hitler years but the large majority of those we saw was young and had obviously been born after the war. We went to a modern Konditorei, a pastry shop. It was almost deserted but the few customers were pre-war Germans in their 80's. The two Kasernes on Lamboystrasse were still there but deserted. As we approached the locked gate, an American guard, an African-American woman, appeared and warned us not to get close to the gate. I tried to explain to her that I had been stationed there in 52-54 during the Korean War. She would not hear of it and became more and more menacing. Marie pulled me away. A bit further, the Jewish Cemetery was walled in and one would require special permission to visit it. We drove away to our hotel in Stuttgart. I felt depressed.

In 1952 a hot café/bar prospered where Mayo would be found each night dancing away. The girls loved him; he was such a smooth dancer. The band would play "On the Sunny Side of the Strasse" and the place was jumping. One evening, I went with Mayo. I saw a young girl that I wanted to dance with. I approached her and asked if she would dance with me. She refused immediately and seeing my quizzical look she drew a downward curve with her finger over her face, to indicate that I had a Jewish nose and she would not dance with a Jew. I was hurt. After all, had I not been baptized Protestant, had my ears fixed? My name was not printed on my uniform. I was in an American uniform. It had been seven years since the war had ended. And still, she would not dance with a Jew!

Some of the other German women were not so particular but these were mostly the professional prostitutes who hung around the *Kasernes* and pursued any soldier as soon as he ventured out into the street. These women were attracted to soldiers regardless of color, creed or origin as long as the color of money was flashed. There was a miserable flotsam of a woman who spent most of her time squatting in the middle of the street or on the sidewalk across from the main gate. She would pull up her short skirt, point her fingers to the space between her thighs and yell "Hey soldier, you *wanna* fuck!" whenever a GI would appear out the gate. It was pitiful and embarrassing. I kept thinking that this poor woman was deranged probably following some war provoked trauma. There was talk of women losing their mind after having been gang raped by Russian soldiers as the Red Army had unfurled across Germany in the last onslaught of the war. After a while, this particular woman disappeared from Lamboystrasse probably as a result of the US Command's need to sanitize Hanau now that West Germany had become an ally of the West. In 1953, it had been decreed that Germany would no longer be considered an enemy country but an ally in the perceived cold war that was being drummed into our heads. The US Command had advised us that whenever possible, US troops should now wear civilian clothes whenever off-duty so as to spare the sensitivity of the German population. Of course, I would have none of that as just seven years after the end of the war it pleased me to parade my uniform in town.

BOGGED DOWN

The Army's concern in the winter of '53 was that the Russian armies were always at the ready to push into West Germany and on to conquer the rest of Europe; whether true or not, the High Command wanted us to be kept on a constant alert footing. It was understood that the fighting units, infantry, artillery, tank corps and the Air Force should constantly be prepared to fight. However, our Refrigeration unit had no idea what readiness meant. So, one morning, Lt. Smith organized a sortie in order to locate a safe "alert" area where our entire company could rendezvous when the emergency would occur. A minimal convoy was assembled and we drove away to the countryside around Hanau. I was driving the Jeep with Smith at my side and Sgt. (Smiley) Gilbert as our rear seat passenger. A quarter/ton vehicle followed me and Cpl. Smalley brought up the rear in his tractor/trailer. We quickly got out of town and Lt. Smith and Sgt Gilbert began to argue about the correct way of reading the map they had brought along. After many detours we found a clearing in the forest that would be our assembly point in case of the anticipated alert. Smith wanted to make sure that I'd remember the place. In case of a general alert, or an actual invasion by an "Enemy", a euphemism for "The Russians", I would be expected to lead our entire 627th to this assigned area to await further instructions. After receiving my assurance, we drove back to Hanau very satisfied with our knowledge. The entire trip, with so many detours, had taken us over 5 hours.

Less than a week later, at 4.30 AM we were roused out of bed by the Officer of the Day. An alert was on! We quickly got dressed and rushed to where our rifles were kept. These were chained in the weapons room, under lock and key, on large multiple racks that no one had keys for. Only one sergeant had the keys but he was stationed off-post where he had managed to rent a small apartment for himself and his wife. We waited over 30 minutes for someone to get in touch with him and bring him back so he could unlock the rifles. Since we were a service unit, no one was issued ammunition and we ran to our vehicles to try to get to our assembly point before the "enemy" could destroy us. It was possible that our CO's had side arms with or without bullets, but I would not recall either Capt. Petersen or Lt. Smith ever wearing any holster.

It had snowed during the night and the entire area was covered with a couple of inches of the white slippery stuff and we had not been provided with chains. As best we could, we organized our convoy and finally drove away as the sun began to rise over the Eastern horizon. We drove away, Jeep in front, followed by our ¼ Ton and the 2 ½ Ton truck. 36 tractor/trailers followed our tracks and closing the convoy, our "wrecker" truck. A few miles away, a railway barrier in the middle of Hanau was down as a freight train kept moving to and fro hooking and unhooking a few freight cars. We waited. This enabled a few laggard tractors to finally rejoin our convoy. I was happy this seemed to be an exercise alert or our entire unit would have been obliterated by then. Once the train got out of the way we continued in the general direction of our assembly point. Apparently, no one had taken the trouble to bring along the map!

As we dashed along the roads, we noticed some other military trucks, apparently lost; they joined our large convoy confident that we knew where we were going and our line began to look like a circus parade several miles long. Suddenly, an opening appeared on my left and I could see the huge clearing in the pine forest that was our assigned assembly point. I lurched left and without slowing down drove in a gigantic circle on the spongy snowy ground. The Jeep slowed down, its tires spinning in the soft snow. Quickly, I threw it into 4-wheel drive and it managed to make the full circle of the clearing, then it sputtered and conked out. In back of me all the trucks, the trailers, the wrecker and all the strays we had picked up along the way followed my tracks and bogged down in the snowy clearing. What I had mistaken for our assembly point was a seedling farm for reforestation of pine trees. Under the snow I had not noticed that there were thousands of growing little pine trees. We were stuck!

It took the wrecker the rest of the day and evening to winch every vehicle out of that tree farm. Somehow a chow truck and mobile oven managed to rejoin us and the company was able to provide us with coffee, sandwiches and doughnuts. I thought that this was something to stash away in my souvenirs but no one else was very amused by the incident; least of all the German government. They fined the US Army a considerable sum of money for having destroyed an entire growth of pine seedlings. Since West Germany was now an ally, the US had no choice but to pay the fine.

SECOND VISIT TO BRUSSELS

Almost daily one of my love letters was mailed out to Rosette. Her last word received by me was full of doubt about the future of our relationship. There was always Roger who she did not want to hurt. In the meantime I was racked by doubts about Rosette and the sincerity of her love. She had written me an amorous letter on the 14th of January but I did not receive it until the 21st. on the very next week-end I had finagled a three day pass. Sgt. Carton would drive his Chevrolet to Brussels with me and my buddy X. I would not even let my Father know that I'd be in Belgium that weekend. The entire trip was to plead my case with Rosette in the hope that she would consent to be my wife. I dropped off Carton and X. in the city center and spent most of Saturday with Rosette. We went to visit her parents and they were very amiable toward me. There were so many mundane things to do that I would not recall if we found time to make love during that lightning

Saturday. I remembered thanking Rosette for having sewn a couple buttons on my uniform and for having taken time to show me "her" Brussels, parts of which I had never seen or known before. Rosette seemed to take a particular and intense pleasure in showing me new things, it seemed to energize her.

We parted early Sunday and drove to the American Embassy to see if we could buy gasoline with our military coupons as we could in Germany. Had they accepted our vouchers gas would have cost us 75 centimes per liter. We pleaded but to no avail even though all three of us were in uniform. As it was, we wound up paying BF. 6.50/liter or nearly nine times the military rate. I showed my buddies the tomb of the Unknown Soldier and the Unilever building where I had first met Rosette and by 11 AM we were en route to return to Hanau where we arrived at 18.30h, a half hour late but nobody paid any attention to our transgression.

We would write again about projects that I hoped that Rosette would share with me. She was vacillating and my letters were more and more pleading, cajoling and pressing for a positive answer. I had it bad and it was good, at least for me.

X. would later talk to me about a woman he had picked up in Brussels and of his concern that although they had intercourse he had felt absolutely nothing. "It was as if I had placed my penis in a void!" He was really worried about this. Carton and X. were concerned that Rosette had been upset by the type of women they had latched on during our stay in Brussels. They had marveled at Rosette and insisted that if I did not marry her and let her go, I would live my entire life regretting her. This was not news to me as I was spending every waking moment trying to convince her that we should get married. Rosette would sometimes reply that she had known other men and that she could not promise that she would remain faithful to me should we get married. Blindly I would try to convince her that the strength of our mutual love would palliate this. I had written to my Mother about my desire to marry Rosette. Frieda had replied that Rosette was indeed a very nice girl and that it seemed like a good idea to her.

Years later, Ruth would express reservations about Frieda's positive opinion, she did not like Rosette and neither did Ruth but they tried to make the best of it. Rosette was always cold to Ruth and whenever Ruth (and Frieda) said something, anything, Rosette always knew more or better.

RECONNOITERING

Back in Hanau the 627th was getting more and more involved in finding new ways to keep its men busy. In reality, only one trailer was in constant use. Since it was basically a large refrigeration unit, someone had the idea to store cases of beer and assorted liquor close to the kitchen area. I did not know who had the use of it or the keys but to me it made no difference as I was very proud of my non-drinking status. Although I had consumed a bit of weak beer as a cadre in Virginia, I had now reverted to being a teetotaler. The rest of the trailers were under constant maintenance and the tractors spent much time at the motor pool being serviced for mostly imaginary troubles; all this in the event of more alerts that would require convoys to pre-assigned wooded areas.

Mayo Sotelo, my Jewish Landsman and I had become very friendly. Mayo could always be found sitting on top of his trailer, feet inside of the front refrigeration unit, seemingly deep in repair mode. Closer scrutiny would reveal that he only appeared to be doing maintenance with his head lowered in the condenser area; actually he was reading a book or simply asleep over the cooling unit.

Mayo would go to unbelievable ends in order to avoid any task that the military required of him. He had been drafted for 24 months and obviously intended to serve his time doing as little as he could get away with, short of being court-martialed. If we had to go on a one mile march, he'd excuse himself for medical reasons and walk over a couple of miles to go on sick-call. He once managed to talk the medic on duty to scrape the bottom of his feet so he would be excused from any marching duties. That night you could find him at the café/music-hall dancing away into the night with all the pretty ladies. Mayo was the smoothest talking guy there and his skills as a dancer were without match. Mayo, with his black wavy hair, olive skin and lack of body hair was just irresistible to the ladies in Hanau, Offenbach and Frankfurt. We became inseparable except for frequenting the dance halls where German girls loathed my Jewish looks yet could not detect Mayo's ancestry. I was to photograph him in front of small shack in Hanau that was dealing in jewelry. On the front, above the door a sign read:" Mayo Schmuck" that in Germany meant "Mayo Jewelry". He delighted in it.

Private Sutherburg, a West Virginia native kept delighting in throwing anti-Semitic slurs my way. He would threaten me with body violence, mumbling that he'd punch this lousy Jew whenever he got the chance. Mostly I stayed clear of him and a couple of his buddies that he hung around with. On one Sunday afternoon, as I was walking toward my room, I saw Sutherburg and one of his buddies hanging around a candy machine in the deserted recreation room. Both had obviously been drinking. Each still had a partial bottle of beer in their hands. This time Sutherburg decided to pass from words to action. With a sudden move he lunged at me, bottle held high, cursing at me. He was quite a bit taller than I was and although he held the bottle high over his head it was easy for me to duck under his blow. His belly showed under his T-shirt and I struck him with my left fist right in the bread-basket as hard as I could. He collapsed like a sack of potato and threw up all over the floor. One blow and I never had to worry again about Sutherburg and his buddies.

Now and then the entire 627th Company would go on an overnight maneuver and I'd delight in driving my Jeep in the German countryside, it gave me a feeling of satisfaction; the freedom of seeing parts of Germany that was once forbidden to me and where my life would have been in extreme danger. At night, everyone would pitch their tent in the woods and sleep until early morning when a field breakfast would be served before we drove back to Lamboystrasse. I'd never pitch my tent as I preferred to sleep sitting in my Jeep, fully clothed, with my blanket covering my body from my feet to my neck. I guess I was too lazy to unpack my tent pegs and half-tent. It was much simpler to take refuge in my Jeep. In that late winter with a covering of snow on my Jeep as insulation against the cold, I was sure that I was cozier in my seat than I'd be lying on the floor under the tent. However, when I awoke all bent over and stiff I knew that I had been wrong.

With the coming of spring, we began to study more routes where the 627th could go on extended maneuvers; however we had to be sure that that our convoys could pass through the narrow streets in small German villages and towns without knocking down the many overhanging rooms that dotted the center sections of the roads. For this, we had set up special trips where I and Sgt. Gilbert would drive the Jeep, followed by Cpl. Jim Haley driving his tractor and trailer. Where we could pass it was assumed that the rest of the company would be safe to follow the same route without wrecking the sleepy villages we had gone through. Often it came down to a matter of an inch or two. Once, on a country road, I came bumper to bumper with an enormous German bus that was not about to leave me any part of the right of way. Quickly I veered off and partway into the ditch on the side of the road and I watched as the bus, horn angrily blaring, disappeared around the next curve. I smiled as I knew that Jim Haley had been close behind me with his rig. Tires screeched and the tail lights of the bus reappeared around the bend, the tractor-trailer angrily forcing it back to where there would be enough space to let the rig pass by. Of course, I gleefully followed with my Jeep while the bus driver cursed and shook his fist at us.

Despite our willing efforts, our convoys would often catch and crumble overhanging rooms as we turned and twisted our parade through the villages. That created angry commotions and unending troubles with the local authorities and fines and compensations to repair the damages caused by the US Army trailers. How conditions had changed in the seven years since Uncle Sam's tanks and bombers had reduced to rubble so much of the countryside with impunity.

Lt. Smith had managed to rent an apartment in Bad Orb, quite a distance from Hanau. His wife had joined him in Germany and they had managed to find space in a "Spa" town, well renowned for its beneficial waters. The first time he had to go home, he ordered me to drive him to Bad Orb at No. 1, Einbahnstrasse. I politely mentioned to him that we would need a better address as "Einbahnstrasse" simply meant "One Way Street". Nevertheless he insisted that it was the street name and we drove around Bad Orb for quite a while until he was able to recognize the villa where his wife was waiting to greet him. German was not his forte. As we had been driving among the many towns around the region, he once remarked "Rosie, where is this Innenstadt? Everywhere we go there are always signs pointing to "Innenstadt" but we never get to it. Where do you think it is?"

Trying very hard not to laugh I explained that there was no such town. Innenstadt simply meant the direction to the center of town, the inner city! Lt. Smith was not convinced and was sure that I was fibbing.

Almost daily I had to drive to Battalion HQ in Darmstadt, about 30 miles away over small roads. It whetted my appetite to speed all the way, cutting corners of the roads, turning into the left corners and shaving a few yards wherever I could. There was not a vehicle that came in my sight that I did not have to pass as quickly as I could. Under the best of circumstances the trip to or from Darmstadt took me a bit over 50 minutes. Capt. Petersen would have been proud of "Barney Oldfield". Then, one day, Captain Petersen was transferred to another unit and Lieutenant Smith became our Commanding Officer now with the rank of Captain. The first thing he told me as he assumed command was "Rosie, from now on it will be 35 mph on the roads, 25 mph in town! If you exceed those limits, I will have your stripes!"

My daily trips to Darmstadt became drudgery. I had to resolve to mental gymnastics so that I would not fall asleep during the round trips. Yet I got used to the speed limit and after a while it entered my head that it was not necessary to have to pass every car that appeared ahead of me on the road. My one way trips now took me 60 to 65 minutes, a scant dozen minutes more than when

I was driving at breakneck speed to shave a few seconds at every curve. I now had time to observe and admire the landscape without risking life, limbs and the loss of my stripes. Once, I had given two GI's a lift in my Jeep. After a while one of them inquired "Why are we driving so slow? Do you have a "governor" on your engine?" A governor was an attachment on or near the carburetor that would kick in to restrict the speed if it exceeded the pre-set limit. "Yes! "I replied. "And he has two bars on his shoulders"

Barney Oldfield would be banished from my driving habits forever and I'd always be indebted to Captain Smith.

Second Lieutenant Floyd came into the 627th as the replacement for Lt. Smith who was now our commanding officer. Floyd was from Alabama and spoke with such a deep southern drawl as to be incomprehensible at time. He knew so little about army protocol that he latched on to me so I could give him a crash course into the workings of the 627th unit. He drove a red and black Oldsmobile and sometimes took me along on his errands around Hanau and Frankfurt. Red haired, Lt. Floyd reminded me of the movie actor Red Skelton both in physical appearance and in his natural ability to get himself into trouble. It would then be "Rosie to the rescue". Poor Floyd was totally ineffectual. The one incident that I would recall about him was a trip we took to a men's tailor shop in Hanau where Floyd wanted to have a tailored "pinks" officer's uniform made to order. He needed me as his interpreter for he spoke not a word of German and his Alabama accent (he liked to say that he was from L.A, Lower Alabama) from around Mobile, had to be heard to be disbelieved. Floyd was rightly worried that the German tailor would not be able to understand his instructions.

We walked into a large dressing room where Lt. Floyd took off his slacks. An unbelievable fetid odor exploded and knocked me back several paces. It was not an odor of anything specific. It was the accumulation of foul aromas of someone who had not washed for at least a couple of weeks or more. *Even as I write these words, my mind fills with the awful memory scents of that day.* I could not understand the inability of the U.S Military training schools to make clean gentlemen out of its officers. In WWII, the US had "90-day wonders"; I could not help but wonder if this officer had not bathed in 90 days!?

<u>COURTSHIP OF ROSETTE, THE</u>

Rosette and I continued to exchange letters and sometimes phone calls during that early 1953. My output was much more prolific than Rosette's as most of those were my desperate attempts to convince her that she should marry me. What follows was written in French with the parts written in English shown in *italics*. Nothing has been changed or omitted. It is straight from the mind, heart and passion of a 22 year old.

February 3, 1953.

My Love,

"You already know the reaction that I felt upon reading your letter. On the telephone I had tried to make you understand how much your efforts were futile. I love you, must I still prove it? If you have not yet understood the nature of my sentiments, how could I convince you? All my being cries out my love for you. You will never know how much your letter tortures me. I am afraid. Never have I seen the path traced in from of me with such clarity.

I think only of you, I stay awake at night torturing myself at the thought of losing you. During the day, everything reminds me of your person, everything hurts; I cannot imagine myself without you. I am exhausted loving you. I think of you as soon as I awake. I love you Cherie! How may I hope, I am so far away. Yet, you are near to me, snuggled in my heart. I do not think of you in carnal terms, you are more than just that for me, you are the companion for the happy days of our youth and our old age. *When I'll fall in love, it will be forever, or I'll never fall in love . . . I have fallen in love with you, forever and a day.*

To live without you, what a Utopia, how can you think of it? I do not know what X. wrote to you, I only know that you received his letter before mime. My love, soon I will see you again and then I want you to be mine body and soul. You torture me making me think of losing you. Above all, do not do anything foolish, if you love me as I love you, we may not escape the call to love. We took a wrong turn once more than three years ago; let us not play with destiny. Life is too short; happy days are rare, happy lovers are rarer still. My strength of which you speak is ephemeral since you are in my life, my strength is you and it is our love. Please love me as I want you to love me.

X. is distressed; he does not understand how you might hesitate. Carton, he gives me the example of his wife and him, happy since forever. Please marry me. Espouse-me Mademoiselle Rosette. The happiness that was ours during the too brief hours of my visit to Brussels may be ours forever; that state of intense and maddening joy, I want it during our lives. Please love me . . . I love you.

It is sweet to think about you, about us, our happiness, I am happy and gay and the world smiles at me. Now I torture myself, I hurt and I am sad. The theme is too cruel, to lose you, always to lose you! Do not render me unhappy.

And still those years of separations! If I believed that you were lost for me, it was because I knew all that was happening in Europe. I was reading your words with pain; friends, friends, friends! What could I have hoped for? I did not know that you loved me. How could I have hoped that you loved me? Me, among all the others. Me, puny little urchin, skinny dog of the street. I had feared of exposing my naked heart, feared of making myself ridicule, to suffer still. I love you, you love me. It is more than what I have the right to hope for. I so much want to marry you.

I will show you New York, you will see Mother again and in the evenings we will walk through the park, eternal lovers, sweethearts reunited by the will of the gods of love. Tell me that I am not dreaming that you will be mine. Yesterday I wrote to Mother, thus she knows what I feel for you; I may not write her about all the details, nor my doubts because it is all so confusing. I get lost in the whirlwind of my anguish. *Tell me that you love me, honey. I love you.*

It is true that I wanted to finish my studies before I'd marry but that was without you. What good is success if you do not have near to you the companion that you love? If you love me, if you want to make me happy, be mine.

All your arguments are without basis, I knock them down like a house of cards. You do not believe in them yourself. *You may not be an angel, but who wants to marry an angel? I want a woman in the true sense of the word.* Your age? My age? Childishness all that, what is it except a birth date? How can you talk about cheating on Roger and later cheating on me also? What is happening is stronger than we are and if someone must suffer, why should it only be us. Life is too short to throw it to the wolves. *Tomorrow was made for some, tomorrow may never come.* If we refuse our chance this time, we will take our regrets to the grave. Let's love!

Are you certain that Roger would be the most unhappy one? Do you realize the immensity of my love? I love you; I am crazy about you, your body, your eyes and the thoughts that traverse your mind. I adore you. I do not want to lose you and if I should lose you, I would be lost too. Let us rescue out lives; being swallowed in quicksand is too easy. Let us love. How could I become mean? You hurt me with the uncertainty in which you are plunging me. I thank you for your sincerity. *Please Rosette, be my wife, for the better and for worse.*

I will see you again soon, I live only for you. I kiss you tenderly,

Your Rudy who loves you.

CORPORAL ROSENBERG

On the 25th of February, 1953, I finally broke Rosette's resistance. Indeed, on that day I received a letter that had been delayed several days by George Washington himself. The army had celebrated Washington's Birthday and no mail had been received over the previous four days. When it finally came, it confirmed that Rosette did love me and would accept to marry me. Actually, she had written a letter to X. a few days earlier but he had refused to let me in on its content. And so I waited and waited and my heart sank with each passing day. Now there were no more doubts. It was there in blue on white paper. We would now have to prepare all the necessary papers to satisfy the US Military that Rosette was an honorable person and could be trusted to marry a member of the US Army. The military was used to having soldiers fall in love with the first prostitute who came along and they would place a vast assortment of obstacles to prevent the USA to be flooded with unsavory women. And for the US Army, that meant just about anyone who had set their eyes on a GI. As for me, I was in seventh heaven and could no wait until the time when Rosette and I would be together again. Rosette had made a singular request that she'd be allowed to continue to go out with Roger when I would not be in Brussels. I could see no danger in that as I considered Roger to be a very nice person and safer than anyone else she might have met while I was still stationed in Germany. Later on it would come to my knowledge that Rosette had renewed her affair with Gustave Bauters and that "Roger" might have served as *poudre aux yeux,* throwing dust in my eyes. A few days hence, I had made an appointment with the US Judge Advocate General in Frankfurt to find out all that was required to obtain the necessary papers and permits to ensure a prompt marriage. The first thing was for Rosette to obtain a certificate of proper character from the mayor of her borough of Koekelberg. That would be a simple but essential formality.

At the same time as Rosette had at long last said "Yes!" Uncle Sam had made me a Corporal again but this time a true Corporal, not an Acting one as when I had been a cadre in Virginia. My life was looking up at long last. I was now making an extra $46 each month that would bring me about an additional $800—for the balance of the 17 months left to serve until July 1954. By now I had passed half of my enlistment and my time in the military had passed the peak with 19 months gone and 17 to go.

A few days later, the US Authorities in Frankfurt confirmed that there would be a series of papers to be filled out both from my part and Rosette's part. All would have to be duly notarized. Again, this was going to be a time consuming process, not so much for me as notarization in the army was a simple matter of confirming that I was who I said I was. On the other hand, to notarize signatures in Belgium would be a much more formal endeavor as Rosette would have to make numerous appointments with a Notary, a court official to achieve the same results. However I had been assured that the entire process should take 4 to 5 months. That would allow us to get married during July/August 1953! In the coming months, during one of my visits to Brussels, Rosette and I would find time to have our banns of matrimony published at the City Hall. Now that we were promised to each other, our meetings would become more frequent and either Rosette would come to visit me in Hanau or I'd take the train to Brussels. Often my buddies and I would organize a car trip during a three-day pass and drive to Brussels. By now I had insisted that Rosette should no longer have dates with "Roger" and she had agreed with me.

Rosette would send me letters telling me that she would arrive in Hanau by train "the following Monday". This would drive me nuts. The APO mail was not the swiftest. By the time I received her letter, a few days had elapsed and I tried in vain to figure out when Rosette would actually show up. I'd plead with her to write me the date of her visit, not a day! I'd call her to ask for a more precise day. She'd laugh and kept telling me that her letters were self-explanatory. On one occasion, Rosette wrote that she was planning to come to see me the Monday of Pentecost. When the hell was Pentecost? In Belgium and France, they would refer to "Easter and Pentecost" during which five or six week stretch not much would be done in schools or businesses. It was somewhat similar to "Spring Break" in the USA but no one could pinpoint the dates with any certainty. So I went around the post in Hanau trying to find out when Pentecost would be celebrated. No one knew. The Germans did not know either. They did not know the word. I was to find out later that in Germany the holiday was known as "Pinkst". Who knew? And I would write Rosette or call her trying to find out when the date of her arrival would be. "Everybody knows when Pentecost is" was her invariably stubborn reply. Well, I did not know and it seemed that nobody in Germany knew either. I would plead with Rosette to "give me a **date**!" She would refuse, stating that her letters were sufficiently clear. It was getting very frustrating. I should have known right there and then that there was something drastically wrong with our relationship. Whenever we met, love and passion would take over and we'd be lovers with eyes blind and mind shrouded in fog and cotton. However, my buddies would warn me: "Rudy, don't you hear? You two never have a conversation, only a confrontation!" But I was blind with love and not aware that Rosette, although only two years older than I was, was bent on having her way with every decision and every talk.

During our frequent trips to Brussels, usually with Jim Haley, Tony Testa, X and Mayo, we had met Maria, a tall, blond and beautiful *Bruxelloise* who had taken a liking to me. I guess she was a *Madame* who had a retinue of pretty young girls whom she would rent by the hour. She would take care of my buddies while I went on my way to be with Rosette. In Brussels we'd arrange to meet them at the terrace of the Hotel Metropole and Maria would parcel out her willing ladies among our group. I was in love with Rosette and I'd always decline her offers even though the girls were always offered to me as a free gift. I'd leave them and spent my days and nights with Rosette. On Sunday mornings we'd hustle back to Germany so we'd be back in Hanau before reveille on Monday morning.

By then it was late spring and the weather had turned very warm in Brussels. Maria wore sleeveless dresses while sipping her drinks on the terrace. Later, Haley asked me "Is it proper for a woman (Maria) to wipe her sweaty armpits with her handkerchief while sitting in a café?" I assured him that it was not the norm but then again, Maria and her girls were not exactly the most distinguished citizens of Brussels, no matter how nice and friendly they were.

Mayo had spent the night with one of Maria's girls in her apartment. He was recalling that they had made love on a tiny bed while the girl's sister lay next to them, reading that day's newspaper; totally oblivious to what was going on between her sister and Mayo. Somehow he felt that it had hindered his performance and his enjoyment of same. I explained that rooms were hard to get and that perhaps he should have invited the sister to join them in their tryst. He shook his head in wonderment.

Back in Hanau, a teary-eyed girl had latched on to me. Chris had an affair with a soldier in our outfit and she was begging me to intercede in her favor to get him to return to her. Tony Trolchio was one of our truck drivers, nice guy, a bit rough-edged but decent. Apparently he had gotten all he wanted out of Chris and had now dumped her. Chris was disconsolate and kept begging me to plead her case with her boyfriend so that he would take her back. I spoke to him a couple of times but it was evident that he had had is fill of her and no longer wanted any part of her affections.

I tried to console her. Chris was blond, a bit on the heavy side but "not altogether unattractive". We began to spend much time together in the evenings and whenever I was not on duty or in Brussels. I spent all our time together bending her ear rhapsodizing about my love for Rosette. I was not even aware that she might be developing a crush on me. One evening, we had wandered into the main Hanau Park. It was early summer and days were getting longer. We walked and walked and if I recall we held hands. By ten it had gotten dark and I suggested that we should leave the park. Much to my surprise the gate had been padlocked and we were shut in. Chris did not seem concerned. I was! We groped around in the dark, trying to find a way out. The park was completely closed in by a tall iron fence. Pushing and pulling we helped each other over the spiked metal bars and managed to get back into the street. It would take me some time to realize that Chris had probably been there with Trolchio and that they might have made love after dark on many occasions. She must have known that the park closed at 10PM and may have had hopes that we would wind up making love in the bushes. As it was, we never did. I would not even remember if we ever as much as kissed. I was so in love with Rosette that I could not consider any other girl, no matter how delicious a dish I might have been offered.

Chris would help me select two gold wedding rings, plain round bands with a slight circular design. We were together when I purchased them in a small jewelry shop in Hanau. It was a strange non-relationship that lasted until shortly after Rosette and I were wed.

APPENDICITIS

On a Wednesday night in late March, while on duty as the driver of the guard I suddenly felt the sharpest pain in my right side that caused me to double up. I had never felt such a pain and found myself unable to straighten up. It was 1 AM and after a couple of hours trying to work through the extreme pain I was driven to the doctor at the Hanau dispensary. Fearing an attack of appendicitis, an ambulance drove me to the Wiesbaden Military Hospital for further examination. Picture a pretzel unable to place one foot ahead of the other and you would have gotten a fair idea of my appearance that early afternoon when I finally got to see the German doctor now working in the military hospital.

The doctor gave me the "Bounce Test"! Not only did it work but I swore that I bounced all the way up the ceiling. A nurse took a blood sample to determine my blood count. Then, the young German doctor withdrew the oral thermometer that had been stuck under my tongue. With a thick German accent he declared:

"Vell, your demperadure iss a liddle ele-va-ded; Butt zen you Chewish beoples alvays havv higher demperadures zen normal beople anyvay!"

I could not help but wonder in what concentration camp this young German doctor had gotten his practical training.

The operation to remove my appendix was performed that very afternoon as it was about to burst. Thus a serious peritonitis had been averted. I never knew who was the surgeon who performed the surgery but the stitches revealed neither German accent nor swastika patterns.

I was to remain in the hospital for a full 15 days until I regained my strength and was allowed to return to Hanau. The army Chaplain in the hospital had informed me that this year, Easter would come on April First and that I'd probably not be discharged until after Easter. All along I would carry on my correspondence with Rosette, lamenting the fact that our planned meeting in Brussels would have to be postponed until after Easter and probably to Pentecost whenever that might turn out to be. Every other day, Xides or Mayo Sotel would bring me my mail and news from the *Kaserne* on Lamboystrasse. Naturally most if not all of my mail would be from Rosette and I pined day and night until Byron or Mayo would appear with those precious missives. Both of them had a fine sense of humor and had the bad habit of painfully doubling me over with their jokes. X. had expressed his desire to serve as my best man when we'd eventually get the permission to marry. This hospital interlude threatened to delay the readiness of all the formalities.

Rosette wrote: Do you feel better or is it the nurse who feels you better? Hmmm!

On the last day of March 1953, Pay-Day, Captain Smith showed up at the hospital and brought me my pay for the month. That was a very nice gesture.

GATHERING PAPERS, ETC.

In early April I was back in Hanau and trying to find time to gather the necessary papers to obtain the Army's permission to marry Rosette. It was weird the minutia the Army was interested in. From Mother and Ruth, I received copies of the few bank accounts I had when I left the US. Ruth and Mother signed declarations that they had an apartment in Brooklyn and that we would be welcome to stay there until we could find our own place. Reams and reams of forms that had to be filled and always, notarized.

Once I went to the American Consulate in Frankfurt to meet with the Judge Advocate General. I sat in the reception room with scores of women and dependents and children. I had been sitting there for a couple of hours when nature reminded me that I had to go to the bathroom. I had been sitting right in front of the restroom marked "MEN". So I got up and walked straight in the bathroom. I did my business, washed my hands and noticed that there were women shoes showing from under the next stall. I felt it strange to be able to see and hear all that was going on in the Lady's room and wondered why they had not closed the space between the men' and women's toilets. All it would have taken was to extend the panels from the floor to the ceiling.

After washing my hands, I exited back into the reception room of the Consulate. All the women were staring at me. Then I noticed that the toilet door did not say MEN, but WOMEN! The hallway door had been open and it was hiding the two first letters of women. Standing there, in my US uniform, I felt so embarrassed. I felt my face blushing. As a 23 year old, unsure of myself, I had no idea how to handle the situation. Luckily, it was soon my turn to enter the Jag's room. I thought that I had just blown my chances to get married.

Captain Smith was as anxious as I was to get the whole matter signed and send onward to Battalion HQ. When we finally had assembled everything, he signed the lot and I had the pleasure of driving the entire dossier to Darmstadt. Now it was up to battalion to review the papers, do an investigation and send it on to 7th Army HQ.

With the coming of May, the 627th was assigned to make a display in the town's square for Armed Forces Day. Jim Haley and I organized an exhibit with posters, weapons and refrigeration trailer. Young German boys in short pants, looking just like the Hitler Youths of the Hitler years came to handle, dismantle and assemble the few weapons we had laid out on a couple of tables. They were obviously fascinated by the rifles and carbines. I felt good that we did not have any bullets to display alongside our weapons.

I did manage to wangle a three day pass from Capt. Smith and took the train to Brussels to meet Rosette. I went to see her parents who were not at all enchanted with the prospect that we'd marry and that Rosette would leave Brussels and Belgium forever. There would still be much work to be done there.

Rosette had found a small hotel near the North Station and we met there each day of my visit, enjoying our time together, making plans and making love. She would leave me late at night to go home to her parent's house. In the morning, someone knocked on the door of my room. Half asleep, I wondered what I should reply. In bilingual Brussels I could have replied "oui" or 'ja", in Germany it would have been "Jah" but in the states and in the army "Yes" would be indicated. In the fog of waking up I lay on my bed confused, not sure what to answer. Eventually, "Yes" was my reply.

What is worse than flies on your piano?

Crabs on your organ!

When I got back to Hanau the next morning I noticed an itching in my crotch. As I went to the bathroom in the morning I saw tiny white balls gathered around some of my pubic hair. The dreaded crabs! How could they have gathered there? Was it the hotel in Brussels? Had I gotten them from Rosette? If I had gotten the crabs from somewhere else, had I passed them on to Rosette? I did not dare to call her and ask "Have I given you the crabs?", or "Did you give me the crabs?" I wasn't even sure what to call them in French, *cancre?*

As it turned out, there was an infestation of crabs among all the army personnel in Hanau. Everybody was infected. You could see the crabs jump from the urinals as you went to urinate. It was terrible. No one knew where they had come from. Was the general population also infected? Did it originate among the prostitutes that serviced the American soldiers and gave them generous helpings of venereal diseases?

The dispensary had long since run out of traditional medication and the GI's were now reduced to treating the infestation with Vicks, whether it worked or not. Anyway it burned like hell when applied to the red welts left by the tenacious crabs. The soldiers were restricted to the barracks and forbidden to socialize with the local ladies. Caruthers, who had an incredible amount of chest and back hair, was covered with crabs from his eyelashes to his crotch. One could see crabs leaping from his chest and back, covered with a veritable mattress of dense curly wiry hair.

Then, suddenly, after a week or so, the infestation went away. Cleanliness returned.

I would never mention it to Rosette. Did she suffer from the crabs? Had I passed it on to her? Did I catch it there or only when I returned to Hanau? I never found out but I never forgot getting the crabs in Hanau in 1953.

MANEUVERS NEAR MUNICH

We had spent the better part of the spring of 1953 getting our betrothal documents together, birth certificates, vaccination records, certificates of good morality and behavior, etc. Rosette would obtain the papers from her birthplace in Belgium and from the City of Brussels and I'd get mine from the periphery of my early life from Charleroi to Brooklyn. We were convinced that the US Army was intent on making it as difficult as possible for us to get married under the theory that any union between GI's and foreign women was suspicious at best. Meanwhile Rosette took every opportunity to come and visit me in Hanau. For my part, I did not miss any chance to travel to Brussels alone or with some of my buddies

There were maneuvers scheduled for the southern area of Germany, around Munich and men were "volunteered" among the various units stationed in Germany. I was picked from the 627th to be part of our QM Battalion force that would participate in the Southern Maneuvers. We drove along the Autobahn in a small convoy of 2½ ton trucks under the command of Sergeant First Class (SFC) King. King, a ramrod of a soldier had apparently been wounded in WWII. Half of his face showed signs of having been hit hard on one side of the skull and had caved in. He obviously had undergone major surgery; I admired him as he was a sharp soldier and I considered that he had gotten his disfiguring injury fighting the Germans while trying to come and liberate us.

After having driven for several hours along the Autobahn, we stopped for lunch along the road in the German equivalent of the 'Howard Johnson' restaurant that could be found along our American roads. Of course, someone had to guard the trucks. "Rosenberg, you will be on truck-watch and we will bring you food when we return! "Ordered King. Somehow, I did not like the sarcastic smile and tone he used.

Forty-five minutes later, the entire group returned to the trucks with Sgt. King holding out a paper-wrapped sandwich for me. As I opened the wrapper I was surprised to find two slices of dark German bread, naked, with absolutely nothing on them. King, with a sarcastic tone in his voice explained that they had nothing to put on the bread but ham. "And of course, *Rosenberg,* you cannot eat ham, can you? So I just brought you the bread" There was something so vicious in his tone that my mind did an immediate recall to "Julius and Ethel Rosenberg" who had recently occupied the news and were under death sentence at the time. I said nothing but promised myself that I would do all I could to steer clear of Sgt. King in the future.

We arrived in a dark forest in the vicinity of Munich and set about getting our individual assignments. I was put in charge of the regimental telephone switchboard for which I had never received any training. I would not remember ever getting a call on that board even though it had been installed in the main regiment tent. I did find out that if I inserted the plug at the proper

Rudy Rosenberg

angle partway into the receptacle, I could hear Radio Moscow. It was weird to be deep in a German forest and to be able to hear Russian music just by placing a key askew in an American telephone system.

Somehow, Captain Petersen was also part of these maneuvers and in the early morning a messenger came to find me. He told me that Petersen was wondering if I had brought my map-reader along on this exercise. I had taken the habit of carrying a pocket wheeler that you ran along a map to determine the exact mileage between cities on maps. Capt. Petersen had remembered this habit of mine and wanted to use the reader. For once, I had left it in Hanau and I was unable to help him. That was the last time I would ever hear from him. I felt I had let him down.

Together with me and my field phone switchboard in the HQ tent, the population consisted primarily of a feeble minded corporal and two of the meanest sergeants it has ever been my displeasure to meet. Sergeants Hunniker and Proust were carrying on a conversation between each other, but within earshot of Corporal "Nitwit" and me as I was hidden behind my phone station. They talked about total nonsense but very convincingly with plausible double talk where one word kept coming up "turd". They went on for a lengthy conversation that caught the ear and attention of "Nitwit". Finally, his curiosity aroused he fell into the trap: "What is a turd?" He asked. Hunniker was ready with a crushing reply: "It is a piece of shit about this long! But I would never shit you, you are my favorite turd!"

Later that afternoon Hunniker and Proust were at it again with the same curious listener. This time they talked at length about a "Swinette" and going to school to learn to play one and being hired in a classical orchestra where they were the primary swinette players. They went on and on until Nitwit, unable to contain himself any longer inquired "What is a swinette?" Hunniker: "It is catgut stretched across a pig's ass!"

And both of the sergeants slapping their thighs at the discomfiture of the dimwitted corporal.

The next day, Nitwit was ready with a joke of his own: "What time is it when the Chinaman goes to the dentist?" Both of the sergeants professed total ignorance. "It is two thirty!" Nitwit yelled out triumphantly!

Hunniker and Proust pretended that they did not understand the joke and Nitwit spent the next fifteen minutes trying to make them understand. Because "Tooth hurt he" Well he is a Chinese person and he cannot pronounce "Tooth hurt him" that is why it is 2.30 when a Chinese goes to the dentist. They still did not get it and Nitwit was losing his cool trying to make them get the joke. After a long while, they pretended that they not only had gotten the joke but that it was the funniest joke they had heard in years; and guffaws and guffaws and laughter.

A short while later, the Major walked in the tent. Hunniker "Major, what time is it when the Chinaman goes to the dentist?" The Major does not know. Hunniker, proudly "Half past two!" The Major did not understand! Nitwit came rushing to Hunniker's side and, very agitated, explained that it was not half past two but two thirty to what Hunniker replied that if made no difference as two thirty and half past two was exactly the same thing. Nitwit then explained that with half past two there was no joke! There then followed a lengthy *Abbott and Costello* argument until Henniker and Proust finally pretended that this time they understood the joke.

The next officer to enter the tent was the Colonel and Hunniker popped him the question. No, the Colonel did not know the time when the Chinaman went to the dentist. Triumphantly, Hunniker replied that it was thirty minutes before three! Nitwit was fit to be tied and the Colonel, not wanting to hear the lengthy explanations ran out of the tent. It has remained one of my favorite joke sequences. These two sergeants were definitely not charitable people.

DELAYS

Little by little, we had gathered most of our papers and these had been blessed by my C.O. These were then forwarded to Battalion HQ in Darmstadt for further processing. It was a voluminous file that I personally delivered to Sergeant Major Weddell for approval by the Colonel and further forwarding to 7th Army Headquarters, wherever they were located. Weddell passed them on to Pfc. Fernandez the Battalion Clerk with instructions to process the matter with all deliberate speed.

Rosette and I had gotten very close to Xides and it had been decided that X. would be my best man whenever the wedding would finally be scheduled. In April, X. had gotten very bad news about his Mother who was extremely ill and expected to be alive not more than about 20 hours. The army was shipping him back to McKeesport Pa. The situation was so critical that he was being flown back by military air transport. Capt. Smith ordered me to drive Xides to the Frankfurt airport where I wished him good luck. I was back in Hanau by 10 PM, exhausted and quite depressed at having lost X. As it was, there had been so many delays that my closest buddies, mostly US enlistees, would reach the end of their 24 months of service well before our wedding papers had gone through the maze of military red tape.

Meanwhile, Rosette had written me that she was having second thoughts about the harm she had done to "Roger". *Actually, I was to find out decades later that this was not the same Roger she had been traveling with but a much more serious "Roger" who would surface again in subsequent decades.* Roger had written a letter to Rosette where he blamed her for doing damage to his heart and bringing him near death if she were to go through with her marriage to me. He even told her that he had rewritten a last will and testament in which he was leaving all his worldly possession to Rosette out of his extreme love for her. "Roger" also cautioned Rosette not to mention any of this to his Mother.

I was able to reason with Rosette that this was a bold-faced attempt at influencing her to break off her engagement with me. Surely, I reasoned, if Roger was that ill that he had made a new last will, it was certain that his Mother would be aware that he was now terminally ill. The whole thing did not sound very good to me. It also sounded as if Rosette had gotten cold feet. In any event, I was able to allay her fears and Rosette changed her mind again and decided to go through with our wedding. The Army had now asked that Frieda give her notarized approval and swear that she had no objection to our marriage. I was beginning to detect a marked reluctance to our marriage on the part of the military. After all, both Rosette and I were in our 20's. It was strange to request that I'd need parental consent at the age of 23. Apparently they did not worry about my Father's consent even as he was still titular head of the family.

Ruth sent me a letter that she planned to be in Belgium in the fall of 1953 and suggesting that we should wait until then to get married. I replied that because it has taken so long to obtain permission from the US Army, I did not want any extra delays and that Rosette and I would marry at the earliest possible date. Thereafter, a letter came to me from Frieda where she told me that she now understood that Rosette was pregnant and that she saw no objection to that nor to the early wedding date. "Yes, so is life" (Ja, so ist das Leben)! She further wrote that when we would return in 1954 we would be welcomed by GrandMother Frieda and Aunt Ruth. I had to write that to Rosette as I did not want her to be the only one who was not yet aware that she was expecting!

When we returned from the Munich maneuvers there were rumors that we would soon leave our quarters in Hanau and be relocated to new facilities. It was on a Sunday late morning, as I was looking out the window toward the entrance gate, I saw two tall officers casually pass through the sentry post, exchanging a smart salute with the GI on guard duty. The two officers proceeded down the walkway to the barracks and made a sharp right turn that put them right under my window. That was when I got a good look at them. They were Russian soldiers, unmistakable with their high flat caps, knee length boots, epaulets and enough "fruit salad" on their chest to go in the catering business.

I rushed into Sgt. Pollard's quarters and told him that two Russian officers had just broken our security and were trespassing onto our compound. As Pollard was incredulous, I insisted and pulled him by the arm toward the window. He was puzzled; how could Russian officers simply walk past our gate control? A quick phone call to headquarters brought a hasty response and a couple of Jeeps soon came driving through the gate after showing proper credentials to the now chastised sentry.

The Jeeps and MP's guns drawn, quickly surrounded the suspected Russian officers. They offered no resistance and surrendered their weapons to the Military Police. On request, they produced identity papers; both were members of the American CID who had been on a mission to test the security of American bases in Germany. Had I not spotted them they would probably have joined the troops at lunch. As it was, we had flunked the test. The fact that they had eventually been spotted and questioned was our only saving grace. That incident may have been a factor in the eventual disbanding of the 627th.

In the meantime, things were going well for me. Lt. Floyd wanted to drive me to Brussels in his big Buick for the week-end and Sgt. Carton was offering me the use of his Chevrolet if and when Rosette would visit me in Hanau. I would not remember if Floyd and I ever did drive to Brussels as I did not want to get to Brussels and find that Rosette was elsewhere. At the time, Rosette held the only charms for me in Belgium and I had no inclination to spend time there if I could not be with her. In June 1953, Lt. Floyd would be reassigned to another unit and replaced by a Lt. Johnson. Later I was to learn that Floyd had made passes at Rosette on more than one occasion.

Mayo and I went to see "April in Paris", an insipid movie with Doris Day and Ray Bolger, an odd romantic couple. The only effect that movie had on me were the kissing scenes when I found myself puckering my lips each time they kissed on screen. That only made me miss Rosette more and more. I did not miss the chance to tell her while begging her to come and visit me frequently. I was still trying to ingratiate myself with her parents and urged her to come and pick up an electric razor that I had purchased at the PX for her Father. We kept arguing that she should travel to Frankfurt in second class accommodations that I would pay for. Rosette insisted that she should travel third class and I found myself rebuffed by her stubborn refusals.

Meanwhile, Mayo had hurt his leg playing touch football and was now unable to perform his duties as a refrigeration mechanic. However, he could be found often in the bar/café on Lamboystrasse dancing away and singing "Pigalle" both in the French version that he had learned from Rosette and the American version that he had learned from me. Mayo never missed an occasion to tell me that I was very lucky to be loved by a girl such as Rosette. Once, when Rosette and I were spending an evening in a nightclub, Mayo talked the band into playing a popular Frankie Lane hit and Mayo sang it in our honor:

> "To spend one night with you.
> In our little rendezvous,
> And reminisce with you
> That's my desire . . . ."

At the time I felt that it spoke so well of Mayo and demonstrated what a great friend he was. When we eventually all returned to the U.S. Mayo would call Rosette regularly after he had moved to California. But I was in love and Mayo was to remain my very good friend.

At the end of June'53 I was advised that I'd soon be permanently transferred to Battalion HQ to assume an I.E. position. Although I was not aware of what the "E" stood for, I knew that this had to do with a sensitive Intelligence job. I was sorry to leave my friends at the 627th QM. However, of my enlisted friends, X. was now back home, Mayo and Testa would soon be discharged and back in the USA. The only two that were still close to me were Sgt. Carton and Cpl. Jim Haley my 6'5" Irishman. The way the Army was processing my papers did not make me optimistic for an early wedding. Sgt. Carton was sad to see me go to Battalion HQ but we both agreed that he would still be my Best Man and he and his wife Vera would partly share our honeymoon trip.

In early July came news that the government had passed new regulations that would make it easier for members of the Armed Forces to become US Citizens. All my marriage papers had finally been sent to Bn. HQ. It was now just a question of time, or was it? During a routine visit to Bn. HQ. I found the Battalion clerk sleeping at his desk, resting his head on the file that held my wedding dossier!

All the papers that I sent to HQ had the nasty habit of engendering additional new requests in a usual proportion of 3 to 1, each new paper to be obtained from Charleroi or New York if from me, from Brussels if from Rosette. And everything in triplicate signed and notarized. Lt. Smith, my new CO was anxious to sign anything I'd place on his desk as he was hoping that I'd soon be able to resume intelligent work instead of being constantly distracted by the mounds of papers that were continuously required of me. I was beginning to wonder if the Army was not trying to discourage us from getting married. Of course the Army was aware that a large percentage of the marriage requests pertained to girls whose professions left something to be desired and whose primary purpose was to hook on to a GI just to get a free ticket to the USA. After all, the war had ended only eight years previously and the German economy was still struggling to find a semblance of stability.

As for Rosette and me, our meetings had been getting more and more frequent, in Brussels, Frankfurt or Hanau. We finally straightened the Pentecost schedules and Mayo and I took the train to Frankfurt to secure a decent hotel room where Rosette and I would spend the two nights during Pentecost. Much to our surprise, the German laws prohibited an unmarried couple to spend or to rent a single room in a German hotel. We did find a lovely little hotel where we were able to rent two rooms but with the firm intention of using only one room at a time.

Rosette told her parents that she was spending the Pentecost weekend in Cologne, Germany with her old school friend Josée and her husband Jacques. Jacques was a Lt. Colonel in the Belgian Army of occupation and stationed in Cologne. I would take the train from Hanau to Frankfurt and then to Cologne and the same evening we'd return to Frankfurt for the remainder of the holiday weekend. Saturday we'd go visit Josée and Colonel Jacques just to consolidate Rosette's alibi. Mayo would spend Sunday afternoon with us in Frankfurt and on Monday I'd take Rosette back to Cologne where she would take the train back to Brussels. What a complex schedule so that Rosette and I could spend a few hours and two nights together. We had even contemplated having Rosette return from Frankfurt to Brussels by plane but in those days there were no flights on Mondays.

Josée would later become a faithful companion to my Father Hilaire in his old age. Carton, Mayo and Testa were smitten by Rosette's beauty and were often hangers-on. In later years, Mayo would often call Rosette from his home in California and try to flirt with her; he did not realize that Rosette was impervious to most men.

We did have our long weekend together in Frankfurt. I remembered bliss but very few details. The weather was beautiful and we did spend some time at the Frankfurt Rhine/Main Airport. We saw the gorgeous Lockheed Constellation with its three vertical tails. The "Pez" seller was flirting with Mayo. As we drove around the area, we had admired an odd shaped tower in the countryside. We dubbed it "coït tower" and took a photo of its suggestive shape that reminded us of an aroused penis. Rosette left by train in the early evening and I remembered following her return to Brussels in my mind; Cologne, Liège, Brussels. In the summer of 1953, Mayo joined Rosette and me for a few days' trip to Paris. On the way, Mayo, ever the smooth fellow, picked up an English girl who decided that she would tag along with Mayo to Paris. As I remember it, her name was Maria and she had a high pitched voice with which she would pipe up a refined though marked accent. The first time Mayo lit up a cigarette, she fluted "Oh, you smoke! How Shocking!"

Later, when Mayo took a drink of Whiskey, she piped "Oh, you drink! How shocking!"

Everything was either shocking or wonderful!

When we checked into a small hotel in Paris, we booked two rooms, one for Rosette and me and Mayo somehow persuaded Maria to share his room "to save her some money". I could only assume that when the time came to retire for the night, Maria must have exclaimed in her high pitched British accent "Oh, you fuck! How shocking!" I never did receive a confirmation.

A local village had a "movie theater", a *Kino* that placed primitive ads in the local news sheet. In this year of 1953 the rage in France and Europe was a movie with Martine Carol as *Lucrece Borgia*. This was a French movie with the luscious Marine Carol that was the talk of France. I had seen it advertised during my visit to Paris but had not had the occasion to go see it either in Paris or in Brussels. And now, there it was, in our own backyard in all of its nudity. Surely we had to go and view this wondrous film.

I gathered about one dozen men who would accompany me to the *Kino* to see this nearly pornographic movie, at least by 1953 standards. I was able to find the phone number of the theatre and made a reservation for twelve of us at the Friday evening showing of "Lucrece Borgia". The theater must have had a name but we had nick-named it *"The Kook-a-Mahl Theatre"* that roughly translated to "Take-a-look Theatre".

On that Friday evening, we rushed through the evening meal and requisitioned a truck that would take this cultured dozen GI's to the theatre. It turned out to be a barn with about ten plain wooden benches. We chose to sit on a center bench from which we would have a decent view of the movie. As we waited for the lights to be dimmed we expected crowds of villagers to join us on the unoccupied benches. Not even a lone cat came to share the space with us. I could now understand the somewhat incredulous tone of the person who had answered my phone call when I had reserved twelve seats.

The film was luscious, in color and Martine Carol was as beautiful as advertised. However the movie had been dubbed from French to German without any subtitles and my group could only grope to make sense of the plot. Ms. Carol was parading around in fashionable period dresses with previously unseen low décolleté that cut just above the aureoles of the nipples. It was all very exciting to our "dirty dozen". On a couple of instances, Martine (by then we were on first name basis) took very deep breaths and her gorgeous nipples popped out of her bodice. The 627th group let out an audible sigh in unison. Things were looking up! Later on, when Lucrece emerged from a long bath scene in full frontal nudity, the clunking of a dozen Adam's apples drowned the movie sound track. From that moment on, no one took note of the hard benches, the bad sound or the lack of customers in the barn. As we returned to our casernes, there was much whooping and hollering and I no longer had to worry that I'd be tarred and feathered that night.

DARMSTADT, BATALLION HEADQUARTERS

In summer of 1953 I was transferred to Battalion HQ. to replace Corporal Fernandez and PFC Bland as Battalion Clerk under the direct supervision of Sergeant Major Weddell the top non-com in the battalion.

There were quite a number of us to arrive in the Battalion courtyard that afternoon; we unloaded from the trucks and lined up in formation in the middle of the large agglomeration of buildings that made up the Battalion compound. As always the accommodations of the *Kasernes* were luxurious when compared with the barracks we had been billeted in back stateside. From a third floor window a voice called out to me "Hey, Rosenberg what squad have you been assigned to?" I looked up and recognized SFC King who I had not seen again since we drove to the Munich maneuvers; the same Sergeant King who had left me in charge of the trucks at the Autobahn stop and had brought me two pieces of dry bread "because all they had was ham, Rosenberg, and you don't want to eat ham, right?."

And now this same King wanted to know what squad I had been assigned to. "I don't know, sir" I replied.

"Well, Rosenberg, who do you sleep with?"

I was a bit sharp in my reply "Sir, I do not sleep with anyone, I sleep by myself".

"Then, Rosenberg, I will have you transferred to my squad!"

Thus, I was transferred to SFC King's squad, in the platoon of 1st Lt. Berg, in the company under Capt. Graham' command. That first evening, King advised me that I should be ready for a full field inspection at 6.30 PM. The last "full" I did was in the Leadership School back in Fort Lee, Va. No sweat! It took me 20 minutes to display all my socks underwear, etc in the prescribed manner and disassemble my M1 rifle and lay out all of its parts on my tightly made bunk. And then, wait for St. King who finally showed up at ten minutes to seven. He made a few unwarranted remarks about my display, told me to reassemble everything and that we would do it all over again at 6.30 the next evening. It took me 30 minutes to replace all my belongings into my footlocker and to clean and reassemble my rifle. There was a movie on post that started at 7 PM. By the time I was finished, it was nearly 7.45 and there was no way I could catch the show. I wrote a letter to Rosette and went to bed.

The following day my "full field" was ready again at 6.30 and Sgt. King showed up just a few minutes before 7. He mumbled a few remarks and left the room with instructions to try it again the following day. Again, by the time I was finished putting everything back, it was way too late to go to the movies.

And this went on for several weeks until I finally went to see Lt. Berg to lodge a complaint about Sgt. King. Lt. Berg was not very encouraging "Well, Rosenberg, you are new in this outfit and Sgt. King wants to make sure that you have all your equipment in order. He is only doing his duty towards a new man. ". Talks with Sgt Major Waddell had the same negative result. Attempts to speak with Captain Graham were blocked by the Sergeant Major. Surely, for whatever reason, Sgt. King had it in for me and no one wanted to do anything about it. It was obvious to me that King wanted me to bolt, take a swing at him or go AWOL; at worst desert. I would not give him that satisfaction.

And then, one day, I found out that the Inspector General was waiting in the mess hall for anyone who might have a complaint of unjust mistreatment in the Battalion. I saw my chance and went to see him without asking permission from anyone. I seem to recall that his name was Friedlander or something like that. We spent maybe 20 minutes. I told him that he should check my previous records, to call or visit Captain Petersen and that he would vouch for my good character and my excellence as a soldier. I reaffirmed that I was not a good-off and that Sgt. King was unjustly riding me.

Two weeks later, Sgt. King was transferred to another unit. I never heard from him again. From that day on, all harassment abruptly stopped. I came under the direct protection of Sergeant Major Weddell. Now, I was his "boy". Any attempt directed toward me Weddell considered a direct slight at him or at his authority. When there was an alert, and these were getting to be more and more frequent, the entire Battalion left with vehicles, cooks, enlisted men, non-coms and officers, but one man had to stay at the Headquarters and that one person was Corporal Rosenberg. I never had to go on alert.

The Colonel, who had never laid eyes on me while Sgt. King was maligning me, now let me use his personal car, a black 1953 Chevrolet, to drive to Brussels or wherever Rosette and I would meet. I was now Battalion clerk, interpreter and court-martial clerk. Suddenly I had it made!

After Fernandez went back to the States and I made mine the Battalion orderly room desk, I checked each of the 5 drawers to get rid of the accumulation of years. In the bottom right drawer, under a pile of unrelated papers, I found my folder, my marriage application folder! I had forwarded all my documents to be approved by Battalion and further submit to Seventh Army Headquarters for final approval and Fernandez, not knowing what to do with my file had simply buried it in the bottom drawer of his desk. Nothing had ever been done with my application! Months had been wasted. Was it Fernandez's sole decision or was it the Army's way of discouraging all marriage applications? As it was, I quickly brought my file to Weddell's attention and within 48 hours they were on the Colonel's desk for approval, signed and dispatched to Seventh Army Headquarters.

I had received news from Xides. His Mother was still lingering on despite her worsening health and X. had been reassigned in the Pittsburgh area pending the inevitable outcome of his Mother's illness. For me, it was now much easier to drive to Brussels at least once a month in the Colonel's Chevrolet. I'd drive down to Hanau and pick up Mayo or Tony Testa and we'd drive overnight to Brussels. On one occasion, we hit upon a fog so dense near the Belgian border that we could not travel on. It was the traditional pea soup but the worst I had ever seen. We decided that we would sleep in the Chevrolet until the next morning. Suddenly we heard the whistle of a train. We could not judge the direction it was coming from but we realized that we must have stopped very close to or maybe on top of the railroad tracks. Not wanting to get sliced in two by a locomotive I got out of the car to grope around and to feel the ground where we had stopped, fully expecting to find that we were stopped right on the railroad tracks and about to get hit. I got on my knees and felt around. Yes, we were still on the road but luckily there were no tracks anywhere around the car. Emboldened, I walked on just a few more steps, still looking for the elusive railroad tracks. As I took another step forward, I emerged from the thick fog into a clear crispy starry night. It was as if I had walked through a white curtain onto a lit stage. In front of my feet, the twin railroad tracks crossed the highway. I found my way back to the car and we drove just a few feet into the clear night and proceeded on to Brussels.

Rosette's parents were becoming reconciled with our marriage to their only daughter. Mrs Wauters, Christine, was making plans for the wedding that she insisted would take place in their apartment in Koekelberg near the huge basilica that loomed South over the city. There would be a civil ceremony, probably at the Brussels City Hall and Mme Wauters would do the cooking. Armand Wauters who was seldom at home was getting more and more friendly. He loved his Belgian beers and fine foods. He had served with courage in the First World War, earning several medals in the trenches near the flooded river Yzer (pronounced E-zair) where the combined forces of Belgium, England and France preserved the only part of Belgian soil that was never occupied by the German forces of Kaiser Wilhelm II from 1914 until the Armistice of November 1918. He used to delight in telling me that in 1915, Herbert Hoover had supplied tens of thousands pairs of American boots to the valiant Belgians fighting in the flooded plains of the River Yzer. The troops had exchanged their soaked leather boots for the new ones. Unfortunately the new footwear was made of tightly rolled cardboard and after a few days in the Yzer muddy trenches they had unraveled and disintegrated.

Father and Gerty, his long time girlfriend, would serve as my parents since neither Mother nor Ruth would be available to travel to Belgium for the ceremonies. I fervently hoped that Frieda would not get angry at us for inviting Hilaire and Gerty. For her part, Mother was convinced that I had gotten Rosette pregnant and that we had to get married. Mother, being down to earth would always imagine what she considered the logical outcome of relationships. "Pregnancy comes quicker than diarrhea!" Frieda would say.

Since Xides had returned to the States and Mayo Sotelo would reach the end of his tour before we'd get married, it would fall to Sgt. Larry Carton and his petite wife Vera to act as our witnesses. Everything was now falling into place; all that was needed was the imprimatur of the US Army. For that, we could only wait and hope.

In mid-Summer 1953, the French public transporters went on strike. Shortages of perishables became severe. Fruit, vegetable and dairy products disappeared from French warehouses especially in the Paris area. This presented a serious problem for the US troops stationed in and around the French capital. An urgent call went out to the 627th and its long neglected fleet of refrigerated trucks and trailers. At last the trailers would be used for more than one lone trailer where the company kept beer and other drinks under refrigeration.

A complete convoy of tractor/trailers loaded with perishables wound its way from Hanau to Paris. I was the only guy in the 627th who spoke any French! The mission was there! And I was no longer in the 627th. They left without me! I was so miffed to have lost my one opportunity to be of use.

I had been brought to the 14th QM BN. to become the I & E clerk. Now there was a new regulation (another one!) that no one would handle I & E material without being cleared first. As an alien, it would take me at least one year to obtain the necessary clearance. Major Haupl offered me all sorts of substitute jobs but none appealed to me and it looked as though I might be sent back to the 627th where I would have felt more at home. These changes of addresses were driving Rosette and me crazy as the APO was juggling our correspondence both ways. I had even heard that although BN. had sent a written request to have me transferred back to the 627th, a phone call had been placed high up to make sure that the transfer would be denied so that I would now remain at Battalion HQ.

By the first of August 1953 I learned that our marriage papers had been sent back to Battalion, not because they were not in order but a new directive gave the authority back to BN. to make the final decision. However there was still a need for the C.I.D to complete a thorough investigation before any approval could be contemplated. Also 2nd Group and the 7th Army were completely opposed to my return to the 627th. Apparently the high scores I accumulated during our maneuvers around Ludwigsburg in July had made me "indispensable" to Major Haupl. I had scored a tie with a Sgt Spade, both with a 68 out of a possible 70 that made me very close to being a genius at least in the eyes of the US Army. Sometime it is better to be an imbecile! By August 4th, I was firmly ensconced in Darmstadt where I would probably spend the balance of my three years of enlistment. At least now I would be able to follow the progress of those papers that would eventually be signed by my new CO, Lt. Colonel Hall.

"No, no, Darling, we were only joking when we talked about a room for three; what would we do three in a room?" Letter September 3, 1953 about our forthcoming trip to Paris, Rosette, me and Mayo.

The month of September 1953 passed too slowly for us. Long letters were exchanged speaking of love and complaining of the extreme slowness of the Army in processing our wedding papers. By the end of the month, Mayo left to return to the States. I would miss him. Ruth would spend a few days in Europe. Ruth would have been a perfect witness for our wedding but it was now certain that she'd be back in New York well before the betrothals. Now it seemed that Sgt. Carton would be my witness and that Vera, his wife, would be Rosette's witness. After the wedding, the Cartons and their Chevrolet would drive us around on our honeymoon. The exact schedule was still unsettled as we were in the dark as to the date our precious papers would finally be granted to us.

In the meantime, reams of paper were being recruited to convey to Rosette how much I loved her, the extent of my passion for her and how much I longed to finally be married to her.

Otherwise, life at the 14 QM BN. in the Ernst Ludwig Kaserne in Darmstadt had settled in a pleasant routine where I was now well appreciated and the untouchable darling of Sgt. Major Weddell. The 627th QM Refrigeration Company had been completely disbanded and its remaining personnel either discharged or spread out to related organizations.

On the first weekend of October 1953, still bereft of our wedding papers, I managed to spend a few days in Brussels. Much to my delight, Mayo had been delayed in his departure back to the States and he was able to join me in Belgium. I had given him a letter and present from Rosette and he was able to thank her in person during our trip. My Sister Ruth had spent some time in Paris and by coincidence we met during this trip to Brussels. Unfortunately Ruth would definitively be back in Brooklyn much before the wedding. I have very little recollection of what we were able to do during this visit; however, we did take a picture together on the Boulevard du Botanique. I seem to recall that it was Mayo who snapped it.

Later in October, while I was away on maneuvers in the southern part of Germany my sister Ruth traveled to Hanau in the hope of seeing me. We missed each other and so, she visited with her long time friend Ed Young, chief engineer for Pan American Airways in Europe. During the third week of October there was a crash of a SABENA flight in Cologne and the papers listed a Rosenberg among the victims. After a few anguished hours I was able to learn that the victim was an Irving Rosenberg, no relative of ours and that Ruth was safe indeed. A couple of days later, Ed Young contacted me for the same reason. He knew me back in 1947 as "Rudy" Rosenberg but wanted to be sure that I did not go under the other name of Irving. I was very glad to reassure him that I was safe and sane and had not perished in that terrible accident. That was to be the last time I heard of Young.

Instead of flying back to Brussels as she had planned, my sister took the train up the Rhine valley and visited in Essen with our grandMother's sister, Tante Mali who, weighing only 85 lbs had survived a concentration camp. Mali cried when seeing Ruth "*Meine gestorbene Schwester!*" My dead sister! *Ruth looked very much like a young Emma, our grandMother who, after about three months in the show-camp of Teresienstadt had been sent to "the final solution" in Auschwitz.*

October 20th, 1953! A long last the papers from the American Embassy arrived in Darmstadt. It had taken a full 10 months for the permission to marry Rosette to materialize. The wedding was fixed for November seventh in Brussels. It was decided that I'd leave Darmstadt the evening of the 3rd, spend the night with Carton and Vera in Hanau and drive on the 4th to arrive later that day in Brussels. We'd then have a couple of days to get oriented before the long awaited day for the marriage on November 7th, 1953.

WEDDING DAY AND HONEYMOON

I would remember very little about the marriage or the following honeymoon. The entire two weeks became cloaked in mist and fog with only dim lights piercing out in moments of perceived lucidity.

We drove to Brussels in Carton's Chevrolet, Sgt Carton dressed in civilian clothes; Vera, his petite wife, neat in her light blue gray raincoat and me in my uniform. We did make a brief stop in Cologne to admire the magnificent Dom and limped into Brussels in the dark of the evening. I probably went to my Father's apartment to greet him and Gerty his longtime German girlfriend. There, I spent the night. It was the 4th of November; we were scheduled to wed on the 7th. I guess that the Cartons took a room in a hotel near the North Station where lodgings were reasonable. On the seventh we had a civil wedding, went to have our picture taken and in the late afternoon we all ended up at Rosette's home where her Mother, Christine Wauters had prepared a splendid wedding dinner for all of us. Armand, Rosette's Father was there. The Cartons, Hilaire and Gerty, Rosette and I completed the gathering. My Mother Frieda could not be there as she was now in New York and my sister Ruth had gone back to the States. Frieda long bore a grudge for being "excluded" from her son's wedding while Gerty, Hilaire's mistress was invited to participate.

Rosette had managed to reserve a room at "Au Berger" where we had first made love the previous Christmas. We would not have to rush and vacate the room as we did eleven months before. This time, we were husband and wife and could enjoy the welcoming room for the entire night.

I resolved to make a present to Rosette on our wedding night. I sat her in a plush armchair, lifted her slip, lowered her panties and after a few caresses proceeded to place my lips and my mouth over her "pussy". I tried to be as skillful and loving as I could but could not detect any response from Rosette. I lifted my eyes and looked at her face: nothing! I remember being shocked by the blank look she had, as if nothing was happening. I gave up my efforts and soon we were rolling in bed where I came too fast, probably feeling that I was a great and wonderful lover.

The next day, with Carton back in his uniform, we drove across the French border and soon got stopped by a French policeman for speeding. When he saw Carton and me in our American uniforms and when we explained that I was on my honeymoon, he gave us a broad mustachioed smile and sent us on our way. A garnished sauerkraut lunch awaited us in Strasbourg and we spent our second honeymoon night in Nancy. Somewhere in our hotel some fleas found me to their liking and for the next few days, one flea ate three meals a day on my body and at my expense. Rosette got along fine with Vera and she flourished and delighted in introducing her to all the sights when we spent the next few days in Paris. It was then time for the Cartons to rejoin their outfit in Hanau and we all drove back to Germany.

The next leg of our honeymoon would take us to southern Germany where we would stay on the Eibsee Lake in the middle of the German Alps, at the Eibsee Hotel. I seem to remember that military personnel had preferential rates and it was a major reason for our choosing to stay there for a week as our finances were still limited.

As US personnel we also had very low train rates and I had ordered two round trip military tickets down to Garmisch, the fabled German ski resort. Much to our dismay and chagrin, the train controller questioned the validity of our tickets; there was no problem with my fare but he objected to Rosette's ticket as Rosette was neither US Military personnel nor an American citizen. If she had to pay regular fare, there was no way we could afford the rest of our honeymoon. We both pleaded and argued our case with the controller who eventually relented and allowed us to continue on our way. I guessed there was a god for honeymooners!

We had purchased a small red portable radio at the PX and we were able to listen to AFN all the way to Garmisch and back on a set of D batteries, I guess much to the displeasure of most of the German burghers that were traveling on the train with us.

Oberammergau was on our way, the small German village where the inhabitants grew beards and put on a passion show every ten years. Unfortunately we were in 1953 and there would not be another show until 1960. In a way, it must have been for the best as the Passion was reputed to be laced with strong anti-Semitism sentiments that carry on to this day.

We had plans to go visit the castle of Ludwig the Mad at Neuschwanstein. We never did see it. Each night, I'd be spending long hours trying to get pictures in the moonlight from the vantage point of the balcony of our room. Rosette would be in bed and I'd take pictures of the mountain, the lake, the sky and the moon. By the time the morning came, we were so tired that we never got up early enough to catch the bus that would have taken us to the Castle. We never did see it. I remember Rosette being upset and cross with me for taking too much time getting ready in the morning. I guess I would never change.

That would be all that I would ever remember of our honeymoon!

SEVEN MONTHS TO GO

Now that we were at long last married, each day that remained in my military service was a day keeping Rosette away from me. She had returned to Brussels and her job at Lever Bros. and I was left to count the days that separated us until the month of July 1954 when I would complete my time in the US Army. In those days, every eligible member of the Armed Forces had to serve a total of 8 years. In the Army, it meant 2 years of active duty and 6 years in the Army Reserves. However, when I enlisted for three full years, it had been stipulated that if one completed the three years to the last day, no reserve would apply. That was a fairly recent regulation. Being on duty in the Battalion orderly room I was well aware of this especially of the provision that if the three years were not completed to the last day a full 5 years of reserve duty would be tacked on to the three years of active service already served. The Army had buried it among other regulations and the majority of its personnel remained unaware of it.

Rosette and I had to submit a new set of papers to the US Embassy in Frankfurt in preparation for our departure to the States around July 1954 when my three years would be up and Rosette would be allowed to emigrate to the US. In the meantime, even though she was now my wife Rosette had to apply for a visa so she could be admitted stateside especially since I had not yet become a US Citizen. And every paper that had to be submitted had to be stamped and notarized. The US Army was not going to welcome us back to the USA without wrapping it in ribbons of red tape!

Naturally, we were anxious to meet and we successfully managed a few times, sometimes in Brussels, sometimes Rosette would take the train to meet me in Germany.

On one of my trips to Brussels Rosette was able to obtain tickets for a concert by Josephine Baker (In French, Josephine Back-hair). We were lucky to purchase two seats front row center. As always, I proudly wore my uniform whenever we traveled, either in Belgium or in Germany. Members of the Armed Forces were encouraged to wear civilian clothes when not on duty but I would have none of that. It was barely eight years since the end of the conflict and the US Military wanted the population to feel comfortable with Uncle Sam's soldiers. The new enemy now was the Soviet Union and we did not want to ruffle feathers, especially in Germany.

So, there I sat in my O.D.'s (olive drab) uniform anticipating a grand performance by Josephine. She came on stage in a gaudy, many-colored African garb and sang "*J'ai Deux Amours*" Two loves have I. She then launched into a succession of French language songs and modern dances that were well received by the public. She sang no songs in English. Josephine would work the audience and banter with the patrons seated in the front rows. I soon noticed that even though I sat in the center of the front row she systematically skipped my seat completely ignoring my presence. It became evident that it was my Yankee uniform that turned her off. I had not realized until then the depth of her resentment to all things American. I would long remember her profound dislike for her native country.

December 11, 1953 "—Mon Amour, before I forget, let me ask you this. You tell me that you will arrive in Frankfurt by the 11.50 flight but you do not tell me the date!? And since there is a slight difference between (celebrating) Noel in Europe and Christmas in the United States, I really do not know when you will be here. Please let me know as soon as possible. Thank you my love."

December 14, 1953 'Mamour!—Darling, as far as your arriving, I think that it is better to let the SABENA take you to town. I know where it is and since I do not know when you will arrive (the date?) I will not b e able to tell you now if I will be free soon enough in the morning to be at the airport. OK?"

December 29, 1953 "Mon Amour—I have no confidence in the news that we hear these past days. It would not surprise me if we (the US) were to send troops in Indo-China (Vietnam). I have feared it for a long time and the events of these last days seem to confirm my fears. But you should not worry about me because I may not go there as I am attached to the European Services. It bothers me because it means still more American lives that will get themselves killed. What a world we live in. I hope that my impressions are without basis but I would not be surprised if we had to go there.

MUNSTER AM URINE. 1954

<u>Seven months to go until discharge and our return to the USA!</u>

We had been told that the Battalion HQ. was soon to leave our quarters at the Ernst Ludwig Kaserne in Darmstadt and move to the village of Münster. A few weeks later, we moved lock, stock and barrel about 25 miles to Münster. A couple of miles outside the village stood an empty factory and warehouses where the Germans had stored poisonous gases after WW I. Since gases were not used in WW II warfare the site had probably been vacated right after the war and that would now become the permanent *Kaserne* of the 14th QM Battalion. Of all my friends from the 627th Refrigeration, only Cpl James (Jim) Haley now remained and was transferred to the new outpost. Münster is German for Mint and wherever money was minted, the town took on the name of Münster. There was at least one other "Münster" in Germany, the better known being Münster in Westphalia. Germans had a habit of identifying some cities by the river that ran through it. Thus you had; Köln am Rhein, Frankfurt am Main, Heidelberg am Neckar etc. A deep ditch filled with brackish filthy muck ran from our compound to the village and we took the habit of referring to Münster as Münster am Urine.

Of our time in that isolated outpost, I would remember one incident only. I had developed a fierce sore throat and cold. Someone recommended that I would benefit from a good stiff drink of whiskey. Being a non-drinker it took a lot of convincing but as I was getting sicker by the day, it was agreed that I would take a large swig of the Scotch. Lisel, the German girl who took care of our modest recreation room on post managed to get a hold of whiskey for the "cure". Most of the company turned out to see me drink alcohol and the medication worked perfectly. After having drunk the whiskey, Jim Haley, wanting to compliment Lisel for having procured the alcohol exclaimed "Lisel, you are a jewel!" Lisel reacted as if she had been bitten by a venomous snake "Me, a Jew? No! No! I am not a Jew!" And, red-faced at the thought that Haley might have mistaken her for a Jewess, she ran out of the room. Jim laughed very loudly. I did not think it was that funny.

Beside my duties as the battalion clerk, translator and court martial clerk kept me quite busy. All the difficulties I had encountered so many months ago were now a thing of the past and I enjoyed all my duties. I stayed in the headquarters whenever there were alerts and there was no dearth of three-day passes and furloughs.

"Put that in your pipe and smoke it!" That was what this PFC impudently told a sergeant! Now, under normal circumstances that would have been a forgivable statement. However, the PFC was a bright young black from Philadelphia and the sergeant was a regular army veteran out of Jackson Mississippi. The recent integration of the Army units did not sit well with him. Thus, charges were pressed against the black PFC and no one had the common sense to simply reprimand him. A Court Martial was convened and the PFC was found guilty, demoted to Private and immediately transferred to another outfit.

A German cab driver had been set upon by a trio of members of our unit. They had felt that the charges for driving them from the train station to Munster had been excessive. Not only did they refuse to pay his fee but they had urinated in his little 1950 VW Beetle, stolen his *oxenschwantz* (bull penis) that this driver kept next to the stick shift for protection. All this he had testified to me in German when I had taken his deposition.

However, at the court martial trial of the three Gi's, the driver developed total amnesia and gave us a blank stare with every question that the tribunal asked. Major Haupl, the presiding officer gave me inquisitive looks with each denial apparently doubting my qualifications as a translator. Case dismissed!

There was once the case of SFC Molloy (not his real name) who had taken a truck through a local German town. The truck had been loaded with German civilians and several GIs. On their way to their assigned duties, Molloy had stopped in a German beer hall and had offered drinks all around. It had been reported that he had become inebriated and that he was quite incapacitated by the time everybody had gotten back in the truck. By the time Molloy and his group returned to the barracks, the officer of the day had become aware of Molloy's drinking while on duty and charges had been pressed against him. Molloy promptly went AWOL. Not only did he go AWOL but we heard nothing from him for the better part of four weeks. There was no other subject of conversation among the Battalion officers than Molloy especially as we neared the 30 days time lapse when the charge of AWOL would automatically become "desertion" carrying with it a much more severe punishment than the then *Absent without Leave* charge that had been laid on him.

Molloy came back to the battalion on the 29th day and the charges were rewritten to reflect the time he had been AWOL, drunk while on duty, misappropriation of a military vehicle, reckless driving through a German town, making lewd remarks at German women from the back of the truck, etc.

As the court martial was about to be convened, I remarked to Major Haupl, the court officer, that Molloy could not be tried by the Battalion court martial because all the judging officers had previous knowledge of his case that had been widely discussed for over a month. Haupl did not entertain my comments with an open mind. "What previous knowledge?" He thundered! "The man is guilty!"

Nevertheless, within a couple of weeks a new court martial panel was nominated from a neighboring battalion and the trial finally got under way. Several witnesses were paraded in front of the judges, each describing his recollection of the events as they had happened almost three months prior to the trial. One soldier could recall very little, having been probably under the influence at the same time as Molloy. However he did remember Molloy standing in the back of the truck as it was careening through the town and holding on to the round metal bars that held the tarp covering the truck. Having emptied a large number of bottles in the beer hall, Molloy had felt the pressing need to relieve himself, unzipped his pants and pissed joyously from the moving truck.

The court did not find Molloy guilty of any of the charges but one! They found him guilty of indecent exposure, "To wit: his penis (sic)", a charge that had not even been brought against him and based solely on the innocent testimony of that one witness. Molloy, now sober, was reduced in rank and transferred to another battalion.

PREPARATIONS FOR THE USA

By now, we were about four months away from our trip back to the USA. One more month and I would be discharged having completed my three year enlistment. Rosette and I were alternating our visits every few weeks. Rosette would send me lists of items she wanted me to purchase at the PX, items that we would then prepare to ship to Brooklyn for our life in America; Sunbeam pressing iron, sewing machine, toaster etc. These would be packed and sent ahead to Bremerhaven where we would soon board an Army transport back to New York.

We did have a few differences now and then as attested by our correspondence. I had noticed Rosette had a tendency to pout for *cherry pits* and sometimes she would write about guilt complexes caused by the weeks when we were not in each other's company. Blinded by my passion for her it was easy for me to dismiss these seemingly black clouds in our relationship and gloss over them.

Now that we were married, the US Army wanted tons of additional papers both from me and from Rosette attesting to her good and decent behavior, moral standing in her community, financial responsibility, "acceptable" political leanings as well as those of her parents and close relatives. Most of these had been provided prior to being granted permission to wed; now we had to provide these all over again so that Rosette could be granted a visa to enter America. Similar affidavits were also required from my Mother; all these in triplicate and notarized. Meanwhile I was trying to maneuver so that both Rosette and I could find passage on the same ship.

There was subtle pressure exerted on me to re-enlist for at least another two years but I was adamant. The end of my enlistment was more attractive with every passing month. One week-end late morning, as I was completing my toilette in the large, square communal bathroom Sgt.Major Waddell came in and pleaded for me to re-enlist and stay in the battalion for another three year period. I had become an asset to the battalion and Waddell had been awarded several special prizes for the way the battalion had been organized. He obviously did not want to go back to the assorted eight-balls who had been BN. Clerks prior to my arrival. He pleaded "Rosie,I know that we gave you a hard time when you first arrived in this outfit, but that is all over now and you should re-up!"

He was crying and looked pitiful and funny standing in his Jockey underwear in the large white bathroom. It was flattering but I would have none of it; I wanted out! The fact that Waddell was *slightly* drunk added a comic touch to the situation.

Of course, the thought of spending another thirteen days being seasick on the way to New York would make me weaken but I'd soon come to my senses weighing 13 days on board ship against the prospect of spending another three years in the service.

Throughout March and early April 1954, we were gathering more household goods from the PX. As soon as these were received, I'd get them crated and shipped with the Army services to Mother and Ruth in Brooklyn. I remembered being amazed that three heavy cases could be shipped for a total of $ 3.52 that included each crate being insured for fifty dollars. I was trying to convince Rosette to come and spend the last few weeks in Germany prior to our departure for the USA. Rosette wanted to continue working at Lever Bros. until the last moment. We were still trying to obtain all the travel papers that would be needed for the trip to the German port of Bremerhaven and the two week sea voyage to America.

Remembering the kindness of Larry Carton and Vera, his wonderful wife, I made a few visits to Hanau where they were still stationed to thank them for all their support in the past year. We would not have occasion to see them again when the time would come to travel to Bremerhaven.

At the Cartons I had been scheduled to meet Sgt. Keator and his wife. Keator had been my *Nazi* tormentor when we were cadres in Fort Lee Va. Unfortunately they never got there, claiming that mechanical problems had prevented them to arrive to Hanau in time.

On or about April first, 1954, Rosette let me know that she was late with her ovulation and that she felt that she had become pregnant. There followed 6 days of total silence, no phone call, no letter until April 6th when Rosette wrote me that it had been a false alarm. Rosette had always maintained that she had an inverted uterus and that it was impossible for her to become pregnant. Because of that we had never taken any precautions except that I'd pull out in time even though a couple of times Rosette had tried mightily to retain me in her as I was about to ejaculate.

In early April of 1954 I received a telegram from my friend Maurice Goldman that he had married a girl named Hugette, I believe. I wrote to Rosette advising her that we should have a dinner with Maurice and his bride on my next visit to Brussels later that month. Hugette came from the Walloon part of Belgium, was French speaking and a Catholic. So, both Maurice and I, Hidden Children of the Holocaust, had avoided marrying a Jewish mate but at that time it did not make any impression on either one of us.

We met in a café near the Stock Exchange where we traded platitudes. I recall being astounded at the lack of solicitude shown by Maurice toward his new bride. Instead he was the same brusque, rough-talking Maurice that I remembered from our school days. An old lady came to our table carrying a large whicker basket overflowing with bouquets of tiny violets. *"Des fleurs pour madame?"* Flowers for Madame? She inquired. I turned to Rosette and asked her if she wanted one of the pretty bunches; Rosette declined. The flower lady next turned to Maurice and repeated *"Des fleurs pour madame?"* "Not for us, we are married" Maurice replied with a dismissing wave of the hand. Both Rosette and I were shocked by his cavalier attitude.

A couple of days later Rosette and her Cabaret group were performing and I was thrilled to go hear Rosette in her singing performance. Rosette had a rough slightly raspy tonality in her voice. It was strangely captivating somewhat reminiscent of the mature Edith Piaf sound and Rosette never really had any need for a microphone. Her interpretation of *Ramundsho*, a song made popular by Luis Mariano the king of the French light opera, left the listener breathless. Rosette was very popular not only with the audiences but also with the other members of her group. She seemed particularly fond of another singer, Roger Van W. and a strong good-looking girl Dedee L. who I had been told was a very vocal Lesbian. The entire group worked at Lever Bros and had formed a good cohesive ensemble. Somehow, I did not feel comfortable with the situation but I felt that once we would be in America they would be forgotten

I could not help but remember that a few months earlier, in Germany, Rosette had sung *"Pigalle"*, the big hit by George Ulmer and she had sung it in the original French. Mayo and Tony Testa had liked her singing. I had then proceeded to sing the English version with a heavy French accent. Testa then declared that he liked my version best. Rosette never quite forgave me! *Later, in the States, Rosette claiming that she had developed nodules on her vocal cords never sang again, at least not in my presence.*

ROSENBERG, US CITIZEN!

The army was now moving fast. My discharge papers were being typed and since I was returning with my wife, a dependent, it involves a new set of regulations especially regarding our joint return to the States. On May 10th (signed May 19th, stamped May 20) we were issued an emergency allotment authorization (not to exceed $120.00) for *the proper care, subsistence and well-being of Rosette to be paid in the event of an emergency declared by proper authority,* whatever that meant. In military jargon we were advised that we would depart Germany on June 12th, 1954, tentatively. It now appeared that we would be leaving by air from Frankfurt Rhein-Main airport for New York. Since we would be allowed only 65 pounds of luggage it was now urgent that Rosette immediately ship our household cases to Darmstadt so I could reroute them to Bremerhaven where these would be placed on board an Army ship to New York.

Seventh Army HQ. had notified me that I was to appear before a naturalization judge in Munich, Germany at 8.30 AM on JUNE 3rd, 1954 to be granted my US citizenship! I felt elated! Now Rosette would no longer be the wife of Rudy Rosenberg, a man without a country, but the wife of Rudy Rosenberg, US citizen! Of course, I needed to bring along two witnesses. Captain Graham and Jim Haley volunteered and Graham would drive us to Munich the day before so we could appear before the military judge the next morning. We drove all day in Captain Graham's red and black Oldsmobile to cover the 250 miles to Munich. Graham kept singing a parody to "Humoresque"

> "When the train is in the Station
> We rely on constipation.
> When the train is moving
> So can you."

We reached Munich in the early evening, checked in a hotel, grabbed a bite and went to a second story bar in a private house. There was an imposing wooden bar and both Graham and Haley ordered a Whiskey while I had a Coca-Cola. Over the next hour or so, they ordered Whiskey twice more while I nurtured another Coke. When the bill came, it was $45.-. We thought it was excessive, $15.00 each and me who only had two Cokes! When we objected, the owner claimed that he had served them double-Whiskeys and insisted that we owed him the $45.00. (This was in 1954!). We refused to pay! The owner called the US Military Police. From the ease with which he had their phone number ready and the quickness of their response, we had the impression that this was a common occurrence. Within just a few minutes, two MP's burst in the bar and demanded to know what the problem was. There was a brief discussion about the discrepancy between single and double Whisky. One MP declared that he would have to arrest us and that we would have to appear before the American Judge sometime the next day. If that was inconvenient, he strongly suggested that we pay the $45—and that we went on our way.

He advised us to go home and to be sure that he would not have to meet up with us again that night. So, we pooled our money and each paid $15.00. I could only mull over the high cost of my two Coca-Colas costing $7.50 each. We did not leave a tip.

The next morning, June 3rd, 1954, at 8.30, I appeared in front of the Judge with my two witnesses all dressed in our spiffy uniforms, shaved, smart and sober. I stood at the bar, flanked by a Captain and a Sergeant. The US Judge, looking down on me from his high lectern wanted to know if I had ever been arrested. For a brief moment, I thought to answer "Not until last night, your Honor" But after a millisecond reasoning that we had only been stopped and questioned by the American MP's, I firmly replied that indeed I had not. The Judge smiled, saluted me and having signed it, presented me with a certificate of US citizenship. It felt so good, after 24 years without any nationality, 24 years being Stateless, Statenlos and Apatride, at long last I now had a real nationality, citizen of the United States of America! That this was happening in Germany, in Munich, one of Adolph Hitler's favorite cities, barely 9 years after the defeat of Germany, made it doubly sweet!

RETURNING HOME

Rosette received my letter that we would be leaving Germany by air and that the predicted date would now be June 14th. I urged her to complete her packing, say good bye to friends and relatives and to come and join me near Frankfurt as soon as possible. I was not sure that she would be comfortable with the thought of flying back to New York. For my part I was ecstatic not to have a two weeks crossing of the Atlantic again; the memory of being so seasick in 1952 still remaining fresh after nearly two years. Should we be delayed in Frankfurt the Army had plans to put us up at the BaselerHof Hotel, free of charge.

Mother and Ruth were sent a letter letting them know that we expected to arrive at New York's Idlewild Airport (now JFK) either on the 15 or 16 June, 1954. They had rented a small furnished apartment for us just a few blocks from where they lived and this time they would help Rosette get settled. From Idlewild we would probably be bussed to the Fort Hamilton Hospital and Army camp in Brooklyn where I would have to stay and serve the final days of my enlistment so as to avoid being strapped with an extra five years of Army Reserve. I had found out from Margot, my Brooklyn friend, that her husband Curtis was working there in the dependent section and I did not anticipate having any problems obtaining a pass to go home each night.

On June 14th, we boarded the flight to New York. The plane was a four engine DC 4, the plane that would briefly replace the DC3. The flight was operated as a civilian line leased to the US Army for special services. Besides the crew, there must have been nearly 100 dependents, mostly war brides and their babies, all on their way to the USA. Rosette and I were lucky to have adjoining seats. We took off from Frankfurt, flew a few hours and landed in Shannon, Ireland. There the plane was refueled while we spent some time souvenirs shopping in the huge hangar build for that purpose. However, having more time than money we just hung around until we could board the plane again and proceed to our next port-of-call. For the rest of the passengers it was a time to change dirty diapers and try to feed the babies before we took off again.

Later that afternoon we took off again; destination Gander, Newfoundland. That was the long flight over the North Atlantic. It would mean seven or eight hour's non-stop to Canada's Northeastern province. By then, all of us were tired, the only ones still full of energy were the babies who cried and cried the entire way. The humming of the four engines did reassure us but neither I nor Rosette had ever flown that long, in a large plane, over an endless ocean and flying into quickly waning daylight. We finally arrived in Gander, refueled again and took off in the night for the last leg of our trip, toward New York and Idlewild where we finally arrived in the early hours of the morning of the 15th. We had been underway over 24 hours!

From there, we were processed by Immigration and put on a bus to Fort Hamilton, Brooklyn. Later that day Rosette found her way to 134 Prospect Place in Brooklyn where Ruth and Frieda had rented us a small furnished apartment. I would not remember if I had to stay on the Army camp or if I was allowed to rejoin my wife on that first day. Ruth would remember Rosette exclaiming "My God, this place is soooo dirty!" That did not sit well with Mother and Ruth who had spent evening after evening cleaning up the place. True, the apartment was kind of dark but with a limited budget and the fact that apartments were hard to find, that was the best that they could do. Rosette's tactless remark would be the first unkind cut that would soon drive a wedge between her, Ruth and Mother.

I and the majority of the temporary personnel in Fort Hamilton were just there waiting to be discharged. I had about 29 days to go and apparently it was the intention of Fort Hamilton to get us processed as soon as possible. Most of the soldiers waiting to be discharged wanted out as soon as possible and they were put through the system very quickly. The few of us who wanted to live out our total three years to the last day seemed specially targeted by the Hamilton processors to persuade us to go home early. This would have tacked on an extra 5 years of reserve duty. Non-commissioned officers were prowling the grounds of the fort looking for soldiers wandering about aimlessly. They would pounce on them and give them *"Shit details"* busy work to discourage them from staying longer in the Army. Headaches were plaguing me and often I would throw up for no apparent reasons. Several nights were spent in the Fort Hamilton hospital; the doctors being unable to diagnose a serious cause. That was a classical case of panic; panic at the uncertainty that was now facing me.

I had befriended another soldier who, like me, was trying to be unnoticed. We had gotten hold of a bedspring that we'd carry all over the post, looking busy. We'd walk it over to the PX, drop the spring by the side of the steps to the PX and go inside for a drink or a bite. After a while we'd come out, grab our bedspring again and walked on to our next hiding place. Non-Coms would see us walking with our burden, figure that we had been instructed by another sergeant and would leave us alone. As the days went on, we'd change our burden, mattress, mops, brooms etc, anything that gave some semblance of being busy. It worked most of the time. Finally, on July 12th, 1954, I was discharged from the service and was able to rejoin Rosette.

Rosette had found a job as a trilingual secretary for a Mr Straight at Amsterdam Overseas on Pine Street, downtown Manhattan. Rosette by then was fluent in French, English and could do correspondence in German and Dutch.

I had gone to several interviews but had been unable to match my limited skills with the jobs that were available on the market. I was having a crisis. At night, I slept fitfully and would wake up drenched in sweat. I realized that I had no formal education, no sellable skills, and very little future. And there I was, without a job, without marketable knowledge, married and facing a bleak future.

On the positive side, I was now a veteran; I had become a US citizen. My wife Rosette was making a living.

I had fallen off of the cocoon of the military. I was in a panic! I was 24 year old.

END OF AN UNORTHODOX LIFE, VOLUME ONE PART THREE

September 5, 2010. Final editing: Tuesday August 25, 2012.

1945. Ruth, 17, Colette Pesh (17?). Brussels or Bruges. Note: "Interpreter's star in coat lapel.

1947, Bois de la Cambre, Brussels. First love. Gilberte Doms, 18; Rudy, 17. Note: US Army officer's coat and scarf.

Brussels, 1949. Rudy, 19;
Ruth, 21; shortly before
Rudy leaves for America.
Photo taken by street
photographer on the Blvd.
Du Botanique

1949. Rudy, 19. Eastern
Parkway, Brooklyn, NY.

Frieda, circa 1950,
48; Ostende
Belgium, by the sea.

Ruth, 24; on route
to USA, on board of
SS. Rijndam of the
Holland-America
Line. July 1952.

10.53 BRUSSELS.

RUTH & RUDY.

Ruth, 25; Rudy, 23; chance meeting in Brussels October 1953. Blvd. Du Botanique. Note: US 7th Army shoulder patch "Seven Steps to Hell".

November 7th, 1953. Brussels, Belgium. Wedding photograph. Rosette, 25; the author, 23 in US Army uniform.

The author, NY. Metropolitan
Museum of Art.

With companion Marie Bonazinga -
at Carnegie Hall, Fall 2007.

1984, Summer. Carle Place, Long Island, N.Y. Four generations. The author, 54; Richard,
5 months; Karen, 4; Rudy Jr., 26; Hilaire, 82.

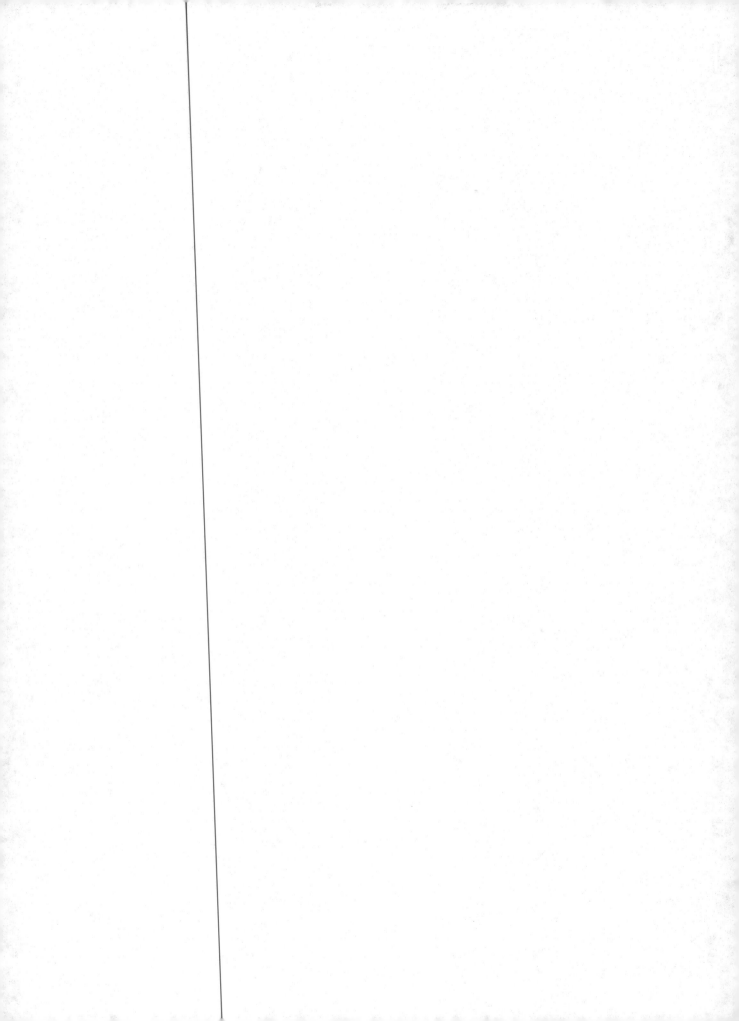